5.00

Family Therapy and Research

An Annotated Bibliography
of Articles and Books Published 1950-1970

IRA D. GLICK, M.D.

Assistant Clinical Professor of Psychiatry,
University of California School of Medicine,
and Chief, Clinical Research Ward,
Langley Porter Neuropsychiatric Clinic,
San Francisco

JAY HALEY

Director of Family Research,
Philadelphia Child Guidance Clinic,
Philadelphia

GRUNE & STRATTON **New York and London**

To Ana, Rachel, and Jonathan

Grune & Stratton, Inc.
757 Third Avenue
New York, New York 10017

Library of Congress Catalog Card Number 72-153577

International Standard Book Number 0-8089-0688-7

Printed in the United States of America (R-R)

Preface

This bibliography of articles and books published from 1950 to 1970 attempts to include all that has been written on family therapy as well as published family research studies relevant to the fields of psychiatry, psychology, and social work. The many papers and books on the family in the area of sociology and anthropology have been excluded. Also excluded are popular books and magazine articles for the nonprofessional. Often the decision of what to include has been a difficult one. In a sense, everything written on the family is relevant, but this bibliography focuses upon a special area of the family field that has developed in the last twenty years.

Almost any paper on therapy that seems to have a family orientation is included. However, the therapy of family members treated individually or in group therapy or the therapy of married couples treated separately is not completely covered, even when articles on the subjects mention the family in passing. Papers on family research are included whenever they deal with family interaction—the actual behavior of family members with one another. Studies of individuals in families or research based upon records, self-report, and individual testing are included only if they deal with differences between types of families within a family orientation. For example, statistical studies of the frequency of divorce in America are not included, but an article giving statistics on frequency of divorce in families containing a schizophrenic member would be listed.

The references are arranged by subject and are followed by an author index. The subject arrangement was designed to meet the needs of readers with diverse interests. Placement of a particular article in a category is sometimes arbitrary. When an article deals with more than one subject, however, the entire annotated reference is repeated under each appropriate subject heading. For example, if an article deals with family therapy of a family with a schizophrenic member, it is listed under both *Family Therapy* and *Family Member Diagnosed Schizophrenic*. A research article contrasting two types of families is listed under each family type as well as under *Contrasting Family Types*.

The annotations for each reference vary in length and completeness; they are intended to give the gist of an article so the reader can determine whether it is relevant to his interests. The length of the abstract does not reflect the quality of the article.

Not only articles from journals are included, but also articles that have appeared in books. Books are listed under the appropriate subject category, and an additional *Books* section provides the reader with a list of entire volumes dealing with family therapy. (If a book contains only one or two relevant articles, it is not listed under *Books*, but the articles are indexed under the appropriate subjects.)

This bibliography is intended to cover the first two decades of family therapy and family interactional research. These were the formative years, and the list of references is as complete as we could make it with the resources available.

We wish to express our gratitude to Norman W. Bell, Ph.D., for his assistance with a number of articles in the social science field.

This bibliography would not have been possible without the dedicated secretarial help of Mrs. Irene Dinkin in New York, Mrs. Helen Morgan in Augusta, Georgia, Miss Sabra Perreten and Miss Judi Yabumoto in San Francisco, and Mrs. Carol Collins in Philadelphia. Also essential was the assistance of numerous librarians who helped find material and of many authors who sent reprints of their work and their own bibliographies of the family field.

IRA D. GLICK, M.D.
JAY HALEY

Contents

Included in this section are papers on the theory of family therapy as well as on special techniques. The emphasis is on the conjoint treatment of the whole family, but the section includes a few references to studies of members treated simultaneously in individual treatment. If the treatment involved several families in a session, the reference is not included here but under *Multiple Family Therapy*. If the focus is only on treating married couples and not on the whole family, the article is listed not here but under *Marriage Therapy*.

This section deals with articles on the treatment of several whole families together as well as references on groups of marital couples. (See also *Family Therapy—Theory and Technique* and *Marriage Therapy*.)

Included here are papers on the treatment of married couples. (Descriptions of marriages which do not emphasize treatment are listed under *Marital Description*.) The emphasis is on conjoint marital therapy, but a few papers are included describing husbands and wives treated in separate interviews. (See also *Family Therapy—Theory and Technique* and *Multiple Family Therapy*.)

Listed here are papers describing family therapy occurring in conjunction with some other procedure, such as placing a child in a foster home, using a day hospital, seeing members in individual or group therapy, or hospitalizing all family members.

This section emphasizes training in the practice of family therapy, but it includes articles on the general teaching of a family orientation.

1.6 Family Therapy Outcome   64

Included here are articles specifically focused on evaluating the results of family therapy, but also included are references to articles in which there is a mention of the outcome of a specific therapy approach.

1.7 Family Consideration in Individual Treatment   71

The papers listed here do not focus on treating the family but on taking the family into account when treating the individual. The need occasionally to see the parents of a child in treatment is emphasized here, as well as the need occasionally to see the spouse of a patient.

1.8 Family Diagnosis—Individual Orientation   77

Listed here are papers that are not about family therapy but are concerned with intake procedures in which the whole family is seen to gather more information about the individual "patient."

2. METHODS OF COLLECTING FAMILY DATA IN RESEARCH

2.1 Family Data—From Records   81

Papers listed here include studies based on government or hospital case records without contact with family members. (Q Sort procedures are included here.)

2.2 Family Data—From Individuals   85

This section includes research procedures in which the information about the family comes from questionnaires given to individuals, projective and other psychological tests of individuals, and interviews with individual family members.

2.3 Family Data—Observation of Group   105

Listed here are reports of studies in which the family members are brought together as a group for observation or testing. included are studies based upon participant observation, such as a conjoint family interview, and family testing, where the interaction is categorized by the use of observers working with actual behavior or tape or film recordings. This section also includes references dealing with home visits.

2.4 Family Data—Experimentation   124

Included here are only those family studies in which the results are obtained by some method other than observation, such as pencil-and-paper results or instrument records.

2.5 Research Theory and Review   127

This section includes articles on the theoretical issues in family research and articles reviewing different research approaches. The sections that include different methods of gathering data also include studies that deal with these issues. (See also *Family Theory*.)

2.6 Family Theory   130

This is a general category for papers about theories of the family. Communication studies of interaction, organizational models applicable to families, articles on stages of family life, family strengths, and kinship theories are listed here. (See also *Ecology of the Family* and *Research Theory and Review*.)

3. FAMILY DESCRIPTION

3.1 Marital Description   159

Included here are papers describing married couples but not the whole family. Some papers on marriage therapy are cross-referenced here, but generally papers describing marriage are listed here and those emphasizing the treatment of marriages are listed under *Marriage Therapy*.

3.2 Sibling Studies   170

Papers listed here deal with the siblings in families in which a member is an "identified patient."

3.3 Family—Multiple Generation   173

Included here are papers dealing with extended kin and other multi-generational involvements. The emphasis is on the network of relatives wider than the nuclear family.

3.4 Family Crisis Studies   178

The emphasis here is on times of crisis in families or on the treatment of crises.

3.5 Ecology of the Family   181

The family in the community is the emphasis in this section. Included are discussions of family involvement with schools, gangs, or a network of helpers; articles on effects of hospitalization of a family member; and studies making cross-cultural comparisons. (See also *Family Theory*.)

4. TYPES OF FAMILIES

4.1 Contrasting Family Types   186

Listed here are papers dealing with the problem of classifying families into types, as well as papers contrasting one type of family with a control type. For example, a comparison of families of good and bad premorbid schizophrenics would be listed here, as would studies contrasting schizophrenic and normal families.

4.2 Family Member Diagnosed Schizophrenic   202

4.3 Family Member Diagnosed as a School Problem   234

This section includes not only papers on school problems but also papers dealing with families of mentally retarded children.

4.4 Family Has a "Personality Disorder" Adolescent   237

Listed here are papers that focus on adolescent problem children and their families. It includes discussions of families with a child defined as delinquent. Suicide is also included in papers listed here.

4.5 Family Member Diagnosed Neurotic   243

Included here are studies of families in which a member is said to be nonpsychotic but a problem and families in which no specific type of pathology is indicated.

4.6 Family—Physical Health   247

Papers listed here deal with family health and medical problems as well as with specific types of physical abnormalities as they relate to the family. Psychosomatic studies are included here.

4.7 Low-Socioeconomic Families   251

5. LITERATURE SURVEYS   253

Listed here are papers that survey the literature of a particular aspect of the family as well as papers that present a large amount of bibliographical material.

6. BOOKS   260

Books, including collections of articles, are listed here and also under the different subject categories.

7. FILMS   270

A number of relevant videotapes and films have been made by individuals or groups. Those listed here are ones easily available for general distribution.

1.1 FAMILY THERAPY — THEORY AND TECHNIQUE

ACKERMAN, N.W., "The Art of Family Therapy," in N. W. Ackerman (Ed.), <u>Family Therapy in Transition</u>, Boston, Little, Brown, 1970.
A brief, personal comment on family interviewing with the emphasis upon using first names with a family, and humor. "The art of family therapy is, in fact, a unique, spontaneous expression of self in the therapeutic role."

ACKERMAN, N.W., "The Emergence of Family Diagnosis and Treatment: A Personal View," <u>Psychotherapy</u>, 4, 125-129, 1967.
An essay on the history of family diagnosis and therapy. The role of the family in the etiology of psychopathology was a long-standing "blind spot." Family psychotherapy is gradually developing as a form of psychotherapy with indications and contraindications of its own. Comparison studies with other forms of psychotherapy should be done.

ACKERMAN, N. W., "Emergence of Family Psychotherapy on the Present Scene," in H. Stein, (Ed.), <u>Contemporary Psychotherapies</u>, New York, Free Press, 1961.
A clinical essay reviewing the development of family therapy, rationale, diagnostic techniques, and methods of treatment. It gives an overview of the field of family therapy, with highlights of the "more important concepts pertinent to the family approach to diagnosis and therapy."

ACKERMAN, N.W., "Eulogy for Don D. Jackson," <u>Fam. Proc.</u>, 9, 117-122, 1970.
A tribute to one of the major figures in the field of family therapy and research.

ACKERMAN, N. W., "The Family Approach to Marital Disorders," in B. Greene (Ed.), <u>The Psychotherapies of Marital Disharmony</u>, New York, Free Press, 1955.
A clinical essay describing rationale and techniques of family therapy. A diagnostic scheme for understanding the problem, treatment goals, and techniques are described.

ACKERMAN, N. W., "Family Focussed Therapy of Schizophrenia," in A. Scher and H. Davis (Eds.), <u>The Outpatient Treatment of Schizophrenia</u>, New York, Grune & Stratton, 1960.
Given at a conference on the outpatient treatment of schizophrenia, this clinical essay is on family therapy and on schizophrenia and the family. The family is relevant not only to the course and outcome but also to the origin of schizophrenia, and treatment should include the whole family together rather than only the identified patient. Techniques of treating the family are described.

ACKERMAN, N. W., "Family Interviewing: The Study Process," in N. W. Ackerman (Ed.), <u>Family Therapy in Transition</u>, Boston, Little, Brown, 1970.
A discussion of family interviewing, indications for family therapy, the process with case examples, and deeper motivation.

ACKERMAN, N. W., "Family Psychotherapy and Psychoanalysis: Implications of Difference," <u>Fam. Proc.</u>, 1, 30-43, 1962.
An essay on the techniques of family psychotherapy, followed by a comparison with psychoanalytic concepts and therapy. The two treatment methods are viewed as complementary -- "psychoanalytic treatment focuses on the internal manifestations of disorder of the individual personality. Family treatment focuses on the behavior disorders of a system of interacting personalities, the family group."

ACKERMAN, N. W., "Family Psychotherapy — Theory and Practice," <u>Amer. J. Psychother.</u>, 20, 405-414, 1966.
A discussion of the theory, history, methods, goals, and future of family therapy. Functions of the therapist are stressed.

ACKERMAN, N. W., "Family Psychotherapy Today: Some Areas of Controversy," <u>Compr. Psychiat.</u>, 7, 375-388, 1966.
A detailed discussion of thirteen controversial areas relating to family therapy, i.e.,

rationale, goals, role of transference, definition, indications and contraindications, "depth" material, acting out, "intimate or secret" matters, relation to other forms of treatment, strength, and weaknesses, and who is qualified to do family treatment.

ACKERMAN, N. W., "Family Therapy," in S. Arieti (Ed.), American Handbook of Psychiatry, Vol. III, New York, Basic Books, 1966.
A chapter in a textbook of psychiatry covering the following aspects of family therapy: theoretical background, homeodynamics, diagnosis and interventions rationale, indications and contraindications.

ACKERMAN, N. W. (Ed.), Family Therapy in Transition, Boston, Little, Brown, 1970.
A two-part book, with the first part a series of papers by different authors on the theory and practice of family therapy. The second part includes critical incidents with discussion by different family therapists.

ACKERMAN, N. W., "A Family Therapy Session," in N. W. Ackerman (Ed.), Expanding Theory and Practice in Family Therapy, New York, Family Service Association of America, 1967.
A transcript of an interview by the therapist with a family of what actually happened as recorded on audiotape, plus the therapist's interpretive comments.

ACKERMAN, N. W., "Further Comments on Family Psychotherapy," in M. Stein (Ed.), Contemporary Psychotherapies, New York, Free Press, 1961.
A clinical essay specifically focussing on techniques of family therapy. Family therapy starts from first contact with the family and a case example is presented in support of some of the theoretical notions. Several contraindications of family therapy are described.

ACKERMAN, N. W., "The Future of Family Psychotherapy," in N. W. Ackerman (Ed.), Expanding Theory and Practice in Family Therapy, New York, Family Service Association of America, 1967.
A clinical essay tracing the development of family therapy, defining it, and pointing out what it is used for. Shortcomings of psychoanalysis are described, as are weaknesses in group therapy and child therapy. Family Therapy is therapy "in vivo, not in vitro." It could become the "very core of the newly emerging community psychiatry."

ACKERMAN, N. W., "To Catch a Thief," in N. W. Ackerman (Ed.), Family Therapy in Transition, Boston, Little, Brown, 1970.
A family interview presented verbatim with comments by the therapist on what was going on.

ACKERMAN, N. W., Treating the Troubled Family, New York, Basic Books, 1966.
A book concerned with techniques of family therapy which includes discussions of family crises, goals, the process of illness developing in the family, functions of the therapist, treatment of husband and wife, treatment when the family includes children, and some special techniques in dealing with the "scapegoat." 306 pp.

ACKERMAN, N. W., BEATMAN, F. L., and SHERMAN, S. N. (Eds.), Expanding Theory and Practice in Family Therapy, New York, Family Service Association of America, 1967.
A collection of new material on family therapy dealing with its future, need for a systems approach, family therapy as a unifying force in social work, intergenerational aspects, family therapy in the home, and multiple impact therapy. There are two panel discussions, one on the classification of family types, and the other on communication within the family. There are also papers on problems and principles, training family therapists through "live" supervision, and an actual family therapy session with comments by the therapists on why certain interventions were made. 182 pp.

ACKERMAN, N. W., BEATMAN, F.L., and SHERMAN, S. N. (Eds.), Exploring the Base for Family Therapy, New York, Family Service Association of America, 1961.

A collection of new material on family therapy including papers on the biosocial unity of the family, concept of the family in casework, family diagnosis and therapy, dynamics, prevention, epidemiology, and research. 159 pp.

ACKERMAN, N. W., and BEHRENS, M., "The Family Approach in Levels of Intervention," Amer. J. Psychother., 22, 5-14, 1968.
Family therapy is seen as complementary to individual therapy. Rationale and applicability are discussed in order to make clear the central thesis of the paper that treatment must be problem-oriented, not technique-oriented; that is, different levels of intervention are used depending on the family and the stage of treatment.

ACKERMAN, N. W., and FRANKLIN, P. F., "Family Dynamics and the Reversibility of Delusional Formation: A Case Study in Family Therapy," in I. Boszormenyi-Nagy and J. L. Framo (Eds.), Intensive Family Therapy, New York, Harper & Row, 1965.
A report on a case of a 16-year-old schizophrenic and her family in which treatment "of the whole family seemed to move toward reversal of the patient's psychotic experience." Interview data and comment are provided.

ALEXANDER, I.E., "Family Therapy," Marriage Fam. Liv., 25, 146-154, 1963.
A review of the history of family therapy followed by a description of the author's experience with family therapy combined with other methods of treatment. Typical processes during family therapy are described, as well as indications for this form of treatment.

ANDERSON, D., "Nursing Therapy with Families," Perspect. Psychiat. Care, 1, 21-27, 1969.
An essay on the use of family therapy with particular focus on its use by nurses in both inpatient and outpatient settings. Theory, rationale, and techniques appropriate are described with liberal use of case examples.

ARLEN, M. S., "Conjoint Therapy and the Corrective Emotional Experience," Fam. Proc., 5, 91-104, 1966.
The use of family therapy with families containing a person with severe character disorder described within a framework of providing a corrective emotional experience.

ATTNEAVE, C. L. "Therapy in Tribal Settings and Urban Network Intervention," Fam. Proc., 8, 192-210, 1969.
A comparison of network therapy and interventions in a network-clan of a tribal minority culture. An example of treatment with an Indian tribe is contrasted with urban network treatment where the clan-like social structure must be reconstituted.

AUGENBRAUN, B., READ, H., and FRIEDMAN, D., "Brief Intervention as a Preventive Force in Disorders of Early Childhood," Amer. J. Orthopsychiat. 37, 697-702, 1967.
A report of a technique used in pediatric practice where the identified patient has a symptom (such as bedwetting, nightmares, etc.) with no apparent organic etiology. It is based on the idea that these may be symptoms indicating underlying family problems. Families are seen together rather than separately. Three family interviews with follow-ups 6 to 9 months later was the technique.

BARDILL, D., "Family Therapy in an Army Mental Hospital Hygiene Clinic," Soc. Casework, 44, 452-457, 1963.

From an outpatient Army mental hygiene clinic, the author presents his experience
in using family therapy with adolescents. Manifest problems represent a breakdown
in the family system. Aims and techniques are discussed and illustrated by clinical
examples.

BARTOLETTI, M., "Conjoint Family Therapy with Clinic Team in a Shopping Plaza," Int.
    J. Soc. Psychiat., 15, 250-257, 1969.
A clinical paper describing the operation of a community mental health clinic which
set up an office in a shopping center. Here conjoint family therapy was done for
brief periods. Personnel included a psychiatrist, psychologist, and social worker.
Treatment plan was divided into a diagnostic treatment period. A variety of interventions use various combinations of family members.

BEATMAN, F. L., "Intergenerational Aspects of Family Therapy," in N. W. Ackerman (Ed.),
    Expanding Theory and Practice in Family Therapy, New York, Family Service Associa-
    tion of America. 1967.
A clinical essay focussing on indications or contraindications for bringing in the third
generation in family therapy. The third generation often incapacitates the nuclear family. Several case examples are presented in support of bringing in the third generation.
The clinical rule of thumb is not on sociologic lines, but rather "lines of meaningful
relationships and conflicts."

BEATMAN, F. L., "The Training and Preparation of Workers for Family-Group Treatment,"
    Soc. Casework, 45, 202-208, 1964.
An essay describing the method of training for social workers learning family therapy
(here called "family-group treatment"). Group processes as a method for supervision
are used in preference to individual supervision because of "the requirements of
treating the family rather than the individual." Specific methods used and discussed
here are group supervision, sitting in on a family session, viewing through a one way
screen, films, and tape recordings.

BEATMAN, F. L., "Trends Toward Preventive Practice in Family Service," in N. W.
    Ackerman, F. L. Beatman, and S. Sherman (Eds.), Exploring the Base for Family
    Therapy, New York, Family Service Association of America, 1961.
A clinical essay with stress on prevention of serious emotional disorder in the family.
The family agency seems the logical agency to do this. Schema includes taking an
"inventory," fortifying the healthy components in the family, and directing the family
for further help where needed.

BEATMAN, F. L., SHERMAN, S., and LEADER, A., "Current Issues in Family Treatment,"
    Soc. Casework, 47, 75-81, 1966.
A clinical essay on controversial issues in family treatment. There is a discussion
of privacy and confidentiality; the effect on children of family therapy (which is felt
to be overstressed in view of the fact that children usually know the problems prior to
therapy); whom to include in sessions; how to formulate a treatment plan, and a discussion of transference reactions.

BECKER, J., "Good Premorbid' Schizophrenic Wives and their Husbands," Fam. Proc.,
    2, 34-51, 1963.
A report of conjoint family therapy with seven married female schizophrenics and their
husbands. Their backgrounds, premorbid marital life, and course of illness are described. Results of treatment were that "five families appeared to benefit substan-
tially, one somewhat, and one not at all."

BEELS, C.C., and FERBER, A.S., "Family Therapy: A View," Fam. Proc., 8, 280-318, 1969.
A "personal view of the literature of family therapy" with an evaluation of the
teaching and practice of different therapists.

BEHRENS, M. and ACKERMAN, N., "The Home Visit as an Aid in Family Diagnosis and
    Therapy," Soc. Casework, 37, 11-19, 1956.

A paper based on the authors' clinical work in which the home visit is used as an aid in family diagnosis and therapy when the identified patient in a child. Observations are based on family interaction patterns, physical environment and atmosphere of the home. A case example is given to illustrate the authors' technique.

BELL, J. E., "The Family Group Therapist: An Agent of Change," Int. J. Group Psychother., 14, 72-83, 1964.
An essay on the therapist's role in family therapy. Indications for whom to include, the theoretical basis for seeing the family as a group, and the task of the therapist with particular emphasis on change (rather than insight).

BELL, J. E., Family Group Therapy, Public Health Monograph No. 64, Dept. of Health, Education and Welfare, 1961.
A manual of family therapy which discusses rationale for and the techniques of family therapy phase by phase from the first conference through the terminal phase. 52 pp.

BELL, J. E., "The Future of Family Therapy," Fam. Proc., 9, 127-141, 1970.
Speculations about the future of family therapy with the emphasis upon the future of the family, different settings for family treatment, and prevention of family problems.

BELL, J. E., "Recent Advances in Family Group Therapy," J. Child Psychol. Psychiat., 3, 1-15, 1962.
A review of family group therapy with various definitions of the family and an emphasis upon the social psychological approach to the unit. Includes a discussion of the development of the family group, its stability, its problems, and the process of bringing about change.

BELL, J. E., "A Theoretical Position for Family Group Therapy," Fam. Proc., 2, 1-14, 1963.
An essay delineating some of the author's thoughts on family therapy over the past eleven years. The author emphasizes that right from the onset of therapy the focus should be on the group rather than the individual. Contrast with group therapy is made, some questions of technique discussed, and a process of family change is set forth.

BODIN, A., "Conjoint Family Therapy," in W. Vinacke (Ed.), Readings in General Psychology, New York, American Book, 1968.
This article is part of a book on general psychology and is written as part of a section on abnormal behavior in therapy. It gives an overview of conjoint family therapy as it is evolved and the theory behind it — focussing on general systems theory, communication theory, social learning, and interactional concepts; its techniques; and comparisons of individual and family therapy. Finally, an attempt is made to give an overview of its place in the fields of psychiatry and psychology. Interpersonal actions are increasingly viewed as the context in which intrapersonal phenomena emerge.

BODIN, A., "Videotape Applications to Training Family Therapists," J. Nerv. Ment. Dis., 148, 25--262, 1969.
Uses of videotape, both in training and in treatment, are described. Training applications include: (1) taping prior to particular courses, (2) tape libraries, (3) splitting audio and visual channels, (4) "on-line" feedback, (5) self-presentation exercises and (6) comparative analysis of a trainee's performance. Several different applications in regard to therapy are also presented.

BOSZORMENYI-NAGY, I., "Intensive Family Therapy as a Process," in I. Boszormenyi-Nagy and J. L. Framo (Eds.), Intensive Family Therapy, New York, Harper & Row, 1965.
"Intensive family therapy differs from all other mental health approaches in its

application of principles and techniques derived from dynamic individual psychotherapy and, to a lesser extent than might be supposed from group therapy, to helping all family members through direct observation and modification of their interactions." A report on the treatment of 50 families is included with case illustrations.

BOSZORMENYI-NAGY, I., and FRAMO, J. L., "Family Concept of Hospital Treatment of Schizophrenia," in J. Masserman (Ed.) Current Psychiatric Therapy, Vol. II, New York, Grune & Stratton, 1962.
An essay describing a research project on an inpatient psychiatric unit investigating schizophrenia. Psychopathology of the family of the schizophrenic has been neglected. To this end, hospital treatment is oriented around a number of techniques involving the family. One of these techniques is conjoint family therapy, which had been conducted with 12 selected families over a three-year period. Responses to these changing forms of treatment are described.

BOSZORMENYI-NAGY, I., and FRAMO, J. L., (Eds.), Intensive Family Therapy: Theoretical and Practical Aspects, New York, Harper and Row, 1965.
A collection of new articles which includes a review of the literature; theory of relationships; rationale, dynamics and techniques; family therapy with schizophrenics in inpatient and outpatient settings; indications and contraindications, countertransference, and research on family dynamics. 507 pp.

BOVERMAN, M., and ADAMS, J. R., "Collaboration of Psychiatrist and Clergyman: A Case Report," Fam. Proc., 3, 251-272, 1964.
A description of a psychotic patient and family treated in collaboration. The different functions of psychiatrist and clergyman are discussed, with each presenting his view of the case.

BOWEN, M., "Family Psychotherapy," Amer. J. Orthopsychiat., 31, 40-60, 1961.
A discussion of the research program where parents and their schizophrenic offspring lived together on a psychiatric ward. The paper includes a description of the history of the project, the sample of families, and the theoretical approach. The emphasis is upon the family as a unit of illness rather than upon individuals in the family group. Principles and techniques of family therapy emphasize utilizing the family leader, avoiding individual relationships with family members, and not accepting the position of omnipotence into which the family attempts to place the therapist. Results are discussed and examples given with case material.

BOWEN, M., "Family Psychotherapy with Schizophrenia in the Hospital and in Private Practice," in I. Boszormenyi-Nagy and J. L. Framo (Eds.), Intensive Family Therapy, New York, Harper & Row, 1965.
A discussion of a theory of the family and of family therapy with sections on differences between family and individual theory, a summary of the family theory of emotional illness with the emphasis upon schizophrenia, the parental transmission of problems to the child, the clinical approach to modify the family transmition process, and principles and techniques of this family therapy approach.

BOWEN, M., "The Use of Family Theory in Clinical Practice," Compr. Psychiat., 7, 345-373, 1966.
An essay based on the author's clinical experience describing the history, current status, and future of the "family movement." The family is discussed as a system of a number of different kinds. The "medical model" is not used. Clinical uses and techniques of family therapy are discussed on the basis of the author's theoretical orientation.

BRANDZEL, E., "Working Through the Oedipal Struggle in Family Unit Sessions," Soc. Casework, 46, 414-422, 1965.
A discussion of the use of family-unit sessions to help a family work through its problems with a young adolescent. Case examples are given.

BRODEY, W. M., Changing the Family, New York, Potter, 1968.
A personal view of families with many styles of family life described. "The stories..
..are little descriptions of families mixed with just enough comment and contrast to
tell their own story and insist that you listen and feel...."

BRODEY, W. M., "A Cybernetic Approach to Family Therapy," in G. H. Zuk and I.
    Boszormenyi-Nagy (Eds.), Family Therapy and Disturbed Families, Palo Alto,
    Science & Behavior Books, 1967.
In this paper "the family is conceptualized as a self-perpetuating organism with a
built-in regulatory system. Family therapy is directed to altering the family's
self regulation...."

BRODEY, W.M., and HAYDEN, M., "Intrateam Reactions: Their Relation to the Conflicts
    of the Family in Treatment," Amer. J. Orthopsychiat., 27, 349-356, 1957.
A clinical report emphasizing the notion that reactions of treating personnel to each
other are in part a reenactment of conflicts of the family. Data were obtained from
an outpatient child guidance clinic team of psychotherapist and caseworker. Five case
examples were given to support this hypothesis. By focusing on the reaction of the
workers, significant dynamics trends can be identified and therapy can be accelerated.
The building of family conflicts that influence the intrateam reactions depends upon
the power of the family conflict and the sensitivity of the team equilibrium to this
particular stress.

BROWN, S., "Family Therapy Viewed in Terms of Resistance to Change," in I.M. Cohen (Ed),
    Psychiatric Research Report 20, Washington. D.C., American Psychiatric Association,
    1966.
Family therapy from a psychoanalytic and "child guidance" point of view with the emphasis on resistance to change. Case examples are given.

BULBULYAN, A., "Psychiatric Nurse as Family Therapist," Perspect. Psychiat. Care,
    7, 58-68, 1969.
From a community mental health center, a psychiatric nurse presents a case in which
she used family therapy. Dynamics and treatment techniques are presented. It is
felt that this is an important technique for psychiatric nurses to use in such a
setting.

BURKS, H., and SERRANO, A., "The Use of Family Therapy and Brief Hospitalization,"
    Dis. Nerv. Syst., 26, 804-806, 1965.
Experience with setting up an inpatient service in conjunction with an outpatient
child guidance clinic (which had a strong bias to family therapy) is described.
Patients were between 12 and 16, and diagnosis varied from neurosis to psychosis.
Hospitalization was short (usually under two months) and was family oriented, using
techniques adapted from the multiple impact therapy technique. Results, including
a one-year follow-up, with 25 patients are described.

CARROLL, E. J., "Family Therapy: Some Observations and Comparisons," Fam. Proc.,
    3, 178-185, 1964.
A discussion of family therapy with comparisons with individual therapy. Differences
between the two methods are listed. Four kinds of operations in the field of family
therapy are noted: emphasis upon the family as individuals, focus upon shifting
dyads such as mother-child and therapist-child, focus upon the family unit with the
patient only as a messenger for the family, and the emphasis upon the family and a
segment of the community as an open system.

CARROLL, E., J., "Treatment of the Family as a Unit," Penn. Med., 63, 57-62, 1960.
A lecture comparing psychotherapy and pscyhoanalysis to family therapy. Rationale
for this form of treatment and techniques for working with a couple as well as with
an entire family are described. One case example is given in illustration.

CARROLL, E. J., CAMBOR, C. G., LEOPOLD, J. V., MILLER, M. D., and REIS, W. J.,
    "Psychotherapy of Marital Couples," Fam. Proc., 2, 25-33, 1963.
A general discussion of indications for, advantages and disadvantages of family
therapy. Two case reports are given. Of six cases seen by the group, four made
significant gains, while the other two were unimproved.

CHARNY, I., "Family Interviews in Redefining a 'Sick' Child's Role in the Family
    Problem," Psychol. Rep., 10, 577-578, 1962.
From a child guidance clinic it is suggested that family therapy offers significant
advantages over individual treatment of parent and child at the beginning of treatment. The problem in the family can then be defined, the child can be released from
the scapegoat role, and the parents allowed to be involved in treatment.

CLOWER, C., and BRODY, L., "Conjoint Family Therapy in Outpatient Practice, "Amer.
    J. Psychother., 18, 670-677, 1964.
This essay, based on the author's clinical work in an outpatient practice, describes
techniques, selection criteria, indications, and treatment goals, for conjoint family
therapy in an outpatient setting. In these respects it is compared to both individual
and group therapy.

COHEN, I. M., (Ed.), Family Structure, Dynamics and Therapy, Psychiatric Research
    Report 20, Washington, D.C., American Psychiatric Association, 1966.
A collection of new material which includes discussions of research methods, family
functioning, communication styles, dynamics, family myths, family relations where
there is a retarded reader, family relations where the patient has 14+6 cps EEG positive spike patterns, family resistances, methods for family work-ups, techniques for
dealing with the low socioeconomic class family, effects of videotape playback on
family members, family therapy as an alternative for psychiatric hospitalization, use
of heterosexual co-therapists, and multiple impact therapy as a teaching device.

CORNWELL, G., "Scapegoating: A Study in Family Dynamics," Amer. J. Nurs., 67, 1862-
    1867, 1967.
In a study of two lower socioeconomic class families which included mother and son,
the following were described: how the scapegoating was done, how each took mutually
reinforcing roles in the scapegoating, and a discussion of how to change the process.

COYLE, G. L., "Concepts Relevant to Helping the Family as a Group," Soc. Casework,
    43, 347-354, 1962.
An essay on the concepts of the family group as the unit of treatment. It is suggested that three trends are being classed together in the family movement: an
increased emphasis on the relationships of the individual with his immediate family
members, the attempt to use concepts about the family drawn from the social sciences,
and research into small group behavior. A framework of the social process within the
family group is offered with six aspects, or dimensions.

CURRY, A. E., "The Family Therapy Situation as a System," Fam. Proc., 5, 131-141,
    1966.
A discussion of the processes which occur between a family unit and the family
therapist which involve neutralizing the therapist, re-establishing the family's pre-
therapy equilibrium, and disrupting the overall family therapy situation. Processes
of coalition, coalescence, and coagulation are presented with examples.

CURRY, A., "Toward the Phenomenological Study of the Family," Existential Psychiat.,
    6, 35-44, 1967.
A paper exploring the theoretical basis for conjoint family therapy from the "phenomenological" point of view (defined as observing the phenomenon as it manifests itself).
Modes of interrelating, affective responses, and methods of communication of both
normal and pathological families are analyzed from this point of view.

CUTTER, A. V., and HALLOWITZ, D., "Diagnosis and Treatment of the Family Unit with
     Respect to the Character-Disordered Youngster," J. Amer. Acad. Child Psychiat.,
     1, 605-618, 1962.
A description of a treatment program of families with children with a diagnosis of
character disorder. There are "56 cases currently active" and the results indicate
that 60% "have been making consistently good progress." Description of the treatment
with case examples is provided.

CUTTER, A. V.; and HALLOWITZ, D., "Different Approaches to Treatment of the Child and
     the Parents," Amer. J. Orthopsychiat., 32, 152-158, 1962.
The authors contrast the point of view of the "child as the patient and the parents
as collaborators" with the "recognition of the importance of familial relationships
and their impact on the developing child." They offer seven treatment approaches
which are different combinations of family members and therapists with the criteria
for their application. Diagnosis and treatment are directed to child, mother, and
father and the pathogenic weaknesses and breakdowns in their relationships with each
other.

DUHRSSEN, A., "Praventive Missnahmen in der Familie," Psychother. Psychosom., 16,
     319-322, 1968.
This article focusses on the preventive aspects of family therapy. Characteristics
of family life in other cultures are first described, and then psychopathology of
specific family types is presented. A case report is presented in support of this
thesis.

DWYER, J. H., MENK, M. C., and VAN HOUTEN, C., "The Caseworker's Role in Family
     Therapy," Fam. Proc. 4, 21-31, 1965.
An approach to family therapy developed in a residential treatment center for children.
The whole family is seen by a psychiatrist and then a caseworker sees the parents while
the psychiatrist sees the child. The caseworker deals with the parents' responses to
the family sessions.

EHRENWALD, J., Neurosis in the Family and Patterns of Psychosocial Defense, New York,
     Harper & Row, 1963.
A collection of some new and some previously published material including chapters on
family traits and attitudes, patterns of family interaction, patterns of sharing and
parent-child symbiosis, a description of a family with obsessive-compulsive personality, dynamics from both an intrapersonal and interpersonal point of view, patterns
of contagion, sections on the Mozart and Picasso families, psychiatric epidemiology,
pattern changeability, and interpersonal dynamics in family therapy. 203 pp.

EIST, H. I., and MANDEL, A.U., "Family Treatment of Ongoing Incest Behavior," Fam.
     Proc., 7, 216-232, 1968.
A description of a case in which there was ongoing incest behavior. Family treatment
was used and the techniques are discussed.

ELLES, G., "Family Treatment from a Therapeutic Community," Confin. Psychiat., 8,
     9-14, 1965.
From an inpatient ward where the identified patient had a personality disorder, some
families were treated with some or all members of the family receiving individual
therapy, while other families were treated by family therapy in the home. Discussion
of experiences, but no data, is presented comparing the two forms of treatment.

EMDE, R., BOYD, C., and MAYO, G., "The Family Treatment of Folie a Deux," Psychiat.
     Quart., 42, 698-711, 1968.
A case report of a mother and daughter who shared delusions. Family dynamics which
explain this phenomenon are presented. Treatment consisted of family therapy,
milieu therapy, and phenothiazines.

ENGLISH, O. S., SCHEFLEN, A. E., HAMPE, W. W., and AUERBACH, A. H., Strategy and
     Structure in Psychotherapy, Behavioral Studies Monograph No. 2, Eastern Penn-
     sylvania Psychiatric Institute, 1965.
A companion volume to Stream and Structure of Communicational Behavior (A. E.
Scheflen) which includes three research studies of the family therapy interview by
Whitaker and Malone.

EPSTEIN, N. B., "Family Therapy", Canad. Ment. Health, 10, 5-9, 1962.
A brief clinical report on the current status of family therapy. There is a review
of transactional vs. interactional dynamics and different techniques of family
therapy. A sound conceptual framework for family therapy based on rigorous research
is urged.

EPSTEIN, N. B. and CLEGHORN, J., "The Family Transactional Approach in General Hospital
     Psychiatry: Experiences, Problems, and Principles," Compr. Psychiat., 7, 389-396,
     1966.
This paper deals with the experiences and problems arising, and principles derived
from, the introduction of concepts of family dynamics and family therapy in the
psychiatry departments of two general hospitals. It was used in the outpatient
department, community department, inpatient service and the day hospital. Ongoing
supervision for family as well as for individual therapy is stressed.

EPSTEIN, N. B., "Treatment of the Emotionally Disturbed Pre-School Child: A Family
     Approach," Canad. Med. Ass. J., 85, 937-940, 1961.
A clinical essay focussing on the assumption that when the identified patient is a
child, the family must be included in the treatment. First a family diagnostic interview is held, followed by a staff discussion of the dynamics and further work-up is
recommended. Possible therapeutic programs prescribed include 1) treatment of the
family as a unit, 2) two or more members of the family are seen as a group, dependency
upon "exigencies" arising as the treatment progresses, 3) treatment as individual
psychotherapy for the identified patient, or 4) treatment including the "significant
dyad", e.g., mother-child, 5) the child may be placed in group, or in individual plus
group therapy. A case example is presented to illustrate the approach.

ERICKSON, M., "The Identification of a Secure Reality," Fam. Proc., 1, 294-303, 1962.
Case report of treatment of an eight-year-old boy who was progressively defiant to
his mother. The author's formulation of the case and treatment with boy and mother
are described.

ESTERSON, A., COOPER, D., and LAING, R., "Results of Family-Oriented Therapy with
     Hospitalized Schizophrenics," Brit. Med. J., 2, 1462-1465, 1965.
A report of a clinical study of 20 male and 22 female schizophrenics treated by conjoint family milieu therapy plus tranquilizers (given in "reduced" doses). No individual psychotherapy or other somatic treatment was used. Results indicated that all
patients were discharged within one year of admission, the average length of stay was
3 months, and 17% were readmitted within a year of discharge. Of 32 patients discharged to jobs, 26 worked for a whole year after discharge, two for from six months
to a year, and four not at all. There was no control group, but the readmission rate
was about the same as with other forms of treatment. During the follow-up period,
less than half of the patients were on psychotropic medication.

FELDMAN, M. J., "Privacy and Conjoint Family Therapy," Fam. Proc., 6, 1-9, 1967.
A discussion of whether greater or lesser degree of privacy effects the nature of
therapeutic disclosures by contrasting individual and conjoint family therapy. There
is no simple relationship between degree of privacy and kind of scope of disclosure,
and the private nature of individual therapy led to an ethical position which elevates an individual's welfare above, and even to the detriment, of others.

FERBER, A. S., and BEELS, C. C., "Changing Family Behavior Programs," in N. W.
     Ackerman (Ed.), Family Therapy in Transition, Boston, Little, Brown, 1970.

A description of an approach to family therapy in which "the family comes to the therapist with a script which they have repeatedly rehearsed, but which they cannot get into production.... His job is to make them aware of the staging, gestures, blocking, and business, and then help them restage it or rewrite it if need be." Case illustrations are provided.

FERREIRA, A. J., "Family Myths," in I. M. Cohen (Ed.), Psychiatric Research Reports 20, American Psychiatric Association, 1966.
A discussion of the myths families develop with an illustration of the contrast of a family's report and their behavior in a test setting. The relevance of family myths in family therapy is discussed.

FERREIRA, A. J., "Family Therapy: A New Era in Psychiatry," Western Med., 8, 83-87, 1967.
A clinical essay focussing on development, rationale, goals, and techniques of family therapy. The difference in orientation from individual therapy is described. Family therapy is seen as more than "a new technique in psychotherapy;" it constitutes, in fact, the beginning of an entirely new chapter on understanding behavior.

FERREIRA, A., "Psychosis and Family Myth," Amer. J. Psychother., 21, 186-197, 1967.
In this essay, several case examples are given in support of the notion that psychotic behavior is a manifestation of not only the individual, but also as an elaboration of preexisting family myths "upon which the preservation of the relationship may depend." Family myths prevent change and are concretizations of the family's interactional patterns. Family therapy is suggested as a method of changing psychotic behavior.

FERREIRA, A., and WINTER, W., "Stability of Interactional Variables in Family Decision-Making," Arch. Gen. Psychiat., 14, 352-355, 1966.
In order to test the stability over time, and after family therapy, of three variables in family decision-making, 23 randomly selected families (10 abnormal and 13 normal) were retested six months after the original research project. The abnormal families had received therapy. Results indicated that there was no significant difference between the means observed in test and retests of the three variables for either normal or abnormal families. It is concluded that these three variables (spontaneous agreement, decision-time, and choice-fulfillment) were consistent over time and were not changed by family therapy.

FLECK, S., "Some General and Specific Indications for Family Therapy," Confin. Psychiat. 8, 27-36, 1965.
From the author's clinical work with in-patient schizophrenic families, indications for family therapy based on the stage of hospitalization are presented. The three phases are the admission phase, period of hospital adjustment, and the final reintegration with the community. Family therapy complements, but does not replace, other treatment modalities.

FLOMENHAFT, K., KAPLAN, D., and LANGSLEY, D. "Avoiding Psychiatric Hospitalization," Soc. Work, 14, 38-46, 1969.
One of a series of articles comparing "outpatient family crisis therapy" with psychiatric hospitalization. The methodology has been previously described. Results achieved by both of these two methods were equivalent. However, the authors stressed outpatient treatment is more economical and less "stigmatizing."

FORREST, T., "Treatment of the Father in Family Therapy," Fam. Proc., 8, 106-118, 1969.
A discussion of family therapy with special emphasis upon dealing with the father. The goals are to provide him emotional support, strengthen his sexual identity, and develop his skills as head of the family group.

FRAMO, J., "My Families, My Family," Voices, 4, 18-27, 1968.
In support of the idea that treating families revives feelings of the therapist toward

his own past and present family, the author has presented material from family sessions followed by his own thoughts and feelings. Material relating to childhood, marriage, parenthood, and adulthood are reviewed.

FRAMO, J. L., "Rationale and Techniques of Intensive Family Therapy," in I. Boszormen-
    yi-Nagy and J. L. Framo (Eds.), Intensive Family Therapy, New York, Harper & Row,
    1965.
A description of the principles derived from the family therapy approach at Eastern Pennsylvania Psychiatric Institute and the techniques found to be useful, promising, limited or anti-therapeutic.

FRAMO, J. L., "The Theory of the Technique of Family Treatment of Schizophrenia," Fam.
    Proc., 1, 119-131, 1962.
A rationale for and experiences with family therapy of schizophrenia is described, based on work with hospitalized young adult female schizophrenics, all of whom were also receiving intensive individual and group psychotherapy. Techniques used by this group are described.

FRANKLIN, P., "Family Therapy of Psychotics," Amer. J. Psychoanal., 29, 50-56, 1969.
A case report of a schizophrenic child and his parents and grandmother who were treated both individually and with family therapy over seven years. The author's thesis is that schizophrenic symptoms are a manifestation of a process that "involves the entire family." The identified patient and the family improved after treatment.

FREEMAN, V. J., "Differentiation of 'Unity' Family Therapy Approaches Prominent in the
    United States," Int. J. Soc. Psychiat., Special Edition 2, 35-46, 1964.
A review and classification of family therapy with six "unit" or "conjoint" methods described, as well as eight closely related approaches. Similarities between methods are discussed in terms of frame of reference, family composition and activity of the therapist. A bibliography of 53 items on family therapy is included.

FREEMAN, V. S., KLEIN, A. F., RIEHMAN, L. M., LUKOFF, I. F., and HEISEG, V. E.,
    "'Family Group Counseling' as Differentiated from Other 'Family Therapies,'" Int.
    J. Group Psychother., 13, 167-175, 1963.
An essay proposing treatment of the family using a "modification of social group work methods" which the authors call "family group counseling." The method focuses on group interactive, rather than individual intrapsychic processes. A schema is presented to differentiate this method from other types of family therapy and from other therapies.

FRIEDMAN, A. S., "Family Therapy as Conducted in the Home," Fam. Proc., 1, 132-140,
    1962.
A discussion of the rationale for, experiences with, and problems resulting from home visits of schizophrenic patients and their families.

FRIEDMAN, A. S., "The Incomplete Family in Family Therapy," Fam. Proc., 2, 288-301,
    1963.
A discussion of the incomplete family in treatment, with emphasis upon obstacles to progress in therapy if all members are not included. A case example is given with verbatim excerpts.

FRIEDMAN, A. S., "The 'Well' Sibling in the 'Sick' Family: A Contradiction," Int.
    J. Soc. Psychiat., Special Edition 2, 47-53, 1964.
A discussion of the function and importance of the sibling in treatment of families with a schizophrenic child. Emphasis is upon the sibling who is absent from the family therapy sessions, and it is said that typically this sibling is in "secret" alliance with one of the parents and the absence affects the outcome of the therapy. Clinical examples are given.

FRIEDMAN, A. S., BOSZORMENYI-NAGY, I., JUNGREIS, J. E., LINCOLN, G., MITCHELL, H., SONNE, J., SPECK, R., and SPIVACK, G., Psychotherapy for the Whole Family: Case Histories, Techniques, and Concepts of Family Therapy of Schizophrenia in the Home and Clinic, New York, Springer, 1965.
A collection of new material based on a research project on treatment of schizophrenia using family therapy done in the home. The papers cover rationale, experience with the study families, results of treatment, and problems and concepts in treatment. There is a section on a search for a conceptual model of family psychopathology. 354 pp.

GEHRKE, S., and KIRSCHENBAUM, M., "Survival Patterns in Family Conjoint Therapy," Fam. Proc., 6, 67-80, 1967.
A discussion of 20 families studied in family therapy with the emphasis upon different patterns of emotional survival myths in the family. Three types of family are contrasted: the repressive family, the delinquent family, and the suicidal family. The survival myth has to do with the illusion of family members that they must continue their existing family ways of relating to survive psychologically.

GERRISH, M., "The Family Therapist is a Nurse," Amer. J. Nurs., 68, 320-323, 1968.
One case example is presented in support of the family approach in treatment of a 52-year-old depressed housewife, her husband, and young daughter. Family therapy was done and it was reported that the family was functioning well "two years following treatment."

GOOLISHIAN, H. A., "A Brief Psychotherapy Program for Disturbed Adolescents," Amer. J. Orthopsychiat., 32, 142-148, 1962.
A report on the multiple impact psychotherapy of the youth development project of the University of Texas Medical Branch. The program is based on the assumptions that "in attempting psychotherapy with adolescents we were dealing with chronic pathological family interaction," and that behavioral changes in adolescents take place rapidly. With intensive brief psychotherapy a family can work toward self rehabilitation. The interdisciplinary team meets with the family group for two or three full days, with follow-up sessions six months and a year later. The procedural pattern is flexible and includes full family sessions, individual and overlapping interviews, and psychological testing. Variations in procedure and treatment goals are discussed.

GRALNICK, A., "Family Psychotherapy: General and Specific Considerations," Amer. J. Orthopsychiat., 32, 515-526, 1962.
A general discussion of family therapy with a partial review of the history. The procedure is described as "any psychotherapeutic approach to the primary patient which consciously includes other members of his family, seen either separately or jointly with the primary patient." The emphasis is upon family treatment of patients in an in-patient setting, with a focus upon the aims and the value of this approach.

GRALNICK, A., and SCHWEEN, P. H., "Family Therapy," in I. M. Cohen (Ed.), Psychiatric Research Report 20, Washington, D. C., American Psychiatric Association, 1966.
The traditional general practitioner "may be looked upon as the forerunner of the present-day psychiatric family-therapist." A discussion of experience leading to seeing the value of treating the family unit. Indications for family therapy, its purposes, and the importance of dealing with the family of the discharged patient are emphasized.

GRALNICK, A., and YELIN, G., "Family Therapy in a Private Hospital Setting," Curr. Psychiat. Ther., 9, 179-180, 1969.
A clinical report of family therapy as used in an inpatient hospital setting. Problems, technique, and rationale are discussed.

GREENBERG, I. M., GLICK, I. D., MATCH, S., and RIBACK, S. S., "Family Therapy: Indications and Rationale," Arch. Gen. Psychiat., 10, 7-25, 1964.

Indications for and results of family therapy with a series of 20 patients, mostly
schizophrenic, in an open hospital, in-patient setting. Indications list diagnostic
as well as therapeutic goals. Six-month follow-up results of 13 cases are presented,
and a rationale using ego, psychological, and group process terms is included. A review of the family therapy literature is presented.

GROSSER, G., and PAUL, N., "Ethical Issues in Family Group Therapy," Amer. J. Ortho-
    psychiat., 34, 875-885, 1964.
This paper is an essay focussed on two aspects of family therapy (1) effects of this
form of therapy on family solidarity and intrafamily relationships and (2) special features in the "doctor-patient" relationship. Therapist should be non-aligned when resolving conflicts, attempting to understand the conflicts and then letting the family
solve them in a more constructive manner than they had previously. Some of the ethical issues raised about family therapy have come from psychiatrists, rather than from
"the public." This may be due to "countertransference" problems of the therapist.

GROTJOHN, M., Psychoanalysis and the Family Neurosis, Norton, 1960.
A book based on clinical experience which combined psychoanalytic as well as interactional factors in the etiology of mental illness. He covers the history and etiology
of the development of family therapy, psychodynamics of health and complementary neurosis of a family, and treatment techniques, including the diagnostic interview, training
analysis, and family treatment, and the dynamics of the therapeutic process. 320 pp.

GROUP FOR THE ADVANCEMENT OF PSYCHIATRY, COMMITTEE ON THE FAMILY, The Field of Family
    Therapy, New York, 1970.
A report on the field of family therapy which is meant to be a "snapshot" taken during
the winter of 1966-67. Data are based upon a questionnaire answered by 312 persons who
considered themselves family therapists, as well as on the opinions of the members of
the family committee. The work deals with the practitioners of family therapy, families typically entering treatment, goals and conceptual approaches, techniques used and
possible ethical problems.

GROUP FOR THE ADVANCEMENT OF PSYCHIATRY, COMMITTEE ON THE FAMILY, Integration and Con-
    flict in Family Behavior, Report No. 27, Topeka, Kansas, 1954.
A report by the Committee on the Family of GAP dealing with organizing data on the
study of the family. It discusses the relation of the family to the social system,
the system of values to which the family is oriented, and Spanish-American family
patterns as well as American middle class family patterns. 67 pp.

GUERNEY, B., and GUERNEY, L. F., "Choices in Initiating Family Therapy," Psychotherapy,
    1, 119-123, 1964.
A discussion of the choices to be made when doing family therapy, such as which members to include, whether to have individual sessions as well, and number of therapists.

HALEY, J., "Approaches to Family Therapy," Int. J. Psychiat., 9, 233-242, 1970.
A description of the differences in premises and approach of the beginning and the experienced family therapist.

HALEY, J. (Ed.) Changing Families: A Family Therapy Reader, New York, Grune &
    Stratton, 1971.
A textbook bringing together 23 articles describing different approaches to family
therapy. Both previously published and new articles are included, as well as an
extensive bibliography.

HALEY, J., "Family Therapy: A Radical Change," in J. Haley (Ed.), Changing Families,
    New York, Grune & Stratton, 1971.
A review of the development of the family therapy field with the emphasis upon the

shift in unit from one person to two to three or more. Consequences to theory and the effect on the professions is described.

HALEY, J., Strategies of Psychotherapy, New York, Grune & Stratton, 1963.
A description of a variety of forms of psychotherapy from an interactional point of view. Includes chapters on marriage therapy and family therapy.

HALEY, J., "Whither Family Therapy," Fam. Proc., 1, 69-100, 1962.
A review of various methods of family therapy with a comparison of family and individual therapy. Similarities and differences and discussed, and it is said that both
methods have in common a series of paradoxes which the patients face as long as they
continue disturbed behavior.

HALEY, J., and GLICK, I., Psychiatry and the Family: An Annotated Bibliography of
     Articles Published 1960-64, Palo Alto, Family Process Monograph, 1965.
An annotated bibliography of papers published from 1960 through 1964. Content includes articles on family therapy as well as family research studies which are relevant to psychiatry and psychology. Papers from the fields of sociology and anthropology were excluded unless they pertained directly to the psychiatric field.

HALEY, J., and HOFFMAN, L., Techniques of Family Therapy, New York, Basic Books, 1967.
A presentation of the work of five family therapists. Interviews were conducted with
Virginia Satir, Don D. Jackson, Charles Fulweiler, Carl Whitaker, and a therapy team
doing crisis therapy. There is intensive examination of a first interview with a
family to illustrate their approaches.

HALLOWITZ, D., "Family Unit Treatment of Character-Disordered Youngsters," Social Work
     Practice, New York, Columbia University Press, 1963.
A report on the family treatment of 38 children with a diagnosis of character disorder.
Procedures and descriptions of the family are offered along with tabular reports of
outcome. 61% had a favorable outcome with the treatment averaging 17 hours per case.

HALLOWITZ, D., and CUTTER, A. V., "The Family Unit Approach in Therapy: Uses Process,
     and Dynamics," Casework Papers, New York, Family Service Association of America,
     1961.
Conjoint family interviewing in a clinic is described in terms of its use as an intake
procedure, during individual treatment of child and parents, and as a continuous form
of treatment. When used as a continuous method of treatment the contraindications are
said to be when the emotional disturbances in the child or the parents "have become
intrapsychically ingrained in the form of a neurosis or psychosis" and when there are
"basic disturbances in the marital relationship." Yet the treatment is effective with
children with character disorders. A case is discussed.

HAMMER, L. I., "Family Therapy with Multiple Therapists," in J. H. Masserman (Ed.),
     Current Psychiatric Therapies, Vol. VII, New York, Grune & Stratton, 1967.
A clinical essay on the use of a technique called "multiple therapy" (defined as more
than one person engaged in the solution of family problems). This technique defines
the family therapist as almost anyone who has contact with the case and who uses a
theoretical framework based on understanding problems from a family viewpoint.
Methods of diagnosis, technique, advantages, and disadvantages are discussed.

HANDLON, J. H., and PARLOFF, M. B., "The Treatment of Patient and Family as a Group:
     Is It Group Psychotherapy?," Int. J. Group Psychother., 12, 132-141, 1962.
Family group therapy differs from conventional group therapy in many important
aspects. The permissive atmosphere of group therapy is difficult in family therapy
because the patient feels unique and lacks equal power status and protection, and
the family comes to therapy with shared mythology and reality distortions.

HANSEN, C., "An Extended Home Visit with Conjoint Family Therapy," Fam. Proc., 7,
        67-87, 1968.
An approach to family therapy which involved staying in the home with the family for
a week to intervene therapeutically in a family's life. Benefits and problems of
this approach are discussed.

HARMS, E., "A Socio-Genetic Concept of Family Therapy," Acta Psychother., 12, 53-60,
        1964.
An essay which criticizes Ackerman's rationale and techniques of family therapy. The
author proposes that family therapy be called "socio-genetic family group therapy,"
because to understand a family one has to understand sociologic as well as genetic
points of view. It also takes into account the concepts of normality. Six points-
of-insight in order to proceed are presented.

HAWKINS, R. P., PETERSON, R. F., SCHWEID, E., and BIJOU, D., "Behavior Therapy in
        the Home: Amelioration of Problem Parent-Child Relations with the Parent in a
        Therapeutic Role," J. Exp. Child Psychol., 4, 99-107, 1966.
A conditioning approach to changing parent-child relations by programming the parents
to deal with the child differently.

HOFFMAN, L., "Deviation Amplifying Processes in Natural Groups," in J. Haley (Ed.),
        Changing Families, New York, Grune & Stratton, 1971.
A theoretical paper on the limitations of a homeostatic theory to deal with change.
The family view, systems theory, and sociological ideas about deviants are brought
together in a discussion of the process of change in systems when a deviation is
amplified.

HOFFMAN, L., and LONG, L., "A Systems Dilemma," Fam. Proc., 8, 211-234, 1969.
A description of a man's breakdown in terms of the social systems within which he
moved, and the attempts to intervene to bring about change. The ecological field of
a person is the area considered.

HORIGAN, F. D., Family Therapy: A Survey of the Literature, Psychiatric Abstracts
        No. 11, Bethesda, Dept. of Health, Education and Welfare, 1964.
This is a selected, annotated bibliography of the literature of family therapy from
1949 up to 1964.

JACKSON, D. D., "Action for Mental Illness -- What Kind?," Stanford Med. Bull., 20,
        77-80, 1962.
An essay discussing the treatment of schizophrenia. It is pointed out that in addition to somatic methods, the family should be involved in family therapy throughout
hospitalization and in the posthospital phase to decrease morbidity. The patient
should be encouraged to leave the hospital from the moment he enters it, and family
therapy should be held in the home.

JACKSON, D. D., "Aspects of Conjoint Family Therapy," in G. H. Zuk and I. Boszor-
        menyi-Nagy (Eds.), Family Therapy and Disturbed Families, Palo Alto, Science &
        Behavior Books, 1967.
A discussion of the difference between the family therapy approach and psychoanalysis
with an example of a "Lolita-type" case. It is argued that the individual and family
are like the wave and particle theories of light and that merging the two is not quite
possible.

JACKSON, D. D., (Ed.), Communication, Family and Marriage, Palo Alto, Science & Be-
        havior Books, 1968.
A collection of previously published papers covering early generalizations on family
dynamics from clinical observations, papers on the double bind theory, communication,
systems and pathology, and research approaches and methods. 289 pp.

JACKSON, D. D., "Conjoint Family Therapy," Mod. Med., 33, 172-198, 1965.
A clinical article discussing the history of, rationale for, and techniques of family
therapy. Schizophrenia is seen as a reaction to a disturbance in family communication.
Families operate in a homeostatic system and the disturbances of one member affect
other members.

JACKSON, D. D., "Family Interaction, Family Homeostasis, and Some Implications for
       Conjoint Family Psychotherapy," in J. Masserman (Ed.), Individual and Familial
       Dynamics, New York, Grune & Stratton, 1959.
A clinical paper focussing on family homeostasis and its importance to the development of pathology. When homeostasis in the family breaks down, it can be expected
that one member of the family will develop symptoms. To treat the system, the entire
family must be involved, therefore offering a distinct advantage over "collaborative"
therapy.

JACKSON, D. D., "Family Therapy in the Family of the Schizophrenic," in H. Stein (Ed.),
       Contemporary Psychotherapies, New York, Free Press, 1961.
A clinical essay dealing with the rationale for the development of family therapy.
Data was based on interviews with 15 schizophrenic families and several delinquent
families. Goals and techniques of family therapy are described by use of an extensive
transcript from a case. Mother, father, siblings, and identified patients are all
caught in a reverberating circuit of pathology. Further research with controls is
needed.

JACKSON, D. D., "The Monad, the Dyad, and Family Therapy," in A. Burton (Ed.),
       Psychotherapy and Psychosis, New York, Basic Books, 1961.
A clinical paper on the treatment of schizophrenics using family therapy. One case
example is used to support a theoretical framework of family therapy, and advantages
and disadvantages of conjoint therapy are discussed. Transference and countertransference problems and the therapist's ability to grasp the data being fed him are
central issues.

JACKSON, D. D. (Ed.), Therapy, Communication and Change, Palo Alto, Science & Behavior
       Books, 1968.
A collection of previously published papers covering psychotic behavior and its interactional context, the interactional context of other kinds of behavior, interactional
views of psychotherapy and conjoint family therapy. 76 pp.

JACKSON, D. D., and SATIR, V., "A Review of Psychiatric Developments in Family
       Diagnosis and Family Therapy," in N. W. Ackerman, F. L. Beatman, and S. Sherman
       (Eds.), Exploring the Base for Family Therapy, New York, Family Service Associa-
       tion of America, 1961.
A discussion of the family point of view in psychiatry with a classification of the
various approaches to treating the family. A review of the historical development and
present attempts to investigate family process.

JACKSON, D. D., and WEAKLAND, J. H., "Conjoint Family Therapy: Some Considerations
       on Theory, Technique, and results, Psychiatry, 24, 30-45, 1961.
A report on conjoint family therapy of families with a schizophrenic member with a
discussion of the theoretical point of view, the procedural arrangements, and typical
problems. Case material is used to illustrate characteristic sequences in the therapy.
The emphasis is upon the current interaction within these families and their resistance
to change. Results are presented, and there is a discussion of countertransference
problems and the shift in psychotherapeutic approach characteristic of therapists who
attempt family psychotherapy.

JACKSON, D. D., and YALOM, I., "Conjoint Family Therapy as an Aid in Psychotherapy,"
       in A. Burton (Ed.), Family Therapy of Schizophrenics in Modern Psychothera-

peutic Practice, Palo Alto, Science & Behavior Books, 1965.
A clinical report presenting one case in support of the notion that family therapy
is useful for breaking an impasse in individual therapy. A case example is presented
in detail and it is shown how the pathology of the family prevented progress in
individual therapy.

JACKSON, D. D., and YALOM, I., "Family Research on the Problem of Ulcerative Colitis,"
     Arch. Gen. Psychiat., 15, 410-418, 1966.
Observations are presented of interaction patterns of ulcerative colitis families
studied during conjoint family therapy sessions. Sample was eight white, middle
class families with the identified patient aged seven to 17. Families were seen to
be restricted in interactions, communicated indirectly, learned restrictive patterns
from grandparents, had fathers of one or both spouses who was absent, and had siblings (of the identified patient) who were also sick.

JACKSON, D. D., and YALOM, I., "Family Homeostasis and Patient Change," in J. Masser-
     man (Ed.), Current Psychiatric Therapies, Vol. IV, New York, Grune & Stratton,
     1964.
By use of a case report of conjoint family therapy, the hypothesis is tested that "The
schizophrenic family is a specific system, which, when altered, results in a change in
the identified patient's symptoms and this change correlates with a noticeable alteration in the behavior of other family members." Specific techniques are described in
detail —— particularly "the therapeutic double bind and prescriptions of behavior."

JENSEN, D., and WALLACE, J. G. , "Family Mourning Process," Fam. Proc., 6, 56-66, 1967.
A discussion of mourning as a family crisis involving all members. Two case examples
are given. Therapy is seen as intervening in maladaptive family interaction patterns
resulting from the loss of a member.

KAFFMAN, M., "Family Diagnosis and Therapy in Child Emotional Pathology," Fam. Proc.,
     4, 241-258, 1965.
A description of families treated in Israel based upon 194 kibbutz families and 126
families living in Haifa. Family treatment is said to be effective and case examples
are given.

KAFFMAN, M., "Short Term Family Therapy," Fam. Proc., 2, 216-234, 1963.
A report on the use of family therapy in a child guidance clinic in Israel with the
emphasis upon short term family treatment. The rationale, methodology, limitations,
and initial evaluations of results are presented for 70 consecutive cases referred
to the clinic.

KANTOR, R. E., and HOFFMAN, L., "Brechtian Theater as a Model for Conjoint Family
     Therapy," Fam. Proc., 5, 218-229, 1966.
A model for family therapy is offered in terms of the theatre with particular emphasis
upon Brecht's approach. Various procedures by Brecht are described as they apply to
the family therapy process.

KARDENER, S., "The Family: Structure, Pattern, and Therapy," Ment. Hyg., 52, 524-
     531, 1968.
Following a review of the concept of the family as an etiologic agent in the development of psychopathology seven types of problem marital constellations, four types of
family interrelationships, and seven danger signals alerting the family to potential
trouble, are described. Role of therapist is outlined to deal with these problems.

KEMPLER, W., "Experiential Family Therapy," Int. J. Group Psychother., 15, 57-72, 1965.
A review of the author's experience in the use of a family approach to both diagnosis
and treatment in the management of psychiatric problems. "Experiential family therapy"
is a psychotherapeutic approach to the treatment of emotionally disturbed individuals
within the framework of the family. Its core is the exploration of the "what and how"
of the "I and thou" in the "here and now."

KEMPLER, W., "Experiential Psychotherapy with Families," Fam. Proc., 7, 88-89, 1968. A description of a particular approach to family therapy with illustrative examples. The emphasis is upon the here and now and upon personal growth for family and therapist.

KEMPLER, W., "Family Therapy of the Future," Int. Psychiat. Clin., 6, 135-158, 1969. An essay on what family therapy will be like in the future. Psychotherapy will be experiential. The orientation will shift from objective-individual to "subjective-interpersonal." The focus will be on the present and there will be no such thing as diagnosis. Rather, only on what is happening at this particular minute. "Focus will be on encounters, not individuals."

KEMPSTER, S. W., and SAVITSKY, E., "Training Family Therapists Through 'Live' Supervision," in N. W. Ackerman, F. L. Beatman, and S. Sherman (Eds.), Expanding Theory and Practice in Family Therapy, New York, Family Service Association of America, 1967. A clinical essay focussing on techniques of supervision of family therapy. A literature review was made, and the method where the supervisor was right in the session is described. Staff and family reaction was "generally favorable, with adverse reactions rare." Family therapy and the process of live supervision should be introduced early in the course of training therapists.

KING, C., "Family Therapy with the Deprived Family," Soc. Casework, 48, 203-208, 1967. From the author's clinical work with delinquent boys at the Wiltwyck School, techniques for working with low socioeconomic class patients and their families are described. Selection, rationale, and scope of family therapy is discussed. Basic techniques consisted of educational and therapeutic maneuvers focussed on clarity of communication and the teaching of parent, and sibling roles.

KNOBLOCHOVA, J., and KNOBLOCH, F., "Family Psychotherapy," in Aspects of Family Mental Health in Europe, Public Health Papers, No. 28, World Health Organization, 1965. A report of the author's experience in a university hospital in Czechoslovakia using family therapy. Theoretical background and techniques are discussed.

KOVACS, L., "A Therapeutic Relationship with a Patient and Family," Perspect. Psychiat. Nurs., 4, 11-21, 1966. A case report where family therapy was used in treatment of a patient from the time of first admission to a private hospital to transfer to a state hospital, and finally reunion with the family post discharge.

KRITZER, H., and PITTMAN, F. S., "Overnight Psychiatric Care in a General Emergency Room", Hosp. Community Psych., 19, 303-306, 1968. A clinical article reviewing the experience with 36 psychiatric patients who came to the emergency room because of a crisis. As alternatives to inpatient hospitalization, overnight hospitalization and the emergency room was used. Rationale was that their presenting problem was often a manifestation of underlying family problems, and by temporarily relieving the crisis and working out the future management, inpatient hospitalization could be avoided. Results indicated that of 36 patients, 11 were essentially sent to a psychiatric hospital, 22 were discharged directly from the emergency room, and three signed out against medical advice.

KWIATKOWSKA, H., "Family Art Therapy," Fam. Proc., 6, 37-55, 1967. A discussion of using art therapy as a therapeutic technique with families. In the previous five years 47 families have participated in family art therapy. The approach is described with a case example.

LANDES, J., and WINTER, W., "A New Strategy for Treating Disintegrating Families," Fam. Proc., 5, 1-20, 1966. A communal therapy procedure in which patient families and the families of therapists

participated in a 48-hour weekend together. The experience, problems and results of
such a weekend are described.

LANGSLEY, D., FLOMENHAFT, K., and MACHOTKA, P., "Followup Evaluation of Family Crisis
      Therapy," Amer. J. Orthopsychiat., 39, 753-759, 1969.
One of a series of papers on a research project in which families were assigned randomly
either to traditional hospital treatment or family crisis therapy with a focus on
family therapy. Six-month follow-up evaluations of 150 family crisis therapy cases and
150 hospital treatment cases demonstrated that patients are less likely to be rehospitalized in the former group.

LANGSLEY, D., and KAPLAN, D., The Treatment of Families in Crisis, Grune & Stratton, New
      York, 1968.
A report of a research project where family crisis therapy was offered as an alternative
to psychiatric hospitalization. Rationale, techniques, data on the patients, results,
and implications of the results are presented. 184 pp.

LANGSLEY, D., PITTMAN, F. S., MACHOTKA, P., and FLOMENHAFT, K., "Family Crisis
      Therapy: Results and Implications," Fam. Proc., 7, 145-159, 1968.
A report on the crisis treatment unit established at Colorado Psychiatric Hospital
in Denver. A total of 186 cases selected randomly were treated by brief family
treatment and compared with control cases hospitalized in the usual way. Preliminary
results are reported.

LANGSLEY, D., PITTMAN, F., and SWANK, G., "Family Crisis in Schizophrenics and Other
      Mental Patients," J. Nerv. Ment. Dis., 149, 270-276, 1969.
A further report on a study using crisis therapy as an alternative to psychiatric
hospitalization. In this study, 50 families which included a schizophrenic patient
and 50 which included a nonschizophrenic mental patient, were studied with the means
of an instrument which quanitified the events leading to a crisis in the family and the
management of such crises. Nonschizophrenic mental patients were better able to
handle crises and interact with their families. Discussion of the findings is presented.

LEADER, A. L., "Current and Future Issues in Family Therapy," Soc. Serv. Rev., 43,
      1-11, 1969.
A clinical essay focussing on current "hot" issues in family therapy. Family therapy
(a way of thinking about emotional problems) is differentiated from family group
treatment techniques (defined as the different techniques of family therapy). At
times the focus should be on the whole family and at other times on individual members. Different ways of using the family interview are discussed.

LEADER, A. L., "The Role of Intervention in Family-Group Treatment," Soc. Casework,
      45, 327-332, 1964.
A clinical essay focussed on techniques of active intervention in family therapy.
Active intervention is indicated because the family interactional patterns are deeply
intrenched and difficult to break, there is a great deal of denial, and usually there
is tremendous diffuseness. By using this technique, the problem can be shifted from
the presenting problem to the underlying problem. Difficulties in being active and
reasons for them are discussed.

LEFER, J., "Counter-Resistance in Family Therapy," J. Hillside Hosp., 15, 205-210,
      1966.
This essay stresses the role of countertransferential feelings of the therapist to
the family being treated. Material was taken from supervision of six residents, who
reported from notes taken during the session or written immediately afterwards. Countertransference is manifested in disturbed feelings toward the family, stereotypy,
love and hate responses, and carrying over affects after the session. The need for
supervision of the therapist and self-knowledge in order to avoid difficulties is
underlined.

LEIK, R. K., and NORTHWOOD, L. K., "Improving Family Guidance Through the Small Group
     Experimental Laboratory," Soc. Work, 9, 18-25, 1965.
A research article on using the experimental laboratory for (1) contributing to
general principles to guide counseling and guidance personnel, (2) providing a diagnostic vehicle for a given case, and (3) treatment evaluation. Interaction research
studies are reviewed and it is pointed out that the laboratory can be useful for
training.

LEVETON, A., "Family Therapy as the Treatment of Choice," Med. Bull. U. S. Army Europe,
     21, 76-79, 1964.
The author discusses his experience with family therapy with 70 families in a military
setting in which family therapy was the initial treatment method employed regardless
of the presenting complaint. Of the 70 families, half involved husband and wife, and
half involved a child and his parents. Rationale for family therapy, as well as
family dynamics, roles and ideologies are discussed and a case history presented. In
general, family therapy, in contrast to individual psychotherapy, deals more with the
present and future, rather than exploration of the individual or collective past.

LEVINE, R., "Treatment in the Home," Soc. Work, 9, 19-28, 1964.
A clinical report of treatment of seven low-income, multiproblem families who came to
a mental hygiene clinic for help with the identified patient, usually a child.
Treatment of the family rather than the individual was begun because it seems more
economical, more family members could be helped, and the therapist could be more
accurate in understanding problems. Treatment was done in the home. Techniques
included "talking," "demonstration," and family activity. The seven families were
rated in terms of improvement, from most improved to least improved.

LEWIS, J., and GLASSER, N., "Evolution of a Treatment Approach to Families: Group
     Family Therapy," Int. J. Group Psychother., 15, 505-515, 1965.
A report of the involvement of families of mentally ill patients in a therapy program
treatment center. Three groups were set up: family members excluding patients,
patients alone, and patients and families together. Impressions of this type of
family involvement are described.

LONG, R., "The Path Toward Psychodrama Family Process," Group Psychother., 19, 43-46,
     1966.
In an inpatient setting, where psychodrama is one of the treatment techniques used, the
author describes his realization that families seemed to be involved in the pathogenesis of mental illness. He suggests that bringing in the real family to the psychodrama
sessions might be useful and describes some problems which arose as a result.

MacGREGOR, R., "Communicating Values in Family Therapy," in G. H. Zuk and I. Boszor-
     menyi-Nagy (Eds.), Family Therapy and Disturbed Families, Palo Alto, Science &
     Behavior Books, 1967.
A discussion of family therapy from the point of view of the therapist attempting to
change a family's system of values. A case illustration defends the advocation of conventional middle-class values. Includes an attempt to differentiate deliberate influence from unwitting culture conflict between therapist and patient.

MacGREGOR, R., "Multiple Impact Psychotherapy with Families," Fam. Proc., 1, 15-29,
     1962.
A description of the treatment approach used by the outpatient psychiatric clinic
staff for adolescents at the University of Texas Medical Branch Hospitals at Galveston.
55 families are described in which an adolescent was the primary patient and the
families were in some sort of crisis. Multiple impact therapy is a form of diagnostic
and therapeutic intervention that uses the entire time and facilities of an ortho-
psychiatric team in different combinations to a family for half a week. The method
and some preliminary results based on six and 18 month follow-up studies are reported.

MacGREGOR, R., "Progress in Multiple Impact Therapy," in N. W. Ackerman, F. L. Beatman,
    and S. Sherman (Eds.), Expanding Theory and Practice in Family Therapy, New York,
    Family Service Association of America, 1967.
A report on the youth development project in Galveston where multiple impact therapy
developed. The approach is described with emphasis upon the bringing together of "a
relatively open system, the team," with "a relatively closed system, the family functioning in a defensive way." Procedures and concepts are described.

MacGREGOR, R., RITCHIE, A.M., SERRANO, A.C., SCHUSTER, F.P., McDANALD, E.C., and
    GOOLISHIAN, H.A., Multiple Impact Therapy With Families, New York, McGraw-Hill,
    1964.
A report of a clinical project using a new technique (one aspect of which is family
therapy) for families who consult a child guidance clinic and who live a great distance away. It includes a section on the development of family therapy, illustrations of the method, discussion of the method, discussion of the family, family dynamics, and therapeutic movement, discussion of the team, and results. 320 pp.

MACHOTKA, P., PITTMAN, F. S., FLOMENHAFT, K., "Incest as a Family Affair," Fam. Proc.
    6, 98-116, 1967.
A discussion of incest from the point of view of the whole family. Two cases of
father-daughter incest and one of sibling incest are discussed with the emphasis upon
the crucial role of the nonparticipating member, the concerted denial of the incest,
and on where the focus of therapy should be.

MACKIE, R., "Family Problems in Medical and Nursing Families," Brit. J. Med. Psychol.,
    40, 333-340, 1967.
From nine cases treated by the author over four years and a review of the literature,
the author presents parts of three of the cases in which the presenting patient was a
doctor or nurse. Of the nine cases, seven improved with family therapy and two did
not. The doctor or nurse will "defend himself against the direct expression of sick
or dependent parts of himself and will instead project these onto the spouse or onto
other relatives."

MARKOWITZ, I., TAYLOR, G., and BOKERT, E., "Dream Discussion as a Means of Reopening
    Blocked Familial Communication," Psychother. Psychosom., 16, 348-356, 1968.
Based on the clinical notion that parents exclude the child in family dialogue, these
family therapists use the dreams of the children "as a focus for familial discussion."
It is thought to be an "indicator of the degree of honesty of communication present in
the family." Numerous case examples are given in support of this view.

MARTIN, B., "Family Interaction Associated with Child Distrubance: Assessment and
    Modification," Psychotherapy, 4, 30-35, 1967.
A report testing the author's notion that disturbances in the interaction between
parents and child can lead to disturbed behavior in the child. An experimental procedure was developed in order to limit communication to just one member of the family
at a time. Sessions were recorded on audiotape and rated according to degree of
blaming. In a pilot study of four families two received modification procedures designed to decondition blaming, and two did not. The experimental families showed a
greater proportion of decrease in blaming scores.

MARX, A., and LUDWIG, A., "Resurrection of the Family of the Chronic Schizophrenic,"
    Amer. J. Psychother., 23, 37-52, 1969.
A careful review of the author's experience treating psychiatric inpatients by systematically involving the family of the patient. Sample was 44 chronic schizophrenic
patients and families over two year period. Family resistances and methods to deal
with these resistances are discussed. The treatment program included family-therapist
meetings, patient-family-therapist sessions, multiple family group meetings, and
multiple family-conjoint therapy sessions. Some of the effects of this treatment
program both positive (patient and family improvement) and negative (member of the
family decompensating) as well as the methods of dealing with these problems and
practical theoretical implications and ethics of this approach are discussed.

MASSERMAN, J. (Ed.), Science and Psychoanalysis, Vol. II: Individual and Family
     Dynamics, New York, Grune & Stratton, 1959.
In this book there is a section on familial and social dynamics. Included are papers
on survey of trends and research in the practice of family therapy, psychoanalytic
approaches to the family, family homeostasis, family dynamics in schizophrenia, cultural aspects of transference and countertransference, techniques of family therapy,
and a panel discussion and review on the family. 218 pp.

McDANALD, E. C., "Out-Patient Therapy of Neurotic Families," in I. M. Cohen (Ed.),
     Psychiatric Research Report 20, Washington, D. C., American Psychiatric Associa-
     tion, 1966.
"Impressions about the psychotherapy of predominately neurotic families on an out-
patient basis." The emphasis is upon considerations for excluding family members,
factors that impede change, and indications for family therapy.

MENDELL, D., and FISCHER, S., "A Multi-Generation Approach to the Treatment of Psycho-
     pathology," J. Nerv. Ment. Dis., 126, 523-529, 1958.
Techniques of treating the family rather than the identified patient for various
problems seen in a private psychiatric population. TAT and Rorschach material were
important parts of the diagnostic evaluation.

MERENESS, D., "Family Therapy: An Evolving Role," Perspect. in Psychiat. Care, 6,
     256-259, 1968.
This essay discusses the role of the psychiatric nurse in family therapy. Rationale
and indications for family therapy are discussed. Nurses are seen as "uniquely well
equipped to accept the role of family therapist." Training for nurses should include
functioning as a co-therapist, being taught the body of knowledge concerning family
dynamics, and learning treatment techniques. Moving outside the "traditional role of
the psychiatric nurse" is suggested.

MESSER, A., "Family Treatment of a School Phobic Child," Arch. Gen. Psychiat., 11, 548-
     555, 1964.
Case report of family treatment over two years of a phobic child and his family. Hypothesis was that the phobia expressed publicly a disruption in the family equilibrium.

MIDELFORT, C. F., The Family in Psychotherapy, New York, McGraw-Hill, 1957.
A report of a clinical project involving family therapy and the use of relatives in the
care of psychiatric patients on both an inpatient and outpatient basis. It discusses
the purpose of the project, and the use of family treatment in schizophrenia, depression, paranoid illness, psychopathic personality, and psychoneurosis. 202 pp.

MIDELFORT, C. F., "Use of Members of the Family in Treatment of Schizophrenia," Fam.
     Proc., 1, 114-118, 1962.
A report of the author's experiences using family members as companions and attendants
for schizophrenic patients hospitalized in a general hospital and treated with family
therapy as well as somatic and pharmacologic agents.

MILLER, S., "A Study in Family Dynamics," Perspect. Psychiat. Care, 1, 9-15, 1963.
From one case example individual, interpersonal, and sociocultural dynamics are
described. Treatment included helping the family to deal with problems of everyday
living, set goals for the future, and accomplish developmental tasks.

MINUCHIN, S., "Conflict-Resolution Family Therapy," Psychiatry, 28, 278-286, 1965.
A description of a method of family therapy developed at Wiltwyck School for Boys in
which the therapist brings members of the family behind the one-way mirror with him
to observe the conversation of the remainder of the family. The procedure is said to

be particularly effective with multiproblem families. The family member is usually
asked in family therapy to be a participant observer and in this method these two
functions are separated. "The one-way mirror maintains the emotional impact of interpersonal experiences, while it does not provide an opportunity for impulsory discharge."
The family members impulse to react with action, which is generally characteristic of
the families treated, is delayed and channeled into verbal forms.

MINUCHIN, S., "Family Structure, Family Language and the Puzzled Therapist," in O.
     Pollak (Ed.), Family Theory and Family Therapy of Female Sexual Delinquency,
     Palo Alto, Science & Behavior Books, 1967.
An approach to family therapy derived from treating low socioeconomic families at the
Wiltwyck School for Boys. "We began to look anew at the meaning and effectiveness of
therapist interventions and to focus on two aspects of the family — family language
and family structure." Ways of challenging the family structure and other procedures
are described with illustrations.

MINUCHIN, S., "Family Therapy: Technique or Theory?" in J. Masserman (Ed.), Science
     and Psychoanalysis, Vol. XIV: Childhood and Adolescence, New York, Grune &
     Stratton, 1969.
A discussion of family therapy with the emphasis upon the need to take into account the
total ecology of the family. "I think that family therapy...will be in danger of ossi-
fication if it fails to move towards an ecological theory of man."

MINUCHIN, S., "Psychoanalytic Therapies and the Low Socioeconomic Population," in J.
     Marmor (Ed.), Modern Psychoanalysis, New York, Basic Books, 1968.
The failure of psychoanalytic therapies and psychotherapy to reach the low socioeconomic
population is discussed in terms of the implicit requirements of those approaches and
the characteristics of the population. Alternate approaches such as living group
therapy, remedial learning therapy, and family therapy are discussed.

MINUCHIN, S., "The Use of an Ecological Framework in the Treatment of a Child," in
     E. J. Anthony and C. Koupernik (Eds.), The Child in His Family, New York, Wiley,
     1970.
A discussion of the three elements in the study of the child: the child as an individual, his environment, and the linkage between. The ecological point of view is
discussed and a case of an adolescent with anorexia nervosa is discussed in terms of
his family and the family therapy approach to the problem.

MINUCHIN, S., AUERSWALD, E., KING, C., and RABINOWITZ, C., "The Study and Treatment of
     Families That Produce Multiple Acting-Out Boys," Amer. J. Orthopsychiat., 34, 125-
     134, 1964.
An early report of experience with families of delinquent boys, social class V, at the
Wiltwyck School for Boys in New York. The report focuses on some aspects of familial
functioning, in particular "the socializing function of parental control, guidance and
nurturance." The group's technique of family diagnosis and therapy with delinquent
families is also presented.

MINUCHIN, S., and BARCAI, A., "Therapeutically Induced Family Crisis," in J. Masserman
     (Ed.), Science and Psychoanalysis, Vol. XIV: Childhood and Adolescence, New York,
     Grune & Stratton, 1969.
A report on a family treatment approach where a crisis is induced and resolved. A
family with a child regularly hospitalized for diabetic acidosis was treated by assigning tasks which induced a crisis situation to which the family members had to respond
by changing.

MINUCHIN, S., and MONTALVO, B., "Techniques for Working with Disorganized Low Socio-
     economic Families," Amer. J. Orthopsychiat., 37, 880-887, 1967.
A paper describing some modifications of family therapy techniques useful for dealing
with some families of "low" socioeconomic class. The techniques include changing the

family composition so that some members observe the family sessions through a one-way mirror, treating various subgroups within the natural family separately (e.g., all adolescents), actively manipulating these subgroups in relation to the whole family group, and finally helpding the family to <u>discuss</u> what they want to <u>act</u> on.

MINUCHIN, S., MONTALVO, B., GUERNEY, B. G., ROSMAN, B. L., and SHUMER, F., <u>Families of the Slums: An Exploration of Their Structure and Treatment</u>, New York, Basic Books, 1967.
A book on a research project dealing with family treatment of low socioeconomic class families where the identified patient was delinquent. Research strategy, rationale, dynamics, techniques and assessment of results are presented. 460 pp.

MITCHELL, C., "A Casework Approach to Disturbed Families," in N. W. Ackerman, F. L. Beatman, and S. Sherman (Eds.), <u>Exploring the Base for Family Therapy</u>, New York, Family Service Association of America, 1961.
The family from the point of view of the caseworker, with emphasis upon family diagnosis and treatment.

MITCHELL, C., "Integrative Therapy of the Family Unit," <u>Soc. Casework</u>, 46, 63-69, 1965.
A discussion of the family-unit therapy approach as practiced at the Jewish Family Service in New York. Concepts are presented with a case example.

MITCHELL, C., "The Use of Family Sessions in the Diagnosis and Treatment of Disturbances in Children," <u>Soc. Casework</u>, 41, 283-290, 1960.
A discussion of family casework where the family as a whole is interviewed in contrast to individual interviews with family members. The family session is supplemented by interviews of family pairs, triads, or individuals. Sessions with the whole family provide unique insights on may levels, help a child accept treatment more readily, lay bare the involvement of all family members in the problem, and further the growth of all family members.

MITCHELL, C., "The Uses and Abuses of Co-Therapy as a Technique in Family Unit Therapy," <u>Bull. Fam. Ment. Health Clin. J. F. S.</u>, 1, 8-10, 1969.
A clinical essay on the advantages vs. the problems of using co-therapists in family therapy. Where the co-therapists fit together well, there are a great number of advantages. Where the co-therapists have trouble in working together, it is better to change one or both therapists.

MIYOSHI, N., and LIEBMAN, R., "Training Psychiatric Residents in Family Therapy," <u>Fam. Proc.</u>, 8, 97-105, 1969.
A report on training psychiatric residents in family therapy at Mercy-Douglass Hospital in Philadelphia. Problems and benefits are discussed.

MOSHER, L. R., "Schizophrenogenic Communication and Family Therapy," <u>Fam. Proc.</u>, 8, 43-63, 1969.
A description of a technique of family therapy with a family of a schizophrenic. The emphsis is upon the structural and process aspects of the family's communication and case material is used for illustration.

MOTTOLA, W., "Family Therapy: A Review," <u>Psychotherapy</u>, 4, 116-124, 1967.
A review of the literature of family therapy to this time, covering problems of definition, history, examinations, issues, and research.

MURNEY, R., and SCHNEIDER, R., "Family Therapy: Understanding and Changing Behavior," in F. McKinney (Ed.), <u>Psychology in Action</u>, New York, Macmillan, 1957.
A review of articles in a book of collected articles for psychologists. It describes rationale, indications, methods and theory of family therapy for the beginner.

MURRELL, S., and STACHOWIAK, J., "The Family Group: Development, Structure, and
     Therapy," J. Marriage Fam., 27, 13-18, 1965.
From the literature, the authors' previous experience and previous research, a theory
of the family is presented. Assumptions in terms of therapy are discussed. Families
are viewed as being unable to problem-solve and as resistant to change.

NATIONAL CLEARINGHOUSE FOR MENTAL HEALTH INFORMATION, Family Therapy: A Selected
     Annotated Bibliography, Bethesda, Public Health Service, 1965.
An annotated bibliography of the literature on family therapy up to 1964, which includes general theoretical articles, therapy with adolescents, child-oriented family
therapy, therapy in the home, therapy with families of psychiatric inpatients, marital
counseling applications, therapy with schizophrenics, and training family therapists.

OSBERG, J. W., "Initial Impressions of the Use of Short-Term Family Group Conferences,"
     Fam. Proc., 1, 236-244, 1962.
A discussion of early experiences with 38 families seen in group treatment over a four-
year period in a psychiatric outpatient clinic. The evaluation, initial session, and
succeeding sessions are described with a case example.

OSTENDORF, M., "The Public Health Nurse Role in Helping a Family to Cope with Mental
     Health Problems," Perspect. Psychiat. Nurs., 5, 208-213, 1967.
A modus operandi for a public health nurse in dealing with a family is described. She
can help the family to strengthen their ability to cope with future mental problems,
help the family deal with daily problems of living, and increase the stability in one
family member ("which will subsequently strengthen the entire family").

PAIDOUSSI, E., "Some Comparisons Between Family Therapy and Individual Therapy," Bull.
     Fam. Ment. Health Clin. J.F.S., 1, 11-12, 1969.
A clinical essay dealing with differences in the two kinds of therapy: family therapy
involves working with interactions, more here and now material, requires more involvement and more leadership on the part of the therapist.

PARLOFF, M. B., "The Family in Psychotherapy," Arch. Gen. Psychiat., 4, 445-451, 1961.
A discussion of the research trends in family therapy with emphasis upon some of the
theoretical modifications which accompany present forms of family therapy. In treatment, a shift has been made from family members seen individually by different therapists to a single therapist treating several family members. The influence of group
therapy provided "the greatest single advance in the interpersonal relationship treatment technique," and from there it was a short step to working with a patient's actual
family rather than his transference family. The child began to be seen less as a victim and more as a part of the organic unit of the family.

PATTERSON, G. R., McNEAL, S., HAWKINS, N., and PHELPS, R., "Reprogramming the Social
     Environment," J. Child Psychol. Psychiat., 8, 181-185, 1967.
A case report in which the hypothesis was that conditioning techniques could be used
to reprogram the parent and the child so that they become mutually reinforcing in
contrast to just conditioning the child alone. The patient was a five-year-old
autistic child. Observation of the new conditioning was done in the home of the patient and both parents. There were 12 conditioning sessions lasting from ten to 20
minutes over a four-week period. Changes in behavior were noted.

PATTERSON, G. R., RAY, R., and SHAW, D., Direct Intervention in Families of Deviant
     Children, Oregon Research Institute, Eugene, 1969.
A description of a conditioning approach in family therapy where the ways parents
deal with children is systematically modified and examined before and after. 70 pp.

PATTERSON, G. R., SHAW, D. A., and EBNER, M. J., "Teachers, Peers, and Parents as
     Agents of Change in the Classroom," in S. A. N. Benson (Ed.), Modifying Deviant

Social Behaviors in Various Classroom Settings, Eugene, University of Oregon, 1969.
An approach to correcting deviant behavior in the classroom by using a combined systems and reinforcement theory approach.

PATTISON, W. M., "Treatment of Alcoholic Families With Nurse Home Visits," Fam. Proc., 4, 75-94, 1965.
The use of public health nurses in making home visits is described in terms of preventive crisis intervention and family therapy. The results in a study of seven families are offered with case examples and it is said the public health nurse can play a decisive role, particularly with lower class, multiproblem families.

PAUL, N. L., "Effects of Playback on Family Members of Their Own Previously Recorded Conjoint Therapy Material," in I.M. Cohen (Ed.), Psychiatric Research Report 20, Washington, D. C., American Psychiatric Association, 1966.
A discussion of the use of playback of tape-recorded conjoint family therapy material to help families "recognize or assess the respective contributions each makes to the maintenance of maladaptive functioning...." Case examples are given with discussion of the responses of the families.

PAUL, N. L., "The Role of a Secret in Schizophrenia," in N. W. Ackerman (Ed.), Family Therapy in Transition, Boston, Little, Brown, 1970.
A case of a family of a schizophrenic with a secret concerning the son's birth. Excerpts from family interviews are included to illustrate decoding the transactions among the family members.

PAUL, N. L., "The Use of Empathy In the Resolution of Grief," Perspect. Biol. Med., 11, 153-169, 1967.
An essay on a technique in family therapy. It is felt that there is a direct relationship between the maladaptive responses to the death of a loved person and the fixity of symbiotic relationships within the family. The patient's symptom is a defense against the grief. Use of empathy by the therapist therefore helps to change the symptomatology.

PAUL, N. L., and GROSSER, G. H., "Family Resistance to Change in Schizophrenic Patients," Fam. Proc., 3, 377-401, 1964.
A description, with case excerpts, of the patterns of family response to schizophrenic patients that develop during the early phase of conjoint family therapy. It is said that families express desire for the patient to change while attempting to maintain the status quo in family relationships in ways that reinforce the patient's symptomatology.

PAUL, N. L., and GROSSER, G., "Operational Mourning and Its Role in Conjoint Family Therapy," Comm. Ment. Health J., 1, 339-345, 1965.
Studies of records of 50 families with a schizophrenic member and 25 families with at least one psychoneurotic member revealed "patterns of inflexible interaction and maladaptive response to object loss." The way the sample was obtained is not stated. It is hypothesized from this data that incomplete mourning after object loss leads to an inability to deal with future object loss and this defect is transmitted to other family members. This is thought to lead to a "fixation of symbiotic relationships in the family." Therefore, "one possible way to dislodge this fixation would be to mobilize those affects which might aid in disrupting this particular kind of equilibrium." "Operational mourning" is the technique evolved by the authors to do this and is believed to "involve the family in a belated mourning experience with extensive grief reactions." A case report is included for illustration.

PERLMUTTER, M., LOEB, D., GUMPERT, G., O'HARA, F., and HIGBIE, I., "Family Diagnosis and Therapy Using Videotape Playback," Amer. J. Orthopsychiat., 37, 900-905, 1967.
A paper describing the uses of videotape in teaching, doing research on family dynamics

and treatment. Videotape was found useful in diagnosis, in getting family consensus on "what happened" and in therapist supervision.

PITTMAN, F., DeYOUNG, C., FLOMENHAFT, K., KAPLAN, D., and LANGSLEY, D., "Crisis Family
     Therapy," in J. Masserman (Ed.), Current Psychiatric Therapies, Vol. VI, New York,
     Grune & Stratton, 1966.
A report of the authors' experiences in using a family approach in dealing with acute
crisis situations, rather than using hospitalization or individual psychotherapy. Setting was an acute treatment facility which hospitalizes about 75% of patients referred.
Of these, 25% were referred to the Family Treatment Unit consisting of a psychiatrist,
social worker and nurse. Fifty cases were referred to this unit and in 42 hospitalization was "avoided completely." Techniques of treatment are discussed.

PITTMAN, F., LANGSLEY, D., and DeYOUNG, C., "Work and School Phobias: A Family Ap-
     proach to Treatment," Amer. J. Psychiat., 124, 1535-1541, 1968.
Eleven cases of work phobia (the patient experienced overt anxiety associated with
having to go to work or staying at work) are thought of as being "the adult form of
school phobia." Treatment goal is to allow the wife or mother to allow the man to
separate. One year follow-up shows that five cases treated with conjoint family
therapy were able to return to work; the six in long-term individual therapy had not.

PITTMAN, F. S., LANGSLEY, D., G., FLOMENHAFT, K., DeYOUNG, C. D., and MACHOTKA, I.,
     "Therapy Techniques of the Family Treatment Unit," in J. Haley (Ed.), Changing
     Families, New York, Grune & Stratton, 1971.
A report on the therapy techniques of the crisis treatment unit in Denver which did
brief family therapy to keep people out of the hospital. Different approaches used
are described.

PITTMAN, F. S., LANGSLEY, D. G., KAPLAN, D. M., FLOMENHAFT, K., and DeYOUNG, C.,
     "Family Therapy as an Alternative to Psychiatric Hospitalization," in I. M.
     Cohen (Ed.), Psychiatric Research Report 20, Washington, D. C., American Psy-
     chiatric Association, 1966.
A report on the crisis treatment team at the Colorado Psychopathic Hospital which
treated a random selection of patients and their families as an alternative to
hospitalization. Case examples are given.

POLLACK, O., and BRIELAND, D., "The Midwest Seminar on Family Diagnosis and Treatment,"
     Soc. Casework, 42, 319-324, 1961.
A description of a project to develop a model for family diagnosis and treatment that
would be useful for the teaching and practice of social work. A discussion of various
aspects of family dynamics, treatment and treatment problems which are important to
case work is presented.

RABINER, E. L., MOLINSKI, H., and GRALNICK, A., "Conjoint Family Therapy in the Inpa-
     tient Setting," Amer. J. Psychother., 16, 618-631, 1962.
A general discussion of the adaptation of family therapy to the inpatient setting with
its advantages and difficulties illustrated by cases.

RABINOWITZ, C., "Therapy for Underprivileged 'Delinquent' Families," in O. Pollack and
     A. S. Friedman (Eds.), Family Dynamics and Female Sexual Delinquency, Palo Alto,
     Science & Behavior Books, 1969.
A report on a family therapy approach to low-socioeconomic families. Includes a de-
tailed description of the process of therapy with such a family based on work at the
Wiltwyck School.

RAKOFF, V., SIGAL, J., and EPSTEIN, N., "Working-Through in Conjoint Family Therapy,"
     Amer. J. Psychother., 21, 782-790, 1967.
Several clinical examples are given in support of the notion that the psychoanalytic

concept of "working-through" is useful in conjoint family therapy. In family therapy
the material is not a specific conflict, rather problems that the family is currently
discussing. In family therapy the therapist must be more persistent than in individual
therapy. In addition "characteristic patterns in the family" are also to be "worked
through."

RASHKIS, H., "Depression as a Manifestation of the Family as an Open System," Arch.
    Gen. Psychiat., 19, 57-63, 1968.
Seven cases are presented in support of the idea that depression in the middle-aged is
regarded as part of a reciprocal relationship involving the adolescent and his parent.
It is treated by "family psychiatry" (simultaneous or consecutive treatment of one or
more family members).

RICHTER, H., "Familientherapie," Psychother. Psychosom., 16, 303-318, 1968.
An essay on the development of family therapy in the last 15 years as an important
new application of "psychoanalysis." An indication for family therapy is "whenever
a family is exposed to a common psychological problem and is capable of making this
problem accessible to a therapeutic approach."

RIESS, F. B. (Ed)., New Directions in Mental Health, Vol. I, New York, Grune & Stratton,
    1968.
A collection of articles on various psychiatric topics including papers on practice of
family treatment in kibbutz and urban child guidance clinics; short-term analytic
treatment of married couples in a group by a therapist couple; the therapeutic field
in the treatment of families in conflict; recurrent themes in literature and clinical
practice; and patterns of interaction in families of borderline patients. 304 pp.

RITCHIE, A., "Multiple Impact Therapy: An Experiment," Soc. Work, 5, 16-21, 1960.
A description of the multiple impact therapy used in the youth development project at
the University of Texas Medical Branch in Galveston. The method consists of a brief,
usually two-day, intensive study and treatment of a family in crises by a guidance team
composed of psychiatrist, psychiatric social worker, and clinical psychologists. The
team deals with a family six or seven hours a day for two days. These families come
from 50 to 450 miles away, and the method was developed for families who could not
regularly visit. There are two basic assumptions to the method: a family facing a
crisis is more receptive to change than at other times, and dramatic change occurs
in early stages of treatment.

ROHDE, I., "The Nurse as a Family Therapist," Nurs. Outlook, 16, 49-52, 1968.
One case example is presented in support of the idea that the nurse can be a valuable
team member in family therapy.

ROSENTHAL, M. J., "The Syndrome of the Inconsistent Mother," Amer. J. Orthopsychiat.,
    32, 637-643, 1962.
A report on a method of treatment of mothers who are inconsistent with regard to matters of discipline of their acting-out problem children. These mothers regard their
disciplinary efforts as proofs of hostility toward the child and exploration of motivations tends to increase guilts. The treatment recommended focusses sharply upon the
disciplinary problem and is oriented toward alleviation of the mother's guilt about
enforcing restrictions by helping her become more consistent and effective in her dis-
ciplining of the child. The procedure is said to be often dramatically effective.

RUBINSTEIN, D., "Family Therapy," Int. Psychiat. Clin., 1, 431-442, 1964.
This essay is oriented toward the teaching of family therapy. Rationale and techniques
are discussed, and it is stressed that this form of family therapy can be taught to
trainees in the same way that other techniques of psychotherapy are taught. Usually
trainees sit in with an experienced staff member as a co-therapist to start.

RUBINSTEIN, D., "Family Therapy," in E. A. Spiegel (Ed.), Progress in Neurology and
      Psychiatry, Vol. XVIII, New York, Grune & Stratton, 1963.
A review article of the literature on family dynamics and therapy for 1961 and 1962.
Articles are grouped in the following categories: (1) theory and research, (2) dy-
namics, (3) technique, and (4) miscellaneous.

RUBINSTEIN, D., "Family Therapy," in E. A. Spiegel (Ed.), Progress in Neurology and
      Psychiatry, Vols. XX, XXI, New York, Grune & Stratton, 1965, 1966.
In these two annual reviews of family therapy, the 1965 review emphasizes a shift to
a concern with the creation of a conceptual framework to understand the dynamics of
the family system. There were 52 references. In the 1966 annual review, there is a
similar emphasis with articles summarized under the following headings: Theory and
Research, Dynamics, Technique, and Miscellaneous. Included are 54 references.

RUBINSTEIN, D., "Family Therapy," in E. A. Spiegel (Ed.), Progress in Neurology and
      Psychiatry, Vol. XXIII, New York, Grune & Stratton, 1968.
In this annual review of family therapy, a trend was noted toward some critical articles on methodology technique such that family studies might have predictive validity
in various forms of psychopathology. There are 63 articles summarized.

RUBINSTEIN, D., and WEINER, O. R., "Co-Therapy Teamwork Relationships in Family Therapy,"
      in G. H. Zuk and I. Boszormenyi-Nagy (Eds.),Family Therapy and Disturbed Families,
      Palo Alto, Science & Behavior Books, 1967.
A description of co-therapy experiences at the Eastern Pennsylvania Psychiatric Institute. "We feel that if one therapist were to deal alone with the intense negative
transference of a family system, the result might be overwhelming for the therapist."
Dynamics of team relationships are discussed.

RYAN, F., "Clarifying Some Issues in Family Group Casework," Soc. Casework, 48, 222-226,
      1967.
An essay attempting to answer some difficult issues in family group casework (defined
as casework with the entire family present rather than just an individual). Seeing the
family together should be the only treatment offered. It does not preclude treatment
of individual members by other therapists. Both historical and here-and-now issues
are important.

SAFER, D. J., "Family Therapy for Children with Behavior Disorders," Fam. Proc., 5,
      243-255. 1966.
  A report on short term therapy of 29 children with behavior disorders and their
  families. All cases were selected because they were either unmotivated or unacceptable for individual psychotherapy. Treatment approach is described, and 40%
  showed improvement.

SAGER, C., "An Overview of Family Therapy," Int. J. Group Psychother., 18, 302-312,
      1968.
This is an essay centered around several issues including a commentary on the development of family therapy, the openness of the therapists in the field, that its approach is interdisciplinary, the implications of research when the identified patient
is schizophrenic and the advantages and disadvantages of co-therapists. Other critical
questions are raised, e.g., is it an effective form of treatment?

SANDER, F. M., "Family Therapy or Religion: A Re-Reading of T. S. Eliot's The Cocktail
      Party," Fam. Proc., 9, 279-296, 1970.
An analysis of the play, The Cocktail Party, from the view of analytic sociology with
the emphasis upon family therapy as a response to changes in the structure of contemporary families.

SATIR, V. M., "Communication as a Tool for Understanding and Changing Behavior," Pro-
        ceedings, Human Growth and Diversity, California Association of School Psycholo-
        gists and Psychometrists, 16th Annual Conference, 1965.
A clinical essay on the notion that communication and its analysis can lead to understanding interactional processes. By using understanding of the participants in a
family and the family system, change can be effected. The basic goal in all therapy
is "to change the self concept from which more appropriate ways of dealing with others
and the objective world can be developed."

SATIR, V. M., Conjoint Family Therapy, A Guide to Theory and Technique, Palo Alto,
        Science & Behavior Books, 1964.
This is a textbook on family therapy covering a theory of normal family function, communication theory, and techniques of family diagnosis and treatment. There is an extensive bibliography. 196 pp.

SATIR, V. M., "The Family as a Treatment Unit," Confin. Psychiat., 8, 37-42, 1965.
A discussion of family therapy with the emphasis on concepts of interaction. The
family is discussed as a closed and open system and "appropriate outcomes" for the
family are said to be "decisions and behavior which fit the age, ability, and the role
of the individuals, which fit the role contracts and the context involved, and which
further the common goals of the family."

SATIR, V. M., "Family Systems and Approaches to Family Therapy," J. Fort Logan Ment.
        Health Center, 4, 81-93, 1967.
An essay focussing on development of the concept of the family as a system. How it
functions and what happens when the family system breaks down are discussed.

SATIR, V. M., "The Quest for Survival, a Training Program for Family Diagnosis and
        Treatment," Acta Psychother., 11, 33-38, 1963.
A review of the training program for family therapists at the Mental Research Institute
given to "psychiatrists, psychologists, and social workers who work in a variety of settings: state hospitals, out-patient clinics, probation departments, and family service
agencies." Setting, goals, and procedures of the training are described.

SCHAFFER, L., WYNNE, L. C., DAY, J., RYCKOFF, I.M. and HALPERIN, A., "On the Nature
        and Sources of the Psychiatrists Experience with the Family of the Schizophrenic,"
        Psychiatry, 25, 32-45, 1962.
A detailed discussion of the experience of the therapist as he performs family therapy
with the family of the schizophrenic, where "nothing has a meaningful relation to any-
thing else." This therapy is said to be different from work with other families. Case
illustrations are given.

SCHEFLEN, A. E., Stream and Structure of Communicational Behavior, Behavioral Series
        Monograph No. 1, Eastern Pennsylvania Psychiatric Institute, Philadelphia, 1965.
A context analysis of a family therapy session of Whitaker and Malone. The examination of the interview is in detail and includes kinesic, linguistic and contextual
description.

SCHOMER, J., "Changing the Matriarchal Family's Perception of the Father," Bull. Fam.
        Ment. Health. Clin. J.F.S., 1, 13-14, 1969.
In working-class families, where the family dynamics are often set up around matriarchal control of the family, the family will often tend to exclude the father from
family therapy. The therapist, by insisting that father attend, showed that in one
case there was improvement in the identified patient. In another case it gave the
family a chance to "ventilate rage," and in another case the family terminated
without improvement.

SCHREIBER, L. E., "Evaluation of Family Group Treatment in a Family Agency," Fam. Proc.,
        5, 21-29, 1966.

A report on the experience of a family service agency in the treatment of 72 families. Within three months, 61% showed improvement in communication processes and 56% in the presenting behavior problem of the child. Of those who continued beyond three months, 96% showed improvement in communication processes and 92% in the behavior of the child.

SCHUSTER, F., "Summary Description of Multiple Impact Psychotherapy," Texas Rep. Bio. Med., 17, 120-125, 1962.
A report of the multiple impact psychotherapy project used at a child guidance clinic in Texas. Families come from great distances and are seen intensively for two days, both individually and in various family situations. The preliminary one-year or one-month follow-ups attest that this method is "at least as effective as individual treatment in many adolescent referrals."

SHELLOW, R. S., BROWN, B. S., and OSBERG, J. W., "Family Group Therapy in Retrospect: Four Years and Sixty Families," Fam. Proc., 2, 52-67, 1963.
A review of experience with family group therapy (author's term for conjoint family therapy) with 60 families in a child guidance clinic over a four-year period. Referral sources were mainly from physicians and school. Several "hidden" factors influenced choice of this form of therapy by staff members: (1) the identified patient was often the oldest child and (2) there was a large proportion of school achievement problems represented

SHERMAN, S. N., "Aspects of Family Interviewing Critical for Staff Training and Education," Soc. Serv. Rev., 40, 302-308, 1966.
An essay focussing on training of social workers in which it is stressed that conjoint family therapy interviews, rather than individual interviews, are helpful in understanding family dynamics, as well as in treating the case. The caseworker can be prepared for group supervision, use of films or videotapes, direct observation, and participation as co-therapist.

SHERMAN, S. N., "The Concept of the Family in Casework Therapy," in N. W. Ackerman, F. L. Beatman, and S. Sherman (Eds.), Exploring the Base for Family Therapy, New York, Family Service Association of America, 1961.
A clinical essay stressing the family when thinking about the individual in casework. Individual behavior is a function of the family group, and the family is in homeostasis. The differences between family therapy and casework are discussed.

SHERMAN, S. N., "Family Therapy as a Unifying Force in Social Work," in N. W. Ackerman (Ed.), Expanding Theory and Practice in Family Therapy, New York, Family Service Association of America, 1967.
Family therapy has changed the way caseworkers practice, not only in terms of seeing families together, but in thinking about the individual from a family point of view. Family therapy may bridge the gap between casework and group work and between social theory and psychological theory.

SHERMAN, S. N., "Family Treatment: An Approach to Children's Problems," Soc. Casework, 47, 368-372, 1966.
A clinical essay focussing on the use of family therapy in treatment where the identified patient is at latency age. Previously the family agencies have not used family treatment for disorders in this age group, preferring individual treatment. Family treatment is seen as helpful in ameliorating both the children's problems and is preferred as a treatment of choice over individual therapy, especially as a "first phase of treatment and to many children's problems in a working-through phase."

SHERMAN, S. N., "Intergenerational Discontinuity and Therapy in the Family," Soc. Casework, 48, 216-221, 1967.
This essay makes the point that the best medium for affecting the rapid social changes that are occurring in our society may be the family. Family casework as a technique to accomplish this is discussed, with several case illustrations.

SHERMAN, S. N., "Joint Interviews in Casework Practice," Soc. Work, 4, 20-28, 1959.
An attempt "to place joint interviews within the methodology of casework." The purpose and concept of family interviewing is discussed with case examples.

SHERMAN, S. N., "Sociopsychological Character of the Family-Group Treatment," Soc.
     Casework, 45, 195-201, 1964.
From a family service agency, this essay makes the point that both interpersonal and
intrafamilial conflicts are being discussed when doing family therapy. Several case
examples are given.

SIGAL, J. J., RAKOFF, V., and EPSTEIN, N. B., "Indications of Therapeutic Outcome
     in Conjoint Family Therapy," Fam. Proc., 6, 215-226, 1967.
A report on a study which attempted to predict the eventual success of family therapy
by examining the degree of family interaction and emotional involvement as described
by therapists in the initial stages of treatment. "The clinical observations in this
study cause some doubts about the value of the interactional frame of reference in
conjoint family therapy."

SKINNER, A., "A Group-Analytic Approach to Conjoint Family Therapy," J. Child Psychol.
     Psychiat., 10, 81-106, 1969.
An essay describing the author's use of group principles and psychoanalytic principles
to doing conjoint family therapy in the setting of a children's psychiatric clinic.
This focus is contrasted to current family approaches with discussion of advantages
and disadvantages in dealing with problems where the identified patient is a child.
A case history and an extensive review of the literature are presented.

SKINNER, A., "Indications and Contraindications for Conjoint Family Therapy," Int.
     J. Soc. Psychiat., 15, 245-249, 1969.
A clinical paper dealing with advantages, disadvantages, indications and contraindications for family therapy. It is useful for diagnostic purposes, for keeping responsibility, and for solving the presenting problem within the family. Family
therapy's primary limitation is that "change is restricted to what is accepted by the
family as a whole, rather than adapted to the needs of any one individual."
Families with paranoid and schizoid mechanisms are most indicated for family therapy;
those using "depressive" symptoms are least indicated.

SLUZKI, C. E., "El Grupo Familiar del Paciente Internado (The Family Group of the
     In-ward Patient)," Acta Psiquiat. Psicolog. Argentina, 9, 304, 1963.
Based on Don D. Jackson's family typology, a description is made of the family group
circumstances and behavior that may favor mental illness in one member and the attitude of the different types of families in regard to the admission of one member to a
mental hosptial and to release from it. Prognosis can be predicted in each case if
one takes into account the type of family and the way of behaving during the onset of
the mental illness. Recommendations for family group therapy simultaneously with the
admission of the single patient are made.

SLUZKI, C. E., "Family Interaction and Symptoms," Interamer. Psicolog., 2, 283-288,
     1968.
Symptoms are seen as having an interactional effect on other family members in causing
as well as explaining other family member symptoms. It is stressed that the identified
patient is not a "victim," but is as much a part of this system as anyone else. The
therapist must maintain equidistance from all members of the group in order to avoid
coalitions.

SMITH, I. W., and LOEB, D., "The Stable Extended Family as a Model in Treatment of
     Atypical Children," Soc. Work, 10, 75-81, 1965.
A report of a multiple impact therapeutic program in the treatment of six severely disturbed children and their families. Three boys and three girls, ages four-seven were
referred as mentally retarded, were intolerable in school and appeared psychotic in

the first interview. Two female therapists, assuming grandmotherly roles, treated the
families conjointly in three overlapping phases: 1) individual treatment for the patient and parents 2) family group therapy 3) peer experiences for all family members.
Patients showed rapid symptomatic recovery.

SMITH, L., and MILLS, B., "Intervention Techniques and Unhealthy Family Patterns,"
     Perspect. Psychiat. Nurs., 7, 112-119, 1969.
A clinical paper describing characteristic family patterns and intervention techniques
that a nurse may take when doing family therapy. One of the main goals is to improve,
clarify, and facilitate communication in the family.

SOCIAL WORK PRACTICE, 1963, SELECTED PAPERS, 90th Annual Forum, National Conference on
     Social Welfare, Cleveland, Ohio, May 19-24, 1963, New York, Columbia University
     Press, 1963.
A collection of papers given at a social work conference which includes a paper on
family diagnosis and treatment, family unit treatment of character-disordered youngsters, and a paper on schizophrenia and family therapy. 255 pp.

SONNE, J. C., "Entropy and Family Therapy: Speculations on Psychic Energy, Thermo-
     dynamics, and Family Interpsychic Communication," in G. H. Zuk and I. Boszormenyi-
     Nagy (Eds.), Family Therapy and Disturbed Families, Palo Alto, Science & Behavior
     Books, 1967.
An attempt to link together concepts from the physical sciences with observations of
schizophrenogenic families in treatment with special emphasis upon the concept of entropy.

SONNE, J. C., and LINCOLN, G., "Heterosexual Co-Therapy Team Experiences During Family
     Therapy," Fam. Proc., 4, 177-197, 1965.
A description of co-therapy experiences when dealing with the family of the schizophrenic. The emphasis is upon clarifying and unifying the male-female co-therapy team
during the treatment.

SONNE, J. C., and LINCOLN, G., "The Importance of a Heterosexual Co-Therapy Relation-
     ship in the Construction of a Family Image," in I. M. Cohen (Ed.), Psychiatric
     Research Report 20, Washington, D. C., American Psychiatric Association, 1966.
A discussion of the use of co-therapy to provide a heterosexual image in the treatment
of the family of the schizophrenic.

SONNE, J. C., SPECK, R. V., and JUNGREIS, J. E., "The Absent-Member Maneuver as a Re-
     sistance in Family Therapy of Schizophrenia," Fam. Proc., 1, 44-62, 1962.
A report of a specific type of resistance encountered while using family treatment in
ten families containing a schizophrenic offspring. The absent-member maneuver, defined
as the absence of a family member from the family sessions, was seen in one form or
another in all ten families. Some of the dynamics of this maneuver are discussed, the
authors believing that the absent member (often seen as "healthy" by the rest of the
family) tends to pathologically maintain unresolved Oedipal problems in the family.

SORRELLS, J., and FORD, F., "Toward an Integrated Theory of Families and Family
     Therapy, Psychotherapy, 6, 150-160, 1969.
A theoretical paper laying out a theory of family functioning and family treatment.
All family members have self-needs, self-wants, and self-concept. The family operates
in a system using certain communication devices which maintain a homeostasis. Concepts
of status quo, decision-making autonomy and distortion of feedback are discussed. Techniques of treatment including making the contract, diagnosis interventions, and goals
are discussed.

SPARK, G. M., "Parental Involvement in Family Therapy," J. Marriage Fam., 30, 111-118,
     1968.

An essay from a child guidance clinic in which family therapy is presented as offering significant advantages over traditional individual therapy with the various family members. There is less tendency for the parents to project onto the children and dependency need and separation fears can be discussed. Relationships between over- and underinvolved parents become more malleable to change, and new homeostasis can be reached.

SPARK, G. M., and BRODY, E. M., "The Aged are Family Members," Fam. Proc., 9, 195-210, 1970.
A discussion of the involvement of older family members and the important roles they play in family dynamics. Including them in treatment can prevent cyclical repetition of pathological relationship patterns.

SPECK, R. V., "Family Therapy in the Home," J. Marriage Fam., 26, 72-76, 1964.
An essay based on the author's clinical experience in doing family therapy in the home. Advantages of this technique are discussed and several new phenomena are described: the absent member, the most disturbed family member, the youngest member, the role of pets, the extended family, and family secrets.

SPECK, R. V., "Family Therapy in the Home," in N. W. Ackerman (Ed.), Expanding Theory and Practice in Family Therapy, New York, Family Service Association of America, 1967.
A clinical paper from a research project in which family therapy was conducted at home. Advantages and disadvantages in techniques are discussed. It is thought to be advantageous over doing therapy in the office, but no definitive experiment has yet been done. At least one home visit should be made to every family.

SPECK, R. V., "Psychotherapy of the Social Network of a Schizophrenic Family," Fam. Proc., 6, 208-214, 1967.
A description of the social network approach to treatment. Procedure, goals and future directions are described.

SPECK, R. V., and ATTNEAVE, C., "Network Therapy," in J. Haley (Ed.), Changing Families, New York, Grune & Stratton, 1971.
A report on network therapy where all of the significant people of a natural group are brought together in relation to a problem. The theory, practice, techniques, and effects of assembling the "tribe" are described.

SPECK, R. V., and RUEVENI, U., "Network Therapy: A Developing Concept," Fam. Proc., 8, 182-191, 1969.
A description of network therapy where all members of the kinship system, all friends of the family, and other significant people are brought together. A description of the method and a case illustration is offered.

SPIEGEL, J., and BELL, N., "The Family of the Psychiatric Patient," in S. Arieti (Ed.), American Handbook of Psychiatry, Vol. I, New York, Basic Books, 1959.
A chapter in a textbook on psychiatry dealing with sections on the history of the role of the family in mental illness, etiologic studies of parent-child interactions and development of various mental illnesses including schizophrenia, psychoneurosis, acting-out disorders; the impact of mental illness upon the family; the family and treatment procedures and new approaches to the family and its pathology, including family therapy. There are 238 references.

STACHOWIAK, J., "Psychological Disturbances in Children as Related to Disturbances in Family Interaction," J. Marriage Fam., 30, 123-127, 1968.
Family therapy is compared to individual psychotherapy, with data from a child guidance clinic. The therapist is portrayed as an active teacher, "whose main concern is that of inducing change in the family's rigid and stereotyped pattern of interactions."

STEIN, M. I. (Ed.), Contemporary Psychotherapies, Glenco, Free Press, 1961.
This book contains a series of lectures about psychotherapy given in a seminar series.
In it are two papers by Ackerman on family therapy, and two papers by Jackson: one a
general paper and the other on family therapy where the identified patient is schizophrenic. 386 pp.

STREAN, H. S., "A Family Therapist Looks at 'Little Hans,' Fam. Proc., 6, 227-234,
      1967.
A re-examination of the case of "little Hans" from the point of view of the family as
the unit of diagnosis and treatment. The case is said to be "an excellent illustration of how a symptom of one member binds and protects and whole family constellation."

STREAN, H. S., "Treating Parents of Emotionally Disturbed Children Through Role Play-
      ing." Psychoanal. Rev., 47, 67-75, 1960.
A procedure for treating mothers of disturbed children by exposing them to a contact
"where the therapist consciously attempted to set an example for the parent-patient."
Case examples are presented. Offers of educational guidance are defeated but accepting
and encouraging the mother's point of view while being firm provides the parent a new
symbolic parent and a corrective emotional experience which she may eventually repeat
with the child.

THARP, R, and OTIS, G., "Toward a Theory for Therapeutic Intervention in Families,"
      J. Consult, Psychol., 30, 426-434, 1966.
Family roles are characterized into five functional entities: solidarity, sexuality,
internal instrumentality, external relations, and division of responsibility. Data
were from the authors' clinical work. A discrepancy between the expectations and the
actual performance can lead to symptoms. Interventions to make the roles more consonant are described with three case illustrations.

THORMAN, G., Family Therapy: Help for Troubled Families, New York, Public Affairs
      Pamphlet No. 356, 1964.
Rationale, indications, family dynamics, techniques, and future trends are described.

TITCHENER, L., and GOLDEN, M., "Predictions of Therapeutic Themes from Observation of
      Family Interaction Evoked by the 'Revealed Differences' Technique," J. Nerv. Ment.
      Dis., 136, 464-474, 1963.
A standard interview procedure with the family discussion observed and classification
of formal content variables attempted. The results are said to be informative for
prediction of the course of therapy.

VASSILIOU, G., "Milieu Specificity in Family Therapy," in N. W. Ackerman (Ed.), Family
      Therapy in Transition, Boston, Little, Brown, 1970.
A description of the Greek family, its historical development, and its problems as
seen from a family therapy point of view.

VIORST, J., "Therapy for the Whole Family," Science News., p. 74, 1963.
A clinical essay defining family therapy and describing indications, advantages, problems, and dangers inherent in the use of "new techniques."

WAIRI, M., "Nurse Participation in Family Therapy," Perspect. Psychiat. Care, 3:
      8-13, 1965.
Based on the idea that the illness of one family member is related to the disturbance
of the total family, this is a clinical essay describing the role of the nurse in
family treatment. The nurse is encouraged to take a role in family treatment along
with other team members.

WARKENTIN, J., "Psychotherapy With Couples and Families," J. Med. Ass., Georgia, 49,

569-570, 1960.
An essay based on the author's clinical work on family psychotherapy as an additional
treatment which can be used in the treatment of emotional disorders. Discussion of
dynamics and problems with a case example.

WEAKLAND, J., "Family Therapy as a Research Arena," Fam. Proc., 1, 63-68, 1962.
A paper emphasizing the appropriateness and importance of using conjoint family therapy
not only for therapeutic purposes, but also for research. Several questions pertinent
to family treatment are raised (such as "what immediate or longer-term results in
family behavior are produced by any given moves on the part of the therapist") and
finding the answers to these questions in the family treatment situation is discussed.

WELLINGTON, J., "A Case for Short-Term Family Therapy," Psychotherapy, 4, 130-132,
      1957.
Based on a case of a 14-year-old female who was treated with family therapy over 12
sessions with good results (she had had five previous years of individual psychotherapy at age 12), it is argued that short-term family therapy is often as effective
as long-term therapy.

WHITAKER, C., "Family Treatment of a Psychopathic Personality," Compr. Psychiat.,
      7, 397-402, 1966.
From part of a summary of treatment of a woman identified as having "eight years of
treatment, three psychotherapists, two near successes of suicide, and two successful
divorces" and her family, the author has evolved a theory of the development of the
psychopathic personality. The child divides a weak parental relationship and then
adopts this approach to all situations in later life. A team approach is suggested.

WHITAKER, C., and BURDY, J., "Family Psychotherapy of a Psychopathic Personality:
      Must Every Member Change?," Compr. Psychiat., 10, 361-364, 1969.
The second of two reports of family treatment where the identified patient was diagnosed a psychopathic personality. The patient was seen with the family for one and
a half years and for six months more she was seen individually. Her brother left
family therapy after "about" six interviews. In this case the identified patient
changed while the other family members did not.

WHITAKER, C., FELDER, R. E., and WARKENTIN, J., "Countertransference in the Family
      Treatment of Schizophrenia," in I. Boszormenyi-Nagy and J. L. Framo (Eds.),
      Intensive Family Therapy, New York, Harper & Row, 1965.
A discussion of family treatment with the emphasis upon the problems that emerge in
the therapist. In the treatment of the schizophrenic family the therapist must be
involved but avoid being absorbed "into their quicksand kind of meshing." Adequate
therapy of the therapist, being part of a professional group, having a satisfying
family life of his own, and supervision help resolve the countertransference problems.

WHITAKER, C., and MILLER, M. H., "A Reevaluation of 'Psychiatric Help' When Divorce
      Impends," Amer. J. Psychiat., 126, 57-64, 1969.
An examination of the effect of therapeutic intervention on one side or another in a
marriage when divorce is being considered. Being neutral is improbable, and the
authors suggest involving the whole family.

WHITIS, P. R., "The Legacy of a Child's Suicide," Fam. Proc., 7, 159-169, 1968.
A discussion of the effect on a family of a child's suicide illustrated with a case
report. Prompt therapeutic intervention is recommended for the bereaved family.

WILKINSON, C., and REED, C., "An Approach to the Family Therapy Process," Dis. Nerv.
      System, 26, 705-714, 1965.
An essay describing experience using family therapy as a new technique in an out-
patient clinic. The rationale, dynamics, and treatment process noted by the author
is described.

WILLIAMS, F., "Family Therapy: A Critical Assessment," Amer. J. Orthopsychiat., 37,
     912-919, 1967.
An essay exploring some of the uses and misuses of family therapy. It is useful for
diagnosis, to help parents to deal with children less than five, to enlist the parents
as allies in treatment of severely psychotic children and in making order out of a
chaotic family situation. Inadequate training and supervision, potential for the
therapist's acting out, and discarding psychoanalytic principles in a premature separation of intrapsychic and interpersonal approaches are dangers discussed.

WORLD HEALTH ORGANIZATION, Aspects of Family Mental Health in Europe, Public Health
     Papers 28, New York, 1965.
Eight papers which were "working papers presented at a Seminar on Mental Health and
the Family held by the WHO Regional Office for Europe at Athens in 1962" and specially
commissioned chapters. These include, "The Mother and the Family", "The Child in the
Family", "Working Women and the Family", "Marriage Problems and their Implications
for the Family", "Family Psychotherapy", "Mental Health and the Older Generation",
"School for Parents," and "The Hampstead Child-Therapy Clinic."

WYATT, G. L. and HERZAN, H. M., "Therapy With Stuttering Children and Their Mothers,"
     Amer. J. Orthopsychiat., 32, 645-659, 1962.
A study of the therapy of stuttering children which indicates that therapy should start
from a sound theory of the interpersonal aspects of language learning in children, the
techniques should be adapted to the age of the child, and the mother should be included
in the treatment program. Twenty-six children were included in the sample with some
children seen in the presence of their mothers and some seen separately. Stuttering
was considered to be the result of a disruption of the complementary patterns of verbal
interaction between mother and child.

WYNNE, L. C., "Some Indications and Contraindications for Exploratory Family Therapy,"
     in I. Boszormenyi-Nagy and J. L. Framo (Eds.), Intensive Family Therapy, New York,
     Harper & Row, 1965.
A discussion of the indications and contraindications "for one form of family therapy:
long-term, exploratory, conjoint family therapy used as a main mode of therapy." This
discussion attempts "to summarize my current views, subject to revision, of some of the
issues pertinent to an appraisal of the place of family therapy in the psychiatric re-
pertory."

WYNNE, L. C., "The Study of Intrafamilial Alignments and Splits in Exploratory Family
     Therapy," in N. W. Ackerman, F. L. Beatman, and S. Sherman (Eds.), Exploring the
     Base for Family Therapy, New York, Family Service Association of America, 1961.
From a clinical research project of 20 schizophrenic families and ten families of nonschizophrenic psychiatric patients it has been observed that schizophrenic families
use as one of their main mechanisms of coping "pseudo-mutuality and pseudo-hostile
mechanisms that disguise but help perpetuate the underlying problems." Conjoint
family therapy based on understanding the family organization and maneuvers in terms
of alignments and splits can benefit the disturbed family.

WYNNE, L. C., RYCKOFF, I., DAY, J., and HIRSCH, S. I., "Pseudo-Mutuality in the Family
     Relations of Schizophrenics," in N. W. Bell, and E. F. Vogel (Eds.), A Modern
     Introduction to the Family, Glencoe, Free Press, 1960.
A description of families of schizophrenics studied with family therapy. Characteristic was pseudo-mutuality in the family; the family supports an illusion of a well-integrated state even when this is not supported by the emotional structure of the members and the strains contribute to the development of schizophrenia.

WYNNE, L., RYCKOFF, I., DAY, J., and HIRSCH, S., "Pseudo-Mutuality in the Family
     Relations of Schizophrenics," Psychiatry, 21, 205-220, 1958.
An essay which postulates that the disturbance in the family is an important causal
factor in schizophrenia. Data was obtained as part of a long-term research project
on schizophrenia in which patients were hospitalized and parents were seen on an out-

patient basis. Most of the data is drawn from clinical work with families. Patients
with schizophrenia have families in which the relations can best be described as
"pseudo-mutual". The acute schizophrenic experience is derived from internalization
of the pathogenic family organization.

ZIERER, E., STERNBERG, D., FINN, R., and FARMER, M., "Family Creative Analysis: Its
      Role in Treatment, Part I," Bull. Art Ther., 5, 47-65, 1966.
A report on the use of creative analysis (which is a technique by which paintings are
used to understand the functioning of the ego) and its application to family treatment.
The family agrees on a project to be done and then the sketch is made by one or many
members of the family. It is then divided into as many sections as there are participants. From an understanding of the painting, the therapist then interprets the family
and their conflicts. Observations are shared with the treatment team of the inpatient
unit it which the identified patients are staying, and also with the members of the
family. Short and long range goals of family treatment are formulated and worked
out in at least 15 projects.

ZIERER, E., STERNBERG, D., FINN, R., and FARMER, M., "Family Creative Analysis: Its
      Role in Treatment, Part II," Bull. Art Ther., 5, 87-104, 1966.
The second in a series of papers describing the use of "creative analysis" in the
treatment of families. A case example is presented demonstrating the method.
Changes in the family were compared with evaluation before treatment, using the interpersonal checklist. Creative analysis is seen as an adjunct of an approach stimulating
a healthy "reingegration of the family as a network of mutually need-gratifying members."

ZUK, G., "Family Therapy," Arch. Gen. Psychiat., 16, 71-79, 1967.   18
A theoretical paper on family therapy in which the author puts forth a model differing from the "insight-centered" psychoanalytic model. The therapist is a go-
between for family members, and attempts to get them to change. Techniques of doing
this as well as the family's defensive reactions are described.

ZUK, G., "Family Therapy: Formulation of a Technique and Its Theory," Int. J. Group   42
      Psychother., 18, 42-57, 1968.
As an alternative to the "insight model" of family therapy, the go-between process is
described. The therapist defines issues, acts as a go-between for family members, and
sides for or against family members. Tactics of the family to forestall this are
listed. The family is thought to change "in order to forestall the therapist's
expected demands for much greater change or in order to foil other attempts of his to
control the relationship."

ZUK, G., "A Further Study of Laughter in Family Therapy," Fam. Proc., 3, 77-89, 1964. 37
A discussion of the function of laughter in the family illustrated with excerpts from
family therapy sessions. It is proposed that laughter is an important means of quali-
fying meaning for the purpose of disguise.

ZUK, G., "The Go-Between Process in Family Therapy," Fam. Proc., 5, 162-178, 1966.
A discussion of family therapy from the point of view of the "go-between process."
Four variations are described with case examples.

ZUK, G., "On the Theory and Pathology of Laughter in Psychotherapy," Psychotherapy, 3   no
      97-101, 1966.
An essay based on the author's previous research, some clinical work, and other notions
on the meaning of laughter. Bizarre laughter in schizophrenics, which often seems
unexplainable, became clear when it was systematically studied in the family setting.
It was found to be due to a "wish to communicate information differentially to members
of the family group." Clinical uses of laughter in therapy are discussed.

ZUK, G., "On the Pathology of Silencing Strategies," Fam. Proc., 4, 32-49, 1965.
A description and categorization of the ways people impose or enforce silence on one
another. "There is a causal relation between silencing strategies and pathological
silence and babbling which may themselves be used as powerful silencing strategies."

ZUK, G., "On Silence and Babbling in Family Psychotherapy with Schizophrenics," Confin.
    Psychiat., 8, 49-56, 1965.
From the author's clinical work, two cases are presented in support of this idea that
both silence and babbling can be understood as attempts to interrupt communication
and silence others' interactions. They are often seen in schizophrenia, but patients
learn these strategies from their parents. Techniques for dealing with this in treatment are discussed.

ZUK, G., "Prompting Change in Family Therapy," Arch. Gen. Psychiat., 19, 727-736, 1968.
An essay describing the author's ideas of why families change and the techniques to
foster it. Families will tend to follow a therapist's direction but will resist it at
the same time. They will also resist the idea that the identified patient's improvement is related to their involvement. A case is reported in support of these observations.

ZUK, G., "The Side-Taking Functioning in Family Therapy," Amer. J. Orthopsychiat., 38,
    553-559, 1968.
One of a series of theoretical papers describing family therapy in terms of the therapist acting as a "go-between" and as a "side-taker." Pros, cons, rationale, and hoped-
for results are discussed.

ZUK, G., "Triadic-Based Family Therapy," Int. J. Psychiat., 8, 539-569, 1969.
A theory that family therapy is more than just a dyadic affair and can be best understood in triadic terms (that is, at least three people involved, some of whom can be
fantasized or introjected). The therapist acts as a "go-between" between two individuals or groups at odds with one another. Techniques of family therapy based on these
theoretical constructs are presented.

ZUK, G., "When the Family Therapist Takes Sides: A Case Report," Psychotherapy, 5, 24-
    28, 1968.
One of series of papers on the "go-between process" (therapist as a facilitator for
communications between family members) as used in family therapy. Previous papers
illustrate when the family therapist does not take sides; in this paper when and how
the therapist takes sides is illustrated. Its purpose is to understand pathogenic
relating of families and to "replace it if possible with a more productive pattern."

ZUK, G., and BOSZORMENYI-NAGY, I. (Eds.), Family Therapy and Disturbed Families, Palo
    Alto, Science & Behavior Books, 1967.
A collection of new material and previously published articles which includes discussions of family theory and psychopathology, relationships between family and sociocultural systems, and specific techniques of family and marriage therapy. 243 pp.

ZUK, G., and RUBINSTEIN, D., "A Review of Concepts in the Study and Treatment of
    Families of Schizophrenics," in I. Boszormenyi-Nagy and J. L. Framo (Eds.),
    Intensive Family Therapy, New York, Harper & Row, 1965.
A review of conceptual trends in family treatment of schizophrenics. Discusses the
shift from parent pathology to nuclear family to three generational involvement.

1.2 MULTIPLE FAMILY THERAPY

BARCAI, A., "An Adventure in Multiple Family Therapy," Fam. Proc., 6, 185-192, 1967.
A discussion of scapegoating as it was dealt with in multiple family therapy with
three families with a schizophrenic son. When the therapist found himself unable to
counteract the dehumanization and disrespect shown to the schizophrenic sons by their
parents, he restructured the group, making the son the group leader.

BERMAN, K.,"Multiple Family Therapy," Ment. Hyg., 50, 367-370, 1966.
Multiple conjoint family therapy (treating two or more families simultaneously) was used
in a large VA hospital for one year. Sample included alcoholics and some "non-severe"
psychotics with sociopaths and "severe" psychotics excluded. Techniques are described.
Preliminary results indicated that no patient has been rehospitalized (30%-40% rehospi-
talization was expected).

BLINDER, M., COLMAN, A., CURRY, A., and KESSLER, D.,"'MCFT': Simultaneous Treatment of
     Several Families," Amer. J. Psychother., 19, 559-569, 1965.
A critique of multiple-conjoint family therapy (a type of group meeting composed of six
to eight family units) done on inpatient service. Stages that the group goes through
are described in achieving the goal of a more healthy equilibrium. It is felt that
this technique is a "potent method" for working through family problems and making the
posthospital adjustment more successful.

BURTON, G., and YOUNG, D., "Family Crisis in Group Therapy," Fam. Proc., 1, 214-223,
     1962.
A report of the experiences of two therapists doing group counseling of twelve couples,
each of which includes an alcoholic husband. The paper is specifically concerned with
the reporting of family crises in the group. It is the author's impression that group
members "use the crisis reports of each other in furthering an understanding of their
own situations and in gaining courage to experiment in modifying their own behavior."

COUGHLIN, F., and WIMBERGER, H. C., "Group Family Therapy," Fam. Proc., 7, 37-50, 1968.
A treatment program using multiple family therapy with ten families seen in a group.
All families were seen together for the first three sessions, and then parts of families were seen in different combinations. It is said to be a useful, short-term treatment technique, and eight of the ten families improved.

CURRY, A., "Therapeutic Management of Multiple Family Group," Int. J. Group Psychother.,
     15, 90-96, 1965.
This is a report on the use of the treatment techniques of having multiple family groups
meeting together. What was discussed and how it was discussed are described. These
techniques appear to be less threatening than conjoint family therapy, but also less
intensive.

DAVIES, Q., ELLENSON, G., and YOUNG, R., "Therapy with a Group of Families in a
     Psychiatric Day Center," Amer. J. Orthopsychiat., 36, 134-147, 1966.
Clinical impressions of treatment of "several" patients with their families all in one
group, meeting weekly and using current concepts of family diagnosis and treatment are
described. Work was done in a day treatment center of a general hospital. Theoretical
principles, objectives, and group process are described. This treatment was found to
be "a useful form of therapy."

DURELL, V., "Adolescents in Multiple Family Group Therapy in a School Setting," Int.
     J. Group Psychother., 19, 44-52, 1969.
A clinical report of four families in multifamily therapy over 11 sessions in a junior
high school setting where the identified patients are having difficulty in school. The
course of a group is discussed. It was felt that the therapy was helpful in terms of
the patient's school performance. Problems with school administration were discussed.

GOTTLIEB, A., and PATTISON, E. M., "Married Couples Group Psychotherapy," <u>Arch. Gen.</u>
     <u>Psychiat.</u>, 14, 143-152, 1966.
A general discussion of group therapy with marital couples with emphasis upon how the
marriage influences group dynamics, how the spouse influences the other spouse's
psychotherapy, and the particular positions of co-therapists in a group of couples.
Arguments for and against the procedure are presented, and a clinical illustration is
offered.

JONES, W., "The Villain and the Victim: Group Therapy for Married Couples," <u>Amer. J.</u>
     <u>Psychiat.</u>, 124, 351-354, 1967.
The author's experience with group therapy where the group is made up of married
couples. One indication for such therapy is when "conjoint marriage therapy" is dead-
locked.

JARVIS, P., ESTY, J., and STUTZMAN, L., "Evaluation and Treatment of Families at Fort
     Logan Mental Health Center," <u>Comm. Ment. Health</u>, 5, 14-19, 1969.
A survey paper of trends in evaluation of treatment of patients from an inpatient facility of a psychiatric hospital. More evaluations are being carried out in the
patient's home or in the community rather than in the hospital itself. There is
greater involvement of "extended families" and of children (and in the case of children, involvement at an earlier age) in evaluation and treatment. There is great use
of multiple-family group therapy rather than conjoint family therapy.

JULIAN, B., VENTOLA, L., and CHRIST, J., "Multiple Family Therapy: The Interaction of
     Young Hospitalized Patients With Their Mothers," <u>Int. J. Group Psychother.</u>, 19,
     501-509, 1969.
A clinical report of multiple family therapy of adolescents, diagnosed as schizophrenic, all of whom are hospitalized. The family group is made up of only the identified patient and the mother. There were four females and two males. The group met
once weekly. Progress and problems are discussed.

KIMBRO, E., TASCHMAN, H., WYLIE, H., and MacLENNAN, B., "Multiple Family Group Approach
     to Some Problems of Adolescence," <u>Int. J. Group Psychother.</u>, 17, 18-24, 1967.
A report of the authors' experience with multiple family groups (three families in each
group). Theoretical considerations, process, problems, goals, and role of the therapist are discussed. This form of therapy is thought to incorporate the advantages of
traditional, group, and family therapy, in addition to adding a dimension of its own.

KLIMENKO, A., "Multifamily Therapy in the Rehabilitation of Drug Addicts," <u>Perspec.</u>
     <u>Psychiat. Care</u>, 6, 220-223, 1968.
A report of experiences at a halfway house for treatment of narcotics addicts, using
multifamily therapy conducted by two co-therapists. Rationale is that "successful
efforts to break the habit are directly related to family cohesiveness." A family
member is loosely defined to include any person with whom an addict is closely involved. Sessions are once a week, lasting one and a half hours. No data are presented, but it is the author's impression that "family disturbances are a major in-
fluencing factor in the life of a drug addict."

LAQUEUR, H. P., "General Systems Theory and Multiple Family Therapy," in W. Gray,
     F. Duhl, and N. Rizzo (Eds.), <u>General Systems Theory and Psychiatry</u>, Boston, Lit-
     tle, Brown, 1969.
A discussion of multiple family therapy from the point of view of systems theory. The
general theoretical base for multiple family therapy is offered within this framework.

LAQUEUR, H. P., "Multiple Family Therapy and General Systems Theory," in N. W. Acker-
     man (Ed.), <u>Family Therapy in Transition</u>, Boston, Little, Brown, 1970.
The family from the point of view of general systems theory with the emphasis upon
treating groups of families. Theory and technique are described with examples.

LAQUEUR, H. P., "Multiple Family Therapy and General Systems Theory," Int. Psychiat.
    Clin., 7, 99-124, 1970.
A discussion of multiple family therapy using the concepts of general systems theory.
The family and its components are viewed as subsystems of a larger field of interre-
lations whose interface problems can be studied and dealt with.

LAQUEUR, H. P., and LaBURT, H. A., "Family Organization on a Modern State Hospital
    Ward," Men. Hyg., 48, 544-551, 1964.
A description of the participation of an auxiliary composed of families of hospitalized
patients. The families raise funds, participate in the ward activities, and are involved in group therapy as family groups. The goal is "to integrate the family into
the patient's treatment plan."

LAQUEUR, H. P., LaBURT, H. A., and MORONG, E., "Multiple Family Therapy," in J. H.
    Masserman (Ed.), Psychoanalysis and Social Process, Current Psychiatric Therapies,
    Vol. IV, New York, Grune & Stratton, 1964.
A description of the treatment of families in group sessions in which a therapist sees
several families at once. The context of the treatment is a therapeutic community ward
in a state hospital. The procedure, its rationale, and impressions of results are
given for a sample of 80 families treated with this method.

LAQUEUR, H. P., LaBURT, H. A., and MORONG, E., "Multiple Family Therapy: Further De-
    velopments," Int. J. Soc. Psychiat., Special Ed. 2, 70-80, 1964.
An expanded discussion of the treatment of families in groups at Creedmoor State Hospital. Setting, objectives, problems and techniques of the method are discussed.

LAQUEUR, H. P., WELLS, C., and AGRESTI, M., "Multiple Family Therapy in a State Hospital,"
    Hosp. and Comm. Psychiat., 20, 13-20, 1969.
This is a report of multiple family therapy in a state hospital setting. Sessions were
held for 75 minutes once a week, with one therapist, throughout hospitalization and
sometimes during aftercare. The sample consisted primarily of young schizophrenics.
Rationale, dynamics, techniques, practical matters, and advantages and disadvantages
over conjoint family therapy are discussed.

LEICHTER, E., and SCHULMAN, G., "Emerging Phenomena in Multi-Family Group Treatment,"
    Int. J. Group Psychother., 18, 59-69, 1968.
This is a case report of three families who met together as a group over nine months.
Some of the dynamics and uses of this technique are discussed.

MARKOWITZ, M., and KADIS, A. L., "Parental Interaction as a Determining Factor in So-
    cial Growth of the Individual in the Family," Int. J. Soc. Psychiat., Special Ed.,
    2, 81-89, 1964.
A general discussion of marriage and the family based upon treatment of married couples
in group therapy. The emphasis is on unresolved problems and conflicts in the parents
leading to unconscious alliances fostered in the child, with a breakdown of the potential for corrective experience. Examples from analytic group therapy are given.

MARX, A., and LUDWIG, A., "Resurrection of the Family of the Chronic Schizophrenic,"
    Amer. J. Psychother., 23, 37-52, 1969.
A careful review of the authors' experience treating psychiatric inpatients by systematically involving the family of the patient. Sample was 44 chronic schizophrenic patients and families over a two-year period. Family resistances and methods of dealing
with these resistances are discussed. The treatment program included family-therapist
meetings, patient-family-therapist sessions, multiple family group meetings, and multiple family-conjoint therapy sessions. Some of the effects of this treatment program,
both positive (patient and family improvement) and negative (member of the family decompensating), as well as the methods of dealing with these problems and practical theoretical implications and ethics of this approach are discussed.

OSTBY, C. H., "Conjoint Group Therapy with Prisoners and Their Families," Fam. Proc.,
    7, 184-201, 1968.
A report on a family treatment program at a correctional institution. The approach
used was multiple family therapy. The special effect of the prison setting and case
examples are described.

PAPANEK, H.,"Group Psychotherapy With Married Couples," in J. H. Masserman (Ed.),
    Psychoanalytic Education, Current Psychiatric Therapies, Vol. V., New York
    Grune & Stratton, 1965.
An essay on the use of group therapy with married couples. The couple is seen together (not in group therapy) only as an introductory phase to gather historical data.

POWELL, M., and MONOGHAN, J., "Reaching the Rejects Through Multifamily Group Therapy,"
    Int. J. Group Psychother., 19, 35-43, 1969.
A clinical report based on use of multifamily therapy (two or more families meeting
together). The setting was a child guidance clinic. Data were obtained from five
groups, each consisting of three families. Each family included mother, father, and
the identified patient, with siblings introduced when it was considered "appropriate."
The families were mostly of low socioeconomic class. One group was reported on, and
the results indicated that communication improved with all family members. Premature
termination was not a problem.

1.3 MARRIAGE THERAPY

ALGER, I., "Joint Psychotherapy of Marital Problems," in J. Masserman (Ed.), Current
    Psychiatric Therapies, Vol. VII, New York, Grune & Stratton, 1967.
A clinical essay on the use of marital psychotherapy for problems which seem to have a
marital rather than an intrapsycnic basis. The author prefers seeing the couple with
a co-therapist. Videotaped playbacks have been used with good results.

ALGER, I., and HOGAN, P., "Enduring Effects of Videotape Playback Experience on Family
    and Marital Relationships,"Amer. J. Orthopsychiat,, 39, 86-96, 1969.
The third in a series of papers describing the use of videotape playbacks in family
and marital therapy. Sample included 75 families from the authors' private practice.
Equipment and techniques are described. Playback is said to be valuable as an adjunct
to therapy in encouraging more "intense emotional involvement" on the part of the patients, in making available more objective data on the therapeutic process, and in
clarifying complex behavior patterns and sequences as well as relating verbal and non-
verbal levels. It is thought to be effective on repeated trials over a period of time
and to have a residual effect lasting over a period of months and "even years."

ALGER, I., and HOGAN, P., "The Use of Videotape Recordings in Conjoint Marital Therapy,"
    Amer. J. Psychiat., 123, 1425-1430, 1967.
A description of some findings obtained using videotape playback of parts of conjoint
marital therapy sessions (i.e., treatment of husband and wife by one or two therapists).
The setting was private practice with over 100 sessions with ten different couples. The
videotape technique is thought to be useful in helping patients to see themselves in new
ways, to understand the concept of multiple levels of messages and to help the marital
partners take a more objective position to understand their interaction and therefore
decrease "blaming."

APPEL, K. E., GOODWIN, H. M., WOOD, H. P., and ASKREN, E. L., "Training in Psychotherapy:
    The Use of Marriage Counseling in a University Teaching Clinic," Amer. J. Psychiat.,
    117, 709-711, 1961.
In the department of psychiatry at the University of Pennsylvania School of Medicine,
residents may participate in a teaching program which includes treatment of married
couples. Marriage counseling is discussed and there is a case example of the sort of
case presentation given to psychiatric residents.

ARD, B. N., and ARD, C. C. (Eds.) Handbook of Marriage Counseling, Palo Alto, Science
     & Behavior Books, 1969.
A collection of previously published material on marriage counseling. There are sections on the place of philosophy on values; theoretical issues; conjoint marriage
counseling; group marriage counseling; premarital counseling; special techniques;
counseling regarding sexual problems; professional issues and ethics in marriage
counseling; counseling divorce; and technical assistance for the marriage counselor.
There is a long annotated bibliography. 474 pp.

BECK, D. F., "Marital Conflict: Its Course and Treatment as Seen by Caseworkers,"
     Soc. Casework, 47, 211-221, 1966.
A clinical essay describing a theory of marital conflict. The data were obtained by
sending an unstructured questionnaire to "400 caseworkers in 104 member agencies throughout the United States" and by "stimulation of local study groups to prepare reports in
depth on such topics." There is a marital balance which helps keep the family in equilibrium, which is derived from courtship and the early years of marriage. The breakdown of the marital conflict and the conflicts resulting are described, including the
point where couples apply for help. Good and bad prognostic factors in terms of casework intervention and treatment of marital conflict are described.

BECKER, J., "'Good Premorbid' Schizophrenic Wives and Their Husbands," Fam Proc., 2,
     34-51, 1963.
A report of conjoint family therapy with seven married female schizophrenics and their
husbands. Their backgrounds, premorbid marital life, and course of illness are described. Results of treatment were that "five families appeared to benefit substan-
tially, one somewhat, and one not at all."

BELL, J. E., "Contrasting Approaches in Marital Counseling," Fam. Proc., 76, 16-26, 1967.
A discussion of marital treatment with the emphasis upon the therapist-marital couple
relationship as a social system. Treatment of the marital partners individually and
together is contrasted.

BELLVILLE, T. P., RATHS, O. N., and BELLVILLE, C. J., "Conjoint Marriage Therapy With
     a Husband-and-Wife Team," Amer. J. Orthopsychiat., 39, 473-483, 1969.
A clinical report of marital therapy where the co-therapists were husband and wife.
Advantages, differentness of transference, identification when the therapists are also
a couple, problems of tension between the therapists, selection of therapist couples,
and the personality patterns of the patients treated are discussed. The sample was 44
couples with the primary complaint of "sexual incompatability." They were treated in
16 weekly sessions. The results indicated that 26 were rated as successfully treated
and 18 as unsuccessful.

BERENSTEIN, I., "On the Psychotherapy of the Marital Couple," Acta Psyquiat. Psicolog.
     Amer. Alt. 14, 301-308, 1968.
From the author's private practice, family therapy of a couple is described. Emphasis
is placed on understanding projective identification, analysis of conflicts, and acting
out. Therapy is based on a psychoanalytic understanding of the patient.

BOLTE, G. L., "A Communications Approach to Marital Counseling," Fam. Coord., 19, 32-40,
     1970.
A clinical essay based on the thesis that communications difficulties provide an important avenue for understanding marital conflict. Therefore an interactional approach is
advised for treating problems. Communication difficulties are outlined and interventions are suggested. Interactional techniques are seen as only one part of the marriage counselor's repertoire.

BRODY, S., "Simultaneous Psychotherapy of Married Couples," in J. Masserman (Ed.),
     Current Psychiatric Therapies, Vol. I, New York, Grune & Stratton, 1961.
Current advances in the field of family interaction and communication indicate many advantages to simultaneous therapy of couples by one psychiatrist rather than by two which
tends to "atomize" family interaction. The author discusses the problems in treating a

married individual and a couple, and points out the great assistance provided to a "dead-locked" therapy by the introduction of the marital partner into concurrent therapy.

CARROLL, E. J., CAMBOR, C. G., LEOPOLD, J. V., MILLER, M. D., and REIS, W. J.,
    "Psychotherapy of Marital Couples," Fam. Proc., 2, 25-33, 1963.
A general discussion of indications for, advantages, and disadvantages of family
therapy. Two case reports are given. Of six cases seen by the group, four made significant gains, while the other two were unimproved.

CHARNY, I. W., "Marital Love and Hate," Fam. Proc., 8, 1-24, 1969.
A discussion of marriage with the emphasis upon how marital fighting is "inevitable,
necessary, and desirable — not simply an unhappy by-product of emotional immaturity
or disturbance."

CHRISTENSEN, H. T. (Ed.), Handbook of Marriage and the Family, Chicago, Rand McNally,
    1964.
A collection of new material on marriage and the family, including sections on theoretical orientation; methodological developments; the family in its social setting; member roles and internal processes; applied and normative interests including family life,
education, and the field of marriage counseling. 1028 pp.

COUCH, E. H., Joint and Family Interviews in the Treatment of Marital Problems, New
    York, Fam. Serv., Association of America, 1969.
A report of a project designed to collect data on rationale and techniques of caseworkers dealing with "troubled marriages." There are sections on special values of
joint and family interviews for diagnosis; special values of joint and family interviews for treatment; conditions considered favorable and unfavorable to the use of
joint interviews and to the use of family interviews; expansion of the circle of treatment participants and related experimental approaches; and a summary and implications.
330 pp.

DICKS, H. V., Marital Tensions: Clinical Studies Toward a Psychological Theory of
    Interaction, New York, Basic Books, 1967.
A clinical research report investigating marital problems. Concepts of the study,
rationale, social setting, individual setting, development of the study, evolution of
concepts, symptomatology, diagnosis, treatment, and treatment results are reported.
354 pp.

ELKIN, M., "Short-Contact Counseling in a Conciliation Court," Soc. Casework, 43, 184-
    190, 1962.
A description of the purpose and procedures of the marital counseling program of the
Conciliation Court of Los Angeles County. The court offers short-contact marital
counseling service for couples on the verge of separation or divorce. The background,
purpose, procedures and effectiveness of the service are presented.

FISHER, E. O., Help for Today's Troubled Marriages, New York, Hawthorn Books, 1968.
A book on marriage counseling that covers the problems of marriage, aspects and procedures of marriage counseling, the problems of divorce and widowhood, and comments on
remarriage. 228 pp.

FITZGERALD, R. V., "Conjoint Marital Psychotherapy: An Outcome and Follow-Up Study,"
    Fam. Proc., 8, 261-271, 1969.
A report on an outcome study of couples seen in conjoint marriage therapy. A sample of
57 couples were followed up after two-and-one-half years with an interview by telephone.
Of the couples who were seen because an individual sought therapy, 76% were improved.
Of those who presented an ongoing marital conflict as the presenting problem, 75% im-
proved.

FOX, R. E., "The Effect of Psychotherapy on the Spouse," Fam. Proc., 7, 7-16, 1968.
A discussion and review of the literature of the effect on a spouse when the partner
is in individual psychotherapy. Problems of gathering data are presented and the
ethical problem of adverse effects upon the spouse are discussed.

FRY, W. F., "The Marital Context of an Anxiety Syndrome," Fam. Proc., 1, 245-252, 1962.
A report from a project studying schizophrenic communication, whose hypothesis is that
"the relationship with the marriage partner is intimately related to the psychopathology
of the patient." The patients in the report had the syndrome of anxiety, phobias, and
stereotyped avoidance behavior. Spouses are described, and it was found that the onset
of symptoms correlated with an important change in the life of the spouse and the symptoms seemed to keep the couple united.

GEHRKE, S., and MOXOM, J., "Diagnostic Classifications and Treatment Techniques in
     Marriage Counseling," Fam. Proc., 1, 253-264, 1962.
A report by two case workers describing a marital counseling method with the diagnostic
classifications and treatment techniques used. Indications for joint interviews with
husband and wife are given.

GEIST, J., and GERBER, N., "Joint Interviewing: Treatment Technique With Marital Part-
     ners," Soc. Casework., 41, 76-83, 1963.
Conjoint family interviewing is indicated: (1) when there is a breakdown in communication; (2) when there is distrust of the other partner's actions; (3) when individual
work does not progress; (4) when there is lack of focus in individual interviews; (5)
when the joint interviews seem to be more constructive than individual. Techniques for
joint interviews are discussed, as are methods of termination and contraindications.

GETTY, C., and SHANNON, A., "Nurses: Co-Therapists in a Family Setting," Perspect.
     Psychiat. Nurs., 5, 36-46, 1967.
A clinical paper using one case example in outpatient marital treatment where the nurses
were co-therapists. Co-therapists can serve as "models of communication."

GOTTLIEB, A., and PATTISON, E. M., "Married Couples Group Psychotherapy," Arch. Gen.
     Psychiat., 14, 143-152, 1966.
A general discussion of group therapy with marital couples with emphasis upon how the
marriage influences group dynamics, how the spouse influences the other spouse's psychotherapy, and the particular positions of co-therapists in a group of couples. Arguments
for and against the procedure are presented as well as a clinical illustration.

GREEN, R., "Collaborative and Conjoint Therapy Combined," Fam. Proc., 3, 80-98, 1964.
A discussion of conjoint and collaborative therapy with families with a recommendation
for a combined approach where the family members are seen both individually and conjointly. A case illustration of a married couple is given.

GREENE, B. L.,"Introduction: A Multioperational Approach to Marital Problems," in B.
     L. Greene (Ed.), The Psychotherapies of Marital Disharmony, New York, Free Press,
     1965.
This essay, serving as an introduction to his book, describes the author's personal experience in prescribing counseling, psychoanalysis, collaborative therapy, current
therapy, conjoint therapy, or some combination of the above approaches. Advantages and
disadvantages are discussed.

GREENE, B. L.,"Management of Marital Problems," Dis. Nerv. Syst., 27, 204-209, 1966.
An essay describing some theoretical principles, classification, and treatment techniques
for marital problems. Indications and contraindications are described of (1) counseling,
(2) classic one-to-one psychotherapy, (3) collaborative treatment (marital partners
treated by different therapists), (4) concurrent treatment (both partners treated by same
therapist), (5) conjoint family therapy, (6) conjoint marital therapy, and (7) combinations of the above.

GREENE, B. L., "Marital Disharmony: Concurrent Analysis of Husband and Wife," Dis. Nerv. Syst., 21, 73-78, 1960.
A preliminary report of the concurrent analysis of 14 couples which the author began following three successive failures in collaborative psychoanalysis (each partner treated by a different analyst). Theoretical considerations, philosophy of treatment, and some results are reported.

GREENE, B. L. (Ed.), The Psychotherapies of Marital Disharmony, New York, Free Press, 1965.
A collection of previously presented material on treatment of marital problems using different approaches. There are papers on a multioperational approach, sociologic and psychoanalytic concepts in family diagnosis, marital counselling, the classical psychoanalytic approach, treatment of marital partners separately where the therapists collaborate, concurrent psychoanalytic treatment for the marital partners, conjoint marital therapy, a combination of approaches, and the family approach to diagnosis. 191 pp.

GREENE, B. L., BROADHURST, B. P., and LUSTIG, N., "Treatment of Marital Disharmony: The Use of Individual, Concurrent and Conjoint Sessions as a Combined Approach," in B. L. Greene (Ed.), The Psychotherapies of Marital Disharmony, New York, Free Press, 1965
This clinical essay describes the use of an approach involving individual, concurrent, and conjoint sessions for marital problems. The indication is when "both triadic and dyadic transactions are necessary either for successful treatment of the marital transaction or of one of the partners." Advantages and disadvantages of this technique compared to other techniques are discussed. No results are offered.

GOODWIN, H. M., and MUDD, E. H., "Marriage Counseling: Methods and Goals," Compr. Psychiat., 7, 450-461, 1966.
This is a clinical essay on marriage counseling, covering values in the contemporary marriage; basic concepts of counseling practice; goals, indications, structure, and process; desirable gains; and the future of marital counseling. Marital counseling works best using an unpressured, unaccusing atmosphere, give and take, catharsis, new perspectives, and the supportive efforts of new and mutually acceptable behavior and interaction patterns.

GULLERUD, E. N., and HARLAN, V. L., "Four-Way Joint Interviewing in Marital Counseling," Soc. Casework, 43, 532-537, 1962.
A clinical report of marital therapy using co-therapists of different sexes. Indications include (1) the inability of the marital partners to agree on common goals, (2) excessive dependence, (3) need for support by the caseworker of the same sex, (4) for diagnostic purposes, and (5) when an impasse is reached in individual sessions. Interview procedures, dynamic considerations, advantages, and evaluations are discussed.

HALEY, J., "Marriage Therapy," Arch. Gen. Psychiat., 8, 213-234, 1963.
A discussion of the treatment of conflicts in marriage. Certain types of marital relationships, the kinds of conflicts which arise, and the ways a therapist intervenes to induce change are discussed. It is suggested that conflicts occur when husband and wife define their relationship in conflicting ways thereby imposing paradoxical situations. The resolution of the conflict can occur when the couple faces paradoxical situations provided by marriage therapists.

HALEY, J., Strategies of Psychotherapy, New York, Grune & Stratton, 1963.
A description of a variety of forms of psychotherapy from an interactional point of view. Includes chapters on marriage therapy and family therapy.

HALLOWITZ, D., CLEMENT, R., and CUTTER, A., "The Treatment Process With Both Parents Together," Amer. J. Orthopsychiat., 27, 587-608, 1957.
Based on clinical experience at a child guidance center, the authors stress the need to see both parents of the identified patient together rather than separately. No sessions with all members of the family together were used.

HANSEN, C., "An Extended Home Visit With Conjoint Family Therapy," Fam. Proc., 7, 67-
    87, 1968.
An approach to family therapy which involved staying in the home with the family for a
week to intervene therapeutically in a family's life. Benefits and problems of this
approach are discussed.

HOEK, A., and WOLLSTEIN, S., "Conjoint Psychotherapy of Married Couples: A Clinical
    Report," Int. J. Soc. Psychiat., 12, 209-216, 1966.
A clinical report of 30 cases where the identified patient was treated using marital
therapy with co-therapists. Indications, objectives, treatment focus, type of cases,
clinical findings, and a case illustration are presented in support of this method of
treatment.

HURVITZ, N., "Marital Problems Following Psychotherapy With One Spouse," J. Consult.
    Psychol., 31, 38-47, 1967.
A discussion of the ways marital problems are complicated or created by individual
treatment of one spouse based upon spouses referred later for marriage counseling.
The problem is not only that individual treatment might break up a marriage but that
"the relationship between the spouses, which should be used to benefit them both, is
further disturbed." Marital treatment approach using the individual therapy as a
problem area in the marriage is described.

JACKSON, D. D., and BODIN, A., "Paradoxical Communication and the Marital Paradox,"
    in S. Rosenbaum and I. Alger (Eds.), The Marriage Relationship, New York, Basic
    Books, 1968.
An attempt to provide a conceptual framework and techniques for dealing with a disturbed
marital relationship. The marital situation is seen as a paradox in itself. As a result of that paradox, some examples of disturbed communication are discussed. In the
treatment of such communication, labelling conflicting levels, encouraging the symptoms,
and actually prescribing them are helpful.

JACKSON, D. D., and LEDERER, W. J., Mirages of Marriage, New York, Norton, 1969.
This book focuses on the nature of marriage, marital problems, and procedures for
bringing about change. Illustrations of different problems are given. Exercises
for a couple to work on their marriage are provided.

JONES, W., "The Villain and the Victim: Group Therapy for Married Couples," Amer. J.
    Psychiat., 124, 351-354, 1967.
The author's experience with group therapy where the group is made up of married couples.
One indication for such therapy is when "conjoint marriage therapy" is deadlocked.

KADIS, A., "A New Approach to Marital Therapy," Int. J. Soc. Psychiat., 10, 261-265, 1964.
An essay on a new technique for marital therapy in which the therapist "rechannels communication so that the therapist becomes primarily the listener and tries to maximize
interpartner communication." Steps to achieve this end are described.

KAYLINA, E., "Psychoanalytic Psychotherapy With a Couple Considered as Brief Therapy,"
    Acta Psyquiat. Psicolog. Amer. Alt., 14, 311-316, 1968.
Several case examples are presented in support of the idea of family therapy as a primary
treatment tool. Diagnosis prior to starting therapy is stressed. The main technical
tool is seen as "the interpretation of the unconscious transference fantasy."

KERN, J., "Conjoint Marital Psychotherapy: An Interim Measure in the Treatment of
    Psychosis," Psychiatry, 30, 283-293, 1967.
A case report of use of family therapy in an in-patient setting where there was a stalemate in individual treatment. In this case, a basically pathological relationship was
re-established for use of family therapy as an alternative to no relationship which was
leading to permanent hospitalization of the identified patient.

KLEMER, R. H., <u>Counseling in Marital and Sexual Problems</u>, Baltimore, Williams & Wilkins,
     1965.
A collection of new material and previously published articles which include discussions of counseling in marital problems; counseling in sexual problems; other marriage
problems; premarital counseling; and marriage counseling instruction in the medical
curriculum. There is an extensive reading list. 309 pp.

LASKIN, E.,"Breaking Down the Walls," <u>Fam. Proc.</u>, 7, 118-125, 1968.
A report on the treatment of a couple by a variety of approaches with a recommendation
that a therapist maintain maximum flexibility and innovativeness in treatment.

LEHRMAN, N. S., "The Joint Interview: An Aid to Psychotherapy and Family Stability,"
     <u>Amer. J. Psychother.</u>, 17, 83-94, 1963.
The author discusses, using parts of transcripts of three cases, some of the principles
and techniques of the joint interview of husband and wife, which he uses as an aid to
psychotherapy in "defining and resolving intrafamilial friction, and at times of
impasse."

LESLIE, G. R., "Conjoint Therapy in Marriage Counseling," <u>J. Marriage Fam.</u>, 26, 65-71,
     1964.
A clinical essay by a sociologist focussing on development of conjoint interviewing in
family therapy and in marital counseling. Marital counselors have not tended to take
full advantage of joint interviewing. Conjoint therapy aids in the identification and
working through of distortions, helps hold transference and counter-transference in
check, quickly brings marital conflicts into the open and into the counseling sessions,
and emphasizes current relationship problems. Contraindications include lack of training by the therapist, inability of the marital partners to use conjoint sessions, and
a strong paranoid system in one partner.

MARTIN, P.A., "Treatment of Marital Disharmony by Collaborative Therapy," in B. L.
     Greene (Ed.), <u>The Psychotherapies of Marital Disharmony</u>, New York, Free Press, 1965.
A clinical paper describing collaborative therapy of marital partners, based on treatment of 50 couples. It is not the reality of the situation which is important, it is
the distortion of reality that provides the clinical material. Advantages and disadvantages of the collaborating psychiatrists meeting regularly are discussed.

MUDD, E. H., <u>The Practice of Marriage Counseling</u>, New York, Association Press, 1951.
A study of the development of marriage and family counseling in the United States, and
a description of its practice with case examples. It includes types of organizations
and professions involved. 336 pp.

MUDD, E. H., and GOODWIN, H. M., "Counseling Couples in Conflicted Marriages," in B. L.
     Greene (Ed.), <u>The Psychotherapies of Marital Disharmony</u>, New York, The Free Press,
     1965.
A clinical essay describing the definition, goals, and techniques of marital counseling
developed over 25 years of work. The aim is to bring about an adequate adaptation to
external reality.

NASHE, E. M., JESSNER, L., and ABSE, D. W. (Eds.), <u>Marriage Counseling in Medical Prac-
     tice</u>, Chapel Hill, University of North Carolina Press, 1964.
A collection of new material and previously published articles which includes discussions
of marriage counseling by the physician; premarital medical counseling; concepts of marital diagnosis and therapy; and marital counseling instruction in the medical school curriculum. There is an annotated book list. 368 pp.

NATIONAL CLEARINGHOUSE FOR MENTAL HEALTH INFORMATION, Family Therapy: A Selected Anno-
    tated Bibliography, Bethesda, Public Health Service, 1965.
An annotated bibliography on the literature on family therapy up to 1964, which includes
general theoretical articles, therapy with adolescents, child-oriented family therapy,
therapy in the home, therapy with families of psychiatric inpatients, marital counseling
applications, therapy with schizophrenics, and training family therapists. 27 pp.

PAPANEK, H., "Group Psychotherapy With Married Couples," in J. Masserman (Ed.), Current
    Psychiatric Therapies, Vol. V, New York Grune & Stratton, 1965.
An essay on the use of group therapy with married couples. The couple is seen together
(not in group therapy) only as an introductory phase to gather historical data.

PATTON, J., BRADLEY, J., and HRONOWSKI, M., "Collaborative Treatment of Marital Partners,"
    N. Carolina Med. J., 19, 523-528, 1958.
A clinical report of three psychiatrists who met regularly over 18 months to discuss
their cases being treated by individual psychotherapy. As the discussions progressed,
conceptualizing the psychiatrists' patients in terms of the patients' thinking shifted
from individual dynamics to the realization that the individual symptomatology was representative of family problems. Treatment of the family is suggested.

PAUL, N. L., "The Role of Mourning and Empathy in Conjoint Marital Therapy," in G. H.
    Zuk and I. Boszormenyi-Nagy (Eds.), Family Therapy and Disturbed Families, Palo
    Alto, Science & Behavior Books, 1967.
A discussion of an experimental technique consisting of the induction of a belated mourning reaction as a way of treating couples. Intense grief, unrecognized and unresolved,
has a latent strength and bringing it out "was as if emotional pus were discharged."

PITTMAN, F. S., and FLOMENHAFT, K., "Treating the Doll's House Marriage," Fam. Proc.,
    9, 143-155, 1970.
Intervention procedures in the type of marriage where one spouse's incompetance is required or encouraged by the other. Therapy works best when the emphasis is upon respect for unique individual needs within the framework of the marriage.

POLLAK, O., "Sociological and Psychoanalytic Concepts in Family Diagnosis," in B. L.
    Greene (Ed.), The Psychotherapies of Marital Disharmony, New York, Free Press,
    1965.
A clinical essay describing a sociologic and psychoanalytic model of marriage problems.
In the marital conflict the therapist must identify the problem, identify the obstacle
to improvement, and then offer himself as an ally.

RAVICH, R., "Game-Testing in Conjoint Marital Psychotherapy", Amer. J. Psychother., 23,
    217-229, 1969.
A report on the "game-test" for both family diagnosis and family therapy. Methodology
is described and four typical patterns of interaction are identified: (1) competitive,
(2) alternating, (3) dominant-submissive, and (4) mixed. Based on these patterns,
techniques for therapy are described.

RAVICH, R., "Short-Term Intensive Treatment of Marital Discord," Voices, 11, 42-48, 1966.
Short-term intensive treatment can give a "reasonably quick resolution of discord." The
couples are given the Deutsch-Krause game as a diagnostic tool (this game is oriented toward the idea that the couple must work together to solve a task.) In this technique,
the couple is seen three or four times a week for two or three weeks together and occasionally separately.

REDING, G. R., CHARLES, L., and HOFFMAN, M., "Treatment of the Couple by a Couple. II.
    Conceptual Framwork, Case Presentation, and Follow-up Study," Brit. J. Med. Psychol.,
    40, 243-252, 1967.
A report of the author's experience using a male and female co-therapist for marital

therapy. Previously the "four-way" treatment was seen as a combination of two individual treatments. This has been given up and extensive use of transference and countertransference interpretation has been made. Discussions of theory, process, and a case
are presented. Telephone follow-up three to 30 months after termination of ten of 15
couples treated by this method are reported.

REDING, G. R., and ENNIS, B., "Treatment of the Couple by a Couple," Brit. J. Med. Psy-
      chol., 37, 325-330, 1964.
A description of a treatment of married couples by two psychotherapists. The dynamics
of the four-way interview are described, with emphasis upon the relationship between the
therapists.

RIESS, F. B. (Ed.), New Directions in Mental Health, Vol. I, New York, Grune & Stratton,
      1968.
A collection of articles on various psychiatric topics including papers on practice of
family treatment in kibbutz and urban child guidance clinics; short term analytic treatment of married couples in a group by a therapist couple; the therapeutic field in the
treatment of families in conflict; recurrent themes in literature and clinical practice;
and patterns of interaction in families of borderline patients. 320 pp.

ROSENBAUM, S., and ALGER, I. (Eds.), The Marriage Relationship: Psychoanalytic Perspec-
      tives, New York, Basic Books, 1967.
A collection of some new and some previously presented papers focussing on the marital
relationship from a family and psychoanalytic point of view. It includes discussions
of communication, monogamy, femininity, resistance to marriage, mate choice, expectations in marriage, changing attitudes of marital partners towards each other, marital
problems of older persons, the effects of children, effects of pathology of parents on
the children, effects of sexual disturbances, effects of marital conflicts on psychoanalysis, different treatment approaches to marital problems including individual psychoanalysis, with different analysts, family therapy, group psychotherapy with couples,
growth and maturation in marriage, and marital dissolution. 366 pp.

RUBINSTEIN, D., "Distortion and Dilemma in Marital Choice," Voices, 2, 60-64, 1966.
From an extensive case example, this essay hypothesizes that in a disturbed marital
relationship there are distortions and dilemmas which can be summarized as follows:
(1) the marital pair do not relate as real persons, (2) they relate through each other
to the internal introjects, (3) they try to change each other into an internal introject to solve longstanding conflicts, (4) they become "bad objects," (5) as long as
there is an externalized "bad object," the idealized "good" introject can be kept alive
and hoped for. Family therapy attempts to uncover these distortions and help the marital pair to see each other realistically.

SAGER, C., "The Conjoint Session in Marriage Therapy," Amer. J. Psychoanal., 27, 139-
      146, 1967.
Diagnostic interviews, therapeutic techniques, as well as indications and contraindications for marital therapy are discussed.

SAGER, C., "The Development of Marriage Therapy: An Historical Review," Amer. J. Or-
      thopsychiat., 36, 458-468, 1966.
An historical review of the literature and marital therapy and an attempt to integrate
current theoretical and therapeutic techniques. Transference from both a transactional
and psychoanalytic frame of reference are discussed and is felt to be a valuable tool
in marital therapy.

SAGER, C., "Marital Psychotherapy," in J. Masserman (Ed.), Current Psychiatric Therapies,
      New York, Grune & Stratton, 1967.
An essay on marital psychotherapy from a clinical viewpoint. Indications, contraindications, diagnostic and treatment techniques (with specific emphasis on the nature and use
of transference), problems, and advantages are presented. Behavioral changes are more
likely if the therapist concentrates on the interrelationship between spouses rather than
on insight.

SAGER, C., "Transference and Conjoint Treatment of Married Couples," Arch. Gen. Psy-
    chiat., 16, 185-193, 1967.
A theoretical paper on transference (defined as transfer of relations exhibited toward
objects in infancy onto contemporary objects). Various types are mentioned, and methods
to utilize the transference in therapy are put forth. Conjoint family therapy offers a
significant advantage over individual therapy in that there are greater possibilities
for transference reactions due to the triangular nature of the situation.

SATIR, V., "Conjoint Marital Therapy," in B. L. Greene (Ed.), The Psychotherapies of
    Marital Disharmony, New York, Free Press, 1965.
A clinical article describing rationale and techniques of family therapy. Interpersonal relationships involve two levels of communication, both of which have to be interpreted and worked on to effect change. In this technique the therapist has to be
more active than in other therapies, and must act as a "model of communication."

SILVERMAN, H. L. (Ed.), Marital Counseling, Springfield, Charles C Thomas, 1967.
A collection of new material on marital counselling which includes discussions of
psychological factors, ideological factors, scientific factors, and a summary of
marital counseling concepts. 530 pp.

SKIDMORE, R. A., and GARRETT, H. V., "The Joint Interview in Marriage Counseling,"
    Marriage Fam. Liv., 17, 349-354, 1955.
A clinical essay suggesting that joint interviews rather than individual interviews
are helpful in marriage counseling. Three cases are presented, and advantages as
well as safeguards before doing such an interview are discussed.

SLUZKI, C., and BLEICHMAR, H., "The Interactional Approach to Marital Therapy," Acta
    Psyquiat. Psicolog. Amer. Alt., 14, 325-328, 1968.
The interactional model of couples in family therapy is stressed and techniques for both
understanding and treating, based on this model, are discussed.

SMITH, V., and ANDERSON, F., "Conjoint Interviews With Marriage Partners," Marriage Fam.
    Liv., 25, 184-188, 1963.
Joint interviews in marriage counseling are seen as an additional technique in the range
of techniques offered. Assumptions, advantages, and disadvantages are discussed. Objectives based on clear-cut clinical needs should be spelled out in advance, rather than
having them come about because of resistance of the client or administrative decision.

STUART, R. B., "Token Reinforcement in Marital Treatment," in P. H. Glasser and L. N.
    Glasser (Eds.), Families in Crisis, New York, Harper & Row, 1970.
"The tasks of the marriage therapist are...to identify the desired ("loving") behaviors
sought by each spouse from the other; second, to identify the contingencies which can be
used to accelerate and maintain these behaviors; and third, to increase the probability
that each of these behaviors will occur." Procedures and results with five couples are
presented.

STURGES, S., "Folie à Deux in a Husband and Wife," Bull. Menninger Clin., 31, 343-351,
    1967.
A case report of a mutually shared well-systemized delusion in a husband and wife. Individual and family dynamics underlying this delusion are discussed.

TERUEL, G., "Considerations for a Diagnosis in Marital Psychotherapy," Brit. J. Med.
    Psychol., 39, 231-237, 1966.
This is an essay describing a method to "understand certain patterns of interrelationships between a man and a wife" in marriage. When a spouse is referred for treatment,
the other spouse is invited for a joint interview, and the therapist tries to get the
marriage partners to present the data in their own words. Five cases and the theory
used to understand what is being seen in the joint interview are presented.

THOMPSON, P., and CHEN, R., "Experiences With Older Psychiatric Patients and Spouses
        Together in a Residential Treatment Setting," Bull. Menninger Clin., 30, 23-31,
        1966.
A report of an experimental program of geriatric treatment in an in-patient psychiatric
hospital setting. Husbands and wives were often hospitalized together. Family dynamics
and treatment approaches are discussed.

TITCHENER, J., "The Problem of Interpretation in Marital Therapy," Compr. Psychiat.,
        7, 321-337, 1966.
A theory of interpretation in marital therapy is advanced based on the author's clinical
experience. Rationale and methods based on the dynamics of the couple is discussed.

VINCENT, C. D., (Ed.), Readings in Marriage Counseling, New York, Thomas Y. Crowell,
        1957.
A collection of 52 articles on marriage counseling. It includes sections on marriage
counseling in an emerging and interdisciplinary profession; premarital counseling; definitions, methods, and principles in marriage counseling; marriage counseling of individuals, couples, and groups; theories of personality formation and change applicable
to marriage counseling; research in marriage counseling; and questions related to marriage counseling as an emerging profession.

WARKENTIN, J., "Psychotherapy With Couples and Families," J. Med. Ass. Georgia, 49, 569-
        570, 1960.
An essay based on the author's clinical work on family psychotherapy as an additional
treatment which can be used in the treatment of emotional disorders. Discussion of
dynamics and problems with a case example.

WARKENTIN, J., and WHITAKER, C., "Marriage — The Cornerstone of the Family System,"
        in O. Pollak and A. S. Friedman (Eds.), Family Dynamics and Female Sexual De-
        linquency, Palo Alto, Science & Behavior Books, 1969.
A description of the inner assumptions and postulates about human nature and marriage
of two experienced therapists. The emphasis is upon the importance of the therapist's
views about life when dealing with a family.

WARKENTIN, J., and WHITAKER, C., "The Secret Agenda of the Therapist Doing Couples
        Therapy," in G. H. Zuk and I. Boszormenyi-Nagy (Eds.), Family Therapy and Dis-
        turbed Families, Palo Alto, Science & Behavior Books, 1967.
A discussion of the treatment of married couples with the emphasis upon the profound
influence of the therapist's own pattern of personal living. Includes the author's
premises about marriage.

WARKENTIN, J., and WHITAKER, C., "Serial Impasses in Marriage," in I. M. Cohen (Ed.),
        Psychiatric Research Report No. 20, American Psychiatric Association, 1966.
A discussion of marriage as both a legal and an emotional commitment with special emphasis upon the times "when we may expect difficulty and even impasse in the development of the emotional marriage." These times include the wedding night, pregnancy,
the second baby, and the "ten year syndrome."

WATSON, A. S., "The Conjoint Psychotherapy of Marriage Partners," Amer. J. Orthopsychiat.,
        33, 912-923, 1963.
A discussion of the premises, technique, technical problems, and technical advantages
of conjoint psychotherapy of marital partners. Several indications for this method are
stated: (1) family relationships where the distortions are gross and reality disrupted,
and (2) cases where problems are largely of an acting-out, characterological nature.

WHITAKER, C., "Psychotherapy With Couples," Amer. J. Psychother., 12, 18-23, 1958.
A clinical report on the use of marital therapy as an alternative to the use of individual psychotherapy with the identified patient. Sample was 30 couples all of whom were
in outpatient treatment. There were no individual meetings during the course of treatment. Results indicated that of the 30 couples, six dropped out. In two cases the mari-

tal therapy was preliminary to individual therapy. Ten couples showed no progress in at least one member, and it is unclear what happened to the other couples.

WHITAKER, C., and MILLER, M. H., "A Reevaluation of 'Psychiatric Help' When Divorce
     Impends," Amer. J. Psychiat., 126, 57-64, 1969.
An examination of the effect of therapeutic intervention on one side or another in a marriage when divorce is being considered. Being neutral is improbable, and the authors suggest involving the whole family.

ZUK, G., and BOSZORMENYI-NAGY, I. (Eds.), Family Therapy and Disturbed Families, Palo
     Alto, Science & Behavior Books, 1967.
A collection of new material and previously published articles which includes the discussions of family theory and psychopathology, relationships between family and sociocultural systems, and specific techniques of family and marriage therapy. 243 pp.

1.4 FAMILY THERAPY COMBINED WITH OTHER METHODS

ARBOGAST, R., "The Effect of Family Involvement on the Day Care Center Treatment of
     Schizophrenia," J. Nerv. Ment. Dis., 149, 277-280, 1969.
A pilot study to assess the relationship between the presence of a seriously disturbed parent or spouse in the home environment, and the effect of treatment in a day hospital setting of a consecutive series of schizophrenic patients. The group without seriously disturbed relatives in their environment improved significantly more in their treatment.

BARTON, W. E., and DAVIDSON, E. M., "Psychotherapy and Family Care," in J. Masserman
     (Ed.), Current Psychiatric Therapies, Vol. I, New York, Grune & Stratton, 1961.
Family care is an alternative to the dilemma of returning patients to their families where they are caught up in a pathological role or remaining in the artificial environment of a hospital with pressures toward regression. Group therapy with after-care patients and similar techniques are said to be appropriate for family care patients with the new environment providing a testing ground for patterns in living and an emotional climate for growth.

BASAMANIA, B. W., "The Emotional Life of the Family: Inferences for Social Casework,"
     Amer. J. Orthopsychiat., 31, 74-86, 1961.
A casework view of the Bowen research project where families with a schizophrenic member were hospitalized. Observations of 11 families are categorized into (1) interrelated personality problems among family members, and (2) interaction problems among family members. Case examples are given. A discussion of family therapy procedures is presented with the emphasis upon relating to more than one individual at a time. Inferences for social casework emphasize the dimension of the emotional life of the family rather than the integration of sociological concepts with casework practice.

BELMONT, L. P., and JASNOW, A., "The Utilization of Co-Therapists and of Group Therapy
     Techniques in a Family Oriented Approach to a Disturbed Child," Int. J. Group
     Psychother., 11, 319-328, 1961.
A case history of the treatment of a nine-year-old disturbed boy and his parents. The boy was first placed in a boys' group and the parents were seen in several joint sessions and then placed in a man's group and a woman's group. Later they were seen together with the child and with the two therapists in joint sessions. The authors suggest that they offered the family a series of controlled therapeutic settings which approximated more and more closely the actual family setting.

BOWEN, M., "A Family Concept of Schizophrenia," in D. D. Jackson (Ed.), The Etiology of
     Schizophrenia, New York, Basic Books, 1960.
Clinical observations based upon a research study of the families of schizophrenics. Includes a report on the project where whole families of schizophrenics were hospitalized.

BOWEN, M., "Family Psychotherapy," Amer. J. Orthopsychiat., 31, 40-60, 1961.
A discussion of the research program where parents and their schizophrenic offspring
lived together on a psychiatric ward. The paper includes a description of the history
of the project, the sample of families, and the theoretical approach. The emphasis is
upon the family as a unit of illness rather than upon individuals in the family group.
Principles and techniques of family therapy emphasize utilizing the family leader, avoiding individual relationships with family members, and not accepting the position of omnipotence into which the family attempts to place the therapist. Results are discussed
and examples given with case material.

BRODY, E., "Modification of Family Interaction Patterns by a Group Interview Technique,"
    Int. J. Group Psychother., 6, 38-47, 1956.
As part of a study of prefrontal lobotomy, family members of 11 patients who would un-
dergo this procedure were seen for five months before the operation until at least one
year after the operation. Frequency was from once weekly during the first few months
to as infrequently as once a month during the last few months. Individual interviews
with family members were also used. The family interviews seemed to result in "an increased capacity for action by the family previously immobilized."

BRODY, E., and SPARK, G., "Institutionalization of the Aged: A Family Crisis," Fam.
    Proc., 5, 76-90, 1966.
A discussion of the importance of involving the family in the decision about institu-
tionalizing an aged person. Case examples are given.

BURKS, H., and SERRANO, A., "The Use of Family Therapy and Brief Hospitalization," Dis.
    Nerv. Syst., 26, 804-806, 1965.
Experience with setting up an in-patient service in conjunction with an out-patient
child guidance clinic (which had a strong bias to family therapy) is described. Patients were aged between 12 and 16, and diagnosis varied from neurosis to psychosis.
Hospitalization was short (usually under two months) and was family oriented, using
techniques adapted from the multiple impact therapy technique. Results, including a
one-year follow-up of 25 patients are described.

BURTON, G., and YOUNG, D., "Family Crisis in Group Therapy," Fam. Proc., 1, 214-223,
    1962.
A report of the experiences of two therapists doing "group counseling" of 12 couples,
each of whom had an alcoholic husband. The paper is specifically concerned with the
reporting of family crises in the group. It is the authors' impression that group members "use the crisis reports of each other in furthering an understanding of their own
situations and in gaining courage to experiment in modifying their own behavior."

CHARNY, I., W., "Integrated Individual and Family Psychotherapy," Fam. Proc., 5, 179-
    198, 1966.
An essay on using individual and family interviews concurrently flexibly as the case
requires. It is said the strengths of both approaches can be utilized. Case examples
are given.

COHAN, M., FREEDMAN, N., ENGELHARDT, D., and MARGOLIS, R., "Family Interaction Pat-
    terns, Drug Treatment, and Change in Social Aggression," Arch. Gen. Psychiat.,
    19, 1950-1956, 1968.
A study testing the notion that family interactional patterns will significantly
modify the effect of phenothiazine treatment. Sample was 54 male and 72 female
shizophrenics in an out-patient setting. Using a double blind procedure, patients were
given chlorpromazine, promazine or a placebo. All got supportive individual psychotherapy. A close relative was the source of the data to measure conflict and patient's
behavior in the home. Results indicated that most patient improvement occurred in patients of chlorpromazine living in "least conflict homes." Medication was less effective where family conflict was high.

DREIKURS, R., "Family Group Therapy in the Chicago Community Child Guidance Center,"
    Ment. Hyg., 35, 291-301, 1951.
From a child guidance center, five different types of group therapy are described.
Included in this classification is family therapy. Family dynamics are discussed.

DWYER, J. H., MENK, M. C., and VAN HOUTEN, C., "The Caseworker's Role in Family Therapy,"
    Fam. Proc,, 4, 21-31, 1965.
An approach to family therapy developed in a residential treatment center for children.
The whole family is seen by a psychiatrist and then a caseworker sees the parents while
the psychiatrist sees the child. The caseworker deals with the parents' responses to
the family sessions.

EPSTEIN, N., and CLEGHORN, J., "The Family Transactional Approach in General Hospital
    Psychiatry: Experiences, Problems, and Principles," Compr. Psychiat., 7, 389-396
    1966.
This paper deals with the experiences and problems arising, and principles derived from,
the introduction of concepts of family dynamics and family therapy in the psychiatry departments of two general hospitals. It was used in the out-patient department, community
department, in-patient service and the day hospital. Ongoing supervision for family as
well as for individual therapy is stressed.

EWING, J. A., LONG, V., and WENZEL, G. G., "Concurrent Group Psychotherapy of Alcoholic
    Patients and Their Wives," Int. J. Group Psychother., 11, 329-338, 1961.
A description of concurrent but separate group psychotherapy meetings of alcoholic outpatients and their wives. The authors find that more husbands continue to attend group
meetings if the wife is involved, and there is greater improvement in alcoholic patients
whose wives also attend group meetings. The participation of the wife in the husband's
drinking is examined. An example is the wife who accidentally put a shot of whiskey into her husband's iced tea after he had stopped drinking. The authors highly recommend
involving the wives of alcoholics in group therapy.

FLECK, S., "Psychotherapy of Families of Hospitalized Patients," in J. Masserman (Ed.),
    Current Psychiatric Therapies, Vol. III, New York, Grune & Stratton, 1963.
An essay describing therapeutic principles and approaches to the families of hospitalized
patients. A crisis somewhere in the family usually precipitates hospitalization, and attention to both patient and family as well as some relatively long-range decisions about
service rendered to the family should be made early in the course of the patient's hospitalization. Flexibility in approach is stressed.

FLECK, S., "Some General and Specific Indications for Family Therapy," Confin. Psychiat.
    8, 27-36, 1965.
From the author's clinical work with in-patient schizophrenic families, indications for
family therapy based on the stage of hospitalization are presented. The three phases
are the admission phase, period of hospital adjustment, and the final reintegration
with the community. Family therapy complements, but does not replace, other treatment
modalities.

FRAMO, J. L., "The Theory of the Technique of Family Treatment of Schizophrenia," Fam.
    Proc., 1, 119-131, 1962.
A rationale for and experiences with family therapy of schizophrenia is described based
on work with hospitalized young adult female schizophrenics all of whom were also receiving intensive individual and group psychotherapy. Techniques used by this group
are described.

GRALNICK, A., "Conjoint Family Therapy: Its Role in Rehabilitation of the Inpatient
    and Family," J. Nerv. Ment. Dis., 136, 500-506, 1963.
Family therapy for in-patients is recommended when a patient is not improving and the
conflict appears related to the family, when the patient cannot communicate his thoughts
and feelings to family without help, when an unusually pathological relationship appears
to exist with family members, a.d when rupture of a marital relationship seems imminent.

GRALNICK, A., and SCHWEEN, P. H., "Family Therapy," in I. M. Cohen (Ed.), Psychiatric
    Research Report No. 20, American Psychiatric Association, 1966.
The traditional general practitioner "may be looked upon as the forerunner of the
present-day psychiatric family-therapist." A discussion of experience leading to
seeing the value of treating the family unit. Indications for family therapy, its
purposes, and the importance of dealing with the family of the discharged patient are
emphasized.

GREEN, R., "Collaborative and Conjoint Therapy Combined," Fam. Proc., 3, 80-98, 1964.
A discussion of conjoint and collaborative therapy with families with a recommendation
for a combined approach where the family members are seen both individually and conjointly. A case illustration of a married couple is given.

GRUNEBAUM, H. U., and WEISS, J. L., "Psychotic Mothers and Their Children: Joint Ad-
    mission to an Adult Psychiatric Hospital," Amer. J. Psychiat., 119, 927-933, 1963.
A description of 12 infants and young children cared for by their mothers on the adult
ward of the Massachusetts Mental Health Center. The mothers were hospitalized for
severe emotional disorders, but were still able to care for their children. Such joint
admissions are said to be practical in selected cases and can make a substantial contribution to the mother's recovery.

HANSEN, C., "An Extended Home Visit With Conjoint Family Therapy," Fam. Proc., 7, 67-
    87, 1968.
An approach to family therapy which involved staying in the home with the family for a
week to intervene therapeutically in a family's life. Benefits and problems of this
approach are discussed.

JARVIS, P., ESTY, J., and STUTZMAN, L., "Evaluation and Treatment of Families at the
    Fort Logan Mental Health Center," Comm. Ment. Health J., 5, 14-19, 1969.
A survey paper of trends in evaluation of treatment of patients from an in-patient facility of a psychiatric hospital. More evaluations are being carried out in the patient's home or in the community rather than in the hospital itself. There is greater
involvement of "extended families" and of children (and of involving them at an earlier
age) in both evaluation and treatment. There is great use of multiple-family group
therapy rather than conjoint family therapy. There is less formal training of family
therapists than other forms of therapy. There were no evaluative procedures of the
various forms of family therapy being used.

KAFKA, J., and McDONALD, J., "The Latent Family in the Intensive Treatment of the
    Hospitalized Schizophrenic Patient," in J. Masserman (Ed.), Current Psychiatric
    Therapies, Vol. V, New York, Grune & Stratton, 1965.
Describes the authors' use of the family in an in-patient setting where the primary
treatment method was individual psychotherapy. Differences of this approach compared
to both family therapy alone or individual therapy alone are discussed.

KERN, J., "Conjoint Marital Psychotherapy: An Interim Measure in the Treatment of
    Psychosis," Psychiatry, 30, 283-293, 1967.
A case report of use of family therapy in an in-patient setting where there was a
stalemate in individual treatment. In this case, a basically pathological relationship
was re-established for use of family therapy as an alternative to no relationship which
was leading to permanent hospitalization of the identified patient.

KLAPMAN, H., and RICE, D., "An Experience With Combined Milieu and Family Group Therapy,"
    Int. J. Group Psychother., 15, 198-206, 1965.
A case report of a family in which the primary patient was a 13 year old boy. The family was thought to be more difficult than usual. Treatment was milieu therapy plus a
once-a-week meeting of the family and members of the treatment team, including psychiatrist, social worker, teacher, occupational therapist, and two ward staff members.

KNOBLOCHOVA, J., and KNOBLOCH, F., "Family Therapy in Czechoslovakia: An Aspect of
    Group-Centered Psychotherapy," in N. W. Ackerman (Ed.), Family Therapy in Transi-
    tion, Boston, Little, Brown, 1970.
A description of a family therapy approach in a therapeutic community outside Prague.
Family therapy in the stricter sense is said to be relatively rare, but some form of
family psychotherapy in a broad sense is an indispensible part of every case. A case
illustrates the approach.

KOHLMEYER, W. A., and FERNANDES, X., "Psychiatry in India: Family Approach in the Treat-
    ment of Mental Disorders," Amer. J. Psychiat., 119, 1033-1037, 1963.
This discussion of the family unit in India precedes a report of the new policy of the
mental health centre of the Christian Medical College in which one or two members of
the family must stay with the patient throughout his treatment as an in-patient. Thus
a relatively small psychiatrically trained staff can handle a large number of patients,
even if acutely disturbed.

LANGDELL, J., "Family Treatment of Childhood Schizophrenia," Ment. Hyg., 51, 387-392,
    1967.
Case report of treatment of a child with childhood schizophrenia using both individual
and family therapy. Improvement in the child followed improvement in parental intrapersonal and interpersonal conflicts.

LANDES, J., and WINTER, W., "A New Strategy for Treating Disintegrating Families," Fam.
    Proc., 5, 1-20, 1966.
A communal therapy procedure in which patient families and the families of therapists
participated in a 48-hour weekend together. The experience, problems and results of such
a weekend are described.

LAQUEUR, H. P., and LaBURT, H. A., "Family Organization on a Modern State Hospital Ward,"
    Ment. Hyg., 48, 544-551, 1964.
A description of the participation of an auxiliary composed of families of hospitalized
patients. The families raise funds, participate in the ward activities, and are involved
in group therapy as family groups. The goal is "to integrate the family into the patient's treatment plan."

LAQUEUR, H. P., LaBURT, H. A., and MORONG, E., "Multiple Family Therapy," in J. Masser-
    man (Ed.), Current Psychiatric Therapies, Vol. IV, New York, Grune & Stratton, 1964.
A description of the treatment of families in group sessions where a therapist sees several families at once. The context of the treatment is a therapeutic community ward
in a state hospital. The procedure, its rationale, and impressions of results are given
for a sample of 80 families treated with this method.

LAQUEUR, H. P., WELLS, C., and AGRESTI, M., "Multiple-Family Therapy in a State Hospital,"
    Hosp. Community Psychiat., 20, 13-20, 1969.
A report of "multiple-family therapy" in a state hospital setting. Sessions were held
for 75 minutes once a week, with one therapist, throughout hospitalization and sometimes
during after-care. Sample consisted primarily of young schizophrenics. Rationale, dynamics, techniques, practical matters, and advantages and disadvantages over conjoint
family therapy are discussed.

LEICHTER, E., and SHULMAN, G., "The Family Interview as an Integrative Device in Group
    Therapy With Families," Int. J. Group Psychother., 13, 335-345, 1963.
A report of the authors' experiences in using the family interview (i.e., a meeting
with the identified patient's family) as an adjunctive treatment process to group
therapy. The family interviews are used in a variety of ways, e.g. diagnosis at the
onset of group treatment, integrating changes achieved in total family functioning, and
at the conclusion of the group therapy.

LIDZ, T., "The Influence of Family Studies on the Treatment of Schizophrenia," Psychia-
     try, 32, 237-251, 1969.
In this lecture, the author attempts to link up his work on schizophrenia as a family
disorder with contributions of Freida Fromm-Reichmann, as well as with new advances
with the tranquillizing drugs and milieu therapy. Dynamics of pathologic families as
well as techniques of working with them are discussed in detail.

LINDBERG, D. R., and WOSMEK, A. W., "The Use of Family Sessions in Foster Home Care,"
     Soc. Casework, 44, 137-141, 1963.
A discussion of the use of family sessions with a foster child and his new foster
family. The therapeutic purpose is to help the family accept the child's needs, to
help the child deal with the problem of attachment to his own family and the foster
family, and to clarify misunderstandings which might arise with the caseworker.

MIDELFORT, C. F., "Use of Members of the Family in Treatment of Schizophrenia," Fam.
     Proc., 1, 114-118, 1962.
A report of the author's experiences using family members as companions and attendants
for schizophrenic patients hospitalized in a general hospital and treated with family
therapy as well as other somatic and pharmacologic agents.

NAKHLA, F., FOLKART, L., and WEBSTER, J., "Treatment of Families as In-Patients," Fam.
     Proc., 8, 79-96, 1969.
A report on work at the Cassel Hospital in England where 35 families were hospitalized
for a period of eight months on the average. The treatment was intensive, analytically oriented psychotherapy against the background of a therapeutic community. Rationale, problems, advantages, and case illustrations are given.

RABINER, E. L., MOLINSKI, H., and GRALNICK, A., "Conjoint Family Therapy in the In-
     patient Setting," Amer. J. Psychother., 16, 618-631, 1962.
A general discussion of the adaptation of family therapy to the in-patient setting
with its advantages and difficulties illustrated with cases.

SCHWEEN, P., and GRALNICK, A., "Factors Affecting Family Therapy in the Hospital Set-
     ting," Compr. Psychiat., 7, 424-431, 1966.
Discusses the modifications necessary when doing family therapy in a hospital setting.
Transference and countertransference problems, administrative problems, and the role
of the other patients in treatment are mentioned.

SEARLES, H. F., "The Contributions of Family Treatment to the Psychotherapy of Schizo-
     phrenia," in I. Boszormenyi-Nagy and J. L. Framo (Eds.), Intensive Family Therapy,
     New York, Harper & Row, 1965.
A discussion of the importance of the family in the treatment of schizophrenia with the
emphasis upon processes which are predominantly intrapsychic differentiated from processes which are predominantly interpersonal.

SMITH, I. W., and LOEB, D., "The Stable Extended Family as a Model in Treatment of
     Atypical Children," Soc. Work, 10, 75-81, 1965.
A report of a multiple-impact therapeutic program in the treatment of six severely
disturbed children and their families. Three boys and three girls, aged four-seven,
were referred as mentally retarded, were intolerable in school, and appeared psychotic
in the first interview. Two female therapists, assuming grandmotherly roles, treated
the families conjointly in three overlapping phases: (1) individual treatment for the
patient and parents, (2) family group therapy, and (3) peer experiences for all family
members. Patients showed rapid symptomatic recovery, enabling them to return to school
and participate in social situations. Parents and siblings, relieved of anxiety, functioned more efficiently and experienced improved interpersonal relationships.

SZALITA, A., "The Combined Use of Family Interviews and Individual Therapy in Schizo-
     phrenia," Amer. J. Psychother., 22, 419-430, 1968.
A discussion of the use of family interviews when doing individual therapy with schizophrenics. New information is provided for both therapist and patient.

TAUBER, G., "Prevention of Posthospital Relapse Through Treatment of Relatives," J.
     Hillside Hosp., 13, 158-169, 1964.
Observations of a caseworker working with families of psychiatric patients discharged
from a voluntary psychiatric hospital. The hypothesis presented is that intensive
casework service with the family as well as the patient is necessary to prevent posthospital relapse. Problems of working with these families as well as techniques of
treatment are described.

VIKERSUND, G., "Family Treatment in Psychiatric Hospitals," Psychother. Psychosom., 16,
     333-338, 1968.
A report of the author's experience in setting up a family treatment center in which an
entire family is admitted into a hospital for family therapy. In-patient treatment of
the entire family is indicated only where out-patient treatment is not feasible. The
report focusses primarily on indications for this form of treatment: (1) hysterical
young married women who develop severe anxiety neurosis after the first or second child,
(2) depressive reactions due to unsuccessful marriages where the partner is mentally ill,
(3) young patients in conflict with their parents, (4) alcoholic patients, (5) sexual
deviates, and (6) neurotic marriages. No results of this form of treatment are indicated as yet.

ZIERER, E., STERNBERG, D., FINN, R., and FARMER, M., "Family Creative Analysis: I: Its
     Role in Treatment," Bull. Art Ther., 5, 47-65, 1966.
A report on the use of creative analysis (which is a technique by which paintings are
used to understand the functioning of the ego) and its application to family treatment.
The family agrees on a project to be done and then the sketch is made by one or many
members of the family. It is then divided into as many sections as there are participants. From an understanding of the painting, the therapist then interprets the family
and their conflicts. Observations are shared with the treatment team of the in-patient
unit in which the identified patients are staying, and also with the members of the
family. Short and long range goals of family treatment are formulated and worked out
in at least 15 projects.

ZWERLING, I., and MENDELSOHN, M., "Initial Family Reactions to Day Hospitalization,"
     Fam. Proc., 4, 50-63, 1965.
A report of a study on the relationship between the course of hospital treatment and
certain family responses at the time of admission of a psychotic member. The sample
consists of 100 patients consecutively admitted to a Day Hospital. It includes responses to admission, to family treatment and to improvement.

1.5 FAMILY THERAPY TRAINING

APPEL, K. E., GOODWIN, H. M., WOOD, H. P., and ASKREN, E., "Training in Psychotherapy:
     The Use of Marriage Counseling in a University Teaching Clinic," Amer. J. Psy-
     chiat., 117, 709-711, 1961.
In the department of psychiatry at the University of Pennsylvania School of Medicine,
residents may participate in a teaching program which includes treatment of married
couples. Marriage counseling is discussed and a case example of the type given to
psychiatric residents.

BARD, M., and BERKOWITZ, B., "A Community Psychology Consultation Program in Police
     Family Crisis Intervention: Preliminary Impressions," Int. J. Soc. Psychiat.,
     15, 209-215, 1969.

The second in a series of reports describing training of police in family crisis intervention with low socioeconomic class patients. Rationale for the program, methods
of selection, and techniques of training (which included use of family crisis laboratory demonstrations and "human relations workshops") are presented.

BEATMAN, F., "The Training and Preparation of Workers for Family-Group Treatment,"
     Soc. Casework, 45, 202-208, 1964.
An essay describing the method of training for social workers learning family therapy.
Group processes as a method for supervision are used in preference to individual supervision because of "the requirements of treating the family rather than the individual." Specific methods used and discussed here are group supervision, sitting in on
a family session, viewing through a one way screen, films and tape recordings.

BEELS, C. C., and FERBER, F., "Family Therapy: A View," Fam. Proc., 8, 280-318, 1969.
A "personal view of the literature of family therapy" with an evaluation of the teaching
and practice of different therapists.

BODIN, A., "Family Therapy Training Literature: A Brief Guide," Fam. Proc., 8, 727-279,
     1969.
The literature on training in family therapy is described and a bibliography of 32
articles listed.

BODIN, A., "Videotape Applications to Training Family Therapists," J. Nerv. Ment. Dis.,
     148, 251-262, 1969.
Uses of videotape, both in training and in treatment, are described. Training applications include: (1) taping prior to particular courses, (2) tape libraries, (3) splitting
audio and visual channels, (4) "on line feedback," (5) self-presentation exercises, and
(6) comparative analysis of a trainee's performance. Several different applications in
regard to therapy are also presented. Trainees themselves may be exposed to a wide
variety of ways of using videotape.

BRYANT, C. M., and GRUNEBAUM, H. U., "The Theory and Practice of the Family Diagnostic:
     I: Practical Aspects and Patient Evaluation. II: Theoretical Aspects and Resident
     Education," in I. M. Cohen (Ed.), Psychiatric Research Report No. 20, American Psy-
     chiatric Association, 1966.
A presentation of a family diagnostic procedure at the Massachusetts Mental Health Center, which includes a description of methodology and of theoretical considerations as
well as resident teaching. Family members are interviewed individually and together
about the subject of what brings the patient to the hospital. The training of the
psychiatric resident is said to be broadened by participation.

BULBULYAN, A., "Psychiatric Nurse as Family Therapist," Perspect. Psychiat. Care, 7, 58-
     68, 1969.
From a community mental health center, a psychiatric nurse presents a case in which she
used family therapy. Dynamics and treatment techniques are presented. It is felt that
this is an important technique for psychiatric nurses to use in such a setting.

COLMAN, A., "The Effect of Group and Family Emphasis on the Role of the Psychiatric Resi-
     dent of an Acute Treatment Ward," Int. J. Group Psychother., 15, 516-525, 1965.
A report of a psychiatric resident on his experiences and impressions on a ward which
stressed group and family dynamics rather than individual approaches. The ward is described, and the resident's self-image is discussed and compared with the staff and patient expectations of the resident.

FERBER, A. and MENDELSOHN, M.,"Training for Family Therapy," Fam. Proc., 8, 25-34, 1969.
A description of the program of training in family therapy at the Albert Einstein College of Medicine in New York. The different levels of the program, the assumptions on
which it is based, and the content is discussed.

FLINT, A. A., and RIOCH, M. J., "An Experiment in Teaching Family Dynamics," Amer. J.
     Psychiat., 119, 940-944, 1963.
A discussion of a course in family dynamics for a group of women with no prior formal
experience or training in the mental health field. The course included tape recordings
of family therapy, literature review, observation of family screening interviews, observation of collateral group therapy, and structural interviews of parents. The students
were able to benefit without having too heavy a therapeutic responsibility in this difficult field, and the program is recommended for training other psychotherapists.

KEMPSTER, S. W., and SAVITSKY, E., "Training Family Therapists Through Live Super-
     vision," in N. W. Ackerman (Ed.), Expanding Theory and Practice in Family Therapy,
     New York, Family Service Association of America, 1967.
A clinical essay focussing on techniques of supervision of family therapy. A literature
review was done, and this method where the supervisor was right in the session is described. Staff and family reaction was "generally favorable, with adverse reactions
rare." Family therapy and the process of live supervision should be introduced early
in the course of training therapists.

KRAFT, I. A., "Multiple Impact Therapy as a Teaching Device," in I. M. Cohen (Ed.),
     Psychiatric Research Report No. 20, American Psychiatric Association, 1966.
A discussion of the value of multiple impact therapy in the training of psychiatric
residents with the emphasis upon experience working with other professionals as well
as family understanding.

MERENESS, D., "Family Therapy: An Evolving Role," Perspect. Psychiat. Care, 6, 256-259,
     1968.
This essay discusses the role of the psychiatric nurse in family therapy. Rationale
and indications for family therapy are discussed. Nurses are seen as "uniquely well
equipped to accept the role of family therapist." Training for nurses should include
functioning as a co-therapist, being taught the body of knowledge concerning family
dynamics, and learning treatment techniques. Moving outside the "traditional role of
the psychiatric nurse" is suggested.

MIYOSHI, N., and LIEBMAN, R., "Training Psychiatric Residents in Family Therapy," Fam.
     Proc., 3, 97-105, 1969.
A report on training psychiatric residents in family therapy at Mercy-Douglass Hospital in Philadelphia. Problems and benefits are discussed.

NATIONAL CLEARINGHOUSE FOR MENTAL HEALTH INFORMATION, Family Therapy: A Selected Anno-
     tated Bibliography, Bethesda, Public Health Service, 1965.
An annotated bibliography on the literature on family therapy up to 1964, which includes
general theoretical articles, therapy with adolescents, child-oriented family therapy,
therapy in the home, therapy with families of psychiatric inpatients, marital counseling applications, therapy with schizophrenics, and training family therapists. 27 pp.

PERLMUTTER, M., LOEB, D., GUMPERT, G., O'HARA, F., and HIGBIE, I., "Family Diagnosis
     and Therapy Using Videotape Playback," Amer. J. Orthopsychiat., 37, 900-905, 1967.
A paper describing the uses of videotape in teaching, doing research on family dynamics
and treatment. Videotape was found useful in diagnosis, in getting family consensus on
"what happened," and in therapist supervision.

RUBINSTEIN, D., "Family Therapy," Int. Psychiat. Clin., 1, 431-442, 1964.
This essay is oriented toward the teaching of family therapy. Rationale and techniques
are discussed, and it is stressed that this form of family therapy can be taught to
trainees in the same way that other techniques of psychotherapy are taught. Trainees
usually sit in with an experienced staff member as a co-therapist to start.

SATIR, V. M., "The Quest for Survival: A Training Program for Family Diagnosis and
     Treatment," Acta Psychother., 11, 33-38, 1963.
A review of the training program for family therapists at the mental research institute

given to "psychiatrists, psychologists, and social workers who work in a variety of settings; state hospitals, out-patient clinics, probation departments, and family service agencies." Setting, goals, and procedures of the training are described.

SCHOPLER, E., FOX, R., and COCHRANE, C., "Teaching Family Dynamics to Medical Students,"
     Amer. J. Orthopsychiat., 37, 906-911, 1967.
In an attempt to orient fourth-year medical students to child psychiatry, each group of six to eight students was assigned to one family for study during their psychiatry rotation. One student was assigned to each family member in addition, and observations of family interaction were made a routine part of the diagnostic procedure. A family interaction situation was set up using the method of Drechsler and Shapiro. Ten families were rated by the students watching through a one-way mirror. This seemed to be a useful way of observing family interaction and of teaching family dynamics to students.

SHERMAN, S., "Aspects of Family Interviewing Critical for Staff Training and Education,"
     Soc. Serv. Rev., 40, 302-308, 1966.
An essay focussing on training of social workers in which it is stressed that conjoint family therapy interviews, rather than individual interviews, are helpful in understanding family dynamics, as well as in treating the case. The caseworker can be prepared for the group supervision, use of films or videotapes, direct observation, and participation as co-therapist.

1.6 FAMILY THERAPY OUTCOME

ARBOGAST, R., "The Effect of Family Involvement on the Day Care Center Treatment of
     Schizophrenia," J. Nerv. Ment. Dis., 149, 277-280, 1969.
A pilot study to assess the relationship between the presence of a seriously disturbed parent or spouse in the home environment and the effect of treatment in a day hospital setting of a consecutive series of schizophrenic patients. The group without seriously disturbed relatives in their environment improved significantly more in their treatment.

BELLVILLE, T. P., RATHS, O. N., and BELLVILLE, C. J., "Conjoint Marriage Therapy With
     a Husband-and-Wife Team," Amer. J. Orthopsychiat., 39, 473-483, 1969.
A clinical report of marital therapy where the co-therapists were husband and wife. Advantages, differences of transference and identification when the therapists are also a couple, problems of tension between the therapists, selection of therapist couples, and the personality patterns of the patients treated are discussed. Sample was 44 couples with the primary complaint of "sexual incompatability." They were treated in 16 weekly sessions. The results indicated that 26 were rated as successfully treated and 18 as unsuccessful.

BURKS, H., and SERRANO, A., "The Use of Family Therapy and Brief Hospitalization," Dis.
     Nerv. Syst., 26, 804-806, 1965.
Experience with setting up an in-patient service in conjunction with an out-patient child guidance clinic (which had a strong bias to family therapy) is described. Patients were between 12 and 16, and diagnosis varied from neurosis to psychosis. Hospitalization was short (usually under two months) and was family oriented, using techniques adapted from the multiple impact therapy technique. Results, including a one-year follow-up, with 25 patients are described.

COUGHLIN, F., and WIMBERGER, H. C., "Group Family Therapy," Fam. Proc., 7, 37-50, 1968.
A treatment program using Multiple Family Therapy with ten families seen in a group. All families were seen together for the first three sessions, and then parts of families were seen in different combinations. It is said to be a useful, short term treatment technique and eight of the ten families improved.

CUTTER, A. V., and HALLOWITZ, D., "Diagnosis and Treatment of the Family Unit With
     Respect to the Character-Disordered Youngster," J. Amer. Acad. Child Psychiat.,
     1, 605-618, 1962.
A description of a treatment program of families with children with a diagnosis of character disorder. There are "56 cases currently active" and the results indicate that 60% "have been making consistently good progress." Descriptions of the treatment with case examples are provided.

ESTERSON, A., COOPER, D., and LAING, R., "Results of Family-Oriented Therapy with Hos-
    pitalized Schizophrenics," Brit. Med. J., 2, 1462-1465, 1965.
A report of a clinical study of 20 male and 22 female schizophrenics treated by conjoint
family milieu therapy plus tranquillizers (given in "reduced" doses). No individual
psychotherapy or other somatic treatment was used. Results indicated that all patients
were discharged within one year of admission, the average length of stay was three months,
and 17% were readmitted within a year of discharge. Of 32 patients discharged to jobs,
26 worked for a whole year after discharge, two for from six months to a year, and four
not at all. There was no control group, but the readmission rate was about the same as
with other forms of treatment. During the follow-up period, less than half of the patients were on psychotropic medication.

FERREIRA, A., and WINTER, W., "Stability of Interactional Variables in Family Decision-
    Making," Arch. Gen. Psychiat., 14, 352-355, 1966.
In order to test the stability over time, and after family therapy, of three variables in
family decision-making, 23 randomly selected families (ten abnormal and 13 normal) were
retested six months after the original research project. The abnormal families had received therapy. Results indicated that there was no significant difference between the
means observed in test and retests of the three variables for either normal or abnormal
families. It is concluded that these three variables (spontaneous agreement, decision-
time, and choice-fulfillment) were consistent over time and were not changed by family
therapy.

FITZGERALD, R. V., "Conjoint Marital Psychotherapy: An Outcome and Follow-Up Study,"
    Fam. Proc., 8, 261-271, 1969.
A report on an outcome study of couples seen in conjoint marriage therapy. A sample of
57 couples were followed up after two-and-one-half years with an interview by telephone.
Of the couples who were seen because an individual sought therapy, 76% were improved.
Of those who presented an ongoing marital conflict as the presenting problem, 75% im-
proved.

FLOMENHAFT, K., KAPLAN, D., and LANGSLEY, D., "Avoiding Psychiatric Hospitalization,"
    Soc. Work, 14, 38-46, 1969.
One of a series of articles comparing "out-patient family crisis therapy" with psychiatric hospitalization. The methodology has been previously described. Results achieved
by both of these two methods were equivalent. However, the authors stressed out-patient
treatment is more economical and less "stigmatizing."

GRAD, J., and SAINSBURG, P., "Mental Illness and the Family," Lancet, 1, 544-547, 1963.
An analysis of the effects on the family of psychiatric illness of one member of the
family before and after treatment. The sample was 410 patients from psychiatric facilities in England. Problems reported by families were analyzed; the sicker or older the
patient the greater the number of problems reported by the family. The number of problems reported by families was reduced significantly after treatment of the patient.

GREENBERG, I. M., GLICK, I. D., MATCH, S., and RIBACK, S. S., "Family Therapy: Indica-
    tions and Rationale," Arch. Gen. Psychiat., 10, 7-25, 1964.
Indications for and results of family therapy with a series of 20 patients, mostly
schizophrenic, in an open hospital, in-patient setting. Indications list diagnostic as
well as therapeutic goals. Six-month follow-up results of 13 cases are presented, and
a rationale using ego psychological and group process terms is included. A review of
the family therapy literature is presented.

HAHN, I., "Family Therapy: A Child-Centered Approach to Disturbed Parent-Child Rela-
    tionships," Penn. Psychiat. Quart., 4, 58-62, 1964.
Family oriented treatment (including "therapist, child and usually both parents") seemed
to offer advantages over the "typical psychoanalytical approach." Sample was 15 families, where the child was the identified patient, referred to either a child guidance
clinic or private practice. All cases improved and telephone follow-up in seven cases
after six months "corroborated the results."

HALLOWITZ, D., "Family Unit Treatment of Character-Disordered Youngsters," Soc. Work. Practice, New York Columbia University Press, 1963.
A report on the family treatment of 38 children with a diagnosis of character disorder. Procedures and descriptions of the family are offered along with tabular reports of outcome. 61% had a favorable outcome with the treatment averaging 17 hours per case.

HAWKINS, R. P., PETERSON, R. F., SCHWEID, E., and BIJOU, S. W., "Behavior Therapy in the Home: Amelioration of Problem Parent-Child Relations With the Parent in a Therapeutic Role," J. Exper. Child Psychol. 4, 99-107, 1966.
A description of the behavior modification approach to bringing about changes in a family. Theory and technique are described as well as outcome.

KAFFMAN, M., "Short Term Family Therapy," Fam. Proc., 2, 216-234, 1963.
A report on the use of family therapy in a child guidance clinic in Israel with the emphasis upon short term family treatment. The rationale, methodology, limitations, and initial evaluations of results are presented for 70 consecutive cases referred to the clinic.

KRITZER, H., and PITTMAN, F. S., "Overnight Psychiatric Care in a General Emergency Room," J. Hosp. Community Psychiat., 19, 303-306, 1968.
A clinical article reviewing the experience with 36 psychiatric patients who came to the emergency room because of a crisis. As alternatives to in-patient hospitalization, overnight hospitalization and the emergency room was used. Rationale was that their presenting problem was often a manifestation of underlying family problems, and by temporarily relieving the crisis and working out the future management, in-patient hospitalization could be avoided. Results indicated that of 36 patients, 11 were essentially sent to a psychiatric hospital, 22 were discharged directly from the emergency room, and three signed out against medical advice.

LANGSLEY, D., FLOMENHAFT, K., and MACHOTKA, P., "Follow-Up Evaluation of Family Crisis Therapy," Amer. J. Orthopsychiat., 39, 753-759, 1969.
One of a series of papers on a research project in which families were assigned randomly either to traditional hospital treatment or family crisis therapy with a focus on family therapy. Six-month follow-up evaluations of 150 family crisis therapy cases and 150 hospital treatment cases demonstrated that patients are less likely to be rehospitalized in the former group.

LANGSLEY, D., and KAPLAN, D., The Treatment of Families in Crisis, New York, Grune & Stratton, 1968.
A report of a research project where family crisis therapy was offered as an alternative to psychiatric hospitalization. Rationale for, techniques, data on the patients, results and implications of the results, are presented. 208 pp.

LANGSLEY, D., PITTMAN, F., and SWANK, G., "Family Crisis in Schizophrenics and Other Mental Patients," J. Nerv. Ment. Dis., 149, 270-275, 1969.
A further report on a study using crisis therapy as an alternative to psychiatric hospitalization. In this study, 50 families which included a schizophrenic patient, and 50 which included a nonschizophrenic mental patient, were studied with the means of an instrument which quantified the events leading to a crisis in the family and the management of such crises. Nonschizophrenic mental patients were better able to handle crises and interact with their families. Discussion of these findings is presented.

LEVINE, R., "Treatment in the Home," Soc. Work, 9, 19-28, 1964.
A clinical report of treatment of seven low-income multiproblem families who came to a mental hygiene clinic for help with the identified patient, usually a child. Treatment of the family rather than the individual was begun because it seemed more economical, more family members could be helped, and the therapist could be more accurate in understanding problems. Treatment was done in the home. Techniques included talking, demonstration, and family activity. The seven families were rated in terms of improvement.

MacGREGOR, R., RITCHIE, A. M., SERRANO, A. C., SCHUSTER, F. P., McDANALD, E. C., and
     GOOLISHIAN, H. A., Multiple Impact Therapy With Families, New York, McGraw Hill,
     1964.
A report of a clinical project using a new technique for families who consult a child
guidance clinic and who live a great distance away. It includes a section on the development of family therapy, illustrations of the method, discussion of the method, discussion of the family, family dynamics, therapeutic movement, discussion of the team
and results. 320 pp.

MACKIE, R., "Family Problems in Medical and Nursing Families," Brit. J. Med. Psychol.,
     40, 333-340, 1967.
From nine cases treated by the author over four years and a review of the literature,
the author presents parts of three of the cases in which the presenting patient was a
doctor or nurse. Of the nine cases, seven improved with family therapy and two did not.
The doctor or nurse will "defend himself against the direct expression of sick or dependent parts of himself and will instead project these onto the spouse or onto other
relatives."

OSBERG, J. W., "Initial Impressions of the Use of Short-Term Family Group Conferences,"
     Fam. Proc., 1, 236-244, 1962.
A discussion of early experiences with 38 families seen in group treatment over a four-
year period in a psychiatric outpatient clinic. The evaluation, initial session, and
succeeding sessions are described with a case example.

PATTERSON, B., McNEAL, S., HAWKINS, N., and PHELPS, R., "Reprogramming the Social En-
     vironment," J. Child Psychol. Psychiat., 8, 181-185, 1967.
A case report in which the hypothesis was that conditioning techniques could be used
to reprogram the parent and the child so that they become mutually reinforcing in contrast to conditioning the child alone. The patient was a five-year-old autistic child.
Observation of the new conditioning was done in the home of the patient and both parents.
There were 12 conditioning sessions lasting from ten to 20 minutes over a four-week
period. Changes in behavior were noted.

PATTERSON, G. R. , RAY, R., and SHAW, D., Direct Intervention in Families of Deviant
     Children, Eugene, Oregon Research Institute, 1969.
A description of a conditioning approach in family therapy where the ways parents deal
with children is systematically modified and examined before and after.

PITTMAN, F., DeYOUNG, C., FLOMENHAFT, K. KAPLAN, D., and LANGSLEY, D., "Crisis Family
     Therapy," in J. Masserman (Ed.), Current Psychiatric Therapies, Vol. VI, New York,
     Grune & Stratton, 1966.
A report of the authors' experiences in using a family approach in dealing with acute
crisis situations, rather than using hospitalization or individual psychotherapy.
Setting was an acute treatment facility which hospitalizes about 75% of patients referred. Of these, 25% were referred to the family treatment unit consisting of a psychiatrist, social worker and nurse. 50 cases were referred to this unit and in 42 hospitalization was "avoided completely." Techniques of treatment are discussed.

PITTMAN, F., LANGSLEY, D., and DeYOUNG, C., "Work and School Phobias: A Family Approach
     to Treatment," Amer. J. Psychiat., 124, 1535-1541, 1968.
11 cases of work phobia (the patient experienced overt anxiety associated with having
to go to work or staying at work) are thought of as being "the adult form of school
phobia." Treatment goal is to allow the wife or mother to allow the man to separate.
One year follow-up shows that five cases treated with conjoint family therapy were
able to return to work; the six in long-term individual therapy had not.

REDING, G., CHARLES, L., and HOFFMAN, M., "Treatment of the Couple by a Couple, II.
     Conceptual Framework, Case Presentation, and Follow-Up Study," Brit. J. Med. Psy-
     chol., 40, 243-252, 1967.
A report of the authors' experience using a male and female co-therapist for marital

therapy. Previously the "four-way" treatment was seen as a combination of two individual treatments. This has been given up and extensive use of transference and countertransference interpretation have been made. Discussions of theory, process and a case
are presented. Telephone follow-up three to 30 months after termination of ten of 15
couples treated by this method are reported.

SAFER, D. J., "Family Therapy for Children With Behavior Disorders," Fam. Proc., 5, 243-
    255, 1966.
A report on short term therapy of 29 children with behavior disorders and their families.
All cases were selected because they were either unmotivated or unacceptable for indivi-
dual psychotherapy. Treatment approach is described and 40% showed improvement.

SAGER, C., GRUNDRACH, R., KRAMER, M., LANZ, R., and ROYCE, J., "The Married in Treatment:
    Effects of Psychoanalysis on the Marital State," Arch. Gen. Psychiat., 19, 205-217,
    1968
In order to ascertain the effects of psychoanalysis on the marital state, a study of 736
married patients (432 women and 304 men), aged 21 to 68 in middle and upper socioeconomic
class who were being treated in psychoanalysis, was done. 79 psychoanalysts supplied
data on any ten consecutive patients. It was obtained through a closed ended questionnaire. 12% of the patients had concurrent group therapy, 2% were in conjoint marital
therapy and about 20% of the patients had one or more conjoint consultations with their
spouse and analyst. Results indicated that marriages rated poor initially improved.
Marriages rated better also improved. There was no evidence that as one marital partner
got better another got worse. Overall individual patient improvement was rated at about
60% of the cases. Of the spouses who were in treatment, good effects were more frequently reported in cases in which both husband and wife were treated by the same psychoanalyst.

SCHREIBER, L. E., "Evaluation of Family Group Treatment in a Family Agency," Fam. Proc.,
    5, 21-29, 1966.
A report on the experience of a family service agency in the treatment of 72 families.
Within three months, 61% showed improvement in communication processes and 56% in the
presenting behavior problem of the child. Of those who continued beyond three months,
96% showed improvement in communication processes and 92% in the behavior of the child.

SCHUSTER, F., "Summary Description of Multiple Impact Psychotherapy," Texas Rep. Bio.
    Med., 17, 120-125, 1962.
A report of the multiple impact psychotherapy project used at a child guidance clinic in
Texas. Families come from great distances and are seen intensively for two days, both
individually and in various family situations. The preliminary one-year and one-month
follow-ups attest that this method is "at least as effective as individual treatment in
many adolescent referrals."

SHELLOW, R. S., BROWN, B. S., and OSBERG, J. W., "Family Group Therapy in Retrospect:
    Four Years and Sixty Families," Fam. Proc., 2, 52-67, 1963.
A review of experience with family group therapy (authors' term for conjoint family
therapy) with 60 families in a child guidance clinic over a four-year period. Referral
sources were mainly from physicians and school. Several "hidden" factors influenced
choice of this form of therapy by staff members: (1) the identified patient was often
the oldest child, and (2) there was a large proportion of school achievement problems
represented.

SIGAL, J. J., RAKOFF, V., and EPSTEIN, N. B., "Indications of Therapeutic Outcome in
    Conjoint Family Therapy," Fam. Proc., 6, 215-226, 1967.

A report on a study which attempted to predict the eventual success of family therapy by examining the degree of family interaction and emotional involvement as described by therapists in the initial stages of treatment. "The clinical observations in this study raise some doubts about the value of the interactional frame of reference in conjoint family therapy."

SMITH, I. W., and LOEB, D., "The Stable Extended Family as a Model in Treatment of
     Atypical Children," Soc. Work, 10, 75-81, 1965.
A report of a multiple-impact therapeutic program in the treatment of six severely disturbed children and their families. Three boys and three girls, aged four-seven were
referred as mentally retarded, were intolerable in school, and appeared psychotic in
the first interview. Two female therapists, assuming grandmotherly roles, treated the
families conjointly in three overlapping phases: (1) individual treatment for the patient and parents, (2) family group therapy, and (3) peer experiences for all family
members. Patients showed rapid symptomatic recovery, enabling them to return to school
and participate in social situations. Parents and siblings, relieved of anxiety, functioned more efficiently and experienced improved interpersonal relationships.

STUART, R. B., "Token Reinforcement in Marital Treatment," in P. H. Glasser and L. N.
     Glasser (Eds.), Families in Crisis, New York, Harper & Row, 1970.
"The tasks of the marriage therapist are...to identify the desired ("loving") behaviors
sought by each spouse from the other; second, to identify the contingencies which can
be used to accelerate and maintain these behaviors; and third, to increase the probability that each of these behaviors will occur." Procedures and results with five
couples are presented.

WAINWRIGHT, W. H., "The Reaction of Mothers to Improvement in Their Schizophrenic
     Daughters," Compr. Psychiat., 1, 236-243, 1960.
At the Payne Whitney Psychiatric Clinic eight mother-schizophrenic daughter combinations
were interviewed and observed for a period ranging from four to 48 months, including up
to 30 months after the patient's hospital discharge. Of these eight mothers, two responded favorably to their daughter's improvement, two showed fluctuation in response which
seemed dependent upon the severity of the daughter's symptoms, and four mothers showed
signs of illness as their daughters improved. The author sees a common need with these
four mothers to keep the daughter partially ill. Where hostility emerges during the
recovery phase, he suggests evaluation for treatment of the mother.

WELLINGTON, J., "A Case for Short Term Family Therapy," Psychotherapy, 4, 130-132, 1957.
Based on a case of a 14-year-old female who was treated with family therapy over 12 sessions with good results (she had had five previous years of individual psychotherapy at
age 12), it is argued that short-term family therapy is often as effective as long-term
therapy.

WHITAKER, C. A., "Psychotherapy With Couples," Amer. J. Psychother., 12, 18-23, 1958.
A clinical report on the use of marital therapy as an alternative to the use of individual psychotherapy with the identified patient. Sample was 30 couples all of whom
were in outpatient treatment, and there were no individual meetings during the course
of treatment. Results indicated that of the 30 couples, six dropped out, in two cases
the marital therapy was preliminary to individual therapy, ten couples showed no progress in at least one member, and it is unclear what happened to the other couples.

ZIERER, E., STERNBERG, D., FINN, R., and FARMER, M., "Family Creative Analysis: Its
     Role in Treatment," Bull. Art. Ther., 5, 87-104, 1966.
The second in a series of papers describing the use of "creative analysis" in the treatment of families. A case example is presented demonstrating the method. Changes in
the family were compared with evaluation before treatment, using the interpersonal checklist. Creative analysis is seen as an adjunct of an approach stimulating a healthy "reintegration of the family as a network of mutually need-gratifying members."

1.7 FAMILY CONSIDERATION IN INDIVIDUAL TREATMENT

ACKERMAN, N. W., "Disturbances of Mothering and Criteria for Treatment," Amer. J. Ortho-
    psychiat., 26, 252-263, 1956.
A clinical paper discussing theory and practice of mothering and its disturbances. Critique of traditional techniques used in the child guidance clinic are presented and suggestions for therapy are made. Disturbances of mothering can be seen as by-products of
intrafamilial difficulties of the mother with other family members as well as a disturbance in individual psychodynamics.

ACKERMAN, N. W.,"Interpersonal Disturbances in the Family," Psychiatry, 17, 359-368,
    1954.
Involves in part an historical review of the handling of family problems by psychotherapeutic means. Previously, family problems have been handled in terms of individual psychotherapy, couple psychotherapy, and by various members of the family being seen separately but simultaneously by different or the same therapists. "Even if every member of a
family were given individual psychotherapy, it still would not constitute a psychotherapy
of the family." Some suggestions for working with family problems are made.

ACKERMAN, N. W., "The Psychoanalytic Approach to the Family in J. Masserman (Ed.), Indi-
    vidual and Familial Dynamics, New York, Grune & Stratton, 1959.
A clinical essay defending the use of some psychoanalytic concepts as a basis for family
therapy: unconscious communication; use of diagnostic family interviews; and an illustration of techniques of family therapy. Conjoint interviews can be an aid to individual
psychoanalysis.

ACKERMAN, N. W., "Toward an Integrative Therapy of the Family," Amer. J. Psychiat., 144,
    727-723, 1958.
Based on the author's clinical experience, a method for understanding family pathology
and a program of prevention is presented and illustrated by case examples. Illness is
a function of the family as well as a manifestation of individual behavior.

ACKERMAN, N. W., and FRANKLIN, P. F., "Family Dynamics and the Reversibility of Delu-
    sional Formation: A Case Study in Family Therapy," in I. Boszormenyi-Nagy and J.
    L. Framo (Eds.), Intensive Family Therapy, New York, Harper & Row, 1965.
A report on a case of a 16-year-old schizophrenic and her family in which treatment "of
the whole family seemed to move toward reversal of the patient's psychotic experience.
Interview data and comment is provided.

ACKERMAN, N. W., and SOBEL, R., "Family Diagnosis," Amer. J. Orthopsychiat., 20, 744-753,
    1950.
To understand the preschool child who is a patient, it is necessary to consider the psychosocial effects of the family members upon each other. Treatment of the young child
should begin with treatment of the family group.

ARLEN, M. S., "Conjoint Therapy and the Corrective Emotional Experience," Fam. Proc.,
    5, 91-104, 1966.
The use of family therapy with families containing a person with severe character disorder described within a framework of providing a corrective emotional experience.

BEATMAN, F. L., "Family Interaction: Its Significance for Diagnosis and Treatment,"
    Soc. Casework, 38, 111-118, 1957.
A discussion of the importance of considering the dynamics of the family illustrated
with a case example.

BENNEY, C., and PECK, H., "The Family as a Factor in the Rehabilitation of the Mentally
    Ill," Ment. Hyg., 47, 372-379, 1963.
A report of the author's experiences in a rehabilitation workshop treating psychiatric
patients. The value of using family dynamics in the individual approach to the patient,
as well as bringing in the whole family is stressed.

BERENSTEIN, I., "On the Psychotherapy of the Marital Couple," Acta Psyquiat. Psicolog.
    Amer. Alt., 14, 301-308, 1968.
Family therapy of a couple is described. Emphasis is placed on understanding projective identification, analysis of conflicts, and acting out, all based on a psychoanalytic understanding of the patient techniques.

BRODY, E., "Modification of Family Interaction Patterns by a Group Interview Technique,"
    Int. J. Group Psychother., 6, 38-47, 1956.
As part of a study of prefrontal lobotomy, family members of 11 patients who would un-
dergo this procedure were seen for five months before the operation until at least one
year after the operation. Frequency was from once weekly during the first few months
to as infrequently as once a month during the last few months. Individual interviews
with family members were also used. The family interviews seemed to result in "an increased capacity for action by the family previously immobilized."

BROOKS, W. B., DEANE, W. N., LAGOV, R. C., and CURTIS, B. B., "Varieties of Family Par-
    ticipation in the Rehabilitation of Released Chronic Schizophrenic Patients," J.
    Nerv. Ment. Dis., 136, 432-444, 1963.
A study of the posthospital course of 170 chronic schizophrenic patients. The data
were abstracted from records. The social, economic and psychiatric outcomes are correlated with various aspects of the family's participation in the rehabilitation process. A major factor in the success of this group is said to be the breaking of
pathological ties with the family and the forming of new, healthier relationships.

BROWN, S., "Family Therapy Viewed in Terms of Resistance to Change," in I. M. Cohen (Ed.),
    Psychiatric Research Report No. 20, Wash., American Psychiatric Association, 1966.
Family therapy from a psychoanalytic and "child guidance" point of view with the emphasis on resistance to change. Case examples are given.

CHANDLER, E., HOLDEN, H., and ROBINSON, M., "Treatment of a Psychotic Family in a Family
    Psychiatry Setting," Psychother. Psychosom., 16, 333-347, 1968.
This case report is in support of an experimental approach to a family by a psychologist, social worker, and psychiatrist working in a psychoanalytically-oriented psychiatric out-patient clinic. Whereas previously each member of the family had had a separate
therapist, in this case the family was seen together by all three therapists, and following the family meeting, each of the two sons would see a therapist and the parents together saw one therapist. Accounts of each of the therapists in their work with each of
the individuals is described. Goals of the family were to regard themselves as separate
individuals.

COOPER, S., "New Trends in Work With Patients: Progress or Change?" Soc. Casework, 42,
    342-347, 1961.
Discusses the notion that treatment of the individual patient often stems from problems
in the family as a whole. Individual dynamics and therapy should be kept in mind along
with consideration of family dynamics. Indications for each type of treatment should be
carefully considered in each case.

DAVIDSON, S., "School Phobia as a Manifestation of Family Disturbance: Its Structure
    and Treatment," J. Child Psychol. Psychiat., 1, 270-288, 1960-61.
30 Cases of school phobia were studied at a child guidance clinic. Data were gathered
from social histories and from individual interviews with patients and their parents.
Family dynamics and methods of individual treatment are discussed.

DELL, N., TRIESCHMAN, A., and VOGEL, E., "A Sociocultural Analysis of Resistances of
    Working-Class Fathers Treated in a Child Psychiatric Clinic," Amer. J. Orthopsy-
    chiat., 31, 388-405, 1961.
The authors' hypothesis is that fathers have been excluded from the treatment process
in the child guidance clinic setting. Ten working-class fathers were seen for periods
ranging from one to four years. It was part of concurrent, simultaneous treatment of
the identified patient (the child) and the mother. Familial dynamics are discussed.
The child's treatment may be facilitated when the father is seen.

DYSINGER, R., "A Family Perspective of the Diagnosis of Individual Members,"Amer. J.
     Orthopsychiat., 31, 61-68, 1961.
Based on the authors' clinical experience and a research project on family groups of
schizophrenic children all living in a ward setting the authors hypothesize that psychiatric illness may be a function of disturbance in the family. Families with schizophrenic members seem to be involved "in an intense emotional process with one another"
and have difficulty in being effective in just about any area. They aren't aware that
their judgment is undependable. A case example supports these hypotheses.

ELLES, G., "Family Treatment from a Therapeutic Community," Confin. Psychiat., 8, 9-14,
     1965.
From an in-patient ward where the identified patient had a personality disorder, some
families were treated with some or all members of the family receiving individual therapy,
while other families were treated by family therapy in the home. Discussion of experiences, but no data is presented comparing the two forms of treatment.

FAUCETT, E., "Multiple Client-Interviewing: A Means of Assessing Family Process," Soc.
     Casework, 43, 114-119, 1962.
One case example is offered in support of the notion that the identified patient in casework is often acting out some of the family problems. "The focus of the therapy of the
patient must be on the family's most burdensome problem."

FOX, R. E., "The Effect of Psychotherapy on the Spouse," Fam. Proc., 7, 7-16, 1968.
A discussion and review of the literature of the effect on a spouse when the partner is
in individual psychotherapy. Problems of gathering data are presented and the ethical
problem of adverse effects upon the spouse are discussed.

FRIEDMAN, T., ROLFE, P., and PERRY, S., "Home Treatment of Psychotic Patients," Amer. J.
     Psychiat., 116, 807-809, 1960.
A report of the first 15 months of operation of the psychiatric home treatment service
of the Boston State Hospital, whose aim was "better management of mental illness at a
time of stress and to see if appropriate alternatives to hospitalization might be possible." Each case was seen by psychiatrist and social worker. 60% of the cases were
able to return home. Families were included in the planning for the identified patient;
no family therapy was done.

GLASSMAN, R., LIPTON, H., and DUNSTAN, P., "Group Discussions With a Hospitalized Schizo-
     phrenic and His Family," Int. J. Group Psychother., 9, 204-212, 1959.
From an in-patient hospital service, this is a case report of treatment of a schizophrenic patient at the time of an acute crisis in his hospitalization. The crisis was
the return of the patient to his family. The crisis was handled through treatment of
the patient and family together in ten one-hour sessions over a period of 17 weeks.

GRAD, J., and SAINSBURG, P., "Mental Illness and the Family," Lancet, 1, 544-547, 1963.
An analysis of the effects on the family of psychiatric illness of one member of the
family before and after treatment. The sample was 410 patients from two psychiatric
facilities in England. Problems reported by families were analyzed; the sicker or older
the patient the greater the number of problems reported by the family. The number of
problems reported by families was reduced significantly after treatment of the patient.

GRALNICK, A., "Conjoint Family Therapy: Its Role in Rehabilitation of the Inpatient
     and Family," J. Nerv. Ment. Dis., 136, 500-506, 1963.
Family therapy for in-patients is recommended when a patient is not improving and the
conflict appears related to the family, when the patient cannot communicate his thoughts
and feelings to family without help, when an unusually pathological relationship appears to exist with family members, and when rupture of a marital relationship seems
imminent.

GRALNICK, A., "The Family in Psychotherapy," in J. Masserman (Ed.), Individual and
    Familial Dynamics, New York, Grune & Stratton, 1959.
From an in-patient unit, diagnostic and treatment techniques involving the family are
described. "The therapeutic community" which integrates the family into the treatment program must be developed.

GROTJAHN, M., "Letter to the Editor," Psychoanal. For., 1, 426, 1966.
In relation to Freud's insight into family dynamics, there is an interview by Freud in
which he advises another analyst not to continue treatment with an alcoholic due to the
"masochism of the wife, which would be an 'obstacle' to the treatment." It is deduced
that Freud realized the wife's "important part in the husband's drinking habits."

HAHN, I., "Family Therapy: A Child-Centered Approach to Disturbed Parent-Child Rela-
    tionships," Penn. Psychiat. Quart., 4, 58-62, 1964.
Family oriented treatment (including "therapist, child and usually both parents") seemed
to offer advantages over the "typical psychoanalytical approach." Sample was 15 families
where the child was the identified patient, referred to either a child guidance clinic or
private practice. All cases improved and telephone follow-up in seven cases six months
"corroborated the results."

HOLLENDER, M. H., MANN, W. A., and DANEHY, J. H., "The Psychiatric Resident and the
    Family of the Hospitalized Patient," Arch. Gen. Psychiat., 2, 125-130, 1960.
Problems of the resident who must deal with the families of patients hospitalized in
acute diagnostic and treatment centers. An examination of the difficulties of residents
in this area, a discussion of the ambiguities in the situation, such as whether the resident represents the patient or the hospital, and comments on whether or not the resident
should be the one who maintains contact with the family.

HOWELLS, J. G., "Child-Parent Separation as a Therapeutic Procedure," Amer. J. Psychiat.,
    19, 922-926, 1963.
A discussion of the idea that separation of child from mother (defined as "the child is
physically apart from its parents") is not always harmful, and in fact can be useful in
treatment. A summary of the author's previous investigations is included and a sharp
differentiation made between separation and deprivation.

HURVITZ, N., "Marital Problems Following Psychotherapy With One Spouse," J. Consult.
    Psychol., 31, 38-47, 1967.
A discussion of the ways marital problems are complicated or created by individual treatment of one spouse based upon spouses referred later for marriage counseling. The problem is not only that individual treatment might break up a marriage but that "the relationship between the spouses, which should be used to benefit them both, is further
disturbed." Marital treatment approach using the individual therapy as a problem area
in the marriage is described.

JACKSON, D. D., and YALOM, I., "Conjoint Family Therapy as an Aid in Psychotherapy," in
    A. Burton (Ed.), Family Therapy of Schizophrenics in Modern Psychotherapeutic Prac-
    tice, Palo Alto, Science & Behavior Books, 1965.
A clinical report presenting one case in support of the notion that family therapy is
useful for breaking an impasse in individual therapy. The case example is presented
in detail and it is shown how the pathology of the family prevented progress in individual therapy.

JACOB, C., "The Value of the Family Interview in the Diagnosis and Treatment of Schizo-
    phrenia," Psychiatry, 30, 162-172, 1967.
Using several case examples, the author's hypothesis is that a single family interview
can be an important additional factor in the evaluation of certain schizophrenic patients, by providing information that would otherwise be unavailable or relatively
inaccessible. This interview can also be therapeutic, and also, by studying the protocol in the interview, it can provide clues to countertransference and other errors
in technique.

JOSSELYN, I., "The Family as a Psychological Unit," Soc. Casework, 34, 336-343, 1953.
Based on the author's clinical experience, the idea is presented that the family can
be viewed as a psychological unit. Not only does the family influence the individual,
but the individual has a crucial impact on the family unit. Thus individual psychopathology can be better understood by understanding the family psychopathology.

KLAPMAN, H., and RICE, D., "An Experience With Combined Milieu and Family Group Therapy,"
    Int. J. Group Psychother., 15, 198-206, 1965.
A case report of a family in which the primary patient was a 13-year-old boy. The family was thought to be more difficult than usual. Treatment was milieu therapy plus a
once-a-week meeting of the family and members of the treatment team, including psychiatrist, social worker, teacher, occupational therapist, and two ward staff members.

LAING, R. D., "Mystification, Confusion and Conflict," in I. Boszormenyi-Nagy and J. L.
    Framo (Eds.), Intensive Family Therapy, New York, Harper & Row, 1965.
The theoretical schema of Marx —— where the exploiter mystifies with a plausible misrep-
resentation of what is going on the exploited —— is applied to the family of the
schizophrenic. The act of mystifying and the state of being mystified are described
with case examples. The therapist's task is to help such a person become demystified.

LEWIS, J., and GLASSER, N., "Evolution of a Treatment Approach to Families: Group Family
    Therapy," Int. J. Group Psychother., 15, 505-515, 1965.
A report of the involvement of families of mentally ill patients in a therapy program
treatment center. Three groups were set up: family members excluding patients, patients
alone, and patients and families together. Impressions of this type of family involvement are described.

LINDON, G., "A Psychoanalytic View of the Family: A Study of Family Member Interactions",
    Psychoanal. For., 3, 11-65, 1968.
A transcript of a panel discussion in which three papers were read and were discussed by
seven panelists. These papers dealt with: (1) a case report on a patient and the effects of the analysis on her family, (2) the simultaneous analysis of father and son
and, (3) a theory of the family which is illustrated by several case vignettes and from
the literature.

LOMAS, P., "Family Role and Identity Formation," Int. J. Psychoanal., 42, 371-380, 1961.
A report of a case of a 30-year-old woman with fears of traveling, being poisoned, blind-
ness, and going insane. Her parents were in conflict over a change in their social situation, and the anxiety over family disintegration was dealt with by a myth of mutual love
and loyalty. The basic marital disharmony resulted in each parent seeing the patient as
a loved object to supplant the marriage partner.

LONG, R., "The Path Toward Psychodrama Family Process," Group Psychother., 19, 43-46,
    1966.
In an in-patient setting, where psychodrama is one of the treatment techniques used, the
author describes his realization that families seemed to be involved in the pathogenesis
of mental illness. He suggests that bringing in the real family to the psychodrama sessions might be useful and describes some problems which arose as a result.

MADDISON, D. C., "The Integrated Therapy of Family Members —— A Case Report," Int. J.
    Group Psychother., 11, 33-48, 1961.
A case report of a mother and daughter dealt with by the joint interview technique with
a brief survey of some of the family therapy reports. An 18-year-old patient with recurrent nightmares was seen individually, then her mother was seen individually, and
finally both were seen conjointly while continuing individual sessions. The emphasis
is upon analytically oriented individual psychotherapy from the same psychiatrist with
occasional combined interviews where every opportunity was taken to analyze the patient's
reactions to the triangular situation.

MARKOWITZ, I., "Family Therapy in a Child Guidance Clinic," Psychiat. Quart., 40, 308-
    319, 1966.
An essay describing some limitations of family therapy. Cases were from a child guidance clinic in which a child was the primary patient. Limitations are "when individual
psychopathology is so severe that the family cannot be harmonious."

MENZIES, M., "The Angry Parent in Family-Oriented Therapy," Canad. Psychiat. Ass. J.,
    10, 405-410, 1965.
A clinical essay focussed on "the hostility of the parent towards the child" with the
data obtained from "working with parents during the past 14 years." Dynamics centering on hostility as a "defensive reaction" are discussed as are principles of treatment.

MITCHELL, C. B., "Family Interviewing in Family Diagnosis," Soc. Casework, 40, 381-
    384, 1959.
A discussion of the importance of family interviews for diagnosis. "In the course of
a series of interviews with the entire family, disturbance in any one individual serves
to illuminate graphically the family disturbance of which it is symptomatic."

MITCHELL, C. B., "Problems and Principles in Family Therapy," in N. W. Ackerman (Ed.),
    Expanding Theory and Practice in Family Therapy, New York, Family Service Associa-
    tion of America, 1967.
A clinical essay by a caseworker using family dynamics to understand individual problems. Problems and benefits from the family approach are outlined and a case example
is given in support of several of the points.

MUNRO, F., and BIDWELL, B., "Joint Interviews in the Treatment of Mothers and Their
    Young Children," J. Child Psychol. Psychiat., 5, 231-239, 1965.
Report of three cases in which the child was the primary patient in which treatment
was done using two therapists, one for the mother and one for the child, and inter-
communicating rooms. Advantages and disadvantages of the technique are discussed.

PATTON, J., BRADLEY, J., and HRONOWSKI, M., "Collaborative Treatment of Marital Part-
    ners," N. Carolina Med. J., 19, 523-528, 1958.
A clinical report of three psychiatrists who met regularly over 18 months to discuss
their cases being treated by individual psychotherapy. As the discussions progressed,
conceptualizing the psychiatrists' patients in terms of the patients' thinking shifted
from individual dynamics to the realization that the individual symptomatology was representative of family problems. Treatment of the family is suggested.

PING-NIE, PAO, "The Use of Patient-Family-Doctor Interview to Facilitate the Schizo-
    phrenic Patient's Return to the Community," Psychiatry, 23, 199-207, 1960.
A discussion of the use of conjoint interviews with family members to ease a schizophrenic patient's move from the hospital to the outside world. After intensive psychotherapy, a crisis may come when the patient is faced with going home. After preparing
both family members and patient, joint interviews are held which allow the family members and patient to deal with each other in preparation for living together with less
distress. Four cases are given as examples, including one where the outcome was unfavorable.

RAUTMAN, A. L., "Meeting a Need in Child Guidance," Fam. Proc., 4, 217-227, 1965.
A procedure for dealing with families with child problems by a marital pair interviewing in their home in "as personal and relaxed a setting as possible consistent with
professional standards."

REIDY, J. J., "An Approach to Family-Centered Treatment in a State Institution," Amer. J.
    Orthopsychiat., 32, 133-141, 1962.
A report on methods of treatment in a state children's psychiatric hospital, the Esther
Loring Richards Children's Center in Maryland. The treatment assumes that the child's

problems are due in part to detrimental family relationships and that the function of
the hospital is "to help the child become well enough to return to the community." A
community agency maintains continuing interest in the child and provides the necessary
help to the family, and the child returns home each week-end. Emphasis is placed upon
parental adjustment to changes in the child and in those cases where a child is discharged to a foster home he is given week-end visits there and a new family unit is
gradually built for him.

RINSLEY, D. B., and HALL, D. D., "Psychiatric Hospital Treatment of Adolescents," _Arch._
      Gen. Psychiat., 7, 286-294, 1962.
A report on a study of the metaphorical communications among patients, parents and
staff members of an in-patient unit for the treatment of psychiatrically-ill adolescents.
Parental resistances to their children's treatment are described as they are expressed
in metaphors to the staff. The child's problem of conflicting loyalties is also discussed. Optimum psychiatric treatment is accomplished only if the parents are meaning-
fully involved in the treatment process.

SCHERZ, F., "Multiple Client-Interviewing: Treatment Implications," _Soc. Casework,_ 43,
      120-124, 1962.
From a family service agency, indications or contraindications for having more than the
identified patient present at interviews is discussed. Individual and group treatment
can be used in various combinations. Techniques for multiple client interviewing are
put forth.

SEARLES, H. F., "The Contributions of Family Treatment to the Psychotherapy of Schizo-
      phrenia," in I. Boszormenyi-Nagy and J. L. Framo (Eds.), _Intensive Family Therapy,_
      New York, Harper & Row, 1965.
A discussion of the importance of the family in the treatment of schizophrenia with the
emphasis upon processes which are predominantly intrapsychic differentiated from processes which are predominantly interpersonal.

SHERESHKY, P., "Family Unit Treatment in Child Guidance," _Soc. Work_, 8, 63-70, 1963.
An essay reviewing concepts about the family and its effect on individual psychopathology with the specific focus on how that concept could be useful to case workers in a
child guidance clinic. Following a brief review of the literature, aims and specific
techniques to accomplish this purpose are discussed. Differences from the traditional
focus on the "mother-child relationship" and individual psychotherapy casework are
pointed out.

SHERMAN, S. N., "Joint Interviews in Casework Practice," _Soc. Work_, 4, 20-28, 1959.
An attempt "to place joint interviews within the methodology of casework." The purpose and concept of family interviewing is discussed with case examples.

SIPORIN, M., "Family-Centered Casework in a Psychiatric Setting," _Soc. Casework_, 37,
      167-174, 1956.
One case is presented in support of the author's notion that casework can be best done
by keeping both individual as well as family dynamics in mind. A review of the family
approach in casework is presented.

SLAVSON, S. R., "Coordinated Family Therapy," _Int. J. Group Psychother._, 15, 177-187,
      1965.
A report on a new plan of family treatment in which the primary patient (here adolescents) were placed in treatment in "para-analytic group psychotherapy," with the group
being derived according to sex and a two year age range. Fathers and mothers of the
primary patient were seen in separate groups.

SOLOMON, A. P., and GREENE, B. L., "Concurrent Psychoanalytic Therapy in Marital Dis-
      harmony," in B. L. Greene (Ed.), _The Psychotherapies of Marital Disharmony_, New
      York, Free Press, 1965.
The authors describe treatment of a marital problem using concurrent psychoanalytic
therapy for both partners by the same therapist. Indications, contraindications and

techniques are discussed and supported by case examples. It is useful in understanding family transactions.

SZALITA, A., "The Combined Use of Family Interviews and Individual Therapy in Schizo-
      phrenia," Amer. J. Psychother., 22, 419-430, 1968.
Seeing the family together as an adjunct to individual, psychoanalytically oriented
psychotherapy with schizophrenic patients is thought to be useful. Data comes from
the author's out-patient private practice. Schizophrenia is not seen as a "disease
of the family."

VAN AMEROGEN, S., "Initial Psychiatric Family Studies," Amer. J. Orthopsychiat., 24,
      73-84, 1954.
Based on treatment failures for a child guidance clinic over the previous three year-
period, it was concluded that the failures were possibly the result of the fact that
the total family dynamics were not taken into consideration. For this reason, the
author presented a revised scheme for initial psychiatric work-up. One or two interviews were held with both parents conjointly, two or three interviews with the child
alone. The child had psychological testing. The family study was terminated by a
final planning conference, usually with both parents. Two cases are presented in
support of this treatment approach.

WHITAKER, C., and BURDY, J., "Family Psychotherapy of a Psychopathic Personality:
      Must Every Member Change?," Compr. Psychiat., 10, 361-364, 1969.
The second of two reports of family treatment where the identified patient was diagnosed a psychopathic personality. The patient was seen with the family for one-and-
a-half years and for six months more she was seen individually. Her brother left
family therapy after about six interviews. In this case the identified patient
changed while the other family members did not.

1.8 FAMILY DIAGNOSIS — INDIVIDUAL ORIENTATION

ACKERMAN, N. W., "A Dynamic Frame for the Clinical Approach to Family Conflict," in
      N. W. Ackerman, F. L. Beatman, and S. Sherman (Eds.), Exploring the Base for
      Family Therapy, New York, Family Service Association of America, 1961.
A paper describing a diagnostic scheme as well as therapeutic principles in dealing
with a disturbed family. The diagnostic task is to establish the specific dynamic
relationship between the family members. Strengths as well as weaknesses should be
carefully delineated.

ACKERMAN, N. W., "Emergence of Family Psychotherapy on the Present Scene," in H. Stein
      (Ed.), Contemporary Psychotherapies, New York, Free Press, 1961.
A clinical essay reviewing the development of family therapy, rationale, diagnostic
techniques, and methods of treatment. It gives an overview of the field of family
therapy with highlights of the "more important concepts pertinent to the family approach to diagnosis and therapy."

ACKERMAN, N. W., "The Family Approach to Marital Disorders," in B. L. Greene (Ed.),
      The Psychotherapies of Marital Disharmony, New York, Free Press, 1956.
A clinical essay describing rationale and techniques of family therapy. A diagnostic
scheme for understanding the problem and treatment goals are described.

ACKERMAN, N. W., "Prejudice and Scapegoating in the Family," in G. H. Zuk and I. Bos-
      zormenyi-Nagy (Eds.), Family Therapy and Disturbed Families, Palo Alto, Science &
      Behavior Books, 1967.
A description of families in terms of the victim who is scapegoated, the destroyer or
persecutor who is specially prejudiced against the victim, and the family healer who
neutralizes the destructive powers of the attack.

ACKERMAN, N., and BEHRENS, M., "The Family Group and Family Therapy: The Practical
     Application of Family Diagnosis," in J. Masserman and J. Mareno (Eds.), Progress
     in Psychotherapy, Vol. III: Techniques of Psychotherapy, New York, Grune & Stra-
     ton, 1958.
A clinical essay pointing out limitations of individual psychotherapy in dealing with
emotional illness. Family diagnosis and evaluating family functioning is emphasized.
Several case examples are given to illustrate clinical procedures.

ACKERMAN, N. W., and BEHRENS, M. L., "A Study of Family Diagnosis," Amer. J. Ortho-
     psychiat., 26, 66-78.
A study of 40 families from the council child development center in New York. Concepts
of the family and a classification of family types is offered. The emphasis is upon
the family context of the developing child.

BEHRENS, M., and ACKERMAN, N., W., "The Home Visit as an Aid in Family Diagnosis and
     Therapy," Soc. Casework, 37, 11-19, 1956.
A paper based on the authors' clinical work in which the home visit is used as an aid
in family diagnosis and therapy when the identified patient is a child. Observations
are based on family interaction patterns, physical environment, and atmosphere of the
home. A case example is given to illustrate the authors' technique.

BEHRENS, M., and SHERMAN, A., "Observations of Family Interaction in the Home," Amer.
     J. Orthopsychiat., 29, 243-248, 1959.
An essay on the authors' previous studies using home visits in evaluating family interactional patterns to differentiate schizophrenic families from nonschizophrenic
families. Difficulties in this type of research are discussed and suggestions for
further data collection are made. It is felt that this is a useful technique for
"diagnostic, treatment, and research purposes."

BRYANT, C. M., and GRUNEBAUM, H. U., "The Theory and Practice of the Family Diagnostic:
     I: Practical Aspects and Patient Evaluation. II: Theoretical Aspects and Resident
     Education," in I. M. Cohen (Ed.), Psychiatric Research Report No. 20, American
     Psychiatric Association, 1966.
A presentation of a family diagnostic procedure at the Massachusetts Mental Health Center which includes a description of methodology and of theoretical considerations as
well as resident teaching. Family members are interviewed individually and together
about the subject of what brings the patient to the hospital. The training of the
psychiatric resident is said to be broadened by participation.

COHEN, R. L., CHARNY, I. W., and LEMBKE, P., "Parental Expectations as a Force in Treat-
     ment," Arch. Gen. Psychiat., 4, 471-478, 1961.
A discussion of parental involvement with severely disturbed children based upon 175
cases referred to the inpatient unit at Oakbourne Hospital. It is suggested that intake-
diagnostic procedures include exploration of parental motivation to anticipate later
parental resistance to the child's treatment.

DAVANZO, H., "The Family Group and Dynamic Psychiatric Diagnosis," Int. J. Group Psycho-
     ther., 12, 496-502, 1962.
Three cases are reported in support of the idea of using the family interview as a diagnostic device. Advantages and disadvantages are discussed.

DRECHSLER, R. J., and SHAPIRO, M. I., "A Procedure for Direct Observation of Family In-
     teraction in a Child Guidance Clinic," Psychiatry, 24, 163-170, 1961.
A procedure for making direct observations of a family as part of the intake procedures
of a child guidance clinic. A psychiatrist interviews the family, the family is observed alone, and the family answers a 20-item questionnaire while being observed. The
procedural aim was to sample family interactions in a way that would fit economically
into ongoing clinic policy. The interview clarifies the presenting problem. A task for
the family provides a stage upon which the family acts out the interactive patterns in
their relationships. Case illustrations are provided.

EHRENWALD, J., "Family Diagnosis and Mechanisms of Psychosocial Defense," Fam. Proc.,
     2, 121-131, 1963.
Second of a series of papers attempting to delineate patterns of family interaction for
the purposes of arriving at a diagnostic schema for the family as a whole. Method used
is an inventory of 30 traits and attitudes "descriptive of interpersonal habitual relationships in family members." Four major patterns have emerged from the author's work
with families and are described.

EPSTEIN, N. B., "Treatment of the Emotionally Disturbed Pre-School Child: A Family
     Approach," Canad. Med. Ass. J., 85, 937-940, 1961.
A clinical essay focussing on the assumption that when the identified patient is a
child, the family must be included in the treatment. First a family diagnostic interview is held, followed by a staff discussion of the dynamics, and further work-up is
recommended. Possible therapeutic programs prescribed include (1) treatment of the
family as a unit, (2) two or more members of the family are seen as a group, dependent
upon "exigencies" arising as the treatment progresses, (3) treatment as individual
psychotherapy for the identified patient, (4) treatment including the "significant dyad,
e.g., mother-child, (5) the child may be placed in group, or (6) in individual plus
group therapy. A case example is presented to illustrate the approach.

GAP Report No. 76: The Case History Method in the Study of Family Process, New York,
     Group for the Advancement of Psychiatry, 1970.
The purpose of this report is to demonstrate a systematic approach to modifying the traditional psychiatric "case history" for use in family diagnosis, treatment, and research.
There are sections on principles for compiling a family case history. A typical case is
presented and contrast made between a Puerto Rican working-class and American middle-
class family. Contrast in values within the nuclear family as well in the extended
family network are described. There is an appendix with a family case history outline
and one with a case history example given. 380 pp.

GREENBAUM, M., "Joint Sibling Interview as a Diagnostic Procedures,"J. Child Psychol.
     Psychiat., 6, 227-232, 1965.
A report of a diagnostic procedure in which two siblings are interviewed jointly, or observed playing together, as part of a family workup. Setting is a children's out-patient
clinic. Techniques are described. It is said to offer the advantages of actually
seeing how the patient interacts with others, lessens the artificial nature of the patient-therapist contact, and gives the therapist a chance to observe the health of at
least one other sibling in the family.

GROTJAHN, M., "Analytic Family Therapy: A Study of Trends in Research and Practice,"
     in J. Masserman (Ed.), Individual and Familial Dynamics, New York, Grune & Strat-
     ton, 1959.
An essay focussing on the "psychoanalytic approach to the dynamics of the family."
Freudian theory dwells heavily on inborn patterning of personality in the first years
of life but not on the importance of the later levels of social participation. Freudian
observations have been based on reconstruction from individual psychoanalysis. A schema
for family diagnosis is outlined and compared to psychoanalytic diagnostic schemes.

JACOB, C., "The Value of the Family Interview in the Diagnosis and Treatment of Schizo-
     phrenia," Psychiatry, 30, 162-172, 1967.
Using several case examples, the author's hypothesis is that a single family interview
can be an important additional factor in the evaluation of certain schizophrenic patients
by providing information that would otherwise be unavailable or relatively inaccessible.
This interview can also be therapeutic, and also, by studying the protocol in the interview, it can provide clues to countertransference and other errors in technique.

JARVIS, P., ESTY, J., and STUTZMAN, L., "Evaluation and Treatment of Families at Fort
     Logan Mental Health Center," Comm. Ment. Health., 5, 14-19, 1969.
A survey paper of trends in evaluation of treatment of patients from an in-patient facility of a psychiatric hospital. More evaluations are being carried out in the patient's home or in the community rather than in the hospital itself. There is greater
involvement of "extended families" and of children (and of involving them at an earlier

age) in evaluation and treatment. There is great use of multiple-family group therapy
rather than conjoint family therapy.

KAFFMAN, M., "Family Diagnosis and Therapy in Child Emotional Pathology," Fam. Proc., 4,
    241-258, 1965.
A description of families treated in Israel based upon 194 kibbutz families and 126 families living in Haifa. Family treatment is said to be effective and case examples are
given.

MARTIN, F., and KNIGHT, J., "Joint Interviews as Part of Intake Procedure in a Child
    Psychiatric Clinic," J. Child Psychol. Psychiat., 3, 17-26, 1962.
An intake procedure for pre-adolescent children in use at the Tavistock Clinic, London,
is described and illustrated with case material. Based upon current concepts of family
dynamics, the procedure entails the use of one or more initial joint interviews between
both parents and members of the psychiatric team (psychiatrist, caseworker and psychologist). The advantages over the traditional procedure include: better contact with
fathers, and increased opportunity for direct observation of family interaction and for
assessment of differing motivations for approaching the clinic.

MENDELL, D., and FISCHER, S., "A Multi-Generation Approach to the Treatment of Psycho-
    pathology," J. Nerv. Ment. Dis., 126, 523-529, 1958.
Techniques of treating the family rather than the identified patient for various problems seen at a private psychiatric population. TAT and Rorschach material were important.

MENZIES, M., BEDLAK, S., and McRAE, L., "An Intensive Approach to Brief Family Diagnosis
    at a Child Guidance Clinic," Canad. Psychiat. J., 6, 295-298, 1961.
Two case examples are given in support of a treatment method of families who come to a
child guidance clinic and are not from the immediate community. It is suggested that
parents and patient come for a two to three day period to participate in both individual
as well as joint interviews.

SERRANO, A. C., McDANALD, E. C., GOOLISHIAN, H. A., MacGREGOR, R., and RITCHIE, A. M.,
    "Adolescent Maladjustment and Family Dynamics," Amer. J. Psychiat., 118, 897-901,
    1962.
A summary of the dynamics of 63 disturbed adolescents and their families. The patients
are said to fall into four diagnostic categories each associated with a type of family
interaction. These categories of maladjustment reaction in adolescence are: the infantile, the childish, the juvenile, and the preadolescent. The adolescent functions as a
stabilizing factor in the family and when his behavior becomes unendurable to himself,
the family or society this precipitates a crisis which mobilizes the family to seek help.

SERRANO, A. C., and WILSON, N. S., "Family Therapy in the Treatment of the Brain Da-
    maged Child," Dis. Nerv. Syst., 24, 732-735, 1963.
The authors review their experiences with 34 children diagnosed as having organic brain
syndromes with behavior disorders. They emphasize including the evaluation of the total
family constellation (here using their multiple impact therapy method previously reported
on), in addition to the more traditional physical and psychological studies of the child.

Social Work Practice, 1963, Selected Papers, 90th Annual Forum National Conference on
    Social Welfare, Cleveland, Ohio, May 19-24, 1963, New York, Columbia University
    Press, 1963.
A collection of papers given at a social work conference which includes a paper on
family diagnosis and treatment, family unit treatment of character-disordered youngsters,
and a paper on schizophrenia and family therapy. 255 pp.

TYLER, E. A., TRUUMAA, A., and HENSHAW, P., "Family Group Intake by a Child Guidance
    Clinic Team," Arch. Gen. Psychiat., 6, 214-218, 1962.
A report on an intake method devised by the Riley Child Guidance Clinic at the Indiana

University Medical Center. The procedure substitutes the family group for the usual
single informant and uses and three man team in place of a single interviewer. Experience with the procedure with 100 cases is described in terms of the main problems,
the teaching aspects, nature of diagnosis, team work, and family responses.

VAN AMEROGEN, S., "Initial Psychiatric Family Studies," Amer. J. Orthopsychiat., 24,
     73-84, 1954.
Based on treatment failures for a child guidance clinic over the previous three-year
period, it was concluded that the failures were possibly the result of the fact that
the total family dynamics were not taken into consideration. For this reason, the author presented a revised scheme for initial psychiatric work-up. One or two interviews
were held with both parents conjointly, two or three interviews with the child alone,
and the child had psychological testing. The family study was terminated by a final
planning conference usually with both parents.

WEISS, V., "Multiple Client Interviewing: An Aid in Diagnosis," Soc. Casework, 43,
     111-113, 1962.
This essay from a family service agency points out that often seeing others in addition to the identified patient is helpful in establishing a diagnosis. Indications
for whom should be included are discussed.

2.1 FAMILY DATA – FROM RECORDS

AHMED, F., "Family and Mental Disorders in Pakistan," Int. J. Social Psychiat., 14,
     290-295, 1968.
To study the effect of the structure of the family on mental illness, 967 cases from a
privately owned psychiatric clinic in Pakistan were studied, using retrospective case
records. Only psychotics and neurotics were used from the larger sample. Results revealed that there were more female psychotics, that psychotic patients were closer in
age to their parents, that more psychotics were the oldest in the family and more neurotics were the youngest in the family. There was more psychopathology in the family of
psychotics than neurotic patients. No relationship was found between mental disorders
and marital status. Siblings, parental loss in childhood, and mother's age at birth.

BECK, S. F., "Families of Schizophrenic and of Well Children: Methods, Concepts, and
     Some Results," Amer. J. Orthopsychiat., 30, 247-275, 1960.
A report on a research study attempting to differentiate and compare families with
schizophrenic children, families with neurotic children, and families with normal children. A list of trait items about individuals in 106 families were Q-sorted by a psychiatrist and three social workers. The clusterings are said to indicate similarities
and differences.

BROOKS, W. B., DEANE, W. N., LAGOV, R. C., and CURTIS, B. B., "Varieties of Family Par-
     ticipation in the Rehabilitation of Released Chronic Schizophrenic Patients," J.
     Nerv. Ment. Dis., 136, 432-444, 1963.
A study of the post-hospital course of 170 chronic schizophrenic patients. The data
were abstracted from records. The social, economic and psychiatric outcomes are correlated with various aspects of the family's participation in the rehabilitation process.
A major factor in the success of this group is said to be the breaking of pathological
ties with the family and the forming of new, healthier relationships.

BROWNING, C. J., "Differential Impact of Family Disorganization on Male Adolescents,"
     Soc. Problems, 8, 37-44, 1960.
Samples of 60 nondelinquent, 60 delinquent-truancy, and 60 delinquent-auto theft (boys
age 15) were identified. Data were obtained from school, police, and probation records,
from interviews with mothers, from family solidarity and marital adjustment scales
filled out by parents, and California test of personality scales filled out by the boys.

The incidence of broken homes is higher in the delinquent groups, but this variable is not a consistently good indicator of family disorganization and needs refinement.

BUCK, C. W., and LADD, K. L., "Psychoneurosis in Marital Partners," Brit. J. Psychiat., 3, 587-590, 1965.
A study of records of physicians' diagnoses from a health insurance plan in a Canadian city. There was a definite association between the occurrence of psychoneurotic illness in husbands and wives who had been married for many years, little association for partners recently married and no association during the pre-marital period. The authors interpret these findings as evidence that a process of contagion rather than mate selection determines the concordance between marital partners is psychoneurotic illness.

DAVIDSON, S., "School Phobia as a Manifestation of Family Disturbance: Its Structure and Treatment," J. Child Psychol. Psychiat., 1, 270-288, 1960-61.
30 cases of school phobia were studied at a child guidance clinic. Data was gathered from social histories and from individual interviews with patients and their parents. Family dynamics and methods of individual treatment are discussed.

HILGARD, J., and NEWMAN, M. F., "Parental Loss by Death in Childhood as an Etiological Factor Among Schizophrenic and Alcoholic Patients Compared With a Non-Patient Community Sample," J. Nerv. Ment. Dis., 137, 14-28, 1963.
Hospital records were examined and a sample of 1,561 schizophrenic patients and 929 alcoholic patients were compared with a control sample of 1,096 cases. Schizophrenics had lost one or both parents more often than the control group. Parent loss is said to be one of the factors associated with an increase in vulnerability in coping with the stresses of adult life.

HILGARD, J., and NEWMAN, M. F., "Early Parental Deprivation as a Function Factor in the Etiology of Schizophrenia and Alcoholism," Amer. J. Orthopsychiat., 33, 409-420, 1963.
A study designed to consider the age at which loss by death was sustained during childhood by hospitalized schizophrenic and alcoholic patients. Comparison was made using hospital admission records of 1521 schizophrenic patients, 929 alcoholic patients and a control group of 1,096 cases selected using an area-sampling technique from an urban community. It was concluded that mother loss among women in both diagnostic categories was earlier than in the control group who lost mothers. Schizophrenic women showed loss of both mother and father at a significantly earlier age than the control subjects.

JACKSON, D. D., BLOCK, J., and PATTERSON, V., "Psychiatrists' Conceptions of the Schizophrenogenic Parent," Arch. Neur. Psychiat., 79, 448-459, 1958.
20 psychiatrists were asked for their conceptions of the mothers and fathers of schizophrenics. Three types of mothers and three types of fathers were described. This data was then compared with Q-Sorts done on 20 mothers and 20 fathers of 20 schizophrenic patients. Two out of three mother types described by psychiatrists correlated highly. None of the father descriptions correlated statistically.

JENKINS, R., "The Varieties of Children's Behavioral Problems and Family Dynamics," Amer. J. Psychiat., 124, 1440-1445, 1968.
1500 children attending a psychiatric clinic were separated into three groups by computer clustering of their symptoms, and correlated with family types. Overanxious children are likely to have an anxious, infantilizing mother. A critical, depreciative, punitive, inconsistent mother or stepmother is typical for the unsocialized, aggressive child. Socialized delinquents are likely to come from large families characterized by parental neglect and delegation of parental responsibilities.

KREITMAN, N., "Mental Disorder in Married Couples," J. Ment. Sci., 108, 438-446, 1962.
To determine the incidence and nature of mental illness in the spouses of psychiatric patients, the records of the Chichester psychiatric service in England were examined. The findings indicate that the incidence of mental illness in spouses of psychiatric patients is higher than among the general population. Various hypotheses to account for this finding are discussed.

LANE, E. A., and ALBEE, G. W., "Early Childhood Differences Between Schizophrenic
    Adults and Their Siblings," J. Abnorm. Soc. Psychol., 68, 193-195, 1964.
The IQ tests which had been taken when they were in the second grade were obtained for
36 men and women who were later hospitalized for schizophrenia. These IQ results were
compared with those of their siblings taken at the same time. The mean IQ of those who
later became schizophrenic was lower than that of the siblings. A control group did not
show such differences.

LEVINGER, G., "Sources of Marital Dissatisfaction Among Applicants for Divorce," in P.
    H. Glasser and L. N. Glasser (Eds.), Families in Crisis, New York, Harper & Row,
    1970.
A study of dissatisfaction in marriage based upon 600 couples, with data derived from
records of marriage counselors doing mandatory interviews as part of the application
for divorce. Spouse complaints are classified and discussed.

McCORD, W., PORTA, J., and McCORD, J., "The Familial Genesis of Psychoses," Psychiatry,
    25, 60-71, 1962.
A study of the influence of early environment on the development of psychosis based
upon data gathered during the childhood of subjects who later became psychotic. In the
middle 1930's in Massachusetts a sample of boys was observed as part of a study on the
prevention of delinquency. These past case histories were examined and 12 prepsychotics
were matched with nonpsychotic controls. The familial environments of the prepsychotics
differed from those of the nonpsychotics in a number of ways. Typically the prepsychotics were raised in an environment directed by an overprotective mother and an absent
or passive father. This "silver cord syndrome" has also been noted by other investiga-
tors who used a retrospective approach.

McCORD, W., McCORD, J., and VERDEN, P., "Familial Correlates of Psychosomatic Symptoms
    in Male Children," J. Health Hum. Behav., 1, 192-199, 1960.
Further study of data from the Cambridge-Somerville Youth Study (1935-1945). Data were
available on the physical condition of youths, their family backgrounds, and delinquent
activities. Hypotheses that children with psychosomatic disorders would have been raised
in families with a high degree of interpersonal stress and with anxious, hypochondriacal, symptom-ridden parents were not confirmed. But when boys are cross-classified as
extropunitive or intropunitive, some regularities are observable. It is concluded that
degree of extropunitiveness and nature of parental "sick-role" models are variables
which affect childhood deseases.

MORRIS, G., and WYNNE, L., "Schizophrenic Offspring, Parental Styles of Communication,"
    Psychiatry, 28, 19-44, 1965.
A study of parental styles of communication and schizophrenic children. Data were selected from excerpts of transcripts of conjoint family sessions with twelve families.
Predictions about the most disturbed offspring were made by a judge blind to the clinical aspects of the case. Predictive criteria were then reformulated using the data
from a parallel study utilizing psychological test material as predictors. These reformulated criteria were then utilized for blind predictions on eight new families.
Results indicated that the style of the family communication can be related to the thought
and affect disorder in schizophrenics.

NOVAK, A. L., and VAN DER VEEN, F., "Family Concepts and Emotional Disturbance in the
    Families of Disturbed Adolescents With Normal Siblings," Fam. Proc., 9, 157-171,
    1970.
A sample of 13 families with an adolescent who had applied to an outpatient clinic for
treatment was contrasted with a group of similar families selected through a school.
A Q-Sort procedure was used with individual family members. "Real family concepts" and
"ideal family concepts" were obtained and differences were found between the two groups
and between disturbed children and their normal siblings.

PAUL, N., and GROSSER, G., "Operational Mourning and Its Role in Conjoint Family Therapy,"
    Comm. Ment. Health J., 1, 339-345, 1965.
Studies of records of 50 families with a schizophrenic member and 25 families with at

least one psychoneurotic member revealed "patterns of inflexible interaction and maladaptive response to object loss." The way the sample was obtained is not stated. It is hypothesized from this data that incomplete mourning after object loss leads to an inability to deal with future object loss and this defect is transmitted to other family members. This is thought to lead to a "fixation of symbiotic relationships in the family."

RABKIN, L. Y., "The Patient's Family: Research Methods," Fam. Proc., 4, 105-132, 1965.
A review of family research with special emphasis upon the family of the schizophrenic. Critical examination is done of case history studies, interviewing studies, psychodiagnostic testing, questionnaire studies, and observational research. A bibliography of 99 references is included.

RYLE, A., and HAMILTON, M., "Neurosis in Fifty Married Couples," J. Ment. Sci., 108, 265-273, 1962.
An investigation of 50 working class marital couples to record the prevalence of neurosis as indicated by the Cornell medical index, the records of the general practitioner with whom the families were registered, and the home interviews of a psychiatric social worker. The information from these sources was compared and the presence of neurosis was correlated with some aspects of adverse childhood experience, marital adjustment, consumer status, and social integration.

SAGER, C., GRUNDRACH, R., KRAMER, M., LANZ, R., and ROYCE, J., "The Married in Treatment: Effects of Psychoanalysis on the Marital State," Arch. Gen. Psychiat., 19, 205-217, 1968.
In order to ascertain the effects of psychoanalysis on the marital state, a study of 736 married patients (432 women and 304 men), aged 21 to 68 in middle and upper socioeconomic class who were being treated in psychoanalysis, was done. 79 psychoanalysts supplied data on any ten consecutive patients. It was obtained through a closed ended questionnaire. 12% of the patients had concurrent group therapy, 2% were in conjoint marital therapy and about 20% of the patients had one or more conjoint consultations with their spouse and analyst. Results indicated that marriages rated poor initially improved. Marriages rated better also improved. There was no evidence that as one marital partner got better another got worse. Overall individual patient improvement was rated at about 60% of the cases. Of the spouses who were in treatment, good effects were more frequently reported in cases in which both husband and wife were treated by the same psychoanalyst.

SANUA, V., "Sociocultural Factors in Families of Schizophrenics: A Review of the Literature," Psychiatry, 24, 246-265, 1961.
A review of the literature on the etiology of schizophrenia. Problems and methodology are looked at and the literature is discussed from the point of view of data from hospital records, from separate interviews with patients and families, from interviews of families together, from studies using personality tests, questionnaires and rating scales, and from studies using the cross-cultural approach. All these studies look at the problem one of four ways: (1) parental troubles transmitted to the children, (2) family structure, (3) disturbed interactional patterns, and, (4) genetic and constitutional factors in the child.

SPITZER, S. P., SWANSON, R. M., and LEHR, R. K., "Audience Reactions and Careers of Psychiatric Patients," Fam. Proc., 8, 159-181, 1969.
A study of the reaction of families and the ways these reactions influence the psychiatric patient career. The histories of 79 first admission patients were examined and patient and a family member were interviewed. Two dimensions of family reaction to deviance are described leading to a typology of eight career patterns which allow for the classification of 95% of the cases reviewed.

WARING, M., RICKS, D., "Family Patterns of Children Who Become Adult Schizophrenics," J. Nerv. Ment. Dis., 140, 351-364, 1965.
A study comparing family variables of three groups of adult patients, who were seen as adolescents at a child guidance center. The three groups were (1) 30 patients, who as

adults developed schizophrenia and remitted (defined as leaving the hospital), (2) 20 patients, who as adults developed schizophrenia and did not remit and, (3) a control group of 50 patients, selected from the clinic population, who did not develop schizophrenia and were never hospitalized. Data were obtained retrospectively from work-ups at the time the patients were adolescents, and also from subsequent follow-ups with schools, hospitals, and other agencies, and finally in some cases with interviews with patient and family. There were significant familial differences between the remitting and unremitting groups, and less significant differences between the total schizophrenia group and the controls.

WEAKLAND, J. H., and FRY, W. F., "Letters of Mothers of Schizophrenics," Amer. J. Orthopsychiat., 32, 604-623, 1962.
Several selected letters to schizophrenic patients from their mothers are presented with a microscopic and macroscopic examination of their characteristic and significant patterns. The letters exhibit similar influential patterns consisting of concealed incongruence between closely related messages. Almost no statement is ever allowed to stand clearly and unambiguously, but is disqualified in a variety of ways. Patient's statements support the hypothesis that the letter induces paralysis or frantic activity in the recipients, which would be reasonable in response to "such a pervasive and general pattern of concealed strong but incompatible influence."

2.2 FAMILY DATA – FROM INDIVIDUALS

ANTHONY, E. J., "The Mutative Impact of Serious Mental and Physical Illness in a Parent on Family Life," in E. J. Anthony and C. Koupernik (Eds.), The Child in His Family, New York, Wiley, 1970.
A study of families where a parent figure has succumbed to a serious mental or physical disorder necessitating hospitalization. Various views are offered of such illness, as a disruption of family roles, as a crisis in accommodation, as a disconnection, and as a challenge. Family members were interviewed individually and in dyads and triads.

BAUMANN, G., and ROMAN, M., "Interaction Testing in the Study of Marital Dominance," Fam. Proc., 5, 230-242, 1966.
A sample of 50 couples was exposed individually and conjointly to the Wechsler Bellevue. In the conjoint testing, the couple was asked to reach agreement on the response. Comparisons of the individual test and the conjoint test were made, as well as measures of dominance in the couple when tested together.

BAXTER, J. C., ARTHUR, S., FLOOD, C., and HEDGEPETH, B., "Conflict Patterns in the Families of Schizophrenics," J. Nerv. Ment. Dis., 135, 419-424, 1962.
Families of 12 male and six female schizophrenics were interviewed individually and as a group to explore conflict patterns in relation to the sex of the child. The amount of conflict is said to be comparable in the two groups while patterns of conflict differ. There is more interparental conflict in the group of families with a male patient and more involvement of the patient in conflict in the group with a female patient.

BAXTER, J. C., and BECKER, J., "Anxiety and Avoidance Behavior in Schizophrenics in Response to Parental Figures," J. Abnorm. Soc. Psychol., 64, 432-437, 1962.
Good and poor premorbid schizophrenics were exposed to TAT cards of parent-child relationships. Poor premorbids were expected to produce more anxiety in response to a mother figure than a father figure, and did. Good premorbids were expected to show the reverse, and did. Avoidance behavior in response to parental figures did not differ.

BAXTER, J. C., BECKER, J., and HOOKS, W., "Defensive Style in the Families of Schizophrenics and Controls," J. Abnorm. Soc. Psychol., 66, 512-518, 1963.
Parents of good and poor premorbid schizophrenics were given Rorschach tests. Parents of poor premorbids showed a greater amount of immature behavior than parents of good premorbids or parents of neurotics.

BEAVERS, W. T., BLUMBERG, S., TIMKEN, D. R., and WEINER, M. F., "Communication Patterns
     of Mothers of Schizophrenics," Fam. Proc., 4, 95-104, 1965.
A study of the ways the mothers of schizophrenics communicate with an interviewer. Nine
mothers of schizophrenics were contrasted with nine mothers of hospitalized nonschizophrenic patients. The mothers of schizophrenics communicated their feelings in a quantitatively more ambiguous fashion.

BECK, S., and NUNNALLY, J., "Parental Attitudes in Families," Arch. Gen. Psychiat., 13,
     208-213, 1965.
Differences in attitudes of parents of schizophrenic children were compared with those
of parents with well children. Eighteen attitudes were measured using the semantic differential test of Osgood (measures concepts like "My Child, Pregnancy," etc.). Schizophrenic families were obtained from 32 families of children resident in a therapeutic
school; well-children families came from the community. Concepts associated with greater
mental health by the well families included "my mother, the kind of father I am, the kind
of mother I am, myself when I was a father, clinic mothers, and clinic our family."
There was no difference between samples in the other nine concepts.

BENTINCK, C., "Opinions About Mental Illness Held by Patients and Relatives," Fam. Proc.,
     6, 193-207, 1967.
The nature of the attitudes at home about mental illness in families of male schizophrenics was studied. A control group of male medical patients was used. The data were gathered by a questionnaire administered in a home interview. The sample was 50 schizophrenics and 50 relatives, and 50 medical patients and 50 relatives. Opinions of relatives of schizophrenics had "more in common with blue collar employees than with mental
health professionals."

BERGER, A., "A Test of the Double Bind Hypothesis of Schizophrenia," Fam. Proc., 4, 198-
     205, 1965.
A sample of 20 schizophrenics, 18 maladjusted nonschizophrenics, 20 hospital employees,
and 40 students were exposed to a questionnaire of items rated for their double bind
nature. Differences were found.

BODIN, A., "Conjoint Family Assessment: An Evolving Field," in P. McReynolds (Ed.), Ad-
     vances in Psychological Assessment, Palo Alto, Science & Behavior Books, 1968.
A resume of testing methods designed for use with families in the fields of both family
therapy and family research. Approaches have been individual, conjoint, and combined.
Subjective techniques include family tasks, family strengths inventory, and family art.
Objective techniques include analysis of communication, games and how conflict is re-
solved. A critique of these methods is presented.

BOSWELL, J., LEWIS, C., FREEMAN, D., and CLARK, K., "Hyperthyroid Children: Individual
     and Family Dynamics," J. Amer. Acad. Child Psychiat., 6, 64-85, 1967.
A retrospective study describing twelve children (ten girls, two boys; six Negro, six
white; four lower, eight middle-class), who developed hyperthyroidism between the ages
of four and 14. Data were gathered from individual psychiatric interviews, psychologic
tests, parents, and from social agencies — but not from family interviews. Parents
were found to have given minimal care and expected maximum self-sufficiency from the
child. Children were found to be fixated at a pregenital stage.

BROWN, B. S., "Home Visiting by Psychiatrists," Arch. Gen. Psychiat., 7, 98-107, 1962.
     As part of an exploration of alternatives to psychiatric hospitalization, an in-
vestigation was done of home visiting by 34 psychiatrists with varied practice patterns.
Data were gathered by interviews on frequency of visit, attitudes, and experiences.
Nine of the psychiatrists had never done a home visit. 13 had done one to five a year,
seven had made six to 25 visits per year, and five had made from 50 to 400 visits yearly.
The type of practice apparently is the greatest determinant. Psychoanalytically oriented
phychiatrists do least. The consensus of the group of psychiatrists is that home visits
have doubtful utility. The movement to break down rigid boundaries between home and
hospital may lead to a renaissance of home visiting.

BROWNING, C. J., "Differential Impact of Family Disorganization on Male Adolescents,"
    Soc. Prob., 8, 37-44, 1960.
Samples of 60 nondelinquent, 60 delinquent-truancy, and 60 delinquent-auto theft boys
aged 15, were identified. Data were obtained from school, police, and probation records,
from interviews with mothers, from family solidarity and marital adjustment scales filled
out by parents, and California test of personality scales filled out by the boys. The
incidence of broken homes is higher in the delinquent groups, but this variable is not
a consistently good indicator of family disorganization and needs refinement.

CAPLAN, G., "Patterns of Parental Response to the Crisis of Premature Birth: A Preli-
    minary Approach to Modifying the Mental Health Outcome," Psychiatry, 23, 365-374,
    1960.
Types of response to the crisis of a premature birth were derived from interview data
on ten cases where the baby weighed less than four pounds, and the records were suf-
ficiently detailed so a case could be assigned unambiguously to an extreme category of
healthy or unhealthy outcome. Cases were classified as "healthy outcome" if all relationships in the family were as healthy or more healthy than before the birth and if
parent-child relationships were healthy at the end of 12 weeks. "Unhealthy outcomes"
were the reverse.

CAPUTO, D. V., "The Parents of the Schizophrenic," Fam. Proc., 2, 339-356, 1963.
A study to assess the role of the parents in the development of schizophrenia, with
particular emphasis upon the passive father and dominating mother notion. Parents
were given individual tests, and after taking a parent attitude inventory they were
asked to discuss the items on which they had disagreed. These discussions were assessed
with the Bales method. Reversal of role was not found to be a significant factor, and
a hostile atmosphere is indicated in the home of the potential schizophrenic.

CHEEK, F. E. "Family Interaction Patterns and Convalescent Adjustment of the Schizo-
    phrenic," Arch. Gen. Psychiat., 13, 138-147, 1965.
In an attempt to examine the relationship between family interaction patterns and outcome in schizophrenia, data were obtained from 51 patients who had been hospitalized
between the ages of 15 and 26, all of whom had living mothers and fathers. Each family
member filled out a questionnaire relating to interaction patterns, and all three
family members together worked on two questionnaire problems. An interview with the
mother on the adjustment of the patient was evaluated by means of a 40-item four point
rating scale. One week later in the home of the patient two more 15-minute discussions
between family members were recorded. Fifty-six normal families were studied with
identical procedures used as with the schizophrenics. Results indicated that it was the
characteristics of the parents, rather than the degree of sickness of the patient
"which was the decisive factor in producing a poor outcome."

CHEEK, F. E., "Family Socialization Techniques and Deviant Behavior," Fam. Proc., 5,
    199-217, 1966.
A study based upon Parsons' theoretical framework in which deviant behavior is related
to imbalance of systems inputs and outputs at various stages of development. A sample
of 120 male adults, from four different groups: schizophrenics, normals, alcoholics,
and reformatory inmates were exposed to a questionnaire on family problem situations.
Differences were found and it is suggested that Parsons' theoretical scheme could be
translated into reinforcement theory.

CHEEK, F. E., "Parental Role Distortions in Relation to Schizophrenic Deviancy," in I.
    M. Cohen (Ed.), Psychiatric Research Report 20, American Psychiatric Association,
    1966.
A study investigating the nature of the schizophrenic interacting in the family, and
the relation of family interaction to the outcome of the schizophrenic. The study combined questionnaire and observational data. The sample included 67 schizophrenics contrasted with 56 nonpsychotic young adults.

CLARK, A. W., and Van SOMMERS, P., "Contradictory Demands in Family Relations and Ad-
     justment to School and Home," Hum. Rel., 14, 97-111, 1961.
Intensive case-studies of families of 20 maladjusted and 20 adjusted children, all families having one or more adults other than the parents living in the family. The concern was with "the process of explaining an unsatisfactory relationship between any two
individuals in terms of the influence of a third individual." Data were obtained by detailed, focussed interviews, questionnaires to school staffs, group interviews with
peers, and tests of ability. School difficulties were associated with unsatisfactory
relationships in the home, such as dependence of one parent upon the other adult.
Unsatisfactory relationships of adults contribute to withdrawal of father from family
activities, difficulties between adults and children, maladjustment of children at home
and school, and to recurrence of symptoms in parents.

COE, W. C., CURRY, A. E., and KESSLER, D. R., "Family Interactions of Psychiatric Pa-
     tients," Fam. Proc., 8, 119-130, 1969.
A study using a questionnaire to examine family interaction patterns with emphasis upon
everyday activities. Forty males and 40 females and their relatives who were psychiatric in-patients were contrasted with 54 husband and wife volunteers. Results include
the finding that more family decision-making is left to the child in the patient families. The members tend not to recognize disagreement in their interactions.

COHAN, M., FREEDMAN, N., ENGELHARDT, D., and MARGOLIS, R., "Family Interaction Patterns,
     Drug Treatment, and Change in Social Aggression," Arch. Gen. Psychiat., 19, 1950-
     1956, 1968.
A study testing the notion that family interactional patterns will significantly modify
the effect of phenothiazine treatment. Sample was 54 male and 72 female schizophrenics
in an out-patient setting. Using a double bind procedure, patients were given chlorpromazine, promazine or a placebo. All got supportive individual psychotherapy. A
"close relative" was the source of the data to measure conflict and patient's behavior
in the home. Results indicated that most patient improvement occurred in patients of
chlorpromazine living in "least conflict homes." Medication was less effective where
family conflict was high.

CORNELISON, A. R., "Casework Interviewing as a Research Technique in a Study of Families
     of Schizophrenic Patients," Ment. Hyg., 44, 551-559, 1960.
A discussion of casework interviewing in family study as experienced by a caseworker
with the Lidz project. The families of 16 cases were studied by individual interviews
with family members. Group interviews have been recently initiated. Caseworker-family
contact begins upon hospital admission, if not sooner, and family patterns are frequently illuminated by the various and varying attitudes displayed toward the caseworker.
A general discussion is offered of the special usefulness of combined casework service
and research, practical aspects of the method, and problems involved.

DAVIDSON, S., "School Phobia as a Manifestation of Family Disturbance: Its Structure
     and Treatment," J. Child Psychol. Psychiat., 1, 270-288, 1960-61.
Thirty cases of school phobia were studied at a child guidance clinic. Data were gathered from social histories and from individual interviews with patients and their
parents. Family dynamics and methods of individual treatment are discussed.

DAVIS, D., "Family Processes in Mental Retardation," Amer. J. Psychiat., 124, 340-350,
     1967.
A lecture pointing out that in addition to genetic factors, mental retardation may result
from failure of the family to give the child protection from stress during critical
periods of learning in early childhood. Data were obtained from 50 cases (36 boys and
14 girls) with I.Q. below 75 (median 55) ── all cases were seen by the author prior to
age seven. Retrospective historical data were obtained from parents ── mothers were
found to be depressed through much of the child's life including the period prior to
recognition of the child's retardation. These mothers were found to have lost their
fathers during adolescence and to have gotten "ineffective lifelong support" from the
maternal grandmother. Prevention and treatment are discussed.

DENIKER, P., DeSAUGY, D., and ROPERT, M., "The Alcoholic and His Wife,"Compr. Psychiat.,
    5, 374-384, 1964.
A study focussing on the relationship between the alcoholic and his wife by studying
three groups of patients: 50 alcoholics with psychiatric disorders called"psychiatric
alcoholics," 50 alcoholics with cirrhosis or gastritis called "digestive alcoholics,"
and 67 in a control group where the husband was matched for age and socioeconomic
status. All couples were interviewed using a questionnaire designed for this study.
Compared with the digestive alcoholics and the controls, the psychiatric alcoholics
showed a relationship to birth order, had fathers who were also alcoholics, made lower
salaries, had dominant wives, and drank relatively little at home. The wife of the
psychiatric alcoholic "tends to unconsciously maintain her husband's alcoholism."

DOWNING, R., COMER, N., and EBERT, J., "Family Dynamics in a Case of Gilles de la Tou-
    rette's Syndrome, J. Nerv. Ment. Dis., 138, 548-557, 1964.
A case report of a patient with Gilles de la Tourette's syndrome in which all the members of the family were interviewed and tested with a WAIS, Rorschach, TAT, and word
association test. A Leary interpersonal check list was done in the home. From this
data a dynamic, genetic, and familial formulation of the case was made.

DUPONT, R., and GRUNEBAUM, H., "Willing Victims: The Husbands of Paranoid Women,"
    Amer. J. Psychiat., 125, 151-159, 1968.
In an attempt to understand the dynamics of spouses of paranoid women, cases with paranoid delusions (both in-patient and out-patient) were evaluated over a three-year period.
Data were collected on nine women with paranoid state, using clinical interviews with
the husband alone, wife alone, and the couple together, plus the MMPI and interpersonal
checklist. Results indicated that the wife expressed the anger and dissatisfaction in
the marriage, while the husband manifested passivity and apparent reasonableness and
thus seemed to be a "willing victim."

ELDER, G. H., "Structural Variations in the Child-Rearing Relationship," Sociometry,
    25, 241-262, 1962.
Seven types of parent-adolescent interdependence, ranging from parental autocracy to
parental ignoring, were identified by focussed interviews. Questionnaires to 7,400
Ohio and North Carolina adolescents reveal that parental dominance is most common in
lower-class, large, Catholic families. Parental autocracy is most likely to be associated with negative evaluations of parental policies by adolescents, and with mutual
rejection of each other.

ELDER, G. H.; and BOWERMAN, C. E., "Family Structure and Child-Rearing Patterns: The
    Effect of Family Size and Sex Composition," Amer. Social Rev., 28, 891-905, 1963.
The effects of family size, sex composition, and social class on the involvement of
the father in child rearing, on the type of parental control exerted, and on the disciplinary techniques used were studied. Data were obtained from a 40% sample (N=1261)
of all seventh grade white Protestant students of unbroken homes in central Ohio and
central North Carolina. Family size and sex composition were found to have effects on
child-rearing methods, but the effects are highly contingent on the sex of the child
and the social class of the family.

EPSTEIN, N. B., and WESTLEY, W. A., "Parental Interaction as Related to the Emotional
    Health of Children," Soc. Prob., 8, 87-92, 1960.
The nine healthiest of 160 university freshmen and their families were evaluated. The
child's emotional health is not related to the parents' sexual adjustment, but is related to the dependency needs of the father and the father's executive ego function.
It is concluded that the parental sexual relationship is a poor indicator of family
health and that the father's family position is important.

FARBER, B., "Perceptions of Crisis and Related Variables in the Impact of a Retarded
    Child on the Mother," J. Health Hum. Behav., 1, 108-118, 1960.
An extension of earlier findings that a retarded child produces a tragic crisis (shock
of diagnosis) or a role organization crisis (inability to develop roles to cope with the

child). A sample of 268 mothers and fathers of retarded children were interviewed and
administered questionnaires. The hypotheses concern the reaction of mothers to the crises, role definitions of mother, and her self-perceived health. The general conclusion
is that health-symptom status of mother is related to the type of crisis experienced.

FARINA, A., "Patterns of Role Dominance and Conflict in Parents of Schizophrenic Pa-
     tients," J. Abnorm. Soc. Psychol., 61, 31-38, 1960.
Parents of 12 good premorbid schizophrenics, 12 poor premorbids, and 12 children hospitalized for tuberculosis were interviewed. They were exposed individually and as
pairs to hypothetical incidents with children. The joint conversations were analyzed
for dominance and conflict. Father dominance was associated with good premorbid adjustment of the son and mother dominance with the poor premorbids. Parents of schizophrenics displayed more conflict than the control parents.

FELDMAN, M. J., "Privacy and Conjoint Family Therapy," Fam. Proc., 6, 1-9, 1967.
A discussion of whether greater or lesser degree of privacy effects the nature of therapeutic disclosures by contrasting individual and conjoint family therapy. There is no
simple relationship between degree of privacy and kind and scope of disclosure. The
private nature of individual therapy led to an ethical position which elevates an individual's welfare above others, which may even be to their detriment.

FERBER, A., KLIGLER, D., ZWERLING, I., and MENDELSOHN, M., "Current Family Structures,"
     Arch. Gen. Psychiat., 16, 659-667, 1967.
The hypothesis was that the family, in order to maintain equilibrium, will extrude to
the hospital certain members (most usually those members functioning peripherally).
Data were obtained from an emergency room psychiatric population of a large municipal
hospital. Nine hundred and thirty-seven patients and/or their "closest companion"
filled out a family information form. Families of psychiatric patients were compared
with families from the general population. Reliability on the raw data was 90%. Findings were that being married (rather than single, widowed, etc.), coming from a family
of procreation, coming from an intact family, and being an emotionally important member
of the household are associated with a lower risk of becoming a patient and of having a
better outcome from treatment.

FERREIRA, A. J., "Decision-Making in Normal and Pathologic Families," Arch. Gen. Psy-
     chiat., 8, 68-73, 1963.
An experiment to find differences between 25 normal and 25 abnormal families using a
decision making test. The family members first make a choice of items on a questionnaire when alone, and then are brought together and asked to reach agreement on the
same items. Their choices separately and together are compared and the agreements are
categorized as unanimous, majority, dictatorial, and chaotic. The two types of families
are found to differ.

FERREIRA, A., and WINTER, W., "Stability of Interactional Variables in Family Decision-
     Making," Arch. Gen. Psychiat., 14, 352-355, 1966.
In order to test the stability over time and after family therapy, of three variables in
family decision-making, 23 randomly selected families (10 abnormal and 13 normal) were
retested six months after the original research project. The abnormal families had received therapy. Results indicated that there was no significant difference between the
means observed in tests and retests of the three variables for either normal or abnormal
families. It is concluded that these three variables (spontaneous agreement, decision-
time, and choice-fulfillment) were consistent over time and were not changed by family
therapy.

FISCHER, A., "The Importance of Sibling Position in the Choice of a Career in Pediatric
     Nursing," J. Health Hum. Behav., 3, 283-288, 1962.
Questionnaires on sibling status and various other background characteristics and attitudes were administered to 109 student nurses in a children's hospital. The hypothesis
that senior siblings are more likely to become pediatric nurses than junior siblings
holds only for sibling groups of four or more. Further analysis shows that sex composi-

tion of the sibling group also affects this career choice. A theory to cover all sibling group sizes, based on opportunities for identification with feminine models is advanced. It is suggested that sibling position, handled more complexly, may be as significant as clinical studies suggest.

FISHER, S., and FISHER, R. L., "The Complexity of Spouse Similarity and Difference,"
      in G. H. Zuk and I. Boszormenyi-Nagy (Eds.), Family Therapy and Disturbed Families,
      Palo Alto, Science & Behavior Books, 1967.
A report on a study of similarities and differences among spouses based upon 119 families. The parents were exposed to a battery of test procedures intended to tap personality, value, and attitudinal dimensions. Measures of multiple levels of response
would seem necessary because "depending upon the variables one chooses to measure,
spouses will appear to be similar, different, or both."

FISHER, S., and MENDELL, D., "The Communication of Neurotic Patterns Over Two and Three
      Generations," in N. W. Bell and E. F. Vogel (Eds.), A Modern Introduction to the
      Family, Glencoe, Free Press, 1960.
A report on a study of similarities in the patterning of fantasy and behavior in two or
more generations of family groups. The data included projective tests and psychiatric
interviews. Six families with three generations of kin and 14 families with two generations of kin were examined and impressions are given.

FISHER, S., and MENDELL, D., "The Spread of Psychotherapeutic Effects from the Patient
      to His Family Group," Psychiatry, 21, 133-140, 1958.
One of a series of papers on the effect of family therapy on an entire family. Some ten
patients in the authors' private practice, who were willing participate in the study,
were given the Rorschach test and the TAT. Data were analyzed based "purely on inspec-
tion, impression, and striking individual correlations of events." The authors conclude that significant changes in the patient are accompanied by clearcut changes in the
other members of the family.

FITZGERALD, R. V., "Conjoint Marital Psychotherapy: An Outcome and Follow-Up Study,"
      Fam. Proc., 8, 261-271, 1969.
A report on an outcome study of couples seen in conjoint marriage therapy. A sample of
57 couples were followed up after two-and-one-half years with an interview by telephone.
Of the couples who were seen because an individual sought therapy, 76% were improved.
Of those who presented an ongoing marital conflict as the presenting problem, 75% im-
proved.

FREEMAN, H. E., "Attitudes Toward Mental Illness Among Relatives of Former Patients,"
      Amer. Social Rev., 26, 59-66, 1961.
The relatives of 649 newly discharged mental hospital patients (of a total population of
714) were successfully interviewed to investigate their attitudes about the etiology of
mental illness, the mental hospital, the normalcy of patients after mental illness, and
the responsibility of patients for their condition. As in other surveys, age and education were associated with attitudes. "Enlightened" attitudes were not associated with
social class measured independently of education, but were associated with verbal skill.
It is suggested that verbal skill may be more important than style of life. However,
attitudes were related to the patients' post-hospital behavior, and appear to be complexly determined and deeply rooted."

FREEMAN, H. E., and SIMMONS, O. G., "Feelings of Stigma among Relatives of Former Mental
      Patients," Soc. Prob., 8, 312-321, 1961.
Feelings of stigma were elicited from the families of 649 of a cohort of 714 functional
psychotics released from hospitals in eastern Massachusetts. Data were gathered by
means of standard items in a structured interview with a relative a month after the patient's release. One-quarter of the sample reported feelings of stigma, while two-
thirds acknowledged management problems. These feelings are associated with the patient's posthospital behavior, the education, class status, and personality characteristics of the relatives. Wives are more likely than other kin to feel stigma.

GANGER, R., and SHUGART, G., "The Heroin Addict's Pseudoassertive Behavior and Family
    Dynamics," Soc. Casework, 57, 643-649, 1966.
A discussion of heroin addiction based upon interviews with addicts and family members.
Addiction is said to have a function within the family and the authors conclude, "Our
clinical observations and our experience with casework treatment provided to the total
family unit, including the addicted person, lead us to the conviction that addiction is
specifically a 'familiogenic' disease; consequently, any attempt to cure it must be undertaken within the context of the family unit."

GARMEZY, N., CLARKE, A. R., and STOCKNER, C., "Child Rearing Attitudes of Mothers and
    Fathers as Reported by Schizophrenic and Normal Patients," J. Abnorm. Soc. Psychol.,
    63, 176-182, 1961.
A group of 15 good premorbid and 15 poor premorbid schizophrenic patients were asked to
think back to when they were 13 or 14 years old and try to remember their mothers and
fathers at that time. The experimenter then presented them with 75 statements describing
various child rearing attitudes and asked the patients if their parents would have agreed
or disagreed with each item. A group of 15 patients hospitalized for medical problems
was used as a control. The results indicate that the subject's level of social maturity
and the extent of attitudinal deviance ascribed to parents are related. Poor premorbids
reveal maternal dominance whereas good premorbids ascribe heightened paternal dominance
in their responses.

GETZELS, J. W., and JACKSON, P. W., "Family Environment and Cognitive Style: A Study
    of the Sources of Highly Intelligent and of Highly Creative Adolescents," Amer.
    Sociol. Rev., 26, 351-359, 1961.
A study of adolescent boys and girls, 28 highly intelligent but not creative and 26
creative but not concomitantly intelligent, chosen from a school population on the basis
of testing. These students proved equally superior in achievement to the remainder of
the student body although they differed both functionally and in their goals. The central issue of this report deals with the role of the family environment in the differentiation of kinds of intellectual ability through interviews with the mothers. Significant group differences were found in parental type education, childhood memories,
reading interests, values, degree of satisfaction with child and school, and so on.
The authors find less anxiety in the highly creative home and therefore more freedom
for "individual divergence."

GOODRICH, W., RYDER, R., and RAUSH, H., "Patterns of Newlywed Marriage," J. Marriage
    Fam., 30, 383-391, 1968.
A report of an exploratory study of 50 average, middle-class marriages examined during
the fourth month with interviews, problem solving situations, and questionnaires.
Eight patterns of marriage are suggested.

GRAD, J., and SAINSBURG, P., "Mental Illness and the Family," Lancet, 1, 544-547, 1963.
An analysis of the effects on the family of psychiatric illness of one member of the
family before and after treatment. The sample was 410 patients from psychiatric facilities in England. Problems reported by families were analyzed: the sicker or older
the patient the greater the number of problems reported by the family. The number of
problems reported by families was reduced significantly after treatment of the patient.

GREENBERG, I. M., and ROSENBERG, G., "Familial Correlates of the 14 and 6 CPS EEG Posi-
    tive Spike Pattern," in I. M. Cohen (Ed.), Psychiatric Research Report 20, Amer.
    Psychiat. Assoc., 1966.
A report on the results of a study of the families of young hospitalized psychiatric
patients in which central nervous system function, individual psychodynamics, cognitive
style, and social and familial factors are considered. A sample of nine patients were
contrasted with ten with no EEG abnormality. Differences were found in the families.

GREENBLUM, J., "The Control of Sick Care Functions in the Hospitalization of a Child:
    Family vs. Hospital," J. Health Hum. Behav., 2, 32-38, 1961.
The author hypothesizes that parents are more willing to give up control of instrumental

functions involved in the sickness situation (medical tasks associated with care and
treatment of illness) than of the associated functions (merging socio-emotional needs
and socializing into desirable behavior). Interviews were conducted with 18 children
suffering from paralytic polio and their parents. Fourteen families participated in
two repeat interviews. The degree of dissatisfaction with various aspects of hospital
care was taken as an index of resistance to transfer of parental control.

HANDEL, G. (Ed.), The Psychosocial Interior of the Family: A Sourcebook for the Study
    of Whole Families, Chicago, Aldine, 1967.
An anthology of previously published articles on the social psychology of the family.
It includes sections on the family as a psychosocial organization, research methods,
the family as mediator of the culture, the meanings of family boundaries, the family
as a universe of cognition and communication, patterning separateness and connected-
ness, and a review of family theories. 560 pp.

HARMS, E., "Defective Parents, Delinquent Children," Correct. Psychiat., 8, 34-42, 1962.
A discussion of the relationship between delinquency and defective parents. In 300 cases
of children stealing and lying, it was found that in 264 of them "at least one parent
was, in one respect or another, deficient." Where the father is the defective factor,
the boys will be found to be lying and the girls stealing. Where the mother is the defective factor, the girls will be found lying and the boys stealing.

HIGGINS, J., "Sex of Child Reared by Schizophrenic Mothers," J. Psychiat. Res., 4, 153-
    167, 1966.
In an attempt to assess the effect of child-rearing by schizophrenic mothers, two groups
of 25 children of schizophrenic mothers were studied. One group was reared by the mothers and the other group was reared from an early age by agents without psychiatric
illness. The sample was tested using a psychiatric interview of the child only, several
psychological tests, and a report from the school. Results failed to support the hypothesis that the mother-reared children would display greater maladjustment on the various
measures than would the reared-apart children.

JOHNSTON, R., and PLANANSKY, K., "Schizophrenia in Men: The Impact on Their Wives,"
    Psychiat. Quart., 42, 146-155, 1968.
A study on an in-patient unit rating 36 wives of chronic in-patients. Data were obtained from independent interviews with spouses by four raters on the unit. As the
patients regressed, about half the spouses rejected (divorced, separated, etc.) their
husbands. Reasons for this are discussed.

KATZ, I., COHEN, M., and CASTIGLIONE, L., "Effect of One Type of Need Complementarity
    on Marriage Partners' Conformity to One Another's Judgments," J. Abnorm. Soc.
    Psychol., 67, 8-14, 1963.
Fifty-five paid volunteer couples were examined using a forced-choice questionnaire to
test the hypothesis that when the husband's need to receive affection is similar in
strength to the wife's complementary need to give affection the tendency of spouses
to be influenced by one another will be significant. Results indicated husbands could
accept wives' judgments; the converse was not true.

KATZ, M., "Agreement on Connotative Meaning in Marriage," Fam. Proc., 4, 64-74, 1965.
A study of marriage based on the assumption that marital happiness is related to the
degree of similarity between the spouses. Two groups of 20 couples, one seeking marriage counselling and one classed as happily married, were exposed to the Osgood semantic differential instrument and differences were found. Troubled couples were more
discrepant in their semantic structures.

KEMPLER, W., IVERSON, R., and BEISSER, A., "The Adult Schizophrenic and His Siblings,"
    Fam. Proc., 1, 224-235, 1962.
Sixty-five siblings in a group of 16 schizophrenic families were interviewed using a
structured protocol to explore parent-child relationships as seen by the siblings.

Findings included distortions in communications by both patients and siblings, and appeared unrelated to the schizophrenic process. Four subjects, all of whom were "favorite" children in the family, showed no such distortions. A transcript from a single family is presented in illustration.

KREITMAN, N., "The Patient's Spouse," Brit. J. Psychiat., 110, 159-174, 1964.
A group of 75 patients and 95 controls, closely matched for sex, social class, father's social class, education, and number of children, were subjects of a mail survey using the Maudsley personality inventory, the Cornell medical index, and biographical details for the purpose of describing spouses of mental patients and their relationship with the marriage partner. Compared with controls the patients' spouses were more neurotic and had more physical and psychological symptoms which increased as the marriage went on. Wives were more likely than husbands to reflect the illnesses of spouses.

LAING, R. D., PHILLIPSON, H., and LEE, A., Interpersonal Perception — A Theory and a
     Method of Research, London, Tavistock, 1966.
A research project oriented toward understanding interaction of two persons. It includes sections on self and other; interaction and interexperience in dyads; the spiral of reciprocal perspective; historical view of the method; the interpersonal perception methods (IPM); disturbed and nondisturbed marriages; study of a dyad; developments; and the IPM questions. 179 pp.

LERNER, P., "Resolution of Intrafamilial Role Conflict in Families of Schizophrenic Pa-
     tients. I. Thought Disturbance," J. Nerv. Ment. Dis., 141, 342-351, 1966.
Hypothesis was that there would be differences in the processes used to solve intrafamilial role conflict in parents with schizophrenic sons with marked thought disorder (12 families), less severe thought disorder (12 families), and control families (12 families). Thought disorder was measured by Rorschach protocol using the Becker genetic level score. Intrafamilial role conflict solving was measured using a situational test with Strodtbeck's "revealed differences" technique. Results supported the hypothesis. Methodology of such research is discussed.

LESLIE, G. R., and JOHNSON, K. P., "Changed Perceptions of the Maternal Role," Amer.
     Social Rev., 28, 919-928, 1963.
The generalization that child-rearing methods have become more permissive is questioned. Several hypotheses relating changed perceptions to the normative patterns receiving authoritative support in that generation, the amount of exposure to the normative pattern at the time the mother role is being enacted, and the explicitness of the norms associated with various areas of child-rearing are set forth. Questionnaire data from 297 of 418 woman graduates of the 1949 class of a midwestern university covered their own and their mothers' practices in several areas: sex and modesty training, aggression toward mother, and the encouragement of self-direction. Predictions are confirmed, thus raising questions about the true nature of change and validity of generalizing from one aspect of the maternal role to another.

LEVINGER, G., "Supplementary Methods in Family Research," Fam. Proc., 2, 357-366, 1963.
A review of methods in family research with a comparison of subjective report and objective observation with a discussion of their strengths and weaknesses. A study is reported of 31 families who were studied with both observation and self report. The results showed gross correspondence between the two methods and it is suggested that both procedures should be used since they supplement each other.

LEVITT, H., and BAKER, R., "Relative Psychopathology of Marital Partners," Fam. Proc.,
     8, 33-42, 1969.
A study examining whether the member of a marriage who seeks treatment is the more disturbed of the spouses. A sample of 25 patients and their spouses were examined with questionnaire and psychological tests. Eleven psychologists served as judges to examine the test results and identify the "sicker" member. In 13 of the 25 cases the identified patient was judged to be sicker.

LEVY, J., and EPSTEIN, N., "An Application of the Rorschach Test in Family Investigation,"
    Fam. Proc., 3, 344-376, 1964.
A description of family testing using the Rorschach as a stimulus for conversation. Includes a detailed presentation of the individual and family responses to a set of cards
by one family.

LEWIS, V. S., and ZEICHNER, A. N., "Impact of Admission to a Mental Hospital on the Pa-
    tient's Family," Ment. Hyg., 44, 503-509, 1960.
A report on a study of the effect on families when a member is hospitalized for mental
illness. The study is based upon interviews with members of the family of 109 patients
admitted to Connecticut's three state mental hospitals. Reported with tables are such
categories as the recognition and acceptance of mental illness, the ways of coping with
the patient's illness, assessment of help of resources tried, and treatment given prior
to hospitalization.

LIDZ, T., CORNELISON, A., FLECK, S., and TERRY, D., "The Intrafamilial Environment of a
    Schizophrenic Patient. I. The Father," Psychiatry, 20, 329-342, 1957.
To understand the role of the family in the etiology and pathogenesis of schizophrenia,
14 families with a hospitalized schizophrenic were studied for periods varying from six
months to over two years. Data collection included interviewing all members of the
family (individually), observations and records of interactions of family members with
each other and with the hospital personnel, home visits, and projective testing of all
family members. Focus was on the fathers, in view of the fact that so much previous
work had focussed on mothers alone. Fathers were found to be "very important, albeit
often extremely disturbing, members of the families, whose presence and influence cannot
be neglected." Five different types of fathers are described.

LIDZ, T., CORNELISON, A., FLECK, S., and TERRY, D., "Intrafamilial Environment of Schizo-
    phrenic Patients. II. Marital Schism and Marital Skew," Amer. J. Psychiat., 114,
    241-248, 1957.
A study of the intrafamilial environment of the schizophrenic patient. In this study
of 14 families, eight were split in two factions by overt schism between the parents.
Thus the identified patient cannot use one parent as a model for identification or as
a love object without losing the support of the other parent. The other six families
were "skewed" (defined as psychopathology in the dominant parent) which was accepted
or shared by the other without trying to change it. Case examples are given.

LIDZ, T., CORNELISON, A. R., FLECK, S., and TERRY, D., "Schism and Skew in the Families
    of Schizophrenics," in N. W. Bell and E. F. Vogel (Eds.), A Modern Introduction to
    the Family, Glencoe, Free Press, 1960.
A discussion of 14 families of schizophrenics where it was found the marital relationships
of the parents were seriously disturbed. There was either an overt schism between the
parents or there was an appearance of harmony but the family environments were badly
distorted or "skewed" because serious psychopathology in the dominant parent was accepted
or share by the other.

LIDZ, T., FLECK, S., ALANEN, Y. O., and CORNELISON, A., "Schizophrenic Patients and
    Their Siblings," Psychiatry, 26, 1-18, 1963.
A study of the siblings of schizophrenics based upon individual interviews of family
members, observation of family members with each other and hospital staff, and projective tests. Sixteen families were studied for periods ranging from six months to six
years. As many siblings were psychotic as were reasonably well adjusted, and all except
five or six of the 24 siblings suffered from severe personality disorders. Siblings of
the same sex as the patient were more disturbed than those of the opposite sex.

LIDZ, T., PARKER, B., and CORNELISON, A., "The Role of the Father in the Family Environ-
    ment of the Schizophrenic Patient," Amer. J. Psychiat., 113, 126-132, 1956.
One of a series of papers on a study of the families of schizophrenic patients. Families in which there was both a mother and father present were interviewed separately, in
pairs, and in groups. The identified patient was an in-patient and came from upper-

class or upper-middle-class families. Sixteen families (of which five identified patients were female and 11 were male) were studied. The fathers are seen as "noxious"
in the development of schizophrenia. Three types are described: (1) fathers of schizophrenic daughters who are constantly battling their wives and seeking to enlist the
support of their daughters, (2) fathers who feel their sons are rivals for their wives,
and (3) passive, withdrawn, and absent fathers.

LINTON, H., BERLE, B. B., GROSS, M., and JACKSON, E., "Reaction of Children Within Fam-
     ily Group as Measured by the Bene-Anthony Tests," J. Ment. Sci., 107, 308-325, 1962.
A study of 69 children in 28 families who were given the Bene-Anthony family relations
test where they were asked to match statements with representations of family members.
The test scores were rated high or low on six qualitative variables in family life. The
child rated as sick by pediatrician and nurse was more involved with parent of the opposite sex, and in families with episodes of illness the children express a marked preference for the mother. Significant patterns were found in boys and girls of different
age groups and in the group as a whole.

LU, Y. C., "Contradictory Parental Expectations in Schizophrenia," Arch. Gen. Psychiat.,
     6, 219-234, 1962.
A report of some preliminary findings of an investigation of the families of schizophrenics. The emphasis is upon a comparison of the parents' relationship with the patient
and with nonschizophrenic siblings in an attempt to explain why one child in a family
develops schizophrenia and not another. The parents expect a higher degree of dependence from the preschizophrenic than from the nonschizophrenic child, and they also expect a higher degree of achievement and responsibility. The author suggests that the
relational pattern of contradictory parental expectations and the child's persistent
effort to fulfill them could be called a "quadruple bind."

LU, Y. C., "Mother-Child Role Relations in Schizophrenia: A Comparison of Schizophrenic
     Patients With Nonschizophrenic Siblings," Psychiatry, 24, 133-142, 1961.
An investigation into why one child in a family develops schizophrenia and another does
not, based upon interviews with 50 chronic schizophrenic patients, their siblings, and
their parents. The patient is largely confined to his parents and especially his mother
while the siblings have several significant other relationships.

LUCKEY, E. B., "Marital Satisfaction and Congruent Self-Spouse Concepts," Soc. Forces,
     39, 153-157, 1960.
Satisfactorily (S) and less satisfactorily (LS) married couples were identified by Locke's
marital adjustment scale from a population of 594 married students. Couples in the two
groups independently completed the Leary interpersonal check list regarding the self and
spouse. The congruence of the husband's perception of himself and his wife's perception
of him was related to satisfaction, but the congruence of the wife's self concept and her
husband's perception of her was not. Some implications and explanations of these results
are offered.

LUCKEY, E. B., "Perceptional Congruence of Self and Family Concepts as Related to Mari-
     tal Interaction," Sociometry, 24, 234-250, 1961.
Forty-one satisfactorily married (S) and 40 less satisfactorily married (LS) couples
completed Leary interpersonal check lists on self, spouse, mother, father, and ideal
self. S and LS subjects were compared on agreement of self concept and spouse's concept of subject, of self and ideal self, of self and parent, of spouse and parent, of
idea self and spouses. The many differences between S and LS subjects are used to refine the proposition that marital satisfaction is related to perceptual congruence, and
to evaluate a theory of marital interaction.

McCONAGHY, N., and CLANCY, M., "Formal Relationships of Allusive Thinking in University
     Students and Parents," Brit. J. Psychiat., 114, 1079-1087, 1968.
The notion was tested that when a person showed allusive thinking (defined as similar
to "loosening of associations" but called "allusive" to avoid the implication of pathology), at least one of his parents would also show this type of thinking. Sample was

38 university students and their parents. Measures used were the object sorting test
and the F-scale of the MMPI. Results showed that the students with allusive thinking
did have parents with similar thoughts, but they did not have schizophrenic pathology.

McCORD, W., McCORD, J., and HOWARD, A., "Early Familial Experiences and Bigotry,"
     Amer. Social. Rev., 25, 717-772, 1960.
The Authoritarian Personality concluded that bigots have experienced stern, moralistic,
rejecting child rearing. The conclusion, much challenged, is evaluated in the light of
data from the Cambridge-Somerville youth study. Ratable data on prejudices are available for 45 of 200 subjects re-interviewed in 1948 and 1956. No relation between degree
of prejudice and family experiences as determined earlier could be established. The
interpretation is suggested that prejudice in the lower class is a part of a generally
stereotyped culture and does not relate to personality needs or family environment.

McGHIE, A., "A Comparative Study of the Mother-Child Relationship in Schizophrenia. I.
     The Interview. II. Psychological Testing," Brit. J. Med. Psychol., 34, 195-221, 1961.
In Part I of this two-part article there is a description of interviews with 20 mothers
of schizophrenics, 20 mothers of neurotics, and 20 mothers of normals. Findings about
families of schizophrenics reported in the literature were generally confirmed. There
is more marital disharmony in the schizophrenic group and the fathers are said to be
weak. However, mothers of schizophrenics do not appear as overprotective as mothers of
neurotics. In Part II, the test findings for the three groups are reported. They were
given a child rearing questionnaire, a sentence completion test, a word connection test,
and the Rorschach test.

MENDELL, D., and CLEVELAND, S., "A Three-Generation View of a School Phobia," Voices,
     3, 16-19, 1967.
A case report in support of the notion that psychopathology is "passed on from generation to generation with a more or less specific way and expectation of handling it.
Three generations of data from the identified patient, a 14-year-old boy, his mother,
and maternal grandmother were obtained from clinical psychiatric interviews and the
Rorschach and thematic apperception tests. School phobia of the identified patient is
seen as an attempt to answer the obsessive concern of a boy's relationship to his mother and her relationship to her mother.

MENDELL, D., CLEVELAND, S. E., CLEVELAND, and FISHER, S., "A Five-Generation Family
     Theme," Fam. Proc., 7, 126-132, 1968.
A study examining projective test fantasies of family members. Five generations of one
family including examination of 27 members, were conducted. It was found that a family
selects one or two central themes which are perpetuated in the responses of family members across generations.

MENDELL, D., and FISHER, S., "An Approach to Neurotic Behavior in Terms of a Three-Ge-
     neration Family Model," J. Nerv. Ment. Dis., 123, 171-180, 1956.
One of a series of papers pointing out that psychotic pathology can be understood in
terms of a three-generational family model. The data were obtained from the author's
clinical experience, other studies in the literature, and projective data from the
Rorschach and TAT.   Data from one case are offered in support of these hypotheses.

MENDELL, D., and FISHER, S., "A Multi-Generation Approach to the Treatment of Psycho-
     pathology," J. Nerv. Ment. Dis., 126, 523-529, 1958.
Techniques of treating the family rather than the identified patient for various problems
seen at a private psychiatric population TAT and Rorschach material were important.

MEYEROWITZ, J. H., and FELDMAN, H., "Transition to Parenthood," in I. M. Cohen (Ed.),
     Psychiatric Research Reports 20, American Psychiatric Association, 1966.
A report based on a study of four hundred couples (individual interviewing). Experiences
during the first pregnancy are described as well as experiences when the child is one
month and five months old.

MEYERS, D., and GOLDFARB, W., "Studies of Perplexity in Mothers of Schizophrenic Child-
    ren," Amer. J. Orthopsychiat., 31, 551-564, 1961.
In order to document the association of parental complexity (defined as passivity, un-
certainty, lack of spontaneity, absence of empathy, with diminished awareness of the
child's needs, bewilderment, and blandness in the fact of unacceptable behavior in the
child, and an absence of parental control), 23 mothers of schizophrenic children and
23 mothers of normal public school children were studied. Techniques included a participant-observation technique, in which the observer spent three hours with the family
at home, and a semistructured open-ended interview of the mothers. Results indicated
that the mothers of the schizophrenic children, without organic involvement, have a
greater difficulty in appropriately structuring their child's environment, while the
mothers of the organic group cannot be differentiated from mothers of the normals.

MILLER, D. R., and WESTMAN, J. C., "Reading Disability as a Condition of Family Stabil-
    ity," Fam. Proc., 3, 66-76, 1964.

A report of a study of the relationship between reading disability in a child and the
condition of the family. The subjects were 18 boys in out-patient care. The family members were given individual tests, data were drawn from individual therapy sessions, and
there were periodic visits to home and school. A matched control group was compared.
It is postulated that parents and children resist change in the reading disability because it contributes to the family's survival.

MITCHELL, H. E., "Application of the Kaiser Method to Marital Pairs," Fam. Proc., 2,
    265-279, 1963.
A discussion of the Leary measurement as used on 20 maritally conflicted alcoholics and
their spouses. Questions concerning resemblances and differences are raised. The major emphasis is "not to be substantive findings but to demonstration of the feasibility
of the Kaiser method as a technique for measuring interpersonal dimensions of marital
and family dynamics."

MITCHELL, H. E., BULLARD, J. W., and MUDD, E. H., "Areas of Marital Conflict in Success-
    fully and Unsuccessfully Functioning Families," J. Health Hum. Behav., 3, 88-93,
    1962.
The nature and frequency of marital disagreements in 200 marriage counseling cases and
in 100 self selected, successful families. Data on both groups were obtained from the
marriage adjustment schedule and from interviews. Both groups rank their problems in
the same order, economic is highest, religious and educational are lowest. No differences in ranking of problems by husbands and wives were apparent, but conflicted families report a greater frequency of problems. Some cultural implications of these
findings are discussed.

NAVRAN, L., "Communication and Adjustment in Marriage," Fam. Proc., 6, 173-184, 1967.
A sample of married couples was exposed to the marital relationship inventory and the
primary communication inventory, two questionnaires which were given to the couples
individually. The 24 couples having a "happy" relationship were contrasted with 24
having an "unhappy" relationship. Differences were found and"marital adjustment was
shown to be positively correlated with capacity to communicate."

NEALON, J., "The Adolescent's Hospitalization as a Family Crisis," Arch. Gen. Psychiat.,
    11, 302-312, 1964.
A study of the reactions of 25 sets of parents to the hospitalization of an adolescent
member of the family. Data were collected from parents' initial interviews with caseworker ("Generally one or two, but ranging up to six"). Interviews were held before admission, or as soon as possible afterward. The hospitalization was defined as a family
crisis because "of the impact of mental illness on the family, family disruption precipitating and following hospitalization, and the parent's expectation of the hospitalization." Family-oriented approach is stressed, and implications for treatment are discussed.

OLSON, D. H., "The Measurement of Family Power by Self-Report and Behavioral Methods,"
     J. Marriage Fam., 31, 545-550, 1969.
A study comparing self report and observed behavior on the question in power in marriage.
Thirty-five couples were given questionnaires and their responses compared with their
behavior in the laboratory dealing with real problems. No relationship was found between what the couples said about the distribution of power in the marriage and what was
observed when they dealt with one another. Explanatory factors are offered, and the conclusion is reached that this research reinforces "the idea that methodological research
of this type should precede, rather than follow, substantive research in the field."

OTTO, H. A., "Criteria for Assessing Family Strength," Fam. Proc., 2, 329-339, 1963.
A discussion of family strengths and resources with the data collected by questionnaire.
Twenty-seven families were queried. Married couples met for group discussions on family
strengths. A set of criteria for assessing family strengths is offered.

PARAD, H. J., and CAPLAN, G., "A Framework for Studying Families in Crises," Soc. Work.,
     5, 3-15, 1960.
An approach to the observation and study of the family in crisis. Family members are
seen individually and as a group in the home while engaged in household activities. The
concepts of family life-style, problem-solving mechanisms, and need-response patterns
are illustrated with a case history. It is suggested that intervention is most effective at the moment the family is in crisis.

PARSONS, A., "Family Dynamics in South Italian Schizophrenics," Arch. Gen. Psychiat.,
     3, 507-518, 1960.
If family factors play an etiological role in schizophrenia, comparative studies of the
family background of schizophrenics in different cultures is important. After observation of south Italian patients in the United States, a sample of 25 patients hospitalized in public hospitals in Naples and vicinity was investigated. Patterns in the families are described in terms of exclusive dyads, imbedded dyads, competitive and unstable situations, and isolates. Comparing pathological family constellations in different cultures, the taboo areas are important, and the problem of differentiating the
normal from the pathological must be resolved. "We would doubt that these problems can
ever be resolved in a framework in which any particular set of social values or conditions is considered as inherently schizogenetic."

PETURSSON, E., "A Study of Parental Deprivation and Illness in 291 Psychiatric Patients,"
     Int. J. Soc. Psychiat., 7, 97-105, 1961.
A group of 291 patients with functional psychiatric illness was observed by the author
and information gathered about their parents from them, from spouses or relatives, or
by direct observation in some instances. The parents suffered from functional psychiatric illness in 77.5% of the cases. The incidence of broken homes was 31.7%. There
appeared to be a high incidence of patients developing the same type of psychiatric
illness as the parents in various categories. Well integrated family units occurred
in the background of patients in only 11.7% of the cases.

POLLACK, M., WOERNER, M., GOLDBERG, P., and KLEIN, D., "Siblings of Schizophrenic and
     Nonschizophrenic Psychiatric Patients," Arch. Gen. Psychiat., 20, 652-658, 1969.
A study which attempts to test the relative power of genetic versus psychogenic etiology in schizophrenia. Sixty-four siblings of 46 schizophrenic patients, 104 siblings
of 68 personality disorder patients, and 16 siblings of 13 index cases with psychoneurotic and affective disorders were compared in terms of their psychiatric status. Method
was clinical interview in most cases, but where siblings could not personally be contacted, descriptions from the family or from other records were used. Results indicated
the siblings of the schizophrenic patients did not differ from those of nonschizophrenic
patients in overall incidence of abnormality. None of the many specific family interaction patterns hypothesized to be pathogenic for schizophrenia have thus far been substantiated by methodologically sound studies.

PURCELL, K., and METZ, S. R., "Distinctions between Subgroups of Asthmatic Children:
     Some Parent Attitude Variables Related to Age of Onset of Asthma," J. Psychosom.
     Res., 6, 251-258, 1962.
A continuation of the authors' previous work with asthmatic children at the Children's
Asthma Research Institute and Hospital in Denver. Previous work had tentatively classified these 86 children as "steroid dependent" and "rapidly remitting" in terms of their
clinical course once at the hospital and separated from home. Parents' attitudes were
measured using the parent attitude research instrument. Positive findings of this study
were that within the group of rapidly remitting children, relatively late age of onset
(after 12-18 months) was associated with autocratic and restrictive attitudes on the
part of their mothers. These findings were not substantiated by the other group.

QUERY, J. M. N., "Pre-Morbid Adjustment and Family Structure: A Comparison of Selected
     Rural and Urban Schizophrenic Men," J. Nerv. Ment. Dis., 133, 333-338, 1961.
A study which reviews schizophrenia in relating to cultural and familial settings. The
hypothesis is that premorbid adjustment of rural schizophrenics will be better than that
of urban subjects because the rural setting includes a more patriarchal family structure,
more emphasis upon individualism, and better sex-role identification. Case history data
were examined in terms of the Phillips' scale and supplemented by family interviews.
Fifty-one families were interviewed and the hypothesis was supported by the evidence.

RABKIN, L. Y., "The Patient's Family: Research Methods," Fam. Proc., 4, 105-132, 1965.
A review of family research with special emphasis upon the family of the schizophrenic.
Critical examination is done of case history studies, interviewing studies, psychodiagnostic testing, questionnaire studies, and observational research. A bibliography of
99 references is included.

RAPOPORT, R., "Normal Crises, Family Structure and Mental Health," Fam. Proc., 2, 68-80,
     1963.
An essay on some of the ideas and methods behind an exploratory study of how the family
handled "the newly married state." Six couples were thus studied via interviews both before and after marriage for variable periods of time.

REISS, P. J., "The Extended Kinship System: Correlates of and Attitudes on Frequency
     of Interaction," Marriage Fam. Liv., 24, 333-339, 1962.
A report of a study of urban middle-class kinship systems with emphasis upon frequency
of contact and attitudes about it. A sample was selected from the metropolitan Boston
area and interviewed. The conclusions are that frequency of interaction are not explained by the sex, ethnic background, or family cycle phase of these respondents.
Degree of kin relationship and distance of residence of kin are the most important
variables. Half of the respondents felt the frequency of contact with kin has been
insufficient and there is a desire for kin to live close but not too close.

ROSENTHAL, M. J., NI, E., FINKELSTEIN, M., and BERKWITZ, G. K., "Father-Child Relation-
     ships and Children's Problems," Arch. Gen. Psychiat., 7, 360-373, 1962.
A group of 405 new patients coming into the Institute for Juvenile Research in Chicago
were examined to determine whether the emotional problems of children were related to
certain types of father-child relationships. The relationship was examined by interviews with parents and children. Certain of the children's problems were found to be
correlated with types of father-child relationships being studied while others were not.

ROSMAN, B., WILD, C., RICCI, J., FLECK, S., and LIDZ, T., "Thought Disorders in the
     Parents of Schizophrenic Patients: A further Study Utilizing the Object Sort-
     ing Test," J. Psychiat. Res., 2, 211-221, 1964.
This is a second replication of a study by McConughy who found that parents of schizophrenic patients received scores in the object sorting test that were indicative of
pathology in conceptual thinking. Sixty-eight parents of schizophrenic patients and
115 control parents were used. The hypothesis of greater frequency of pathological
scores in the patient-parent group was supported only with subjects from higher levels
of intelligence, education and occupation.

RUTTER, M., "Sex Differences in Children's Responses to Family Stress," in E. J. An-
     thony and C. Koupernik (Eds.), The Child in His Family, New York, Wiley, 1970.
A questionnaire study investigating the impact on the child of marital problems and
parental psychiatric disorders. Antisocial behavior in boys is associated with disturbance in family relationships but the marriage rating bore no relation to the rate
of disorder in girls. Theoretical discussion is offered.

RYLE, A., and HAMILTON, M., "Neurosis in Fifty Married Couples," J. Ment. Sci., 108,
     265-273, 1962.
An investigation of 50 working-class marital couples to record the prevalence of neurosis as indicated by the Cornell medical index, the records of the general practitioner
with whom the families were registered, and the home interviews of a psychiatric social
worker. The information from these sources was compared and the presence of neurosis
was correlated with some aspects of adverse childhood experience, marital adjustment,
consumer status and social integration.

SAFILIOS-ROTHSCHILD, C., "Deviance and Mental Illness in the Greek Family," Fam. Proc.,
     7, 100-117, 1968.
A study of spouses of hospitalized mental patients in Greece to determine attitudes
about deviance and mental illness. The defining of behavior as deviant will depend
upon cultural definitions. Whether the deviance is defined as mental illness depends
upon other factors. Here the "degree of marital satisfaction seems to be the determining factor as to whether or not the normal spouse will" label the deviance as mental illness.

SAGER, C., GRUNDRACH, R., KRAMER, M., LANZ, R., and ROYCE, J., "The Married in Treat-
     ment: Effects of Psychoanalysis on the Marital State," Arch. Gen. Psychiat., 19,
     205-217, 1968.
In order to ascertain the effects of psychoanalysis on the marital state, a study of 736
married patients (432 women and 304 men), aged 21 to 68, in middle and upper socioeconomic class who were being treated in psychoanalysis, was done. Seventy-nine psychoanalysts supplied data on "any ten consecutive patients" and it was obtained through a
closed ended questionnaire. Twelve percent of the patients had concurrent group therapy,
two percent were in conjoint marital therapy, and about 20% of the patients had one or
more conjoint consultations with their spouse and analyst. Results indicated that marriages rated poor initially improved. Marriages rated better also improved. There was
no evidence that as one marital partner got better another got worse. Overall individual
patient improvement was rated at about 60%. Of the spouses who were in treatment, good
effects were more frequently reported in cases in which both husband and wife were
treated by the same psychoanalyst.

SAMPSON, H., MESSINGER, S., and TOWNE, R. D., "Family Processes and Becoming a Mental
     Patient," Amer. J. Social., 68, 88-96, 1962.
Accommodation of the family to the deviant behavior of the future patient, and the disruption of this accommodation which leads to hospitalization are described for a series
of 17 married mothers. Patients were located at time of first admission and extensive
data collected by interviews with family members, by professionals involved at any stage,
and by direct observation in home and hospital. Types of accommodation found were (1)
spouses isolated, emotionally distant from each other, and (2) family not self-contained
but revolved about a maternal figure who took over wife's duties. Each type has characteristic ways of disrupting, resulting in different implications to hospitalization.

SAMPSON, H., MESSINGER, S., and TOWNE, R. D., "The Mental Hospital and Family Adaptations,"
     Psychiat. Quart., 36, 704-719, 1962.
The authors' purpose was to examine the effects of hospitalization on the family, not
only during the hospitalization but also after discharge. Seventeen families in which
the wife-mother was hospitalized for the first time and was diagnosed by the state hospital as schizophrenic, were studied using interviews and records up to two years after
release. Emphasis is placed on a more deliberate therapeutic intervention based on study
of the crisis that precipitated hospitalization, and ways in which these crises are
coped with by the family.

SANUA, V., "Sociocultural Factors in Families of Schizophrenics: A Review of the Litera-
    ture," Psychiatry, 24, 246-265, 1961.
A review of the literature on the etiology of schizophrenia. Problems and methodology
are looked at and the literature is discussed from the point of view of data from hospital records; from separate interviews with patients and families; from interviews with
families together; from studies using personality tests, questionnaires and rating
scales; and from studies using the cross-cultural approach. All these studies boil
down to looking at the problem one of 4 ways: (1) parental troubles transmitted to the
children, (2) family structure, (3) disturbed interactional patterns, and (4) genetic
and constitutional factors in the child.

SCOTT, R. D., and ASHWORTH, P. L., "The 'Axis Value' and the Transfer of Psychosis,"
    Brit. J. Med. Psychol., 38, 97-116, 1965.
A report of a study of seven families with a schizophrenic member using a self report
test in which parents and child mark a check list of 42 items. The family members check
off what applies to themselves and to each of the others, then what each thinks the other
will check off about him. Contrasts are made between "shadow parents," (the parent who
is most involved with the patient and also had a significant involvement with a mad an-
cestor), and non-shadow parents. Differences are said to be found, and descriptions of
the families are offered.

SINGER, M. T., and WYNNE, L. C., "Communication Styles in Parents of Normals, Neurotics,
    and Schizophrenics: Some Findings Using a New Rorschach Scoring Manual," in I.
    M. Cohen (Ed.), Psychiatric Research Report 20, American Psychiatric Association,
    1966.
A report of a study of 250 families in which the Rorschach was used as a stimulus for
individual family members. Styles of parental communication are described and findings
reported.

SINGER, M. T., and WYNNE, L. C., "Differentiating Characteristics of Parents of Child-
    hood Schizophrenics, Childhood Neurotics, and Young Adult Schizophrenics," Amer.
    J. Psychiat., 120, 234-243, 1963.
A study where parents of 20 autistic children were blindly differentiated at a statistically significant level of accuracy from parents of 20 neurotic children. The data
were TAT and Rorschach tests of the parents. Additionally, the parents of adolescent
and young adult schizophrenics were compared with the parents of autistic children and
differences were found.

SINGER, M., and WYNNE, L., "Principles for Scoring Communication Defects and Deviances
    in Parents of Schizophrenics: Rorschach and TAT Scoring Manuals," Psychiatry, 29,
    260-289, 1966.
A continuation of previous studies in which the authors have predictively related parental behavior on psychological tests with psychiatric diagnosis of their offspring. Two
scoring manuals for use with the Rorschach and with the TAT are presented in an effort
to pinpoint certain selective features of parental behavior which can be quickly scored
(previous studies used inferences which required a great deal of time in analyzing a
battery of tests). A discussion of the tests and their clinical correlates in the
family of schizophrenics is also provided.

SINGER, M. T., and WYNNE, L. C., "Thought Disorder and Family Relations of Schizophrenics.
    III. Methodology Using Projective Techniques. IV. Results and Implications,"
    Arch. Gen. Psychiat., 12, 187-212, 1965.
A continuation of the study of families through the use of projective tests with the emphasis upon predicting the form of thinking and degree of disorganization of each patient
from the tests of other members of his family, and the blind matching of patients and
their families. The series includes a full discussion of various aspects of schizophrenia and the family.

SPITZER, S. P., SWANSON, R. M., and LEHR, R. K., "Audience Reactions and Careers of
    Psychiatric Patients," Fam. Proc., 8, 159-181, 1969.
A study of the reaction of families and the ways these reactions influence the psychiat-

ric patient career. The histories of 79 first admission patients were examined and the
patient and a family member were interviewed. Two dimensions of family reaction to deviance are described leading to a typology of eight career patterns which allow for the
classification of 95% of the cases reviewed.

STABENAU, J. R., TUPIN, J., WERNER, M., and POLLIN, W., "A Comparative Study of Families
    of Schizophrenics, Delinquents, and Normals," Psychiatry, 28, 45-59, 1965.
A report of a comparison of five families with a schizophrenic, five families with a delinquent, and five normal families tested with the revealed differences test, the object
sorting test, and the thematic apperception test. "Data from the three different tests
suggest that in the schizophrenic and delinquent families there were both individual disturbances in thought process and impaired communication at the family level." "There was
relatively little evidence of communication impairment at the individual or family level
in the normal families."

STENNETT, R., "Family Diagnosis: MMPI and CIP Results," J. Clin. Psychol., 22, 165-167,
    1966.
MMPI and CIP (California test of personality) tests were done on 230 families over a
five-year period in an out-patient clinic to answer several questions about family dynamics. Families were urban, Protestant, and white, with wide socioeconomic status.
The CIP was given to children from age four up to 13. Findings were that a significant
number of family members other than the identified patient had personality problems of
their own, that there was a significant correlation in the level of psychopathology
between the parents of troubled families, but no evidence was found of conflicting or
complementary personality characteristics in the parents.

VAN der VEEN, F., HUEBNER, B., JORGENS, B., and NEJA, P., "Relationship Between the
    Parents' Concept of the Family and Family Adjustment," Amer. J. Orthopsychiat.,
    34, 45-55, 1964.
To study the "significance of the family unit for the well-being of the individual" and
"the perceptions of the family unit by each individual," two groups of ten families
each were selected. One group was composed of families from the community which functioned well (called the higher adjustment group). The other group was composed of families which had applied to a guidance center for help with one of their children.
They were matched as to sex and position of the child and size of family. Tests used
were the family concept Q-Sort, family semantic test, and a marital questionnaire.
Results indicated that the adjustment of the families was a function of: (1) the amount
of agreement between the "real" family concept of the parent and "ideal" family concept
as determined by professionals, (2) the agreement between the "real" and "ideal" family
concepts of the parent, and (3) the agreement between the "real" family concepts of the
mother and father.

WAINWRIGHT, W. H., "The Reaction of Mothers to Improvement in Their Schizophrenic Daugh-
    ters," Compr. Psychiat., 1, 236-243, 1960.
At the Payne Whitney psychiatric clinic eight mother-schizophrenic daughter combinations
were interviewed and observed for a period ranging from four to 48 months, including up
to 30 months after the patient's hospital discharge. Of these eight mothers, two responded favorably to their daughter's improvement, two showed fluctuation in response
which seemed dependent upon the severity of the daughter's symptoms, and four mothers
showed signs of illness as their daughters improved. The author sees a common need
with these four mothers to keep the daughter partially ill. Where hostility emerges
during the recovery phase, he suggests evaluation for treatment of the mother.

WARING, M., and RICKS, D., "Family Patterns of Children who Become Adult Schizophrenics,"
    J. Nerv. Ment. Dis., 140, 351-364, 1965.
A study comparing family variables of three groups of adult patients, who were seen as
adolescents at a child guidance center. The three groups were (1) 30 patients, who as
adults developed schizophrenia and remitted (defined as leaving the hospital), (2) 20
patients, who as adults developed schizophrenia and did not remit, and (3) a control
group of 50 patients, selected from the clinic population, who did not develop schizophrenia and were never hospitalized. Data were obtained retrospectively from work-ups
at the time the patients were adolescents, and also from subsequent follow-ups with

schools, hospitals, and other agencies, and finally in some cases with interviews with patient and family. There were significant familial differences between the remitting and unremitting groups, and less significant differences between the total schizophrenia group and the controls.

WEISMAN, I., "Exploring the Effect of the Marital Relationship on Child Functioning and
     Parental Functioning," Soc. Casework, 44, 330-334, 1963.
A report on a study investigating the relationship between child functioning and marital patterns. A sample was drawn of clients from the community service society of New York. The data consisted of the judgements of the caseworkers who used a rating scale to indi- cate severity and persistence of conflict in several areas of child functioning and paren- tal patterns.

WESTLEY, W. A., and EPSTEIN, N. B., "Report on the Psychosocial Organization of the Fa-
     mily and Mental Health," in D. Willner (Ed.), Decisions, Values and Groups, New
     York, Pergamon Press, 1960.
A report of a study designed to investigate the relationship between family functioning and development of either mental health or pathology. The sample was 531 students of the first year class at a university who were given a Rorschach, Gordon-Personality test, and interviewed by a psychiatrist. Out of these, 20 were classified as being the most emotionally healthy and of these, 17 were in the study, in view of the fact that they were available and their families agreed to participate. There is a schema for descrip- tion, analysis, and evaluation of the family which is extensively illustrated using a case example. Common features of these emotionally healthy families are described.

WILLI, J., "Joint Rorschach Testing of Partner Relationship," Fam. Proc., 8, 64-78, 1969.
A test of marital partners by the conjoint Rorschach procedure. A sample of 80 pairs was examined with each person administered the Rorschach individually and then again ad- ministered it conjointly with the partner. The goal was to measure the relative strength of the partners and how the personality of the subject changes in the discussion with the other.

WINTER, W. D., and FERREIRA, H. J., Research in Family Interaction, Palo Alto, Science
     & Behavior Books, 1969.
A collection of some new and some previously published material dealing with studies and research on family interaction. There are sections on methodological issues in family interaction research; studies of individual family members; studies of family interaction decision-making; studies of family attitudes, power, and behavior and studies of intra- family communication. There is a lengthy bibliography attached.

WOLMAN, B. B., "The Fathers of Schizophrenic Patients," Acta Psychother. Psychosom.,
     9, 193-210, 1961.
Observations on the fathers of schizophrenic patients based upon 33 patients seen in in- dividual and group therapy, and interviews with their family members. Although some fathers performed adequately outside the family circle, each demonstrated child-like dependency upon the wife and inability to play the role of father. Fathers are grouped as sick, prodigies, rebellious, and runaways.

YARROW, M. R., CAMPBELL, J. D., and BURTON, R. V., "Reliability of Maternal Retrospec-
     tion: A Preliminary Report," Fam. Proc., 3, 207-218, 1964.
An examination of the retrospective method of family research where the data are based on self report of family members about the past. A study is reported where retrospec- tion of mothers is obtained through interview methods and these data are compared with the reports of those mothers at the earlier period. The results "demonstrate a very large error in retrospective interview data on parent-child relations."

2.3 FAMILY DATA — OBSERVATION OF GROUP

ACKERMAN, N. W., "Prejudicial Scapegoating and Neutralizing Forces in the Family Group, with Special Reference to the Role of Family Healer," Int. J. Soc. Psyciat., Special Edition 2, 90-96, 1964.
A discussion of conflict in the family based upon films of family diagnostic sessions. The emphasis is upon prejudicial scapegoating within a pattern of interdependent roles: those of the persecutor, the scapegoat, and the family healer. It is said that disturbed families break up into warring factions with a leader of each faction, a victim of prejudicial attack, and a person who provides the emotional antidote. The health-sickness continuum is influenced by the shifting balance of the struggle.

BASAMANIA, B. W., "The Emotional Life of the Family: Inferences for Social Casework," Amer. J. Orthopsychiat., 31, 74-86, 1961.
A casework view of the Bowen research project where families with a schizophrenic member were hospitalized. Observations of 11 families are categorized into (1) interrelated personality problems among family members, and (2) interaction problems among family members. Case examples are given. A discussion of family therapy procedures is presented with the emphasis upon relating to more than one individual at a time. Inferences for social casework emphasize the dimension of the emotional life of the family rather than the integration of sociological concepts with casework practice.

BAUMANN, G., and ROMAN, M., "Interaction Testing in the Study of Marital Dominance," Fam. Proc., 5, 230-242, 1966.
A sample of 50 couples was exposed individually and conjointly to the Wechsler Bellevue. In the conjoint testing, the couple was asked to reach agreement on the response. Comparisons of the individual test and the conjoint test were made, as well as measures of dominance of the couple tested together.

BAXTER, J. C., and ARTHUR, S. C., "Conflict in Families of Schizophrenics as a Function of Premorbid Adjustment and Social Class," Fam. Proc., 3, 273-279, 1964.
A group of 16 hospitalized male schizophrenics were grouped into four classes on the basis of the patients' premorbid adjustment and social class. Standard interviews with the parents were rated for conflict. "Results indicate that the amount of conflict expressed by the parents varies jointly with the premorbid level of the patient and the social class of the family."

BAXTER, J. C., ARTHUR, S., FLOOD, C., and HEDGEPETH, B., "Conflict Patterns in the Families of Schizophrenics," J. Nerv. Ment. Dis., 135, 419-424, 1962.
Families of 12 male and six female schizophrenics were interviewed individually and as a group to explore conflict patterns in relation to the sex of the schizophrenic child. The amount of conflict is said to be comparable in the two groups while patterns of conflict differ. There is more interparental conflict in the group of families with a male patient and more involvement of the patient in conflict in the group with a female patient.

BECKER, J., TATSUOKA, M., and CARLSON, A., "The Communicative Value of Parental Speech in Families with Disturbed Children," J. Nerv. Ment. Dis., 141, 359-364, 1966.
Hypothesis was the communicativeness of parents with emotionally disturbed children (11 sets of parents who had children coming to a clinic) would be lower than that of parents with normal children (12 parent sets who were paid volunteers). Communicativeness was assessed by Taylor's cloze procedure. The speech of nonclinic mothers was significantly more communicative than that of nonclinic fathers, clinic mother, and clinic fathers. The latter three groups did not differ among themselves.

BEHRENS, M., "Brief Home Visits by the Clinic Therapist in the Treatment of Lower-Class Patients," Amer. J. Psychiat., 124, 371-375, 1967.
A paper reviewing the author's experience with home visits. The sample was 80 patients attending an out-patient clinic. These were chronic schizophrenics, the majority black and female of socioeconomic class IV or V with certain exceptions. Home visits were made on the average of one some visit per year per patient, usually in the late afternoon and lasting 30 to 40 minutes. At first they were done only at time of crisis situations, later routinely. The visits have been found useful in obtaining data about the

patient and family, improving the relationship between patient and therapist, and in decreasing rehospitalizations.

BEHRENS, M., and ACKERMAN, N., "The Home Visit As An Aid in Family Diagnosis and Ther-
     apy," Soc. Casework, 37, 11-19, 1956.
A paper based on the author's clinical work in which the home visit is used as an aid in
family diagnosis and therapy when the identified patient is a child. Observations are
based on family interaction patterns, physical environment and atmosphere of the home.
A case example is given to illustrate the author's technique.

BEHRENS, M., and GOLDFARB, W., "A Study of Patterns of Interaction of Families of Schizo-
     phrenic Children in Residential Treatment," Amer. J. Orthopsychiat., 28, 300-312,
     1958.
An attempt to differentiate families of schizophrenic children from those of nonschizophrenic children with a sample of 20 families who had a child diagnosed as schizophrenic
and with five with a behavior disorder, all of whom were in-patients. There were ten
normals, all children living at home. Data were collected using family interaction
scales, and observations were recorded in the homes for both the normals and the patients
when they were home on a visit. One person made all the observations. This observer
knew which families had a schizophrenic child and which did not. Results indicate that
the schizophrenic families were more pathologic than the normal families and the families
with behavior disorders.

BEHRENS, M., MEYERS, D. I., GOLDFARB, W., GOLDFARB, N., and FIELDSTEEL, N. D., "The
     Henry Ittleson Center Family Interaction Scales," Genet. Psychol. Monogr., 80,
     203-295, 1969.
A report of the manual used for the use of the family interaction scales. The scales
appraise the functioning of family groups, and derive from a clinical interest in the
relationship between the identified patient and the family. Data are obtained through
a three-hour home visit at mealtime. Scales have been used to evaluate the functioning
of the family with a schizophrenic child, to compare families which include children
with various diagnoses with normal families and to determine the nature of changes in
family functioning over a specified length of time. A description of scales and scoring instructions, and three-family illustrations are described.

BEHRENS, M., ROSENTHAL, A. J., and CHODOFF, P., "Communication in Lower Class Families
     of Schizophrenics," Arch. Gen. Psychiat., 18, 689-696, 1968.
Part II, observation and findings, of a study of low-socioeconomic families of schizophrenics. The study was done in the home where the family was focussed upon a task,
particularly the Rorschach. Raters were asked to predict type of family from written
transcripts. Results indicate that communication and interaction patterns of lower
class families with a schizophrenic differ from families whose class background is
similar.

BEHRENS, M., and SHERMAN, A., "Observations of Family Interaction in the Home," Amer. J.
     Orthopsychiat., 29, 243-248, 1959.
An essay on the author's previous studies using home visits in evaluating family interactional patterns to differentiate schizophrenic families from nonschizophrenic families.
Difficulties in this type of research are discussed and suggestions for further data
collection are made. It is felt that this is a useful technique for diagnostic, treatment, and research purposes."

BELL, N. W., "Extended Family Relations of Disturbed and Well Families," Fam. Proc., 1,
     175-193, 1962.
The author's thesis is that "disturbed families have been unable to resolve conflicts
with the extended kin outside the nuclear family" and that "well" families have
achieved resolution of the problems of ties to extended kin. Most of the data were
collected from observation and interviews in the home. Findings were that the "pathological" families used the extended family to (1) shore up group defenses, (2) act as
stimuli of conflict, (3) act as screens for the projection of conflicts, and (4) act as
competing objects of support.

BERMAN, G., "Communication of Affect in Family Therapy," Arch. Gen. Psychiat., 17, 154-
     158, 1967.
An experiment attempting to determine how affect is communicated in family sessions.
The method was to take tape-recorded dialogue between three subjects in family therapy,
transcribe it, and give the typewritten dialogue to seven observers (four social workers
and three psychiatric residents). They were asked to rate the affective content of each
speech. Findings were that verbal affect correlates with written dialogue, the preceding
written and verbal dialogue will influence the raters' judgment of the affect of the subsequent speech, and that nonverbal affect will more strongly influence the raters' judgment than verbal affect. Methodology and application of the findings are discussed.

BING, E., "The Conjoint Family Drawing," Fam. Proc., 9, 173-194, 1970.
To assess family functioning, the family is asked to do a conjoint drawing. A sample
of 14 families with a problem child was given the task and the results are reported.

BOWEN, M., "A Family Concept of Schizophrenia," in D. D. Jackson (Ed.), The Etiology of
     Schizophrenia, New York, Basic Books, 1960.
Clinical observations based upon a research study of the families of schizophrenics.
The book includes a report on the project where whole families of schizophrenics were
hospitalized.

BRODY, E., "Modification of Family Interaction Patterns by a Group Interview Technique,"
     Int. J. Group Psychother., 6, 38-47, 1956.
As part of a study of prefrontal lobotomy, family members of 11 patients who would un-
dergo this procedure were seen for five months before the operation until at least one
year after the operation. Frequency was from once weekly during the first few months
to as infrequently as once a month during the last few months. Individual interviews
with family members were also used. The family interviews seemed to result in "an increased capacity for action by the family previously immobilized."

BRODEY, W., "Some Family Operations in Schizophrenia," Arch. Gen. Psychiat., 1, 379-402,
     1959.
One of a series of papers from a research project in which entire families, all of which
have a schizophrenic member, are hospitalized and observed for periods of six months to
two-and-one-half years. Data were collected from five families. Description of the family and of staff-family relationships are reported. Based on the family histories, an
attempt is made to understand the pathology presented.

BROWN, B. S., "Home Visiting by Psychiatrists," Arch. Gen. Psychiat., 7, 98-107, 1962.
As part of an exploration of alternatives to psychiatric hospitalization, an investigation was done of home visiting by 34 psychiatrists with varied practice patterns. Data
were gathered by interviews on frequency of visit, attitudes, and experiences. Nine of
the psychiatrists had never done a home visit, 13 had done one to five a year, seven
had made six to 25 visits per year, and five had made from 50 to 400 visits yearly.
The type of practice apparently is the greatest determinant. Psychoanalytically oriented psychiatrists do least. The consensus of the group of psychiatrists is that home
visits have doubtful utility. The movement to break down rigid boundaries between home
and hospital may lead to a renaissance of home visiting.

CAPUTO, D. V., "The Parents of the Schizophrenic," Fam. Proc., 2, 339-356, 1963.
A study to assess the role of the parents in the development of schizophrenia, with particular emphasis upon the passive father and dominating mother notion. Parents were
given individual tests and after taking a parent attitude inventory they were asked to
discuss the items on which they had disagreed. These discussions were assessed with
the Bales method. Reversal of role was not found to be a significant factor, and a
hostile atmosphere is indicated in the home of the potential schizophrenic.

CHEEK, F., "Family Interaction Patterns and Convalescent Adjustment of the Schizo-
     phrenic," Arch. Gen. Psychiat., 13, 138-147, 1965.
In an attempt to examine the relationship between family interaction patterns and out-

come in schizophrenia, data were obtained from 51 patients who had been hospitalized
between the ages of 15 and 26, all of whom had living mothers and fathers. Each family
member filled out a questionnaire relating to interaction patterns, all three family
members together worked on two questionnaire problems. An interview with the mother
on the adjustment of the patient was evaluated by means of a 40-item four point rating
scale. One week later in the home of the patient two more 15-minute discussions between
family members were recorded. Fifty-six normal families were studied with identifical
procedures used as with the schizophrenics. Results indicated that it was the characteristics of the parents, rather than the degree of sickness of the patient "which was
the decisive factor in producing a poor outcome."

CHEEK, F., "The Father of the Schizophrenic: The Function of a Peripheral Role," Arch.
    Gen. Psychiat., 13, 336-345, 1965.
In view of the absence of data on the role of the father in the intrafamilial environment of the schizophrenic, Bales' interaction process analysis technique and the social
system theoretical framework of Parsons are used for studying the interaction of 67 families of young adult schizophrenics (40 male and 27 female). This was compared to 56
families with nonpsychotic young adults (31 male and 25 female). Outcome in schizophrenia was evaluated a year and a half following discharge from the inpatient setting.
All discussions were tape-recorded and coded, using the Bales interaction categories.
Additionally, each of the three families were asked to fill in a questionnaire examining
expectations and perceptions of how the other three might behave in relation to one another in certain typical family problems. Schizophrenic fathers occupy a peripheral position in the family in which the mother and patient are closest by default. Profiles
of mothers of schizophrenics however, differed more widely from those of normals than
fathers'.

CHEEK, F., "Parental Role Distortions in Relation to Schizophrenic Deviancy," in I. M.
    Cohen (Ed.), Psychiatric Research Report No. 20, Wash. D. C., American Psychiatric
    Association, 1966.
A study investigating the nature of schizophrenic interaction in the family, and the relation of family interaction to the outcome of the schizophrenic. The study combined
questionnaire and observational data. The sample included 67 schizophrenic contrasted
with 56 nonpsychotic young adults.

CHEEK, F., "The 'Schizophrenic Mother' in Word and Deed," Fam. Proc., 3, 155-177, 1964.
A study of the mothers of schizophrenics by direct observation of their behavior in a
standard conversation with spouse and schizophrenic offspring. The data were analyzed
with a revised version of the Bales process analysis. Sixty-seven families of schizophrenics were contrasted with 56 normal families. Differences in the characteristics
of the mothers were found.

CHEEK, F., "A Serendipitous Finding: Sex Roles in Schizophrenia," J. Abnorm. Soc. Psy-
    chol., 69, 392-400, 1964.
One of a series of reports on an ongoing research project studying the family environment
in schizophrenia. Interaction profiles of 67 young adult schizophrenics (40 male and
27 female) were compared with those of 56 normals (31 male and 25 female). Profiles
were derived from 48 minutes of recorded interaction between father, mother, and patient with a variation of the Bales interaction categories. Male schizophrenics presented an interaction equivalent of withdrawal, with low total activity rates and low
dominance behaviors. In contrast, female schizophrenics proved to be more active than
female normals.

DAY, J., and KWIATKOWSKA, H., "The Psychiatric Patient and His Well Sibling: A Compari-
    son Through Their Art Productions," Bull. Art. Ther., 2, 51-66, 1962.
A clinical paper comparing the "well" sibling to the "sick" sibling in a schizophrenic
family. The setting was an in-patient ward, and observations were taken from the art
work of the paired siblings during art therapy. The data from three families reveals
that the sick sibling art productions are quite disorganized, while the well sibling
productions are more normal, but often "incongruous or unusual."

DRECHSLER, R. J., and SHAPIRO, M. I., "A Procedure for Direct Observation of Family In-
     teraction in a Child Guidance Clinic." Psychiatry, 24, 163-170, 1961.
A procedure for making direct observations of a family as part of the intake procedures
of a child guidance clinic. A psychiatrist interviews the family, the family is observed
alone, and the family answers a 20-item questionnaire while being observed. The procedural aim was to sample family interactions in a way that would fit economically into
ongoing clinic policy. The interview clarifies the presenting problem. A task for the
family provides a stage upon which the family acts out the interactive patterns in their
relationships. Case illustrations are provided.

DRECHSLER, R. J., and SHAPIRO, M. I., "Two Methods of Analysis of Family Diagnostic Data,"
     Fam. Proc., 2, 367-379, 1963.
A description of the conjoint use of clinical and statistical analysis of the same data.
Thirteen families were interviewed and also given a standard family task (discussing a
questionnaire) to perform alone. Samples of the tape recordings were extracted and frequency count made of how often one person spoke to another. Clinical impressions were
compared and similarities found.

DUPONT, R., and GRUNEBAUM, H., "Willing Victims: The Husbands of Paranoid Women," Amer.
     J. Psychiat., 125, 151-159, 1968.
In an attempt to understand the dynamics of spouses of paranoid women, cases with paranoid delusions (both in-patient and out-patient) were evaluated over a three-year period.
Data were collected on nine women with paranoid state, using clinical interviews with
the husband alone, wife alone, and the couple together, plus the MMPI and interpersonal
checklist. Results indicated that the wife expressed the anger and dissatisfaction in
the marriage, while the husband manifested passivity and apparent reasonableness and
thus seemed to be a "willing victim."

ELBERT, S., ROSMAN, B., MINUCHIN, S., and GUERNEY, F., "A Method for the Clinical Study
     of Family Interaction," Amer. J. Orthopsychiat., 34, 885-894, 1964.
Two methods are described to obtain data on family interactions which were developed by
the family research unit at the Wiltwick School for Boys. Families were from low socioeconomic status with more than one delinquent child. The family interaction apperception test is a TAT style test consisting of ten pictures showing family members in different activities. The family task is designed to permit observations of the family relations and their interactions. The family is seated in a room and by operating a tape
recorder they hear six different tasks, which they must all discuss and answer together.
During the time they are discussing the tasks, a continuous report on nonverbal behavior
is being dictated by an observer (looking through a one way mirror). Verbal behavior is
recorded by a tape recorder.

ENGLISH, O. S., SCHEFLEN, A. E., HAMPE, W. W., and AUERBACH, A. H., Strategy and Struc-
     ture in Psychotherapy, Behavioral Studies Monograph No. 2, Philadelphia, Eastern
     Pennsylvania Psychiatric Institute, 1965.
A companion volume to Stream and Structure of Communicational Behavior (A. E. Scheflen)
which includes three research studies of a family therapy interview by Whitaker and
Malone.

FARINA, A., "Patterns of Role Dominance and Conflict in Parents of Schizophrenic Pa-
     tients," J. Abnorm. Soc. Psychol., 61, 31-38, 1960.
Parents of 12 good premorbid schizophrenics, 12 poor premorbids, and 12 children hospitalized for tuberculosis were interviewed. They were exposed individually and as pairs
to hypothetical incidents with children. The joint conversation was analyzed for dominance and conflict. Father dominance was associated with good premorbid adjustment of
the son and mother dominance with the poor premorbids. Parents of schizophrenics displayed more conflict than the control parents.

FARINA, A., and DUNHAM, R. M., "Measurement of Family Relationships and Their Effects,"
     Arch. Gen. Psychiat., 9, 64-73, 1963.
A group of families of male hospitalized schizophrenic patients, divided into good premorbid and poor premorbid, were given a structural situation test. Each family member

is exposed to some hypothetical problem situations with children, and the family is
then brought together and exposed to the same situation. Indices of dominance, such as
length of speeches, and indices of conflict were constructed. Immediately following
this, a group of the patients were given a visual task individually and contrasted with
a group given the same task a week after the situation test. The conclusions are that
fathers are more dominant in good premorbid cases and mothers more dominating in bad
premorbids. Conflict scores are higher for good premorbids.

FERREIRA, A. J., "Decision-Making in Normal and Pathologic Families," Arch. Gen. Psy-
    chiat., 8, 68-73, 1963.
An experiment to find differences between 25 normal and 25 abnormal families using a
decision making test. The family members first make a choice of items on a questionnaire when alone and then are brought together and asked to reach agreement on the same
items. Their choices separately and together are compared and the agreements are categorized as unanimous, majority, dictatorial, and chaotic. The two types of families
are found to differ.

FERREIRA, A. J., WINTER, W. D., "Decision-Making in Normal and Abnormal Two-Child Fa-
    milies," Fam. Proc., 7, 17-36, 1968.
A report of a study of 85 families, 36 normal and 49 abnormal (composed of parents and
two children), were tested in a procedure similar to that previously used in a test of
family triads. Differences were found between the two groups on measures of "spontaneous agreement," "decision time," and "choice fulfillment."

FERREIRA, A. J., and WINTER, W. D., "Family Interaction and Decision-Making," Arch. Gen.
    Psychiat., 13, 214-223, 1965.
A report of a study contrasting 50 normal families, and 75 families with an abnormal
child. The abnormal group included 15 schizophrenics, 16 delinquents, and 44 maladjusted children. The family members were asked to fill out a neutral questionnaire
separately, and then they were brought together and asked to fill out the same questionnaire while reaching agreement on the items as a group. Generally this report is
concerned with the extent of agreement when family members make their choices separately, how much time is necessary to reach group decisions, and the appropriateness of the
family decisions in fulfilling the wishes of the individual family members. Eighteen
hypotheses are described and the results reported in terms of the differences found
between the groups.

FERREIRA, A. J., and WINTER, W. D., "Information Exchange and Silence in Normal and
    Abnormal Families," Fam. Proc., 7, 251-278, 1968.
A comparison of normal and abnormal families which measured exchange of information and
amount of time spent in silence in doing a task. A sample of 30 normal and 45 abnormal
families were contrasted by a rater judgment of tape recordings. Differences were found.

FERREIRA, A. J., and WINTER, W. D., "Stability of Interactional Variables in Family De-
    cision-Making," Arch. Gen. Psychiat., 14, 352-355, 1966.
In order to test the stability over time and after family therapy, of three variables
in family decision-making, 23 randomly selected families (10 abnormal and 13 normal)
were retested six months after the original research project. The abnormal families
had received therapy. Results indicated that there was no significant difference between the means observed in test and retests of the three variables for either normal
or abnormal families. It is concluded that these three variables (spontaneous agreement, decision-time, and choice-fulfillment) were consistent over time, and were not
changed by family therapy.

FERREIRA, A. J., WINTER, W. D., and POINDEXTER, E. J., "Some Interactional Variables
    in Normal and Abnormal Families," Fam. Proc., 5, 60-75, 1966.
A study contrasting normal and abnormal families, with the abnormals including schizophrenic, delinquent, and maladjusted children. The families were exposed to three TAT
cards at a time, and asked to make up a story tying them together. Differences were
found between the types of families.

FISCH, R., "Home Visits in a Private Psychiatric Practice," Fam. Proc., 3, 114-126, 1964.
A discussion of home visiting with the merits described in terms of involving the entire
family, decreasing family defensiveness, gaining new information about the patient's
setting, and preventing hospitalization. Examples of experiences in home visits are
given.

FRIEDMAN, A. S., "Family Therapy as Conducted in the Home," Fam. Proc., 1, 132-140, 1962.
A discussion of the rationale for, experiences with, and problems resulting from home
visits of schizophrenic patients and their families.

FRIEDMAN, C. J., and FRIEDMAN, A. S., "Characteristics of Schizogenic Families During
     a Joint Story-Telling Task," Fam. Proc., 9, 333-353, 1970.
A comparison of families with a schizophrenic, and normal families in the task of telling
a story. Observer ratings were used for the interaction and judges ratings for the final
joint family story. Differences were found.

GARMEZY, N., FARINA, A., and RODNICK, E. H., "The Structured Situation Test: A Method
     for Studying Family Interaction in Schizophrenia," Amer. J. Orthopsychiat., 30,
     445-451, 1960.
A group of 36 sets of parents composed of parents of good and poor premorbids, or parents
of sons with TB ("normals"), were exposed to 12 hypothetical misbehaviors of a son. Individually and then together they were asked to indicate how to handle the situation.
From tape recordings of the interviews, measures of dominance behavior and conflict were
made, such as who spoke first and last, acceptance of another's solution, amount of interruption, and so on. Fathers of good premorbids were dominant, as were mothers of poor
premorbids. The parents of normals share dominance. Poor premorbids show greater conflict than normals.

GLASSER, P. H., "Changes in Family Equilibrium During Psychotherapy," Fam. Proc., 2, 245-
     264, 1963.
A report on a study of role changes in three families when a parent undergoes psychotherapy. Family members were interviewed, families were observed and interviewed as a
group during home visits, reports of therapists and psychiatric and social work records
were examined. Case examples are given and the reaction of the family to the process of
treatment is described in terms of the changes in family equilibrium.

GOLDSTEIN, M., JUDD, L., RODNICK, E., ALKIRE, A., and GOULD, E., "A Method for Studying
     Social Influence and Coping Patterns Within Families of Disturbed Adolescents," J.
     Nerv. Ment. Dis., 127, 233-252, 1968.
The first report of a project dealing with family interaction patterns between parents
and adolescents. Twenty families with the identified patient aged 13 to 19 were seen
for five sessions at the UCLA psychology clinic. Data collected included psychological
testing (TAT and a partial WAIS), psycho-physiological recordings, and videotape recordings of both actual and simulated verbal interaction. The results of simulated interactions indicated that social power usage among family members was related to type of
psychopathology manifested by the adolescents.

GOODRICH, W., and BOOMER, D. S., "Experimental Assessment of Modes of Conflict Resolu-
     tion," Fam. Proc., 2, 15-24, 1963.
A report of an experimental technique for studying the coping behavior of husband and
wife when they attempt to resolve a marital conflict. Fifty paid volunteer couples
between 18 and 27 years of age were asked to match colors — some unmatchable — to see
how the couple coped with puzzling or ambiguous situations. A general discussion of results is given relating the "ability to achieve perspective on the situation and maintenance of self-esteem" to adequacy of coping.

GOODRICH, W., RYDER, R., and RAUSH, H., "Patterns of Newlywed Marriage," J. Marriage
     Fam., 30, 383-391, 1968.
A report of an exploratory study of 50 average, middle-class marriages examined during
the fourth month with interviews, problem solving situations, and questionnaires.
Eight patterns of marriage are suggested.

HALEY, J., "Cross-Cultural Experimentation: An Initial Attempt," Hum. Organ., 3, 110-
     117, 1967.
A comparison of Caucasian middle-class American families and Japanese-born families in
an experimental setting where the measure is speech sequences. Differences are found.

HALEY, J., "The Family of the Schizophrenic: A Model System," J. Nerv. Ment. Dis., 129,
     357-374, 1959.
A description of the family of the schizophrenic as a governed system with a verbatim
excerpt from a family interview for illustration.

HALEY, J., "Observation of the Family of the Schizophrenic," Amer. J. Orthopsychiat.,
     30, 460-467, 1960.
A report on a research project examining families containing a schizophrenic child by
observation of conjoint family therapy sessions, filmed structured interviews, and experimental situations. The family is seen as a self-corrective system which is governed
by the behavior of each family member. The limited range of a family system can be described in terms of rules and prohibitions which, when infringed, activate family members to behave in such a way as to reinforce the system. The general communicative behavior of the schizophrenic family is described.

HALEY, J., "Research on Family Patterns: An Instrument Measurement," Fam. Proc., 3, 41-
     65, 1964.
A report of an investigation of patterns of interchange in families. The questions are
whether families follow patterns, whether "normal" and "abnormal" families differ, and
whether patterns change over time. A group of 40 normal and 40 abnormal families were
given a standard stimulus for conversation and a frequency count was made of the order
in which family members speak. Families were found to follow patterns and differences
were found between the normal and abnormal groups.

HALEY, J., "Speech Sequences of Normal and Abnormal Families with Two Children Present,"
     Fam. Proc., 6, 81-97, 1967.
A sample of 50 abnormal and 40 normal families were contrasted in an experimental setting
where a measurement was made of the sequence in which family members speak. Differences
had been found in a previous study where the families were tested in triads. In this
study, where the sibling was included as well as the index child, differences were not
found between the two groups.

HENRY, J., "The Study of Families by Naturalistic Observation," in I. M. Cohen (Ed.),
     Psychiatric Research Report No. 20, American Psychiatric Association, 1966.
A discussion of the observation of psychotic children in the home with the emphasis
upon the methodology and the experience of such observation. An illustration is given,
and "when such observations are undertaken, it quickly becomes apparent that the data
are so rich as to compel re-examination of old theories and suggest hypotheses leading
to new ones."

JACKSON, D. D., RISKIN, J., and SATIR, V., "A Method of Analysis of a Family Interview,"
     Arch. Gen. Psychiat., 5, 321-339, 1961.
The authors examined the first five minutes of a family therapy interview without know-
ing the diagnosis of the child in the family. This "blind" analysis included a prediction of the psychopathology of the patient and some character traits of his brother.
The information available was only the parents' conversation which was examined from
the point of view of their communicative behavior, their needs and defenses, and possible early life experiences which would lead them to interact in this way. The purpose of the study was to illustrate a method of analyzing a family system.

JACKSON, D. D., and YALOM, I., "Family Research on the Problem of Ulcerative Colitis,"
     Arch. Gen. Psychiat., 15, 410-418, 1966.
A study attempting to correlate parental behavior and the onset of ulcerative colitis.
Eight patients were intensively studied using four to 20 conjoint family therapy ses-
sions which were tape-recorded. Identified patients were all children ranging in age

from seven to 17. Sociality of the family was limited, and they related in a "pseudo-mutual" fashion. Suggestions for further study were made.

JONES, D. M., "Binds and Unbinds," Fam. Proc., 3, 323-331, 1964.
A description of a family, with excerpts of verbatim conversation, which discusses the processes of the family members binding and unbinding in relation to one another.

KADUSHIN, P., CUTLER, C., WAXENBERG, S., and SAGER, C., "The Family Story Technique and
     Intrafamily Analysis," J. Project. Techn., 33, 438-450, 1969.
A report of a new technique — the family story technique (FST) -- to assess affect, in-teractional patterns, and future outlook in the family. The FST is said to be useful as a diagnostic tool, as a research tool, and in comparing separate families with one ano-ther once normative data have been accumulated on a wide variety of families.

KAUFMAN, I., FRANK, T., HEIMS, L., HERRICK, S., REISER, D., and WILLER, L., "Treatment
     Implications of a New Classification of Parents of Schizophrenic Children," Amer.
     J. Psychiat., 116, 920-924, 1960.
A report of a study of the personalities of 80 schizophrenic children's parents. Ma-terial was gathered from psychotherapy, psychological testing, and direct observation of parent-child interaction. Parent personalities are classified as "psychoneurotic," "somatic," "pseudodelinquent," and "overly psychotic." The first two types of person-alities were found more frequently in an out-patient setting, while the last two were found more frequently in a state hospital setting. Treatment for these parents is dis-cussed.

LEIK, R. K., "Instrumentality and Emotionality in Family Interaction," Sociometry, 26,
     131-145, 1963.
A comparison of discussion groups where nine families composed of father, mother, and daughter participated in triadic sessions. One third of the discussion groups were made up of all fathers, all mothers, or all daughters. Another third were composed of a father, a mother, and a daughter not of the same family. The final third was of natu-ral families. The three groups were exposed to standard questions and observed. Cate-gories of acts were derived from the Bales system with an emphasis upon instrumentality versus emotionality. It was found that sex role differentiation tends to disappear in family groups and the relevance of instrumentality and emotionality is quite different for family interaction than for interaction among strangers.

LENNARD, H. L., BEAULIEU, M. R., and EMBREY, N. G., "Interaction in Families with a
     Schizophrenic Child," Arch. Gen. Psychiat., 12, 166-183, 1965.
A study contrasting ten families with a schizophrenic child and seven normal families. The families have a 15-minute discussion of three topics related to a child's life. The conversations are recorded, transcribed, and coded along 12 dimensions. Differ-ences are found between the two groups, and there is a discussion of the theoretical background and methodological problems.

LERNER, P., "Resolution of Intrafamilial Role Conflict in Families of Schizophrenic
     Patients. I. Thought Disturbance," J. Nerv. Ment. Dis., 141, 342-351, 1966.
Hypothesis was that there would be differences in the processes used to solve intra-familial role conflict in parents with schizophrenic sons with marked thought disorder (12 families), less severe thought disorder (12 families), and control families (12 families). Thought disorder was measured by Rorschach protocol using the genetic level score of Becker. Intrafamilial role conflict solving was measured using a situational test with Strodtbeck's "revealed differences" technique. Results supported the hypo-thesis. Methodology of such research is discussed.

LERNER, P., "Resolution of Intrafamilial Role Conflict in Families of Schizophrenic
     Patients. II. Social Maturity," J. Nerv. Ment. Dis., 4, 336-341, 1967.
A study attempting to evaluate the relationship between resolution of intrafamilial role conflict and premorbid level of social competence in schizophrenics. Sample and methods were the same as in a previous study except that here social competence was

measured by a scale developed by Zigler and Phillips. Findings were that control families compromised and acknowledged disagreement, while schizophrenic families did not
but let the mother or father decide.

LEVIN, G., "Communicator-Communicant Approach to Family Interaction Research," Fam.
    Proc., 5, 105-116, 1966.
A family experiment in which the experimenter asks the subject to make a tape recording
which might be played subsequently to some specific other person in his family. The
recording includes specific instructions about a simple task. Individuals from families
containing a schizophrenic (a sample of 33) were contrasted with normal individuals.
The recordings were not actually played to family members, but the instructions were
analyzed and classified with differences found between the two groups.

LEVINE, R., "Treatment in the Home," Soc. Work, 9, 19-28, 1964.
A clinical report of treatment of seven low-income, multiproblem families who came to a
mental hygiene clinic for help with the identified patient, usually a child. Treatment
of the family rather than the individual was begun because it seemed more economical,
more family members could be helped, and the therapist could be more accurate in understanding problems. Treatment was done in the home. Techniques included "talking,"
"demonstration," and family activity. The seven families were rated in terms of improvement.

LEVINGER, G., "Supplementary Methods in Family Research," Fam. Proc., 2, 357-366, 1963.
A review of methods in family research with a comparison of subjective report and objective observation with a discussion of their strengths and weaknesses. A study is reported of 31 families who were studied with both observation and self report. The results showed gross correspondence between the two methods and it is suggested that both
procedures should be used since they supplement each other.

LEVINGER, G., "Task and Social Behavior in Marriage," Sociometry, 27, 433-448, 1964.
This study hypothesized that in a family, task-behavior (designated as subject-object
activity) is specialized while social behavior (designated as subject-subject activity)
is mutual. Sample is 60 middle-class couples with children interviewed clinically
(separately and together) and performing together on several tasks: a vocabulary test,
a color symbol test, and an adaptation of the Wechsler-Bellevue digit-symbol test. Social-behavior performance is the essence of marital relations as seen by both spouses
and it is mutual, rather than specialized.

LEVY, J., and EPSTEIN, N., "An Application of the Rorschach in Family Investigation,"
    Fam. Proc., 3, 344-376, 1964.
A description of family testing using the Rorschach as a stimulus for conversation.
Includes a detailed presentation of the individual and family responses to a set of
cards by one family.

LIDZ, T., CORNELISON, A., FLECK, S., and TERRY, D., "The Intrafamilial Environment of
    a Schizophrenic Patient. I. The Father," Psychiatry, 20, 329-342, 1957.
To understand the role of the family in the etiology and pathogenesis of schizophrenia,
14 families with a hospitalized schizophrenic were studied for periods varying from six
months to over two years. Data collection included interviewing all members of the
family (individually), observations and records of interactions of family members with
each other and with the hospital personnel, home visits, and projective testing of all
family members. Focus was on the fathers, in view of the fact that so much previous
work had focussed on mothers alone. Fathers were found to be "very important, albeit
often extremely disturbing, members of the families whose presence and influence cannot
be neglected."

LIDZ, T., CORNELISON, A., FLECK, S., and TERRY, D., "Intrafamilial Environment of Schizo-
    phrenic Patients. II. Marital Schism and Marital Skew," Amer. J. Psychiat., 114,
    241-248, 1957.
A study of the intrafamilial environment of the schizophrenic patient. In this study of

14 families, eight were split in two factions by "overt schism between the parents."
Thus the identified patient cannot use one parent as a model for identification or as
a love object without losing the support of the other parent. The other six families
were "skewed" (defined as psychopathology in the dominant parent) which was accepted
or shared by the other without trying to change it. Case examples are given.

LIDZ, T., FLECK, S., ALANEN, Y. O., and CORNELISON, A., "Schizophrenic Patients and
     Their Siblings," Psychiatry, 26, 1-18, 1963.
A study of the siblings of schizophrenics based upon individual interviews of family
members, observation of family members with each other and hospital staff, and projective tests. Sixteen families were studied for periods ranging from six months to
six years. As many siblings were psychotic as were reasonably well adjusted, and all
except five or six of the 24 siblings suffered from severe personality disorders. Siblings of the same sex as the patient were more disturbed than those of the opposite sex.

LIDZ, T., PARKER, B., and CORNELISON, A., "The Role of the Father in the Family Environ-
     ment of the Schizophrenic Patient," Amer. J. Psychiat., 113, 126-132, 1956.
One of a series of papers on a study of the families of schizophrenic patients. Families in which there was both a mother and father present were interviewed separately,
in pairs, and in groups. The identified patient was an in-patient and came from upper-
class or upper middle-class families. Sixteen families (of which five identified patients were female and 11 were male) were studied. The fathers are seen as "noxious"
in the development of schizophrenia. Three types are described: (1) fathers of schizophrenic daughters who are constantly battling their wives and seeking to enlist the
support of their daughters, (2) fathers who feel their sons are rivals for their wives,
and (3) passive, withdrawn, and absent fathers.

LOVELAND, N. T., "The Family Rorschach: A New Method for Studying Family Interaction,"
     Fam. Proc., 2, 187-215, 1963.
A report of a study in which the Rorschach was used as a standardized stimulus for family
conversations. The procedure is described, the advantages and disadvantages are discussed, and excerpts from a family Rorschach are presented.

MANNING, J., and GLASSER, B., "The Home Visit in the Treatment of Psychiatric Patients
     Awaiting Hospitalization," J. Health Hum. Behav., 3, 97-104, 1962.
As an experimental project, 16 patients on a waiting list for hospitalization were visited in their homes by a social worker and/or a nurse, psychologist, or psychiatrist.
Case materials are presented to demonstrate the reasons for home visiting, and the benefits that were seen. It is felt that home visits are helpful both diagnostically and
in terms of treatment.

MARTIN, B., "Family Interaction Associated with Child Disturbances Assessment and Modi-
     fication," Psychotherapy, 4, 30-35, 1967.
A report testing the author's notion that disturbances in the interaction between
parents and child can lead to disturbed behavior in the child. An experimental procedure was developed in order to limit communication to just one member of the family at
a time. Sessions were recorded on audiotape and rated according to degree of blaming.
In a pilot study of four families, two received modification procedures designed to
decondition blaming, and two did not. The experimental families showed a greater proportion of decrease in blaming scores.

MEYERS, D., and GOLDFARB, W., "Studies of Perplexity in Mothers of Schizophrenic Child-
     ren," Amer. J. Orthopsychiat., 31, 551-564, 1961.
In order to document the association of parental complexity (defined as passivity, un-
certainty, lack of spontaneity, absence of empathy, with diminished awareness of the
child's needs, bewilderment, blandness in the face of unacceptable behavior in the
child, and an absence of parental control), 23 mothers of schizophrenic children and
23 mothers of normal public school children were studied. Techniques included a participant-observation technique, in which the observer spent three hours with the family
at home, and a semistructured open-ended interview of the mothers. Results indicated
that the mothers of the schizophrenic children without organic involvement have a

greater difficulty in appropriately structuring their child's environment, while the
mothers of the organic group cannot be differentiated from mothers of the normals.

MINUCHIN, S., and MONTALVO, B., "An Approach for Diagnosis of the Low Socioeconomic
     Family," in I. M. Cohen (Ed.), Psychiatric Research Report No. 20, Washington,
     D. C., American Psychiatric Association, 1966.
A report on the diagnostic techniques used in appraising the individual and the family
at the Wiltwyck School for Boys. The emphasis is upon communication style and affect.
Clinical illustrations are provided.

MINUCHIN, S., MONTALVO, B., GUERNEY, B. G., ROSMAN, B. L., and SHUMER, F., Families of
     the Slums: An Exploration of Their Structure and Treatment, New York, Basic Books,
     1967.
A book on a research project dealing with family treatment of low socioeconomic class
families where the identified patient was delinquent. Research strategy, rationale,
dynamics, techniques, and assessment of results are presented. 460 pp.

MISHLER, E., "Families and Schizophrenia: An Experimental Study," Ment. Hyg., 50, 552-
     556, 1966.
A discussion of a way of testing families with a schizophrenic member and contrasting
them with normal families. Findings are not given, but illustrations are offered of
ways the families respond in the test situation.

MISHLER, E., and WAXLER, N., "Family Interaction in Schizophrenia," Arch. Gen. Psychiat.,
     15, 64-75, 1966.
A study which describes only methodology used in an experimental study of family interactions in schizophrenia. Subjects were 30 schizophrenic families (in which a schizophrenic child was hospitalized) and 16 normal families recruited from the community.
Schizophrenic patients were newly admitted to the hospital, unmarried, white, living in
the Boston area, living at home with both parents (who had to be alive and living together), and had one unmarried sibling of the same sex. Experimental procedure was Strodtbeck's revealed differences test. Coding and data analysis procedures are described.

MORGAN, R. W., "The Extended Home Visit in Psychiatric Research and Treatment," Psychia-
     try, 26, 168-175, 1963.
A report of some data on 14 cases and techniques involved in the extended home visit by
the social worker. The material presented is said to give support to the idea that
highly relevant data pertinent to psychiatric research and treatment is obtained and
is worth the time, cost, and emotional expense involved.

MORRIS, G., and WYNNE, L., "Schizophrenic Offspring and Parental Styles of Communica-
     tion," Psychiatry, 28, 19-44, 1965.
One of a series of papers reporting a study of parental styles of communication and
schizophrenic children. Data were selected from excerpts of transcripts of conjoint
family sessions with 12 families. Predictions about the most disturbed offspring were
made by a judge blind to the clinical aspects of the case. Predictive criteria were
then reformulated using the data from a parallel study utilizing psychological test
material as predictors. These reformulated criteria were then utilized for blind predictions on eight new families. Results indicated that the style of the family communication can be related to the thought and affect disorder in schizophrenics.

MURRELL, S., and STACHOWIAK, J., "Consistency, Rigidity, and Power in the Interaction
     Patterns of Clinic and Non-Clinic Families," J. Abnorm. Psychol., 72, 265-272,
     1967.
To study interaction patterns in families, 11 families, each having at least two children who were attending a child guidance clinic were matched with 11 control families,
whose names were obtained from school, who were thought to be normal. Families were
observed by two raters through a one-way mirror and were asked to (1) plan something
together as a family, (2) answer a list of 11 questions about the families and agree
on the answers, (3) list adjectives regarding their family, and (4) make up stories

to seven TAT pictures. Results indicated that in all 22 families, the pattern of who talks to whom was consistent. Secondly, the control patients had more rigidity in speaking than the "sick" families. Thirdly, in the sick families the older child had more power within the family than in the controls, and fourthly, the sick families were not as productive as the well families.

NIELSON, J., "Home Visits by Psychiatrists," Compr. Psychiat., 4, 442-461, 1963.
The author reports on another aspect of the Samsø Project (Samsø is an island off the Danish mainland), that is the home visits of psychiatrists for diagnostic and thera-peutic purposes. It is felt that one home visit is of diagnostic importance in nearly all types of mental illness, and of therapeutic importance in all elderly and all psy-chotic, except paranoid patients. A home visit is advised for neurotic patients when supportive and dynamic family therapy is used.

OLSON, D. H., "The Measurement of Family Power by Self-Report and Behavioral Methods,"
      J. Marriage Fam., 31, 545-550, 1969.
A study comparing self report and observed behavior on the question of power in mar-riage. Thirty-five couples were given questionnaires and their responses compared with their behavior in the laboratory dealing with real problems. No relationship was found between what the couples said about the distribution of power in the marriage and what was observed when they dealt with one another. Explanatory factors are of-fered, and the conclusion is reached that this research reinforces "the idea that methodological research of this type should precede, rather than follow, substantive research in the field."

PARAD, H. J., and CAPLAN, G., "A Framework for Studying Families in Crises," Soc. Work,
      5, 3-15, 1960.
An approach to the observation and study of the family in crisis. Family members are seen individually and as a group in the home while engaged in household activities. The concepts of family life-style, problem-solving mechanisms, and need-response pat-terns are illustrated with a case history. It is suggested that intervention is most effective at the moment the family is in crisis.

RAVICH, R., "Game-Testing in Conjoint Marital Psychotherapy," Amer. J. Psychother., 23,
      217-229, 1969.
A report on the "game-test" for both family diagnosis and family therapy. Methodology is described and four typical patterns of interaction are identified: (1) competitive, (2) alternating, (3) dominant-submissive, and (4) mixed. Based on these patterns tech-niques for therapy are described.

REISS, D., "Individual Thinking and Family Interaction. III. An Experimental Study of
      Categorization Performance in Families of Normals, Those with Character Disorders,
      and Schizophrenics," J. Nerv. Ment. Dis., 146, 384-404, 1968.
The second of a series of studies to measure the relationship between individual family interaction and individual thinking, and to determine what differences in this relation-ship exist among families of normals, personality disorders, and schizophrenics. Method was to give the families a puzzle, tape their discussion, and to code verbal responses. Sample has been previously described; there were five families in each group. Results indicated that normals could solve the puzzle, while the others could not. The data on why they could not was felt to be consistent with the hypothesis that interpersonal problems in families significantly interfere with their collaborative problem-solving efforts.

REISS, D., "Individual Thinking and Family Interaction. IV. A Study of Information
      Exchange in Families of Normals, Those with Character Disorders, and Schizophren-
      ics," J. Nerv. Ment. Dis., 149, 473-490, 1969.
The third in a series of papers on interrelationships of family interaction and thinking and perception of family members. This experiment was developed to test the family's efficiency in exchanging information within itself. Families of normals and schizo-phrenics were more sensitive than those with character disorders to cues from within the family. Families of schizophrenics appeared to represent a group of families who utilize cues from within but not from without the family.

RISKIN, J., "Family Interaction Scales: A Preliminary Report," Arch. Gen. Psychiat.,
    11, 484-494, 1964.
A report on a research project where nine families were given a structured interview
and the conversation categorized. Two minute segments of the conversation are categorized by the coder as clear, change of topic, commitment, and so on. At attempt is
then made to describe the family from the coding sheets blindly. "Results suggest that
it is possible to make clinically meaningful and accurate descriptions of the whole
family and of its various members, based on the coded speeches and without focussing
on the content."

RISKIN, J., "Methodology for Studying Family Interaction," Arch. Gen. Psychiat., 8, 343-
    348, 1963.
A report of a pilot study with five families designed to develop a conceptual framework
and methods for investigating the relationship between family interaction and personality
formation. Family members are brought together in standardized structured interviews
with the tape recorded conversations analyzed by a set of categories which include
clarity, content, agreement, commitment, congruency, intensity, and attack or acceptance
of the other person.

ROSENTHAL, A. J., BEHRENS, M. I., and CHODOFF, P., "Communication in Lower Class Fa-
    milies of Schizophrenics," Arch. Gen. Psychiat., 18, 464-470, 1968.
This is the first part, methodological problems, of a two-part report on low socioeconomic families of schizophrenics. Groups compared were 17 black schizophrenics and
their families, 11 black families in a control group, and 11 white schizophrenics and
their families. The procedure included observation in the home with tasks requiring
the family to maintain a focus of attention on a specific topic. (For Part II of this
study see Behrens, M. I., "Communication in Lower Class Families of Schizophrenics,"
Arch. Gen. Psychiat., 18, 689-696, 1968.)

RYDER, R. G., "Husband-Wife Dyads vs. Married Strangers," Fam. Proc., 7, 233-238, 1968.
A comparison of the behavior of spouses with each other and with strangers by use of
the color matching test which induces a conflict situation. Sixty-four married dyads
and 56 unmarried dyads were contrasted. Few differences were found, but persons
"treat strangers more gently, and generally more nicely than they do their spouses."

RYDER, R. G., "Two Replications of Color Matching Factors," Fam. Proc., 5, 43-48, 1966.
A replication of the color matching test of Goodrich and Boomer. The test was applied
to 64 married couples and 56 split couples defined as a male and female pair not married. Comparisons with the original sample, and between the married and unmarried
groups are made.

RYDER, R. G., and GOODRICH, D. W., "Married Couples Responses to Disagreement," Fam.
    Proc., 5, 30-42, 1966.
A report on the color matching test administered to 49 recently married couples. Husband and wife are exposed to colors and asked to match them when some of them do not
match. Ways of handling the conflict are categorized and described.

SCHEFLEN, A. E., Stream and Structure of Communicational Behavior, Behavioral Series
    Monograph No. 1, Philadelphia, Eastern Pennsylvania Psychiatric Institute, 1965.
A context analysis of a family therapy session by Whitaker and Malone. The examination of the interview is in detail and includes kinesic, linguistic and contextual
description.

SCHULMAN, R. E., SHOEMAKER, D. J., and MOELIS, I., "Laboratory Measurement of Parental
    Behavior," J. Consult. Psychol., 26, 109-114, 1962.
Families were told to make up stories about a scene which included a variety of buildings and people with the hypothesis that in families with a conduct problem child,
parents would exhibit more control over behavior of the child, and that in these families there would be significantly more aggression between parents. Parents and one
son, age eight to 12, of 41 families were tested. In 20 families the child was con-

sidered a conduct problem while the other 21 had no reported conduct problems. Parents'
behavior was rated by observers who found that parents of conduct problem children were
more rejecting and hostile than parents of children without problems. It was concluded
that there is a cause-effect relation between parental hostility and rejection and aggressive behavior in children.

SHARAN, SHLOMO, "Family Interaction with Schizophrenics and Their Siblings," J. Abnorm.
    Psychol., 71, 345-353, 1966.
An experimental study contrasting the behavior of parents of schizophrenics with the patient and with a sibling. Twenty-four families were asked to solve collectively the
questions from the comprehension and similarities subtests of the Wechsler-Bellvue intelligence scale. The conversations were compared for problem-solving efficiency, mutual support patterns, and parent-child sex role alignments. Parents and patient worked
as efficiently as parents and siblings, parents supported both children equally and
fathers and mothers were equally dominant. The patients were more supportive of their
parents than were the siblings, and parental discord was more prominent when the patient
was present than when the sibling was present.

SHERMAN, M. H., ACKERMAN, N. W., SHERMAN, S. N., and MITCHELL, C., "Non-Verbal Cues in
    Family Therapy," Fam. Proc., 4, 133-162, 1965.
A discussion of non-verbal cues in family therapy with excerpts from an interview. Non-
verbal expressions tend to occur in inverse proportion to verbal expressions which are
ineffective, give clues to attitudes and traits, and act as hidden cues to shared emotional conflicts.

SIGAL, J. J., RAKOFF, V., and EPSTEIN, N. B., "Indications of Therapeutic Outcome in
    Conjoint Family Therapy," Fam. Proc., 6, 215-226, 1967.
A report on a study which attempted to predict the eventual success of family therapy
by examining the degree of family interaction and emotional involvement as described
by therapists in the initial stages of treatment. "The clinical observations in this
study raise some doubts about the value of the interactional frame of reference in
conjoint family therapy."

SNELL, J., ROSENWALD, R., and ROBEY, A., "The Wifebeater's Wife, A Study of Family In-
    teraction," Arch. Gen. Psychiat., 11, 107-113, 1964.
A study of 37 families in which men were charged by their wives with assault and battery and who were referred to one of the psychiatric clinics which serve the courts of
Massachusetts. Twelve of the families were studied in detail (both husband and wife
were seen for three or more interviews). Four wives were in individual psychotherapy
for more than 18 months. In addition some group therapy and couple therapy were attempted. A typical family structure is described: husband is passive, indecisive, and
sexually inadequate; wife aggressive, masculine, frigid, and masochistic; relationship
between the two characterized by alternation of passive and aggressive roles. An adolescent son may upset the equilibrium.

SOJIT, C. M., "Dyadic Interaction in a Double Bind Situation," Fam. Proc., 8, 235-260,
    1969.
Marital couples were exposed to a "double bind situation" to contrast parents of delinquents, ulcerative colitis patients, and normal controls. The couples were exposed
to the proverb "a rolling stone gathers no moss" and were asked to reach agreement
about its meaning. The responses were categorized and differences found.

SPECK, R., "Family Therapy in the Home," J. Marriage Fam., 26, 72-76, 1964.
An essay based on the author's clinical experience in doing family therapy in the home.
Advantages of this technique are discussed and several new phenomena are described:
the absent member, the most disturbed family member, the youngest member, the role of
pets, the extended family, and family secrets.

SPECK, R., "Family Therapy in the Home," in N. W. Ackerman (Ed.), Expanding Theory and
     Practice in Family Therapy, New York, Family Service Association of America, 1967.
A clinical paper from a research project in which family therapy was conducted at home.
Advantages and disadvantages in techniques are discussed. It is thought to be advanta-
geous over doing therapy in the office, but no definitive experiment "has yet been done".
At least one home visit should be made to every family.

STABENAU, J. R., TUPIN, J., WERNER, M., and POLLIN, W., "A Comparative Study of Families
     of Schizophrenics, Delinquents, and Normals," Psychiatry, 28, 45-59, 1965.
A report of a comparison of five families with a schizophrenic, five families with a
delinquent, and five normal families tested with the revealed differences test, the
object sorting test, and the thematic apperception test. "Data from the three different tests suggest that in the schizophrenic and delinquent families there were both
individual disturbances in thought process and impaired communication at the family
level....There was relatively little evidence of communication impairment at the individual or family level in the normal families."

STACHOWIAK, J., "Decision-Making and Conflict Resolution in the Family Group," in C. Lar-
     son and F. Dance (Eds.), Perspectives on Communication, Milwaukee, University of
     Wisconsin Press, 1968.
The author discusses his previous research summarizing major findings on (1) family
productivity ——which is decreased in "sick families," (2) influence of individual
members ——maladaptive families showed distinct hierarchal ordering of members, (3)
conflict in which maladaptive families showed more aggression and hostility than adaptive, and (4) communication, which was disturbed in maladaptive families. Implications
for future research are discussed.

STRODTBECK, F., "The Family as a Three-Person Group," Amer. Sociol. Rev., 23-29, 1954.
     A research study attempting to replicate the findings of Mills in relation to
three-person groups. The sample was 48 cases including father, mother, and adolescent
son. They were asked to fill out alternatives to 47 items. The study was done in the
family homes and tape recorded. Decision-making power was associated with high participation and when the two most active members show "solidarity" in their relation to
one another, the stability of their rank participation is high. When the two most active members were in conflict, stability was as low for these families as for the other
families.

STRODTBECK, F., "Husband-Wife Interaction Over Revealed Differences," Amer. Sociol.
     Rev., 23, 468-473, 1951.
A field study of ten Navajo, ten Texan, and ten Mormon couples. Balance of power can
be shown using the revealed differences. The technique depends both on power elements
in a larger cultural organization and amount of participation in the small group situation.

STRODTBECK, F., "The Interaction of a Henpecked Husband with His Wife," Marriage Fam.
     Liv., 14, 305-308, 1952.
A clinical case report on the psychodynamics of being "henpecked." Method was the revealed differences test. Compared to other couples, although the wife was more dominant, it was "not so painful in practice as the community gossip would lead one to believe." Interaction sequence is a more accurate way of assessing family dynamics than
community observation.

TAYLOR, W. R., "Research on Family Interaction. I: Static and Dynamic Models," Fam.
     Proc., 9, 221-232, 1970.
A comparison of static and dynamic models of family structure illustrated with a clinical
example. The emphasis is upon the Markov process where a state is succeeded by other
possible states.

TERRILL, J. M., and TERRILL, R. E., "A Method for Studying Family Communication," Fam.
    Proc., 4, 259-290, 1965.
A description of the application of the Leary interpersonal system to family interaction.
Rather than use a check list, the system is applied to the actual interchange between
family members in a standard interview.

TITCHENER, J. L., D'ZMURA, T., GOLDEN, M., and EMERSON, R., "Family Transaction and
    Derivation of Individuality," Fam. Proc., 2, 95-120, 1963.
A report of an experimental method in research on family interaction. Subjects were
families of patients who applied because of neurotic symptoms. Task was for the family
to "reconcile their differences in opinion previously revealed in a questionnaire administered to each family member." The observers used tapes, films and notes of direct
observation to record the family transactions. The authors believe that "a young person elaborates an identity and develops his sense of it from the communicative interplay of the family." A case is presented in detail to illustrate.

TITCHENER, L., and GOLDEN, M., "Predictions of Therapeutic Themes from Observation of
    Family Interaction Evoked by the Revealed Differences Technique," J. Nerv. Ment.
    Dis., 136, 464-474, 1963.
A standard interview procedure with the family discussion observed and classification of
formal content variables attempted. The results are said to be informative for prediction of the course of therapy.

TITCHENER, J., VANDER HEIDE, C., and WOODS, E., "Profiles in Family Interaction Sys-
    tems," J. Nerv. Ment. Dis., 143, 473-483, 1966.
A report of a study designed to measure family interaction systems. Data were collected using Riskin's interaction scales which were then modified. Advantages of this
technique are discussed. Methods of sampling and data analysis are described and several profiles of family interaction are exemplified with discussion of variables in
family interaction systems. Flow of information and quality of the flow are key variables to measure how families function.

WATZLAWICK, P., "A Structured Family Interview," Fam. Proc., 5, 256-271, 1966.
A report on the use of a standard interview developed in the Bateson project and applied
at the mental research institute on samples of families. The family is placed in a room
and asked a series of standard questions, or given tasks to do together. It is said
to be a simple and effective teaching and training aid and helpful to the therapist
who is going to deal with the family. The procedure is given with examples.

WAXLER, N. E., and MISHLER, E. G., "Scoring and Reliability Problems in Interaction
    Process Analysis: A Methodological Note," Sociometry, 29, 28-40, 1966.
A discussion of rater reliability when using Bales' interaction process analysis. Comparisons of tape recordings, typescripts, and combinations of both are given and comparisons are made of different ways of summarizing agreements between coders.

WESTLEY, W., and EPSTEIN, N., "Patterns of Intra-Familial Communication," Psychiatric
    Research Report No. 11, American Psychiatric Association, 1959.
A research report attempting to describe intrafamily communication patterns. Nine healthy families with an adolescent were studied using clinical interview, the Rorschach,
and the TAT. Nine categories of family function are described and patterns of overt
communication versus other types of communication are described.

WILD, C., "Disturbed Styles of Thinking," Arch. Gen. Psychiat., 13, 464-470, 1966.
Examiner's reactions to giving the object sorting test to parents of schizophrenics
are described. Findings here are taken from the Wynne and Singer papers on "Thought
Disorder and Family Relations of Schizophrenics." Examiners felt "frustrated and
hopeless" in dealing with schizophrenic parents' inability to maintain a consistent
task, inability to maintain role of subject being tested, and general negativism.
Theoretical, tentative implications of the findings are discussed.

WILD, C., SINGER, M., ROSMAN, G., RICCI, J., and LIDZ, T., "Measuring Disordered Styles
    of Thinking," Arch. Gen. Psychiat., 13, 471-476, 1966.
Forty-four parents whose child was a schizophrenic in-patient were matched for age and
education with 46 control parents (community volunteers) on the object sorting test.
A scoring manual is described. Patient-parents scores differed significantly from
controls. The object scoring test seems to discriminate between parents of schizophrenic patients and controls who do not have children with psychiatric pathology.

WILLI, J., "Joint Rorschach Testing of Partner Relationship," Fam. Proc., 8, 64-78, 1969.
A test of marital partners by the conjoint Rorschach procedure. A sample of 80 pairs
was examined with each person administered the Rorschach individually and then again
administered it conjointly with the partner. The goal was to measure the relative
strength of the partners and how the personality of the subject changes in the discussion with the other.

WING, J., "Ratings of Behavior of Patient and Relative," J. Psychosom. Res., 8, 223-228,
    1964.
A report of a test of the hypothesis that (1) high emotional involvement of patient and
relative should lead to deterioration of the patient, and (2) that the amount of face-
to-face contact between patient and relative would be related to outcome. Patients
were evaluated by means of two raters' description and a checklist. Relatives were
evaluated by means of scheduled ratings. Patients were hospitalized schizophrenics.
Results indicated that if there was a high index of emotional involvement of relative
with patient there was a high percentage of deterioration. In the case of patients
who were moderately or severely ill at time of discharge, and who were living with
relatives rated as showing a high degree of emotional involvement, relatively few hours
of contact were associated with relatively better outcome.

WINTER, W. D., and FERREIRA, A. J., "Interaction Process Analysis of Family Decision-
    Making," Fam. Proc., 6, 155-172, 1967.
A sample of 90 triads of father, mother, and child were tested to contrast normals with
abnormals. The families were exposed to a set of three TAT cards and asked to make up
a story they all agreed upon which linked the three cards together. The protocols
were scored with the Bales IPA system. It is concluded that "the Bales IPA system, in
its present form, is not suited for work with families."

WINTER, W. D., and FERREIRA, A. J., "Talking Time as an Index of Intrafamilial Simi-
    larity in Normal and Abnormal Families," J. Abnorm. Psychol., 74, 574-575, 1969.
A study testing the hypothesis that normal families correlate more highly with each
other than do abnormal families in terms of talking at length in extemporaneous speech.
127 family triads were tested. Of these, 77 were abnormals with identified patients
being "emotionally disturbed maladjusted," and 50 were normals. The families took the
group thematic apperception test. Results are given.

WINTER, W. D., FERREIRA, A. J., and OLSON, J., "Hostility Themes in the Family TAT,"
    J. Project. Tech., 30, 270-275, 1966.
The second of a series describing a diagnostic test adapted for use with families. Results were obtained from use of three TAT stories based on three cards each produced
conjointly by 126 three-member families. Stories were scored for hostility in the story
themes. Fifty families had normal children, 44 had neurotic children, 16 had schizophrenic children, and 16 had delinquent children. Normal and schizophrenic groups produced stories low in hostility, neurotics produced stories high in hostility, and delinquents scored high on one hostility variable and low on another.

WINTER, W. D., FERREIRA, A. J., and OLSON, J. L., "Story Sequence Analysis of Family
    TATS," J. Project. Techn., 29, 392-397, 1965.
A group of 126 families, composed of parents and one child, were asked to produce TAT
stories conjointly. The families were to make up a story based upon three TAT cards
presented simultaneously to them. Three stories based on nine cards were composed by
each family and scored by the Arnold system of story sequence analysis. In the sample there were 50 families with normal children. The abnormal group consisted of 44

emotionally maladjusted, 16 delinquent, and 16 schizophrenic children. The procedure
successfully differentiated normal from abnormal families but the three abnormal group=
did not differ from each other. The stories of abnormal families are said to be characterized by negative attitudes toward achievement, morality, responsibility, human relationships, and reaction to adversity.

WYNNE, L. C., "The Study of Intrafamilial Alignments and Splits in Exploratory Family
    Therapy," in N. W. Ackerman, F. L. Beatman, and S. Sherman (Eds.), Exploring the
    Base for Family Therapy, New York, Family Service Association of America, 1961.
A discussion of families studied during family therapy with the emphasis upon alignments and splits as structural points of reference. Includes experiences with the family
therapy of 30 families at NIMH with case examples and verbatim transcripts.

ZIERER, E., STERNBERG, D., FINN, R., and FARMER, M., "Family Creative Analysis. I. Its
    Role in Treatment," Bull. Art Ther., 5, 47-65, 1966.
A report on the use of creative analysis (which is a technique by which paintings are
used to understand the functioning of the ego) and its application to family treatment.
The family agrees on a project to be done and then the sketch is made by one or many
members of the family. It is then divided into as many sections as there are participants. From an understanding of the painting, the therapist then interprets the
family and their conflicts. Observations are shared with the treatment team of the
in-patient unit in which the identified patients are staying, and also with the members of the family. Short and long range goals of family treatment are formulated
and worked out in at least 15 projects.

ZUK, G. H., "A Further Study of Laughter in Family Therapy," Fam. Proc., 3, 77-89, 1964.
A discussion of the function of laughter in the family illustrated with excerpts from
family therapy sessions. It is proposed that laughter is an important means of quali-
fying meaning for the purpose of disguise.

ZUK, G., "On the Pathology of Silencing Strategies," Fam. Proc., 4, 32-49, 1965.
A description and categorization of the ways people impose or enforce silence on one
another. "There is a causal relation between silencing strategies and pathological
silence and babbling which may themselves be used as powerful silencing strategies."

ZUK, G., "On Silence and Babbling in Family Psychotherapy with Schizophrenics," Con-
    fin. Psychiat., 8, 49-56, 1965.
From the author's clinical work, two cases are presented in support of the idea that
both silence and babbling can be understood as attempts to interrupt communication and
silence others' interactions. They are often seen in schizophrenia, but patients learn
these strategies from their parents. Techniques for dealing with this in treatment are
discussed.

ZUK, G., "On the Theory and Pathology of Laughter in Psychotherapy," Psychotherapy, 3,
    97-101, 1966.
An essay based on the author's previous research, some clinical work, and other notions
on the meaning of laughter. Bizarre laughter in schizophrenics, which often seems unexplainable, became clear when it was systematically studied in the family setting. It
was found to be due to a "wish to communicate information differentially to members of
the family group." Clinical uses of laughter in therapy are discussed.

ZUK, G. H., BOSZORMENYI-NAGY, I., and HEIMAN, E., "Some Dynamics of Laughter During
    Family Therapy," Fam. Proc., 2, 302-314, 1963.
An examination of the frequency of laughter in family therapy sessions with parents and
a schizophrenic girl. Frequency of laughter was totalled for different intervals during
the sessions. A correlation is suggested between tension or anxiety and laughter and it
was found that the parents laughed most in the first interval of a session. Significantly more laughter of the daughter occurred in the third of four intervals, thus
showing a reversal of patterns of laughter between parents and daughter over thirteen
sessions.

2.4 FAMILY DATA — EXPERIMENTATION

BAUMANN, G., and ROMAN, M., "Interaction Testing in the Study of Marital Dominance,"
    Fam. Proc., 5, 230-242, 1966.
A sample of 50 couples was exposed individually and conjointly to the Wechsler Bellevue.
In the conjoint testing, the couple was asked to reach agreement on the response. Comparisons of the individual test and the conjoint test were made, as well as measures of
dominance in the couple when tested together.

FERREIRA, A. M., "Decision-Making in Normal and Pathologic Families," Arch. Gen. Psy-
    chiat., 8, 68-73, 1963.
An experiment to find differences between 25 normal and 25 abnormal families using a
decision making test. The family members first make a choice of items on a questionnaire when alone and then are brought together and asked to reach agreement on the same
items. Their choices separately and together are compared and the agreements are categorized as unanimous, majority, dictatorial, and chaotic. The two types of families
are found to differ.

FERREIRA, A. J., "Interpersonal Perceptivity Among Family Members," Amer. J. Orthopsy-
    chiat., 34, 64-71, 1964.
A report of a study investigating interpersonal perceptivity among members of families
in terms of the individual's ability to guess the rejecting behavior of the other two
family members. The sample consisted of "25 normal and 30 pathologic families." The
families were asked to color a number of flags on pieces of cardboard and asked to
"throw away, i.e., to reject, the productions of the other family members: which they
didn't like for any reason. They were also asked to guess how many of their own flags
would be thrown away by other family members. Interpersonal perceptivity is greater
in children than in adults.

FERREIRA, A. J., "Rejection and Expectancy of Rejection in Families," Fam. Proc., 2,
    235-244, 1963.
A report of a study to investigate overt rejection and expectancy of rejection in normal and abnormal families. The sample was "25 normal and 30 pathologic families."
The families were asked to color a number of flags on pieces of cardboard and asked to
"throw away, i.e., to reject the productions of the other family members" which they
didn't like for any reason. They were also asked to guess how many of their own flags
would be thrown away by other family members. Differences were found between the two
groups and there was a marked discrepancy between rejecting and expecting to be rejected in pathological families.

FERREIRA, A. J., and WINTER, W. D., "Decision-Making in Normal and Abnormal Two-Child
    Families," Fam. Proc., 7, 17-36, 1968.
A report of a study of 85 families, 36 normal and 49 abnormal (composed of parents and
two children), were tested in a procedure similar to that previously used in a test of
family triads. Differences were found between the two groups on measures of "spontaneous agreement," "decision time," and "choice fulfillment."

FERREIRA, A. J., and WINTER, W. D., "Family Interaction and Decision-Making," Arch. Gen.
    Psychiat., 13, 214-223, 1965.
A report of a study contrasting 50 normal families and 75 families with an abnormal child.
The abnormal group included 15 schizophrenics, 16 delinquents, and 44 maladjusted children. The family members were asked to fill out a neutral questionnaire separately, and
then they were brought together and asked to fill out the same questionnaire while reaching agreement on the items as a group. Generally this report is concerned with the extent of agreement when family members make their choices separately, how much time is
necessary to reach group decisions, and the appropriateness of the family decisions in
fulfilling the wishes of the individual family members. Eighteen hypotheses are described
and the results reported in terms of the differences found between the groups.

FERREIRA, A., WINTER, W. D., and POINDEXTER, E. J., "Some Interactional Variables in
    Normal and Abnormal Families," Fam. Proc., 5, 60-75, 1966.
A study contrasting normal and abnormal families with the abnormals including schizo-

phrenic, delinquent, and maladjusted children. The families were exposed to three TAT
cards at a time and asked to make up a story tying them together. Differences were
found between the types of families.

GOODRICH, D. W., and BOOMER, D. S., "Experimental Assessment of Modes of Conflict Reso-
    lution," Fam. Proc., 2, 15-24, 1963.
A report of an experimental technique for studying the coping behavior of husband and
wife when they attempt to resolve a marital conflict. Fifty paid volunteer couples
between 18 and 27 years of age were asked to match colors -- some unmatchable -- to see
how the couple coped with puzzling or ambiguous situations. A general discussion of
results is given, with the authors relating the "ability to achieve perspective on the
situation and maintenance of self-esteem" to adequacy of coping.

HALEY, J., "Cross-Cultural Experimentation: An Initial Attempt," Hum. Organ., 3, 110-
    117, 1967.
A comparison of Caucasian middle-class American families and Japanese-born families in
an experimental setting where the measure is speech sequences. Differences are found.

HALEY, J., "Experiment with Abnormal Families," Arch. Gen. Psychiat., 17, 53-63, 1967.
A comparison of abnormal and normal families in an experimental setting where family
members speak to each other from different rooms. Measures are who chooses to speak
with whom and patterns of speech sequence.

HALEY, J., "Family Experiments: A New Type of Experimentation," Fam. Proc., 1, 265-
    293, 1962.
A report on a research project in which parents and schizophrenic children were contrasted with parents and normal children in an experimental game to test hypotheses about
coalition patterns in normal and abnormal families. Differences were found between the
30 families in each group. There is a genreal discussion of the uniqueness of experimenting with families in theoretical, methodological, and sampling problems.

HALEY, J., "Research on Family Patterns: An Instrument Measurement," Fam. Proc., 3,
    41-65, 1964.
A report of an investigation of patterns of interchange in families. The questions are
whether families follow patterns, whether normal and abnormal families differ, and whether patterns change over time. A group of 40 normal and 40 abnormal families were
given a standard stimulus for conversation and a frequency count was made of the order
in which family members speak. Families were found to follow patterns and differences
were found between the normal and abnormal groups.

HALEY, J., "Speech Sequences of Normal and Abnormal Families with Two Children Present,"
    Fam. Proc., 1, 81-97, 1967.
A comparison of families with an abnormal child and families with normal children in an
experimental setting with parents and two children present. The measure is speech sequences.

HALEY, J., "Testing Parental Instructions to Schizophrenic and Normal Children: A Pilot
    Study," J. Abnorm. Psychol., 73, 559-566, 1968.
An experiment to test the hypothesis that parents communicate to their schizophrenic
children in conflicting ways. Parental instructions were given from a separate room
and tape recorded so that they could be played to matched children. On this small sample, the indications were that parents of schizophrenics do not communicate in more conflicting ways than parents of normal children when the measurement is the success of a
child in following their instructions.

LEVIN, G., " Communicator-Communicant Approach to Family Interaction Research," Fam.
    Proc., 5, 105-116, 1966.
A family experiment in which the experimenter asks the subject to make a tape recording
which might be played subsequently to some specific other person in his family. The re-

cording includes specific instructions about a simple task. Individuals from families
containing a schizophrenic (a sample of 33) were contrasted with normal individuals.
The recordings were not actually played to family members, but the instructions were
analyzed and classified with differences found between the two groups.

RAVICH, R., "Game-Testing in Conjoint Marital Psychotherapy," Amer. J. Psychother., 23,
     217-229, 1969.
A report on the "game-test" for both family diagnosis and family therapy. Methodology
is described and four typical patterns of interaction are identified: (1) competitive,
(2) alternating, (3) dominant-submissive, and (4) mixed. Based on these patterns, techniques for therapy are described.

RAVICH, R., DEUTSCH, M., and BROWN, B., "An Experimental Study of Marital Discord and
     Decision Making," in I. M. Cohen (Ed.), Psychiatric Research Report No. 20, Wash.,
     D. C., American Psychiatric Association, 1966.
A report on a study of 38 couples tested with a game in which the partners imagine that
they are operating a truck and can effect each other's truck when they meet a one-lane
road. Behavior is described in terms of sharing, dominating and submitting, being inconsistent, being competitive, and being dysjunctive.

REISS, D., "Individual Thinking and Family Interaction: Introduction to an Experimental
     Study of Problem-Solving in Families of Normals, Character Disorders, and Schizo-
     phrenics," Arch. Gen. Psychiat., 16, 80-93, 1967.
A report of an experimental study of the relationship between individual thinking and
family interaction. Experimental procedures and methods of analysis are discussed.
Subjects were families of five normals, five character disorders, and six schizophrenics.
The test used was a puzzle that required active use of cognitive and conceptual capa-
cities. The method of analysis was derived from the work of Riley which developed a
systematic approach of computing scores from the raw data and rules concerning inferences.

REISS, D., "Individual Thinking and Family Interaction. II. A Study of Pattern Recog-
     nition and Hypothesis Testing in Families of Normals, Character Disorders, and
     Schizophrenics," J. Psychiat. Res., 5, 193-211, 1967.
The second in a series of studies of the relationship of family process and individual
thinking. Results indicate that following a period of family interaction, members of
normal families showed improvement in pattern recognition; members of families of schizophrenics showed deterioration or no change; members of character disorder families showed
results in between the other two.

RYDER, R. G., "Husband-Wife Dyads vs. Married Strangers," Fam. Proc., 7, 233-238, 1968.
A comparison of the behavior of spouses with each other and with strangers by use of
the color matching test which induces a conflict situation. Sixty-four married dyads
and 56 unmarried dyads were contrasted. Few differences were found, but persons "treat
strangers more gently, and generally more nicely than they do their spouses."

RYDER, R. G., "Two Replications of Color Matching Factors," Fam. Proc., 5, 43-48, 1966.
A replication of the color matching test of Goodrich and Boomer. The test was applied
to 64 married couples and 56 split couples (defined as a male and female pair not married). Comparisons with the original sample, and between the married and unmarried
groups are made.

RYDER, R. G., and GOODRICH, D. W., "Married Couples Responses to Disagreement," Fam.
     Proc., 5, 30-42, 1966.
A report on the color matching test administered to 49 recently married couples. Husband and wife are exposed to colors and asked to match them when some of them do not
match. Ways of handling the conflict are categorized and described.

SHARAN, SHLOMO, "Family Interaction with Schizophrenics and Their Siblings," J. Abnorm.
    Psychol., 71, 345-353, 1966.
An experimental study contrasting the behavior of parents of schizophrenics with the
patient and with a sibling. Twenty-four families were asked to solve collectively the
questions from the comprehension and similarities subtests of the Wechsler-Bellevue intelligence scale. The conversations were compared for problem-solving efficiency, mutual support patterns, and parent-child sex role alignments. Parents and patient worked
as efficiently as parents and siblings, parents supported both children equally, and
fathers and mothers were equally dominant. The patients were more supportive of their
parents than were the siblings, and parental discord was more prominent when the patient
was present than when the sibling was present.

2.5 RESEARCH THEORY AND REVIEW

BEHRENS, M. L., BATESON, G., LEICHTER, H. J., LENNARD, H. L., and COTTRELL, L. S., Jr.,
    "The Challenge of Research in Family Diagnosis and Therapy ——Summary, Parts I-IV,"
    in N. W. Ackerman, F. L. Beatman, and S. Sherman (Eds.), Exploring the Base for
    Family Therapy, New York, Family Service Association of America, 1961.
Discussions about research by Bateson, Lennard, Cottrell and Leichter following an introductory summary by Behrens.

BELL, N. W., "Terms of a Comprehensive Theory of Family Psycopathology Relationships,"
    in G. H. Zuk and I. Boszormenyi-Nagy (Eds.), Family Therapy and Disturbed Families,
    Palo Alto, Science & Behavior Books, 1967.
A discussion of the current status of family ideas and the work that needs to be done.
There is a lack of shared language, of coordination with other sciences, of adequate
scientific method in the research, and lack of consensus on the components of the systems investigated.

BODIN, A., "Conjoint Family Assessment: An Evolving Field," in P. McReynolds (Ed.),
    Advances in Psychological Assessment, Palo Alto, Socience & Behavior Books, 1968
A resume of testing methods designed for use with families in the fields of family therapy and family research. Approaches have been individual, conjoint, and combined. Subjective techniques include family tasks, family strengths inventory, and family art.
Objective techniques include analysis of communication, games, and how conflict is resolved. A critique of these methods is presented.

CORNELISON, A. R., "Casework Interviewing as a Research Technique in a Study of Families
    of Schizophrenic Patients," Ment. Hyg., 44, 551-559, 1960.
A discussion of casework interviewing in family study as experienced by a caseworker
with the Lidz project. The families of sixteen cases were studied by individual interviews with family members. Group interviews have been recently initiated. Caseworker-
family contact begins upon hospital admission if not sooner and family patterns are
frequently illuminated by the various and varying attitudes displayed toward the caseworker. A general discussion is offered of the special usefulness of combined casework service and research, practical aspects of the method, and problems involved.

DRECHSLER, R. J., and SHAPIRO, M. I., "Two Methods of Analysis of Family Diagnostic
    Data," Fam. Proc., 2, 367-379, 1963.
A description of the conjoint use of clinical and statistical analysis of the same data.
Thirteen families were interviewed and also given a standard family task (discussing a
questionnaire) to perform alone. Samples of the tape recordings were extracted and frequency count made of how often one person spoke to another. Clinical impressions were
compared and similarities found.

FONTANA, A. F., "Familial Etiology of Schizophrenia: Is a Scientific Methodology Pos-
        sible?," Psycho. Bull., 66, 214-227, 1966.
A review of methodology in family research on schizophrenia, emphasizing clinical observation, retrospective recall, and direct observation of family interaction. The former
two approaches are said to be unsuitable "for a scientific body of etiological facts":
the latter approach should be used with caution. Findings of various studies are reviewed. The author concludes the greatest value so far is in the guidelines provided
for longitudinal research, but sufficient knowledge is not yet available to warrant the
great expenditure involved in longitudinal research at the present time.

FRAMO, J. L., "Systematic Research on Family Dynamics," in I. Boszormenyi-Nagy and J.
        L. Framo (Eds.), Intensive Family Therapy, New York, Harper & Row, 1965.
A review of family research relevant to family dynamics. Includes a discussion of small
group research, family interaction studies, and methodological problems.

GOLDBERG, E., "Difficulties Encountered in Assessing Family Attitudes," J. Psychosom.
        Res., 8, 229-234, 1964.
A discussion of studies made which attempted to assess family organization and functioning in relation to disease (such as chronic ulcers, schizophrenia, etc.). Problems of
methodology include interrelatedness of variables, objective assessment, comparisons,
and measurement in relation to the family.

HILL, R., "Marriage and Family Research: A Critical Evaluation," Eugen. Quart., 1, 58-
        63, 1954.
An essay undertaking a critical review of the literature on marriage and the family,
covering trends in research, contemporary emphasis, and prospects for the future research. The essay covers primarily the sociologic literature.

HILL, R., "Methodological Issues in Family Development Research," Fam. Proc., 3, 186-
        206, 1964.
A review of family study oriented toward a family development frame of reference and the
special requirements of the longitudinal method of data collection. Concepts of the
family frame of reference are said to be developmental, structure-function, learning
theory, personality development, and household-economic. Difficulties in, and alternatives to, the longitudinal study are discussed.

HILL, R., and HANSEN, D., "Identification of Conceptual Frameworks Utilized in Family
        Study," Marriage Fam. Liv., 22, 299-326, 1960.
An article which reports on a ten-year study attempting to inventory research on the
family in terms of (1) findings, (2) research procedures, and (3) theoretical proposi-
tions derived from the research. Five different research approaches (interactional,
structure-function, situational, institutional, and developmental) and the disciplines
they are developed in are presented and discussed.

LEVINGER, G., "Supplementary Methods in Family Research," Fam. Proc., 2, 357-366, 1963.
A review of methods in family research with a comparison of subjective report and objective observation with a discussion of their strengths and weaknesses. A study is
reported of 31 families who were studied with both observation and self report. The
results showed gross correspondence between the two methods, and it is suggested that
both procedures should be used since they supplement each other.

NYE, F. I., and MAYER, A. E., "Some Recent Trends in Family Research," Soc. Forces, 41,
        290-301, 1963.
The research literature on the family in four leading sociological journals from 1947-
61 (N = 456) was analyzed. Changes in methodological aspects and substantive content
are documented. Problems remain regarding the failure to use research competence fully,
inadequate communication among researchers, and lack of attention to methodological research per se. Special attention is given problems, and potentials in the utilization
of theory, in control of extraneous variables, in the validity of data, in using third
variables as contingent conditions, and in longitudinal design.

POST, F., and WARDLE, J., "Family Neurosis and Family Psychosis: A Review of the Prob-
    lem," J. Ment. Sci., 108, 147-158, 1962.
A review of some of the work that has been done in social psychiatry——the psychiatry
of relationships. After discussing early studies investigating families of various
types of orientation the authors review the studies of the current families of child
and adult patients. They conclude that even those studies of family events and interactions occurring shortly before the patient became ill, and not years previously, are
prematurely concerned with proving some basic theoretical construct. It is essential
to discover the proportion and type of psychiatric cases in which there is a clear link
between emotional characteristics in relatives and friends and the patient's breakdown.
A bibliography of 57 references is included.

RABKIN, L., "The Patient's Family: Research Methods," Fam. Proc., 4, 105-132, 1965.
A review of family research with special emphasis upon the family of the schizophrenic.
Critical examination is done of case history studies, interviewing studies, psychodiagnostic testing, questionnaire studies, and observational research. A bibliography of
99 references is included.

SINGER, M., and WYNNE, L., "Principles for Scoring Communication Defects and Deviances
    in Parents of Schizophrenics: Rorschach and TAT Scoring Manuals," Psychiatry, 29,
    260-289, 1966.
A continuation of previous studies in which the authors have predictively related parental behavior on psychological tests with psychiatric diagnosis of their offspring.
Two scoring manuals for use with the Rorschach and with the TAT are presented in an effort to pinpoint certain selective features of parental behavior which can be quickly
scored (previous studies used inferences which required a great deal of time in analyzing a battery of tests). A discussion of the tests and their clinical correlates in
the family of schizophrenics is also provided.

TITCHENER, J., VANDER HEIDE, C., and WOODS, E., "Profiles in Family Interaction Systems,"
    J. Nerv. Ment. Dis., 143, 473-483, 1966.
A report of a study designed to measure family interaction systems. Data were collected
using Riskin's interaction scales which were then modified. Advantages of this technique are discussed. Methods of sampling and data analysis are described and several
profiles of family interaction are exemplified with discussion of variables in family
interaction systems. Flow of information and quality of the flow are key variables to
measure how families function.

WAXLER, N. E., and MISHLER, E. G., "Sequential Patterning in Family Interaction: A
    Methodological Note," Fam. Proc., 9, 211-220, 1970.
A discussion of different ways of analyzing participation rates in family conversations
when the measure is who speaks after whom.

WINTER, W. and FERREIRA, A., Research in Family Interaction, Palo Alto, Science & Be-
    havior Books, 1969.
A collection of some new and some previously published material dealing with studies
and research on family interaction. There are sections on methodological issues in
family interaction research; studies of individual family members; studies of family
interaction: decision-making; studies of family interaction: studies, attitudes, and
power; studies of family interaction: behavior; and studies of family interaction:
intrafamily communication. There is a lengthy bibliography.

YARROW, M. R., CAMPBELL, J. D., and BURTON, R. V., "Reliability of Maternal Retrospec-
    tion: A Preliminary Report," Fam. Proc., 3, 207-218, 1964.
An examination of the retrospective method of family research where the data is self
report of family members about the past. A study is reported where retrospection of
mothers is obtained through interview methods and these data are compared with the reports of those mothers at the earlier period. The results "demonstrate a very large
error in retrospective interview data on parent-child relations."

2.6 FAMILY THEORY

ACKERMAN, N. W., "Child and Family Psychiatry Today: A New Look at Some Old Problems,"
Ment. Hyg., 47, 540-545, 1963.
A paper evaluating some basic concepts of child psychiatry, which finds these concepts incomplete without amending them "so that child and family may be treated as a single entity, rather than piecing them apart." Some basic family dynamics are discussed in support of that idea.

ACKERMAN, N. W., "Prejudice and Scapegoating in the Family," in G. H. Zuk and I. Bos-
zormenyi-Nagy (Eds.), Family Therapy and Disturbed Families, Palo Alto, Science
& Behavior Books, 1967.
A description of families in terms of the victim who is scapegoated, the destroyer or persecutor who is specially prejudiced against the victim, and the family healer who neutralizes the destructive powers of the attack.

ACKERMAN, N. W., "Prejudicial Scapegoating and Neutralizing Forces in the Family Group,
with Special Reference to the Role of Family Healer," Int. J. Soc. Psychiat., Special Edition No. 2, 90-96, 1964.
A discussion of conflict in the family based upon films of family therapy sessions. The emphasis is upon prejudicial scapegoating within a pattern of interdependent roles: those of the persecutor, the scapegoat, and the family healer. It is said that dis-turbed families break up into warring factions with a leader of each faction, a victim of prejudicial attack, and a person who provides the emotional antidote.

ACKERMAN, N. W., "Toward an Integrative Therapy of the Family," Amer. J. Psychiat., 144,
727-723, 1958.
Based on the author's clinical experience in family therapy, a method for understanding family pathology and a program of prevention is presented and illustrated by case exam-ples. Illness is a function of the family as well as a manifestation of individual be-havior.

ACKERMAN, N. W., and BEHRENS, M. L., "A Study of Family Diagnosis," Amer. J. Orthopsychiat., 26, 66-78, 1956.
A study of 40 families from the council child development center in New York. Concepts of the family and a classification of family types are offered. The emphasis is upon the family context of the developing child.

ACKERMAN, N. W., PAPP, P., and PROSKY, P., "Childhood Disorders and Interlocking Pathology in Family Relationships," in E. J. Anthony and C. Koupernik (Eds.), The Child
in His Family, New York, Wiley, 1970.
A discussion of the concept of studying the child by moving from the dynamic study of the whole family back to the child. Case examples are given.

ACKERMAN, N. W., and SOBEL, R., "Family Diagnosis," Amer. J. Orthopsychiat., 20, 744-
753, 1950.
It is necessary to consider the psychosocial effects of the family members upon each other to understand the preschool child who is a patient. Treatment of the young child should begin with treatment of the family group.

ALANEN, Y. O., "Round Table Conference of Family Studies and Family Therapy of Schizophrenic Patients," Acta Psychiat. Scand., Supplement No. 169, 39, 420-426, 1963.
A report of a panel discussion oriented toward family dynamics and therapy held at the Thirteenth Congress of Scandinavian Psychiatrists in 1962. Topics described include the Yale studies on families, parental interaction and the resulting disturbed body images of schizophrenic patients, reactions of the family when the patient is in indi-vidual psychotherapy, and families of schizophrenics in relation to the "larger fami-lies" of our contemporary societies.

ANTHONY, E. J., "The Mutative Impact of Serious Mental and Physical Illness in a Parent
      on Family Life," in E. J. Anthony and C. Koupernik (Eds.), The Child in His Family,
      New York, Wiley, 1970.
A report of a study of families where a parent figure has succumbed to a serious mental
or physical disorder necessitating hospitalization. Various views are offered of such
illness as a disruption of family roles, as a crisis in accommodation, as a disconnection,
and as a challenge. Family members were interviewed individually and in dyads and triads.

ANTHONY, E. J., and KOUPERNIK, C. (Eds.), The Child in His Family, New York, Wiley, 1970.
Volume 1 in the series of the International Yearbook for Child Psychiatry and Allied Disciplines. Included are papers from a variety of authors of different nations. The sections include family dynamics, family vulnerability and crisis, chronic family pathology,
and mental health and families in different cultures. 492 pp.

ARCHIBALD, H., "The Disturbed Child-Disturbed Family," Arch. Pediat., 67, 128-133, 1950.
An essay, based on the author's clinical practice, which describes presenting signs and
symptoms of emotional nature seen in a pediatric practice. The emotional symptoms are
seen as related to a disturbed family. The child is in a "vicious cycle." Suggestions
for dealing with this problem are made.

ARNOLD, A., "The Implications of Two-Person and Three-Person Relationships for Family
      Psychotherapy," J. Health Hum. Behav., 3, 94-97, 1962.
An essay on the disinclinations of psychotherapists to work directly with families. A
sociological formulation is offered in terms of the differences in the dynamics of dyadic and triadic relationships and how they impinge on the therapist.

AUERSWALD, E. H., "Interdisciplinary vs. Ecological Approach," Fam. Proc., 7, 202-215,
      1968.
A discussion of the difference between approaching a problem from the viewpoint of different disciplines or using an ecological systems approach. A case of a runaway girl
is used for exploring this difference.

BATESON, G., "The Biosocial Integration of Behavior in the Schizophrenic Family," in N.
      W. Ackerman, F. L. Beatman, and S. Sherman (Eds.), Exploring the Base for Family
      Therapy, New York, Family Service Association of America, 1961.
A description of families and other systems in terms of feedback and calibration where
calibration is at the "setting" level. Families of schizophrenics are described in
terms of difficulties at the calibration level.

BATESON, G., "Minimal Requirements for a Theory of Schizophrenia," Arch. Gen. Psychiat.,
      2, 477-491, 1960.
An essay on developing a theory of schizophrenia. The role of learning theory, genetics,
and evolution is discussed. The double-bind model may be used in part to explain the
symptoms of schizophrenia and perhaps other behavioral disorders.

BATESON, G., and JACKSON, D. D., "Some Varieties of Pathogenic Organization," Disorders
      of Communication No. 42, Research Publications, Association for Research in Ner-
      vous and Mental Disease, 1964.
A discussion of symmetrical and complementary relationships, analogic and digital communication models, and the relation of such ideas to pathological organization.

BATESON, G., JACKSON, D. D., HALEY, J., and WEAKLAND, J., "Towards a Theory of Schizo-
      phrenia," Behav. Sci., 1, 251-264, 1956.
Based on the authors' previous clinical experience, experimental data, the theory of logical types (defined as a discontinuity between a class and its members), and communication theory, the authors hypothesize that schizophrenic symptoms may results from being
caught in a double bind. This is defined as a situation in which no matter what a person does, he can't "win". Therapeutic implications are discussed — many therapeutic
gambits are "borderline double binds".

BAXTER, J., "Family Relationship Variables in Schizophrenia," Acta Psychiat. Scand.,
    42, 362-391, 1966.
A review of the literature from 1892 to the present with the focus on variables related
to the family and child development. Topics covered are: (1) sibling position of the
patient, (2) loss of one or both parents, (3) presence of a distressed childhood in the
patient's background, (4) atypical mother-child relationship, (5) atypical father-child
relationship, (6) emotional immaturity in the parents, (7) dominance and disturbances
between the parents, (8) interpersonal conflict in the family, (9) family-centered
pathological behavior, and (10) special position of sibling set for the patient.

BELL, N. W., "Extended Family Relations of Disturbed and Well Families," Fam. Proc., 1,
    175-193, 1962.
The author's thesis is that "disturbed families have been unable to resolve conflicts
with the extended kin outside the nuclear family" and that "well" families have achieved
resolution of the problems of ties to extended kin. Most of the data were collected
from observation and interviews in the home. Findings were that the "pathological"
families used the extended family to (1) shore up group defenses, (2) act as stimuli
of conflict, (3) act as screens for the projection of conflicts, and (4) act as competing objects of support.

BELL, N. W., "Terms of a Comprehensive Theory of Family Psychopathology Relationships,"
    in G. H. Zuk and I. Boszormenyi-Nagy (Eds.), Family Therapy and Disturbed Fami-
    lies, Palo Alto, Science & Behavior Books, 1967.
A discussion of the current status of family ideas and the work that needs to be done.
There is a lack of shared language, of coordination with other sciences, of adequate
scientific method in the research, and lack of consensus on the components of the systems investigated.

BELL, N. W., and VOGEL, E. S. (Eds.), A Modern Introduction to the Family, Glencoe,
    Free Press, 1961.
A collection of new material and previously published articles by multiple authors
which attempts to provide a "sociology of the family." It includes a framework for a
functional analysis of family behavior, study of different family systems, papers on
the family and economy, the family and community, and the family and value systems.
It also includes a section on how normal families function and how family function relates to personality development and maldevelopment. 691 pp.

BENNIS, W., SCHEINE, E., BERLEW, D., and STEELE, F. (Eds.), Interpersonal Dynamics,
    Homewood, Dorsey Press, 1964.
A collection of previously published material which includes discussions of the family
scapegoat, the family theory of schizophrenia, interpersonal relationships within the
family, and role conflict.

BERGLER, E., Parents Not Guilty! Of Their Children's Neuroses, New York, Liveright,
    1964.
A clinical report based on the notion that "there is no direct connection between acts,
words, or attitudes of parents on the child's behavior and later development." 283 pp.

BIRDWHISTELL, R. L., "An Approach to Communication," Fam. Proc., 1, 194-201, 1962.
An essay on communication processes in general, emphasizing types and multi-functions
of messages with particular applicability to the child receiving "messages" in growing
up.

BOSZORMENYI-NAGY, I., "The Concept of Schizophrenia from the Perspective of Family Treat-
    ment," Fam. Proc., 1, 103-113, 1962.
A discussion of "the problems and mechanisms of family relationships." The author's hypothesis is that "schizophrenic personality development may in part be perpetrated by
reciprocal interpersonal need complementaries between parent and offspring." Observations were collected from intensive psychotherapy of young female schizophrenics and
concurrent conjoint therapy of their relatives at a psychiatric hospital.

BOSZORMENYI-NAGY, I., "From Family Therapy to a Psychology of Relationships: Fictions
        of the Individual and Fictions of the Family," Compr. Psychiat., 7, 408-423, 1966.
A theoretical paper examining some of the questions posed by having a "family orientation" to psychiatric problems. A comprehensive psychology of relationships would include both internal experience and observable behavior. Theories of family dynamics
and other theories of psychology are discussed.

BOSZORMENYI-NAGY, I., "Relational Modes and Meaning," in G. H. Zuk and I. Boszormenyi-
        Nagy (Eds.), Family Therapy and Disturbed Families, Palo Alto, Science & Behavior
        Books, 1967.
An essay on the determinents and meaning of relationships. "Existential freedom is a
dialectical process; it is not love through merger. It is a capacity for symmetrical
self-other delineations and continuous new resolutions of opposing positions in relationships."

BOSZORMENYI-NAGY, I., "A Theory of Relationships: Experience and Transaction," in I.
        Boszormenyi-Nagy and J. L. Framo (Eds.), Intensive Family Therapy, New York, Har-
        per & Row, 1965.
A discussion of relationships from the point of view of a dialectical theory of personality and relatedness, alternate choices of self-delineation, and an object model of the
formation of relational systems.

BOWEN, M., "Family Psychotherapy with Schizophrenia in the Hospital and in Private Prac-
        tice," in I. Boszormenyi-Nagy and J. L. Framo (Eds.), Intensive Family Therapy,
        New York, Harper & Row, 1965.
A discussion of a theory of the family and of family therapy with sections on differences between family and individual theory, a summary of the family theory of emotional
illness with the emphasis upon schizophrenia, the parental transmission of problems
to the child, the clinical approach to modify the family transmission process, and
principles and techniques of this family therapy approach.

BOWEN, M., DYSINGER, R., and BASAMANIA, B., "Role of the Father in Families with a Schi-
        zophrenic Patient," Amer. J. Psychiat., 115, 1017-1020, 1959.
One of a series of papers on a study of families with schizophrenics in which the entire
family was all hospitalized in the psychiatric research ward for periods of "up to two
and a half years." Four families were hospitalized while an additional six families
were seen in out-patient family therapy for periods of up to two years. The most frequent family dynamic observed was "emotional divorce" between mother and father and an
intense relationship between mother and patient in which father was excluded.

BRITTAIN, C. V., "Adolescent Choices and Parent-Peer Cross-Pressures," Amer. Sociol.
        Rev., 28, 385-391, 1963.
Adolescent choices when peers and parents indicate different courses were investigated
as to variation by content area. Two hundred and eighty high school girls in two
southern states responded to hypothetical dilemmas. On two occasions interviews were
also held with 42 subjects. The data indicate that choice depended upon the area, and
that a complex process of perception of and identification with peers and parents is
involved.

BRODEY, W. M., Changing the Family, New York, Potter, 1968.
A personal view of families with many styles of family life described. "The stories...
are little descriptions of families mixed with just enough comment and contrast to tell
their own story and insist that you listen and feel...."

BRODEY, W. M., "A Cybernetic Approach to Family Therapy," in G. H. Zuk and I. Boszor-
        menyi-Nagy (Eds.), Family Therapy and Disturbed Families, Palo Alto, Science &
        Behavior Books, 1967.
In this paper "the family is conceptualized as a self-perpetuating organism with a built-
in regulatory system. Family therapy is directed to altering the family's self regulation..."

BRODEY, W., "The Family as the Unit of Study of Treatment: Image, Object, and Nar-
     cissistic Relationships," Amer. J. Orthopsychiat., 31, 69-73, 1961.
An essay which attempts to outline the dynamics of family relationships starting from
the intrapsychic point of view and moving to interactional models. Externalization,
object relationships, image relationships and narcissism are all discussed in the family context in terms of building a conception of how a family operates.

BRODEY, W. M., "The Need for a Systems Approach," in N. W. Ackerman (Ed.), Expanding
     Theory and Practice in Family Therapy, New York, Family Service Association of
     America, 1967.
A clinical essay pointing out that there is still a great lack of a standardized method to evaluate complex intervention into complex systems. Further study and methods
are needed.

BRODSKY, C. M., "The Social Recovery of Mentally Ill Housewives," Fam. Proc., 7, 170-
     183, 1968.
A report on a study of the relationship between social recovery and role among mentally
ill housewives. A sample of 38 housewives admitted to an acute treatment research unit
were examined and followed up. The housewife's role is said to be conducive to recovery.

BROFENBRENNER, U., "The Changing American Child — A speculative Analysis," J. Soc.
     Issues, 17, 6-18, 1961.
A variety of studies show that American parents have changed their child-rearing techniques in the past 25 years. No solid comparative data exist, but one may infer existence of changes from known relationships between socialization techniques and outcome.
Outcome varies by sex of child and authority-nurturance division between parents. Many
signs point to the conclusion that a generation lacking initiative, inner direction,
and responsibility has been produced. Recent changes suggest that parents may now be
raising a more achievement-oriented generation, the motivation being inculcated by mothers in a family atmosphere of "cold democracy".

BRUCH, H., "Changing Approaches to the Study of the Family," in I. M. Cohen (Ed.) Psy-
     chiatric Research Report No. 20, American Psychiatric Association, 1966.
A general discussion of family influence with the emphasis upon the salient aspects of
family transactions centering on the continuous interaction of biological endorsement
with environmental forces.

BURSTEN, B., "Family Dynamics, The Sick Role, and Medical Hospital Admissions," Fam.
     Proc., 4, 206-216, 1965.
A discussion of how the medical hospital may be used in the service of family patterns.
There may be no organic difficulty or an organic difficulty can be combined with psycho-
social factors to resolve a family conflict. Case examples are given.

CHRISTENSEN, H. T., (Ed.), Handbook of Marriage and the Family, Chicago, Rand McNally,
     1964.
A collection of new material on marriage and the family, including sections on theoretical orientation; methodological developments; the family in its social setting; member roles and internal processes; applied and normative interests including family life,
education, and the field of marriage counseling.

CLARK, A. W., and VAN SOMMERS, P., "Contradictory Demands in Family Relations and Adjust-
     ment to School and Home," Hum. Rel. 14, 97-111, 1961.
Intensive case-studies of families of 20 maladjusted and 20 adjusted children, all families having one or more adults other than the parents living in the family. The concern
was with "the process of explaining an unsatisfactory relationship between any two individuals in terms of the influence of a third individual." Data were obtained by detailed,
focussed interviews, questionnaires to school staffs, group interviews with peers, and
tests of ability. School difficulties were associated with unsatisfactory relationships
in the home, one of which was dependence of one parent upon the other adult. Unsatisfac-

tory releeationships of adults contribute to withdrawal of father from family activities, difficulties between adults and children, maladjustment of children at home and school, and recurrence of symptoms in parents.

COLLVER, A., "The Family Cycle in India and the United States," Amer. Sociol. Rev., 26, 86, 1963.
Systematic comparisons of age at marriage, interval before birth of the first child, total child-bearing period, and other stages of family cycle are made between the United States and a rural-Indian area. The stages are less clearly defined in India. The meaning in terms of kinship system and the ramifications for the society are explored.

COUNTS, R., "Family Crisis and the Impulsive Adolescent," Arch. Gen. Psychiat., 17, 64-74, 1967.
A case example is presented in support of the hypothesis that the acting out of an adolescent can best be understood by seeing it as acting out of a family crisis. The adolescent is used as a scapegoat of the family and he acts out somebody else's impulses, which helps to stabilize his own internal operations while it stabilizes the family.

DAVIS, D., "Interventions Into Family Affairs," Brit. J. Med. Psychol., 41, 73-79, 1968.
An essay using a case example from Ibsen's play, The Lady From The Sea. How the family problem was resolved in the play and how it might be resolved using present psychiatric treatment methods (ECT, behavior therapy, family therapy, and so forth) are discussed. Emphasis is placed on finding the "right" treatment course by an appraisal covering the entire family.

DELL, N., TRIESCHMAN, A., and VOGEL, E., "A Sociocultural Analysis of Resistances of Working-Class Fathers Treated in a Child Psychiatric Clinic," Amer. J. Orthopsychiat., 31, 388-405, 1961.
The authors' hypothesis is that fathers have been excluded from the treatment process in the child guidance clinic setting. Ten "working-class" fathers were seen for periods ranging from one to four years. It was part of concurrent, simultaneous treatment of the identified patient (the child) and the mother. Familial dynamics are discussed. The child's treatment may be facilitated when the father is seen.

DUHRSSEN, A., "Preventive Missnahmen in der Familie," Psychother. Psychosom., 16, 319-322, 1968.
The preventive aspects of family therapy. Characteristics of family life in other cultures are described and the psychopathology of specific family structures is presented with a case example.

DUNHAM. R. M., "Ex Post Facto Reconstruction of Conditioning Schedules in Family Interaction," in I. M. Cohen (Ed.), Psychiatric Research Report No. 20, Wash., D. C., American Psychiatric Association, 1966.
A discussion of family behavior from the point of view of learning theory. Given some of the descriptions of families of schizophrenics, "have the patients been exposed to a chronic pattern of aversive conditioning that has inhibited the development of ego strength and left them passive?"

DUVALL, E., Family Development, Philadelphia, Lippincott, 1967.
A book on the family for "preprofessionals" who work with the family. It focusses on family life style, tasks, how families reflect social changes, how families change with the introduction of children, and how families change after the children leave the family. 532 pp.

EHRENWALD, J., Neurosis in the Family and Patterns of Psychosocial Defense, New York, Harper & Row, 1963.
A collection of some new and some previously published material including chapters on family traits and attitudes, patterns of family interaction, patterns of sharing and

parent-child symbiosis, a description of a family with obsessive-compulsive personality, dynamics from both an intrapersonal and interpersonal point of view, patterns of contagion, sections on the Mozart and Picasso families, psychiatric epidemiology, and interpersonal dynamics in family therapy. 203 pp.

ELDER, G. H., "Structural Variations in the Child-Rearing Relationship," Sociometry,
    25, 241-262, 1962.
Seven types of parent-adolescent interdependence, ranging from parental autocracy to parental ignoring, were identified by focussed interviews. Questionnaires to 7,400 Ohio and North Carolina adolescents reveal that parental dominance is most common in lower-class, large, Catholic families. Parental autocracy is most likely to be associated with negative evaluations of parental policies by adolescents and with mutual rejection of each other.

ELDER, G. H., and BOWERMAN, C. E., "Family Structure and Child-Rearing Patterns: The
    Effect of Family Size and Sex Composition," Amer. Social. Rev., 28, 891-905, 1963.
The effects of family size, sex composition and social class on the involvement of the father in child rearing, on the type of parental control exerted, and on the disciplinary techniques used were studied. Data were from a 40% sample (N = 1261) of all seventh grade white Protestant students of unbroken homes in central Ohio and central North Carolina. Family size and sex composition were found to have effects on child-rearing methods, but the effects are highly contingent on the sex of the child and the social class of the family.

ENGLISH, O. S., SCHEFLEN, A. E., HAMPE, W. W., and AUERBACH, A. H., Strategy and Struc-
    ture in Psychotherapy, Behavioral Studies Monograph No. 2, Philadelphia, Eastern
    Pennsylvania Psychiatric Institute, 1965.
A companion volume to Stream and Structure of Communicational Behavior (A. E. Scheflen) which includes three research studies of a family therapy interview by Whitaker and Malone.

EPSTEIN, N., and WESTLEY, W., "Parental Interaction as Related to the Emotional Health
    of Children," Soc. Prob., 8, 87-92, 1960.
One of a series of papers concerned with the parents' relationship with, and emotional health of, their children. Methodology was previously described. Results indicated that there was no firm relationship between the level of the parental sexual relationship and the average level of emotional health among the children, but a clearcut degree of dependency needs in the father was directly related to unhealthiness in the children. The level of the father's unresolved dependency needs does not seem to affect the children's health as long as the father is stronger than the mother.

FARBER, S. M., MUSTACCHI, P., and WILSON, R. H. L. (Eds.), Man and Civilization: The
    Family's Search for Survival, New York, McGraw-Hill, 1965.
A collection of new material given at a conference concerned with the changes in the family secondary to changes in society. It includes articles concerned with the "necessity of the family," sacrifice of family structure, the family role, and new paths. 210 pp.

FELDMAN, M. J., "Privacy and Conjoint Family Therapy," Fam. Proc., 6, 1-9, 1967.
A discussion of whether greater or lesser degree of privacy effects the nature of therapeutic disclosures by contrasting individual and conjoint family therapy. There is no simple relationship between degree of privacy and kind and scope of disclosure.
The private nature of individual therapy led to an ethical position which elevates an individual's welfare above others, which may even be to their detriment.

FERREIRA, A., "Family Myth and Homeostasis," Arch. Gen. Psychiat., 9, 457-463, 1963.
A discussion of a particular aspect of the family relationship, the family myth, which is defined as "a series of fairly well integrated beliefs shared by all family members, concerning each other and their mutual position in the family life"——beliefs that go unchallenged despite reality distortions which they imply. Three family case reports

are presented in support of the discussion; the author believes that the family myth
is to the relationship what the defense is to the individual.

FERREIRA, A. J., "Family Myths," in I. M. Cohen (Ed.), Psychiatric Research Report No.
    20, Wash., D. C., American Psyciatric Association, 1966.
A discussion of the myths families develop with an illustration of the contrast of a family's report and their behavior in a test setting. The relevance of family myths in
family therapy is discussed.

FERREIRA, A. J., "Family Myths: The Covert Rules of the Relationship," Confin. Psychiat.,
    8, 15-20, 1965.
A general discussion of the myths in families which express covert rules of family relationships. These well-systematized fabrications perform an important part as homeostatic mechanisms. "In fact, it seems that the family myth is to the family what the defense is to the individual." From family therapy observations, the author says that
"pathologic families" can be overburdened with their own mythology and "seem to retain
very little freedom for unrehearsed action, and to suffer in their ability to deal with
new situations, and unexpected events."

FERREIRA, A., "Psychosis and Family Myth," Amer. J. Psychother., 21, 186-197, 1967.
Two vignettes are reported in support of the thesis that "psychotic behavior may be
regarded not simply as a product of the individual but rather as an expression of the
family interaction, that is, as a relationship event." Family myths (defined as a series
of beliefs, which are untrue, held by members of the family about each other and their
relationship) are to the family what the defense is to the individual. Treatment considerations are discussed.

FLECK, S., "An Approach to Family Pathology," Compr. Psychiat., 7, 307-320, 1966.
Functions and tasks of normal families, as well as an approach to understanding family
pathology based on deficiencies in performing their functions and tasks are outlined.
Suggestions for research on the family are made.

FRAMO, J. L., "Symptoms from a Family Transactional Viewpoint," in N. W. Ackerman (Ed.),
    Family Therapy in Transition, Boston, Little, Brown, 1970.
A discussion of symptoms in terms of irrational role assignments, projective transference
distortions, and internalized objects which become subidentities. Case examples illustrate symptom choice, symptom maintenance, and pseudosymptoms.

FREEDMAN, D. S., FREEDMAN, R., and WHELPTON, P. K., "Size of Family and Preference for
    Children of Each Sex," Amer. J. Sociol., 66, 141-146, 1960.
An investigation of 889 white couples with two, three, or four children, to determine
whether the question of American family size is influenced by a desire of parents to
have at least one child of each sex.

GALDSTON, I. (Ed.), The Family in Contemporary Society, New York, International Univer-
    sities Press, 1958.
A collection of material given at a conference on the family with discussions of the
previous conference on the family given in 1956, the history of the family as a social
and cultural institution, changing dynamics of the contemporary family: social and economic basis, behavioral trends and disturbances of the contemporary family, homeostatic
mechanisms within the family, and emotionally disturbed and healthy adolescents and
their family backgrounds. 147 pp.

GALDSTON, I. (Ed.), The Family: A Focal Point in Health Education, New York, Interna-
    tional Universites Press, 1961.
A collection of material previously given at a conference with sections on the family in
general, profile of the American family, psychological dynamics of the "familial organism," an approach to the study of family mental health, education for personal and familial living, education for parenthood, family and physician, social worker and family,

family health maintenance, the anthropology of the American family, ethnic differences
in behavior and health practices, and social differences in health practices. 216 pp.

GALDSTON, I., "The Need for an Epidemiology of Psychiatric Disorders of the Family," in
     N. W. Ackerman, F. L. Beatman, and S. Sherman (Eds.), Exploring the Base for Family
     Therapy, New York, Family Service Association of America, 1961.
A clinical essay, which points out that although there are strong biases to the contrary,
there is very little information about the epidemiology of either normal or pathologic
families. Such information cannot be obtained during treatment. In addition to data
about normal families, follow-up data of normal families must also be obtained.

GAP Report No. 76: The Case History Method in the Study of Family Process, New York,
     Group for the advancement of Psychiatry, 1970.
The purpose of this report is to demonstrate a systematic approach to modifying the traditional psychiatric "case history" for use in family diagnosis, treatment, and research.
There are sections on principles for compiling a family case history, a typical case is
presented, and contrast made between a Puerto Rican working-class and American middle-
class family. Contrast in values within the nuclear family as well as in the extended
family network are described. There is an appendix with a family case history outline.
380 pp.

GEHRKE, S., and KIRSCHENBAUM, M., "Survival Patterns in Family Conjoint Therapy," Fam.
     Proc., 6, 67-80, 1967.
A discussion of 20 families studied in family therapy with the emphasis upon different
patterns of emotional survival myths in the family. Three types of family are contrasted: the repressive family, the delinquent family, and the suicidal family. The survival myth has to do with the illusion of family members that they must continue their
existing family ways of relating to survive psychologically.

GEISMAR, L. L., "Family Functioning as an Index of Need for Welfare Services," Fam. Proc.,
     3, 99-113, 1964.
A discussion of the need to have an objective means of assessing the need for welfare
services. A standardized method of evaluating family functioning is offered with a
report of a study of families.

GLASSER, P. H., "Changes in Family Equilibrium During Psychotherapy," Fam. Proc., 2,
     245-264, 1963.
A report on a study of the ways in which role changes occur in a family when a parent
is mentally ill and undergoes psychotherapy. The case study method was used with three
families seen in interviews. Stages of family equilibrium are delineated.

GLASSER, P., and GLASSER, L., "Adequate Family Functioning," in I. M. Cohen (Ed.), Psy-
     chiatric Research Report No. 20, American Psychiatric Association, 1966.
A report of a study of families in which at least one member was undergoing psychotherapy.
The emphasis is upon five criteria of adequate family functioning: internal role consistency, consistency of role and actual performance, compatibility of roles, meeting
psychological needs, and the ability of the family to respond to change.

GLASSER, P. H, and GLASSER, L. (Eds.), Families in Crisis, New York, Harper & Row, 1970.
A collection of new material and previously published articles which include discussions
of families in poverty, disorganization of marriages and families, and families in terms
of physical and mental health. 405 pp.

GLASSER, P. H., and NAVARRE, E. L., "The Problems of Families in the AFDC Program," in
     P. H. Glasser and L. N. Glasser (Eds.), Families in Crisis, New York, Harper & Row,
     1970.
The effects of poverty on the family presented from the point of view of the mother,
the social worker, a sociological view, and psychological factors.

GOODE, W., The Family, Englewood Cliffs, Prentice Hall, 1964.
The author discusses sociological theory as applied to family relationships. He describes the complex relationships between family systems and the larger social structure,
the biological basis of the family, legitimacy and illegitimacy, mate selection and marriage, forms of the household, organized descent groupings, role relations, stratification, dissolution of family role systems, and changes in the family patterns. 120 pp.

HADER, M., "The Importance of Grandparents in Family Life," Fam. Proc., 4, 228-240, 1965.
A discussion of the significance of grandparents in the life of young people and their
significance to young people. The literature is reviewed on grandparents with a division between the positive and negative influences.

HALEY, J. (Ed.), Changing Families: A Family Therapy Reader, New York, Grune & Stratton,
A textbook bringing together 21 articles describing different approaches to family therapy. Both previously published and new articles are included, and there is an extensive
bibliography.

HALEY, J., "Family Therapy: A Radical Change," in J. Haley (Ed.), Changing Families,
     New York, Grune & Stratton, 1971.
A review of the development of the family therapy field with the emphasis upon the
shift in unit from one person to two to three or more. Consequences to theory and the
effect on the professions are described.

HALEY, J., "Observation of the Family of the Schizophrenic," Amer. J. Orthopsychiat.,
     30, 460-467, 1960.
A report on a research project examining families containing a schizophrenic child by
observation of conjoint family therapy sessions, filmed structured interviews, and
experimental situations. The family is seen as a self-corrective system which is
"governed" by the behavior of each family member. The limited range of a family system can be described in terms of rules and prohibitions which, when infringed, activate family members to behave in such a way as to reinforce the system. The general
communicative behavior of the schizophrenic family is described and a film is shown
for illustration.

HALEY, J., "The Perverse Triangle," in G. Zuk and I. Boszormenyi-Nagy (Eds.), Family
     Therapy and Disturbed Families, Palo Alto, Science & Behavior Books, 1967.
A discussion of cross-generational coalitions as a cause of disturbance in family and
other organizations.

HALEY, J., Strategies of Psychotherapy, New York, Grune & Stratton, 1963.
A description of a variety of forms of psychotherapy from an interactional point of
view. Includes chapters on marriage therapy and family therapy.

HANDEL, G. (Ed.), The Psychosocial Interior of the Family: A Sourcebook for the Study
     of Whole Families, Chicago, Aldine, 1967.
An anthology of previously published articles on the social psychology of the family.
It includes sections on the family as a psychosocial organization, research methods,
the family as mediator of the culture, the meanings of family boundaries, the family
as a universe of cognition and communication, patterning separateness and connected-
ness, and a review of family theories. 560 pp.

HENRY, J., "Family Structure and the Transmission of Neurotic Behavior," Amer. J. Ortho-
     psychiat., 21, 800-818, 1951.
Based on analysis of interaction patterns of one family attending a child guidance clinic, the author makes the following hypotheses: "(1) individuals learn relatively rigid
patterns of interaction which they then tend to project upon the world in such a way as
to expect reciprocal patterns from others, (2) from the standpoint of intrafamilial interaction, neurosis may be considered originating in rigid interaction patterns of pathogenic, quality, (3) family interaction patterns may be described with relative precision

that will enable therapists to state the general psychological characteristic of families, and (4) the transmission of a neurosis in a family line is a transmission of a
rigid interactional pattern of pathogenic quality."

HENRY, J., "The Study of Families by Naturalistic Observation," in I. M. Cohen (Ed.),
    Psychiatric Research Report No. 20, American Psychiatric Association, 1966.
A discussion of the observation of psychotic children in the home with the emphasis upon
the methodology and the experience of such observation. An illustration is given, and
"when such observations are undertaken it quickly becomes apparent that the data is so
rich as to compel reexamination of old theories and suggest hypotheses leading to new
ones."

HOFFMAN, L., "Deviation Amplifying Processes in Natural Groups," in J. Haley (Ed.),
    Changing Families, New York, Grune & Stratton, 1971.
A theoretical paper on the limitations of a homeostatic theory to deal with change.
The family view, systems theory, and sociological ideas about deviants are brought
together in a discussion of the process of change in systems when a deviation is amplified.

HOFFMAN, L., and LONG, L., "A Systems Dilemma," Fam. Proc., 8, 211-234, 1969.
A description of a man's breakdown in terms of the social systems within which he moved,
and the attempts to intervene to bring about change. The ecological field of a person
is the area considered.

HOWELLS, J. G., Family Psychiatry, Springfield, Charles C Thomas, 1963.
A collection of some new and some previously published material intended to be a textbook of family psychiatry. There are sections on theory and practice of family psychiatry; illustrations of the dimensions of the family; individual, relationship, group,
maternal circumstances, and community interaction; and finally, illustrations from clinical practice, divided into organization, the presenting patient, clinical syndromes,
and therapy itself. There is an extensive bibliography. 953 pp.

HOWELLS, J. G., "The Nuclear Family as the Functional Unit in Psychiatry," J. Ment. Sci.,
    108, 675-684, 1962.
A discussion of the family, the nuclear family (defined as a sub-system of the social
system and consisting of two adults of different sexes who undertake a parenting role
to one or more children), and family psychiatry.

HOWELLS, J..G., (Ed.), Theory and Practice of Family Psychiatry, Edinburgh and London,
    Oliver & Boyd, 1968.
A collection of new material and previously published articles which include discussions
of the theory and practice of family psychiatry; the dimensions of the family from the
individual dimension, the relationship dimension, the group properties dimension, the
material circumstances dimension, and the community interaction dimension; and illustrations of clinical practice, including organization, the presenting patient, clinical
syndromes, and therapy. There is an extensive bibliography. 953 pp.

JACKSON, D. D., "Aspects of Conjoint Family Therapy," in G. H. Zuk and I. Boszormenyi-
    Nagy (Eds.), Family Therapy and Disturbed Families, Palo Alto, Science & Behavior
    Books, 1967.
A discussion of the difference between the family therapy approach and psychoanalysis
with an example of a "Lolita type" case. It is argued that the individual and family
are like the wave and particle theories of light and that merging the two is not quite
possible.

JACKSON, D. D. (Ed.), Communication, Family and Marriage, Palo Alto, Science & Behivior
    Books, 1968.
A collection of previously published papers covering generalizations on family dynamics
from clinical observations, papers on the double bind theory, communication, systems
and pathology, and research approaches and methods. 289 pp.

JACKSON, D. D. (Ed.), <u>The Etiology of Schizophrenia</u>, New York, Basic Books, 1960.
A collection of new material dealing with the etiology of schizophrenia. It includes
a section on an overview of the problem, genetic aspects, biochemical aspects, physiologic aspects, psychological studies, and family theories of schizophrenia. 456 pp.

JACKSON, D. D., "Family Rules: Marital, Quid Pro Quo," <u>Arch. Gen. Psychiat.</u>, 12, 589-
      594, 1965.
A clinical paper in which a theory of marriage is proposed based on the relationship
rather than the individuals. Similarities and differences between spouses comprise
the "bargain" on which the marriage relationship is based. Advantages and disadvantages
of this scheme of understanding the marital relationship are discussed.

JACKSON, D. D., "The Individual and the Larger Contexts," <u>Fam. Proc.</u>, 6, 139-154, 1967.
An essay on the contexts in which individuals function. The emphasis is upon the system and includes a discussion of the individual in his family as well as any entity,
such as a nation, in systematic relationship with other entities. The article is followed by discussions by George Vassiliou, Nathan B. Epstein, and Lyman C. Wynne.

JACKSON, D. D., "The Study of the Family," <u>Fam. Proc.</u>, 4, 1-20, 1965.
An essay on the family emphasizing the family as a rule-governed, homeostatic system.
It includes problems of family theory and research.

JACKSON, D. D., (Ed.), <u>Therapy, Communication and Change</u>, Palo Alto, Science & Behavior
      Books, 1968. 276 pp.
A collection of previously published papers covering psychotic behavior and its interactional context, the interactional context of other kinds of behavior, interactional
views of psychotherapy, and conjoint family therapy. 76 pp.

JACKSON, D. D., RISKIN, J., and SATIR, V., "A Method of Analysis of a Family Interview,"
      <u>Arch. Gen. Psychiat.</u>, 5, 321-339, 1961.
The authors examined the first five minutes of a family therapy interview without know-
ing the diagnosis of the child in the family. This "blind" analysis included a prediction of the psychopathology of the patient and some character traits of his brother.
The information available was only the parents' conversation which was examined from
the point of view of their communicative behavior, their needs and defenses, and possible
early life experiences which would lead them to interact in this way. The purpose of
the study was to illustrate a method of analyzing a family system.

JACKSON, D. D., and SATIR, V., "A Review of Psychiatric Developments in Family Diagnosis
      and Therapy," in N. W. Ackerman, F. L. Beatman and S. Sherman (Eds.), <u>Exploring the</u>
      <u>Base for Family Therapy</u>, New York, Family Service Association of America, 1961.
A clinical essay describing the development of family therapy. Clinical trends from
psychiatry, social work, anthropology, and psychoanalysis as well as the literature are
carefully reviewed in seeing a gradual development of a way of thinking about the individual patient as a reflection of a disturbed family. Family therapy offers an impres-
sive laboratory for studying growth and change available to the researcher. Behavior
that had formerly been thought of as "constitutional" could now be seen as interactional
in etiologic terms.

JACKSON, D. D., and WEAKLAND, J., "Schizophrenic Symptoms in Family Interaction," <u>Arch.</u>
      <u>Gen. Psychiat.</u>, 1, 618-621, 1959.
Based on psychological, sociological, and anthropological information about families,
data collection from individual interviews of family members, and treatment of the family
together, the authors hypothesize that schizophrenic behavior can be seen as (1) "re-
sembling the behavior of other family members, though it may be exaggerated almost to
a caricature," and (2) "appearing to subserve important functions within the family."
Two case examples are given in support of this view.

KANTOR, R. E., "Schizophrenia and Symbolic Interactionism," Fam. Proc., 3, 402-414, 1964.
A general discussion of the "basic assumptions of interactionism" presented in the form
of seven issues: processes, contemporary causality, dynamic fields, self-concepts,
emergents, and molarity and systems.

KELLNER, R., Family Ill Health: An Investigation in General Practice, Springfield,
        Charles C Thomas, 1963.
A report by a general practitioner concerning the incidence of physical and emotional
illness and its relationship to family dynamcis. The book includes a plan of the investigation, description of the cases, method of analyzing the data, results, and a
summary. 112 pp.

KOHL, R. N., "Pathologic Reactions of Marital Partners to Improvement of Patients,"
        Amer. J. Psychiat., 118, 1036-1041, 1962.
A discussion of the precipitation of a psychiatric illness in a marital partner when a
patient shows clinical improvement based upon observation of 39 in-patients treated at
the Payne Whitney psychiatric clinic over a period of ten years. In all cases it was
necessary to include both spouses in the treatment plan to maintain the patient's improvement or recovery. Commonly there was denial of marital conflict as etiologically
significant by both partners at the time of hospitalization and emphasis upon the "ideal"
nature of the marriage with mutual denial of resentment or hostility. With improvement
in the patient, the spouses displayed the first observable signs of psychopathology.

LaBARRE, W., "The Biosocial Unity of the Family," in N. W. Ackerman, F. L. Beatman, and
        S. Sherman (Eds.), Exploring the Base for Family Therapy, New York, Family Service
        Association of America, 1961.
A clinical essay by an anthropologist on the role of the family. The nuclear family is
a "human universal," which is not culturally contingent, but rather biologically fundamental. All attempts at therapy, including individual psychotherapy, are essentially
restructuring of the family.

LAING, R. D., "Mystification, Confusion and Conflict," in I. Boszormenyi-Nagy and J. L.
        Framo (Eds.), Intensive Family Therapy, New York, Harper & Row, 1965.
The theoretical schema of Marx — where the exploiter mystifies with a plausible misrep-
resentation of what is going on with the exploited — is applied to the family of the
schizophrenic. The act of mystifying and the state of being mystified are described with
case examples. The therapist's task is to help such a person become demystified.

LAING, R. D., and ESTERSON, A., Sanity, Madness and the Family, Vol. I, Families of
        Schizophrenics, London, Tavistock, 1964.
A book describing a research project investigating 11 families in which the identified
patient was a female schizophrenic. The data were obtained from clinical interviews
with family members both individually and together. "The behavior of schizophrenics is
much more socially intelligible than has come to be supposed by most psychiatrists."
Rather than indicating an illness, the symptoms are seen as a "strategy" invented by
the person to live in an "unlivable" situation. 272 pp.

LAING, R. D.,"PHILLIPSON, H., and LEE, A., Interpersonal Perception: A Theory and a
        Method of Research, London, Tavistock, 1966.
A research project oriented toward understanding interaction of two persons. It includes sections on self and other; interaction and interexperience in dyads; the spiral
of reciprocal perspective; historical view of the method; the interpersonal perception
methods (IPM); disturbed and nondisturbed marriages; study of a dyad; developments;
and the IPM questions. 179 pp.

LANGSLEY, D., and KAPLAN, D., The Treatment of Families in Crisis, New York, Grune &
        Stratton, 1968.
A report of a research project in which family crisis therapy was offered as an alternative to psychiatric hospitalization. Rationale, techniques of therapy, data on the
patients, and results and implications are presented. 184 pp.

LAQUEUR, H. P., "General Systems Theory and Multiple Family Therapy," in W. Gray, F.
     Duhl, and N. Rizzo (Eds.), General Systems Theory and Psychiatry, Boston, Little,
     Brown, 1969.
A discussion of multiple family therapy from the point of view of systems theory. The
general theoretical base for multiple family therapy is offered within this framework.

LAQUEUR, H. P., "Multiple Family Therapy and General Systems Theory," in N. W. Ackerman
     (Ed.), Family Therapy in Transition, Boston, Little, Brown, 1970.
The family from the point of view of general systems theory with the emphasis upon treating groups of families. Theory and technique are described with examples.

LAQUEUR, H. P., "Multiple Family Therapy and General Systems Theory," Int. Psychiat.
     Clin., 7, 99-124, 1970.
A discussion of multiple family therapy using the concepts of general systems theory.
The family and its components are viewed as subsystems of a larger field of interre-
lations whose interface problems can be studied and dealt with.

LEBOVICI, S., "The Psychoanalytic Theory of the Family," in E. J. Anthony and C. Kouper-
     nik (Eds.), The Child in His Family, New York, Wiley, 1970.
The psychoanalytic view of a child's development in his family and his fantasy life.

LEHRMAN, N. S., "Anarchy, Dictatorship, and Democracy Within the Family: A Biosocial
     Hierarchy," Psychiat. Quart., 36, 455-474, 1962.
An essay in which the author proposes "that the backbone of the family structure in most
human societies, including our own, is basically a linear hierarchy of roles arranged
along the ordinal of intrafamilial power." The hierarchy is headed by father followed
by mother, followed by children in order of birth. A discussion of roles and of types
of families is also presented.

LENNARD, H., and BERNSTEIN, A., Patterns in Human Interaction, San Francisco, Jossey-
     Bass, 1969.
A textbook on "clinical sociology" which discusses interaction processes, methodological
problems in describing interaction processes, interaction patterns in the family, psychotherapeutic interaction, and functions of human interaction. Patterns of schizophrenic
and control families are described. 224 pp.

LESLIE, G. R., and JOHNSON, K. P., "Changed Perceptions of the Maternal Role," Amer. So-
     ciol. Rev., 28, 919-928, 1963.
The generalization that child-rearing methods have become more permissive is questioned
and several hypotheses relating changed perceptions to the normative patterns receiving
authoritative support in that generation, the amount of exposure to the normative pattern at the time the mother role is being enacted, and the explicitness of the norms
associated with various areas of child-rearing are set forth. Questionnaire data from
297 of 418 woman graduates of the 1949 class of a Midwestern university covered their
own and their mothers' practices in several areas: sex and modesty training, aggression toward mother, and the encouragement of self-direction. Predictions are confirmed,
thus raising questions about the true nature of change and validity of generalizing from
one aspect of the maternal role to another.

LEVINGER, G., "Marital Cohesiveness and Dissolution: An Integrative Review," in P. H.
     Glasser and L. N. Glasser (Eds.), Families in Crisis, New York, Harper & Row, 1970.
A discussion of cohesiveness in marriage as a special case of group cohesiveness in general. The framework is based upon two components: attractions toward or repulsions
from a relationship, and barriers against its dissolution. Includes a review of factors associated with divorce.

LEVINGER, G., "Supplementary Methods in Family Research," Fam. Proc., 2, 357-366, 1963.
A review of methods in family research with a comparison of subjective report and objective observation, with a discussion of their strengths and weaknesses. A study is reported of 31 families who were studied with both observation and self-report. The results

showed gross correspondence between the two methods and it is suggested that both procedures should be used since they supplement each other.

LEVINGER, G., "Task and Social Behavior in Marriage," Sociometry, 27, 433-448, 1964.
This study hypothesized that in a family, "task-behavior" (designated as subject-object activity) is specialized, while "social behavior" (designated as subject-subject
activity) is mutual. Sample is 60 middle-class couples with children, interviewed
clinically (separately and together) and performing together on several tasks: a vocabulary test, a color symbol test, and an adaptation of the Wechsler-Bellevue Digit-
Symbol Test. Social-behavior performance is the essence of marital relations as seen
by both spouses and it is mutual, rather than specialized.

LIDZ, T., "The Family as the Developmental Setting," in E. J. Anthony and C. Koupernik
     (Eds.), The Child in His Family, New York, Wiley, 1970.
A description of child development in terms of the family with the emphasis upon the
parental nurturant function, the dynamic organization of the family, the social roles
learned in the family and the parental transmition of the culture.

LIDZ, T., The Family and Human Adaption, New York, International Universities Press, 1963.
A collection of three lectures dealing with the role of the family in normal development,
the role of the family in a changing society, and specific requisites for successful family functioning: the parents' ability to form a coalition, maintain boundaries between
generations, and adhere to their appropriate sex-linked role. Finally, the author covers the family's capacity to transmit the basic adaptive techniques of the culture by
means of communication. Failures in these functions are explored in terms of an etiologic theory for schizophrenia. 120 pp.

LIDZ, T., "The Psychoanalytic Theory of Development and Maldevelopment: Recapitulation,"
     Amer. J. Psychoanal., 27, 115-127, 1967.
An attempt to integrate both psychoanalytic and family concepts in developing a theory
of normal family functioning and malfunctioning. "When the family organization is dis-
urbed, there can be a multiplicity of ways in which things can go wrong." However when
the parents can form a coalition, the child "can develop a reasonably firm and satisfac-
tory gender identity."

LIDZ, T., CORNELISON, A., FLECK, S., and TERRY, D., "Intrafamilial Environment of Schizo-
     phrenic Patients. II. Marital Schism and Marital Skew," Amer. J. Psychiat., 114,
     241-248, 1957.
A study of the intrafamilial environment of the schizophrenic patient. In this study of
14 families, eight were split in two factions by "overt schism between the parents."
Thus the identified patient cannot use one parent as a model for identification or as a
love object without losing the support of the other parent. The other six families were
"skewed" (defined as psychopathology in the dominant parent) which was accepted or shared
by the other without trying to change it. Case examples are given.

LIDZ, T., CORNELISON, A., TERRY, D., and FLECK, S., "Intrafamilial Environment of the
     Schizophrenic Patient. VI. The Transmission of Irrationality," Arch. Neurol.
     Psychiat., 79, 305-316, 1958.
A study of families of schizophrenics in which nine of the 15 patients had at least one
parent who could be called schizophrenic. Their "irrational" behavior was transmitted
through disturbed communication to the children who were reared in intrafamilial systems of communication which distort or deny reality. The implications of these findings
in terms of the etiology of schizophrenia are discussed.

LIDZ, T., and FLECK, S., "Some Explored and Partially Explored Sources of Psychopatholo-
     gy," in G. H. Zuk and I. Boszormenyi-Nagy (Eds.), Family Therapy and Disturbed Fa-
     milies, Palo Alto, Science & Behavior Books, 1967.
An essay on the problem of how the infant develops as a person in relation to significant
family members and the family as a social system. Six sources of psychopathological development in offspring are presented.

LIDZ, T., FLECK, S., and CORNELISON, A. R., <u>Schizophrenia and the Family</u>, New York,
     International Universities Press, 1965.
A collection of new material and previously published articles by the Yale research
group concerning their investigations of the intrafamilial environment in which schizophrenic patients grow up. It includes the rationale for the study, some articles on
the family environment of schizophrenic patients, a number of articles on the 17 study
families (including aspects of casework techniques, family interaction the hospital
staff, familial dynamics, and psychological testing), and the implications of this
data for a new theory of schizophrenia based on a disturbed intrafamilial environment.
There is also a section documenting the type of thought disorder found in families with
schizophrenic patients as seen on the object sorting test. There is an extensive bibliography. 477 pp.

LINDSAY, J., "The Structure Within Groups," <u>Brit. J. Soc. Clin. Psychol.</u>, 6, 195-203,
     1967.
An analysis of a group therapy session with the emphasis upon the formal characteristics of the sequences in the conversation. "Without any concern with the content of
the conversation, it has been possible to demonstrate significant dyadic, triadic, and
other multiple person situations, and of the effect of the therapist's remarks and of
silences."

LINDSAY, J., "Types of Family and Family Types," <u>Fam. Proc.</u>, 7, 51-66, 1968.
A discussion of the application of the theory of logical types to family descriptions.
Confusions between the monad, the dyad, and the triad are described and a hypothesis
for schizophrenia is presented.

LITWAK, E., "Geographic Mobility and Family Cohesion," <u>Amer. Sociol. Rev.</u>, 25, 385-394,
     1960.
A second paper reporting a study of the families of 920 married white women living in
a middle-class urban area. Several hypotheses about the relationship of identification
with extended kin and occupational mobility are tested. The data indicate that extended
families do not hinder, but rather aid geographical, and hence, occupational mobility.

LOMAS, P., (Ed.), <u>The Predicament of the Family</u>, New York, International University Press,
     1967.
A collection of new material oriented toward psychoanalytic concepts of the family.
There are articles on family relationships in contemporary society; mirror-role of mother and family in child development; family interaction and adolescent therapy; the
family pattern of distress; simultaneous analysis of mother and child; the family and
individual structure; and a study of marriage as a critical transition for personality
and family development. 219 pp.

LUSTIG, N., DRESSEN, J., SPELLMAN, S., and MURRAY, T., "Incest," <u>Arch. Gen. Psychiat.</u>,
     14, 31-41, 1966.
Family constellations in six cases of father-daughter incest are reported. Data were
gathered from clinical interviews with the families. From the cases and from reviewing
the literature, intrapsychic and transactional dynamics are hypothesized which contribute to choice of father-daughter incest as a family defense. Incest is seen as a
"tension reducing defence within a dysfunctional family serving to maintain the integrity of the family unit."

MABREY, J. H., "Medicine and the Family," in P. H. Glasser and L. N. Glasser (Eds.),
     <u>Families in Crisis</u>, New York, Harper & Row, 1970.
A consideration of family relationships in the promotion of health and the treatment
of illness. Topics include medicine and family functioning; the family as a unit in
medical care; and the family's nursing function.

MacGREGOR, R., "Each Family Member Experiences a Different Environment," in I. H. Cohen
     (Ed.), <u>Psychiatric Research Report No. 20</u>, American Psychiatric Association, 1966.
A view of the family emphasizing the basic notion that much of psychiatric illness can

be viewed as an arrest in development of a family unit. Four types of families have
been diagnosed: those with infantile, childish, juvenile, and preadolescent functioning.

MacGREGOR, R., "The Family Constellation from the Standpoint of Various Siblings," in
     O. Pollak and A. S. Friedman (Eds.), Family Dynamics and Female Sexual Delinquency,
     Palo Alto, Science & Behavior Books, 1969.
A typology of families in relation to delinquency with case illustrations.

MACHOTKA, P., PITTMAN, F. S., III, and FLOMENHAFT, K., "Incest as a Family Affair," Fam.
     Proc., 6, 98-116, 1967.
A discussion of incest from the point of view of the whole family. Two cases of father-
daughter incest and one of sibling incest are discussed with the emphasis upon the crucial role of the nonparticipating member, the concerted denial of the incest, and where
the focus of therapy should be.

MASSERMAN, J. (Ed.), Science and Psychoanalysis, Vol. II: Individual and Family Dynamics,
     New York, Grune & Stratton, 1959.
In this book there is a section on familial and social dynamics. Included are papers on
survey of trends and research in the practice of family therapy, psychoanalytic approaches to the family, family homeostasis, family dynamics in schizophrenia, cultural aspects
of transference and countertransference, techniques of family therapy, and a panel discussion and review on the family. 218 pp.

MAYER, J. E., "People's Imagery of Other Families, Fam. Proc., 6, 27-36, 1967.
A discussion of the ways people's ideas about other families significantly affect their
familial relationships. The emphasis is upon the need for research in this area and a
classification scheme.

MEISSNER, W. W., "Family Dynamics and Psychosomatic Processes," Fam. Proc., 5, 142-161,
     1966.
A discussion of the impact of patterns of family interaction on patterns of physical
health and illness, with a review of the literature.

MEISSNER, W. W., "Thinking About the Family: Psychiatric Aspects," Fam. Proc., 3, 1-40,
     1964.
A review of the ideas and the literature produced by the shift from individual orientation to a specifically family-centered orientation. The family studies are reviewed in
terms of what has been said about mothers, fathers, parental interaction, and total family constellations. The ideas of the major research groups are presented and analyzed.
A bibliography of 135 references is included.

MENDELL, D., and CLEVELAND, S., "A Three-Generation View of a School Phobia," Voices,
     3, 16-19, 1967.
A case report in support of the notion that psychopathology is "passed on from generation to generation with a more or less specific way and expectation of handling it."
Three generations of data from the identified patient (a 14-year-old boy), his mother,
and maternal grandmother were obtained from clinical psychiatric interviews and the
Rorschach and thematic apperception tests. School phobia of the identified patient
is seen as an attempt to answer the obsessive concern of a boy's relationship to his
mother and her relationship to her mother.

MENDELL, D., CLEVELAND, S., and FISHER, S., "A Five-Generation Family Theme," Fam. Proc.,
     7, 126-132, 1968.
A study examining projective test fantasies of family members. Five generations of one
family, including examination of 27 members, were conducted. It was found that a family
selects one or two central themes which are perpetuated in the responses of family members across generations.

MILLER, D. R., and WESTMAN, J. C., "Family Teamwork and Psychotherapy," Fam. Proc., 5,
    49-59, 1966.
A discussion of primary questions about etiology and treatment developed in a study of
functional retardation in reading. In one type of reading difficulty the problem can
be explained by poor teaching or traumatic experiences, and in the other there is a
function in the family. The roots of the symptom in family relationships is described
with an emphasis upon family teamwork in maintaining the difficulty.

MINUCHIN, S., "Family Therapy: Technique or Theory?," in J. Masserman (Ed.), Science
    and Psychoanalysis, Vol. XIV, Childhood and Adolescence, New York, Grune & Strat-
    ton, 1969.
A discussion of family therapy with the emphasis upon the need to take into account the
total ecology of the family. "I think that family therapy...will be in danger of ossi-
fication if it fails to move towards an ecological theory of man."

MINUCHIN, S., "The Use of an Ecological Framework in the Treatment of a Child," in E.
    J. Anthony and C. Koupernik (Eds.), The Child in His Family, New York, Wiley, 1970.
A discussion of the three elements in the study of the child: as an individual, in his
environment, and the linkage between the two. A case of an adolescent with anorexia nervosa is dealt with in terms of his family and the family therapy approach to the problem.

MINUCHIN, S., MONTALVO, B., BUERNEY, B. G., ROSMAN, B. L., and SHUMER, F., Families of
    the Slums: An Exploration of Their Structure and Treatment, New York, Basic Books,
    1967.
A book on a research project dealing with family treatment of low socioeconomic-class
families where the identified patient was delinquent. Research strategy, rationale,
dynamics, techniques, and assessment of results are presented. 460 pp.

MISHLER, E., and WAXLER, N., "Family Interaction Processes and Schizophrenia," Int. J.
    Psychiat., 2, 375-430, 1966.
A critical and extensive review of the theories of the relationship between family interaction and schizophrenia, with major space devoted to the work of the Bateson, Lidz,
and Wynne groups. The purpose of the review was to see how the theories could be tested and used as guidelines for research. The major contributions of these groups are
to the theory of the etiology of schizophrenia, by focussing on the family and its methods of interactions, rather than on the individual. Critical evaluations by Bateson,
Lidz, Spiegel, and Wynne of the article and the various theories contained in it are
included.

MISHLER, E., and WAXLER, N., (Eds.), Family Process and Schizophrenia, New York, Science
    House, 1968.
A collection of previously published articles which includes discussions of current
theories; experimental studies; parents of the schizophrenic; dyadic interaction; parents with a schizophrenic child: pathogenic triad; parent and sibling: the family
tetrad; and finally, commentaries, which is a discussion by four family therapy theoreticians on the articles. 323 pp.

MORRIS, G., and WYNNE, L., "Schizophrenic Offspring, Parental Styles of Communication,"
    Psychiatry, 28, 19-44, 1965.
One of series of papers reporting a study of parental styles of communication and schizophrenic children. Data were selected from excerpts of transcripts of conjoint family
sessions with 12 families. Predictions about the most disturbed offspring were made
by a judge blind to the clinical aspects of the case. Predictive criteria were then
reformulated using the data from a parallel study utilizing psychological test material
as predictors. These reformulated criteria were then utilized for blind predictions on
eight new families. Results indicated that the style of the family communication can be
related to the thought and affect disorder in schizophrenics.

MURRELL, S., and STACHOWIAK, J., "The Family Group: Development, Structure, and Therapy," J. Marr. Fam., 27, 13-18, 1965.
From the literature, authors' previous experience, and previous research, a theory of
the family is presented. Assumptions in terms of therapy are discussed. Families are
viewed as being unable to problem-solve and as resistant to change.

NIMKOFF, M. F., and MIDDLETON, R., "Types of Family and Types of Economy," Amer. J.
   Sociol., 66, 215-225, 1961.
The relationship between family types and subsistence patterns is explored with reference
to 549 societies in the World Ethnographic Survey. Two family types — the independent
(normally only one nuclear or polygamous family) and the extended (whether laterally,
vertically, or both), and 11 subsistence types (e.g., hunting and gathering dominant,
agriculture dominant) are distinguished. The independent family is found to be associated with hunting and the extended family with agriculture. The associations are
accounted for in terms of food supply, demand for family labor, physical mobility and
property.

OPLER, M. K., "Social and Cultural Influences on the Psychopathology of Family Groups,"
   in G. H. Zuk and I. Boszormenyi-Nagy (Eds.), Family Therapy and Disturbed Families,
   Palo Alto, Science & Behavior Books, 1967.
An essay considering the social context of the family as related to mental health.
Examples from different cultures are given.

OTTO, H. A., "Criteria for Assessing Family Strength," Fam. Proc., 2, 329-339, 1963.
A discussion of family strengths and resources with the data collected by questionnaire.
Twenty-seven families were queried. Married couples met for group discussions on family
strengths. A set of criteria for assessing family strengths is offered.

PARSONS, A., "Family Dynamics in South Italian Schizophrenics," Arch. Gen. Psychiat., 3,
   507-518, 1960.
If family factors play an etiological role in schizophrenia, comparative studies of the
family background of schizophrenics in different cultures is important. After observation of south Italian patients in the United States, a sample of 25 patients hospitalized
in public hospitals in Naples and vicinity was investigated. Patterns in the families
are described in terms of exclusive dyads, imbedded dyads, competitive and unstable situations, and isolates. Comparing pathological family constellations in different cultures
the taboo areas are important, and the problem of differentiating the normal from the
pathological must be resolved. "We would doubt that these problems can ever be resolved
in a framework in which any particular set of social values or conditions is considered
as inherently schizogenic."

PARSONS, T., and BALES, R. F., Family, Socialization and Interaction Process, Glencoe,
   Free Press, 1955.
A collection of papers organized around the family and its relation to personality development, social structure, child socialization, role differentiation in a nuclear
family and small groups, and the role of the family in the general culture.

PENISTON, D. H., "The Importance of 'Death Education' in Family Life," Fam. Life Coord.,
   11, 15-18, 1962.
A discussion by a pastor of the need to educate families for preparation for a possible
death in the family. Includes discussions of death as a taboo area like sex; disruption of family life caused by death; and the importance of preparing professional men
to deal wisely with bereaved families.

POLLAK, O., "Developmental Difficulties and the Family System," in O. Pollak and A.S.
   Friedman (Eds.), Family Dynamics and Female Sexual Delinquency, Palo Alto, Science
   & Behavior Books, 1969.
A discussion of the development and growth of family members as a person moves from the
family unit in which he is born, to the family he creates through marriage, to the family
of his children to which he eventually relates as a dependent.

POLLAK, O., "Family Structure: Its Implications for Mental Health," in O. Pollak and
    A. S. Friedman (Eds.),Family Dynamics and Female Sexual Delinquency, Palo Alto,
    Science & Behavior Books, 1969.
A discussion of the implications for mental health of various types of family structure.
Compared are middle-class families, fatherless families, and three-generation families.

POLLAK, O., and FRIEDMAN, A. (Eds.), Family Dynamics and Female Sexual Delinquency,
    Palo Alto, Science & Behavior Books, 1968.
A collection of new material and previously published articles on sexual delinquency
which includes articles on family theory, socioeconomic and cultural factors, and
family therapy applications. 210 pp.

PRINCE, A. J., "A Study of 194 Cross-Religion Marriages," Fam. Life Coord., 11, 3-7, 1962.
A report on a study of 142 interfaith marriages and 52 marriages between protestants of
different denominations. Data were obtained with questionnaires. Topics of interest
are cross-religion marriages, major areas of conflict, changes in church attendance
patterns, degree of satisfaction with marriage, and attitudes about cross-religion
marriages for children.

PULVER, S. E., and BRUNT, M. Y., "Deflection of Hostility in Folie à Deux," Arch. Gen.
    Psychiat., 5, 257-265, 1961.
Three cases are presented to illustrate a description of the psychodynamics of the
transfer of delusions. The partners are divided into the primary and secondary with
the primary partner strongly dependent upon the secondary. As the primary partner
begins to feel taken advantage of and increasingly angry, his anger against the secondary partner is projected onto an outsider as paranoid delusion. When the secondary
partner does not support the delusion, the direct hostility toward the secondary partner becomes intolerable and the secondary partner deflects it by accepting the delusion and joining in the projection.

RABKIN, R., Inner and Outer Space, New York, Norton, 1970.
A book on social psychiatry with the emphasis on the shift from the inner space of the
individual to social organisms. 215 pp.

RABKIN, R., "Uncoordinated Communication Between Marriage Partners," Fam. Proc., 6.
    10-15, 1967.
A discussion of communication codes unique to particular family systems. Examples of
couples' problems in developing mutual codes are given.

RAPOPORT, R., "The Family and Psychiatric Treatment," Psychiatry, 23, 53-62, 1960.
A conceptual framework for analyzing family relationships and role performance of
psychiatric patients applied to a case. Three areas are considered important in conceptualizing role difficulties: familial position, personal and social norms, and
personality factors. This framework is applied to a case presented in detail.

RAVICH, R. A., "A System of Dyadic Interaction," Fam. Proc., 9, 297-300, 1970.
A description of a notation for two-person interaction based upon the I Ching, or Book
of Changes.

RICHARDSON, H. B., "A Family as Seen in the Hospital," in P. H. Glasser and L. N. Glas-
    ser (Eds.), Families in Crisis, New York, Harper & Row, 1970.
Families who are involved with a medical hospital are studied from various points of
view. The family is discussed as seen by staff, the records, the patient, and the
conversation of individual family members.

RIESS, F. B. (Ed.), New Directions in Mental Health, Vol. I, New York, Grune & Stratton, 1968.
A collection of articles on various psychiatric topics including papers on practice of family treatment in kibbutz and urban child guidance clinics; short-term analytic treatment of married couples in a group by a therapist couple; the therapeutic field in the treatment of families in conflict; recurrent themes in literature and clinical practice; and patterns of interaction in families of borderline patients. 320 pp.

RISKIN, J., "Family Interaction Scales: A Preliminary Report," Arch. Gen. Psychiat., 11, 484-494, 1964.
A report on a research project where nine families were given a structured interview and the conversation categorized. Two minute segments of the conversation are categorized by the coder as clear, change of topic, commitment, and so on. An attempt is then made to describe the family from the coding sheets blindly. "Results suggest that it is possible to make clinically meaningful and accurate descriptions of the whole family and of its various members based on the coded speeches and without focussing on the content."

RISKIN, J., "Methodology for Studying Family Interaction," Arch. Gen. Psychiat., 8, 343-348, 1963.
A report of a pilot study with five families designed to develop a conceptual framework, including methods for investigating the relationship between family interaction and personality formation. Family members are brought together in standardized structured interviews with the tape recorded conversations analyzed by a set of categories which include clarity, content, agreement, commitment, congruency, intensity, and attack or acceptance of the other person.

ROSENBAUM, C. P., "Patient-Family Similarities in Schizophrenia," Arch. Gen. Psychiat., 5, 120-126, 1961.
A discussion of the family of the schizophrenic based upon conjoint interviews with such families on several research projects. It is suggested that the disordered thinking and interpersonal relations of the schizophrenic have recognized counterparts in his family. Such primary symptoms of schizophrenia as disorders of association, selective inattention, and ambivalence, as described by Bleuler, are compared with similar thought patterns in the family, and illustrated with case material. A review and synthesis is made of research in the field of the schizophrenic family with the emphasis upon the appropriateness of schizophrenic symptoms in this context.

ROSENTHAL, D., The Genian Quadruplets — A Case Study and Theoretical Analysis of Heredity and Environment in Schizophrenia, New York, Basic Books, 1963.
A case study in schizophrenia of a family in which quadruplets were schizophrenic. The book is divided into sections dealing with the case history, tests and studies dealing with basic characteristics in response processes, projective tests and their analysis, systematic analysis of observations of the family by the research staff and the community, conceptualization of the family members in their interrelationships, and finally a theoretical analysis of the heredity-environment problem in schizophrenia. 609 pp.

ROSENTHAL, M. J., NI, E., FINKELSTEIN, M., and BERKWITZ, G. K., "Father-Child Relationships and Children's Problems," Arch. Gen. Psychiat., 7, 360-373, 1962.
A group of 405 new patients coming into the Institute for Juvenile Research in Chicago were examined to determine whether the emotional problems of children were related to certain types of father-child relationships. The relationship was examined by interviews with parents and children. Certain of the children's problems were found to be correlated with types of father-child relationships being studied while others were not.

RUTTER, M., "Sex Differences in Children's Responses to Family Stress," in E. J. Anthony and C. Koupernik (Eds.), The Child in His Family, New York, Wiley, 1970.
A questionnaire study investigating the impact on the child of marital problems and parental psychiatric disorders. Antisocial behavior in boys is associated with disturbance in family relationships, but the marriage rating bore no relation to the rate of disorder in girls. Theoretical discussion is offered.

RYLE, A., Neurosis in the Ordinary Family: A Psychiatric Survey, London, Tavistock, 1967.
A report of the author's study of the psychiatric health and personal relationships of
112 working-class families with children of primary school age. The study was done
while the author was a general practitioner. The book covers the methods of collecting
data, social circumstances and characteristics of the population, parents' childhood,
parents' psychodynamics, their parents' marriages, child rearing practices and their
relation to other parental attributes, psychological disturbances in the children, parental factors associated with the disturbance in the children, family diagnosis, consultation and treatment, and evaluation and conclusions. 153 pp.

SAFILIOS-ROTHSCHILD, C., "Deviance and Mental Illness in the Greek Family," Fam. Proc.,
     7, 100-117, 1968.
A study of spouses of hospitalized mental patients in Greece to determine attitudes about
deviance and mental illness. The defining of behavior as deviant will depend upon cultural definitions. Whether the deviance is defined as mental illness depends upon
other factors. Here the "degree of marital satisfaction seems to be the determining
factor as to whether or not the normal spouse will..." label the deviance as mental
illness.

SANDER, F. M., "Family Therapy or Religion: A Re-Reading of T.S. Eliot's The Cocktail
     Party," Fam. Proc., 9, 279-296, 1970.
An analysis of the play, The Cocktail Party, from the view of analytic sociology, emphasizing family therapy as a response to changes in the structure of contemporary families.

SANUA, V., "The Sociocultural Aspects of Childhood Schizophrenia," in G. H. Zuk and I.
     Boszormenyi-Nagy (Eds.), Family Therapy and Disturbed Families, Palo Alto, Science
     & Behavior Books, 1967.
A discussion of methodological issues, research strategies, and the problems inherent in
studying parent-child relationships and interaction as an etiological factor in schizophrenia. Includes a review of the literature.

SANUA, V., "Sociocultural Factors in Families of Schizophrenics: A Review of the Litera-
     ture," Psychiatry, 24, 246-265, 1961.
A review of the literature on the etiology of schizophrenia. Problems and methodology
are looked at and the literature is discussed from the point of view of data from hospital records, from separate interviews with patients and families, from interviews of
families together, from studies using personality tests, from questionnaires and rating
scales, and from studies using the cross-cultural approach. All these studies boil down
to looking at the problem one of four ways: (1) parental troubles transmitted to the
children, (2) family structure, (3) disturbed interactional patterns, and (4) genetic
and constitutional factors in the child.

SATIR, V. M., "The Family as a Treatment Unit," Confin. Psychiat., 8, 37-42, 1965.
A discussion of family therapy with the emphasis on concepts of interaction. The family
is discussed as a closed and open system and "appropriate outcomes" for the family are
said to be "decisions and behavior which fit the age, ability, and role of the individuals, which fit the role contracts and the context involved, and which further the common
goals of the family."

SATIR, V., "Family Systems and Approaches to Family Therapy," J. Fort Logan Ment. Health
     Center, 4, 81-93, 1967.
An essay focussing on development of the concept of the family as a system. How it functions and what happens when the family system breaks down are discussed.

SCHEFLEN, A. E., "Regressive One-To-One Relationships," Psychiat. Quart., 34, 692-709,
     1960.
A description of regressive attachments between two individuals. The characteristics
of these "gruesome twosomes" are: limitations of relatedness to others, decreasing
gratification within the relationships, and the maintenance of the attachment by mutual
exploitation of the partner's anxieties by such means as threats of desertion and arousal of guilt. Several variations of this type of relationship are presented and illus-

trated with four case histories involving differing sex and age combinations. There
is a discussion of differentiating between neurotic and non-neurotic one-to-one relationships.

SHERZ, F., "The Crisis of Adolescence in Family Life," Soc. Casework, 48, 209-215, 1967.
Adolescence is seen as a time of crisis for the family in addition to the patient.
When behavioral symptoms appear, family treatment is indicated. The influence of grand-
parents in the chain of family communication is discussed.

SCOTT, R., "Perspectives on the American Family Studies in Schizophrenia," Confin. Psy-
     chiat., 8, 43-48, 1965.
A review of the American literature on family studies of schizophrenia with questions
and criticisms. There is a selective bias in leaving out family histories of schizophrenics and focussing on interactional aspects. The concept of the double bind is
questioned and explained.

SHAPIRO, R. L., "The Origin of Adolescent Disturbances in the Family: Some Considera-
     tions in Theory and Implications for Therapy," in G. H. Zuk and I. Boszormenyi-
     Nagy (Eds.), Family Therapy and Disturbed Families, Palo Alto, Science & Behavior
     Books, 1967.
The study of the current family relations of the adolescent helps to identify the nature of determinants in his developmental experience. Verbatim excerpts from interviews are presented and therapeutic design is discussed.

SHERMAN, S., BEATMAN, F. L., and ACKERMAN, N. W., "Concepts of Family Striving and
     Family Distress: The Contribution of M. Robert Gomberg," Soc. Casework, 39,
     383-391, 1958.
A review of the ideas of M. Robert Gomberg with emphasis upon his writings on family
process, family stability and instability, and therapeutic intervention.

SHOHAN, S., and RAHAV, G., "Social Stigma and Prostitution," Ana. Int.de Criminolog.,
     6, 479-513, 1967.
An attempt to relate the "stigma theory of crime and deviation to the etiology of prostitution in authoritarian oriental families." The population examined are the Jewish
North-African immigrants to Israel and the conclusion is that "the processes of differential identification and association leading the girl to a full-fledged life of
prostitution are the final stages of a dynamic process initiated by the girl's com-
pliance with a stigmatizing role cast on her within the family."

SLUZKI, C., "Transactional Disqualification: Research on the Double Bind," Arch. Gen.
     Psychiat., 16, 494-504, 1967.
One of a series of papers connected with a research project on communication in families
with schizophrenic patients. Transactional disqualification is a form of communication
in which the subject can verbally or nonverbally deny the previous communication. This
kind of persistent relating can lead to schizophrenic symptoms.

SLUZKI, C., and BEAVIN, J., "Simetria y Complementariada: Una Definición Operacional
     y Una Tipologia de Parejas," Acta Psiquiat. Psicolog. Amer. Lat., 11, 321-330, 1965.
A discussion of classifying relationships in terms of symmetry and complementarity,
with a review of the literature on the subject. The variables are operationally defined and a speech score is derived based upon analysis of the transactional unit. A
typology of couples and other dyads is proposed composed of seven possible configurations based upon these modalities of interaction.

SONNE, J. C., "Entropy and Family Therapy: Speculations on Psychic Energy, Thermodynam-
     ics, and Family Interpsychic Communication," in G. H. Zuk and I. Boszormenyi-Nagy
     (Eds.), Family Therapy and Disturbed Families, Palo Alto, Science & Behavior Books,
     1967.
An attempt to link together concepts from the physical sciences with observations of
schizophrenic families in treatment with special emphasis upon the concept of entropy.

SORRELLS, J., and FORD, F., "Toward an Integrated Theory of Families, and Family Therapy,"
    Psychotherapy, 6, 150-160, 1969.
A theoretical paper describing a theory of family functioning and family treatment.
All family members have self-needs, self-want and self-concepts. The family operates
in a system using certain communication devices which maintain a homeostasis. Concepts
of status quo, decision-making autonomy and distortion of feedback are discussed. Techniques of treatment including making the contract, diagnosis, interventions, and goals
are discussed.

SPARK, G. M., and BRODY, E. M., "The Aged are Family Members," Fam. Proc., 9, 195-210,
    1970.
A discussion of the involvement of older family members and the important roles they
play in family dynamics. Including them in treatment can prevent cyclical repetition
of pathological relationship patterns.

SPECK, R., "Family Therapy in the Home," J. Marriage Fam., 26, 72-76, 1964.
An essay based on the author's clinical experience in doing family therapy in the home.
Advantages of this technique are discussed and several new phenomena are described:
the absent member, the most disturbed family member, the youngest member, the role of
pets, the extended family, and family secrets.

SPECK, R., and ATTNEAVE, C., "Network Therapy," in J. Haley (Ed.), Changing Families,
    New York, Grune & Stratton, 1971.
A report on"network therapy" where all of the significant people of a natural group are
brought together in relation to a problem. The theory, practice, techniques, and effects of assembling the "tribe" are described.

SPEER, D. C., "Family Systems: Morphostasis and Morphogenesis, or 'Is Homeostasis
    Enough?'" Fam. Proc., 9, 259-278, 1970.
It is argued that homeostasis is insufficient as a basic explanatory principle for
family systems. The needs for considering positive feedback processes and variety
are emphasized.

SPIEGEL, J., "Interpersonal Influence Within the Family," in B. Schaffner (Ed.), Group
    Processes: Transactions of the Third Conference, New York, Josiah Macy, Jr. Foun-
    dation, 1956.
A group discussion of the findings from the author's research project (which had been
previously reported in a series of papers) of an interdisciplinary study of the effects
of conflicts between cultural-value orientations of the processes of interaction within
the family, and consequently the development of health or pathology of the individual
members of the family. There are discussions of normal and pathological equilibrium
in the family and a classification of social roles.

SPIEGEL, J., "Mental Health and the Family," New Eng. J. Med., 251, 843-846, 1954.
"Complex psychological, social, and somatic forces are interwoven in the dynamics of
family adjustment." Family dynamics and a model of family relationships are discussed.

SPIEGEL, J., "New Perspectives in the Study of the Family," Marriage Fam. Liv., 16, 4-
    12, 1954.
A clinical essay attempting to formulate a dynamic model for understanding the whole
family rather than individuals. There are marked value clashes and role conflicts
within variant families that are in transition towards the dominant middle-class model.
Family dynamics as well as individual dynamics must be taken into account to understand
families. More information on values, and role and value conflicts encountered in
various family systems are also needed.

SPIEGEL, J., "The Resolution of Role Conflict Within the Family," Psychiatry, 20, 1-16,
    1957.
An offshoot of a study between cultural value conflict and the emotional adjustment of

the identified patient, this essay analyzes the concept of social role and its relation
to the functional or dysfunctional behavior in the family. "Equilibrium — disequilibrium balance and its relationship to role" is examined, as well as how role modification is achieved. Disequilibrium can lead to symptoms in the patient.

SPIEGEL, J., "Some Cultural Aspects of Transference and Counter-Transference," in J.
      Masserman (Ed.), Science and Psychoanalysis, Vol. II, Individual and Family Dy-
      namics, New York, Grune & Stratton, 1959.
A clinical essay based on work with "working-class" Irish-American, Italian-American, and
so-called "old American" families from two groups. The first were "well" families; the second were "sick" families. Data were gathered from clinic visits as well as home visits.
Countertransference difficulties vary as to the cultural population. Having an entire
family involved helps break the impasse that often develops. The family and the community
are seen as important variables in the functioning of an individual.

SPIEGEL, J., and BELL, N., "The Family of the Psychiatric Patient," in S. Arieti (Ed.),
      American Handbook of Psychiatry, New York, Basic Books, 1959.
A chapter in a textbook on psychiatry dealing with sections on the history of the role
of the family in mental illness; etiologic studies of parent-child interactions and development of various mental illnesses including schizophrenia, psychoneurosis, and acting-out disorders; the impact of mental illness upon the family; the family and treatment procedures; and new approaches to the family and its pathology, including family
therapy. There are 238 references.

STACHOWIAK, J., "Decision-Making and Conflict Resolution in the Family Group," in C.
      Larson and F. Dance (Eds.), Perspectives on Communication, Milwaukee, Speech Com-
      munication Center, University of Wisconsin, 1968.
The author discusses his previous research summarizing major findings on: (1) family
productivity — which is decreased in "sick families," (2) influence of individual members — maladaptive families showed distinct hierarchal ordering of members, (3) conflict in which maladaptive families showed more aggression and hostility than adaptive
families, and (4) communication, which was disturbed in maladaptive families. Implications for future research are discussed.

STENNETT, R., "Family Diagnosis: MMPI and CTP Results," J. Clin. Psychol., 22, 165-167,
      1966.
MMPI and CTP (California Test of Personality) tests were done on 230 families over a
five-year period in an out-patient clinic to answer several questions about family dynamics. Families were urban, Protestant, whites with wide socioeconomic status. The
CTP was given to children from age four up to 13. Findings were that a significant
number of family members other than the identified patient had personality problems of
their own, that there was a significant correlation in the level of psychopathology
between the parents of troubled families, but no evidence was found of conflicting
or complementary personality characteristics in the parents.

STREAN, H. S., "A Family Therapist Looks at 'Little Hans,'" Fam. Proc., 6, 227-234, 1967.
A reexamination of the case of Little Hans from the point of view of the family as the
unit of diagnosis and treatment. The case is said to be "an excellent illustration of
how a symptom of one member binds and protects a whole family constellation."

STRODTBECK, F. L., "The Family as a Three-Person Group.," Amer. Sociol. Rev., 23-29, 1954.
A research study attempting to replicate findings of Mills in relation to three-person
groups. The sample was 48 cases including father, mother, and adolescent son. They were
asked to fill out alternatives to 47 items. The study was done in the family homes and
tape recorded. Decision-making power was associated with high participation and when
the two most active members show "solidarity" in their relation to one another, the
stability of their rank participation is high. When the two most active members were
in conflict, stability was as low for these families as for the other families.

STRODTBECK, F. L., "The Interaction of a 'Henpecked' Husband with his Wife," Marriage
     Fam. Liv., 14, 305-308, 1952.
A clinical case report on the psychodynamics of being "henpecked." Method was the revealed differences test. Compared to other couples, although the wife was more dominant, it was "not so painful in practice as the community gossip would lead one to believe." Interaction sequence is a more accurate way of assessing family dynamics than
community observation.

SUSSMAN, M. B., "Adaptive, Directive, and Integrative Behavior of Today's Family," Fam.
     Proc., 7, 239-250, 1968.
A discussion of the relationship between the nuclear family and its kinship structure,
as well as between other social institutions. It is said that the kin network acquires
commitments by rewards perceived as superior to those offered by other social structures
and so establishes tradition-laden obligations among family members.

TAYLOR, W. R., "Research on Family Interaction. I. Static and Dynamic Models," Fam.
     Proc., 9, 221-232, 1970.
A comparison of static and dynamic models of family structure illustrated with a clinical
example. The emphasis is upon the Markov process where a state is succeeded by other
possible states.

TESSMAN, L. H., and KAUFMAN, I., "Variations on a Theme of Incest," in O. Pollak and
     A. S. Friedman (Eds.), Family Dynamics and Female Sexual Delinquency, Palo Alto,
     Science & Behavior Books, 1969.
A discussion of incest occuring in families with young girls, either in fantasy or fact,
with case examples.

THARP, R., and OTIS, G., "Toward a Theory for Therapeutic Intervention in Families," J.
     Consult, Psychol., 30, 426-434, 1966.
Family roles are characterized into five functional entities: solidarity, sexuality,
internal instrumentality, external relations, and division of responsibility. Data
were obtained from the authors' clinical work. A discrepancy between the expectations
and the actual performance can lead to symptoms. Interventions to make the roles more
consonant are described with three case illustrations presented in support of these concepts.

TITCHENER, J. L., "Family System as a Model for Ego System," in G. H. Zuk and I. Boszor-
     menyi-Nagy (Eds.), Family Therapy and Disturbed Families, Palo Alto, Science & Be-
     havior Books, 1967.
A discussion of the importance of an intrapsychic point of view in the comprehension of
family process, the family system phase of ego development, and how family life influences the maturing ego.

TOMAN, W., The Family Constellation: Its Effects on Personality and Social Behavior,
     New York, Springer, 1969.
A book describing a theory of the effects of the family constellation on personality
and social behavior. The theory is described, as well as the major types of sibling
positions, and the major types of relations of the parents. Prediction of behavior is
illustrated with six case examples. 280 pp.

TOWNE, R. D., MESSINGER, S. L., and SAMPSON, H., "Schizophrenia and the Marital Family:
     Accommodations to Symbiosis," Fam. Proc., 1, 304-318, 1962.
Another in a series of reports by this group of their study of 17 women who as young
adults had experienced severe difficulties in their marital families, and were hospitalized with a diagnosis of schizophrenia. Here the focus was on the "symbiotic" nature of
the family relationships which seem to serve to keep the families together, and when broken down led to hospitalization of the wife. Three patterns are described.

TYLER, E. A., "The Process of Humanizing Physiological Man," Fam. Proc., 3, 280-301, 1964.
A general discussion of how "man, the physiological animal, becomes man, the social human" is presented as a social theory of human behavior. The individual is traced through various stages of socialization development from infancy to old age.

VERON, E., KORNBLIT, A., MALFE, R., and SLUZKI, C. E., "Estructures de Conducta y Sistemas de Comunicacion Social (Conduct Structures and Systems of Social Communication)," Acta Psiquiat. y Psicolog. Argentina, 9, 297, 1963.
A conceptual model for the sociological study of psychoneurosis is described, which includes three strategic levels: individual; familial (group structure); and social stratification, including cultural structures. The recurrence of certain conduct structures in an individual, that is, of generalized ways of interaction, is the result of of a meta-communicative process of learning, i.e., deutero-learning. The presence of recurrent ways of learning in a family group is a function of the family organization as communication system. The persistence of certain types of communication within the family group is a function of the socio-cultural context which influences the family.

VINCENT, C. E., "Mental Health and the Family," in P. H. Glasser and L. N. Glasser (Eds.) Families in Crisis, New York, Harper & Row, 1970.
A selective review of broad developments and trends in the emerging role of the federal government in the mental health field. The relevance of the family to mental health and community mental health centers is discussed with a review. Present needs are discussed.

VOGEL, E. F., and BELL, N. W., "The Emotionally Disturbed Child as the Family Scapegoat," in N. W. Bell and E. F. Vogel (Eds.), A Modern Introduction to the Family, Glencoe, Free Press, 1960.
A discussion of families with disturbed children in terms of the child's function as a scapegoat. Topics include selection of the child for scapegoating, the induction of him into this role, and the rationalizations.

WALLACE, A. F., and FOGELSON, R. D., "The Identity Struggle," in I. Boszormenyi-Nagy and J. L. Framo (Eds.), Intensive Family Therapy, New York, Harper & Row, 1965.
Anthropological observers of a family therapy program discuss "representative instances of identity struggle" observed in the treatment of the family of the schizophrenic.

WARKENTIN, J., "Marriage: The Cornerstone of the Family System," in O. Pollak and A. S. Friedman (Eds.), Family Dynamics and Female Sexual Delinquency, Palo Alto, Science & Behavior Books, 1969.
A description of the inner assumptions and postulates about human nature and marriage of two experienced therapists. The emphasis is upon the importance of the therapist's views about life when dealing with a family.

WARKENTIN, J., and WHITAKER, C., "Serial Impasses in Marriage," in I. M. Cohen (Ed.), Psychiatric Research Report No. 20, American Psychiatric Association, Washington, 1966.
A discussion of marriage as both a legal and an emotional commitment with special emphasis upon the times "when we may expect difficulty and even impasse in the development of the emotional marriage." These times include the wedding night, pregnancy, the second baby, and the"ten year syndrome."

WATZLAWICK, P., An Anthology of Human Communication, Palo Alto, Science & Behavior Books, 1964.
A textbook and tape dealing with family dynamics, interaction, and communication patterns. Communication theory is outlined and there are sections on agreement and disagreement, type relationships, disqualifications, schizophrenic communication, double binds, coalitions, and a suggested reading list. 63 pp. plus an audiotape.

WATZLAWICK, P., "A Review of the Double Bind Theory," Fam. Proc., 2, 132-153, 1963.
A presentation of the comments on the double bind theory occurring in the literature
from 1957-1961. The comments are discussed and excerpts presented.

WATZLAWICK, P., BEAVIN, H., and JACKSON, D. D., Pragmatics of Human Communication: A
     Study of Interactional Patterns, Pathologies, and Paradoxes, New York, Norton, 1967.
A book dealing with "behavioral effects of human communication with special attention
to behavior disorders." There are discussions of the frame of reference of the book;
some axioms of communication; pathological communication; the organization of family
interaction; analysis of the play, Who's Afraid of Virginia Woolf, paradoxical communication; paradoxes in psychotherapy; and existentialism and the theory of human communication. 296 pp.

WEAKLAND, J. H., "The Double Bind Hypothesis of Schizophrenia and Three-Party Interac-
     tion," in D. D. Jackson (Ed.), The Etiology of Schizophrenia, New York, Basic Books,
     1960.
A discussion of the double bind as it applies to three party situations. Described are
mother, father, child relationships and such institutional relationships as administrator-
therapist-patient and doctor-nurse-patient.

WELLER, L., "The Relationship of Birth Order to Anxiety: A Replication of the Schacter
     Findings, Sociometry, 25, 415-417, 1962.
Schacter (The Psychology of Affiliation) showed that first-born and only-children became
more anxious in threatening situations than later-born children. Schacter's experimental procedures were repeated with 234 female undergraduates. Anxiety was assessed by an
adjective check list and a questionnaire. No relationship of birth order and anxiety
appear, contradicting Schacter's findings. The author suggests that birth order in itself may be too simple and needs to be considered in conjunction with other variables.

WEST, S. S., "Sibling Configurations of Scientists," Amer. J. Sociol., 66, 268-274, 1960.
Birth order and the number of siblings of 813 scientists were obtained as part of a study
of six research organizations. The aim was to determine what type of family experience
is associated with choice of research as a career. First, fifth, and sixth birth ranks
are over-represented; second, third, and fourth are under-represented. Siblings are
distributed randomly as regards sex. Comparison with data on the general population indicates that a sibship size increases, probability of a scientist coming from family decreases. Isolation in childhood is said to be important in developing the characteristics of a scientist. Data support either a hypothesis that relative isolation is necessary for research career, or the hypothesis that mothers of scientists have fewer
children than normal.

WESTLEY, W., and EPSTEIN, N., "Family Structure and Emotional Health: A Case Study Ap-
     proach," Marriage Fam. Liv., 22, 25-27, 1960.
One of a series of papers from a study of the emotional health of nine families, each of
which contained at least one emotionally healthy adolescent. In studying the grandmo-
thers of these emotionally healthy families, it was found that they were seen as "cold
and manipulative," while the fathers were seen as "warm and supportive." The attitude
of these mothers, as towards their husbands, was one of seeing husbands as they had seen
their fathers. The marital relationship was "warm and well adjusted." The mental health
of the subjects was influenced more by the organization of the nuclear families, than
by the mental health of the grandparents.

WESTLEY, W., and EPSTEIN, N., "Patterns of Intra-Familial Communication," Psychiatric
     Research Report No. 11, American Psychiatric Association, Washington, 1959.
A research report attempting to describe intrafamily communication patterns. Nine
healthy families with an adolescent were studied using clinical interview, the Rorschach
and the TAT. Nine categories of family function are described and patterns of overt
communication versus other types of communication are described.

WESTMAN, J. C., MILLER, D. R., and ARTHUR, B., "Psychiatric Symptoms and Family Dynamics
      as Illustrated by the Retarded Reader," in I. M. Cohen (Ed.), Psychiatric Research
      Report No. 20, American Psychiatric Association, Washington, 1966.
A discussion of the family of the retarded reader to illustrate how individual psychopathology can be linked with interpersonal relationships through symptoms and signs.

WHITTAKER, C. (Ed.), Psychotherapy of Chronic Schizophrenic Patients, Boston, Little,
      Brown, 1958.
A transcript of a conference on schizophrenia in which there were eight sessions, each
oriented toward a particular topic in which no formal presentation is made, but rather
a general discussion with a moderator for each section was held. It includes sections
on diagnosis and prognosis, schizophrenic distortion of communication, orality, anality,
family and sexuality, countertransference, management of the patient, and family management. 219 pp.

WORLD HEALTH ORGANIZATION, "Aspects of Family Mental Health in Europe," Public Health
      Papers No. 28.
Eight papers which were "working papers presented at a seminar on mental health and the
family held by the WHO Regional Office for Europe at Athens in 1962" and specially commissioned chapters. These include "The Mother and the Family", "The Child in the Family", "Working Women and the Family", "Marriage Problems and their Implications for the
Family", "Family Psychotherapy", "Mental Health and the Older Generation", "School for
Parents", and "The Hampstead Child-Therapy Clinic".

WYNNE, L., RYCKOFF, I., DAY, J., and HERSCH, S., "Pseudo-Mutuality in the Family Rela-
      tions of Schizophrenics," Psychiatry, 21, 205-220, 1958.
An essay which postulates that the disturbance in the family is an important causal
factor in schizophrenia. Data was obtained as part of a long-term research project
on schizophrenia in which patients were hospitalized and parents were seen on an out-
patient basis. Most of the data are drawn from clinical work with families. Patients
with schizophrenia have families in which the relations can best be described as "pseudo-mutual." The acute schizophrenic experience is derived from internalization of the
pathogenic family organization.

WYNNE, L. C., RYCKOFF, I. M., DAY, J., and HERSCH, S., "Pseudo-Mutuality in the Family
      Relations of Schizophrenics," in N. W. Bell, and E. F. Vogel, A Modern Introduc-
      tion to the Family, Glencoe, Free Press, 1960.
A description of families of schizophrenics studied with family therapy. Characteristic was pseudo-mutuality in the family; the family supports an illusion of a well-integrated state even when this is not supported by the emotional structure of the members
and the strains contribute to the development of schizophrenia.

ZUCKERMAN, M., "Save the Pieces!," Psychol. Bull, 66, 78-80, 1966.
A brief comment correcting factual mistakes in Frank's review of the method and results
of a study by Zuckerman, Oltean, and Moashkin. There is also an argument that the retrospective statistical approach to the study of the family's relation to psychopathology is valid and has contributed to the discovery of etiology in other disorders. Methodology involved in dealing with multiple factors and lack of reliability of instruments
is discussed.

ZUK, G., "On the Pathology of Silencing Strategies," Fam. Proc., 4, 32-49, 1965.
A description and categorization of the ways people impose or enforce silence on one
another. "There is a causal relation between silencing strategies and pathological silence and babbling which may themselves be used as powerful silencing strategies."

ZUK, G., and RUBINSTEIN, D., "A Review of Concepts in the Study and Treatment of Families
      of Schizophrenics," in I. Boszormenyi-Nagy and J. L. Framo (Eds.), Intensive Family
      Therapy, New York, Harper & Row, 1965.
A review of conceptual trends in family treatment of schizophrenics. Discusses the shift
from parent pathology to nuclear family to three generational involvement.

3.1 MARITAL DESCRIPTION

ACKERMAN, N. W., "The Diagnosis of Neurotic Marital Interaction," Soc. Casework, 35, 139-147, 1954.
A lecture based on the author's clinical work in which he lays out a theory of family pathology and marital disharmony. There is an extensive schema for evaluating the marital relationship, divided into 7 categories: (1) goals, (2) performance, (3) achievement, (4) dynamic interrelations, (5) neurotic interactions, (6) consequences of Neurotic interactions, and (7) patterns of compensation.

ARD, B. N., and ARD, C. C. (Eds.), Handbook of Marriage Counseling, Palo Alto, Science & Behavior Books, 1969.
A collection of previously published material on marriage counseling. There are sections on the place of philosophy on values; theoretical issues; conjoint marriage counseling; group marriage counseling; premarital counseling; special techniques; counseling regarding sexual problems; professional issues and ethics in marriage counseling; counseling divorce; and technical assistance for the marriage counselor. There is a long annotated bibliography. 474 pp.

BAILEY, M. B., "Alcoholism and Marriage," Quart. J. Stud. Alcohol., 22, 81-97, 1961.
A review paper summarizing and discussing the major literature relating to alcoholism and marriage. Further research is said to be needed to attempt an integration of the two hypotheses that regard the course of an alcoholic marriage as a manifestation of a personality disorder or as a response to a particular kind of stress. "The past few years have witnessed a general growth of psychiatric interest in total family diagnosis and treatment, but this new emphasis has hardly begun to manifest itself in respect to alcoholism." A bibliography of 46 references is included.

BAUMANN, G. and ROMAN, M., "Interaction Testing in the Study of Marital Dominance," Fam. Proc., 5, 230-242, 1966.
A sample of 50 couples was exposed individually and conjointly to the Wechsler Bellevue. In the conjoint testing, the couple was asked to reach agreement on the response. Comparisons of the individual test and the conjoint test were made as well as measures of dominance of the couple tested together.

BECK, D. F., "Marital Conflict: Its Course and Treatment as Seen by Caseworkers," Soc. Casework, 47, 211-221, 1966.
A clinical essay describing a theory of marital conflict. Data were obtained by sending an unstructured questionnaire to "four hundred caseworkers in 104 member agencies throughout the United States" and "stimulation of local study groups to prepare reports in depth on such topics." There is a "marital balance" which helps keep the family in equilibrium and which is derived from courtship and the early years of marriage. The breakdown of the marital conflict and the conflicts resulting are described, including the point where couples apply for help. Good and bad prognostic factors in terms of casework intervention and treatment of marital conflict are described.

BEUKENKAMP, C., "Parental Suicide as a Source of Resistance to Marriage," Int. J. Group Psychother., 11, 204-208, 1961.
A review of 45 former patients seen in private practice who had remained unmarried despite their efforts to the contrary. Because 25 of them had later married and 20 had not, the author renewed contact to explore the difference. He learned that of the 25 who had married, the fathers of eight had committed suicide and the fathers of 17 had made attempts or implied they might do so. The author concludes that the 25 who married resolved in therapy an unhealthy identification with a suicidal father which was related to their reluctance to marry.

BOLTE, G. L., "A Communications Approach to Marital Counseling," Fam. Coord., 19, 32-40, 1970.
A clinical essay based on the hypothesis that communications difficulties provide an important avenue for understanding marital conflict. Therefore an interactional approach is advised for treating problems. Communication difficulties are outlined and interventions are suggested. Interactional techniques are seen as only one part of the marriage counselor's repertoire.

BUCK, C. W., and LADD, K. L., "Psychoneurosis in Marital Partners," Brit. J. Psychiat.,
     3, 587-590, 1965.
A study of records of physicians' diagnoses from a health insurance plan in a Canadian
city. There was a definite association between the occurrence of psychoneurotic illness in husbands and wives who had been married for many years, little association for
partners recently married and no association during the pre-marital period. The authors
interpret these findings as evidence that a process of contagion rather than mate selection determines the concordance between marital partners in psychoneurotic illness.

BURCHINAL, L., and CHANCELLOR, L. E., "Age at Marriage, Occupations of Grooms, and In-
     terreligious Marriage Rates," Soc. Forces, 40, 343-354, 1962.
The effects of age at marriage, status of the groom, and their interaction effects, on
the propensity for intra- or inter-religious marriage were tested in all Iowa first
marriages, 1953 to 1957 (N = 17,636). Protestants are less likely to contract inter-
religious marriages than Catholics. Interreligious marriages are more frequent with
higher age of marriage and higher status of the groom. There are also joint effects
which vary by group. The data are interpreted as indicating that the saliance of religion varies in relation to the reference group experience specific to age and status
levels.

BURCHINAL, L. and CHANCELLOR, L. E., "Survival Rates among Religiously Homogeneous and
     Interreligious Marriages," Soc. Forces, 41, 353-362, 1963.
All first marriages of white Iowa residents between 1953 and 1959 which lasted at least
12 months were recorded (N = 72,488). Divorces in such marriages during the period
were also identified. Homogamous marriages had a higher survival rate than interreligious marriages, but the age of the bride at marriage and the husband's occupational
status are even stronger variables. Among Protestants, denominationally-homogamous marriages are less stable than denominationally-mixed marriages. Homogamous Catholic marriages survive better than denominationally homogamous Protestant marriages. In mixed
marriages survival varies widely depending on the denomination of the Protestant spouse.

CHARNY, I. W., "Marital Love and Hate," Fam. Proc., 8, 1-24, 1969.
A discussion of marriage with the emphasis upon how marital fighting is "inevitable,
necessary, and desirable — not simply an unhappy byproduct of emotional immaturity
or disturbance."

DENIKER, P., deSAUGY, D., and ROPERT, M., "The Alcoholic and His Wife," Compr. Psychiat.,
     5, 374-384, 1964.
A study focussing on the relationship between the alcoholic and his wife by studying
three groups of patients: 50 alcoholics with psychiatric disorders called psychiatric
alcoholics, 50 alcoholics with cirrhosis or gastritis called digestive alcoholics, and
67 in a control group where the husband was matched for age and socioeconomic status.
All couples were interviewed using a questionnaire designed for this study. Compared
with the digestive alcoholics and the controls, the psychiatric alcoholics showed a relationship to birth order, had fathers who were also alcoholics, made lower salaries,
had dominant wives, and drank relatively little at home. The wife of the psychiatric
alcoholic "tends to unconsciously maintain her husband's alcoholism."

DICKS, H. V., Marital Tensions: Clinical Studies Toward a Psychological Theory of In-
     teraction, New York, Basic Books, 1967.
A clinical research report investigating marital problems. Concepts of the study, rationale, social setting, individual setting, development of the study, evolution of
concepts, symptomatology, diagnosis, treatment, and treatment results are reported.
354 pp.

DUPONT, R., and GRUNEBAUM, H., "Willing Victims: The Husbands of Paranoid Women,"
     Amer. J. Psychiat., 125, 151-159, 1968.
In an attempt to understand the dynamics of spouses of paranoid women, cases with paranoid delusions (both in-patient and out-patient) were evaluated over a three-year period.
Data were collected on nine women with paranoid state, using clinical interviews with
the husband alone, wife alone, and the couple together, plus the MMPI and interpersonal

checklist. Results indicated that the wife expressed the anger and dissatisfaction in
the marriage, while the husband manifested passivity and apparent reasonableness and
thus seemed to be a "willing victim."

DYER, W. G., "Analyzing Marital Adjustment Using Role Theory," Marriage Fam. Liv., 24,
    371-375, 1962.
Marriage partners enter marriage with certain ideas about their roles and how they should
behave in this new position, and each also has certain expectations of how the other
should behave in his role. Conflicts may come when one's self perception does not agree
with the perception of the partner, when the norms and personal preferences of the husband are in conflict with those of the wife, and when the role performance of one does
not agree with role expectations of the other.

EISENSTEIN, V. (Ed.), Neurotic Interaction in Marriage, New York, Basic Books, 1956.
A collection of new material which includes discussions mostly from the psychoanalytic
point of view, on a cultural perspective on marriage, the effects of marital conflicts
on child development, neurotic choices of mate, analysis of interaction patterns, psychological assessment in marital maladjustment, changes as a result of treatment of one
member, case work with a disturbed family, approaches to treatment of marital problems,
and problems of prediction of marital adjustment. 352 pp.

EWING, J. A., LONG, V., and WENZEL, G. G., "Concurrent Group Psychotherapy of Alcoholic
    Patients and Their Wives," Int. J. Group Psychother., 11, 329-338, 1961.
A description of concurrent but separate group psychotherapy meetings of alcoholic outpatients and their wives. The authors find that more husbands continue to attend group
meetings if the wife is involved, and there is greater improvement in alcoholic patients
whose wives also attend group meetings. The participation of the wife in the husband's
drinking is examined. An example is the wife who accidentally put a shot of whiskey
into her husband's iced tea after he had stopped drinking. The authors highly recommend involving the wives of alcoholics in group therapy.

FALLDING, H., "The Family and The Idea of a Cardinal Role," Hum. Rel., 14, 329-350, 1961.
Thirty-eight Melbourne, Australia, intact families were studied intensively by group and
individual interviews. Three types of families were distinguished on the basis of the
extent to which members' external involvements are made relevant or necessary to the
group: (1) Adaptation type — Husband and wife seek different satisfactions from life,
but adapt to each other by giving independence to other to follow personal interests
without accountability to the family. (2) Identification type — Husband's and wife's
satisfactions largely derived from family life. Satisfactions independently derived
from outside are incidental. (3) False identification type — Husband and wife have
conflicting aims, individually and/or together. They strive to control conflicts by
acting as if the family is of cardinal importance to both, resulting in dissatisfaction.
Some of the external controls on family conduct and the nature of the unit provided by
the cardinal role are explored.

FISCHER, S., and FISCHER, R. L., "The Complexity of Spouse Similarity and Difference,"
    in G. H. Zuk and I. Boszormenyi-Nagy (Eds.), Family Therapy and Disturbed Fami-
    lies, Palo Alto, Science & Behavior Books, 1967.
A report on a study of similarities and differences among spouses based upon a sample
of 119 families. The parents were exposed to a battery of test procedures intended to
tap personality, value, and attitudinal dimensions. Measures of multiple levels of response would seem necessary, because "depending upon the variables one chooses to measure, spouses will appear to be similar, different, or both."

FOX, R. E., "The Effect of Psychotherapy on the Spouse," Fam. Proc., 7, 7-16, 1968.
A discussion and review of the literature of the effect on a spouse when the partner
is in individual psychotherapy. Problems of gathering data are presented and the
ethical problem of adverse effects upon the spouse are discussed.

FRY, W. F., "The Marital Context of an Anxiety Syndrome," Fam. Proc., 1, 245-252, 1962.
A report from a project for the study of schizophrenic communication, whose hypothesis
is that "the relationship with the marriage partner is intimately related to the psychopathology of the patient." The patients in the report had the syndrome of anxiety,
phobias, and stereotyped avoidance behavior. Spouses are described, and it was found
that the onset of symptoms correlated with an important change in the life of the spouse.
The symptoms seemed to keep the couple united.

GEHRKE, S., and MOXOM, J., "Diagnostic Classifications and Treatment Techniques in Mar-
      riage Counseling," Fam. Proc., 1, 253-264, 1962.
A report by two case workers describing a marital counseling method with the diagnostic
classifications and treatment techniques used. Indications for joint interviews with
husband and wife are given.

GOODE, W. J., "Marital Satisfaction and Instability: A Cross-Cultural Class Analysis
      of Divorce Rates," in P. H. Glasser and L. N. Glasser (Eds.), Families in Crisis,
      New York, Harper & Row, 1970.
A discussion of marital stability with the emphasis upon forms of instability and disorganization in families. Divorce is described in terms of class and across cultures
with divorce rates given for different countries.

GOODRICH, D. W., and BOOMER, D. S., "Experimental Assessment of Modes of Conflict Reso-
      lution," Fam. Proc., 2, 15-24, 1963.
A report of an experimental technique for studying the coping behavior of husband and
wife when they attempt to resolve a marital conflict. Fifty paid volunteer couples between 18 and 27 years of age were asked to match colors——some unmatchable — to see
how the couple coped with puzzling or ambiguous situations. A general discussion of
results is given, with the authors relating the "ability to achieve perspective on the
situation and maintenance of self-esteem" to adequacy of coping.

GOODRICH, D. W., RYDER, R., and RAUSH, H., "Patterns of Newlywed Marriage," J. Marriage
      Fam., 30, 383-391, 1968.
A report of an exploratory study of 50 average, middle-class marriages examined during
the fourth month with interviews, problem solving situations, and questionnaires.
Eight patterns of marriage are suggested.

GREEN, K. A., "The Echo of Marital Conflict," Fam. Proc., 2, 315-328, 1963.
A study of the characteristics of couples coming to the Conciliation Court of the Superior Court of Los Angeles County. In 1960, 500 consecutive cases of couples apply-
ing to the conciliation service were examined. The sociocultural characteristics are
presented.

GREENE, B. L. (Ed.), The Psychotherapies of Marital Disharmony, New York, Free Press, 1965.
A collection of previously presented material on treatment of marital problems using
different approaches. There are papers on a multioperational approach, sociologic and
psychoanalytic concepts in family diagnosis, marital counselling, the classical psychoanalytic approach, treatment of marital partners separately where the therapists collaborate, concurrent psychoanalytic treatment for the marital partners, conjoint marital
therapy, a combination of approaches, and the family approach to diagnosis. 191 pp.

HALEY, J., "Marriage Therapy," Arch. Gen. Psychiat., 8, 213-234, 1963.
A discussion of the treatment of conflicts in marriage. Certain types of marital relationships, the kinds of conflicts which arise, and the ways a therapist intervenes to
induce change are discussed. It is suggested that conflicts occur when husband and wife
define their relationship in conflicting ways thereby imposing paradoxical situations.
The resolution of the conflict can occur when the couple faces paradoxical situations
provided by marriage therapists.

HILL, R., "Marriage and Family Research: A Critical Evaluation," Eugen. Quart., 1, 58-
     63, 1954.
An essay undertaking a critical review of the literature on marriage and the family,
covering trends in research, contemporary emphasis, and prospects for the future research. It covers primarily the sociologic literature.

JACKSON, D. D., "Family Rules: Marital, Quid Pro Quo," Arch. Gen. Psychiat., 12, 589-
     594, 1965.
A clinical paper in which a theory of marriage is proposed based on the relationship
rather than the individuals. Similarities and differences between spouses comprise
the "bargain" on which the marriage relationship is based. Advantages and disadvantages
of this scheme of understanding the marital relationship are discussed.

JACKSON, D. D., and BODIN, A., "Paradoxical Communication and the Marital Paradox," in
     S. Rosenbaum, and I. Alger (Eds.), The Marriage Relationship, New York, Basic Books,
     1968.
An attempt to provide a conceptual framework and techniques for dealing with a disturbed
marital relationship. The marital situation is seen as a paradox in itself. As a result of that paradox, some examples of disturbed communication are discussed. In the
treatment of such communication, labelling conflicting levels, encouraging the symptoms,
and actually prescribing them are helpful.

JACKSON, D. D., and LEDERER, W. J., Mirages of Marriage, New York, Norton, 1969.
A book which focusses on the nature of marriage, marital problems, and procedures for
bringing about change. Illustrations of different problems are given. Exercises for
a couple to work on their marriage are provided.

KARDENER, S., "The Family: Structure, Pattern, and Therapy," Ment. Hyg., 52, 524-531,
     1968.
Following a review of the concept of the family as an etiologic agent in the development
of psychopathology, seven types of problem marital constellations, four types of family
interrelationships, and seven danger signals alerting the family to potential trouble,
are described. Role of therapist is outlined to deal with these problems.

KATZ, I., COHEN, M., and CASTIGLIONE, L., "Effect of One Type of Need Complementarity
     on Marriage Partners' Conformity to One Another's Judgments," J. Abnorm. Soc. Psy-
     chol., 67, 8-14, 1963.
Fifty-five paid volunteer couples were examined using a forced-choice questionnaire to
test the hypothesis that when the husband's need to receive affection is similar in
strength to the wife's complementary need to give affection the tendency of spouses to
be influenced by one another will be significant. Results indicated husbands could
accept wives' judgments; the converse was not true.

KATZ, M., "Agreement on Connotative Meaning in Marriage," Fam. Proc., 4, 64-74, 1965.
A study of marriage based on the assumption that marital happiness is related to the degree of similarity between the spouses. Two groups of 20 couples, one seeking marriage
counselling and one classed as happily married, were exposed to the Osgood semantic differential instrument and differences were found. Troubled couples were more discrepant
in their semantic structures.

KERCKHOFF, A., and DAVIS, K. E., "Value Consensus and Need Complementarity in Mate Se-
     lection," Amer. Sociol. Rev., 27, 295-303, 1962.
Approximately 100 college couples seriously considering marriage were studied on two occasions, seven months apart. Their need complementarity (measured by Schutz's FIRO
scales) and value consensus (by Farber's index) were measured and related to length of
association and progress toward a permanent union. The hypothesis that consensus relates
to progress toward a permanent union holds only for short-term couples. The hypothesis
that need complementarity is related to progress holds only for long-term couples. The
findings are interpreted to mean that different factors are salient at different stages
of mate selection.

KLEMER, R. H., Counseling in Marital and Sexual Problems, Baltimore, Williams & Wilkins,
    1965.
A collection of new material and previously published articles which includes discussions
of counseling in marital problems; counseling in sexual problems; other marriage problems; premarital counseling; and marriage counseling instruction in the medical curriculum. There is an extensive reading list. 309 pp.

KOHL, R. N., "Pathologic Reactions of Marital Partners to Improvement of Patients," Amer.
    J. Psychiat., 118, 1036-1041, 1962.
A discussion of the precipitation of a psychiatric illness in a marital partner when a
patient shows clinical improvement based upon observation of 39 in-patients treated at
the Payne Whitney Psychiatric Clinic over a period of ten years. In all cases it was
necessary to include both spouses in the treatment plan to maintain the patient's improvement or recovery. Commonly there was denial of marital conflict as etiologically
significant by both partners at the time of hospitalization and emphasis upon the "ideal"
nature of the marriage with mutual denial of resentment or hostility. With improvement
in the patient, the spouses displayed the first observable signs of psychopathology.

KREITMAN, N., "Mental Disorder in Married Couples," J. Ment. Sci., 108, 438-446, 1962.
To determine the incidence and nature of mental illness in the spouses of psychiatric
patients, the records of the Chichester Psychiatric Service in England were examined.
The findings indicate that the incidence of mental illness in spouses of psychiatric
patients is higher than among the general population. Various hypotheses to account
for this finding are discussed.

KRIETMAN, N., "The Patient's Spouse," Brit. J. Psychiat., 110, 159-174, 1964.
A group of 75 patients and 95 controls, closely matched for sex, social class, father's
social class, education, and number of children, were subjects of a mail survey using
the Maudsley personality inventory, the Cornell medical index, and biographical details for the purpose of describing spouses of mental patients and their relationship
with the marriage partner. Compared with controls the patients' spouses were more
neurotic and had more physical and psychological symptoms which increased as the marriage went on. Wives were more likely than husbands to reflect the illnesses of
spouses.

KUNSTADTER, P., "A Survey of the Consanguine or Matrifocal Family," Amer. Anthropolog.,
    65, 56-66, 1963.
A review and critique of historical, value-system, and functional explanations of the
existence of the matrifocal family. It is concluded that "matrifocal families develop
as a result of the division of labor separating adult males and adult females in a community" when other solutions to an unbalanced sex ratio of adults are unavailable.

LAING, R. D., PHILLIPSON, H., and LEE, A., Interpersonal Perception: A Theory and a
    Method of Research, London, Tavistock, 1966.
A research project oriented toward understanding interaction of two persons. It includes sections on self and other; interaction and interexperience in dyads; the spiral
of reciprocal perspective; historical view of the method; the interpersonal perception
methods (IPM); disturbed and nondisturbed marriages; study of a dyad; developments; and
the IPM questions. 179 pp.

LEVINGER, G., "Marital Cohesiveness and Dissolution: An Integrative Review," in P. H.
    and L. N. Glasser (Eds.), Families in Crisis, New York, Harper & Row, 1970.
A discussion of cohesiveness in marriage as a special case of group cohesiveness in
general. The framework is based upon two components: attractions toward or repulsions
from a relationship, and barriers against its dissolution. Includes a review of factors
associated with divorce.

LEVINGER, G., "Sources of Marital Dissatisfaction Among Applicants for Divorce," in P.
    H. Glasser and L. N. Glasser (Eds.), Families in Crisis, New York, Harper & Row,
    1970.
A study of dissatisfaction in marriage based upon 600 couples with data derived from

records of marriage counselors doing mandatory interviews as part of the application
for divorce. Spouse complaints are classified and discussed.

LEVITT, H., and BAKER, R., "Relative Psychopathology of Marital Partners," Fam. Proc.,
    8, 33-42, 1969.
A study examining whether the member of a marriage who seeks treatment is the more disturbed of the spouses. A sample of 25 patients and their spouses were examined with
questionnaire and psychological tests. Eleven psychologists served as judges to examine the test results and identify the "sicker" member. In 13 of the 25 cases the identified patient was judged to be the "sicker".

LICHTENBERG, J. D., and PIN-NIE PAO, "The Prognostic and Therapeutic Significance of
    the Husband-Wife Relationship for Hospitalized Schizophrenic Women," Psychiatry,
    23, 209-213, 1960.
A discussion of the types of husbands of hospitalized schizophrenic women and the importance of taking the spouse into account in psychotherapy. Observation of 43 patients
indicated the husbands fell into certain groups, although no prototype personality was
found. In terms of prognosis, the husbands are classified as constructively active,
obstructively active, rejecting, maintaining the previous pathological relationship,
and vacillating. Ways to include the husband in the therapeutic program were attempted
and are recommended.

LUCKEY, E. B., "Marital Satisfaction and Congruent Self-Spouse Concepts," Soc. Forces,
    39, 153-157, 1960.
Satisfactorily (S) and less satisfactorily (LS) married couples were identified by Locke's
marital adjustment scale from a population of 594 married students. Couples in the two
groups independently completed the Leary Interpersonal checklist regarding the self and
spouse. The congruence of the husband's perception of himself and his wife's perception
of him was related to satisfaction, but the congruence of the wife's self concept and her
husband's perception of her was not. Some implications and explanations of these results
are offered.

LUCKEY, E. B., "Perceptional Congruence of Self and Family Concepts as Related to Mari-
    tal Interaction," Sociometry, 24, 234-250, 1961.
Forty-one satisfactorily married (S) and 40 less satisfactorily married (LS) couples
completed Leary interpersonal check lists on self, spouse, mother, father, and ideal
self. S and LS subjects were compared on agreement of self concept and spouse's concept
of subject, of self and ideal self, of self and parent, of spouse and parent, of ideal
self and spouses. The many differences between S and LS subjects are used to refine
the proposition that marital satisfaction is related to perceptual congruence, and to
evaluate a theory of marital interaction.

MARKOWITZ, M., and KADIS, A. L., "Parental Interaction as a Determining Factor in Social
    Growth of the Individual in the Family," Int. J. Soc. Psychiat., Special Ed. 2, 81-
    89, 1964.
A general discussion of marriage and the family based upon treatment of married couples
in group therapy. The emphasis is upon unresolved problems and conflicts in the parents
leading to unconscious alliances fostered in the child with a breakdown of the potential
for corrective experience. Examples from analytic group therapy are given.

MEYEROWITZ, J. H., and FELDMAN, H., "Transition to Parenthood," in I. M. Cohen (Ed.),
    Psychiatric Research Reports No. 20, Washington, American Psychiatric Association,
    1966.
A report of a study of 400 couples based on interviews of individuals. Experiences
during the first pregnancy are described as well as when the child is one month and
five months old.

MITCHELL, H. E., "Application of the Kaiser Method to Marital Pairs," Fam. Proc., 2,
    265-279, 1963.
A discussion of the Leary measurement as used on 20 maritally conflicted alcoholics and
their spouses. Questions concerning resemblances and differences are raised. The major

emphasis is "not to the substantive findings but to demonstration of the feasibility of the Kaiser method as a technique for measuring interpersonal dimensions of marital and family dynamics."

MITCHELL, H. E., BULLARD, J. W., and MUDD, E. H., "Areas of Marital Conflict in Success-fully and Unsuccessfully Functioning Families," J. Health Hum. Behav., 3, 88-93, 1962.
The nature and frequency of marital disagreements in 200 marriage counseling cases and in 100 self selected, successful families. Data on both groups were obtained from the marriage adjustment schedule and from interviews. Both groups rank their problems in the same order: economic is highest, religious and educational are lowest. No differences in ranking of problems by husbands and wives were apparent, but conflicted families report a greater frequency of problems. Some cultural implications of these findings are discussed.

MUDD, E. H., The Practice of Marriage Counseling, New York, Association Press, 1951.
A study of the development of marriage and family counseling in the United States, and a description of its practice with case examples. It includes types of organizations and professions involved. 336 pp.

NASHE, E. M., JESSNER, L., and ABSE, D. W. (Eds.), Marriage Counseling in Medical Prac-tice, Chapel Hill, University of North Carolina Press, 1964.
A collection of new material and previously published articles which includes discussions of marriage counseling by the physician; premarital medical counseling; concepts of mari-tal diagnosis and therapy; and marital counseling instruction in the medical school cur-riculum. There is an annotated book list. 368 pp.

NAVRAN, L., "Communication and Adjustment in Marriage", Fam. Proc., 6, 173-184, 1967.
A sample of married couples was exposed to the marital relationship inventory and the primary communication inventory, two questionnaires given to the couples individually. The 24 couples having a "happy" relationship were contrasted with 24 having an "unhappy" relationship. Differences were found and marital adjustment was shown "to be positively correlated with capacity to communicate."

OLSON, D. H., "The Measurement of Family Power by Self-Report and Behavioral Methods," J. Marriage Fam., 31, 545-550, 1969.
A study comparing self report and observed behavior on the question of power in marriage. Thirty-five couples were given questionnaires and their responses compared with their behavior in the laboratory dealing with real problems. No relationship was found be-tween what the couples said about the distribution of power in the marriage and what was observed when they dealt with one another. Explanatory factors are offered, and the conclusion is reached that this research reinforces "the idea that methodological research of this type should precede, rather than follow, substantive research in the field."

PATTERSON, G. R., RAY, R., and SHAW, D., Direct Intervention in Families of Deviant Children, Eugene, Oregon Research Institute, 1969.
A description of a conditioning approach in family therapy where the ways parents deal with children is systematically modified and examined before and after.

PITTMAN, F. S., and FLOMENHAFT, K., "Treating the Doll's House Marriage," Fam. Proc., 9, 143-155, 1970.
Intervention procedures in the type of marriage where one spouse's incompetance is re-quired or encouraged by the other. Therapy works best when the emphasis is upon re-spect for unique individual needs within the framework of the marriage.

PRINCE, A. J., "A Study of 194 Cross-Religion Marriages," Fam. Life Coord., 11, 3-7, 1962.
A report on a study of 142 interfaith marriages and 52 marriages between protestants of different denominations. Data were obtained with questionnaires. Topics of interest

are cross-religion marriages, major areas of conflict, changes in church attendance patterns, degree of satisfaction with marriage, and attitudes about cross-religion marriages for children.

RABKIN, R., "Uncoordinated Communication Between Marriage Partners," Fam. Proc., 6, 10-15, 1967.
A discussion of communication codes unique to particular family systems. Examples of couples' problems in developing mutual codes are given.

RAPOPORT, R., "Normal Crises, Family Structure and Mental Health," Fam. Proc., 2, 68-80, 1963.
An essay on some of the "ideas and methods" behind an exploratory study of how "the family handled "the newly married state." Six couples were thus studied via interviews both before and after marriage for variable periods of time.

RAPOPORT, R., and RAPOPORT, R. N., "New Light on the Honeymoon," Hum. Rel., 17, 33-56, 1964.
A general discussion of the honeymoon followed by a task description illustrated with a case example. The honeymoon ritual is described as part of the life-cycle transition point of marriage.

RAVICH, R., "Game-Testing in Conjoint Marital Psychotherapy," Amer. J. Psychother., 23, 217-229, 1969.
A report on the "game-test" for both family diagnosis and family therapy. Methodology is described and four typical patterns of interaction are identified: (1) competitive, (2) alternating, (3) dominant-submissive, and (4) mixed. Based on these patterns, techniques for therapy are described.

RAVICH, R., DEUTSCH, M., and BROWN, B., "An Experimental Study of Marital Discord and Decision Making," in I. M. Cohen (Ed.), Psychiatric Research Report No. 20, American Psychiatric Association, Washington, 1966.
A report on a study of 38 couples tested with a game in which the partners imagine that they are operating a truck and can effect each other's truck when they meet a one-lane road. Behavior is described in terms of sharing, dominating and submitting, being inconsistent, being competitive, and being dysjunctive.

ROSENBAUM, S., and ALGER, I. (Eds.), The Marriage Relationship: Psychoanalytic Perspectives, New York, Basic Books, 1967.
A collection of some new and some previously presented papers focussing on the marital relationship from a family and a psychoanalytic point of view. It includes discussions of communication; monogamy; femininity; resistance to marriage; mate choice; expectations in marriage; changing attitudes of marital partners towards each other; marital problems of older persons; the effects of children; effects of pathology of parents on the children; effects of sexual disturbances; effects of marital conflicts on psychoanalysis; different treatment approaches to marital problems including individual psychoanalysis; with different analysts; family therapy; group psychotherapy with couples; growth and maturation in marriage; and marital dissolution. 366 pp.

RUBINSTEIN, D., "Distortion and Dilemma in Marital Choice," Voices, 2, 60-64, 1966.
From an extensive case example, this essay hypothesizes that in a disturbed marital relationship there are distortions and dilemmas which can be summarized as follows: (1) the marital pair does not relate as real persons, (2) they relate through each other to the internal introjects, (3) they try to change each other into an internal introject to solve longstanding conflicts, (4) they become "bad objects," and (5) as long as there is an externalized "bad object," the idealized "good" introject can be kept alive and hoped for. Family therapy attempts to uncover these distortions and help the marital pair to see each other realistically.

RYDER, R. G., "Husband-Wife Dyads vs. Married Strangers," Fam. Proc., 7, 233-238, 1968. A comparison of the behavior of spouses with each other and with strangers by use of the color matching test which induces a conflict situation. Sixty-four married dyads and 56 unmarried dyads were contrasted. Few differences were found, but persons "treat strangers more gently, and generally more nicely than they do their spouses."

RYDER, R. G., "Two Replications of Color Matching Factors," Fam. Proc., 43-48, 1966. A replication of the color matching test of Goodrich and Boomer. The test was applied to 64 married couples and 56 split couples (defined as a male and female pair not married). Comparisons with the original sample, and between the married and unmarried groups are made.

RYDER, R. G., and GOODRICH, D. W., "Married Couples Responses to Disagreement," Fam. Proc., 5, 30-42, 1966. A report on the color matching test administered to 49 recently married couples. Husband and wife are exposed to colors and asked to match them when some of them do not match. Ways of handling the conflict are categorized and described.

RYLE, A., and HAMILTON, M., "Neurosis in Fifty Married Couples," J. Ment. Sci., 108, 265-273, 1962. An investigation of 50 working-class marital couples to record the prevalence of neurosis as indicated by the Cornell medical index, the records of the general practitioner with whom the families were registered, and the home interviews of a psychiatric social worker. The information from these sources was compared and the presence of neurosis was correlated with some aspects of adverse childhood experience, marital adjustment, consumer status and social integration.

SAGER, C., GRUNDRACH, R., KRAMER, M. LANZ, R., and ROYCE, J., "The Married in Treatment: Effects of Psychoanalysis on the Marital State," Arch. Gen. Psychiat., 19, 205-217, 1968. In order to ascertain the effects of psychoanalysis on the marital state, a study of 736 married patients (432 women and 304 men), aged 21 to 68, in middle and upper socioeconomic class who were being treated in psychoanalysis, was done. Seventy-nine psychoanalysts supplied data on "any ten consecutive patients." The data were obtained through a closed ended questionnaire. Twelve percent of the patients had concurrent group therapy, two percent were in conjoint marital therapy, and about twenty percent of the patients had one or more conjoint consultations with their spouse and analyst. Results indicated that marriages rated poor initially improved and marriages rated better also improved. There was no evidence that as one marital partner got better another got worse. Overall individual patient improvement was rated at about 60% of the cases. Of the spouses who were in treatment, good effects were more frequently reported in cases in which both husband and wife were treated by the same psychoanalyst.

SILVERMAN, H. L. (Ed.), Marital Counseling, Springfield, Charles C Thomas, 1967. A collection of new material on marital counseling which includes discussions of psychological factors, ideological factors, scientific factors, and a summary of marital counseling concepts. 530 pp.

SLUZKI, C. E., and BEAVIN, J., "Simetria y Complementariada: Una Definicion Operacional y Una Tipologia de Parejas," Acta Psiquiat. Psicolog. Amer. Lat., 11, 321-330, 1965. A discussion of classifying relationships in terms of symmetry and complementarity with a review of the literature on the subject. The variables are operationally defined and a speech score is derived based upon analysis of the transactional unit. A typology of couples and other dyads is proposed, composed of seven possible configurations based upon these modalities of interaction.

SNELL, J., ROSENWALD, R., and ROBEY, A., "The Wifebeater's Wife: A Study of Family Interaction," Arch. Gen. Psychiat., 11, 107-113, 1964. A study of 37 families in which men were charged by their wives with assault and battery and who were referred to one of the psychiatric clinics which serve the courts of Massachusetts. Twelve of the families were studied in detail (both husband and wife being

seen for three or more interviews). Four wives were in individual psychotherapy for
"more than 18 months." In addition, some group therapy and "couple therapy" was attempted. A typical family structure is described: husband is passive, indecisive,
and sexually inadequate; wife aggressive, masculine, frigid, and masochistic; relationship between the two characterized by alternation of passive and aggressive roles.
An adolescent son may upset the equilibrium.

STRODTBECK, F., "Husband-Wife Interaction Over Revealed Differences," Amer. Sociol. Rev.,
     23, 468-473, 1951.
A field study of ten Navajo, ten Texan, and ten Mormon couples. Balance of power can
be revealed using this technique, and it depends both on power elements in a larger
cultural organization and amount of participation in the small group situation.

THARP, R., "Marriage Roles, Child Development and Family Treatment," Amer. J. Orthopsy-
     chiat., 35, 531-538, 1965.
Previous research on marriage has given "a small grain of knowledge" according to the
author. He proposes a tentative structure of marriage roles: solidarity, sexuality,
external relations, internal instrumentality, and division of responsibility. Disturbed
marriage roles may result in disturbed parent-child relations within the same role function. Advances of this theory as well as applications to treatment of the family are
discussed.

TOWNE, R. D., MESSINGER, S. L., and SAMPSON, H., "Schizophrenia and the Marital Family:
     Accommodations to Symbiosis," Fam. Proc., 1, 304-318, 1962.
Another in a series of reports by this group of their study of 17 women who as young
adults had experienced severe difficulties in their marital families, and were hospitalized with a diagnosis of schizophrenia. Here the focus was on the "symbiotic" nature
of the family relationships which seem to serve to keep the families together, and
when broken down led to hospitalization of the wife. Three patterns are described.

VAN DEN BERGHE, P., "Hygergamy, Hypergenation and Miscegenation," Hum. Rel., 13, 83-91,
     1960.
The author suggests that marriage or mating of women upward in the status hierarchy is
widespread, and that it occurs under, and leads to, certain specific conditions. The
hypothesis of maximization of status is suggested to account for the marriage, mating,
and also miscegenation patterns. Data from a variety of societies give support to the
hypothesis.

VINCENT, C. D. (Ed.), Readings in Marriage Counseling, New York, Thomas Y. Crowell, 1957.
A collection of 52 articles on marriage counseling, the book includes sections on marriage counseling in an emerging and interdisciplinary profession; premarital counseling;
definitions, methods, and principles in marriage counseling; marriage counseling of individuals, couples and groups; theories of personality formation and change applicable
to marriage counseling; research in marriage counseling; and questions related to marriage counseling as an emerging profession.

VOGEL, E. F., "The Marital Relationship of Parents of Emotionally Disturbed Children:
     Polarization and Isolation," Psychiatry, 23, 1-12, 1960.
In a study of 18 families seen by an interdisciplinary team, nine families with emotionally disturbed children were matched with nine families with relatively healthy children.
The marriage relationship in all families with an emotionally disturbed child was found
to be more disturbed; the parents behaved as if they were polar opposites and each partner contended that his standards were right and the spouse's wrong. In the control families the parents had less physical separation, shared activities with each other more,
and exhibited more flexibility in the handling of money.

WARKENTIN, J., and WHITAKER, C., "Marriage -- The Cornerstone of the Family System," in
     O. Pollak and A. S. Friedman (Eds.), Family Dynamics and Female Sexual Delinquency,
     Palo Alto, Science & Behavior Books, 1969.
A description of the inner assumptions and postulates about human nature and marriage
of two experienced therapists. The emphasis is upon the importance of the therapist's
views about life when dealing with a family.

WARKENTIN, J., and WHITAKER, C. A., "The Secret Agenda of the Therapist Doing Couples
      Therapy," in G. H. Zuk and I. Boszormenyi-Nagy (Eds.), Family Therapy and Dis-
      turbed Families, Palo Alto, Science & Behavior Books, 1967.
A discussion of the treatment of married couples with the emphasis upon the profound
influence of the therapist's own pattern of personal living. Includes the authors'
premises about marriage.

WARKENTIN, J., and WHITAKER, C., "Serial Impasses in Marriage," in I. M. Cohen (Ed.),
      Psychiatric Research Report No. 20, Washington, American Psychiatric Association,
      1966.
A discussion of marriage as both a legal and an emotional commitment with special emphasis upon the times "when we may expect difficulty and even impasse in the development
of the emotional marriage." These times include the wedding night, pregnancy, the
second baby, and the"ten year syndrome."

WEISMAN, I., "Exploring the Effect of the Marital Relationship on Child Functioning
      and Parental Functioning," Soc. Casework, 44, 330-334, 1963.
A report on a study investigating the relationship between child functioning and marital patterns. A sample was drawn of clients from the Community Service Society of New
York and the data consisted of the judgments of the caseworkers who used a rating scale
to indicate severity and persistence of conflict in several areas of child functioning
and parental patterns.

WESTLEY, W. A., and EPSTEIN, N. B., "Report on the Psycho-Social Organization of the
      Family and Mental Health," in D. Willner (Ed.), Decisions, Values, and Groups,
      New York, Pergamon Press, 1960.
A report of a study designed to investigate the relationship between family functioning
and development of either mental health or pathology. The sample was 531 students of
the first-year class at a university who were given a Rorschach, a Gordon-Personality
test, and interviewed by a psychiatrist. Twenty were classified as being the most emotionally healthy, and of these, 17 were in the study. There is a schema for description, analysis, and evaluation of the family using a case example. Common features
of these emotionally healthy families are described.

WILLI, J., "Joint Rorschach Testing of Partner Relationships," Fam. Proc., 8, 64-78,
      1969.
A test of marital partners by the conjoint Rorschach procedure. A sample of 80 pairs
was examined with each person administered the Rorschach individually, and then again
administered it conjointly with the partner. The goal was to measure the relative
strength of the partners and how the personality of the subject changes in the discussion with the other.

YOUNG, T. L., "Family Neuropsychiatry," Dis. Nerv. Syst., 24, 243-246, 1963.
A report by a physician, trained in both neurology and psychiatry, of impressions gained
from treating 114 cases from 43 families for neurologic, psychotic, and psychoneurotic
states. Numerous cases are cited in support of the author's impressions that mental disturbances run in families, and that one family member's illness has significant effect on
other family members.

3.2 SIBLING STUDIES

BAXTER, J., "Family Relationship Variables in Schizophrenia, Acta Psychiat. Scand., 42,
      362-391, 1966.
A complete review of the literature starting from 1892 up to the present, with the focus
on variables related to the family and child development. Topics covered are: (1) sibling position of the patient, (2) loss of one or both parents, (3) presence of a distressed childhood in the patient's background, (4) atypical mother-child relationship,

(5) atypical father-child relationship, (6) emotional immaturity in the parents, (7) dominance and disturbances between the parents, (8) interpersonal conflict in the family (9) family-centered pathological behavior, and (10) special position of sibling set for the patient.

DAY, J., and KWIATKOWSKA, H., "The Psychiatric Patient and His 'Well' Sibling: A Comparison Through Their Art Productions," Bull. Art. Ther., 2, 51-66, 1962.
A clinical paper comparing the "well" sibling to the "sick" sibling in a schizophrenic family. The setting was an in-patient ward, and observations were taken from the art work of the paired siblings, during art therapy. The data from three families reveal that the "sick" sibling's art productions are quite disorganized, while the "well" sibling's productions are more normal, but often "incongruous or unusual."

FISCHER, A., "The Importance of Sibling Position in the Choice of a Career in Pediatric Nursing," J. Health Hum. Behav., 3, 283-288, 1962.
Questionnaires on sibling status and various other background characteristics and attitudes were administered to 109 student nurses in a children's hospital. The hypothesis that senior siblings are more likely to become pediatric nurses than junior siblings holds only for sibling groups of four or more. Further analysis shows that sex composition of the sibling group also affects this career choice. A theory to cover all sibling group sizes, based on opportunities for identification with feminine models is advanced. It is suggested that sibling position, handled more complexly, may be as significant as clinical studies suggest.

FOX, J. R., "Sibling Incest," Brit. J. Sociol., 13, 128-150, 1962.
A consideration of what motivates incestuous and non-incestuous behavior, i.e., the conditions under which incestuous behavior between siblings does and does not occur. Two types of pattern exist: when there is physical separation before puberty, desire is strong after puberty and temptation must be controlled by strong sanctions; when there is physical interaction before puberty, there will be aversion after puberty and little temptation, anxiety or strong sanctions. Ethnological evidence is introduced to support the hypothesis.

FRIEDMAN, A. S., "The 'Well' Sibling in the 'Sick' Family: A Contradiction," Int. J. Soc. Psychiat., Special Edition 2, 47-53, 1964.
A discussion of the function and importance of the sibling in treatment of families with a schizophrenic child. Emphasis is upon the sibling who is absent from the family therapy sessions, and it is said that typically this sibling is in "secret" alliance with one of the parents and the absence affects the outcome of the therapy. Clinical examples are given.

GREENBAUM, M., "Joint Sibling Interview as a Diagnostic Procedure," J. Child Psychol. Psychiat., 6, 227-232, 1965.
A report of a diagnostic procedure in which two siblings are interviewed jointly, or observed playing together, as part of a family work-up. Setting is a children's out-patient clinic. Techniques are described. It is said to offer the advantages of actually seeing how the patient interacts with other, lessens the artificial nature of the patient-therapist contact, and gives the therapist a chance to observe the health of at least one other sibling in the family.

JENSEN, S., "Five Psychotic Siblings," Amer. J. Psychiat., 119, 159-163, 1962.
Case report of a family in which five of seven siblings and ten of 17 members of the last two generations have had psychotic episodes. Genetic, environmental, and psychodynamic theories of etiology are discussed.

KEMPLER, W., IVERSON, R., and BEISSER, A., "The Adult Schizophrenic and His Siblings," Fam. Proc., 1, 224-235, 1962.
Sixty-five siblings in a group of 16 schizophrenic families were interviewed using a

structured protocol to explore parent-child relationships as seen by the siblings. Findings included distortions in communications by both patients and siblings and appeared unrelated to the schizophrenic process. Four subjects, all of whom were "favorite" children in the family, showed no such distortions. A transcript from a single family is presented.

LANE, E. A., and ALBEE, G. W., "Early Childhood Differences Between Schizophrenic Adults and Their Siblings," J. Abnorm. Soc. Psychol., 68, 193-195, 1964.
The IQ tests which had been taken when they were in the second grade were obtained for 36 men and women who were later hospitalized for schizophrenia. These IQ results were compared with those of their siblings taken at the same time. The mean IQ of those who later became schizophrenic was lower than that of the siblings. A control group did not show such differences.

LIDZ, T., FLECK, S., ALANEN, Y. O., and CORNELISON, A., "Schizophrenic Patients and Their Siblings," Psychiatry, 26, 1-18, 1963.
A study of the siblings of schizophrenics based upon individual interviews of family members, observation of family members with each other and hospital staff, and projective tests. Sixteen families were studied for periods ranging from six months to six years. As many siblings were psychotic as were reasonably well adjusted, and all except five or six of the 24 siblings suffered from severe personality disorders. Siblings of the same sex as the patient were more disturbed than those of the opposite sex.

LU, Y. C., "Contradictory Parental Expectations in Schiozphrenia," Arch. Gen. Psychiat., 6, 219-234, 1962.
A report of some preliminary findings of an investigation of the families of schizophrenics. The emphasis is upon a comparison of the parents' relationship with patient and with nonschizophrenic siblings in an attempt to explain why one child in a family develops shcizophrenia and not another. The parents expect a higher degree of dependence from the preschizophrenic than from the nonschizophrenic child, and they also · expect a higher degree of achievement and responsibility. The author suggests that the relational pattern of contradictory parental expectations and the child's persistent effort to fulfill them could be called a "quadruple bind."

LU, Y. C., "Mother-Child Role Relations in Schizophrenia: A Comparison of Schizophrenic Patients With Non-Schizophrenic Siblings," Psychiatry, 24, 133-142, 1961.
An investigation into why one child in a family develops schizophrenia and another does not, based upon interviews with 50 chronic schizophrenic patients, their siblings, and their parents. The patient is largely confined to his parents, especially his mother, while the siblings have several significant others.

NEWMAN, G., "Younger Brothers of Schizophrenics," Psychiatry, 29, 146-151, 1966.
As a contribution to intrafamilial dynamics in schizophrenic families, three cases are reported of siblings who had an older brother who was schizophrenic and who developed emotional disorder themselves. The cases were studied by the author in the course of psychotherapy. All three had great guilt from three sources — "letting the older brother bear the burden of the parent's demands, for not saving the older brother from mental illness, and for exercising his own perception, judgment, and initiative."

POLLAK, M., WOERNER, M., GOLDBERG, P., and KLEIN, D., "Siblings of Schizophrenic and Nonschizophrenic Psychiatric Patients," Arch. Gen. Psychiat., 20, 652-658, 1969.
A study attempting to test the relative power of genetic versus psychogenic etiology in schizophrenia. Sixty-four siblings of 46 schizophrenic patients, 104 siblings of 68 personality disorder patients, and 16 siblings of 13 index cases with psychoneurotic and affective disorders were compared in terms of their psychiatric status. Method was clinical interview in most cases, but where siblings could not personally be contacted, descriptions from the family or from other records were used. Results indicated the siblings of the schizophrenic patients did not differ from those of nonschizophrenic patients in overall incidence of abnormality. None of the many specific family interaction patterns hypothesized to be pathogenic for schizophrenia have thus far been substantiated by methodologically sound studies.

ROSENTHAL, D., "Confusion of Identity and the Frequency of Schizophrenia in Twins,"
    Arch. Gen. Psychiat., 3, 297-304, 1960.
The author sought to test the hypothesis that if the etiology of schiozphrenia is on
a familial basis, with genetic as well as psychodynamic factors playing equal roles,
then schizophrenia should occur more frequently among twins than among nontwins and
among monozygotic than among dizygotic twins. Case material is from two previously
reported studies in which the proportions of twins to nontwins with various psychotic
illness could be calculated. Findings were that neither schizophrenic nor psychotic
illness requiring hospitalization occurred more frequently in twins than in nontwins
or in monozygotic than dizygotic twins. The finding suggests that "confusion of ego
identity" said to occur more commonly among twins does not have etiological value with
respect to schizophrenia.

SHARAN (SINGER), SHLOMO, "Family Interaction with Schizophrenics and Their Siblings,"
    J. Abnorm. Psychol., 71, 345-353, 1966.
An experimental study contrasting the behavior of parents of schizophrenics with the
patient and with a sibling. Twenty-four families were asked to solve collectively the
questions from the comprehension and similarities subtests of the Wechsler-Bellvue Intelligence Scale. The conversations were compared for problem-solving efficiency, mutual support patterns, and parent-child sex role alignments. Parents and patient
worked as efficiently as parents and siblings, parents supported both children equally,
and fathers and mothers were equally dominant. The patients were more supportive of
their parents than were the siblings, and parental discord was more prominent when the
patient was present than when the sibling was present.

WEST, S. S., "Sibling Configurations of Scientists," Amer. J. Sociol., 66, 268-274,
    1960.
Birth order and the number of siblings of 813 scientists were obtained as part of a
study of six research organizations. The aim was to determine what type of family experience is associated with choice of research as a career. First, fifth, and sixth
birth ranks are over-represented; second, third, and fourth are under-represented.
Siblings are distributed randomly as regards sex. Comparison with data on the general
population indicates that as sibship size increases, probability of a scientist coming
from family decreases. Isolation in childhood is said to be important in developing
the characteristics of a scientist. Data support either a hypothesis that relative
isolation is necessary for research career, or the hypothesis that mothers of scientists
have fewer children than normal.

WYNNE, L. C., and SINGER, M. T., "Thought Disorder and Family Relations of Schizophren-
    ics: I. A Research Strategy. II. A Classification of Forms of Thinking," Arch.
    Gen. Psychiat., 9, 191-206, 1963.
A general discussion of the approach of the Wynne project. Families with schizophrenic
members are contrasted with families of nonschizophrenic psychiatric patients, and siblings are contrasted with patients. The emphasis is upon the links between family patterns and schizophrenic thought disorder, defined broadly to include experience. The
first part outlines the clinical and conceptual basis, the setting, and the kinds of research data. The second part presents a classification of schizophrenic thought disorders, including discrimination among varieties of schizophrenic and paranoid thinking.

3.3 FAMILY — MULTIPLE GENERATION

ATTNEAVE, C. L., "Therapy in Tribal Settings and Urban Network Intervention," Fam. Proc.
    8, 192-210, 1969.
A comparison of network therapy and interventions in a network-clan of a tribal minority
culture. An example of treatment with an Indian tribe is contrasted with urban network
treatment where the clan-like social structure must be reconstituted.

BEATMAN, F. L., "Intergenerational Aspects of Family Therapy," in N. W. Ackerman (Ed.),
      Expanding Theory and Practice in Family Therapy, New York, Family Service Associa-
      tion of America, 1967.
A clinical essay focussing on indications or contraindications for bringing in the third
generation in family therapy. The third generation often incapacitates the nuclear family. Several case examples are presented in support of bringing in the third generation. The clinical rule of thumb is not on sociologic lines, but rather "lines of
meaningful relationships and conflicts."

BELL, N. W., "Extended Family Relations of Disturbed and Well Families," Fam. Proc., 1,
      175-193, 1962.
The author's thesis is that "disturbed families have been unable to resolve conflicts
with the extended kin outside the nuclear family" and that "well" families have achieved
resolution of the problems of ties to extended kin. Most of the data were collected
from observation and interviews in the home. Findings were that the "pathological" families used the extended family to (1) shore up group defenses, (2) act as stimuli of
conflict, (3) act as screens for the projection of conflicts, and (4) act as competing
objects of support.

BRODY, E. H., and SPARK, G., "Institutionalization of the Aged: A Family Crisis," Fam.
      Proc., 5, 76-90, 1966.
A discussion of the importance of involving the family in the decision about institution-
alizing an aged person. Case examples are given.

EHRENWALD, J., "Neurosis in the Family," Arch. Gen. Psychiat., 3, 232-242, 1960.
Assuming that it is maladjusted attitudes rather than specific nosological entities
which are subject to psychological contagion, this article discusses the potentially
communicable nature of disturbed interpersonal attitudes. Examples are given of a family
covering four generations, and three smaller family groups, presenting obsessive-compulsive, psychosomatic, and hysteric features. Epidemiologically, the emphasis is upon
"elementary units of behavior as are included in our inventory of traits and attitudes"
rather than on the manifest symptoms.

EIST, H. I., and MANDEL, A. U., "Family Treatment of Ongoing Incest Behavior," Fam. Proc.,
      7, 216-232, 1968.
A description of a case in which there was ongoing incest behavior. Family treatment
was used and the techniques are discussed.

FISHER, S., and MENDELL, D., "The Communications of Neurotic Patterns Over Two and Three
      Generations," in N. W. Bell, and E. F. Vogel (Eds.), A Modern Introduction to the
      Family, Glencoe, Free Press, 1960.
A report on a study of similarities in the patterning of fantasy and behavior in two or
more generations of family groups. The data included projective tests and psychiatric
interviews. Six families with three generations of kin, and fourteen families with two
generations of kin, were examined and impressions are given.

FRANKLIN, P., "Family Therapy of Psychotics," Amer. J. Psychoanal., 29, 50-56, 1969.
A case report of a schizophrenic child and his parents and grandmother who were treated
both individually and with family therapy over seven years. The author's thesis is that
schizophrenic symptoms are a manifestation of a process that "involves the entire family."
The identified patient and the family improved after treatment.

GAP Report No. 76: The Case History Method in the Study of Family Process, New York,
      Group for the Advancement of Psychiatry, 1970.
The purpose of this report is to demonstrate a systematic approach to modify the traditional psychiatric case history for use in family diagnosis, treatment, and research.
There are sections on principles for compiling a family case history. A typical case
is presented and contrast made between a Puerto Rican working-class and American middle-
class family. Contrast in values within the nuclear family as well as within the extended family network are described. There is an appendix with a family case history outline. 380 pp.

HADER, M., "The Importance of Grandparents in Family Life," Fam. Proc., 4, 228-240,
     1965.
A discussion of the significance of grandparents in the life of young people and their
significance to young people. The literature is reviewed on grandparents with a division between the positive and negative influences.

HENRY, J., "Family Structure and the Transmission of Neurotic Behavior," Amer. J. Ortho-
     psychiat., 21, 800-818, 1951.
Based on analysis of interaction patterns of one family attending a child guidance clinic, the author makes the following hypothesis: "(1) Individuals learn relatively rigid patterns of interaction, which they then tend to project upon the world in such a
way as to expect reciprocal patterns from others," (2) "From the standpoint of intrafamilial interaction, neurosis may be considered originating in rigid interaction patterns of pathogenic quality," (3) "Family interaction patterns may be described with
relative precision that will enable us to state the general psychological characteristic of families," and (4) "The transmission of a neurosis in a family line is a transmission of a rigid interactional pattern of pathogenic quality."

JENSEN, S., "Five Psychotic Siblings," Amer. J. Psychiat., 119, 159-163, 1962.
Case report of a family in which five of seven siblings and ten of 17 members of the
last two generations have had psychotic episodes. Genetic, environmental, and psychodynamic theories of etiology are discussed.

KIERMAN, I. R., and PORTER, M. E., "A Study of Behavior-Disorder Correlations between
     Parents and Children," Amer. J. Orthopsychiat., 33, 539-541, 1963.
A report of three cases of youthful offenders who had been institutionalized, seemingly
reformed, and later married and reared children who eventually were referred to a child
guidance clinic. In all cases, an almost perfect correlation was found between the behavior of the preadolescent child and that of his parent at the time he or she was a
youthful offender.

LITWAK, E., "Geographic Mobility and Family Cohesion," Amer. Sociol. Rev., 25, 385-394,
     1960.
A second paper reporting a study of the families of 920 married white women living in
a middle class urban area. Several hypotheses about the relationship of identification
with extended kin and occupational mobility are tested. The data indicate that extended families do not hinder, but rather aid geographical, and hence, occupational mobility.

LITWAK, E., "Occupational Mobility and Extended Family Cohesion," Amer. Sociol. Rev.,
     25, 9-21, 1960.
Parson's view that occupational mobility is antithetical to the extended family system
is questioned. In this study of visiting and identification patterns in the families of
920 married white women living in a middle-class urban area, the findings support the
modified view that the extended family in a mature industrial society can provide aid
across class lines without hindering mobility.

MACHOTKA, P., PITTMAN, F. S., and FLOMENHAFT, K., "Incest as a Family Affair," Fam. Proc.,
     6, 98-116, 1967.
A discussion of incest from the point of view of the whole family. Two cases of father-
daughter incest and one of sibling incest are discussed with the emphasis upon the crucial role of the nonparticipating member, the concerted denial of the incest, and on
where the focus of therapy should be.

MENDELL, D., and CLEVELAND, S., "A Three-Generation View of a School Phobia," Voices,
     3, 16-19, 1967.
A case report in support of the notion that psychopathology is "passed on from generation to generation with a more or less specific way and expectation of handling it."
Three generations of data from the identified patient, a 14-year-old boy, his mother,
and maternal grandmother were obtained from clinical psychiatric interviews and the
Rorschach and thematic apperception tests. The school phobia of the identified patient
is seen as an attempt to answer the "obsessive concern" of the boy's relationship to
his mother and her relationship to her mother.

MENDELL, D., CLEVELAND, S., and FISHER, S., "A Five-Generation Family Theme," Fam. Proc., 7, 126-132, 1968.
A study examining projective test fantasies of family members. Five generations of one family were examined, including examination of 27 members. It was found that a family selects one or two central themes which are perpetuated in the responses of family members across generations.

MENDELL, D., and FISHER, S., "An Approach to Neurotic Behavior in Terms of a Three-Generation Family Model," J. Nerv. Ment. Dis., 123, 171-180, 1956.
One of a series of papers explaining that psychotic pathology can be understood in terms of a three-generational family model. The data were obtained from the author's clinical experience, other studies of the literature, and projective data from the Rorschach and TAT. Data from one case are offered in support of those hypotheses.

MENDELL, D., and FISCHER, S., "A Multi-Generation Approach to the Treatment of Psycho-pathology," J. Nerv. Ment. Dis., 126, 523-529, 1958.
An essay describing techniques of treating the family rather than the identified patient for various problems seen in a private psychiatric setting. TAT and Rorschach material were important parts of the diagnostic evaluation.

PETURSSON, E., "A Study of Parental Deprivation and Illness in 291 Psychiatric Patients," Int. J. Soc. Psychiat., 7, 97-105, 1961.
A group of 291 patients with functional psychiatric illness was observed by the author and information gathered about their parents from them, from spouses or relatives, or by direct observation in some instances. The parents suffered from functional psychiatric illness in 77.5% of the cases. The incidence of broken homes was 31.7%. There appeared to be a high incidence of patients developing the same type of psychiatric illness as the parents in various categories. Well integrated family units occurred in the background of patients in only 11.7% of the cases.

REISS, P. J., "The Extended Kinship System: Correlates of and Attitudes on Frequency of Interaction, Marriage Fam. Liv., 24, 333-339, 1962.
A report of a study of urban middle-class kinship systems with emphasis upon frequency of contact and attitudes about it. A sample was selected from the metropolitan Boston area and interviewed. The conclusions are that frequency of interaction are not explained by the sex, ethnic background, or family cycle phase of the respondents. Degree of kin relationship and distance of residence of kin are the most important variables. Half of the respondents felt the frequency of contact with kin has been insufficient and there is a desire for kin to live close but not too close.

SCHERZ, F., "The Crisis of Adolescence in Family Life," Soc. Casework, 48, 209-215, 1967.
Adolescence is seen as a time of crisis for the family in addition to the patient. When behavioral symptoms come up, family treatment is indicated. The influence of grandparents in the chain of family communication is discussed.

SCOTT, R., and ASHWORTH, P., "Closure at the First Schizophrenic Breakdown: A Family Study," Brit. J. Med. Psychol., 40, 109-146, 1967.
One of a series of papers on the preillness familial relationships of schizophrenics with their families at the time of the first decompensation. Sample included 23 families (19 female patients and four male patients), average age 26, who were seen over two and a half years, with an average number of interviews totalling 27 and lasting three hours apiece. Using a three-generational hypothesis, one or both parents has had a significant traumatic event (such as death or insanity of a parent). Their feelings about this event are studied pertinent to the development of a schizophrenic reaction in their children. "Signs of disturbance in the child are regarded by the parent as if a catastrophic event is occurring again" and their reaction often then seems inappropriate.

SOBEL, D. E., "Children of Schizophrenic Patients: Preliminary Observations on Early
    Development," Amer. J. Psychiat.,118, 512-517, 1961.
A report on observations of the early development of children whose parents are both
schizophrenic. Four infants were raised by their schizophrenic parents and four raised
by foster parents. Three of the four children raised by their original schizophrenic
parents developed clear signs of depression and irritability in infancy. None of the
four infants raised by foster parents developed any such clear signs of emotional disorder. The three schizophrenic mothers engaged in relatively little active play with
their infants or showed pleasurable responsiveness. Case details are presented.

STUCKERT, R. P., "Occupational Mobility and Family Relationships," Soc. Forces, 41, 301-
    307, 1963.
Conflicting theories as to whether the extended family is compatible with mobility have
been advanced. To resolve this issue and determine whether mobility affects other forms
of interaction, 266 white married couples in Milwaukee were interviewed. Current status
was assessed by occupation. Mobility was assessed relative to parental occupations.
Mobility is shown to be conversely related to frequency of contacts, lesser identification with extended family, lesser tendency to use the extended family as a reference
group, lesser tendency to use neighbors as a reference group, and higher participation
of wives in voluntary associations. It is concluded that mobility is detrimental to
extended family relations, and tends to produce social isolation of married women.

SUSSMAN, M. B., "Adaptive, Directive, and Integrative Behavior of Today's Family," Fam.
    Proc., 7, 239-250, 1968.
A discussion of the relationship between the nuclear family and its kinship structure,
as well as between other social institutions. It is said that the kin network acquires
commitments by rewards perceived as superior to those offered by other social structures and so establishes tradition-laden obligations among family members.

SWEETSER, D. A., "Mother-Daughter Ties Between Generations in Industrial Societies,"
    Fam. Proc., 3, 332-343, 1964.
A report of cross-generational family relations in Finland and Sweden. Though the nuclear family is relatively independent, strong kinship ties are maintained most frequently, with the married couples sharing a household with wives' parents rather than
husbands'.

TRIBBEY, J. A., "Like Father, Like Son: A Projection-Displacement Pattern," Bull. Men-
    ninger Clin., 28, 244-251, 1964.
A study concerned with the frequency with which a son begins to take up the behavior of
an antisocial father. Case material was from 55 boys referred for treatment to the psychiatric diagnostic unit of a children's receiving home. Of the 55, ten were judged by
the author to have histories similar to that of the father. The overall family picture
is "that of a boy whose parents are divorced, and whose father had a long-standing history of antisocial behavior. Before long, as the mother had always 'known,' the son
begins to get into trouble." Dynamics are discussed. Poor treatment results with these
cases are pointed out.

WAHL, C. W., "The Psychodynamics of Consummated Maternal Incest," Arch. Gen. Psychiat.,
    3, 188-193, 1960.
This is a report of two cases of hospitalized schizophrenic men who had sexual relations
with their mothers. The author discusses dynamics of maternal incest, and states that
his case material supports the view that incestuous problems in schizophrenic patients
play a role in the development of schizophrenia.

YOUNG, M., and GEERTZ, H., "Old Age in London and San Francisco: Some Families Compared,"
    Brit. J. Sociol., 12, 124-141, 1961.
A British and an American suburb are compared as to family attitudes of older people. No
differences were found in the frequency of contact with adult children and the tendency
to live close by, or in the greater importance of adult daughters in parents' lives.
But the American respondents had more knowledge of and pride in their ancestors. Larger
national samples confirmed the last finding. The finding is explained in terms of the
prestige of ancestry and the openness of the class system in the United States.

YOUNG, T. L., "Family Neuropsychiatry," Dis. Nerv. Syst., 24, 243-246, 1963.
A report by a physician, trained in both neurology and psychiatry, of impressions gained
from treating 114 cases from 43 families for neurologic, psychotic, and psychoneurotic
states. Numerous cases are cited in support of the author's impressions that mental
disturbances run in families, and that one family member's illness has significant effect on other family members.

3.4 FAMILY CRISIS STUDIES

ANTHONY, E. J., and KOUPERNIK, C. (Eds.), The Child in His Family, New York, Wiley, 1970.
Volume 1 in the series of the International Yearbook for Child Psychiatry and Allied
Disciplines. Included are papers from a variety of authors of different nations. The
sections include family dynamics, family vulnerability and crisis, chronic family pathology, and mental health and families in different cultures. 492 pp.

BARD, M., and BERKOWITZ, B., "A Community Psychology Consultation Program in Police
     Family Crisis Intervention: Preliminary Impressions," Int. J. Soc. Psychiat., 15,
     209-215, 1969.
The second in a series of reports describing training of police in family crisis intervention with low socioeconomic-class patients. Rationale for the program, methods of
selection, and techniques of training (which included use of family crisis laboratory
demonstrations and "human relations workshops") are presented.

BARD, M., and BERKOWITZ, B., "Training Police As Specialists in Family Crisis Interven-
     tion: A Community Psychology Action Program," Comm. Ment. Health J., 3, 315-337,
     1967.
A description of a project to train policemen in doing family crisis intervention based
on the idea that family crises often precipitate criminal acts or that policemen are often called as a first line of defense during family crisis. During the preparatory
phase, volunteers were given lectures, field trips, and "learning by doing" demonstrations. An evaluation of the program is planned.

BOLMAN, W., "Preventive Psychiatry for the Family: Theory, Approaches, and Programs,"
     Amer. J. Psychiat., 125, 458-472, 1968.
A detailed paper attempting to integrate the ideas on preventive psychiatry for the family with systems theory. Goals, approaches, and specific programs are given for
various types of populations, e. g., families in crisis due to loss of a member.

BRODY, E. H., and SPARK, G., "Institutionalization of the Aged: A Family Crisis," Fam.
     Proc., 5, 76-90, 1966.
A discussion of the importance of involving the family in the decision about institu-
tionalizing an aged person. Case examples are given.

CAPLAN, G., "Patterns of Parental Response to the Crisis of Premature Birth: A Prelimi-
     nary Approach to Modifying the Mental Health Outcome," Psychiatry, 23, 365-374,
     1960.
Types of response to the crisis of a premature birth were derived from interview data
on ten cases where the baby weighed less than four pounds and the records were suffi-
ciently detailed so a case could be assigned unambiguously to an extreme category of
healthy or unhealthy outcome. Cases were classified as "healthy outcome" if all relationships in the family were as healthy or more healthy than before the birth and if
parent-child relationships were healthy at the end of 12 weeks. "Unhealthy outcomes"
were the reverse. It is hoped that further studies will help professional people recognize extreme patterns associated with poor outcome to a crisis so they can intervene
promptly.

COUNTS, R., "Family Crisis and the Impulsive Adolescent," Arch. Gen. Psychiat., 17, 64-74, 1967.
A case example is presented in support of the hypothesis that the acting out of an adolescent can best be understood by seeing it as acting out of a family crisis. The adolescent is used as a scapegoat of the family and he acts out somebody else's impulses, which helps to stabilize his own internal operations while it stabilizes the family.

FLOMENHAFT, K., KAPLAN, D., and LANGSLEY, D., "Avoiding Psychiatric Hospitalization," Soc. Work, 14, 38-46, 1969.
One of a series of articles comparing "out-patient family crisis therapy" with psychiatric hospitalization. The methodology has been previously described. Results achieved by both of these two methods were equivalent. However, the authors stressed out-patient treatment treatment as more economical and less "stigmatizing."

GLASSMAN, R., LIPTON, H., and DUNSTAN, P., "Group Discussions With A Hospitalized Schizophrenic and His Family," Int. J. Group Psychother., 9, 204-212, 1959.
From an in-patient hospital service, this is a case report of treatment of a schizophrenic patient at the time of an acute crisis in his hospitalization. The crisis was the return of the patient to his family. The crisis was handled through treatment of the patient and family together in ten one-hour sessions over a period of 17 weeks.

Group for the Advancement of Psychiatry, Committee on the Family, Integration and Conflict in Family Behavior, Report No. 27, Topeka, 1954.
A report by the committee on the family of GAP dealing with organizing data on the study of the family. It discusses the relation of the family to the social system, the system of values to which the family is oriented, and Spanish-American family patterns as well as American middle-class family patterns. 67 pp.

JENSEN, D., and WALLACE, J. G., "Family Mourning Process," Fam. Proc., 6, 56-66, 1967.
A discussion of mourning as a family crisis involving all members. Two case examples are given. Therapy is seen as intervening in maladaptive family interaction patterns resulting from the loss of a member.

KAPLAN, D. M., and MASON, E. A., "Maternal Reactions to Premature Birth Viewed as an Acute Emotional Disorder," Amer. J. Orthopsychiat., 30, 539-552, 1960.
A study of the maternal reaction to premature birth being carried out in the Harvard School of Public Health Family Guidance Center. Examination of 60 families following the premature birth indicates a typical psychological experience for the mother. The maternal stress begins with the onset of labor and continues through delivery and after. Case examples are given of more and less successful resolution of the situation.

KRITZER, H., and PITTMAN, F. S., "Overnight Psychiatric Care in a General Emergency Room," J. Hosp. Comm. Psychiat., 19, 303-306, 1968.
A clinical article reviewing the experience with 36 psychiatric patients who came to the emergency room because of a crisis. As alternatives to in-patient hospitalization, overnight hospitalization and the emergency room were used. Rationale was that the patients' presenting problems were often a manifestation of underlying family problems, and by temporarily relieving the crisis and working out the future management, in-patient hospitalization could be avoided. Results indicated that of 36 patients, 11 were essentially sent to a psychiatric hospital, 22 were discharged directly from the emergency room, and three signed out against medical advice.

LANGSLEY, D., FLOMENHAFT, K., and MACHOTKA, P., "Followup Evaluation of Family Crisis Therapy," Amer. J. Orthopsychiat., 39, 753-759, 1969.
One of a series of papers on a research project in which families were assigned randomly either to traditional hospital treatment or family crisis therapy with a focus on family therapy. Six-month follow-up evaluations of 150 family crisis therapy cases and 150 hospital treatment cases demonstrated that patients are less likely to be rehospitalized in the former group.

LANGSLEY, D. G., PITTMAN, F., MACHOTKA, P., and FLOMENHAFT, K., "Family Crisis Therapy:
    Results and Implications," Fam. Proc., 7, 145-159, 1968.
A report on the crisis treatment unit established at Colorado Psychiatric Hospital in
Denver. A total of 186 cases randomly selected were treated by brief family treatment
and compared with control cases hospitalized in the usual way. Preliminary results
are reported.

LANGSLEY, D., PITTMAN, F., and SWANK, G., "Family Crisis in Schizophrenics and Other
    Mental Patients," J. Nerv. Ment. Dis., 149, 270-276, 1969.
A further report on a study using crisis therapy as an alternative to psychiatric hospitalization. In this study, 50 families which included a schizophrenic patient, and
50 which included a nonschizophrenic mental patient, were studied using an instrument
which quanitified the events leading to a crisis in the family and the management of
such crises. Nonschizophrenic mental patients were better able to handle crisis and
interact with their families. Discussion of these findings is presented.

MORRISON, G., and COLLIER, J., "Family Treatment Approaches to Suicidal Children and
    Adolescents," J. Amer. Acad. Child Psyciat., 8, 140-154, 1969.
A study of 34 patients referred to a child psychiatry emergency service because of a
suicide attempt. There were 28 girls and six boys in the sample, with 65% of the group
between the ages of 15 and 17. They were seen with their families by a psychiatrist
and social worker. Rationale was that the suicide attempt was an effort on the part
of the child to reveal underlying family disruption. After the acute crisis was resolved
using family therapy, 30 of the 34 patients were referred for further therapy. Of
these 30, 28 accepted the recommendation, but only eight made further interviews and
only two were in treatment one year after the suicide attempt.

NEALON, J., "The Adolescent's Hospitalization as a Family Crisis," Arch. Gen. Psychiat.,
    11, 302-312, 1964.
A study of the reactions of 25 sets of parents to the hospitalization of an adolescent
member of the family. Data were collected from parents' initial interviews with caseworker. Interviews were held before admission, or as soon as possible afterward. The
hospitalization was defined as a family crisis because "of the impact of mental illness
on the family, family disruption precipitating and following hospitalization, and the
parent's expectation of the hospitalization." Family-oriented approach is stressed,
and implications for treatment are discussed.

PARAD, H. J., and CAPLAN, G., "A Framework for Studying Families in Crises," Soc. Work.,
    5, 3-15, 1960.
An approach to the observation and study of the family in crisis. Family members are
seen individually and as a group in the home, while engaged in household activities.
The concepts of family life-style, problem-solving mechanisms, and need-response patterns are illustrated with a case history. It is suggested that intervention is most
effective at the moment the family is in crisis.

PATTISON, W. M., "Treatment of Alcoholic Families with Nurse Home Visits," Fam. Proc.,
    4, 75-94, 1965.
The use of public health nurses in making home visits is described in terms of preventive crisis intervention and family therapy. The results in a study of seven families
are offered with case examples and it is said the public health nurse can play a decisive role, particularly with lower-class, multiproblem families.

PITTMAN, F., DeYOUNG, C., FLOMENHAFT, K., KAPLAN, D., and LANGSLEY, D., "Crisis Family
    Therapy," in J. Masserman (Ed.), Current Psychiatric Therapies, Vol. VI, New York,
    Grune & Stratton, 1966.
A report of the authors' experiences in using a family approach in dealing with acute
crisis situations, rather than using hospitalization or individual psychotherapy. Setting was an acute treatment facility which hospitalizes about 75% of patients referred.
Of these, 25% were referred to the family treatment unit consisting of a psychiatrist,
social worker, and nurse. Fifty cases were referred to this unit and in 42 cases hospitalization was "avoided completely." Techniques of treatment are discussed.

PITTMAN, F., LANGSLEY, D., FLOMENHAFT, K., DeYOUNG, D., and MACHOTKA, P., "Therapy
    Techniques of the Family Treatment Unit," in J. Haley (Ed.), Changing Families,
    New York, Grune & Stratton, 1971.
A report on the therapy techniques of the crisis treatment unit in Denver which did
brief family therapy to keep people out of the hospital. Different approaches used
are described.

PITTMAN, F., LANGSLEY, D., KAPLAN, D., FLOMENHAFT, K., and DeYOUNG, C., "Family Therapy
    as an Alternative to Psychiatric Hospitalization," in I. M. Cohen (Ed.), Psychiat-
    ric Research Report No. 20, Washington, American Psychiatric Association, 1966.
A report on the crisis treatment team at the Colorado Psychopathic Hospital which
treated a random selection of patients and their families as an alternative to hospitalization. Case examples are given.

RAPOPORT, R., and RAPOPORT, R. N., "New Light on the Honeymoon," Hum. Rel., 17, 33-56,
    1964.
A general discussion of the honeymoon followed by a task description illustrated with
a case example. The honeymoon ritual is described as part of the life-cycle transition point of marriage.

SAMPSON, H., MESSINGER, S., and TOWNE, R. D., "Family Processes and Becoming a Mental
    Patient," Amer. J. Sociol., 68, 88-96, 1962.
The accommodation of the family to the deviant behavior of the future patient, and the
disruption of this accommodation which leads to hospitalization are described for a
series of 17 married mothers. Patients were located at time of first admission and extensive data collected by interviews with family members, by professionals involved
at any stage, and by direct observation in home and hospital. Types of accommodation
found were: (1) spouses isolated, emotionally distant from each other, and (2) family
not self-contained but revolved about a maternal figure who took over wife's duties.
Each type has characteristic ways of disrupting, resulting in different implications
to hospitalization.

SAMPSON, H., MESSINGER, S., and TOWNE, R. D., "The Mental Hospital and Family Adapta-
    tions," Psychiat. Quart., 36, 704-719, 1962.
The authors' purpose was to examine the effects of hospitalization on the family, not
only during the hospitalization but also after discharge. Seventeen families in which
the wife-mother was hospitalized for the first time and was diagnosed by the state hospital as schizophrenic, were studied using interviews and records up to two years after release. Emphasis is placed on a more deliberate therapeutic intervention based
on study of the crisis that precipitated hospitalization, and ways in which these crises are coped with by the family.

WHITIS, P. R., "The Legacy of a Child's Suicide," Fam. Proc., 7, 159-169, 1968.
A discussion of the effect on a family of a child's suicide illustrated with a case
report. Prompt therapeutic intervention is recommended for the bereaved family.

3.5 ECOLOGY OF THE FAMILY

ACKERMAN, N. W., "Adolescent Problems: A Symptom of Family Disorder," Fam. Proc., 1,
    202-213, 1962.
An essay based on the thesis that adolescent problems represent in part not only a disorder of a particular stage of growth, but also a symptom of a parallel disorder in the
family, society, and culture. Clinical examples are given.

ANTHONY, E. J., and KOUPERNIK, C., (Eds.), The Child in His Family, New York, Wiley, 1970.
Volume 1 in the series of the International Yearbook for Child Psychiatry and Allied Disciplines. Papers included are from a variety of authors of different nations. The sections include family dynamics, family vulnerability and crisis, chronic family pathology, and mental health and families in different cultures. 492 pp.

ARONSON, J., and POLGAR, S., "Pathogenic Relationships in Schizophrenia," Amer. J. Psychiat., 119, 222-227, 1962.
While investigating 13 soldiers who developed overtly schizophrenic psychoses in the army, the authors interviewed 185 individuals on 11 army posts to gather data. Work performance and overt psychotic symptoms are said to depend upon the type of relationship established with significant others. Three types of relationship were distinguished: the quasitherapeutic, the pseudotherapeutic, and the contratherapeutic. The authors suggest the data indicate that groups other than the family can be pathogenic.

BERTRAND, A. L., "School Attendance and Attainment: Function and Dysfunction of School and Family Social Systems," Soc. Forces, 40, 228-233, 1962.
The hypothesis is advanced that the dropping out of school of capable youths is dysfunctional for the society but functional for family, school, and other primary social systems. Data were gathered in Louisiana from 369 students and 68 dropouts, and from 125 and 68 of their parents, respectively. The families of dropouts are found to be farmlaborers rather than owners and managers, have less education, less involvement in school affairs, place a low value on education, and were of lower status. Dropouts also are geographically distant from schools, have low grades, participate little in school activities, and do not find the school system compatible.

BOLMAN, W., "Preventive Psychiatry for the Family: Theory, Approaches and Programs," Amer. J. Psychiat., 125, 458-472, 1968.
A detailed paper attempting to integrate the ideas on preventive psychiatry for the family with systems theory. Goals, approaches, and specific programs are given for various types of populations, e. g., families in crisis due to loss of a member.

BRODEY, W., and HAYDEN, M., "Intrateam Reactions: Their Relation to the Conflicts of the Family in Treatment," Amer. J. Orthopsychiat., 27, 349-356, 1957.
A clinical report emphasizing the notion that reactions of treating personnel to each other are in part a reenactment of conflicts of the family. Data were obtained from an out-patient child guidance clinic team of psychotherapist and caseworker. Five case examples were given to support this hypothesis. By focussing on the reactions of the workers, significant dynamics trends can be identified and therapy can be accelerated. The building of family conflicts that influence the intrateam reactions depends upon the power of the family conflict and the sensitivity of the team equilibrium to this particular stress.

BURSTEN, B., "Family Dynamics, The Sick Role, and Medical Hospital Admissions," Fam. Proc., 4, 206-216, 1965.
A discussion of how the medical hospital may be used in the service of family patterns. There may be no organic difficulty, or an organic difficulty can be combined with psychosocial factors to resolve a family conflict. Case examples are given.

CAREK, D. J., and WATSON, A. S., "Treatment of a Family Involved in Fratricide," Arch. Gen. Psychiat., 11, 533-543, 1964.
Case report of a family where the eldest male sibling (age ten) shot and killed the youngest male sibling. The parents were treated with conjoint family therapy, and the oldest sibling was hospitalized. Data were collected from the conjoint family meetings and from observations of the hospitalized patient. Formulation and treatment is discussed. The data are related to "society's philosophical view of illegal behavior and treatment, and some speculations about therapeutic implementation."

CHOPE, H. D., and BLACKFORD, L., "The Chronic Problem Family: San Mateo County's Ex-
     perience," Amer. J. Orthopsychiat., 33, 462-469, 1963.
A report summarizing ideas developed by the San Mateo Department of Health and Welfare
in dealing with the chronic, multiproblem family and their multiple agency services.
They point out that the agencies helping the chronic, multiproblem family cannot function independently and suggest one worker to "represent the family."

CLARK, A. W., and Van SOMMERS, P.,"Contradictory Demands in Family Relations and Adjust-
     ment to School and Home," Hum. Rel., 14, 97-111, 1961.
Intensive case-studies of families of 20 maladjusted and 20 adjusted children: all
families had one or more adults other than the parents living in the family. The concern was with "the process of explaining an unsatisfactory relationship between any two
individuals in terms of the influence of a third individual." Data were obtained by
detailed, focussed interviews, questionnaires to school staffs, group interviews with
peers, and tests of ability. School difficulties were associated with unsatisfactory
relationships in the home, one of which was dependence of one parent upon the other
adults. Unsatisfactory relationships of adults contribute to withdrawal of father from
family activities, difficulties between adults and children, maladjustment of children
at home and school, and recurrence of symptoms in parents.

COLLOMB, H., and VALANTIN, S., "The Black African Family," in E. J. Anthony and C. Kou-
     pernik (Eds.), The Child in His Family, New York, Wiley, 1970.
A description of the black African family with the emphasis upon demographic data, cultural and social frameworks, filiation and lineage, and intrafamilial relationships.

CURRY, A. E., "The Family Therapy Situation as a System," Fam. Proc., 5, 131-141, 1966.
A discussion of the processes which occur between a family unit and the family therapist
which involve neutralizing the therapist, reestablishing the family's pre-therapy equilibrium, and disrupting the overall family therapy situation. Processes of coalition,
coalescence, and coagulation are presented with examples.

EPSTEIN, N., and CLEGHORN, J., "The Family Transactional Approach in General Hospital
     Psychiatry: Experiences, Problems, and Principles," Compr. Psychiat., 7, 389-
     396, 1966.
A paper dealing with the experiences and problems arising, and principles derived from,
the introduction of concepts of family dynamics and family therapy in the psychiatry departments of two general hsopitals. The concepts were used in the out-patient department,community department, in-patient service, and the day hospital. Ongoing supervision for family as well as for individual therapy is stressed.

FLECK, S., CORNELISON, A., NORTON, N., and LIDZ, T., "The Intrafamilial Environment of
     the Schizophrenic Patient. III. Interaction Between Hospital Staff and Families,"
     Psychiatry, 20, 343-350, 1957.
One of a series of papers on the effect of the family on the etiology and pathogenisis
of schizophrenia. The role of the patient's family with the hospital staff was examined.
Neglecting the relationship of the family to the staff can affect the patient's hospital
course "deleteriously or even catastrophically."

GARDNER, R. A., "A Four-Day Diagnostic-Therapeutic Home Visit in Turkey," Fam. Proc., 9,
     301-317, 1970.
A report of a four-day visit in Istanbul to consult with a family of a 20-year-old Turkish patient. A Greek and a Turkish psychiatrist comment on the article.

GLASSER, P. H., and NAVARRE, E. L., "The Problems of Families in the AFDC Program," in
     P. H. Glasser and L. N. Glasser (Eds.), Families in Crisis, New York, Harper & Row,
     1970.
The effects of poverty on the family presented sociologically and psychologically, and
from the point of view of the mother, and the social worker.

GOODE, W. J., "Marital Satisfaction and Instability: A Cross-Cultural Class Analysis
     of Divorce Rates," in P. H. Glasser and L. N. Glasser (Eds.), Families in Crisis,
     New York, Harper & Row, 1970.
A discussion of marital stability with the emphasis upon forms of instability and disorganization in families. Divorce is described in terms of class and across cultures,
with divorce rates given for various countries.

HALEY, J., "Cross-Cultural Experimentation: An Initial Attempt," Hum. Organ., 3, 110-
     117, 1967.
A comparison of Caucasion middle-class American families and Japanese-born families in
an experimental setting where the measure is speech sequences. Differences are found.

HOFFMAN, L., and LONG, L., "A Systems Dilemma," Fam. Proc., 8, 211-234, 1969.
A description of a man's breakdown in terms of the social systems within which he moved
and the attempts to intervene to bring about change. The ecological field of a person
is the area considered.

JEFFERS, C., "Living Poor: Providing the Basic Necessities, Priorities and Problems,"
     in P. H. Glasser and L. N. Glasser (Eds.), Families in Crisis, New York, Harper
     & Row, 1970.
A description of low-income families and the problems of a mother providing decent food,
clothing, and shelter.

KAFFMAN, M., "Family Diagnosis and Therapy in Child Emotional Pathology," Fam. Proc.,
     4, 241-258, 1965.
A description of families treated in Israel based upon 194 kibbutz families and 126
families living in Haifa. Family treatment is said to be effective. Case examples are
given.

KHATRI, A. A., "Personality and Mental Health of Indians (Hindus) in the Context of
     Their Changing Family Organization," in E. J. Anthony and C. Koupernik (Eds.),
     The Child in His Family, New York, Wiley, 1970.
A discussion of the Hindu patrilineal family and its impact on personality and mental
health. The effects of social change are emphasized.

LANCASTER, L., "Some Conceptual Problems in the Study of Family and Kin Ties in the
     British Isles," Brit. J. Sociol., 12, 317-333, 1961.
A critique of studies of family and kinship in contemporary societies, with emphasis
upon clarifying structural categories such as kinship systems, networks, sets, groups,
and households.

McCORD, W., McCORD, J., and HOWARD, A., "Early Familial Experiences and Bigotry," Amer.
     Sociol. Rev., 25, 717-772, 1960.
The Authoritarian Personality concluded that bigots have experienced stern, moralistic,
rejecting child rearing. The conclusion, much challenged, is evaluated in the light
of data from the Cambridge-Somerville Youth Study. Ratable data on prejudices are
available for 45 of 200 subjects re-interviewed in 1948 and 1956. No relation between
degree of prejudice and family experiences as determined earlier could be established.
The interpretation is suggested that prejudice in the lower class is a part of a generally stereotyped culture and does not relate to personality needs or family environment.

MINUCHIN, S., "The Use of an Ecological Framework in the Treatment of a Child," in E. J.
     Anthony and C. Koupernik (Eds.), The Child in His Family, New York, Wiley, 1970.
A discussion of the three elements in the study of the child: as an individual, in his
environment, and the linkage between the two. The ecological point of view is discussed.
A case of an adolescent with anorexia nervosa is examined in terms of his family and the
family therapy approach to the problem.

NARAIN, D., "Growing Up in India," Fam. Proc., 3, 127-154, 1964.
A review of research on the socialization of the child in India with a detailed review
of the studies on child rearing and parent-child relationships.

OPLER, M. K., "Social and Cultural Influences on the Psychopathology of Family Groups,"
    in G. H. Zuk and I. Boszormenyi-Nagy (Eds.), Family Therapy and Disturbed Fami-
    lies, Palo Alto, Science & Behavior Books, 1967.
An essay considering the social context of the family as related to mental health. Examples from different cultures are given.

OSTBY, C. H., "Conjoint Group Therapy with Prisoners and Their Families," Fam. Proc.,
    7, 184-201, 1968.
A report on a family treatment program at a correctional institution. The approach
used was multiple family therapy. The special effect of the prison settings are given.
Case examples are described.

POLLAK, O., "Family Structure: Its Implications for Mental Health," in O. Pollak and
    A. S. Friedman (Eds.), Family Dynamics and Female Sexual Delinquency, Palo Alto,
    Science & Behavior Books, 1969.
A discussion of the implications for mental health of various types of family structure.
Compared are middle-class families, fatherless families, and three-generation families.

SAMPSON, H., MESSINGER, S. L., and TOWNE, R. D., "The Mental Hospital and Marital Family
    Ties," Soc. Prob., 9, 141-155, 1961.
The social processes affecting the marital family of 17 first admissions to a California state hospital and their families are described. Hospitalization for these cases
did not interrupt ties to the community, but did provide a moratorium which allowed a
reestablishment of outside ties.

SCHWEEN, P., and GRALNICK, A., "Factors Affecting Family Therapy in the Hospital Setting,"
    Compr. Psychiat., 7, 424-431, 1966.
An article discussing the modifications necessary when doing family therapy in a hospital setting. Transference and countertransference problems, administrative problems,
and the role of the other patients in treatment are mentioned.

SPECK, R. V., "Psychotherapy of the Social Network of a Schizophrenic Family," Fam.
    Proc., 6, 208-214, 1967.
A description of the social network approach to treatment. Procedure, goals, and future
directions are described.

SPIEGEL, J. P., "Some Cultural Aspects of Transference and Counter-Transference," in J.
    Masserman (Ed.), Science and Psychoanalysis, Vol. II, Individual and Family Dynam-
    ics, New York, Grune & Stratton, 1959.
A clinical essay based on work with working class Irish-American, Italian-American, and
so-called "old American" families from two groups. The first were "well" families; the
second were "sick" families. Data were gathered from clinic visits as well as home visits. Countertransference difficulties vary as to the cultural population. Having an
entire family involved helps break the impasse that often develops. The family and the
community are seen as important variables in the functioning of an individual.

SPITZER, S. P., SWANSON, R. M., and LEHR, R. K., "Audience Reactions and Carrers of
    Psychiatric Patients," Fam. Proc., 8, 159-181, 1969.
A study of the reaction of families and the ways these reactions influence the psychiatric patient career. The histories of 79 first admission patients were examined, and
patient and a family member were interviewed. Two dimensions of family reaction to
deviance are described leading to a typology of eight career patterns which allow for
the classification of 95% of the cases reviewed.

STRODTBECK, F., "Husband-Wife Interaction over Revealed Differences," Amer. Sociol. Rev.,
      23, 468-473, 1951.
A field study of ten Navajo, ten Texan and ten Mormon couples. Balance of power can be
revealed using this technique. The technique depends both on power elements in a larger cultural organization and amount of participation in the small group situation.

SUMER, E. A., "Changing Dynamic Aspects of the Turkish Culture and Its Significance
      for Child Training," in E. J. Anthony and C. Koupernik (Eds.), The Child in His
      Family, New York, Wiley, 1970.
A description of families in Turkey based upon "intensive psychiatric work with large
numbers of families" who have applied at out-patient services. Child rearing, sexual
education, and discipline are discussed.

SUSSMAN, M. B., "Adaptive, Directive, and Integrative Behavior of Today's Family," Fam.
      Proc., 7, 239-250, 1968.
A discussion of the relationship between the nuclear family and its kinship structure
as well as other social institutions. It is said that the kin network acquires commitments by rewards perceived as superior to those offered by other social structures
and so establishes tradition-laden obligations among family members.

VASSILIOU, G., "Milieu Specificity in Family Therapy," in N. W. Ackerman (Ed.), Family
      Therapy in Transition, Boston, Little, Brown, 1970.
A description of the Greek family, its historical development, and its problems as seen
from a family therapy point of view.

VINCENT, C. E., "Mental Health and the Family," in P. H. Glasser and L. N. Glasser (Eds.),
      Families in Crisis, New York, Harper & Row, 1970.
A selective review of broad developments and trends in the emerging role of the federal
government in the mental health field. The relevance of the family to mental health
and community mental health centers is discussed with a review. Present needs are examined.

VINCENT, C. E., "Mental Health and the Family," J. Marriage Fam., 29, 18-38, 1967.
A clinical essay by a sociologist focussing on creating a new specialty. The adaptation
of the family to community and society, as well as to its own members, is crucial in the
development of individual psychopathology.

WARKENTIN, J., and WHITAKER, C. A., "The Secret Agenda of the Therapist doing Couples
      Therapy," in G. H. Zuk and I. Boszormenyi-Nagy (Eds.), Family Therapy and Disturbed
      Families, Palo Alto, Science & Behavior Books, 1967.
A discussion of the treatment of married couples with the emphasis upon the profound influence of the therapist's own pattern of personal living. Includes the authors' premises about marriage.

4.1 CONTRASTING FAMILY TYPES

AHMED, F., "Family and Mental Disorders in Pakistan," Int. J. Soc. Psychiat., 14, 290-
      295, 1968.
In order to study the effect of the structure of the family on mental illness, 967 cases
from a privately owned psychiatric clinic in Pakistan were studied, using retrospective
case records. Only psychotics and neurotics were used from the larger sample. Results
revealed that there were more female psychotics, that psychotic patients were closer in
age to their parents, that father was usually less than 25 years of age for the psychotics and more than 25 for the neurotics. That more psychotics were the oldest in the
family and more neurotics were the youngest. There was more psychopathology in the
family of psychotics than in that of neurotics. No relationship was found between men-

tal disorders and marital status, sibling order, parental loss in childhood, and mother's age at birth.

BAXTER, J. C., and ARTHUR, S., "Conflict in Families of Schizophrenics as a Function
        of Premorbid Adjustment and Social Class," Fam. Proc., 3, 273-279, 1964.
A group of 16 hospitalized male schizophrenics was classified into four groups on the basis of the patients' premorbid adjustment and social class. Standard interviews with the parents were rated for conflict. "Results indicate that the amount of conflict expressed by the parents varies jointly with the premorbid level of the patient and the social class of the family."

BAXTER, J. C., ARTHUR, S., FLOOD, C., and HEDGEPETH, B., "Conflict Patterns in the
        Families of Schizophrenics," J. Nerv. Ment. Dis., 135, 419-424, 1962.
Families of 12 male and six female schizophrenics were interviewed individually and as a group to explore conflict patterns in relation to the sex of the child. The amount of conflict is said to be comparable in the two groups while patterns of conflict differ. There is more interparental conflict in the group of families with a male patient and more involvement of the patient in conflict in the group with a female patient.

BAXTER, J. C., and BECKER, J., "Anxiety and Avoidance Behavior in Schizophrenics in
        Response to Parental Figures," J. Abnorm. Soc. Psychol., 64, 432-437, 1962.
Good and poor premorbid schizophrenics were exposed to TAT cards of parent-child relationships. Poor premorbids produced more anxiety in response to a mother figure than a father figure. Good premorbids showed the reverse. Avoidance behavior in response to parental figures did not differ.

BAXTER, J. C., BECKER, J., and HOOKS, W., "Defensive Style in the Families of Schizo-
        phrenics and Controls," J. Abnorm. Soc. Psychol., 66, 512-518, 1963.
Parents of good and poor premorbid schizophrenics were given Rorschach tests. Parents of poor premorbids showed a greater amount of immature behavior than parents of good premorbids or parents of neurotics.

BEAVERS, W. T., BLUMBERG, S., TIMKEN, D. R., and WEINER, M. F., "Communication Patterns
        of Mothers of Schizophrenics," Fam. Proc., 4, 95-104, 1965.
A study of the ways the mothers of schizophrenics communicate with an interviewer. Nine mothers of schizophrenics were contrasted with nine mothers of hospitalized non-schizophrenic patients. The mothers of schizophrenics communicated their feelings in a quantitatively more ambiguous fashion.

BECK, S. F., "Families of Schizophrenic and of Well Children: Methods, Concepts, and
        Some Results," Amer. J. Orthopsychiat., 30, 247-275, 1960.
A report on a research study attempting to differentiate and compare families with schizophrenic children, families with neurotic children and families with normal children. A list of trait items about individuals in 106 families were Q-sorted by a psychiatrist and three social workers. The clusterings are said to indicate similarities and differences.

BECK, S., and NUNNALLY, J., "Parental Attitudes in Families," Arch. Gen. Psychiat., 13,
        208-213, 1965.
Differences in "attitudes" of parents of schizophrenic children were compared with those with well children. Eighteen attitudes were measured using the semantic differential test of Osgood (measures concepts like "my child, pregnancy," etc.). Schizophrenic families were obtained from 32 families of children resident in a therapeutic school; well children families came from the community. Concepts associated with greater mental health by the well families included "my mother, the kind of father I am, the kind of mother I am, myself when I was a father, clinic mothers, and clinic our family." There was no difference between samples in the other nine concepts.

BECKER, J., TATSUOKA, M., and CARLSON, A., "The Communicative Value of Parental Speech
    in Families with Disturbed Children," J. Nerv. Ment. Dis., 141, 359-364, 1966.
Hypothesis was the communicativeness of parents with emotionally disturbed children (11
sets of parents who had children coming to a clinic) would be lower than that of parents
with normal children (12 parent sets who were paid volunteers). Communicativeness was
assessed by Taylor's cloze procedure. The speech of nonclinic mothers was significantly
more communicative than that of nonclinic fathers, clinic mother, and clinic fathers.
The latter three groups did not differ among themselves.

BEHRENS, M., and GOLDFARB, W., "A Study of Patterns of Interaction of Families of Schizo-
    phrenic Children in Residential Treatment," Amer. J. Orthopsychiat., 28, 300-312,
    1958.
An attempt to differentiate families of schizophrenic children from those of nonschizophrenic children with a sample of 20 families who had a child diagnosed as schizophrenic
and five with a behavior disorder, all of whom were in-patients. There were ten normals,
all children living at home. Data were collected using family interaction scales; observations were recorded in the homes for both the normals and the patients when they were
home on a visit. Results indicate that the schizophrenic families were more pathologic
than the normal families and the families with behavior disorders.

BEHRENS, M., MEYERS, D. I., GOLDFARB, W., GOLDFARB, N., and FIELDSTEEL, N. D., "The
    Henry Ittleson Center Family Interaction Scales," Genet. Psychol. Monogr., 80,
    203-295, 1969.
A report on the manual used for the family interaction scales. The scales appraise
the functioning of family groups, and derive from a clinical interest in the relationship between the identified patient and the family. Data are obtained through a three-
hour home visit at mealtime. Scales have been used to evaluate the functioning of the
family with a schizophrenic child, to compare families which include children with various diagnoses with normal families, and to determine the nature of changes in family
functioning over a specified length of time. A description of scales and scoring instructions, and three family illustrations are included.

BEHRENS, M., ROSENTHAL, A. J., and CHODOFF, P., "Communication in Lower-Class Families
    of Schizophrenics," Arch. Gen. Psychiat., 18, 689-696, 1968.
The second part of a study of low-socioeconomic families of schizophrenics. The study
was done in the home where the family was focussed upon a task, particularly the Rorschach. Raters were asked to predict type of family from written transcripts. Results
indicate that communication and interaction patterns of lower-class families with a
schizophrenic differ from families whose class background is similar.

BEHRENS, M., and SHERMAN, A., "Observations of Family Interaction in the Home," Amer. J.
    Orthopsychiat., 29, 243-248, 1959.
An essay on the author's previous studies using home visits in evaluating family interactional patterns to differentiate schizophrenic families from nonschizophrenic families.
Difficulties in this type of research are discussed and suggestions for further data collection are made. It is felt that this is a useful technique for "diagnostic, treatment,
and research purposes."

BENTINCK, C., "Opinions About Mental Illness Held by Patients and Relatives," Fam. Proc.,
    6, 193-207, 1967.
A study inquiring into the nature of the attitudes at home about mental illness in families of male schizophrenics. A control group of male medical patients was used. The
data were gathered by a questionnaire administered in a home interview. The sample was
50 schizophrenics and 50 relatives, and 50 medical patients and 50 relatives. Opinions
of relatives of schizophrenics had "more in common with blue collar employees than with
mental health professionals."

BROWNING, C. J., "Differential Impact of Family Disorganization on Male Adolescents,"
    Soc. Prob., 8, 37-44, 1960.
Samples of 60 nondelinquent, 60 delinquent-truancy, and 60 delinquent-auto theft boys
(aged 15) were identified. Data were obtained from school, police, and probation re-

cords; from interviews with mothers; from family solidarity and marital adjustment
scales filled out by parents; and California test of personality scales filled out by
the boys. The incidence of broken homes is higher in the delinquent groups, but this
variable is not a consistently good indicator of family disorganization and needs
refinement.

CHEEK, F., "Family Interaction Patterns and Convalescent Adjustment of the Schizophrenic,"
     Arch. Gen. Psychiat., 13, 138-147, 1965.
An attempt to examine the relationship between family interaction patterns and outcome
in schizophrenia. Data were obtained from 51 patients who had been hospitalized between
the ages of 15 and 26, all of whom had living mothers and fathers. Each family member
filled out a questionnaire relating to interaction patterns; all three family members
together worked on two questionnaire problems; an interview with the mother on the adjustment of the patient was evaluated by means of a 40-item four point rating scale. One
week later, in the home of the patient, two more 15-minute discussions between family
members were recorded. Fifty-six normal families were studied with identical procedures
used as with the schizophrenics. Results indicated that it was the characteristics of
the parents, rather than the degree of sickness of the patient "which was the decisive
factor in producing a poor outcome."

CHEEK, F., "Family Socialization Techniques and Deviant Behavior," Fam. Proc., 5, 199-
     217, 1966.
A study based upon Parsons' theoretical framework in which diviant behavior is related
to imbalance of systems inputs and outputs at various stages of development. A sample
of 120 male adults from four different groups — schizophrenics, normals, alcoholics,
and reformatory inmates — were exposed to a questionnaire on family problem situations.
Differences were found and it is suggested that Parsons' theoretical scheme could be
translated into reinforcement theory.

CHEEK, F., "The Father of the Schizophrenic: The Function of a Peripheral Role," Arch.
     Gen. Psychiat., 13, 336-345, 1965.
In view of the absence of data on the role of the father in the intrafamilial environment of the schizophrenic, Bales' interaction process analysis technique and the social
system theoretical framework of Parsons are used for studying the interaction of 67 families of young adult schizophrenics (40 male and 27 female). This sample was compared to
56 families with nonpsychotic young adults (31 male and 25 female). Outcome in schizophrenia was evaluated a year and a half following discharge from the in-patient setting.
All discussions were tape-recorded and coded, using the Bales interaction categories.
Additionally, each member of the families was asked to fill in a questionnaire examining
expectations and perceptions of how the others might behave in relation to one another
in certain typical family problems. Schizophrenic fathers occupy a peripheral position
in the family in which the mother and patient are closest by default. Profiles of
mothers of schizophrenics however differed more widely from those of normals than
fathers.

CHEEK, F., "Parental Role Distortions in Relation to Schizophrenic Deviancy," in I. M.
     Cohen (Ed.), Psychiatric Research Report No. 20, Washington, American Psychiatric
     Association, 1966.
A study investigating the nature of the schizophrenic interacting in the family, and
the relation of family interaction to the outcome of the schizophrenic. The study combined questionnaire and observational data. The sample included 67 schizophrenic contrasted with 56 nonpsychotic young adults.

CHEEK, F., "A Serendipitous Finding: Sex Roles in Schizophrenia," J. Abnorm. Soc. Psy-
     chol., 69, 392-400, 1964.
One of a series of reports on an ongoing research project studying the family environment in schizophrenia. Interaction profiles of 67 young adults schizophrenics (40 male
and 27 female) were compared with those of 56 normals (31 male and 25 female). Profiles
were derived from 48 minutes of recorded interaction between father, mother, and patient
with a variation of the Bales interaction categories. Male schizophrenics presented an
interaction equivalent of withdrawal, with low total activity rates and low dominance
behaviors. In contrast, female schizophrenics proved to be more active than female normals.

CLARK, A. W., and Van SOMMERS, P., "Contradictory Demands in Family Relations and Adjust-
        ment to School and Home," Hum. Rel., 14, 97-111, 1961.
Intensive case-studies of families of 20 maladjusted and 20 adjusted children. All families had one or more adults other than the parents living in the family. The concern
was with "the process of explaining an unsatisfactory relationship between any two individuals in terms of the influence of a third individual." Data were obtained by detailed, focussed interviews, questionnaires to school staffs, group interviews with
peers, and tests of ability. School difficulties were associated with unsatisfactory
relationships in the home, one of which was dependence of one parent upon the other
adult. Unsatisfactory relationships of adults contribute to withdrawal of father from
family activities, difficulties between adults and children, maladjustment of children
at home and school, and recurrence of symptoms in parents.

COE, W. C., CURRY, A. E., and KESSLER, D. R., "Family Interaction of Psychiatric Pa-
        tients," Fam. Proc., 8, 119-130, 1969.
A study using a questionnaire to examine family interaction patterns with emphasis upon
everyday activities. Forty males and 40 females and their relatives who were psychiatric in-patients were contrasted with 54 husband and wife volunteers. Results include
the finding that more family decision-making is left to the child in the patient families. In these families the members tend not to recognize disagreement in their interactions.

CUMMING, J. H., "The Family and Mental Disorder: An Incomplete Essay," in Causes of
        Mental Disorders: A Review of Epidemiological Knowledge, 1959, New York, Milbank
        Memorial Fund, 1961.
An essay called incomplete because it reviews only a portion of the very large number of
studies which attempt to relate mental disorder with the family. After a review of
ideas about the functions of the family unit, an attempt is made to provide a typology
of family studies by surveying studies in the field with emphasis upon the structure
and function of socialization processes. Relating the various studies to each other,
the author concludes, "It is clear that organized study of the area of the family and
mental illness is in a state of chaos."

CURRY, A., "Toward the Phenomenological Study of the Family," Exist. Psychiat., 6, 35-
        44, 1967.
A paper exploring the theoretical basis for conjoint family therapy from the "phenomenological" point of view (defined as observing the phenomenon as it manifests itself).
Modes of interrelating, affective responses, and methods of communication of both normal and pathological families are analyzed from this point of view.

DENIKER, P., deSAUGY, D., and ROPERT, M., "The Alcoholic and His Wife," Compr. Psychiat.,
        5, 374-384, 1964.
A study focussing on the relationship between the alcoholic and his wife by studying
three groups of patients: 50 alcoholics with psychiatric disorders called psychiatric
alcoholics, 50 alcoholics with cirrhosis or gastritis called digestive alcoholics, and
67 in a control group where the husband was matched for age and socioeconomic status.
All couples were interviewed using a questionnaire designed for this study. Compared
with the digestive alcoholics and the controls, the psychiatric alcoholics showed a relationship to birth order, had fathers who were also alcoholics, made lower salaries,
had dominant wives, and drank relatively little at home. The wife of the psychiatric alcoholic "tends to unconsciously maintain her husband's alcoholism."

FARINA, A., "Patterns of Role Dominance and Conflict in Parents of Schizophrenic Pa-
        tients," J. Abnorm. Soc. Psycol., 61, 31-38, 1960.
Parents of 12 good premorbid schizophrenics, 12 poor premorbids, and 12 children hospitalized for turberculosis were interviewed. They were exposed individually and as pairs
to hypothetical incidents with children. The joint conversation was analyzed for dominance and conflict. Father dominance was associated with good premorbid adjustment of
the son and mother dominance with poor premorbid adjustment. Parents of schizophrenics
displayed more conflict than the control parents.

FARINA, A., and DUNHAM, R. M., "Measurement of Family Relationships and Their Effects,"
    Arch. Gen. Psychiat., 9, 64-73, 1963.
A group of families of male hospitalized schizophrenic patients, divided into good premorbid and poor premorbid, was given a structural situation test. Each family member
is exposed to some hypothetical problem situations with children, and the family is then
brought together and exposed to the same situation. Indices of dominance, such as length
of speeches, and indices of conflict were constructed. Immediately following this, a
group of the patients was given a visual task individually and contrasted with a group
given the same task a week after the situation test. The conclusions are that fathers
are more dominant in good premorbid cases and mothers more dominant in bad premorbid
cases. Conflict scores are higher for good premorbids.

FERBER, A., KLIGLER, D., ZWERLING, I., and MENDELSOHN, M., "Current Family Structure,"
    Arch. Gen. Psychiat., 16, 659-667, 1967.
Hypothesis was that the family, in order to maintain equilibrium, will extrude to the
hospital certain members (most usually those members functioning peripherally). Data
were obtained from an emergency room psychiatric population of a large municipal hospital. Nine hundred and thirty-seven patients and/or their "closest companion" filled
out a family information form. Families of psychiatric patients were compared with
families from the general population. Reliability on the raw data was 90%. Findings
were that being married (rather than single, widowed, etc.), coming from family of
procreation, coming from an intact family, and being an emotionally important member
of the household are associated with a lower risk of becoming a patient and of having
a better outcome from treatment.

FERREIRA, A. J., "Decision-Making in Normal and Pathologic Families," Arch. Gen. Psy-
    chiat., 8, 68-73, 1963.
An experiment to find differences between 25 normal and 25 abnormal families using a
decision-making test. The family members first make a choice of items on a questionnaire when alone and then are brought together and asked to reach agreement on the same
items. Their choices separately and together are compared and the agreements are categorized as unanimous, majority, dictatorial, and chaotic. The two types of families
are found to differ.

FERREIRA, A. J., "Interpersonal Perceptivity Among Family Members," Amer. J. Orthopsy-
    chiat., 34, 64-71, 1964.
A report of a study investigating interpersonal perceptivity among members of families
in terms of the individual's ability to guess the rejecting behavior of the other two
family members. The sample consisted of "25 normal and 30 pathologic families." The
families were asked to color a number of flags on pieces of cardboard and asked to
"throw away, i.e., to reject, the productions of the other family members" which they
didn't like for any reason. They were also asked to guess how many of their own flags
would be thrown away by other family members. Interpersonal perceptivity is greater
in children than in adults.

FERREIRA, A. J., "Rejection and Expectancy of Rejection in Families," Fam. Proc., 2,
    235-244, 1963.
A report of a study to investigate overt rejection and expectancy of rejection in normal and abnormal families. The sample was "25 normal and 30 pathologic families."
The families were asked to color a number of flags on pieces of cardboard and asked to
"throw away, i.e., to reject, the productions of the other family members" which they
didn't like for any reason. They were also asked to guess how many of their own flags
would be thrown away by other family members. Differences were found between the two
groups and there was a marked discrepancy between rejecting and expecting to be rejected in pathological families.

FERREIRA, A. J., and WINTER, W. D., "Decision-Making in Normal and Abnormal Two-Child
    Families," Fam. Proc., 7, 17-36, 1968.
A report of a study of 85 families, 36 normal and 49 abnormal, composed of parents and
two children. The families were tested in a procedure similar to that previously used
in a test of family triads. Differences were found between the two groups on measures
of "spontaneous agreement," "decision time," and "choice fulfillment."

FERREIRA, A. J., and WINTER, W. D., "Family Interaction and Decision-Making," <u>Arch. Gen.</u>
    <u>Psychiat.</u>, 13, 214-223, 1965.
A report of a study contrasting 50 normal families and 75 families with an abnormal
child. The abnormal group included 15 schizophrenic, 16 delinquent, and 44 maladjusted children. The family members were asked to fill out a neutral questionnaire separately, and then they were brought together and asked to fill out the same questionnaire while reaching agreement on the items as a group. Generally this report is concerned with the extent of agreement when family members make their choices separately,
how much time to reach group decisions is necessary, and the appropriateness of the
family decisions in fulfilling the wishes of the individual family members. Eighteen
hypotheses are described and the results reported in terms of the differences found
between the groups.

FERREIRA, A. J., and WINTER, W. D., "Information Exchange and Silence in Normal and Ab-
    normal Families," <u>Fam. Proc.</u>, 7, 251-278, 1968.
A comparison of normal and abnormal families which measured exchange of information and
amount of time spent in silence in doing a task. A sample of 30 normal and 45 abnormal
families were contrasted by a rater judgement of tape recordings. Differences were
found.

FERREIRA, A., and WINTER, W. D., "Stability of Interactional Variables in Family De-
    cision-Making," <u>Arch. Gen. Psychiat.</u>, 14, 352-355, 1966.
In order to test the stability over time, and after family therapy, of three variables
in family decision-making, 23 randomly selected families (10 abnormal and 13 normal)
were retested six months after the original research project. The abnormal families
had received therapy. Results indicated that there was no significant difference between the means observed in tests and retests of the three variables for either normal or abnormal families. It is concluded that these three variables (spontaneous
agreement, decision-time, and choice-fulfillment) were consistent over time and were
not changed by family therapy.

FISHER, S., and MENDELL, D., "The Communication of Neurotic Patterns Over Two and Three
    Generations," in N. W. Bell, and E. F. Vogel (Eds.), <u>A Modern Introduction to the</u>
    <u>Family</u>, Glencoe, Free Press, 1960.
A report on a study of similarities in the patterning of fantasy and behavior in two or
more generations of family groups. The data included projective tests and psychiatric
interviews. Six families with three generations of kin and 14 families with two generations of kin were examined and impressions are given.

FLECK, S., LIDZ, T., and CORNELISON, A., "Comparison of Parent-Child Relationships of
    Male and Female Schizophrenic Patients," <u>Arch. Gen. Psychiat.</u>, 8, 1-7, 1963.
A study of 17 families containing a schizophrenic child emphasizing the differences
between families containing schizophrenic sons and those with schizophrenic daughters.
Schizophrenic males often come from skewed families with passive, ineffectual fathers
and disturbed, engulfing mothers. Schizophrenic girls typically grow up in schismatic
families with narcissistic fathers and emotionally distant mothers.

FRIEDMAN, C. J., and FRIEDMAN, A. S., "Characteristics of Schizogenic Families During
    a Joint Story-Telling Task," <u>Fam. Proc.</u>, 9, 333-353, 1970.
A comparison of families with a schizophrenic and normal families in the task of telling
a story. Observer ratings were used for the interaction and judges ratings for the
final joint family story. Differences were found.

GARMEZY, N., CLARKE, A. R., and STOCKNER, C., "Child Rearing Attitudes of Mothers and
    Fathers as Reported by Schizophrenic and Normal Patients," <u>J. Abnorm. Soc. Psy-</u>
    <u>chiat.</u>, 63, 176-182, 1961.
A group of 15 good premorbid and 15 poor premorbid schizophrenic patients were asked
to think back when they were 13 or 14 years old and try to remember mother and father
at that time. The experimenter then presented them with 75 statements describing various
child-rearing attitudes and asked the patients if their parents would have agreed or

disagreed with each item. A group of 15 patients hospitalized for medical problems
was used as a control. The results indicate that the subject's level of social maturity and the extent of attitudinal deviance ascribed to parents are related. Poor
premorbids reveal maternal dominance whereas good premorbids ascribe heightened paternal dominance in their responses.

GARMEZY, N., FARINA, A., and RODNICK, E. H., "The Structured Situation Test: A Method
        for Studying Family Interaction in Schizophrenia," Amer. J. Orthopsychiat., 30,
        445-451, 1960.
A group of 36 sets of parents composed of parents of good and poor premorbids and of
sons with tuberculosis ("normals") were exposed to 12 hypothetical misbehaviors of a
son. Individually and then together they were asked to indicate how to handle the situation. From tape recordings of the interviews, measures of dominance behavior and
conflict were made, such as who spoke first and last, acceptance of another's solution,
amount of interruption, and so on. With good premorbids the fathers were dominant and
in poor premorbids the mothers were. The "normals" share dominance. Poor premorbids
show greater conflict than "normals".

GEHRKE, S., and KIRSCHENBAUM, M., "Survival Patterns in Family Conjoint Therapy," Fam.
        Proc., 6, 67-80, 1967.
A discussion of 20 families studied in family therapy with the emphasis upon different
patterns of emotional survival myths in the family. Three types of family are contrasted: the repressive family, the delinquent family, and the suicidal family. The survival myth has to do with the illusion of family members that they must continue their
existing family ways of relating to survive psychologically.

GETZELS, J. W., and JACKSON, P. W., "Family Environment and Cognitive Style: A Study
        of the Sources of Highly Intelligent and of Highly Creative Adolescents," Amer.
        Sociol. Rev., 26, 351-359, 1961.
A study of adolescent boys and girls, 28 highly intelligent but not creative and 26
creative but not concomitantly intelligent, chosen from a school population on the basis of testing. These students proved equally superior in achievement to the remainder of the student body although they differed both functionally and in their goals.
The central issue of this report deals with the role of the family environment in the
differentiation of kinds of intellectual ability through interviews with the mothers.
Significant group differences were found in parental type education, childhood memories, reading interests, values, degree of satisfaction with child and school, etc.
The authors find less anxiety in the highly creative home and therefore more freedom
for "individual divergence."

GREENBERG, I. M., and ROSENBERG, G., "Familial Correlates of the 14 and 6 CPS EEG Posi-
        tive Spike Pattern," in I. M. Cohen (Ed.), Psychiatric Research Report No. 20,
        Washington, American Psychiatric Association, 1966.
A report on the results of a study of the families of young hospitalized psychiatric
patients in which central nervous system function, individual psychodynamics, cognitive style, and social and familial factors are considered. A sample of nine patients
were contrasted with ten with no EEG abnormality. Differences were found in the families.

HALEY, J., "Cross-Cultural Experimentation: An Initial Attempt," Hum. Org., 3, 110-117,
        1967.
A comparison of Caucasion middle-class American families and Japanese-born families in
an experimental setting where the measure is speech sequences. Differences are found.

HALEY, J., "Experiment with Abnormal Families," Arch. Gen. Psychiat., 17, 53-63, 1967.
A comparison of abnormal and normal families in an experimental setting where family members speak to each other from different rooms. Measures are who chooses to speak with
whom and patterns of speech sequence.

HALEY, J., "Family Experiments: A New Type of Experimentation," Fam. Proc., 1, 265-293, 1962.
A report on a research project in which parents and schizophrenic child were contrasted with parents and normal child in an experimental game to test hypotheses about coalition patterns in normal and abnormal families. Differences were found between the 30 families in each group. There is a general discussion of the uniqueness of experimenting with families in theoretical,methodological, and sampling problems.

HALEY, J., "Research on Family Patterns: An Instrument Measurement," Fam. Proc., 3, 41-65, 1964.
A report of an investigation of patterns of interchange in families. The questions are whether families follow patterns, whether "normal" and "abnormal" families differ, and whether patterns change over time. A group of 40 normal and 40 abnormal families were given a standard stimulus for conversation and a frequency count was made of the order in which family members speak. Families were found to follow patterns and differences were found between the normal and abnormal groups.

HALEY, J., "Speech Sequences of Normal and Abnormal Families with Two Children Present," Fam. Proc., 6, 81-97, 1967.
A sample of 50 "abnormal" and 40 "normal" families were contrasted in an experimental setting where a measurement was made of the sequence in which family members speak. Differences had been found in a previous study where the families were tested in triads. In this study, where the sibling was included as well as the index child, differences were not found between the two groups.

HALEY, J., "Testing Parental Instructions to Schizophrenic and Normal Children: A Pilot Study," J. Abnorm. Soc. Psychol., 73, 559-566, 1968.
An experiment to test the hypothesis that parents communicate to their schizophrenic children in conflicting ways. Parental instructions were given from a separate room and tape recorded so that they could be played to matched children. On this small sample, the indications were that parents of schizophrenics do not communicate in more conflicting ways than parents of normal children when the measurement is the success of a child in following their instructions.

HILGARD, J., and NEWMAN, M. F., "Early Parental Deprivation as a Function Factor in the Etiology of Schizophrenia and Alcoholism," Amer. J. Orthopsychiat., 33, 409-420, 1963.
A study designed to consider the age at which loss by death was sustained during childhood by hospitalized schizophrenic and alcoholic patients. Comparison was made using hospital admission records of 1521 schizophrenic patients, 929 alcoholic patients, and a control group of 1096 cases selected using an area-sampling technique from an urban community. It was concluded that mother loss among women in both diagnostic categories was earlier than in the control group members who lost mothers. Schizophrenic women showed loss of both mother and father at a significantly earlier age than the control subjects.

HILGARD, J., and NEWMAN, M. F., "Parental Loss by Death in Childhood as an Etiological Factor Among Schizophrenic and Alcoholic Patients Compared with a Non-Patient Community Samples," J. Nerv. Ment. Dis., 137, 14-28, 1963.
Hospital records were examined and a sample of 1,561 schizophrenic patients and 929 alcoholic patients were compared with a control sample of 1,096 cases. Schizophrenics had lost one or both parents more often than the control group members. Parent loss is said to be one of the factors associated with an increase in vulnerability in coping with the stresses of adult life.

JENKINS, R., "The Varieties of Children's Behavioral Problems and Family Dynamics," Amer. J. Psychiat., 124, 1440-1445, 1968.
1500 children attending a psychiatric clinic were separated into three groups by computer clustering of their symptoms and correlated with family types. Overanxious children are likely to have an anxious, infantilizing mother. A critical, depreciative, punitive, inconsistent mother or stepmother is typical for the unsocialized, aggressive child. Socialized delinquents are likely to come from large families characterized by parental neglect and delegation of parental responsibilities.

LERNER, P., "Resolution of Intrafamilial Role Conflict in Families of Schizophrenic
      Patients. I. Thought Disturbance," J. Nerv. Ment. Dis., 141, 342-351, 1966.
Hypothesis was that there would be differences in the processes used to solve intrafamilial role conflict in parents with schizophrenic sons with marked thought disorder
(12 families), less severe thought disorder (12 families), and control families (12 families). Thought disorder was measured by Rorschach protocol using the genetic level
score of Becker. Intrafamilial role conflict solving was measured using a situational
test with Strodtbeck's "revealed differences" technique. Results supported the hypothesis. Methodology of such research is discussed.

LEARNER, P., "Resolution of Intrafamilial Role Conflict in Families of Schizophrenic
      Patients. II. Social Maturity," J. Nerv. Ment. Dis., 4, 336-341, 1967.
A study attempting to evaluate the relationship between resolution of intrafamilial role
conflict and premorbid level of social competence in schizophrenics. Sample and methods
were the same as in a previous study except that here social competence was measured by
a scale developed by Zigler and Phillips. Findings were that control families compromised and acknowledged disagreement, while schizophrenic families did not but let mother or father decide.

LEIK, R. K., "Instrumentality and Emotionality in Family Interaction," Sociometry, 26,
      131-145, 1963.
A comparison of discussion groups where nine families composed of father, mother, and
daughter participated in triadic sessions. One third of the discussion groups were
made up of all fathers, all mothers, or all daughters. Another third were composed of
a father, a mother, and a daughter not of the same family. The final third was of natural families. The three groups were exposed to standard questions and observed.
Categories of acts were derived from the Bales system with an emphasis upon instrumentality versus emotionality. It was found that sex role differentiation tends to disappear in family groups and the relevance of instrumentality and emotionality is quite
different for family interaction than for interaction among strangers.

LENNARD, H. L., BEAULIEU, M. R., AND EMBREY, N. G., "Interaction in Families with a
      Schizophrenic Child," Arch. Gen. Psychiat., 12, 166-183, 1965.
A study contrasting ten families with a schizophrenic child and seven normal families.
The families have a 15-minute discussion of three topics related to a child's life.
The conversations are recorded, transcribed, and coded along 12 dimensions. Differences
are found between the two groups. There is a discussion of the theoretical background
and methodological problems.

LEVIN, G., "Communicator-Communicant Approach to Family Interaction Research," Fam. Proc.,
      5, 105-116, 1966.
A family experiment in which the experimenter asks the subject to make a tape recording
which might be played subsequently to some specific other person in his family. The recording includes specific instructions about a simple task. Individuals from families
containing a schizophrenic (a sample of 33) were contrasted with normal individuals.
The recordings were not actually played to family members, but the instructions were
analyzed and classified with differences found between the two groups.

LIDZ, T., CORNELISON, A., FLECK, S., and TERRY, D., "Intrafamilial Environment of Schizo-
      phrenic Patients. II. Marital Schism and Marital Skew," Amer. J. Psychiat., 114,
      241-248, 1957.
A study of the intrafamilial environment of the schizophrenic patient. In this study
of 14 families, eight were split in two factions by "overt schism between the parents."
Thus the identified patient cannot use one parent as a model for identification or as
a love object without losing the support of the other parent. The other six families
were "skewed" (defined as psychopathology in the dominant parent) which was accepted or
shared by the other without trying to change it. Case examples are given.

MALMQUIST, C., "School Phobia: A Problem in Family Neurosis," J. Amer. Acad. Child Psy-
      chiat., 4, 293-319, 1965.
In contrast to the traditional approach to school phobia, this essay puts forth the clini-

nical notion that it can be seen as a reaction to family pathology. Four types for
characterizing disordered families that have been reported in the literature are: (1)
the perfectionistic family, (2) the inadequate family, (3) the egocentric family, and
(4) the unsocial family. How these family types relate to the symptom are discussed.
There is an extensive review of the literature.

McCORD, J., McCORD, W., and HOWARD, A., "Family Interaction as Antecedent to the Direc-
        tion of Male Aggressiveness," J. Abnorm. Soc. Psychol., 66, 239-242, 1963.
A continuation of earlier studies in delinquency in which the question is asked, "What
family environments tend to produce antisocial as opposed to socialized aggressiveness?"
Results suggest that extreme neglect and punitiveness, coupled with a deviant-aggressive
paternal model, produce the former, while moderate neglect and punitiveness and ineffectual controls produce the latter.

McGHIE, A., "A Comparative Study of the Mother-Child Relationship in Schizophrenia: I.
        The Interview. II. Psychological Testing," Brit. J. Med. Psychol., 34, 195-221,
        1961.
In Part I of this two-part article there is a description of interviews with 20 mothers
of schizophrenics, 20 mothers of neurotics, and 20 mothers of normals. Findings about
families of schizophrenics reported in the literature were generally confirmed. There
is more marital disharmony in the schizophrenic group and the fathers are said to be
weak. However, mothers of schizophrenics do not appear as overprotective as mothers
of neurotics. In Part II, the test findings for the three groups are reported. They
were given a child rearing questionnaire, a sentence completion test, a word connection
test, and the Rorschach.

MEYERS, D., and GOLDFARB, W., "Studies of Perplexity in Mothers of Schizophrenic Child-
        ren," Amer. J. Orthopsychiat., 31, 551-564, 1961.
In order to document the association of parental complexity (defined as passivity, un-
certainty, lack of spontaneity, absence of empathy; with diminished awareness of the
child's needs, bewilderment, and blandness in the face of unacceptable behavior in the
child, and an absence of parental control), 23 mothers of schizophrenic children and
23 mothers of normal children were studied. Techniques included a participant-observation technique (in which the observer spent three hours with the family at home),
and a semistructured open-ended interview of the mothers. Results indicated that the
mothers of the schizophrenic children without organic involvement have a greater difficulty in appropriately structing their child's environment, while the mothers of
the organic group cannot be differentiated from mothers of the normals.

MINUCHIN. S., MONTALVO, B., GUERNEY, B. G., ROSMAN, B. L., and SHUMER, F., Families
        of the Slums: An Exploration of Their Structure and Treatment, New York, Basic
        Books, 1967.
A book on a research project dealing with family treatment of low-socioeconomic class
families where the identified patient was delinquent. Research strategy, rationale,
dynamics, techniques, and assessment of results are presented. 460 pp.

MISHLER, E., "Families and Schizophrenia: An Experimental Study," Ment. Hyg., 50, 552-
        556, 1966.
A discussion of a way of testing families with a schizophrenic member and contrasting
them with normal families. Findings are not given, but illustrations are offered of
ways the families respond in the test situation.

MISHLER, E., and WAXLER, N., "Family Interaction in Schizophrenica," Arch. Gen. Psy-
        chiat., 15, 64-75, 1966.
A paper describing only methodology used in an experimental study of family interactions
in schizophrenia. Subjects were 30 schizophrenic families (in which a schizophrenic
child was hospitalized) and 16 normal families recruited from the community. Schizophrenic patients were newly admitted to the hospital, unmarried, white, living in the
Boston area, living at home with both parents (who had to be alive and living together),
and had one unmarried sibling of the same sex. Experimental procedure was Strodtbeck's
revealed differences test. Coding and data analysis procedures are described.

MITCHELL, H. E., BULLARD, J. W., and MUDD, E. H., "Areas of Marital Conflict in Success-
     fully and Unsuccessfully Functioning Families," J. Health Hum. Behav., 3, 88-93,
     1962.
The nature and frequency of marital disagreements in 200 marriage counseling cases and
in 100 self selected, successful families. Data on both groups were obtained from the
marriage adjustment schedule and from interviews. Both groups rank their problems in
the same order: economic is highest, religious and educational are lowest. No differences in ranking of problems by husbands and wives was apparent, but conflicted families
report a greater frequency of problems. Some cultural implications of these findings
are discussed.

MORRIS, G., and WYNNE, L., "Schizophrenic Offspring, Parental Styles of Communication,"
     Psychiatry, 28, 19-44, 1965.
One of series of papers reporting a study of parental styles of communication and schizophrenic children. Data were selected from excerpts of transcripts of conjoint family
sessions with 12 families. Predictions about the most disturbed offspring were made by
a judge blind to the clinical aspects of the case. Predictive criteria were then reformulated using the data from a parallel study, utilizing psychological test material as
predictors. These reformulated criteria were then utilized for blind predictions on
eight new families. Results indicated that the style of the family communication can
be related to the thought and affect disorder in schizophrenics.

MURRELL, S., and STACHOWIAK, J., "Consistency, Rigidity, and Power in the Interaction
     Patterns of Clinic and Non-Clinic Families," J. Abnorm. Psychol., 72, 265-272, 1967.
To study interaction patterns in families, 11 families (each having at least two children who were attending a child guidance clinic) were matched with 11 control families
whose names were obtained from school (who were thought to be normal). Families were
observed by two raters through a one-way mirror and were asked to (1) plan something
together as a family, (2) answer a list of 11 questions about the families and agree on
the answers, (3) list adjectives regarding their family, and (4) make up stories to
seven TAT pictures. Results indicated that in all 22 families, the pattern of who
talks to whom was consistent. Secondly, the control patients had more rigidity in speaking than the "sick" families. Thirdly, in the sick families the older child had more
power within the family than in the controls. Fourthly, the sick families were not as
productive as the well families.

NOVAK, A. L., and VAN der VEEN, F., "Family Concepts and Emotional Disturbance in the
     Families of Disturbed Adolescents with Normal Siblings," Fam. Proc., 9, 157-171,
     1970.
A sample of 13 families with an adolescent who had applied to an out-patient clinic for
treatment were contrasted with a group of similar families selected through a school.
A Q-sort procedure was used with individual family members. "Real family concepts" and
"ideal family concepts" were obtained and differences were found between the two groups
and between disturbed children and their normal siblings.

PAUL N., and GROSSER, G., "Operational Mourning and Its Role in Conjoint Family Therapy,"
     Comm. Ment. Health J., 1, 339-345, 1965.
Studies of records of 50 families with a schizophrenic member and 25 families with at
least one psychoneurotic member revealed "patterns of inflexible interaction and maladaptive response to object loss." The way the sample was obtained is not stated. It
is hypothesized from this data that incomplete mourning after object loss leads to an
inability to deal with future object loss and this defect is transmitted to other family
members. This is thought to lead to a "fixation of symbiotic relationships in the family."
Therefore, "one possible way to dislodge this fixation would be to mobilize those affects
which might aid in disrupting this particular kind of equilibrium." "Operational mourning" is the technique evolved by the authors to do this and is believed to "involve the
family in a belated mourning experience with extensive grief reactions." A case report
is included for illustration.

QUERY, J. M. N., "Pre-Morbid Adjustment and Family Structure: A Comparison of Selected
     Rural and Urban Schizophrenic Men," J. Nerv. Ment. Dis., 133, 333-338, 1961.
A study which reviews schizophrenia in relation to cultural and familial settings. The
hypothesis is that premorbid adjustment of rural schizophrenics will be better than that

of urban subjects because the rural setting includes a more patriarchal family structure,
more emphasis upon individualism, and better sex-role identification. Case history
data were examined in terms of the Phillips' scale and supplemented by family interviews. Fifty-one families were interviewed and the hypothesis was supported by the evidence.

REISS, D., "Individual Thinking and Family Interaction: Introduction to an Experimen-
      tal Study of Problem-Solving in Families of Normals, Character Disorders, and Schi-
      zophrenics," Arch. Gen. Psychiat., 16, 80-93, 1967.
A report of an experimental study of the relationship between individual thinking and
family interaction. Experimental procedures and methods of analysis are discussed.
Subjects were families of five normals, five character disorders, and six schizophrenics.
The test used was a puzzle that required active use of cognitive and conceptual capaci-
ties. The method of analysis was derived from the work of Riley which developed a systematic approach of computing scores from the raw data and rules concerning inferences.

REISS, D., "Individual Thinking and Family Interaction. II. A Study of Pattern Recog-
      nition and Hypothesis Testing in Families of Normals, Character Disorders, and
      Schizophrenics," J. Psychiat. Res., 5, 193-211, 1967.
The second in a series of studies of the relationship of family process and individual
thinking. Results indicate that following a period of family interaction, members of
normal families showed improvement in pattern recognition; members of families of schizophrenics showed deterioration or no change; and results of members of character disorder families were in between the two.

REISS, D., "Individual Thinking and Family Interaction. III. An Experimental Study of
      Categorization Performance in Families of Normals, Those with Character Disorders,
      and Schizophrenics," J. Nerv. Ment. Dis., 146, 384-404, 1968.
The second of a series of studies to measure the relationship between individual family
interaction and individual thinking and to determine what differences in this relationship exist among families of normals, personality disorders, and schizophrenics. Method
was to give the families a puzzle, tape their discussion, and to code verbal responses.
Sample has been previously described; there were five families in each group. Results
indicated that normals could solve the puzzle, while the others could not. The data on
why they could not were felt to be consistent with the hypothesis that interpersonal
problems in families significantly interfere with their collaborative problem-solving
efforts.

REISS, D., "Individual Thinking and Family Interaction. IV. A Study of Information
      Exchange in Families of Normals, Those with Character Disorders, and Schizophrenics,"
      J. Nerv. Ment. Dis., 149, 473-490, 1969.
The third in a series of papers on interrelationships of family interaction and thinking
and perception of family members. The experiment was developed to test the family's efficiency in exchanging information within itself. Families of normals and schizophrenics
were more sensitive than those with character disorders to cues from within the family.
Families of schizophrenics appeared to represent a group of families who utilize cues
from within but not from without the family.

ROSENTHAL, A. J., BEHRENS, M. I., and CHODOFF, P., "Communication in Lower Class Fami-
      lies of Schizophrenics," Arch. Gen. Psychiat., 18, 464-470, 1968.
Part I, Methodological Problems, of a two-part report on low-socioeconomic families of
schizophrenics. Groups compared were 17 black schizophrenics and their families, 11 in
a black control group, and 11 white schizophrenics and their families. The procedure
included observation in the home with tasks requiring the family to maintain a focus of
attention on a specific topic. (For Part II of this study see Behrens, M. I., "Communication in Lower Class Families of Schizophrenics," Arch. Gen. Psychiat., 18, 689-696,
1968.)

SCHULMAN, R. E., SHOEMAKER, D. J., and MOELIS, I., "Laboratory Measurement of Parental
      Behavior," J. Consult. Psychol., 26, 109-114, 1962.
Families were told to make up stories about a scene which included a variety of buildings
and people with the hypothesis that in families with a conduct problem child, parents

would exhibit more control over behavior of the child, and that in these families there
would be significantly more aggression between parents. Parents and one son (age eight-
twelve) of 41 families were tested. In 20 families the child was considered a conduct
problem while the other 21 had no reported conduct problem while the other 21 had no
reported conduct problems. Parents' behavior was rated by observers who found that
parents of conduct problem children were more rejecting and hostile than parents of
children without problems. It was concluded that there is a cause-effect relation
between parental hostility and rejection and aggressive behavior in children.

SHARP, V., GLASNER, S., LEDERMAN, I., and WOLFE, S., "Sociopaths and Schizophrenics —
    A Comparison of Family Interactions," Psychiatry, 27, 127-134, 1964.
To test the hypothesis that there would be differences in the family interaction of
matched groups of sociopaths and schizophrenics, 20 subjects of each group were examined.
These included every patient admitted to the authors' case load at the Philadelphia Naval
Hospital. Sources of data were social service questionnaires, parental visits, and interviews with parents. Findings were that sociopaths joined the service "to escape from
home," had shorter hospitalizations, and their families were much more unconcerned and
rejecting than the schizophrenic families, who visited more.

SINGER, M. T., and WYNNE, L. C., "Communication Styles in Parents of Normals, Neurotics,
    and Schizophrenics: Some Findings Using a New Rorschach Scoring Manual," in I. M.
    Cohen (Ed.), Psychiatric Research Report No. 20, Washington, American Psychiatric
    Association, 1966.
A report of a study of 250 families in which the Rorschach was used as a stimulus for
individual family members. Styles of parental communication are described and findings
reported.

SINGER, M. T., and WYNNE, L. C., "Differentiating Characteristics of Parents of Child-
    hood Schizophrenics, Childhood Neurotics, and Young Adults Schizophrenics," Amer.
    J. Psychiat., 120, 234-243, 1963.
A study in which parents of 20 autistic children were blindly differentiated at a statistically significant level of accuracy from parents of 20 neurotic children. The data
were TAT and Rorschach tests of the parents. Additionally, the parents of adolescent
and young adult schizophrenics were compared with the parents of autistic children and
differences were found.

SOJIT, C. M., "Dyadic Interaction in a Double Bind Situation," Fam. Proc., 8, 235-260,
    1969.
Marital couples were exposed to a "double bind situation" to contrast parents of delinquents, ulcerative colitis patients, and normal controls. The couples were exposed to
the proverb "a rolling stone gathers no moss" and were asked to reach agreement about
its meaning. The responses were categorized and differences found.

SPITZER, S. P., SWANSON, R. M., and LEHR, R. K., "Audience Reactions and Careers of Psy-
    chiatric Patients," Fam. Proc., 8, 159-181, 1969.
A study of the reaction of families and the ways these reactions influence the psychiatric patient career. The histories of 79 first admission patients were examined, and
patient and a family member were interviewed. Two dimensions of family reaction to deviance are described leading to a typology of eight career patterns which allow for the
classification of 95% of the cases reviewed.

STABENAU, J. R., TUPIN, J., WERNER, M., and POLLIN, W., "A Comparative Study of Families
    of Schizophrenics, Delinquents, and Normals," Psychiatry, 28, 45-59, 1965.
A report of a comparison of five families with a schizophrenic, five families with a delinquent, and five normal families tested with the revealed differences test, the object
sorting test, and the thematic apperception test. "Data from the three different tests
suggest that in the schizophrenic and delinquent families there were both individual disturbances in thought process and impaired communication at the family level...There was
relatively little evidence of communication impairment at the individual or family level
in the normal families."

STACHOWIAK, J., "Decision-Making and Conflict Resolution in the Family Group," in C.
      Larson and F. Dance (Eds.), Perspectives on Communication, Milwaukee, Speech Com-
      munication Center, University of Wisconsin, 1968.
The author discusses his previous research summarizing major findings on (1) family productivity — which is decreased in "sick families," (2) influence of individual members
— maladaptive families showed distinct hierarchal ordering of members, (3) conflict in
which maladaptive families showed more aggression and hostility than adaptive, and (4)
communication, which was disturbed in maladaptive families. Implications for future
research are discussed.

VAN DER VEEN, F., HUEBNER, B., JORGENS, B., and NEJA, P., "Relationship Between the
      Parents' Concept of the Family and Family Adjustment," Amer. J. Orthopsychiat.,
      34, 45-55, 1964.
To study the "significance of the family unit for the well-being of the individual" and
"the perceptions of the family unit by each individual," two groups of ten families each
were selected. One group was composed of families from the community which functioned
well (called the higher adjustment group). The other group was composed of families
which had applied to a guidance center for help with one of their children. They were
matched as to sex and position of the child and size of family. Tests used were the
family concept Q-sort, family semantic test, and a marital questionnaire. Results indicated that the adjustment of the families was a function of: (1) the amount of agreement between the "real" family concept of the parent and "ideal" family concept as determined by professionals, (2) the agreement between the "real" and "ideal" family concepts of the parent, and (3) the agreement between the "real" family concepts of the
mother and the father.

VIDAL, G., PRECE, G., and SMULEVER, M., "Convivencia y Trastorno Mental," Acta Psiquiat.
      Psicolog. Amer. Lat., 15, 55-65, 1969.
A sample of 1,322 patients were studied for family size, birth order of the patient,
and family integrity (number of years the offspring lived together with both parents).
The hypothesis was that "the higher the amount of the family relationship the lower the
severity of the mental disorder." Neurotics were expected to show smaller families,
first birth order positions, and intact families, while psychotics would show larger
families, last birth order positions, and disrupted families. The hypothesis about neurotics was confirmed but that about psychotics was only partially confirmed.

VOGEL, E. F., "The Marital Relationship of Parents of Emotionally Disturbed Children:
      Polarization and Isolation," Psychiatry, 23, 1-12, 1960.
In a study of 18 families seen by an interdisciplinary team, nine families with emotionally disturbed children were matched with nine families with relatively healthy children. The marriage relationship in all families with an emotionally disturbed child was
found to be more disturbed; the parents behaved as if they were polar opposites and each
partner contended that his standards were right and the spouse's wrong. In the control
families the parents had less physical separation, shared activities with each other
more, and exhibited more flexibility in the handling of money.

VOGEL, E. F., and BELL, N. W., "The Emotionally Disturbed Child as a Family Scapegoat,"
      Psychoan. Psychoanal. Rev., 47, 21-42, 1960.
Based upon intensive study of nine families with a disturbed child matched with a group
of "well" families, this report emphasizes the use of the child as a scapegoat for the
conflicts between the parents. In all the disturbed families a particular child was
involved in the tensions existing between parents, while in the "well" families the
tensions were less severe or were handled in such a way that the child did not become
pathologically involved.

WESTLEY, W. A., and EPSTEIN, N. B., "Report on the Psychosocial Organization of the Fam-
      ily and Mental Health," in D. Willner (Ed.), Decisions, Values and Groups, No. I,
      New York, Pergamon Press, 1960.
A report of a study designed to investigate the relationship between family functioning
and development of either mental health or pathology. The sample was 531 students of
the first-year class at a university who were given a Rorschach, a Gordon personality
test, and interviewed by a psychiatrist. Out of these, 20 were classified as being the
most emotionally healthy, and of these, 17 were in the study. There is a schema for de-

scription, analysis, and evaluation of the family. Common features of these emotionally
healthy families are described.

WILD, C., SINGER, M., ROSMAN, G., RICCI, J., and LIDZ, T., "Measuring Disordered Styles
     of Thinking," Arch. Gen. Psychiat., 13, 471-476, 1966.
Forty-four parents whose child was a schizophrenic in-patient were matched for age and
education with 46 control parents (community volunteers) on the object sorting test. A
scoring manual is described. Patient-parents scores differed significantly from controls. The object scoring test seems to discriminate between parents of schizophrenic
patients and controls who do not have children with psychiatric pathology.

WINTER, W. D., and FERREIRA, A. J., "Interaction Process Analysis of Family Decision-
     Making," Fam. Proc., 6, 155-172, 1967.
A sample of 90 triads of father, mother, and child were tested to contrast "normals"
with "abnormals." The families were exposed to a set of three TAT cards and asked to
make up a story they all agreed upon which linked the three cards together. The protocols were scored with the Bales IPA system. It is concluded that "the Bales IPA system,
in its present form, is not suited for work with families."

WINTER, W. D., and FERREIRA, A., Research in Family Interaction, Palo Alto, Science &
     Behavior Books, 1969.
A collection of some new and some previously published material dealing with studies
and research on family interaction. There are sections on methodological issues in
family interaction research; studies of individual family members; studies of family
interaction: decision-making; studies of family interaction: studies, attitudes, and
power; studies of family interaction: behavior; and studies of family interaction:
intrafamily communication. There is a lengthy bibliography attached.

WINTER, W. D., and FERREIRA, A. J., "Talking Time as an Index of Intrafamilial Similarity
     in Normal and Abnormal Families," J. Abnorm. Psychol., 74, 574-575, 1969.
A study testing the hypothesis that normal families correlate more highly with each
other than do abnormal families in terms of talking at length in extemporaneous speech.
127 family triads were tested. Of these, 77 were abnormals with identified patients
being "emotionally disturbed maladjusted;" 50 were normals. The families took the
group thematic apperception test and the total number of seconds of speech of each of
them indicated that members of abnormal families resembled each other more than do members of normal families.

WINTER, W. D., FERREIRA, A. J., and OLSON, J., "Hostility Themes in the Family TAT,"
     J. Project. Techn. Person. Ass., 30, 270-275, 1966.
Second of a series describing a diagnostic test adapted for use with families. Results
were obtained from use of three TAT stories based on three cards, each produced conjointly
by 126 three-member families. Stories were scored for hostility in the story themes.
Fifty families had normal children, 44 had neurotic children, 16 had schizophrenic children, and 16 had delinquent children. Normal and schizophrenic groups produced stories
low in hostility, neurotics produced stories high in hostility, and delinquents scored
high on one hostility variable and low on another.

WINTER, W. D., FERREIRA, A. J., and OLSON, J. L., "Story Sequence Analysis of Family
     TATs", J. Project. Techn. Person. Ass., 29, 392-397, 1965.
A group of 126 families, composed of parents and one child, were asked to produce TAT
stories conjointly. The families were to make up a story based upon three TAT cards
presented simultaneously to them. Three stories based on nine cards were composed by
each family and scored by the Arnold system of story sequence analysis. In the sample
there were 50 families with normal children. The abnormal group consisted of 44 emotionally maladjusted, 16 delinquent, and 16 schizophrenic children. The procedure
successfully differentiated normal from abnormal families but the three abnormal groups
did not differ from each other. The stories of abnormal families are said to be characterized by negative attitudes toward achievement, morality, responsibility, human relationships, and reaction to adversity.

WYNNE, L. C., "The Study of Intrafamilial Alignments and Splits in Exploratory Family
        Therapy," in N. W. Ackerman, F. L. Beatman, and S. Sherman (Eds.), Exploring the
        Base for Family Therapy, New York, Family Service Association of America, 1961.
From a clinical research project of 20 schizophrenic families and ten families of nonschizophrenic psychiatric patients, it has been observed that schizophrenic families
use, as one of their main mechanisms of coping, "pseudomutuality and pseudo-hostile
mechanisms that disguise but help perpetuate the underlying problems." Conjoint family
therapy based on understanding the family organization, and maneuvers in terms of alignments and splits, can benefit the disturbed family.

WYNNE, L. C., and SINGER, M. T., "Thought Disorder and Family Relations of Schizophren-
        ics. I. A Research Strategy. II. A Classification of Forms of Thinking," Arch.
        Gen. Psychiat., 9, 191-206, 1963.
A general discussion of the approach of the Wynne project. Families with schizophrenic
members are contrasted with families of nonschizophrenic psychiatric patients, and siblings are contrasted with patients. The emphasis is upon the links between family patterns and schizophrenic thought disorder, defined broadly to include experience. The
first part outlines the clinical and conceptual basis, the setting, and the kinds of
research data. The second part presents a classification of schizophrenic thought disorders, including discrimination among varieties of schizophrenic and paranoid thinking.

YOUNG, M., and GEERTZ, H., "Old Age in London and San Francisco: Some Families Compared,"
        Brit. J. Sociol., 12, 124-141, 1961.
A British and an American suburb are compared as to family attitudes of older people.
No differences were found in the frequency of contact with adult children, the tendency
to live close by, or in the greater importance of adult daughters in parents' lives.
But the American respondents had more knowledge of and pride in their ancestors. Lar-
ger national samples confirmed the last finding.

4.2 FAMILY MEMBER DIAGNOSED SCHIZOPHRENIC

ACKERMAN, N. W., "Family Focussed Therapy of Schizophrenia," in A. Scher, and H. Davis
        (Eds.), The Out-Patient Treatment of Schizophrenia, New York, Grune & Stratton,
        1960.
Given at a conference on the out-patient treatment of schizophrenia, this clinical essay is on family therapy, schizophrenia, and the family. The family is relevant not
only to the course and outcome but also to the origin of schizophrenia, and treatment
should include the whole family together rather than only the identified patient. Techniques of treating the family are described.

ACKERMAN, N. W., "The Schizophrenic Patient and His Family Relationships," in M. Green-
        blatt, D. J. Levinson, and G. L. Klerman (Eds.), Mental Patients in Transition,
        Steps in Hospital-Community Rehabilitation, Springfield, Thomas C Charles, 1961.
A discussion of the influence of the family on the patient discharged from the hospital.

ACKERMAN, N. W., and FRANKLIN, P. F., "Family Dynamics and the Reversibility of Delusion-
        al Formation: A Case Study in Family Therapy," in I. Boszormenyi-Nagy and J. L.
        Framo (Eds.), Intensive Family Therapy, New York, Harper & Row, 1965.
A report on a case of a 16-year-old schizophrenic and her family in which treatment "of
the whole family seemed to move toward reversal of the patient's psychotic experience."
Interview data and comment is provided.

AHMED, F., "Family and Mental Disorders in Pakistan," Int. J. Soc. Psychiat., 14, 290-
        295, 1968.
In order to study the effect of the structure of the family on mental illness, 967 cases from a privately owned psychiatric clinic in Pakistan were studied, using retrospective case records. Only psychotics and neurotics were used from the larger sample. Results revealed that there were more female psychotics, that psychotic patients were

closer in age to their parents, that father was usually less than 25 years of age for
the psychotics and more than 25 for the neurotics, that more psychotics were the oldest
in the family and more neurotics were the youngest. There was more psychopathology in
the family of psychotics than neurotic patients. No relationship was found between
mental disorders and marital status, sibling order, parental loss in childhood, and
mother's age at birth.

ALANEN, Y., "Round Table Conference of Family Studies and Family Therapy of Schizophren-
      ic Patients," Acta Psychiat. Scand., Supplement No. 169, 39, 420-426, 1963.
A report of a panel discussion oriented toward family dynamics and therapy held at the
Thirteenth Congress of Scandinavian Psychiatrists in 1962. Topics discussed included
findings of the Yale studies on families, parental interaction and the resulting disturbed body images of schizophrenic patients, reactions of the family when the patient
is in individual psychotherapy, and families of schizophrenics in relation to the "larger families" of our contemporary societies."

ALANEN, Y., "Some Thoughts on Schizophrenia and Ego Development in the Light of Family
      Investigations," Arch. Gen. Psychiat., 3, 650-656, 1960.
Noting a divergence between the studies of family environment of the schizophrenic and
classical psychoanalytical conceptions, the author reviews the problem and attempts to
bring the ideas closer together with four main points in the pathological ego development of the schizophrenic.

ALBERT, R. S., "Stages of Breakdown in the Relationships and Dynamics Between the Mental
      Patient and His Family," Arch. Gen. Psychiat., 3, 682-690, 1960.
Since a family is a social system of many different interlocking roles, the absence or
illness of a member produces a reaction throughout the family. Two guiding premises
are: (1) with disruption, the ongoing dynamics move patient and family into a poorer
state with less possibility of a return to earlier, healthier stages of interaction,
and (2) in the earlier stages other members of the family are equally ill and suscep-
tible candidates for becoming the patient. Given a description of stages as a model,
there could be better prediction and preparation for dealing with cases.

ANTHONY, E. J., "The Mutative Impact of Serious Mental and Physical Illness in a Parent
      on Family Life," in E. J. Anthony and C. Koupernik (Eds.), The Child in His Family,
      New York, Wiley, 1970.
A report of a study of families where a parent figure has succumbed to a serious mental
or physical disorder necessitating hospitalization. Various views are offered of such
illness as a disruption of family roles, as a crisis in accommodation, as a disconnection, and as a challenge. Family members were interviewed individually and in dyads
and triads.

ARBOGAST, R., "The Effect of Family Involvement on the Day Care Center Treatment of Schi-
      zophrenia," J. Nerv. Ment. Dis., 149, 277-280, 1969.
A pilot study to assess the relationship between the presence of a seriously disturbed
parent or spouse in the home environment and the effect of treatment in a day hospital
setting of a consecutive series of schizophrenic patients. The group without seriously
disturbed relatives in their environment improved significantly more in their treatment.

ARONSON, J., and POLGAR, S., "Pathogenic Relationships in Schizophrenia," Amer. J. Psy-
      chiat., 119, 222-227, 1962.
Investigating 13 soldiers who developed overtly schizophrenic psychoses in the army,
the authors interviewed 185 individuals on eleven army posts to gather data. Work performance and overt psychotic symptoms are said to depend upon the type of relationship
established with significant others. Three types of relationship were distinguished:
The quasitherapeutic, the pseudotherapeutic and the contratherapeutic. The authors suggest the data indicate the groups other than the family can be pathogenic.

AUERBACK, A. (Ed.), Schizophrenia: An Integrated Approach, New York, Ronald Press, 1959.
A collection of papers oriented toward research in schizophrenia. Included is a paper
by Bateson on cultural problems posed by studying the schizophrenic process, and a paper
by Bowen on family relationships in schizophrenia. 224 pp.

AUERSWALD, E. H., "Interdisciplinary vs. Ecological Approach," Fam. Proc., 7, 202-215,
    1968.
A discussion of the difference between approaching a problem from the viewpoint of different disciplines or using an ecological systems approach. A case of a runaway girl
is used for exploring this difference.

BASAMANIA, B., W., "The Emotional Life of the Family: Inferences for Social Casework,"
    Amer. J. Orthopsychiat., 31, 74-86, 1961.
A casework view of the Bowen research project where families with a schizophrenic member were hospitalized. Observations of 11 families are categorized into (1) interrelated personality problems among family members, and (2) interaction problems among family
members. Case examples are given. A discussion of family therapy procedures is presented with the emphasis upon relating to more than one individual at a time. Inferences
for social casework emphasize the dimension of the emotional life of the family rather
than the integration of sociological concepts with casework practice.

BATESON, G., "The Bisocial Integration of Behavior in the Schizophrenic Family," in N.
    W. Ackerman, F. L. Beatman, and S. Sherman (Eds.), Exploring the Base for Family
    Therapy, New York, Family Service Association of America, 1961.
A description of families and other systems in terms of feedback and calibration, where
calibration is at the "setting" level. Families of schizophrenics are described in
terms of difficulties at the calibration level.

BATESON, G., "Minimal Requirements for a Theory of Schizophrenia," Arch. Gen. Psychiat.,
    2, 477-491, 1960.
An essay on developing a theory of schizophrenia. The role of learning theory, genetics,
and evolution is discussed. The double-bind model may be used in part to explain the
symptoms of schizophrenia and perhaps other behavioral disorders.

BATESON, G., JACKSON, D. D., HALEY, J., and WEAKLAND, J. H., "A Note on the Double Bind
    — 1962," Fam. Proc., 2, 154-161, 1963.
A brief comment by the Bateson group on the context of their 1956 paper on the double
bind and further developments after that time. Includes a bibliography of project members arranged by subject with 70 references.

BATESON, G., JACKSON, D. D., HALEY, J., and WEAKLAND, J., "Toward a Theory of Schizo-
    phrenia," Behav. Sci., 1, 251-264, 1956.
Based on the authors' previous clinical experience, experimental data, the theory of
logical types (defined as a discontinuity between a class and its members), and communication theory, the authors hypothesize that schizophenic symptoms may result from being caught in a double bind. This is defined as a situation in which no matter what a
person does, he can't "win." Therapeutic implications are discussed — many therapeutic gambits are "borderline double binds."

BAXTER, J. C., "Family Relations and Variables in Schizophrenia," in I. M. Cohen (Ed.),
    Psychiatric Research Report No. 20, American Psychiatric Association, 1966, Wash.
An article reviewing the variables used in the study of family relationships of schizophrenics. Whether child or family is "causal" is discussed and the merits of one interpretation or the other is ambiguous at present.

BAXTER, J. C., "Family Relationship Variables in Schizophrenia," Acta Psychiat. Scand.,
    42, 362-391, 1966.
A complete review of the literature from 1892 up to the present, with the focus on variables related to the family and child development. Topics covered are: (1) sibling position of the patient, (2) loss of one or both parents, (3) presence of a distressed
childhood in the patient's background, (4) atypical mother-child relationship, (5) atypical father-child relationship, (6) emotional immaturity in the parents, (7) dominance
and disturbances between the parents, (8) interpersonal conflict in the family, (9)
family-centered pathological behavior, and (10) special position of sibling set for the
patient.

BAXTER, J. C., and ARTHUR S., "Conflict in Families of Schizophrenics as a Function of
    Premorbid Adjustment and Social Class," Fam. Proc., 3, 273-279, 1964.
A group of 16 hospitalized male schizophrenics was classified into four groups on the
basis of the patients' premorbid adjustment and social class. Standard interviews with
the parents were rated for conflict. "Results indicate that the amount of conflict expressed by the parents varies jointly with the premorbid level of the patient and the
social class of the family."

BAXTER, J. C., ARTHUR, S., FLOOD, C., and HEDGEPETH, B., "Conflict Patterns in the Fami-
    lies of Schizophrenics," J. Nerv. Ment. Dis., 135, 419-424, 1962.
Families of 12 male and six female schizophrenics were interviewed individually and as
a group to explore conflict patterns in relation to the sex of the child. The amount of
conflict is said to be comparable in the two groups while patterns of conflict differ.
There is more interparental conflict in the group of families with a male patient and
more involvement of the patient in conflict in the group with a female patient.

BAXTER, J. C., and BECKER, J., "Anxiety and Avoidance Behavior in Schizophrenics in Re-
    sponse to Parental Figures," J. Abnorm. Soc. Psychol., 64, 432-437, 1962.
Good and poor premorbid schizophrenics were exposed to TAT cards of parent-child relationships. Poor premorbids produced more anxiety in response to a mother figure than
a father figure. Good premorbids showed the reverse. Avoidance behavior in response
to parental figures did not differ.

BAXTER, J. C., BECKER, J., and HOOKS, W., "Defensive Style in the Families of Schizophren-
    ics and Controls," J. Abnorm. Soc. Psychol., 66, 512-518, 1963.
Parents of good and poor premorbid schizophrenics were given Rorschach tests. Parents
of poor premorbids showed a greater amount of immature behavior than parents of good
premorbids or parents of neurotics.

BEAVERS, W. T., BLUMBERG, S., TIMKIN, D. R., and WEINER, M. F., "Communication Patterns
    of Mothers of Schizophrenics," Fam. Proc., 4, 95-104, 1965.
A study of the ways the mothers of schizophrenics communicate with an interviewer. Nine
mothers of schizophrenics were contrasted with nine mothers of hospitalized non-schizophrenic patients. The mothers of schizophrenics communicated their feelings in a quantitatively more ambiguous fashion.

BECK, S., "Families of Schizophrenic and of Well Children: Methods, Concepts, and Some
    Results," Amer. J. Orthopsychiat., 30, 247-275, 1960.
A report on a research study attempting to differentiate and compare families with schizophrenic children, families with neurotic children, and families with normal children.
A list of trait items about individuals in 106 families were Q-sorted by a psychiatrist
and three social workers. The clusterings are said to indicate similarities and differences.

BECK, S., and NUNNALLY, J., "Parental Attitudes in Families," Arch. Gen. Psychiat., 13,
    208-213, 1965.
Differences in "attitudes" of parents of schizophrenic children were compared with those
with well children. Eighteen attitudes were measured using the semantic differential
test of Osgood (measures concepts like "my child, pregnancy," etc.). Schizophrenic families were obtained from 32 families of children resident in a therapeutic school; well
children families came from the community. Concepts associated with greater mental health
by the well families included "my mother, the kind of father I am, the kind of mother I
am, myself when I was a father, clinic mothers, and clinic our family." There was no
difference between samples in the other nine concepts.

BEHRENS, M., and GOLDFARB, W., "A Study of Patterns of Interaction of Families of Schizo-
    phrenic Children in Residential Treatment," Amer. J. Orthopsychiat., 28, 300-312,
    1958.
An attempt to differentiate families of schizophrenic children from those of nonschizophrenic children with a sample of 20 families who had a child diagnosed as schizophrenic,
and five who had a child with a behavior disorder, all of whom were in-patients. There

were 10 normals, all children living at home. Data were collected using family interaction scales, and observations were recorded in the homes for both the normals and
the patients when they were home on a visit. Results indicate that the schizophrenic
families were more pathologic than the normal families and the families with bahavior
disorders.

BEHRENS, M., MEYERS, D. I., GOLDFARB, W., GOLDFARB, N., and FIELDSTEEL, N. D., "The Hen-
     ry Ittleson Center Family Interaction Scales," Genet. Psychol. Monogr., 80, 203-
     295, 1969.
A report of a manual used for the family interaction scales. The scales appraise the
functioning of family groups, and derive from a clinical interest in the relationship
between the identified patient and the family. Data are obtained through a three-hour
home visit at mealtime. Scales have been used to evaluate the functioning of the family
with a schizophrenic child, to compare families which include children with various diagnoses with normal families, and to determine the nature of changes in family functioning
over a specified length of time. A description of scales and scoring instructions, and
three family illustrations are included.

BEHRENS, M., ROSENTHAL, A. J., and CHODOFF, P., "Communication in Lower Class Families
     of Schizophrenics," Arch. Gen. Psychiat., 18, 689-696, 1968.
The second part of a study of low-socioeconomic families of schizophrenics. The study
was done in the home where the family was focussed upon a task, particularly the Rorschach. Raters were asked to predict type of family from written transcripts. Results
indicate that communication and interaction patterns of lower-class families with a
schizophrenic differ from families whose class background is similar.

BENNIS, W., SCHEINE, E., BERLEW, D., and STEELE, F. (Eds.), Interpersonal Dynamics,
     Homewood, Dorsey Press, 1964.
A collection of previously published material which includes discussions of the family
scapegoat, the family theory of schizophrenia, interpersonal relationships within the
family, and role conflict.

BENTINCK, C., "Opinions About Mental Illness Held by Patients and Relatives," Fam. Proc.,
     6, 193-207, 1967.
A study inquiring into the nature of the attitudes at home about mental illness in families of male schizophrenics. A control group of male medical patients was used. The
data were gathered by a questionnaire administered in a home interview. The sample was
50 schizophrenics and 50 relatives, and 50 medical patients and 50 relatives. Opinions
of relatives of schizophrenics had "more in common with blue collar employees than with
mental health professionals."

BERGER, A., "A Test of the Double Bind Hypothesis of Schizophrenia," Fam. Proc., 4, 198-
     205, 1965.
A sample of 20 schizophrenics, 18 maladjusted nonschizophrenics, 20 hospital employees,
and 40 students were exposed to a questionnaire of items rated for their double bind
nature. Differences were found.

BOSZORMENYI-NAGY, I., "The Concept of Schizophrenia from the Perspective of Family Treat-
     ment," Fam. Proc., 1, 103-113, 1962.
A discussion of "the problems and mechanisms of family relationships." The author's
hypothesis is that "schizophrenic personality development may in part be perpetrated by
reciprocal interpersonal need complementaries between parent and offspring. Observations
were collected from intensive psychotherapy of young female schizophrenics and concurrent
conjoint therapy of their relatives at a psychiatric hospital.

BOSZORMENYI-NAGI, I., and FRAMO, J. L. (Eds.), Intensive Family Therapy: Theoretical
     and Practical Aspects, New York, Harper & Row, 1965.
A collection of new material which includes a review of the literature; theory of relationships; rationale, dynamics and techniques; family therapy with schizophrenics in
in-patient and out-patient settings; indications and contraindications, countertransference; and research on family dynamics. 507 pp.

BOVERMAN, M., and ADAMS, J. R., "Collaboration of Psychiatrist and Clergyman: A Case
    Report," Fam. Proc., 3, 251-272, 1964.
A description of a psychotic patient and family treated in collaboration. The different
functions of psychiatrist and clergyman are discussed, each presenting his view of the
case.

BOWEN, M., "A Family Concept of Schizophrenia," in D. D. Jackson (Ed.), The Etiology of
    Schizophrenia, New York, Basic Books, 1960.
Clinical observations based upon a research study of the families of schizophrenics.
Includes a report on the project in which whole families of schizophrenics were hospi-
talized.

BOWEN, M., "Family Psychotherapy," Amer. J. Orthopsychiat., 31, 40-60, 1961.
A discussion of the research program in which parents and their schizophrenic offspring
lived together on a psychiatric ward. The paper includes a description of the history
of the project, the sample of families, and the theoretical appraoch. The emphasis is
upon the family as a unit of illness rather than upon individuals in the family group.
Principles and techniques of family therapy emphasize utilizing the family leader,
avoiding individual relationships with family members, and not accepting the position
of omnipotence into which the family attempts to place the therapist. Results are
discussed and examples given with case material.

BOWEN, M., "Family Psychotherapy with Schizophrenia in the Hospital and in Private Prac-
    tice," in I. Boszormenyi-Nagy and J. L. Framo (Eds.), Intensive Family Therapy,
    New York, Harper & Row, 1965.
A discussion of a theory of the family and of family therapy with sections on differences
between family and individual theory; a summary of the family theory of emotional illness
with the emphasis upon schizophrenia; the parental transmission of problems to the child;
the clinical approach to modify the family transmition process; and principles and techniques of this family therapy approach.

BOWEN, M., DYSINGER, R., and BASAMANIA, B., "Role of the Father in Families with a
    Schizophrenic Patient," Amer. J. Psychiat., 115, 1017-1020, 1959.
One of a series of papers on a study of families with schizophrenics in which the entire
family (mother, father, identified patient, and well sibling) were all hospitalized in
the psychiatric research ward for periods of "up to two and a half years." Four families filled this criteria while an additional six families were seen in out-patient
family therapy for periods of up to two years. The most frequent family dynamic observed was "emotional divorce" between mother and father and an intense relationship
between mother and patient in which father was excluded.

BRODEY, W., "Image, Object and Narcissistic Relationships," Amer. J. Orthopsychiat., 31,
    69-73, 1961.
A discussion of the family unit with a conceptualization involving externalization,
the narcissistic relationship, and the image relationship. It is suggested that the
psychotic member has escaped from the bizarre pseudologicalness and stereotype of the
family, but his astonishingly perceptive comments are dismissed by the family as entirely crazy.

BRODEY, W., "Some Family Operations in Schizophrenia," Arch. Gen. Psychiat., 1, 379-
    402, 1959.
One of a series of papers from a research project in which entire families (all of which
have a schizophrenic member) are hospitalized and observed for periods of six months to
two-and-one-half years. Data were collected from five families. Descriptions of the
family and of staff-family relationships are reported. Based on the family histories,
an attempt is made to understand the pathology presented.

BRODSKY, C. M., "The Social Recovery of Mentally Ill Housewives," Fam. Proc., 7, 170-
    183, 1968.
A report on a study of the relationship between social recovery and role among mentally
ill housewives. A sample of 38 housewives admitted to an acute treatment research unit
were examined and followed-up. The housewife's role as said to be conducive to recovery.

CAPUTO, D. V., "The Parents of the Schizophrenic," Fam. Proc., 2, 339-356, 1963.
A study to assess the role of the parents in the development of schizophrenia, with particular emphasis upon the concept of the passive father and dominating mother. Parents
were given individual tests and after taking a parent attitude inventory they were asked
to discuss the items on which they had disagreed. These discussions were assessed with
the Bales method. Reversal of role was not found to be a significant factor, and a hostile atmosphere is indicated in the home of the potential schizophrenic.

CHEEK, F., "Family Interaction Patterns and Convalescent Adjustment of the Schizophrenic,"
     Arch. Gen. Psychiat., 13, 138-147, 1965.
An attempt to examine the relationship between family interaction patterns and outcome
in schizophrenia. Data were obtained from 51 patients who had been hospitalized between
the ages of 15 and 26, all of whom had living mothers and fathers. Each family member
filled out a questionnaire relating to interaction patterns; all three family members
together worked on two questionnaire problems; an interview with the mother on the adjustment of the patient was evaluated by means of a 40-item four point rating scale. One
week later, in the home of the patient, two more 15-minute discussions between family
members were recorded. Fifty-six normal families were studied with identical procedures
used as with the schizophrenics. Results indicated that it was the characteristics of
the parents, rather than the degree of sickness of the patient, "which was the decisive
factor in producing a poor outcome."

CHEEK, F., "Family Socialization Techniques and Deviant Behavior," Fam. Proc., 5, 199-
     217, 1966.
A study based upon Parsons' theoretical framework in which deviant behavior is related
to imbalance of systems inputs and outputs at various stages of development. A sample
of 120 male adults from four different groups — schizophrenics, normals, alcoholics,
and reformatory inmates — were exposed to a questionnaire on family problem situations.
Differences were found and it is suggested that Parsons' theoretical scheme could be
translated into reinforcement theory.

CHEEK, F., "The Father of the Schizophrenic: The Function of a Peripheral Role," Arch.
     Gen. Psychiat., 13, 336-345, 1965.
In view of the absence of data on the role of the father in the intrafamilial environment of the schizophrenic, Bales' interaction process analysis technique and the social
system theoretical framework of Parsons are used for studying the interaction of 67 families of young adult schizophrenics (40 male and 27 female). This sample was compared to
56 families with nonpsychotic young adults (31 male and 25 female). Outcome in schizophrenia was evaluated a year and a half following discharge from the in-patient setting.
All discussions were tape-recorded and coded, using the Bales interaction categories.
Additionally, each member of the families was asked to fill in a questionnaire examining
expectations and perceptions of how the others might behave in relation to one another
in certain typical family problems. Schizophrenic fathers occupy a peripheral position
in the family in which the mother and patient are closest by default. Profiles of
mothers of schizophrenics however differed more widely from those of normals than
fathers.

CHEEK, F., "Parental Role Distortions in Relation to Schizophrenic Deviancy," in I. M.
     Cohen (Ed.), Psychiatric Research Report No. 20, Washington, American Psychiatric
     Association, 1966.
A study investigating the nature of the schizophrenic interacting in the family, and
the relation of family interaction to the outcome of the schizophrenic. The study combined questionnaire and observational data. The sample included 67 schizophrenic
contrasted with 56 nonpsychotic young adults.

CHEEK, F., "The 'Schizophrenogenic Mother' in Word and Deed," Fam. Proc., 3, 155-177,
     1964.
A study of the mothers of schizophrenics by direct observation of their behavior in a
standard conversation with spouse and schizophrenic offspring. The data were analyzed
with a revised version of the Bales process analysis. Sixty-seven families of schizophrenics were contrasted with 56 normal families. Differences in the characteristics
of the mothers were found.

CHEEK, F., "A Serendipitous Finding: Sex Roles in Schizophrenia," J. Abnorm. Soc. Psy-
      chol., 69, 392-400, 1964.
One of a series of reports on an ongoing research project studying the family environment
in schizophrenia. Interaction profiles of 67 young adult schizophrenics (40 male and 27
female) were compared with those of 56 normals (31 male and 25 female). Profiles were
derived from 48 minutes of recorded interaction between father, mother, and patient with
a variation of the Bales interaction categories. Male schizophrenics presented an interaction equivalent of withdrawal, with low total activity rates, and low dominance behaviors. In contrast, female schizophrenics proved to be more active than female normals.

COE, W. C., CURRY, A. E., and KESSLER, D. R., "Family Interaction of Psychiatric Patients,"
      Fam. Proc., 8, 119-130, 1969.
A study using a questionnaire to examine family interaction patterns with emphasis upon
everyday activities. Forty males and 40 females and their relatives who were psychiatric
in-patients were contrasted with 54 husband and wife volunteers. Results include the
finding that more family decision-making is left to the child in the patient families.
In these families the members tend not to recognize disagreement in their interactions.

DAVIS, D. R., "The Family Triangle in Schizophrenia," Brit. J. Med. Psychol., 34, 53-63,
      1961.
An attempt to answer the question "What contribution to the etiology of schizophrenia in
young males is made by conflicts arising out of the Oedipus complex?" with emphasis upon
the patient's attitude toward parents. A review of the literature and a discussion of
actual incest and patricide are presented. The author discusses 15 schizophrenic patients with emphasis upon the onset of illness. He concludes that the onset occurs during a crisis between the patient and his mother when anxiety becomes intense. Frustra-
tion of incestuous wishes contributes to this anxiety. Hatred for the father was clearly
shown in a minority of the cases.

DAVIS, D. R., "A Re-Appraisal of Ibsen's Ghosts," Fam. Proc., 2, 81-94, 1963.
A critical analysis of Ibsen's play, Ghosts: A Domestic Drama, in light of modern therapy
on family psychopathology. Current ideas about the family of the schizophrenic are applied to this family drama.

DAY, J., and KWIATKOWSKA, H., "The Psychiatric Patient and His 'Well' Sibling: A Com-
      parison Through Their Art Productions," Bull. Art. Ther., 2, 51-66, 1962.
A clinical paper comparing the "well" sibling to the "sick" sibling in a schizophrenic
family. The setting was an in-patient ward, and observations were taken from the art
work of the paired siblings, during art therapy. The data from three families reveal
that the "sick" sibling art productions are quite disorganized, while the "well" sibling's productions are more normal.

DUNHAM, R. M., "Ex Post Facto Reconstruction of Conditioning Schedules in Family Inter-
      action," in I. M. Cohen (Ed.), Psychiatric Research Report No. 20, Washington,
      American Psychiatric Association, 1966.
A discussion of family behavior from the point of view of learning theory. Given some
of the descriptions of families of schizophrenics, "have the patients been exposed to
a chronic pattern of aversive conditioning that has inhibited the development of ego
strength...?"

DUPONT, R., and GRUNEBAUM, H., "Willing Victims: The Husbands of Paranoid Women," Amer.
      J. Psychiat., 125, 151-159, 1968.
In an attempt to understand the dynamics of spouses of paranoid women, cases with paranoid delusions (both in-patient and out-patient) were evaluated over a three-year period.
Data were collected on nine women with paranoid state, using clinical interviews, with
the husband alone, wife alone, and the couple together, plus the MMPI and interpersonal
checklist. Results indicated that the wife expressed the anger and dissatisfaction in
the marriage, while the husband manifested passivity and apparent reasonableness and
thus seemed to be a "willing victim."

DYSINGER, R. H., "A Family Perspective on the Diagnosis of Individual Members," Amer.
    J. Orthopsychiat., 31, 61-68, 1961.
A discussion of the characteristic view of health matters by members of families containing a hospitalized schizophrenic as part of the Bowen study. Typically mother,
father, and identified patient are intensely involved emotionally over health issues.
Siblings are not included in the same way. Confusion over feelings, physical symptoms,
and definite illness exists, and attempts to do something effective about a health matter are often stalemated. Intense emotional problems in the parental relationship are
handled through a set of mechanisms that operate to support an inaccurate assumption
that the problem is the health of one child. The development of psychosis in the child
demonstrates the inefficiency of this displacement and also can become a focus for the
perpetuation of the family mechanism.

EVANS, A. S., BULLARD, D. M., Jr., and SOLOMON, M. H., "The Family as a Potential Resource
    in the Rehabilitation of the Chronic Schizophrenic Patient: A Study of 60 Patients
    and Their Families," Amer. J. Psychiat., 117, 1075-1083, 1961.
A study of the relative value of drugs on social therapies in the treatment of chronic
schizophrenia. The success or failure of plans for discharge was often found to be dependent upon the relationship between the patient and his family. This descriptive report summarizes some of the findings about these families, including the discovery that
a surprising number of families maintained an active interest in the patient and regularly visited him after years of hospitalization. The need for psychiatric social workers and additional community resources is emphasized as imported for facilitating discharge.

FARINA, A., "Patterns of Role Dominance and Conflict in Parents of Schizophrenic Pa-
    tients," J. Abnorm. Soc. Psychol., 61, 31-38, 1960.
Parents of 12 good premorbid schizophrenics, 12 poor premorbids, and 12 children hospitalized for tuberculosis were interviewed. They were exposed individually and as pairs
to hypothetical incidents with children. The joint conversation was analyzed for dominance and conflict. Father dominance was associated with good premorbid adjustment of
the son and mother dominance with poor premorbid adjustment. Parents of schizophrenics
displayed more conflict than the control parents.

FARINA, A., and DUNHAM, R. M., "Measurement of Family Relationships and Their Effects,"
    Arch. Gen. Psychiat., 9, 64-73, 1963.
A group of families of male hospitalized schizophrenic patients, divided into good premorbid and poor premorbid, was given a structural situation test. Each family member
is exposed to some hypothetical problem situations with children, and the family is then
brought together and exposed to the same situation. Indices of dominance, such as length
of speeches, and indices of conflict were constructed. Immediately following this, a
group of the patients was given a visual task individually and contrasted with a group
given the same task a week after the situation test. The conclusions are that fathers
are more dominant in good premorbid cases and mothers more dominant in bad premorbid
cases. Conflict scores are higher for good premorbid.

FERBER, A., KLIGLER, D., ZWERLING, I., and MENDELSOHN, M., "Current Family Structure,"
    Arch. Gen. Psychiat., 16, 659-667, 1967.
Hypothesis was that the family, in order to maintain equilibrium, will extrude to the
hospital certain members (most usually those members functioning peripherally). Data
were obtained from an emergency room psychiatric population of a large municipal hospital. Nine hundred and thirty-seven patients and/or their "closest companion" filled
out a family information form. Families of psychiatric patients were compared with
families from the general population. Reliability on the raw data was 90%. Findings
were that being married (rather than single, widowed, etc.) coming from family of procreation, coming from an intact family, and being an emotionally important member of
the household are associated with a lower risk of becoming a patient and of having a better outcome from treatment.

FERREIRA, A., "Psychosis and Family Myth," Amer. J. Psychother., 21, 186-197, 1967.
Two vignettes are reported in support of the thesis that "psychotic behavior may be
regarded not simply as a product of the individual but rather as an expression of the

family interaction, that is, as a relationship-event." Family myths (defined as a
series of beliefs, which are untrue, held by members of the family about each other
and their relationship) are to the family what the defense is to the individual.
Treatment considerations are discussed.

FERREIRA, A. J., and WINTER, W. D., "Family Interaction and Decision-Making," Arch. Gen.
    Psychiat., 13, 214-223, 1965.
A report of a study contrasting 50 normal families and 75 families with an abnormal
child. The abnormal group included 15 schizophrenic, 16 delinquent, and 44 maladjusted
children. The family members were asked to fill out a neutral questionnaire separately
and then they were brought together and asked to fill out the same questionnaire while
reaching agreement on the items as a group. Generally this report is concerned with
the extent of agreement when family members make their choices separately, how much time
is necessary to reach group decisions, and the appropriateness of the family decisions
in fulfilling the wishes of the individual family members. Eighteen hypotheses are described and the results reported in terms of the differences found between the groups.

FERREIRA, A. J., and WINTER, W. D., and POINDEXTER, E. J., "Some Interactional Variables
    in Normal and Abnormal Families," Fam. Proc., 5, 60-75, 1966.
A study contrasting normal and abnormal families, with the abnormals including schizophrenics, delinquents, and maladjusted. The families were exposed to TAT cards three
at a time and asked to make up a story tying them together. Differences were found between the types of families and are described.

FLECK, S., "Family Dynamics and Origin of Schizophrenia," Psychosom. Med., 22, 333-344,
    1960.
A comprehensive review of the Lidz project with a discussion of the findings and of the
general problem of investigating the family of the schizophrenic. All of the 16 families studied were severely disturbed. Typical characteristics include a failure to form
a nuclear family; family schisms; family skews; blurring of generation lines; pervasion
of the entire atmosphere with irrational, usually paranoid ideation; persistence of conscious incestuous preoccupation; and sociocultural isolation. Case examples are presented.

FLECK, S., CORNELISON, A., NORTON, N., and LIDZ, T., "The Intrafamilial Environment of
    the Schizophrenic Patient. III. Interaction Between Hospital Staff and Families,"
    Psychiatry, 20, 343-350, 1957.
One of a series of papers on the effect of the family in the etiology and pathogenesis
of schizophrenia. The role of the patient's family with the hospital staff was examined.
Neglecting the relationship of the family to the staff can affect the patient's hospital
course "deleteriously or even catastrophically."

FLECK, S., LIDZ, T., and CORNELISON, A., "Comparison of Parent-Child Relationships of
    Male and Female Schizophrenic Patients," Arch. Gen. Psychiat., 8, 1-7, 1963.
A study of 17 families containing a schizophrenic child, emphasizing the differences
between families containing schizophrenic sons and those with schizophrenic daughters.
Schizophrenic males often come from skewed families with passive, ineffectual fathers
and disturbed, engulfing mothers. Schizophrenic girls typically grow up in schismatic
families with narcissistic fathers and emotionally distant mothers.

FLECK, S., LIDZ, T., CORNELISON, A., SCHAFER, S., and TERRY, D., "The Intrafamilial En-
    vironment of the Schizophrenic Patient," in J. Masserman (Ed.), Science and Psycho-
    analysis, Vol. II, Individual and Familial Dynamics, New York, Grune & Stratton,
    1959.
One of a series of papers on a study of schizophrenic families focussing on problems of
incest in the understanding and treatment of schizophrenic patients. Essential requisites of normal family function and organization are described along with consistent disturbances in schizophrenic families.

FONTANA, A. F., "Familial Etiology of Schizophrenia: Is a Scientific Methodology Pos-
     sible?," Psychol. Bull., 66, 214-227, 1966.
A review of methodology in family research on schizophrenia emphasizing clinical observation, retrospective recall, and direct observation of family interaction. The former
two approaches are said to be unsuitable "for a scientific body of etiological facts";
the latter approach should be used with caution. Findings of various studies are reviewed. The author concludes the greatest value so far is in the guidelines provided
for longitudinal research, but sufficient knowledge is not yet available to warrant the
great expenditure involved in longitudinal research at the present time.

FOUDRAINE, J., "Schizophrenia and the Family: A Survey of the Literature 1956-1960 on
     the Etiology of Schizophrenia," Acta Psychother., 9, 82-110, 1961.
In a thorough review of the literature, the author describes the development of the
family point of view of schizophrenia and summarizes the works of authors who have published on the subject during this period. He explores the problems of attempting to
conceptualize the function of the family as a whole, and to connect pathological family
structure with schizophrenia in the individual. A bibliography of 97 items is included.

FRANK, G. H., "The Role of the Family in the Development of Psychopathology," Psychol.
     Bull., 64, 191-205, 1965.
A review of some of the literature on family influence as it relates to personality development and psychopathology. Studies of schizophrenia and neurotic problems are examined in terms of method of collecting data on family influence, including case history,
psychiatric interview, psychological evaluation, and observation. The review concludes
"we have not been able to find any unique factors in the family of the schizophrenic
which distinguishes it from the family of the neurotic or from the family of controls,
who are ostensibly free from evidence of patterns of gross psychopathology."

FRANKLIN, P., "Family Therapy of Psychotics," Amer. J. Psychoanal., 29, 50-56, 1969.
A case report of a schizophrenic child and his parents and grandmother who were treated
both individually and with family therapy over seven years. The author's thesis is
that schizophrenic symptoms are a manifestation of a process that "involves the entire
family." The identified patient and the family improved after treatment.

FREEMAN, H. E., "Attitudes Toward Mental Illness Among Relatives of Former Patients,"
     Amer. Sociol. Rev., 26, 59-66, 1961.
The relatives of 649 newly discharged mental hospital patients (of a total population
of 714) were successfully interviewed to investigate their attitudes about the etiology
of mental illness, the mental hospital, the normalcy of patients after mental illness,
and the responsibility of patients for their condition. As in other surveys, age and
education were associated with attitudes. "Enlightened" attitudes were not associated
with social class measured independently of education, but were associated with verbal
skill. It is suggested that verbal skill may be more important than "style of life."
However, attitudes were related to the patients' posthospital behavior, and appear to
be complexly determined and deeply rooted.

FREEMAN, H. E., and SIMMONS, O. G., "Feelings of Stigma Among Relatives of Former Men-
     tal Patients," Soc. Prob., 8, 312-321, 1961.
Feelings of stigma were elicited from the families of 649 members of a group of 714
functional psychotics released from hospitals in eastern Massachusetts. Data were gathered by means of standard items in a structured interview with a relative a month
after the patient's release. One-quarter of the sample reported feelings of stigma,
while two-thirds acknowledged management problems. These feelings are associated with
the patient's posthospital behavior, the education, class status, and personality characteristics of the relatives. Wives are more likely than other kin to feel stigma.

FRIEDMAN, A. S., BOSZORMENYI-NAGY, I., JUNGREIS, J. E., LINCOLN, G., MITCHELL, H., SONNE,
     J., SPECK, R., and SPIVACK, G., Psychotherapy for the Whole Family: Case Histories,
     Techniques, and Concepts of Family Therapy of Schizophrenia in the Home and Clinic,
     New York, Springer, 1965.
A collection of new material based on a research project involving treatment of schizo-

phrenia using family therapy done in the home. The papers cover rationale, experience
with the study families, results of treatment, and problems and concepts in treatment.
There is a section on a search for a conceptual model of family psychopathology. 354 pp.

FRIEDMAN, C. J., and FRIEDMAN, A. S., "Characteristics of Schizogenic Families During
     a Joint Story-Telling Task," Fam. Proc., 9, 33-353, 1970.
A comparison of families with a schizophrenic and normal families in the task of telling
a story. Observer ratings were used for the interaction and judges ratings for the
final joint family story. Differences were found.

GARDNER, R. A., "A Four-Day Diagnostic-Therapeutic Home Visit in Turkey," Fam. Proc.,
     9, 301-317, 1970.
A report of a four-day visit in Istanbul to consult with a family of a 20-year-old Turkish patient. A Greek and a Turkish psychiatrist comment on the article.

GARMEZY, N., CLARKE, A. R., and STOCKNER, C., "Child Rearing Attitudes of Mothers and
     Fathers as Reported by Schizophrenic and Normal Patients," J. Abnorm. Soc. Psy-
     chol., 63, 176-182, 1961.
A group of 15 good premorbid and 15 poor premorbid schizophrenic patients were asked to
think back when they were 13 or 14 years old and try to remember mother and father at
that time. The experimenter then presented them with 75 statements describing various
child rearing attitudes and asked the patients if their parents would have agreed or
disagreed with each item. A group of 15 patients hospitalized for medical problems was
used as a control. The results indicate that the subject's level of social maturity
and the extent of attitudinal deviance ascribed to parents are related. Poor premorbids reveal maternal dominance whereas good premorbids ascribe heightened paternal dominance in their responses.

GARMEZY, N., FARINA, A., and RODNICK, E. H., "The Structured Situation Test: A Method
     for Studying Family Interaction in Schizophrenia," Amer. J. Orthopsychiat., 30,
     445-451, 1960.
A group of 36 sets of parents composed of parents of good and poor premorbids and of
sons with tuberculosis ("normals") were exposed to 12 hypothetical misbehaviors of a
son. Individually and then together they were asked to indicate how to handle the situation. From tape recordings of the interviews, measures of dominance behavior and conflict were made, such as who spoke first and last, acceptance of another's solution,
amount of interruption, and so on. With good premorbids the fathers were dominant and
in poor premorbids the mothers were. The "normals" share dominance. Poor premorbids
show greater conflict than "normals."

GLICK, I., "The 'Sick' Family and Schizophrenia — Cause and Effect?," Dis. Nerv. Syst.,
     29, 129-132, 1968.
A critique on the hypothesis that there is a cause and effect relationship between disturbed family functioning and schizophrenia. A summary of a theory is presented, and
questions raised by it are discussed. Data culled from other etiologic theories (bio-
logic, genetic, and intrapsychic) pertinent to family theory are reviewed. Data obtained
thus far are insufficient to form a unitary hypothesis for the etiology of schizophrenia.

GODUCO-AGULAR, C., and WINTROB, R., "Folie à Famille in the Phillipines," Psychiat. Quart.,
     38, 278-292, 1964.
A case report of folie à famille (defined as psychotic behavior in each of eight members
of the family reported) in a Philippine family. A review of the literature and a sociocultural formulation of the case are presented.

GOLDFARB, W., "The Mutual Impact of Mother and Child in Childhood Schizophrenia," Amer.
     J. Orthopsychiat., 31, 738-747, 1961.
Childhood schizophrenia is a psychiatric classification which does not delineate a single and specific clinical entity but describes a broad diversity of serious ego impair-
ments. Etiological diversity is hypothesized as well with a "continuum of causal factors
ranging from primary somatic dificiencies within the child to a primary psychosocial disturbance within the family." In clinical practice it has been feasible to identify two

general classes of disorder: children with abnormal organic status and the class of
nonorganic children. The organic cluster contains children derived from families similar to those of normal children. A case of each type is presented and discussed with
emphasis upon the complex mutual and reciprocating impact of the child on the family
and the family on the child.

GRUNEBAUM, H. U., and WEISS, J. L., "Psychotic Mothers and Their Children: Joint Ad-
     mission to an Adult Psychiatric Hospital," Amer. J. Psychiat., 119, 927-933, 1963.
A description of 12 infants and young children cared for by their mothers on the adult
ward of the Massachusetts Mental Health Center. The mothers were hospitalized for severe emotional disorders, but were still able to care for their children. Such joint
admissions are said to be practical in selected cases and can make a substantial contribution to the mother's recovery.

HALEY, J., "The Art of Being Schizophrenic," Voices, 1, 133-142, 1965.
A description of the schizophrenic with special emphasis upon family and hospital context.

HALEY, J., "Experiment with Abnormal Families," Arch. Gen. Psychiat., 17, 53-63, 1967.
A comparison of abnormal and normal families in an experimental setting where family
members speak to each other from different rooms. Measures are who chooses to speak
with whom and patterns of speech sequence.

HALEY, J., "Family Experiments: A New Type of Experimentation," Fam. Proc., 1, 265-
     293. 1962.
A report on a research project in which parents and schizophrenic child were contrasted
with parents and normal child in an experimental game to test hypotheses about coalition patterns in normal and abnormal families. Differences were found between the 30
families in each group. There is a general discussion of the uniqueness of experimenting with families in theoretical, methodological, and sampling problems.

HALEY, J., "The Family of the Schizophrenic: A Model System," J. Nerv. Ment. Dis.,
     129, 357-374, 1959.
A description of the family of the schizophrenic as a governed system with a verbatim
excerpt from a family interview for illustration.

HALEY, J., "Observation of the Family of the Schizophrenic," Amer. J. Orthopsychiat.,
     30, 460-467, 1960.
A report on a research project examining families containing a schizophrenic child by
observation of conjoint family therapy sessions, filmed structured interviews, and experimental situations. The family is seen as a self-correction system which is "governed" by the behavior of each family member. The limited range of a family system
can be described in terms of rules and prohibitions which, when infringed, activate
family members to behave in such a way as to reinforce the system. The general communicative behavior of the schizophrenic family is described and a film is shown for illustration.

HALEY, J., "The Perverse Triangle," in J. Zuk and I. Boszormenyi-Nagy (Eds.), Family
     Therapy and Disturbed Families, Palo Alto, Science & Behavior Press, 1967.
A discussion of cross-generational coalitions as a cause of disturbance in family and
other organizations.

HALEY, J., Strategies of Psychotherapy, New York, Grune & Stratton, 1963.
A description of a variety of forms of psychotherapy from an interactional point of view.
Includes chapters on marriage therapy and family therapy.

HALEY, J., "Testing Parental Instructions to Schizophrenic and Normal Children: A Pilot
     Study," J. Abnorm. Psychol., 73, 559-566, 1968.
An experiment to test the hypothesis that parents communicate to their schizophrenic child-

ren in conflicting ways. Parental instructions were given from a separate room and tape recorded so that they could be played to matched children. On this small sample, the indications were that parents of schizophrenics do not communicate in more conflicting ways than parents of normal children when the measurement is the success of a child in following their instructions.

HALEY, J., and HOFFMAN, L., Techniques of Family Therapy, New York, Basic Books, 1967. A presentation of the work of five family therapists. Interviews were done with Virginia Satir, Don D. Jackson, Charles Fulweiler, Carl Whitaker, and a therapy team doing crisis therapy. There is intensive examination of a first interview with a family to illustrate their approaches.

HAYWARD, M., "Schizophrenia in a Double Bind," Psychiat. Quart., 34, 89-91, 1960. A case example illustrating the use of the double bind in the development of schizophrenia. Understanding this concept is helpful in understanding schizophrenic behavior.

HENRY, J., "The Study of Families by Naturalistic Observation," in I. M. Cohen (Ed.), Psychiatric Research Report No. 20, Washington, American Psychiatric Association, 1966. A discussion of the observation of psychotic children in the home with the emphasis upon the methodology and the experience of such observation. An illustration is given. "When such observations are undertaken it quickly becomes apparent that the data are so rich as to compel reexamination of old theories and suggest hypotheses leading to new ones."

HIGGINS, J., "Sex of Child Reared by Schizophrenic Mothers," J. Psychiat. Res., 4, 153-167, 1966. In an attempt to assess the effect of child-rearing by schizophrenic mothers, two groups of 25 children of schizophrenic mothers were studied. One group was reared by the mothers and the other group was reared from an early age by agents without psychiatric illness. The sample was tested using a psychiatric interview of the child only, several psychological tests and a report from the school. Results failed to support the hypothesis that the mother-reared children would display greater maladjustment on the various measures than would the reared-apart child.

HILGARD, J., and NEWMAN, M. F., "Early Parental Deprivation as a Function Factor in the Etiology of Schizophrenia and Alcoholism," Amer. J. Orthopsychiat., 33, 409-420, 1963. A study designed to consider the age at which loss by death was sustained during childhood by hospitalized schizophrenic and alcoholic patients. Comparison was made using hospital admission records of 1521 schizophrenic patients, 929 alcoholic patients, and a control group of 1,096 cases selected using an area-sampling technique from an urban community. It was concluded that mother loss among women in both diagnostic categories was earlier than in the control group members who lost mothers. Schizophrenic women showed loss of both mother and father at a significantly earlier age than the control subjects.

HILGARD, J., and NEWMAN, M. F., "Parental Loss by Death in Childhood as an Etiological Factor Among Schizophrenic and Alcoholic Patients Compared with a Non-Patient Community Sample, " J. Nerv. Ment. Dis., 137, 14-28, 1963. Hospital records were examined and a sample of 1,561 schizophrenic patients and 929 alcoholic patients were compared with a control sample of 1,096 cases. Schizophrenics had lost one or both parents more often than the control group members. Parent loss is said to be one of the factors associated with an increase in vulnerability in coping with the stresses of adult life.

HOOVER, C., "The Embroiled Family: A Blueprint for Schizophrenia," Fam. Proc., 4, 291-310, 1965. An essay on the emotionally entangled family with an adolescent who becomes schizophrenic at adolescence. Schizophrenia is said to arise in the family when there is a combination of factors involving emotional "embroilment."

JACKSON, D. D., (Ed.), Communication, Family and Marriage, Palo Alto, Science & Behavior
    Books, 1968.
A collection of previously published papers covering early generalizations on family
dynamics from clinical observations, the double bind theory, communication, systems
and pathology, and research approaches and methods. 289 pp.

JACKSON, D. D., "Conjoint Family Therapy," Mod. Med., 33, 172-198, 1965.
A clinical article discussing the history of, rationale for, and techniques of family
therapy. Schizophrenia is seen as a reaction to a disturbance in family communication.
Families operate in a homeostatic system and the disturbances of one member affect other
members.

JACKSON, D.D. (Ed.), The Etiology of Schizophrenia, New York, Basic Books, 1960.
A collection of new material dealing with the etiology of schizophrenia. The book includes a section on an overview of the problem, genetic aspects, biochemical aspects.
physiologic aspects, psychological studies, and family theories of schizophrenia. 456 pp.

JACKSON, D. D., Myths of Madness, New York, Macmillan, 1964.
A discussion of madness emphasizing the different mythologies about it and expressing a
more social view.

JACKSON, D. D., BLOCK, J., and PATTERSON, V., "Psychiatrists' Conceptions of the Schizo-
    phrenogenic Parent," Arch. Neurol. Psychiat., 79, 448-459, 1958.
Twenty psychiatrists were asked for their conceptions of the mothers and fathers of schizophrenics. Three types of mothers and three types of fathers were described. This data
were then compared with Q-sorts done on 20 mothers and 20 fathers of 20 schizophrenic patients. Two out of three mother types described by psychiatrists correlate highly. None
of the father descriptions correlated statistically.

JACKSON, D. D., and WEAKLAND, J. H., "Conjoint Family Therapy: Some Considerations on
    Theory, Techniques, and Results," Psychiatry, 24, 30-45, 1961.
A report on conjoint family therapy of families with a schizophrenic member with a discussion of the theoretical point of view, the procedural arrangements, and typical problems. Case material is used to illustrate characteristic sequences in the therapy. The
emphasis is upon the current interaction within these families and their resistance to
change. Results are presented, and there is a discussion of countertransference problems and the shift in psychotheapeutic approach characteristic of therapists who attempt family psychotherapy.

JACKSON, D. D., and WEAKLAND, J., "Schizophrenic Symptoms in Family Interaction," Arch.
    Gen. Psychiat., 1, 618-621, 1959.
Based on psychological, sociological, and anthropological information about families,
data collection from individual interviews of family members, and treatment of the family
together, the authors hypothesize that schizophrenic behavior can be seen as (1) "re-
sembling the behavior of other family members, though it may be exaggerated almost to a
caricature," and (2) "appearing to subserve important functions within the family." Two
case examples are given in support of this view.

JOHNSTON, R., and PLANANSKY, K., "Schizophrenia in Men: The Impact on Their Wives," Psy-
    chiat. Quart., 42, 146-155, 1968.
A study on an in-patient unit rating 36 wives of chronic in-patients. Data were gathered
from interviews with spouses obtained independently by four raters on the unit. As the
patients regressed, about half the spouses rejected (divorced, spearated, etc.), their
husbands. Reasons for this are discussed.

KAUFMAN, I., FRANK, T., HEIMS, L., HERRICK, S., REISER, D., and WILLER, L., "Treatment
    Implications of a New Classification of Parents of Schizophrenic Children," Amer.
    J. Psychiat., 116, 920-924, 1960.
A report of a study of the personalities of 80 schizophrenic children's parents. Material was gathered from psychotherapy, psychological testing, and direct observation of

parent-child interaction. Parent personalities are classified as "psychoneurotic,"
"somatic," "pseudodelinquent," and "overtly psychotic." The first two types of personalities were found more frequently in an out-patient setting, while the last two
were found more frequently in a state hospital setting. Treatment for these parents
is discussed.

KEMPLER, W., IVERSON, R., and BEISSER, A., "The Adult Schizophrenic and His Siblings,"
     Fam. Proc., 1, 224-235, 1962.
Sixty-five siblings in a group of 16 schizophrenic families were interviewed using a
structured protocol to explore "parent-child relationships" as seen by the siblings.
Findings included distortions in communications by both patients and siblings and appeared unrelated to the schizophrenic process. Four subjects, all of whom were "favorite" children in the family, showed no such distortions. A transcript from a single
family is presented in illustration.

KIND, H., "The Psychogenesis of Schizophrenia," Int. J. Psychiat., 3, 383-403, 1967.
A review article covering the data bearing on psychogenic factors in the etiology of
schizophrenia. The literature is covered in five headings: (1) findings based on psychotherapy of schizophrenic patients, (2) investigations on interpersonal relationships
in the earlier family life of schizophrenics (3) statistical investigations on the frequency of particular traumatic situations, (4) investigations by various methods on the
attitudes of important figures to the children, and (5) social and cultural circumstances.
The author concludes that a purely psychogenic theory of schizophrenia is just as unten-
able as a purely genetic one. Five critical evaluations by various authors are included.

LAING, R. D., The Divided Self, London, Tavistock, 1960.
A clinical book focussing on a theory of schizophrenia in existential terms. There are
sections on the existential foundation for understanding this phenomenon, the prepsy-
chotic role of the schizophrenic, and the psychotic role of the schizophrenic — all
related to the social context of this symptomatology.

LAING, R. D., "Mystification, Confusion and Conflict," in I. Boszormenyi-Nagy and J. L.
     Framo (Eds.), Intensive Family Therapy, New York, Harper & Row, 1965.
The theoretical schema of Marx — where the exploiter mystifies with a plausible misrep-
resentation of what is happening to the exploited — is applied to the family of the
schizophrenic. The act of mystifying and the state of being mystified are described
with case examples. The therapist's task is to help such a person become demystified.

LAING, R. D., and ESTERSON, A., "Families and Schizophrenia," Int. J. Psychiat., 4, 65-
     71, 1967.
A paper describing the authors' theoretical position for their work studying families
with a schizophrenic member. Schizophrenia is seen as a social event — "a set of clinical attributions made by certain persons about the experience and behavior of others"—
not as a disease. "Family" includes the extra-familial personal networks of family members. The authors' study is directed to observable interactions between these members
and the family system itself and not to unconscious or inferred motives. Schizophrenia
is seen as a reaction to family behavior.

LAING, R. D., and ESTERSON, A., Sanity, Madness and the Family, Vol. I, Families of Schi-
     zophrenics, London, Tavistock, 1964.
A book describing a research project investigating 11 families in which the identified
patient was a female with schizophrenia. The data were obtained from clinical interviews
with family members both individually and together. "The Behavior of schizophrenics
is much more socially intelligible than has come to be supposed by most psychiatrists."
Rather than having an illness, the symptoms are seen as a "strategy" invented by the
person to live in an "unlivable" situation. 272 pp.

LANGSLEY, D., PITTMAN, F., and SWANK, G., "Family Crisis in Schizophrenics and Other
     Mental Patients," J. Nerv. Ment. Dis., 149, 270-276, 1969.
A further report on a study using crisis therapy as an alternative to psychiatric

hospitalization. In this study, 50 families which included a schizophrenic patient,
and 50 which included a nonschizophrenic mental patient, were studied using an instrument which quantified the events leading to a crisis in the family and the management
of such crises. Nonschiophrenic mental patients were better able to handle crisis and
interact with their families. A discussion of these findings is presented.

LASEQUE, C., and FALRET, J., "La Folie à Deux ou Folie Communiquee," transl. R. Michaud,
     Amer. J. Psychiat., Supplement No. 121, 1964. (Originally published in Ann. Medico
     Psychol., p. 18, November, 1877.)
The first English translation of the classical paper written in 1877. It represents an
attempt to delineate and understand the relationship between emotionally ill people and
those who live in close contact with them. "Insanity" is not contagious (that is the
passing of a delusion from a "sick" to a "healthy" person) except in the following circumstances: (1) the more sick individual is also more intelligent, the other more dependent, (2) both individuals must have lived together for a long time isolated from
outside influences, (3) the delusion is within the realm of probability for both individuals. It is more common among women. Treatment is to separate the two patients;
in the secondary patient the psychopathology is reversible. Case material is presented
in support of the above ideas.

LENNARD, H., BEAULIEU, M. R., and EMBREY, N. G., "Interaction in Families with a Schizo-
     phrenic Child," Arch. Gen. Psychiat., 12, 166-183, 1965.
A study contrasting ten families with a schizophrenic child and seven normal families.
The families have a 15-minute discussion of three topics related to a child's life. The
conversations are recorded, transcribed, and coded along 12 dimensions. Differences are
found between the two groups. There is a discussion of the theoretical background and
methodological problems.

LENNARD, H., and BERNSTEIN, A., Patterns in Human Interaction, San Francisco, Jossey-
     Bass, 1969.
A textbook on "clinical sociology" which discusses interaction processes, methodological
problems in describing interaction processes, interaction patterns in the family, psychotherapeutic interaction, and functions of human interaction. Patterns of schizophrenic
and control families are described. 224 pp.

LEVIN, G., "Communicator-Communicant Approach to Family Interaction Research," Fam. Proc.,
     5, 105-116, 1966.
A family experiment in which the experimenter asks the subject to make a tape recording
which might be played subsequently to some specific other person in his family. The recording includes specific instructions about a simple task. Individuals from families
containing a schizophrenic (a sample of 33) were contrasted with normal individuals.
The recordings were not actually played to family members, but the instructions were
analyzed and classified with differences found between the two groups.

LEWIS, V. S., and ZEICHNER, A. N., "Impact of Admission to a Mental Hospital on the Pa-
     tient's Family," Ment. Hyg., 44, 503-509, 1960.
A report on a study of the effect on families when a member is hospitalized for mental
illness. The study is based upon interviews with members of the families of 109 patients
admitted to Connecticut's three state mental hospitals. Reported with tables are such
categories as the recognition and acceptance of mental illness, the ways of coping with
the patient's illness, assessment of help of resources tried, and treatment given prior
to hospitalization.

LICHTENBERG, J. D., and PING-NIE, PAO, "The Prognostic and Therapeutic Significance of
     the Husband-Wife Relationship for Hospitalized Schizophrenic Women," Psychiatry,
     23, 209-213, 1960.
A discussion of the types of husbands of hospitalized schizophrenic women and the importance of taking the spouse into account in psychotherapy. Observation of 43 patients
indicated the husbands fell into certain groups, although no prototype personality was
found. In terms of prognosis, the husbands are classified as constructively active,
obstructively active, rejecting, maintaining the previous pathological relationships,
and vacillating. Ways to include the husband in the therapeutic program were attempted
and are recommended.

LIDZ, R., and LIDZ, T., "Homosexual Tendencies in Mothers of Schizophrenic Women," J.
     Nerv. Ment. Dis., 149, 229-235, 1969.
From four case studies of schizophrenic women whose mothers were also interviewed, the
authors' thesis is that "incestuous homosexual tendencies of schizophrenic patients reflect similar proclivities in their parents." In therapy, the mothers attempt to focus
on the therapist rather than on the process of therapy.

LIDZ, T., The Family and Human Adaption, New York, International Universities Press,
     1963.
A collection of three lectures dealing with the role of the family in normal development, the role of the family in a changing society, and specific requisites for successful family functioning: the parents' ability to form a coalition, maintain boundaries
between generations, and adhere to their appropriate sex-linked role. Finally, he covers the family's capacity to transmit the basic adaptive techniques of the culture by
means of communication. Failures in these functions are explored in terms of an etiologic theory for schizophrenia. 120 pp.

LIDZ, T., "The Influence of Family Studies on the Treatment of Schizophrenia," Psychi-
     atry, 32, 237-251, 1969.
The author attempts to link his work studying schizophrenia as a family disorder with
contributions of Freida Fromm-Reichmann, as well as with new advances with the tranquillizing drugs and milieu therapy. Dynamics of pathologic families as well as techniques
of working with the families are discussed in detail.

LIDZ, T., "Schizophrenia and the Family," Psychiatry, 21, 21-27, 1958.
An essay dealing with the etiology of schizophrenia. The role of the family in the
etiology is discussed with particular emphasis on how pathological family development
can lead to different syndromes. The author's studies of schizophrenia are described
briefly.

LIDZ, T., CORNELISON, A., FLECK, S., and TERRY, D., "The Intrafamilial Environment of
     a Schizophrenic Patient. I. The Father," Psychiatry, 20, 329-342, 1957.
To understand the role of the family in the etiology and pathogenesis of schizophrenia,
14 families with a hospitalized schizophrenic were studied for periods varying from six
months to over two years. Data collection included interviewing all members of the family (individually), observations and records of interactions of family members with
each other and with the hospital personnel, home visits, and projective testing of all
family members. Focus was on the fathers, in view of the fact that so much previous
work had focussed on mothers alone. Fathers were found to be "very important, albeit
often extremely disturbing, members of the families whose presence and influence cannot
be neglected." Five different types of fathers are described.

LIDZ, T., CORNELISON, A., FLECK, S., and TERRY, D., "Intrafamilial Environment of Schi-
     zophrenic Patients. II. Marital Schism and Marital Skew," Amer. J. Psychiat.,
     114, 241-248, 1957.
A study of the intrafamilial environment of the schizophrenic patient. In this study
of 14 families, eight were split in two factions by "overt schism between the parents."
Thus the identified patient cannot use one parent as a model for identification or as
a love object without losing the support of the other parent. The other six families
were "skewed" (defined as psychopathology in the dominant parent) which was accepted or
shared by the other without trying to change it. Case examples are given.

LIDZ, T., CORNELISON, A., FLECK, S., and TERRY, D., "Schism and Skew in the Families
     of Schizophrenics," in N. W. Bell and E. F. Vogel (Eds.), A Modern Introduction
     to the Family, Glencoe, Free Press, 1960.
A discussion of 14 families of schizophrenics where it was found that the marital relationships of the parents were seriously disturbed. There was either an overt schism
between the parents or there was an appearance of harmony. The family environments were
badly distorted or "skewed" because serious psychopathology in the dominant parent was
accepted or shared by the other.

LIDZ, T., CORNELISON, A., TERRY, D., and FLECK, S., "Intrafamilial Environment of the
     Schizophrenic Patient. VI. The Transmission of Irrationality," Arch. Neurolo.
     Psychiat., 79, 305-316, 1958.
A study of families of schizophrenics in which nine of the 15 patients had at least one
parent who could be called schizophrenic. Their "irrational" behavior was transmitted
through disturbed communication to the children who were reared in intrafamilial systems of communication which distort or deny reality. The implications of these findings
in terms of the etiology of schizophrenia are discussed.

LIDZ, T., and FLECK, S., "Schizophrenia, Human Integration, and the Role of the Family,"
     in D. D. Jackson (Ed.), The Etiology of Schizophrenia, New York, Basic Books, 1960.
A discussion of the deficiencies in families of schizophrenic patients as a way of clarifying the ego weakness of schizophrenic patients.

LIDZ, T., FLECK, S., ALANEN, Y. O., and CORNELISON, A., "Schizophrenic Patients and
     Their Siblings," Psychiatry, 26, 1-18, 1963.
A study of the siblings of schizophrenics based upon individual interviews of family
members, observation of family members with each other and hospital staff, and projective tests. Sixteen families were studied for periods ranging from six months to six
years. As many siblings were psychotic as were reasonably well adjusted, and all except five or six of the 24 siblings suffered from severe personality disorders. Siblings of the same sex as the patient were more disturbed than those of the opposite sex.

LIDZ, T., FLECK, S., and CORNELISON, A., Schizophrenia and the Family, New York, Inter-
     national Universities Press, 1965.
A collection of new material and previously published articles by the Yale research
group concerning their investigations of the intrafamilial environment in which schizophrenic patients grow up. The book includes the rationale for the study, some articles
on the family environment of schizophrenic patients, a number of articles on the 17 study
families (including aspects of casework techniques, family interaction with the hospital
staff, familial dynamics, and psychological testing), and the implications of this data
for a new theory of schizophrenia based on a disturbed intrafamilial environment. There
is also a section documenting the type of thought disorder found in families with schizophrenic patients as seen on the object sorting test. There is an extensive bibliography. 477 pp.

LIDZ, T., FLECK, S., CORNELISON, A., and TERRY, D., "The Intrafamilial Environment of
     the Schizophrenic Patient. IV. Parental Personalities in Family Interaction,"
     Amer. J. Orthopsychiat., 28, 764-776, 1958.
One of a series of papers dealing with observations from an intensive study of the intrafamilial environments of schizophrenic patients. A long case report is presented in
support of the hypothesis that the nature of the parental personalities will determine
family interaction and will bear on the development or nondevelopment of schizophrenia
in siblings.

LIDZ, T., PARKER, B., and CORNELISON, A., "The Role of the Father in the Family Environ-
     ment of the Schizophrenic Patient," Amer. J. Psychiat., 113, 126-132, 1956.
One of a series of papers on a study of the families of schizophrenic patients. Families
in which there was both a mother and father present were interviewed separately, in pairs,
and in groups. The identified patient was an in-patient and came from upper-class or
upper-middle-class families. Sixteen families (of which five identified patients were
female and 11 were male) were studied. The fathers are seen as "noxious" in the development of schizophrenia. Three types are described: (1) fathers of schizophrenic daughters who are constantly battling their wives and seeking to enlist the support of their
daughters, (2) fathers who feel their sons are rivals for their wives, and (3) passive,
withdrawn, and absent fathers.

LINDSAY, J. S. B., "Types of Family and Family Types," Fam. Proc., 7, 51-66, 1968.
A discussion of the application of the theory of logical types to family descriptions.
Confusions between the monad, the dyad, and the triad are described and a hypothesis
for schizophrenia is presented.

LOVELAND, N. T., "The Family Rorschach: A New Method for Studying Family Interaction,"
    Fam. Proc., 2, 187-215, 1963.
A report of a study in which the Rorschach was used as a standardized stimulus for family
conversations. The procedure is described, the advantages and disadvantages are discussed, and excerpts from a family Rorschach are presented.

LU, Y. C., "Contradictory Parental Expectations in Schizophrenia," Arch. Gen. Psychiat.,
    6, 219-234, 1962.
A report of some preliminary findings of an investigation of the families of schizophrenics. The emphasis is upon a comparison of the parents' relationship with patient
and with nonschizophrenic siblings in an attempt to discover why one child in a family
develops schizophrenia and not another. The parents expect a higher degree of dependence from the preschizophrenic than from the nonschizophrenic child, and they also expect a higher degree of achievement and responsibility. The author suggests that the
relational pattern of contradictory parental expectations and the child's persistent
effort to fulfill them could be called a "quadruple bind."

LU, Y. C., "Mother-Child Role Relations in Schizophrenia: A Comparison of Schizophrenic
    Patients with Non-Schizophrenic Siblings," Psychiatry, 24, 133-142, 1961.
An investigation into why one child in a family develops schizophrenia and another does
not, based upon interviews with 50 chronic schizophrenic patients, their siblings, and
their parents. The patient is largely confined to his parents, especially his mother,
while the siblings have several significant others.

MARX, A., and LUDWIG, A., "Resurrection of the Family of the Chronic Schizophrenic,"
    Amer. J. Psychother., 23, 37-52, 1969.
A careful review of the authors' experience treating psychiatric in-patients by systematically involving the family of the patient. Sample was 44 chronic schizophrenic patients and families studied over a two-year period. Family resistances and methods to
deal with these resistances are discussed. The treatment program included family therapist meetings, patient-family-therapist sessions, multiple family group meetings, and
multiple family-conjoint therapy sessions. Some of the effects of this treatment program, both positive (patient and family improvement) and negative (member of the family
decompensating), as well as methods of dealing with these problems, pracitcal theoretical implications, and ethics of this approach are discussed.

McCORD, W., PORTA, J., and McCORD, J., "The Familial Genesis of Psychoses," Psychiatry,
    25, 60-71, 1962.
A study of the influence of early environment on the development of psychosis based upon
data gathered during the childhood of subjects who later became psychotic. In the middle 1930's in Massachusetts, a sample of boys was observed as part of a study on the
prevention of delinquency. These past case histories were examined and twelve prepsychotics were matched with nonpsychotic controls. The familial environments of the prepsychotics differed from those of the nonpsychotics in a number of ways. Typically the
prepsychotics were raised in an environment directed by an overprotective mother and an
absent or passive father. This "silver cord syndrome" has also been noted by other in-
vestigators who used a retrospective approach.

McGHIE, A., "A Comparative Study of the Mother-Child Relationship in Schziophrenia. I.
    The Interview. II. Psychological Testing," Brit. J. Med. Psychol., 34, 195-221,
    1961.
In Part I of this two-part article there is a description of interviews with 20 mothers
of schizophrenics, 20 mothers of neurotics, and 20 mothers of normals. Findings about
families of schizophrenics reported in the literature were generally confirmed. There
is more marital disharmony in the schizophrenic group and the fathers are said to be

weak. However, mothers of schizophrenics do not appear as overprotective as mothers of
neurotics. In Part II, the test findings for the three groups are reported. They were
given a child rearing questionnaire, a sentence completion test, a word connection test,
and the Rorschach.

MEYERS, D., and GOLDFARB, W., "Studies of Perplexity in Mothers of Schizophrenic Child-
    ren," Amer. J. Orthopsychiat., 31, 551-564, 1961.
In order to document the association of parental complexity (defined as passivity, un-
certainty, lack of spontaneity, absence of empathy, with diminished awareness of the
child's needs, bewilderment, and blandness in the face of unacceptable behavior in the
child, and an absence of parental control) 23 mothers of schizophrenic children and 23
mothers of normal children were studied. Techniques included a participant-observation
technique (in which the observer spent three hours with the family at home), and a semistructured open-ended interview of the mothers. Results indicated that the mothers of
the schizophrenic children without organic involvement have a greater difficulty in appropriately structuring their child's environment, while the mothers of the organic
group cannot be differentiated from mothers of the normals.

MIDELFORT, C. F., The Family in Psychotherapy, New York, McGraw-Hill, 1957.
A report of a clinical project involving family therapy and the use of relatives in the
care of psychiatric patients, on both an in-patient and out-patient basis. The report
discusses the purpose of the project, and the use of family treatment in schizophrenia,
depression, paranoid illness, psychopathic personality, and psychoneurosis. 202 pp.

MISHLER, E. G., "Families and Schizophrenia: An Experimental Study," Ment. Hyg.,
    552-556, 1966.
A discussion of a way of testing families with a schizophrenic member and contrasting
them with normal families. Findings are not given, but illustrations are offered of
ways the families respond in the test situation.

MISHLER, E. G., and WAXLER, N. E., "Family Interaction Processes and Schizophrenia,"
    Int. J. Psychiat., 2, 375-430, 1966.
A critical and extensive review of the theories of the relationship between family interaction and schizophrenia, with major space devoted to the work of the Bateson, Lidz,
and Wynne groups. The purpose of the review was to see how the theories could be tested
and used as guidelines for research. The major contributions of these groups are to the
theory of the etiology of schizophrenia by focussing on the family and its methods of
interactions, rather than on the individual. Critical evaluations by Bateson, Lidz,
Spiegel, and Wynne of the article and the various theories contained in it are included.

MISHLER, E. G., and WAXLER, N. E., "Family Interaction Processes and Schizophrenia: A
    Review of Current Theories," Merrill-Palmer Quart., 11, 269-315, 1965.
A review of the theories of schizophrenia and the family with special emphasis upon differences and similarities between the Bateson, Lidz and Wynne groups. A selected bibliography is included.

MISHLER, E. G., and WAXLER, N. E. (Eds.), Family Process and Schizophrenia, New York,
    Science House, 1968.
A collection of previously published articles which includes discussions of current
theories; experimental studies; parents of the schizophrenic; dyadic interaction; parents
with a schizophrenic child: pathogenic triad; parent and sibling: the family tetrad;
and commentaries; a discussion by four family therapy theoreticians on the articles.
323 pp.

MISHLER, E. G., and WAXLER, N. E., Interaction in Families, New York, Wiley, 1968.
A report on a research project with the aim of systematically identifying distinctive
patterns of interaction in families of schizophrenic patients. The book includes background and aims of the study; research design; measurement techniques, strategy for
data analysis; research findings focussed on expressiveness, power, disruptions in communication, and responsiveness; case examples of findings; and a review and implications of the study. 436 pp.

MORRIS, G., and WYNNE, L., "Schizophrenic Offspring Parental Styles of Communication,"
    Psychiatry, 28, 19-44, 1965.
One of series of papers reporting a study of parental styles of communication and schizophrenic children. Data were selected from excerpts of transcripts of conjoint family
sessions with 12 families. Predictions about the most disturbed offspring were made
by a judge blind to the clinical aspects of the case. Predictive criteria were then
reformulated using the data from a parallel study, utilizing psychological test material
as predictors. These reformulated criteria were then utilized for blind predictions on
eight new families. Results indicated that the style of the family communication can be
related to the thought and affect disorder in schizophrenics.

MOSHER, L. R., "Schizophrenogenic Communication and Family Therapy," Fam. Proc., 8, 43-
    63, 1969.
A description of a technique of family therapy with a family of a schizophrenic. The
emphasis is upon the structural and process aspects of the family's communication. Case
material is used for illustration.

NEWMAN, G., "Younger Brothers of Schizophrenics," Psychiatry, 29, 146-151, 1966.
As a contribution to intrafamilial dynamics in schizophrenic families, three cases are
reported of siblings who had an older brother who was schizophrenic and who developed
emotional disorder themselves. The cases were studied by the author in the course of
psychotherapy. All three had great guilt from three sources — "letting the older brother bear the burden of the parent's demands, for not saving the older brother from
mental illness, and for exercising his own perception, judgment and initiative."

PAUL, N. L., "The Role of a Secret in Schizophrenia," in N. W. Ackerman (Ed.), Family
    Therapy in Transition, Boston, Little, Brown, 1970.
A case of a family of a schizophrenic with a secret concerning the son's birth. Excerpts from family interviews are included to illustrate decoding of the transactions
among the family members.

PAUL, N. L., and GROSSER, G. H., "Family Resistance to Change in Schizophrenic Patients,"
    Fam. Proc., 3, 377-401, 1964.
A description, with case excerpts, of the patterns of family response to schizophrenic
patients that develop during the early phase of conjoint family therapy. It is said
that families express desire for the patient to change while attempting to maintain the
status quo in family relationships in ways that reinforce the patient's symptomatology.

PAUL, N. L., and GROSSER, G. H., "Operational Mourning and Its Role in Conjoint Family
    Therapy," Comm. Ment. Health J., 1, 339-345, 1965.
Studies of records of 50 families with a schizophrenic member and 25 families with at
least one psychoneurotic member revealed "patterns of inflexible interaction and maladaptive response to object loss." The way the sample was obtained is not stated. It
is hypothesized from this data that incomplete mourning after object loss leads to an
inability to deal with future object loss, and this defect is transmitted to other family
members. This is thought to lead to a "fixation of symbiotic relationships in the family."

PARSONS, A., "Family Dynamics in South Italian Schizophrenics," Arch. Gen. Psychiat., 3,
    507-518, 1960.
If family factors play an etiological role in schizophrenia, comparative studies of the
family background of schizophrenics in different cultures is important. After observation of south Italian patients in the United States, a sample of 25 patients hospitalized
in public hospitals in Naples and vicinity was investigated. Patterns in the families
are described in terms of exclusive dyads, imbedded dyads, competitive and unstable situations, and isolates. Comparing pathological family constellations in different cultures, the taboo areas are important, and the problem of differentiating the normal from
the pathological must be resolved. "We would doubt that these problems can ever be resolved in a framework in which any particular set of social values or conditions is considered as inherently schizogenic."

PETURSSON, E., "A Study of Parental Deprivation and Illness in 291 Psychiatric Patients,"
     Int. J. Soc. Psychiat., 7, 97-105, 1961.
A group of 291 patients with functional psychiatric illness was observed by the author
and information gathered about their parents from them, from spouses or relatives, or
by direct observation in some instances. The parents suffered from functional psychiatric illness in 77.5% of the cases. The incidence of broken homes was 31.7%. There appeared to be a high incidence of patients developing the same type of psychiatric illness as the parents in various categories. Well-integrated family units occurred in
the background of patients in only 11.7% of the cases.

POLLACK, M., WOERNER, M., GOLDBERG, P., and KLEIN, D., "Siblings of Schizophrenic and
     Nonschizophrenic Psychiatric Patients," Arch. Gen. Psychiat., 20, 652-658, 1969.
A study attempting to test the relative power of genetic versus psychogenic etiology
in schizophrenia. Sixty-four siblings of 46 schizophrenic patients, 104 siblings of
68 personality disorder patients, and 16 siblings of 13 index cases with psychoneurotic
and affective disorders were compared in terms of their psychiatric status. Method was
clinical interview in most cases, but where siblings could not personally be contacted,
descriptions from the family or from other records were used. Results indicated the siblings of the schizophrenic patients did not differ from those of nonschizophrenic patients in overall incidence of abnormality. None of the many specific family interaction patterns hypothesized to be pathogenic for schizophrenia have thus far been substantiated by methodologically sound studies.

PULVER, S. E., and BRUNT, M. Y., "Deflection of Hostility in Folie a Deux," Arch. Gen.
     Psychiat., 5, 257-265, 1961.
Three cases are presented to illustrate a description of the psychodynamics of the transfer of delusions. The partners are divided into the primary and secondary, with the
primary partner strongly dependent upon the secondary. As the primary partner begins
to feel taken advantage of and increasingly angry, his anger against the secondary partner is projected onto an outsider as paranoid delusion. When the secondary partner does
not support the delusion, the direct hostility toward the secondary partner becomes intolerable and the secondary partner deflects it by accepting the delusion and joining
in the projection.

QUERY, J.M.N., "Pre-Morbid Adjustment and Family Structure: A Comparison of Selected
     Rural and Urban Schizophrenic Men," J. Nerv. Ment. Dis., 133, 333-338, 1961.
A study which reviews schizophrenia in relation to cultural and familial settings. The
hypothesis is that premorbid adjustment of rural schizophrenics will be better than
that of urban subjects because the rural setting includes a more patriarchal family
structure, more emphasis upon individualism, and better sex-role identification. Case
history data were examined in terms of the Phillips' scale and supplemented by family
interviews. Fifty-one families were interviewed and the hypothesis was supported by
the evidence.

RABKIN, L. Y., "The Patient's Family: Research Methods," Fam. Proc., 4, 105-132, 1965.
A review of family research with special emphasis upon the family of the schizophrenic.
Critical examination is done of case history studies, interviewing studies, psychodiagnostic testing, questionnaire studies, and observational research. A bibliography of
99 references is included.

RAVICH, R. A., "A System of Dyadic Interaction," Fam. Proc., 9, 297-300, 1970.
A description of a notation for two-person interaction based upon the I Ching, or Book
of Changes.

REISS, D., "Individual Thinking and Family Interaction: Introduction to an Experimental
     Study of Problem-Solving in Families of Normals, Character Disorders, and Schizo-
     phrenics," Arch. Gen. Psychiat., 16, 80-93, 1967.
A report of an experimental study of the relationship between individual thinking and
family interaction. Experimental procedures and methods of analysis are discussed.
Subjects were families of five normals, five character disorders, and six schizophrenics.
The test used was a puzzle that required active use of cognitive and conceptual capa-
cities. The method of analysis was derived from the work of Roley, which developed a
systematic approach of computing scores from the raw data and rules concerning inferences.

REISS, D., "Individual Thinking and Family Interaction. II. A Study of Pattern Recog-
     nition and Hypothesis Testing in Families of Normals, Character Disorders, and
     Schizophrenics," J. Psychiat. Res., 5, 193-211, 1967.
The second in a series of studies of the relationship of family process and individual
thinking. Results indicate that following a period of family interaction, members of
normal families showed improvement in pattern recognition; members of families of schizophrenics showed deterioration or no change; and results of members of character disorder families were in between the two.

REISS, D., "Individual Thinking and Family Interaction. III. An Experimental Study of
     Categorization Performance in Families of Normals, Those with Character Disorders,
     and Schizophrenics," J. Nerv. Ment. Dis., 146, 384-404, 1968.
The third of a series of studies to measure the relationship between individual family
interaction and individual thinking, and to determine what differences in this relationship exist among families of normals, personality disorders, and schizophrenics. Method
was to give the families a puzzle, tape their discussion, and to code verbal responses.
Sample has been previously described; there were five families in each group. Results
indicated that normals could solve the puzzle, while the others could not. The data on
why they could not were felt to be consistent with the hypothesis that interpersonal
problems in families significantly interfere with their collaborative problem-solving
efforts.

REISS, D., "Individual Thinking and Family Interaction. IV. A study of Information
     Exchange in Families of Normals, Those With Character Disorders, and Schizophrenics,"
     J. Nerv. Ment. Dis., 149, 473-490, 1969.
The fourth in a series of four papers on interrelationships of family interaction and
thinking, and perception of family members. Methodology has been discussed in the earlier papers. This experiment was developed to test the family's efficiency in exchanging information within itself. Families of normals and schizophrenics were more sensitive than those with character disorders to cues from within the family. Families of
schizophrenics appeared to represent a group of families who utilize cues from within
but not from without the family.

RETTERSTOL, N., "Paranoid Psychosis Associated with Impending or Newly Established
     Fatherhood," Acta Psychiat. Scand., 44, 51-61, 1968.
A study of 169 consecutive male psychiatric patients with a diagnosis of paranoid psychosis, admitted over a 20-year period to an in-patient service. Follow-ups averaged
five years, but went up to 20 years in some cases. There were four cases where the pre-
cipitant appeared to be impending fatherhood. A shift of the homeostasis between the
father and the mother of the baby appeared to have been caused.

RICHMOND, A. H., and LANGA, A., "Some Observations Concerning the Role of Children in
     the Disruption of Family Homeostasis," Amer. J. Orthopsychiat., 33, 757-759, 1963.
A report from a day-hospital of observations on families and patients whose psychiatric
illness had led the families to request removal of the patient from the community. The
authors noted three patterns of family dynamics in which the child, by its (1) birth,
(2) maturation, and (3) efforts to achieve independence, served to disrupt family homeostasis.

ROSENBAUM, C. P., "Patient-Family Similarities in Schizophrenia," Arch. Gen. Psychiat.,
     5, 120-126, 1961.
A discussion of the family of the schizophrenic based upon conjoint interviews with
such families during several research projects. It is suggested that the disordered
thinking and interpersonal relations of the schizophrenic have recognized counterparts
in his family. Such preimary symptoms of schizophrenia as disorders of association,
selective inattention, and ambivalence, as described by Bleuler, are compared with similar thought patterns in the family, illustrated with case material. A review and synthesis is made of research in the field of the schizophrenic family with the emphasis
upon the appropriateness of schizophrenic symptoms in this context.

ROSENTHAL, A. J., BEHRENS, M. I., and CHODOFF, P., "Communication in Lower-Class Fami-
     lies of Schizophrenics," Arch. Gen. Psychiat., 18, 464-470, 1968.
The first part of a two-part report on low-socioeconomic families of schizophrenics.
Groups compared were 17 black schizophrenics and their families, 11 in a black control
group, and 11 white schizophrenics and their families. The procedure included observation in the home with tasks requiring the family to maintain a focus of attention on
a specific topic. (For Part II of this study see Behrens, M. I., "Communication in
Lower Class Families of Schizophrenics," Arch. Gen. Psychiat., 18, 689-696, 1968.)

ROSENTHAL, D., "Confusion of Identity and the Frequency of Schizophrenia in Twins," Arch.
     Gen. Psychiat., 3, 297-304, 1960.
The author sought to test the hypothesis that if the etiology of schizophrenia is on a
familial basis, with genetic as well as psychodynamic factors playing equal roles, then
schizophrenia should occur more frequently among twins than among nontwins and among
nonzygotic than among dizygotic twins. Case material is from two previously reported
studies in which the proportions of twins to nontwins with various psychotic illness
could be calculated. Findings were that neither schizophrenic nor psychotic illness
requiring hospitalization occurred more frequently in twins than in nontwins or in monozygotic than dizygotic twins. The finding suggests that "confusion of ego identity"
said to occur more commonly among twins does not have etiological value with respect
to schizophrenia.

ROSENTHAL, D., The Genian Quadruplets — A Case Study and Theoretical Analysis of
     Heredity and Environment in Schizophrenia, New York, Basic Books, 1963.
A case study in schizophrenia of a family in which quadruplets were schizophrenic. The
book is divided into sections dealing with the case history, tests and studies dealing
with basic characteristics in response processes, projective tests and their analysis,
systematic analysis of observations of the family by the research staff and the community, conceptualization of the family members in their interrelationships, and finally a theoretical analysis of the heredity-environment problem in schizophrenia. 609 pp.

ROSMAN, B., WILD, C., RICCI, J., FLECK, S., and LIDZ, T., "Thought Disorders in the Pa-
     rents of Schizophrenic Patients: A Further Study Utilizing the Object Sorting
     Test," J. Psychiat. Res., 2, 211-221, 1964.
A second replication of a study by McConaghy who found that parents of schizophrenic
patients received scores in the object sorting test that were indicative of pathology
in conceptual thinking. Sixty-eight parents of schizophrenic patients and 115 control
parents were used. The hypothesis of greater frequency of pathological scores in the
patient-parent group was supported only with subjects from higher levels of intelligence, education, and occupation.

RYCKOFF, I., DAY, J., and WYNNE, L., "Maintenance of Stereotyped Roles in the Families
     of Schizophrenics," Arch. Gen. Psychiat., 1, 93-99, 1959.
One of a series of papers on a study of family relationships and schizophrenia. Data
were collected from a study of the identified patient who was a hospitalized schizophrenic. Parents were seen twice weekly on an out-patient basis. Schizophrenic family
dynamics are described in terms of "role patterns" in an attempt to understand identity
development. Unconscious determinants of these roles are discussed through the use of
clinical examples.

SAFILIOS-ROTHSCHILD, C., "Deviance and Mental Illness in the Greek Family," Fam. Proc.,
     7, 100-117, 1968.
A study of spouses of hospitalized mental patients in Greece to determine attitudes
about deviance and mental illness. The defining of behavior as deviant will depend upon
cultural definitions. Whether the deviance is defined as mental illness depends upon
other factors. Here the "degree of marital satisfaction seems to be the determining
factor as to whether or not the normal spouse will" label the deviance as mental illness.

SAMPSON, H., MESSINGER, S., and TOWNE, R., "Family Processes and Becoming a Mental Pa-
      tient," Amer. J. Sociol., 68, 88-96, 1962.
The accommodation of the family to the deviant behavior of the future patient, and the
disruption of this accommodation which leads to hospitalization are described for a
series of 17 married mothers. Patients were located at time of first admission and extensive data collected by interviews with family members, by professionals involved at
any stage, and by direct observation in home and hospital. Types of accommodation found
were: (1) spouses isolated, emotionally distant from each other, and (2) family not
self-contained but revolved about a maternal figure who took over wife's duties. Each
type has characteristic ways of disrupting, resulting in different implications to hospitalization.

SAMPSON, H., MESSINGER, L, and TOWNE, R., Schizophrenic Women: Studies in Marital Cri-
      ses, New York, Atherton Press, 1963.
A book on a research project studying family relations of 17 schizophrenic women who had
to be hospitalized. It discusses the crisis that led up to hospitalization, its context,
the process of separation, becoming a mental patient in terms of family processes, and
crisis resolution in the hospital and posthospital period. Implications of this study
are discussed. 174 pp.

SANUA, V. D., "The Sociocultural Aspects of Childhood Schizophrenia," in G. H. Zuk and
      I. Boszormenyi-Nagy (Eds.), Family Therapy and Diturbed Families, Palo Alto, Sci-
      ence & Behavior Books, 1967.
A discussion of methodological issues, research strategies, and the problems inherent
in studying parent-child relationships and interaction as an etiological factor in schizophrenia. Includes a review of the literature.

SANUA, V. D., "Sociocultural Factors in Families of Schizophrenics: A Review of the
      Literature," Psychiatry, 24, 246-265, 1961.
A review of family studies which includes problems of methodology, studies using hospital records, interviews with relatives, data from psychotherapy, studies using tests,
cross-cultural comparisons of the schizophrenic environment and that of other pathologies. The author concludes that etiological factors fall into four general categories:
(1) undesirable traits in the parents, (2) family structure — early parental or sibling
deaths or broken families, (3) undesirable interpersonal patterns, and (4) genetic or
constitutional factors. He points out the inconsistency and wide variation in methodology
and sampling and the neglect of social variables, and suggests an international research
organization to coordinate research in mental illness.

SCHAFFER, L., WYNNE, L. C., DAY, J., RYCKOFF, I. M., and HALPERIN, A., "On the Nature
      and Sources of the Psychiatrist's Experience with the Family of the Schizophrenic,"
      Psychiatry, 25, 32-45, 1962.
A detailed discussion of the experience of the therapist as he performs family therapy
with the family of the schizophrenic where "nothing has a meaningful relation to any-
thing else." It is said to be different from work with other families, and case illustrations are given.

SCOTT, R., "Perspectives on the American Family Studies in Schizophrenia," Confin. Psy-
      chiat., 8, 43-48, 1965.
A review of the American literature on family studies of schizophrenia with questions
and criticisms. There is a selective bias in leaving out family history of schizophrenics and focussing on interactional aspects. The concept of the double bind is questioned and explained in a different way.

SCOTT, R., and ASHWORTH, P., "The 'Axis Value' and the Transfer of Psychosis," Brit. J.
      Med. Psychol., 38, 97-116, 1965.
A report of a study of seven families with a schizophrenic member using a self report
test in which parents and child mark a check list of 42 items. The family members check
off what applies to themselves and to each of the others, then what each thinks the other
will check off about him. Contrasts are made between "shadow parents" (the parent who
is most involved with the patient and also had a significant involvement with a mad an-

cestor), and non-shadow parents. Differences are said to be found, and descriptions of the families are offered.

SCOTT, R., and ASHWORTH, P., "Closure at the First Schizophrenic Breakdown: A Family
    Study," Brit. J. Med. Psychol., 40, 109-146, 1967.
One of a series of papers on the preillness familial relationships of schizophrenics with their families at the time of the first decompensation. Sample included 23 families (19 female patients and four male patients), average age 26, who were seen over two and a half years, with an average number of interviews totalling 27 and lasting three hours apiece. Using a three-generational hypothesis, one or both parents has had a significant traumatic event (such as death or insanity of a parent). Their feelings about this event are studied pertinent to the development of a schizophrenic reaction in their children. "Signs of disturbance in the child are regarded by the parent as if a catastrophic event is occurring again," and their reaction often then seems inappropriate.

SHARAN (SINGER), S., "Family Interaction with Schizophrenics and Their Siblings," J.
    Abnorm. Psychol., 71, 345-353, 1966.
An experimental study contrasting the behavior of parents of schizophrenics with the patient and with a sibling. Twenty-four families were asked to solve collectively the questions from the comprehension and similarities subtests of the Wechsler-Bellvue intelligence scale. The conversations were compared for problem-solving efficiency, mutual support patterns, and parent-child sex role alignments. Parents and patient worked as efficiently as parents and siblings, parents supported both children equally, and fathers and mothers were equally dominant. The patients were more supportive of their parents than were the siblings, and parental discord was more prominent when the patient was present than when the sibling was present.

SHARAN (SINGER), S., "Family Interaction with Schizophrenics and Their Siblings," in
    E. G. Mischler, and N.E. Waxler (Eds.), Family Interaction Processes and Schizo-
    phrenia, New York, Science House, 1968.
A report of a research investigation discussing three aspects of family theory: (1) problem-solving within the family (2) the formation of rival intrafamilial dyads, and (3) parental role reversals and the crossing of sex-generation boundaries. The sample was 24 schizophrenic patients, including both parents and a normal child in addition to the identified patient. The interaction testing technique was used as a research instrument. Results indicated that parents were equally supportive of the identified patient as well as the well sibling. The patient was associated with greater interparental conflict than was the normal child. Implications of these findings in comparison with other research are discussed.

SHARP, V., GLASNER, S., LEDERMAN, I., and WOLFE, S., "Sociopaths and Schizophrenics —
    A Comparison of Family Interactions," Psychiatry, 27, 127-134, 1964.
To test the hypothesis that there would be differences in the family interaction of matched groups of sociopaths and schizophrenics, 20 subjects of each group were examined. These included every patient admitted to the authors' case load at the Philadelphia Naval Hospital. Sources of data were social service questionnaires, parental visits, and interviews with parents. Findings were that sociopaths joined the service "to escape from home," had shorter hospitalizations, the families were much more unconcerned and rejecting than the schizophrenic families, who visited more.

SINGER, M. T., and WYNNE, L. C., "Communication Styles in Parents of Normals, Neurotics,
    and Schizophrenics: Some Findings Using a New Rorschach Scoring Manual," in I. M.
    Cohen (Ed.), Psychiatric Research Report No. 20, Washington, American Psychiatric
    Association, 1966.
A report of a study of 250 families in which the Rorschach was used as a stimulus for individual family members. Styles of parental communication are described and findings reported.

SINGER, M. T., and WYNNE, L. C., "Differentiating Characteristics of Parents of Child-
     hood Schizophrenics, Childhood Neurotics, and Young Adults Schizophrenics," Amer.
     J. Psychiat., 120, 234-243, 1963.
A study in which parents of 20 autistic children were blindly differentiated at a statistically significant level of accuracy from parents of 20 neurotic children. The data
were TAT and Rorschach tests of the parents. Additionally, the parents of adolescent
and young adult schizophrenics were compared with the parents of autistic children and
differences were found.

SINGER, M. T., and WYNNE, L. C., "Thought Disorder and Family Relations of Schizophren-
     ics. III. Methodology Using Projective Techniques, IV. Results and Implications,"
     Arch. Gen. Psychiat., 12, 187-212, 1965.
A continuation of the study of families through the use of projective tests with the emphasis upon predicting the form of thinking and degree of disorganization of each patient from the tests of other members of his family, and the blind matching of patients
and their families. The series includes a full discussion of various aspects of schizophrenia and the family.

SLUZKI, C., "Transactional Disqualification: Research on the Double Bind," Arch. Gen.
     Psychiat., 16, 494-504, 1967.
One of a series of papers connected with a research project on communication in families
with schizophrenic patients. Transactional disqualification is a form of communication
in which the subject can verbally or nonverbally deny the previous communication. This
kind of persistent relating can lead to schizophrenic symptoms.

SOBEL, D. E., "Children of Schizophrenic Patients: Preliminary Observations on Early
     Development," Amer. J. Psychiat., 118, 512-517, 1961.
A report on observations of the early development of children whose parents are both
schizophrenic. Four infants were raised by their schizophrenic parents and four raised
by foster parents. Three of the four children raised by their original schizophrenic
parents developed clear signs of depression and irritability in infancy. None of the
four infants raised by foster parents developed any such clear signs of emotional disorder. The three schizophrenic mothers engaged in relatively little active play with
their infants or showed pleasurable responsiveness. Case details are presented.

SONNE, J. C., and LINCOLN, G., "The Importance of a Heterosexual Co-Therapy Relationship
     in the Construction of a Family Image," in I. M. Cohen (Ed.), Psychiatric Research
     Report No. 20, Washington, American Psychiatric Association, 1966.
A discussion of the use of co-therapy to provide a heterosexual image in the treatment
of the family of the schizophrenic.

SONNE, J. C., SPECK, R. V., and JUNGREIS, J. E., "The Absent-Member Maneuver as a Resis-
     tance in Family Therapy of Schizophrenia," Fam. Proc., 1, 44-62, 1962.
A report of a specific type of resistance encountered while using family treatment in
ten families containing a schizophenic offspring. The absent-member maneuver, defined
as the absence of a family member from the family sessions, was seen in one form or
another in all ten families. Some of the dynamics of this maneuver are discussed, the
authors believing that the absent member (often seen as "healthy" by the rest of the family) tends to pathologically maintain unresolved Oedipal problems in the family.

SPECK, R. V., and RUEVENI, U., "Network Therapy: A Developing Concept," Fam. Proc., 8,
     182-191, 1969.
A description of network therapy where all members of the kinship system, all friends of
the family, and other significant people are brought together. A description of the method and a case illustration are offered.

SPIEGEL, J., and BELL, N., "The Family of the Psychiatric Patient," in S. Asieti (Ed.),
     American Handbook of Psychiatry, Vol. I, New York, Basic Books, 1959.
A chapter in a textbook on psychiatry dealing with sections on the history of the role of
the family in mental illness; etiologic studies of parent-child interactions and development of various mental illnesses including schizophrenia, psychoneurosis, and acting-out

disorders; the impact of mental illness upon the family; the family and treatment procedures; and new approaches to the family and its pathology, including family therapy.
There are 238 references.

SPITZER, S. P., SWANSON, R. M., and LEHR, R. K., "Audience Reactions and Careers of Psy-
      chiatric Patients," Fam. Proc., 8, 159-181, 1969.
A study of the reaction of families and the ways these reactions influence the psychiatric patient's career. The histories of 79 first admission patients were examined and
patient and a family member were interviewed. Two dimensions of family reaction to deviance are described leading to a typology of eight career patterns which allow for the
classification of 95% of the cases reviewed.

STABENAU, J. R., TUPIN, J., WERNER, M., and POLLIN, W., "A Comparative Study of Families
      of Schizophrenics, Delinquents, and Normals," Psychiatry, 28, 45-59, 1965.
A report of a comparison of five families with a schizophrenic, five families with a delinquent, and five normal families tested with the revealed differences test, the object
sorting test, and the thematic apperception test. "Data from the three different tests
suggest that in the schizophrenic and delinquent families there were both individual
disturbances in thought process and impaired communication at the family level...There
was relatively little evidence of communication impairment at the individual or family
level in the normal families."

TOWNE, R. D., MESSINGER, S. L., and SAMPSON, H., "Schizophrenia and the Marital Family:
      Accommodations to Symbiosis," Fam. Proc., 1, 304-318, 1962.
Another in a series of reports by this group of their study of 17 women who as young
adults had experienced severe difficulties in their marital families and were hospitalized with a diagnosis of schizophrenia. Here the focus was on the "symbiotic" nature
of the family relationships which seem to serve to keep the families together, and when
broken down led to hospitalization of the wife. Three patterns are described.

VIDAL, G., PRECE, G., and SMULEVER, M., "Convivencia y Trastorno Mental," Acta Psiquiat.
      Psicolog. Amer. Lat., 15, 55-65, 1969.
A sample of 1322 patients was studied for family size, birth order of the patient, and
family integrity (number of years the offspring lived together with both parents). The
hypothesis was that "the higher the amount of the family relationship the lower the severity of the mental disorder." Neurotics were expected to show smaller families, first
birth order positions, and intact families, while psychotics would show larger families,
last birth order positions, and disrupted families. The hypothesis about neurotics was
confirmed but that about psychotics was only partially confirmed.

WAHL, C. W., "The Psychodynamics of Consummated Maternal Incest," Arch. Gen. Psychiat.,
      3, 186-193, 1960.
A report of two cases of hospitalized schizophrenic men who had sexual relations with
their mothers. The author discusses dynamics of maternal incest and states that his
case material supports the view that incestuous problems in schizophrenic patients play
a role in the development of schizophrenia.

WAINWRIGHT, W. H., "The Reaction of Mothers to Improvement in Their Schizophrenic Daugh-
      ters," Compr. Psychiat., 1, 236-243, 1960.
At the Payne Whitney Psychiatric Clinic eight mother-schizophrenic daughter combinations
were interviewed and observed for a period ranging from four to 48 months, including up
to 30 months after the patient's hospital discharge. Of these eight mothers, two responded favorably to their daughter's improvement, two showed fluctuation in response
which seemed dependent upon the severity of the daughter's symptoms, and four mothers
showed signs of illness as their daughters improved. The author sees a common need
with these four mothers to keep the daughter partially ill. Where hostility emerges
during the recovery phase, he suggests evaluation for treatment of the mother.

WARING, M., and RICKS, D., "Family Patterns of Children Who Become Adult Schizophrenics,"
      J. Nerv. Ment. Dis., 140, 351-364, 1965.
A study comparing family variables of three groups of adult patients, who were seen as

adolescents at a child guidance center. The three groups were (1) 30 patients, who as
adults developed schizophrenia and remitted (defined as leaving the hospital), (2) 20
patients, who as adults developed schizophrenia and did not remit, and (3) a control
group of 50 patients, selected from the clinic population, who did not develop schizophrenia and were never hospitalized. Data were obtained retrospectively from work-ups
at the time the patients were adolescents, and also from subsequent follow-ups with
schools, hosptials, and other agencies, and finally in some cases with interviews with
patient and family. There were significant familial differences between the remitting
and unremitting groups, and less significant differences between the total schizophrenia
group and the controls.

WATSON, D., BROWN, E., and BEURET, L., "A Family of Five Schizophrenic Children," Dis.
     Nerv. Syst., 30, 189-193, 1969.
A case report of a family of seven children in which five were clearly schizophrenic.
Neither parents had schizophrenia. Genetic and family dynamic explanations are offered
and the etiology remained unclear.

WATZLAWICK, P., An Anthology of Human Communication (text and two-hour tape), Palo Alto,
     Science & Behavior Books, 1964.
A textbook and tape dealing with family dynamics, interaction, and communication patterns.
Communication theory is outlined and there are sections on agreement and disagreement,
type relationships, disqualifications, schizophrenic communication, double binds, coalitions, and a suggested reading list are included in the text. 63 pp. plus an audiotape.

WATZLAWICK, P., "A Review of the Double Bind Theory," Fam. Proc., 2, 132-153, 1963.
A presentation of the comments on the double bind theory occurring in the literature
from 1957-1961. The comments are discussed and excerpts presented.

WEBLIN, J., "Communication and Schizophrenic Behavior," Fam. Proc., 1, 5-14, 1962.
An essay in which the author's hypothesis is that "schizophrenic communication is a
highly goal-directed activity towards avoiding almost any clearly defined relationships."
This mode of relating is learned from the family — particularly from the parents. Several segments of tapes from two schizophrenic families are given.

WEAKLAND, J. H., "The Double-Bind Hypothesis of Schizophrenia and Three-Party Interaction,"
     in D. D. Jackson (Ed.), The Etiology of Schizophrenia, New York, Basic Books, 1960.
A discussion of the double bind as it applies to three party situations. Described are
mother, father, child relationships, and such institutional relationships as administra-
tor-therapist-patient and doctor-nurse-patient.

WEAKLAND, J. H., and FRY, W. F., "Letters of Mothers of Schizophrenics," Amer. J. Ortho-
     psychiat., 32, 604-623, 1962.
Several selected letters to schizophrenic patients from their mothers are presented with
a microscopic and macroscopic examination of their characteristic and significant patterns. The letters exhibit similar influential patterns consisting of concealed incongruence between closely related messages. Almost no statement is ever allowed to stand
clearly and unambiguously but is disqualified in a variety of ways. Patients' statements
support the hypothesis that the letters induce paralysis or frantic activity in the recipients, which would be reasonable in response to "such a pervasive and general pattern of
concealed strong but incompatible influence."

WHITTAKER, C. (Ed.), Psychotherapy of Chronic Schizophrenic Patients, Boston, Little,
     Brown, 1958.
A transcript of a conference on schizophrenia in which there were eight sessions, each
oriented toward a particular topic in which no formal presentation is made, but rather
a general discussion was held with a moderator for each section. The book includes sections on diagnosis and prognosis, schizophrenic distortion of communication, orality,
anality, family and sexuality, countertransference, management of the patient, and family
management. 219 pp.

WIEDORN, W. S., "Intra-Family Adaptive Significance of Disordered Communication and Re-
     ality Misperception in Families of Schizophrenic Persons," in I. M. Cohen (Ed.),
     Psychiatric Research Report No. 20, Washington, American Psychiatric Association,
     1966.
A discussion of why families of schizophrenics show disordered communications and reality misperceptions, based upon psychoanalytical therapy with psychotic schizophrenic
in-patients. It is said to represent an adaptive attempt in the family to maintain a
symbiotic pairing. Case illustrations are offered.

WILD, C., "Disturbed Styles of Thinking," Arch. Gen. Psychiat., 13, 464-470, 1966.
Examiner's reactions to giving the object sorting test to parents of schizophrenics are
described. Findings here are taken from the Wynne and Singer papers on "Thought Disorder
and Family Relations of Schizophrenics." Examiners felt "frustrated and hopeless" in
dealing with schizophrenic parents' inability to maintain a consistent task, inability
to maintain role of subject being tested, and general negativism. Theoretical, tentative implications of the findings are discussed.

WILD, C., SINGER, M., ROSMAN, G., RICCI, J., and LIDZ, T., "Measuring Disordered Styles
     of Thinking," Arch. Gen. Psychiat., 13, 471-476, 1966.
Forty-four parents whose child was a schizophrenic in-patient were matched for age and
education with 46 control parents (community volunteers) on the object sorting test.
A scoring manual is described. Patient-parents scores differed significantly from controls. The object scoring test seems to discriminate between parents of schizophrenic
patients and controls who do not have children with psychiatric pathology.

WING, J., "Ratings of Behavior of Patient and Relative," J. Psychosom. Res., 8, 223-228,
     1964.
A report of a test of the hypothesis that (1) high emotional involvement of patient and
relative should lead to deterioration o f the patient, and (2) that the amount of face-
to-face contact between patient and relative would be related to outcome. Patients were
evaluated by means of two rater's description, and a checklist. Relatives were evaluated by means of scheduled ratings. Patients were hospitalized schizophrenics. Results
indicated that if there was a high index of "emotional involvement" of relative with
patient there was a high percentage of deterioration. In the case of patients who were
moderately or severely ill at time of discharge, and who were living with relatives
rated as showing a high degree of emotional involvement, relatively few hours of contact were associated with relatively better outcome.

WINTER, W., FERREIRA, A., and OLSON, J., "Hostility Themes in the Family TAT," J. Pro-
     ject. Techn. Person. Ass., 30, 270-275, 1966.
Second of a series describing a diagnostic test adapted for use with families. Results
were obtained from use of three TAT stories based on three cards, each produced conjointly
by 126 three-member families. Stories were scored for hostility in the story themes.
Fifty families had normal children, 44 had neurotic children, 16 had schizophrenic children and 16 had delinquent children. Normal and schizophrenic groups produced stories low
in hostility, neurotics produced stories high in hostility, and delinquents scored high
on one hostility variable and low on another.

WOLMAN, B. B., "The Fathers of Schizophrenic Patients," Acta Psychother. Psychosom., 9,
     193-210, 1961.
Observations on the fathers of schizophrenic patients based upon 33 patients seen in individual and group therapy and interviews with their family members. Although some
fathers performed adequately outside the family circle, each demonstrated child-like
dependency upon the wife and inability to play the role of father. Fathers are grouped
as sick, prodigies, rebellious, and runaways.

WYNNE, L. C., "The Study of Intrafamilial Alignments and Splits in Exploratory Family
     Therapy," in N. W. Ackerman, F. L. Beatman, and S. Sherman (Eds.), Exploring the
     Base for Family Therapy, New York Family Service Association of America, 1961.
From a clinical research project of 20 schizophrenic families and ten families of nonschizophrenic psychiatric patients, it has been observed that schizophrenic families use,

as one of their main mechanisms of coping "pseudo-mutuality and pseudo-hostile mechanisms that disguise but help perpetuate the underlying problems." Conjoint family therapy
based on understanding the family organization, and maneuvers in terms of alignments and
splits, can benefit the disturbed family.

WYNNE, L., RYCKOFF, I. M., DAY, J., and HERSCH, S. I., "Pseudo-Mutuality in the Family
    Relations of Schizophrenics," Psychiatry, 21, 205-220, 1958.
An essay which postulates that the disturbance in the family is an important causal factor in schizophrenia. Data were obtained as part of a long-term research project on
schizophrenia in which patients were hospitalized and parents were seen on an out-patient
basis. Most of the data are drawn from clinical work with families. Patients with schizophrenia have families in which the relations can best be described as "pseudo-mutual."
The acute schizophrenic experience is derived from internalization of the pathogenic family organization.

WYNNE, L. C., RYCKOFF, I. M., DAY, J., and HERSCH, S. I., "Pseudo-Mutuality in the Family
    Relations of Schizophrenics," in N. W. Bell, and E. F. Vogel (Eds.), A Modern Intro-
    duction to the Family, Glencoe, Free Press, 1960.
A description of families of schizophrenics studied with family therapy. Chracteristic
was pseudo-mutuality in the family; the family supports an illusion of a well-integrated
state even when this is not supported by the emotional structure of the members. The
strains contribute to the development of schizophrenia.

WYNNE, L. C., and SINGER, M. T., "Thought Disorder and Family Relations of Schizophrenics.
    I. A Research Strategy. II. A Classification of Forms of Thinking," Arch. Gen.
    Psychiat., 9, 191-206, 1963.
A general discussion of the approach of the Wynne project. Families with schizophrenic
members are contrasted with families of nonschizophrenic psychiatric patients, and siblings are contrasted with patients. The emphasis is upon the links between family patterns and schizophrenic thought disorder, defined broadly to include experience. The
first part outlines the clinical and conceptual basis, the setting, and the kinds of
research data. The second part presents a classification of schizophrenic thought disorders, including discrimination among varieties of schizophrenic and paranoid thinking.

ZUK, G., "On Silence and Babbling in Family Psychotherapy with Schizophrenics," Confin.
    Psychiat., 8, 49-56, 1965.
From the author's clinical work, two cases are presented in support of the idea that
both silence and babbling can be understood as attempts to interrupt communication and
silence others' interactions. They are often seen in schizophrenia, but patients learn
these strategies from their parents. Techniques for dealing with this in treatment are
discussed.

ZUK, G., "On the Theory and Pathology of Laughter in Psychotherapy," Psychotherapy, 3,
    97-101, 1966.
An essay based on the author's previous research, some clinical work, and other notions
on the meaning of laughter. Bizarre laughter in schizophrenics, which often seems unexplainable, became clear when it was systematically studied in the family setting. It
was found to be due to a "wish to communicate information differentially to members
of the family group." Clinical uses of laughter in therapy are discussed.

ZUK, G., "The Victim and His Silencers: Some Pathogenic Strategies Against Being Si-
    lenced," in G. H. Zuk and I. Boszormenyi-Nagy (Eds.), Family Therapy and Disturbed
    Families, Palo Alto, Science & Behavior Books, 1967.
A discussion of the strategies family members use to silence a member and the reciprocal
relationship between the silencer and the victim. "Silencing strategies contribute to
the development of paranoid, delusional, or hallucinatory states."

ZUK, G., BOSZORMENYI-NAGY, I., and HEIMAN, E., "Some Dynamics of Laughter During Family
    Therapy," Fam. Proc., 2, 302-314, 1963.
An examination of the frequency of laughter in family therapy sessions with parents and

a schizophrenic girl. Frequency of laughter was totalled for different intervals during the sessions. A correlation is suggested between tension or anxiety and laughter and it was found that the parents laughed most in the first interval of a session. Significantly more laughter of the daughter occurred in the third of four intervals, thus showing a reversal of patterns of laughter between parents and daughter over 13 sessions.

ZUK, G., and RUBINSTEIN, D., "A Review of Concepts in the Study and Treatment of Families of Schizophrenics," in I. Boszormenyi-Nagy and J. L. Framo (Eds.), <u>Intensive Family Therapy</u>, New York, Harper & Row, 1965.
A review of conceptual trends in family treatment of schizophrenics. Discusses the shift from parent pathology to nuclear family to three generational involvement.

ZWERLING, I., and MENDELSOHN, M., "Initial Family Reactions to Day Hospitalization," <u>Fam. Proc.</u>, 4, 50-63, 1965.
A report of a study on the relationship between the course of hospital treatment and certain family responses at the time of admission of a psychotic member. The sample consists of 100 patients consecutively admitted to a day hospital. It includes responses to admission, to family treatment and to improvement.

4.3 FAMILY MEMBER DIAGNOSED AS A SCHOOL PROBLEM

DAVIS, D., "Family Processes in Mental Retardation," <u>Amer. J. Psychiat.</u>, 124, 340-350, 1967.
A lecture pointing out that in addition to genetic factors, mental retardation may result from failure of the family to give the child protection from stress during critical periods of learning in early childhood. Data were obtained from 50 cases (36 boys and 14 girls) with I.Q. below 75 (median 55) — all cases seen by the author prior to age seven. Retrospective historical data was obtained from parents — mothers were found to be depressed through much of the child's life including the period prior to recognition of the child's retardation. These mothers were found to have lost their fathers during adolescence and to have gotten "ineffective lifelong support" from the maternal grandmother. Prevention and treatment are discussed.

DURELL, V., "Adolescents in Multiple Family Group Therapy in a School Setting," <u>Int. J. Group Psychother.</u>, 19, 44-52, 1969.
A clinical report of four families in multifamily therapy studied in over 11 sessions in a junior high school setting where the identified patients are having difficulty in school. The course of a group is discussed, and it was felt that a group was helpful in terms of the patient's school performance. Problems with school administration were discussed.

FARBER, B., "Perceptions of Crisis and Related Variables in the Impact of a Retarded Child on the Mother," <u>J. Health Hum. Behav.</u>, 1, 108-118, 1960.
An extension of earlier findings that a retarded child produces a tragic crisis (shock of diagnosis) or a role organization crisis (inability to develop roles to cope with the child). A sample of 268 mothers and fathers of retarded children were interviewed and administered questionnaires. The hypotheses concern the reaction of mothers to the crises, relating type of crisis, role definitions of mother, and her self-perceived health. The general conclusion is that health-symptom status of mother is related to the type of crisis experienced.

FOWLE, C., "The Effect of the Severely Mentally Retarded Child on His Family," <u>Amer. J. Ment. Defic.</u>, 73, 468-473, 1968.
In order to test the effect of a severely mentally retarded child on the family a group of 35 families who had institutionalized their child were compared with 35 families who had kept their child in the home. There were 20 males and 15 females in each group. They were predominantly white middle- and lower-class families. Marital and sibling

tension was measured using the Forbes sibling role tension index. Results indicated
that there was no significant difference in "marital integration," but that there was
a significant increase in "role tension" of the siblings if the child was not placed.

GRUNEBAUM, M. G., HURWITZ, I., PRENTICE, N. M., and SPERRY, B. M., "Fathers of Sons
     With Primary Neurotic Learning Inhibitions," Amer. J. Orthopsychiat., 32, 462-
     472, 1962.
An investigation which includes the treatment of 18 elementary school boys with severe
learning difficulties. The resistance to therapeutic modification "persuaded us that
this symptom was deeply embedded in the total family organization." The fathers are
described in terms of their self image of inadequacy and resignation, their passive or
explosively demanding orientation to their wives, their views of their sons as competi-
tors for mother's support and admiration, and their unconscious subversion of the child's
achievement in the face of their conscious wish that the child succeed. The mothers
maintain an image of masculinity that was dangerous or devalued and limit the son's
attempt to form an achieving masculine identification. The parents' neurotic attitudes
are internalized by the child and the conflict is displaced to the school situation.

GUERNEY, B., and GUERNEY, L., "Analysis of Interpersonal Relationships as an Aid to
     Understanding Family Dynamics, a Case Report," J. Clin. Psychol., 17, 225-228, 1961.
A case of a nine-year-old girl who refused to go to school and had fears of death is
presented in terms of the traditional evaluation and in terms of interpersonal family
dynamics. The interpersonal analysis is based upon "a few of the non-quantitative
conceptualizations of Leary's system," particularly "interpersonal reflexes" and the
principle of "reciprocal interpersonal relations."

HECKEL, R. V., "The Effects of Fatherlessness on the Preadolescent Female," Ment. Hyg.,
     47, 69-73, 1963.
A discussion of five fatherless preadolescent girls referred for treatment because of
school problems, excessive sexual interest, daydreaming, and acting-out behavior. The
girls responded more seductively to male staff members and more indifferently to females.
Interviews were conducted with both mother and child. Developmental similarities, treatment, and follow-up information are discussed.

MALMQUIST, C., "School Phobia: A Problem in Family Neurosis," J. Amer. Acad. Child Psy-
     chiat., 4, 293-319, 1965.
In contrast to the traditional approach to school phobia, this essay puts forth the
clinical notion that phobia can be seen as a reaction to family pathology. Four types
for characterizing disordered families that have been reported in the literature are:
(1) the perfectionistic family, (2) the inadequate family, (3) the egocentric family,
and (4) the unsocial family. How these family types relate to the symptom are discussed.
There is an extensive review of the literature.

MENDELL, D., and CLEVELAND, S., "A Three-Generation View of a School Phobia," Voices,
     3, 16-19, 1967.
A case report in support of the notion that psychopathology is "passed on from generation to generation with a more or less specific way and expectation of handling it."
Three generations of data from the identified patient (a 14-year-old boy), his mother,
and maternal grandmother were obtained from clinical psychiatric interviews and the
Rorschach and thematic apperception tests. School phobia of the identified patient
is seen as an attempt to answer the obsessive concern of a boy's relationship to his
mother and her relationship to her mother.

MESSER, A., "Family Treatment of a School Phobic Child," Arch. Gen. Psychiat., 11, 548-
     555, 1964.
Case report of family treatment over two years of a phobic child and his family. Hypothesis was that the phobia expressed publicly a disruption in the family equilibrium.

MILLAR, T. P., "The Child who Refuses to Attend School," Amer. J. Psychiat., 118, 398-
        404, 1961.
The child who doesn't attend school with the knowledge of the parent, but beyond the
parent's control, appears to be less fearful of school than concerned over separation
from the mother. The child is protective of the mother and also able to manipulate and
control his parents through mobilizing and exploiting guilt feelings. Treatment must
be instituted promptly and must include early return to regular school attendance.

MILLER, D. R., and WESTMAN, J. C., "Family Teamwork and Psychotherapy," Fam. Proc., 5,
        49-59, 1966.
A discussion of primary questions about etiology and treatment developed in a study of
functional retardation in reading. In one type of reading difficulty the problem can
be explained by poor teaching or traumatic experiences, and in the other there is a
function in the family. The roots of the symptom in family relationships are described
with an emphasis upon family teamwork in maintaining the difficulty.

MILLER, D. R., and WESTMAN, J. C., "Reading Disability as a Condition of Family Stabi-
        lity," Fam. Proc., 3, 66-76, 1964.
A report of a study of the relationship between reading disability in a child and the
condition of the family. The subjects were 18 boys in out-patient care. The family
members were given individual tests, data were drawn from individual therapy sessions,
and there were periodic visits to home and school. A matched control group was compared. It is postulated that parents and children resist change in the reading disability because it contributes to the family's survival.

PATTERSON, G. R., SHAW, D. A., and EBNER, M. J., "Teachers, Peers, and Parents as Agents
        of Change in the Classroom," in S. A. N. Benson (Ed.), Modifying Deviant Social Be-
        haviors in Various Classroom Settings, Eugene, University of Oregon Press, 1969.
An approach to correcting deviant behavior in the classroom by using a combined systems
and reinforcement theory approach.

PITTMAN, F., LANGSLEY, D., and DeYOUNG, C., "Work and School Phobias: A Family Approach
        to Treatment," Amer. J. Psychiat., 124, 1535-1541, 1968.
Eleven cases of work phobia (the patient experiencing overt anxiety associated with having to go to work or staying at work) are thought of as being "the adult form of school
phobia." Treatment goal is to allow the wife or mother to allow the man to separate.
One-year follow-up shows that five cases treated with conjoint family therapy were able
to return to work; the six in long-term individual therapy had not.

SHELLOW, R. S., BROWN, B. S., and OSBERG, J. W., "Family Group Therapy in Retrospect:
        Four Years and Sixty Families," Fam. Proc., 2, 52-67, 1963.
A review of experience with family group therapy (authors' term for conjoint family
therapy) with 60 families in a child guidance clinic over a four-year period. Referral
sources were mainly from physicians and school. Several "hidden" factors influenced
choice of this form of therapy by staff members: (1) the identified patient was often
the oldest child, and (2) there was a large proportion of school achievement problems
represented.

SMITH, I. W., and LOEB, D., "The Stable Extended Family as a Model in Treatment of Atypi-
        cal Children," Soc. Work, 10, 75-81, 1965.
A report of a multiple-impact therapeutic program in the treatment of six severely disturbed children and their families. Three boys and three girls, aged four-seven, were
referred as mentally retarded, were intolerable in school, and appeared psychotic in
the first interview. Two female therapists, assuming grandmotherly roles, treated the
families conjointly in three overlapping phases: (1) individual treatment for the patient and parents, (2) family group therapy, and (3) peer experiences for all family members. Patients showed rapid symptomatic recovery, enabling them to return to school and
participate in social situations. Parents and siblings, relieved of anxiety, functioned
more efficiently and experienced improved interpersonal relationships.

WESTMAN, J. C., MILLER, D. R., and ARTHUR, B., "Psychiatric Symptoms and Family Dyanmics
     as Illustrated by the Retarded Reader," in I. M. Cohen (Ed.), Psychiatric Research
     Report No. 20, Washington, American Psychiatric Association, 1966.
A discussion of the family of the retarded reader to illustrate how individual psychopathology can be linked with interpersonal relationships through symptoms and signs.

4.4 FAMILY HAS A "PERSONALITY DISORDER" ADOLESCENT

ACKERMAN, N. W., "Adolescent Problems: A Symptom of Family Disorder," Fam. Proc., 1,
     202-213, 1962.
An essay based on the thesis that adolescent problems represent in part not only a disorder of a particular stage of growth, but also a symptom of a parallel disorder in the
family, society, and culture. Clinical examples are given.

BARDILL, D., "Family Therapy in an Army Mental Hospital Hygiene Clinic," Soc. Casework,
     44, 452-457, 1963.
From an out-patient Army mental hygiene clinic, the author presents his experience in
using family therapy with adolescents. Manifest problems represent a breakdown in the
family system. Aims and techniques are discussed and illustrated by clinical examples.

BRANDZEL, E., "Working Through the Oedipal Struggle in Family Unit Sessions," Soc. Case-
     work, 46, 414-422, 1965.
A discussion of the use of family-unit sessions to help a family work through its problems with a young adolescent. Case examples are given.

BRITTAIN, C. V., "Adolescent Choices and Parent-Peer Cross-Pressures," Amer. Sociol.
     Rev., 28, 385-391, 1963.
Adolescent choices when peers and parents indicate different courses were investigated
as to variation by content area. Two hundred and eighty high school girls in two southern states responded to hypothetical dilemmas. On two occasions interviews were also
held with 42 subjects. The data indicate that choice depended upon the area and that
a complex process of perception of and identification with peers and parents is involved.

BROWNING, C. J., "Differential Impact of Family Disorganization on Male Adolescents,"
     Soc. Prob., 8, 37-44, 1960.
Samples of 60 nondelinquent, 60 delinquent-auto theft boys (aged 15) were identified.
Data were obtained from school, police, and probation records; from interviews with
mothers; from family solidarity and marital adjustment scales filled out by parents;
and California test of personality scales filled out by the boys. The incidence of
broken homes is higher in the delinquent groups, but this variable is not a consistently
good indicator of family disorganization and needs refinement.

CAREK, D. J., HENDRICKSON, W. J., and HOLMES, D. J., "Delinquency Addiction in Parents,"
     Arch. Gen. Psychiat., 4, 357-362, 1961.
A discussion of parental participation in the cause and cure of delinquency traits. These
parentally sanctioned traits "have been observed with regular frequency in some 400 cases"
of hospitalized adolescents who had not been admitted primarily for delinquency in the
legal sense. It is suggested that a rough analogy for parental participation is to be
found in the drug addict. Clinical examples are used to illustrate seven mechanisms
parents use to communicate unconscious approval. Complete separation is advised with
anticipation of the parental anxiety which occurs if the child abandons delinquency.

CAREK, D. J., and WATSON, A. S., "Treatment of a Family Involved in Fratricide," Arch.
     Gen. Psychiat., 11, 533-543, 1964.
Case report of a family where the eldest male sibling (age ten) shot and killed the youngest male sibling. The parents were treated with conjoint family therapy, and the oldest

sibling was hospitalized. Data were collected from the conjoint family meetings and from observations of the hospitalized patient. Formulation and treatment is discussed. The data are related to "society's philosophical view of illegal behavior and treatment, and some speculations about therapeutic implementation."

CHEEK, F., "Family Socialization Techniques and Deviant Behavior," Fam. Proc., 5, 199-
      217, 1966.
A study based upon Parsons' theoretical framework in which deviant behavior is related to imbalance of systems inputs and outputs at various stages of development. A sample of 120 male adults from four different groups — schizophrenics, normals, alcoholics, and reformatory inmates — were exposed to a questionnaire on family problem situations. Differences were found and it is suggested that Parsons' theoretical scheme could be translated into reinforcement theory.

COUNTS, R., "Family Crisis and the Impulsive Adolescent," Arch. Gen. Psychiat., 17, 64-
      74, 1967.
A case example is presented in support of the hypothesis that the acting out of an ado- lescent can best be understood by seeing it as acting out of a family crisis. The ado- lescent is used as a scapegoat of the family and he acts out somebody else's impulses, which helps to stabilize his own internal operations while it stabilizes the family.

DIETZ, C. R., "Implications for the Therapeutic Process of a Clinical Team Focus on
      Family Interaction, Amer. J. Orthopsychiat., 32, 395-398, 1962.
A discussion of the treatment of children and adolescents with an emphasis upon the contrast with adult patients. Psychotherapy with adolescent patients is not a simple contractual relationship between therapist and patient but in the family oriented ap- proach the goal is to strengthen the family equilibrium. Parents carry leadership in family affairs, and decisions about therapy with the child should be oriented within that framework. Initiating therapy, the content of the interviews, and termination should be done with the rights and responsibilities of the parents in mind.

EASSON, W. M., and STEINHILBER, R. M., "Murderous Aggression by Children and Adoles-
      cents," Arch. Gen. Psychiat., 4, 27-35, 1961.
A review of murderous agression in families, with a detailed discussion of seven boys who had made murderous assaults and one boy who had committed murder. The background family psychopathology varied in character and malignancy but showed definite psycho- dynamic patterns. All cases demonstrated that one or both parents had fostered and condoned murderous assault. Typically the boys were emotionally tied to mother in a hostile way, the fathers were not available for healthy identification, and the boys were allowed to retain weapons even after episodes of violent and menacing behavior. In each case the child was informed of parental expectations that he would be violent even to the point of murder.

EHRLICH, S. S., "The Family Structure of Hospitalized Adolescents," J. Health Hum. Be-
      hav., 3, 121-124, 1962.
A descriptive study of the family structure of 55 hospitalized adolescents. Character- istics studied were socioeconomic status (religion, ethnicity, father's occupation, and employment of mother), family composition (family intactness and separations, ordinal position), and family roles (mental conflict, role of grandparents).

FERREIRA, A. J., "The 'Double Bind' and Delinquent Behavior," Arch. Gen. Psychiat., 3,
      359-367, 1960.
A discussion of the double-bind theory as it relates to delinquency. Double-binds are not confined to schizophrenic relationships but appear in the genesis of delinquent be- havior. In delinquency, the source of messages is split; messages of distinct logical type, conflicting in themselves, emanate from two equally important parental figures. The child is a "victim" in that he is caught, for example, between a message emanating from father which requires certain behavior from him and a message from mother which is a destructive comment about that message. A case history is presented, and formal se- quences of this delinquent pattern are diagrammed in symbolic logic style.

FERREIRA, A. J., and WINTER, W. D., "Family Interaction and Decision-Making," <u>Arch. Gen.</u>
    <u>Psychiat.</u>, 13, 214-223, 1965.
A report of a study contrasting 50 normal families and 75 families with an abnormal child.
The abnormal group included 15 schizophrenic, 16 delinquent, and 44 maladjusted children.
The family members were asked to fill out a neutral questionnaire separately, and then
they were brought together and asked to fill out the same questionnaire while reaching
agreement on the items as a group. Generally this report is concerned with the extent
of agreement when family members make their choices separately, how much time is necessary to reach group decision, and the appropriateness of the family decisions in fulfilling the wishes of the individual family members. Eighteen hypotheses are described
and the results reported in terms of the differences found between the groups.

FERREIRA, A. J., WINTER, W. D., and POINDEXTER, E. J., "Some Interactional Variables in
    Normal and Abnormal Families," <u>Fam. Proc.</u>, 5, 60-75, 1966.
A study contrasting normal and abnormal families with the abnormals including schizophrenic, delinquent, and maladjusted. The families were exposed to TAT cards three at
a time, and asked to make up a story tying them together. Differences were found between the types of families and are described.

FRIEDMAN, A. S., "Delinquency and the Family System," in O. Pollak and A. S. Friedman
    (Eds.), <u>Family Dynamics and Female Sexual Delinquency</u>, Palo Alto, Science & Be-
    havior Books, 1969.
A review article of what has been written about delinquency in relation to the family.

FRIEDMAN, A. S., "The Family and the Female Delinquent: An Overview," in O. Pollak and
    A. S. Friedman (Eds.), <u>Family Dynamics and Female Sexual Delinquency</u>, Palo Alto,
    Science & Behavior Books, 1969.
A discusssion of young female delinquents and what has been written about the cause,
with illustrations from treatment of families of such girls.

GETZELS, J. W., and JACKSON, P. W., "Family Environment and Cognitive Style: A Study
    of the Sources of Highly Intelligent and of Highly Creative Adolescents," <u>Amer.</u>
    <u>Sociol. Rev.</u>, 26, 351-359, 1961.
A study of adolescent boys and girls, 28 highly intelligent but not creative and 26 creative but not concomitantly intelligent, chosen from a school population on the basis
of testing. These students proved equally superior in achievement to the remainder of
the student body although they differed both functionally and in their goals. The central issue of this report deals with the role of the family environment in the differentiation of kinds of intellectual ability through interviews with the mothers. Significant group differences were found in parental type education, childhood memories,
reading interests, values, degree of satisfaction with child and school, etc. The authors find less anxiety in the highly creative home and therefore more freedom for
"individual divergence."

GOLDSTEIN, M., JUDD, L., RODNICK, E., ALKIRE, A., and GOULD, E., "A Method of Studying
    Social Influence and Coping Patterns Within Families of Disturbed Adolescents,"
    <u>J. Nerv. Ment. Dis.</u>, 127, 233-252, 1968.
The first report of a project dealing with family interaction patterns between parents
and adolescents. Twenty families with the identified patient aged 13 to 19 were seen
for five sessions at the UCLA psychology clinic. Data collected included psychological
testing (TAT and a partial WAIS), psycho-physiological recordings, and videotape recordings of both actual and simulated verbal interaction. The results of simulated
interactions indicated that social power usage among family members was related to type
of psychopathology manifested by the adolescents.

HALLOWITZ, D., "Family Unit Treatment of Character-Disordered Youngsters," <u>Soc. Work</u>
    <u>Practice</u>, Columbia University Press, 1963.
A report on the family treatment of 38 children with a diagnosis of character disorder.
Procedures and descriptions of the family are offered along with tabular reports of outcome. Sixty-one percent had a favorable outcome, with the treatment averaging 17 hours
per case.

HARMS, E., "Defective Parents, Delinquent Children," Correct. Psychiat., 8, 34-42, 1962.
A discussion of the relationship between delinquency and defective parents. In 300 cases of children stealing and lying, it was found that in 264 of them "at least one parent
was, in one respect or another, deficient." Where the father is the defective factor,
the boys will be found to be lying and the girls stealing. Where the mother is the defective factor, the girls will be found lying and the boys stealing.

KIERMAN, I. R., and PORTER, M. E., "A Study of Behavior-Disorder Correlations Between
     Parents and Children," Amer. J. Orthopsychiat., 33, 539-541, 1963.
A report of three cases of youthful offenders who had been institutionalized, seemingly
reformed, later married and reared children who eventually were referred to a child guidance clinic. In all cases, an almost perfect correlation was found between the behavior
of the preadolescent child and that of his parent at the time he or she was a youthful
offender.

KING, C., "Family Therapy with the Deprived Family," Soc. Casework, 48, 203-208, 1967.
From the author's clinical work with delinquent boys at the Wiltwyck School, techniques
with working with low-socioeconomic class patients and their families are described.
Selection, rationale, and scope of family therapy is discussed. Basic techniques consisted of educational and therapeutic maneuvers focussed on clarity of communication,
and the teaching of parent and sibling roles.

LUSTIG, N., DRESSEN, J., SPELLMAN, S., and MURRAY, T., "Incest," Arch Gen. Psychiat.,
     14, 31-41, 1966.
Family constellations in six cases of father-daughter incest are reported. Data were
gathered from clinical interviews with the families. From the cases and from reviews of
the literature, intrapsychic and transactional dynamics are hypothesized which contribute to choice of father-daughter incest as a family defense. Incest is seen as a
"tension reducing defense within a dysfunctional family, serving to maintain the integrity of the family unit."

McCONAGHY, N., and CLANCEY, M., "Formal Relationships of Allusive Thinking in University
     Students and Parents," Brit. J. Psychiat., 114, 1079-1087, 1968.
A study testing the notion that when a person showed allusive thinking (defined as similar to "loosening of associations" but called "allusive" to avoid the implication of
pathology), at least one of his parents would also show this type of thinking. Sample
was 38 university students and their parents. Measures used were the object sorting
test and the F-scale of the MMPI. Results showed that the students with allusive
thinking did have parents with similar thoughts, but they did not have schizophrenic
pathology.

McCORD, J., McCORD, W., and HOWARD, A., "Family Interaction as Antecedent to the Direc-
     tion of Male Aggressiveness," J. Abnorm. Soc. Psycol., 66, 239-242, 1963.
A continuation of earlier studies on delinquency, exploring the question, "What family
environments tend to produce antisocial as opposed to socialized aggressiveness?" Results suggest that extreme neglect and punitiveness, coupled with a deviant-aggressive
paternal model, produce the former, while moderate neglect and punitiveness and ineffectual controls produce the latter.

MacGREGOR, R., "The Family Constellation from the Standpoint of Various Siblings," in
     O. Pollak and A. S. Friedman (Eds.), Family Dynamics and Female Sexual Delinquency,
     Palo Alto, Science & Behavior Books, 1969.
A typology of families in relation to delinquency with case illustrations.

MacGREGOR, R., "Progress in Multiple Impact Therapy," in N. W. Ackerman, F. L. Beatman,
     and S. Sherman (Eds.), Expanding Theory and Practice in Family Therapy, New York,
     Family Service Association of America, 1967.
A report on the youth development project in Galveston where multiple impact therapy developed. The approach is described with emphasis upon the bringing together of "a relatively open system, the team," with "a relatively closed system, the family functioning
in a defensive way." Procedures and concepts are described.

MINUCHIN, S., AUERSWALD, E., KING, C., and RABINOWITZ, C., "The Study and Treatment of
     Families that Produce Multiple Acting-Out Boys," Amer. J. Orthopsychiat., 34, 125-
     134, 1964.
An early report of experience with families of delinquent boys at the Wiltwyck School
for Boys in New York. The report focusses on some aspects of familial functioning, in
particular "the socializing function of parental control, guidance and nurturance."
The group's technique of family diagnosis and therapy with delinquent families is also
presented.

MINUCHIN, S., MONTALVO, B., GUERNEY, B. G., ROSMAN, B. L., and SHUMER, F., Families of
     the Slums: An Exploration of Their Structure and Treatment, New York, Basic Books,
     1967.
A book on a research project dealing with family treatment of low-socioeconomic class
families where the identified patient was delinquent. Research strategy, rationale,
dynamics, techniques, and assessment of results are presented. 460 pp.

MORRISON, G., and COLLIER, J., "Family Treatment Approaches to Suicidal Children and
     Adolescents," J. Amer. Acad. Child Psychiat., 8, 140-154, 1969.
A study of 34 patients referred to a child psychiatry emergency service because of a
suicide attempt. There were 28 girls and 6 boys in the sample, with 65% of the group
between the ages of 15 and 17. They were seen with their families by a psychiatrist
and social worker. Rationale was that the suicide attempt was an effort on the part
of the child to reveal underlying family disruption. After the acute crisis was resolved using family therapy, 30 of the 34 patients were referred for further therapy.
Of these 30, 28 accepted the recommendation, but only eight made further interviews
and only two were in treatment one year after the suicide attempt.

POLLAK, O., and FRIEDMAN, A., (Eds.), Family Dynamics and Female Sexual Delinquency,
     Palo Alto, Science & Behavior Books, 1968.
A collection of new material and previously published articles on sexual delinquency
which includes articles on family theory, socioeconomic and cultural factors, and
family therapy applications. 210 pp.

RABINOWITZ, C., "Therapy for Underprivileged Delinquent Families," in O. Pollak and
     A.S. Friedman (Eds.), Family Dynamics and Female Sexual Delinquency, Palo Alto,
     Science & Behavior Books, 1969.
A report on a family therapy approach to low-socioeconomic families. Includes a de-
tailed description of the process of therapy with such a family based on work at the
Wiltwyck School.

RASHKIS, H., "Depression as a Manifestation of the Family as an Open System," Arch. Gen.
     Psychiat., 19, 57-63, 1968.
Seven cases are presented in support of the idea that depression in the middle-aged is
regarded as part of a reciprocal relationship involving the adolescent and his parent.
It is treated by "family psychiatry" (simultaneous or consecutive treatment of one or
more family members).

RINSLEY, D. B., and HALL, D. D., "Psychiatric Hospital Treatment of Adolescents," Arch.
     Gen. Psychiat., 7, 286-294, 1962.
A report on a study of the metaphorical communications among patients, parents, and staff
members of an in-patient unit for the treatment of psychiatrically ill adolescents.
Parental resistances to their children's treatment are described as they are expressed
in metaphors to the staff. The child's problem of conflicting loyalties is also discussed. Optimum psychiatric treatment is accomplished only if the parents are meaning-
fully involved in the treatment process.

ROBEY, A., ROSENWALD, R., SNELL, J., and LEE, R., "The Runaway Girl: A Reaction to Fam-
     ily Stress," Amer. J. Orthopsychiat., 34, 762-768, 1964.
A study of 42 adolescent girls who were brought before the Framingham Court Clinic.
These 42 girls were referred by the court for further study and treatment. Their ages

ranged from 13 to 17½. Data were obtained from "at least three interviews with parents and the girl...in some cases from data from treatment for as long as two years...and where the father was uncooperative, information was gathered from the probation officer." Typical family constellations are described. The authors state that the family dynamics revolve around "a threatened unconscious incestuous relationship with the father incited by the mother. Subsequent acting out of the unresolved Oedipal conflict through running away represents an attempted solution."

RUTTER, M., "Sex Differences in Children's Responses to Family Stress," in E. J. Anthony
    and C. Koupernik (Eds.), The Child in His Family, New York, Wiley, 1970.
A questionnaire study investigating the impact on the child of marital problems and parental psychiatric disorders. Antisocial behavior in boys is associated with disturbance in family relationships but the marriage rating bore no relation to the rate of disorder in girls. Theoretical discussion is offered.

SCHERZ, F., "The Crisis of Adolescence in Family Life," Soc. Casework, 48, 209-215, 1967.
Adolescence is seen as a time of crisis for the family as well as the patient. When behavioral symptoms come up, family treatment is indicated. The influence of grandparents in the chain of family communication that result from the sum total of all these factor's is discussed.

SERRANO, A. C., McDANALD, E. C., GOOLISHIAN, H. A., MacGREGOR, R., and RITCHIE, A. M.,
    "Adolescent Maladjustment and Family Dynamics," Amer. J. Psychiat., 118, 897-901,
    1962.
A summary of the dynamics of 63 disturbed adolescents and their families. The patients are said to fall into four diagnostic categories each associated with a type of family interaction. These categories of maladjustment reaction in adolescence are: the infantile, the childish, the juvenile, and the preadolescent. The adolescent functions as a stabilizing factor in the family and when his behavior becomes unendurable to himself, the family, or society this precipitates a crisis which mobilizes the family to seek help.

SHAPIRO, R. L., "The Origin of Adolescent Disturbances in the Family: Some Considera-
    tions in Theory and Implications for Therapy," in G. H. Zuk and I. Boszormenyi-Nagy
    (Eds.), Family Therapy and Disturbed Families, Palo Alto, Science & Behavior Books,
    1967.
The study of the current family relations of the adolescent helps to identify the nature of determinants in his developmental experience. Verbatim excerpts from interviews are presented and therapeutic design is discussed.

SOJIT, C. M., "Dyadic Interaction in a Double Bind Situation," Fam. Proc., 8, 235-260,
    1969.
Marital couples were exposed to a double-bind situation to contrast parents of delinquents, ulcerative colitis patients, and normal controls. The couples were exposed to the proberb "a rolling stone gathers no moss" and were asked to reach agreement about its meaning. The responses were categorized and differences found.

STABENAU, J. R., TUPIN, J., WERNER, M., and POLLIN, W., "A Comparative Study of Families
    of Schizophrenics, Delinquents, and Normals," Psychiatry, 28, 45-59, 1965.
A report of a comparison of five families with a schizophrenic, five families with a delinquent, and five normal families tested with the revealed differences test, the object sorting test, and the thematic apperception test. "Data from the three different tests suggest that in the schizophrenic and delinquent families there were both individual disturbances in thought process and impaired communication at the family level...There was relatively little evidence of communication impairment at the individual or family level in the normal families."

TESSMAN, L. H., and KAUFMAN, I., "Variations on a Theme of Incest," in O. Pollak and A.
    S. Friedman (Eds.) Family Dynamics and Female Sexual Delinquency, Palo Alto, Science
    & Behavior Books, 1969.
A discussion of incest occuring in families with young girls, either in fantasy or fact, with case examples.

TRIBBEY, J. A., "Like Father, Like Son: A Projection-Displacement Pattern," Bull. Men-
     ninger Clin., 28, 244-251, 1964.
A study concerned with the frequency with which a son begins to take up the behavior
pattern of an antisocial father. Case material was from 55 boys referred for treatment
to the psychiatric diagnostic unit of a children's receiving home. Of the 55, ten were
judged by the author to have histories similar to that of their fathers. The overall
family picture is "that of a boy whose parents are divorced, and whose father had a long-
standing history of antisocial behavior. Before long, as the mother had always 'known,'
the son begins to get into trouble." Dynamics are discussed. Poor treatment results
with these cases are pointed out.

VOGEL, E. F., and BELL, N. W., "The Emotionally Disturbed Child as the Family Scapegoat,"
     in N.W. Bell, and E. F. Vogel (Eds.), A Modern Introduction to the Family, Glencoe,
     Free Press, 1960.
A discussion of families with disturbed children in terms of the child's function as a
scapegoat. Included is the selection of the child for scapegoating, the induction of
him into this role, and the rationalizations.

WHITIS, P. R., "The Legacy of a Child's Suicide," Fam. Proc., 7, 159-169, 1968.
A discussion of the effect on a family of a child's suicide, illustrated by a case report. Prompt therapeutic intervention is recommended for the bereaved family.

WINTER, W. D., FERREIRA, A. J., and OLSON, J. L., "Hostility Themes in the Family TAT,"
     J. Project. Techn. Person. Ass., 30, 270-275, 1966.
Second of a series describing a diagnostic test adapted for use with families. Results
were obtained from use of three TAT stories based on three cards each, produced conjointly by 126 three-member families. Stories were scored for hostility in the story
themes. Fifty families had normal children, 44 had neurotic children, 16 had schizophrenic children, and 16 had delinquent child. Normal and schizophrenic groups produced stories low in hostility, neurotics produced stories high in hostility, and delinquents scored high on one hostility variable and low on another.

WINTER, W. D., FERREIRA, A. J., and OLSON, J. L., "Story Sequence Analysis of Family
     TATs," J. Project. Techn. Person. Ass., 29, 392-397, 1965.
A group of 126 families, composed of parents and one child, were asked to produce TAT
stories conjointly. The families were to make up a story based upon three TAT cards
presented simultaneously to them. Three stories based on nine cards were composed by
each family and scored by the Arnold system of story sequence analysis. In the sample
there were 50 families with normal children. The abnormal group consisted of 44 emotionally maladjusted, 16 delinquent, and 16 schizophrenic children. The procedure successfully differentiated normal from abnormal families but the three abnormal groups
did not differ from each other. The stories of abnormal families are said to be characterized by negative attitudes toward achievement, morality, responsibility, human relationships, and reaction to adversity.

4.5 FAMILY MEMBER DIAGNOSED NEUROTIC

ACKERMAN, N. W., "The Diagnosis of Neurotic Marital Interaction," Soc. Casework, 35,
     139-147, 1954.
A lecture based on the author's clinical work in which he lays out a theory of family
pathology and marital disharmony. There is an extensive schema for evaluating the marital relationship, divided into 7 categories: (1) goals, (2) performance, (3) achievement, (4) dynamic interrelations, (5) neurotic interactions, (6) consequences of neurotic interactions, and (7) patterns of compensation.

ANASTASIADIS, Y. S., "A Study on Psychopathological Influence of Parental Environment
     in Neurotic and Schizoid Patients," Acta Psychother., 11, 370-391, 1963.
A report from Istanbul "aiming to prove to what extent the neurotic and schizoid forms

of personality defects are due to familial conflicts." Sample was 50 normals contrasted with 30 neurotic and 30 schizoid mental patients. The research method was psychotherapy and/or narcosis. Parents of mental patients are reported to be "a problem" and certain factors relating to the parent-child intervention are discussed.

ARLEN, M. S., "Conjoint Therapy and the Corrective Emotional Experience," Fam. Proc., 5, 91-104, 1966.
The use of family therapy with families containing a person with severe character disorder described within a framework of providing a corrective emotional experience.

BAILEY, M. B., "Alcoholism and Marriage," Quart. J. Stud. Alcohol, 22, 81-97, 1961.
A review paper summarizing and discussing the major literature relating to alcoholism and marriage. Further research is said to be needed to attempt an integration of the two hypotheses that regard the course of an alcoholic marriage as a manifestation of a personality disorder or as a response to a particular kind of stress. "The past few years have witnessed a general growth of psychiatric interest in total family diagnosis and treatment, but this new emphasis has hardly begun to manifest itself in respect to alcoholism." A bibliography of 46 references is included.

BROWN, D. G., "Homosexuality and Family Dynamics," Bull. Menninger Clin., 27, 227-232, 1963.
A review of the literature and review of the author's experiences in treating male homosexuality points to a consistent pattern of family dynamics. That is, a combination of a dominating, overly intimate mother plus a detached, hostile, or weak father.

BUCK, C. W., and LADD, K. L., "Psychoneurosis in Marital Partners," Brit. J. Psychiat., 3, 587-590, 1965.
A study of records of physicians' diagnoses from a health insurance plan in a Canadian city. There was a definite association between the occurrence of psychoneurotic illness in husbands and wives who had been married for many years, little association for partners recently married and no association during the pre-marital period. The authors interpret these findings as evidence that a process of contagion rather than mate selection determines the concordance between marital partners in psychoneurotic illness.

CHEEK, F., "Family Socialization Techniques and Deviant Behavior," Fam. Proc., 5, 199-217, 1966.
A study based upon Parsons' theoretical framework in which deviant behavior is related to imbalance of systems inputs and outputs at various stages of development. A sample of 120 male adults from four different groups — schizophrenics, normals, alcoholics, and reformatory inmates — were exposed to a questionnaire on family problem situations. Differences were found and it is suggested that Parsons' theoretical scheme could be translated into reinforcement theory.

DOWNING, R., COMER, N., and EBERT, J., "Family Dynamics in a Case of Gilles de la Tourette's Syndrome," J. Nerv. Ment. Dis., 138, 548-557, 1964.
A case report of a patient with Gilles de la Tourette's syndrome in which all the members of the family were interviewed and tested with a WAIS, Rorschach, TAT, and word association test. A Leary interpersonal checklist was done in the home. From this data a dynamic, genetic, and familial formulation of the case was made.

EWING, J. A., LONG, V., and WENZEL, G. G., "Concurrent Group Psychotherapy of Alcoholic Patients and Their Wives," Int. J. Group Psychother., 11, 329-338, 1961.
A description of concurrent but separate group psychotherapy meetings of alcoholic outpatients and their wives. The authors find that more husbands continue to attend group meetings if the wife is involved, and there is greater improvement in alcoholic patients whose wives also attend group meetings. The participation of the wife in the husband's drinking is examined. An example is the wife who accidentally put a shot of whiskey into her husband's iced tea after he had stopped drinking. The authors highly recommend involving the wives of alcoholics in group therapy.

FERREIRA, A. J., "Family Myth and Homeostasis," Arch. Gen. Psychiat., 9, 457-463, 1963.
A discussion of a particular aspect of the family relationship: the family myth, which
is defined as "a series of fairly well integrated beliefs shared by all family members,
concerning each other and their mutual position in the family life" — beliefs that go
unchallenged despite reality distortions which they imply. Three family case reports
are presented in support of the discussion; the author believes that the family myth is
to the relationship what the defense is to the individual.

FERREIRA, A. J., "Family Myths: The Covert Rules of the Relationship," Confin. Psychiat.,
  8, 15-20, 1965.
A general discussion of the myths in families which express covert rules of family relationships. These well systematized fabrications perform an important part as homeostatic mechanisms. "In fact, it seems that the family myth is to the family what the
defense is to the individual." From family therapy observations, the author says that
"pathologic families" can be overburdened with their own mythology and "seem to retain
very little freedom for unrehearsed action, and to suffer in their ability to deal with
new situations, and unexpected events."

GANGER, R., and SHUGART, G., "The Heroin Addict's Pseudoassertive Behavior and Family
  Dynamics," Soc. Casework, 57, 643-649, 1966.
A discussion of heroin addiction based upon interviews with addicts and family members.
Addiction is said to have a function within the family. The authors conclude, "Our
clinical observations and our experience with casework treatment provided to the total
family unit, including the addicted person, lead us to the conviction that addiction is
specifically a 'familiogenic' disease; consequently, any attempt to cure it must be
undertaken within the context of the family unit."

GEHRKE, S., and KIRSCHENBAUM, M., "Survival Patterns in Family Conjoint Therapy," Fam.
  Proc., 6, 67-80, 1967.
A discussion of 20 families studied in family therapy with the emphasis upon different
patterns of emotional survival myths in the family. Three types of family are contrasted: the repressive family, the delinquent family, and the suicidal family. The survival myth has to do with the illusion of family members that they must continue their
existing family ways of relating to survive psychologically.

MACHOTKA, P., PITTMAN, F.S., and FLOMENHAFT, K., "Incest as a Family Affair," Fam. Proc.,
  6, 98-116, 1967.
A discussion of incest from the point of view of the whole family. Two cases of father-
daughter incest and one of sibling incest are discussed with the emphasis upon the crucial role of the nonparticipating member, the concerted denial of the incest, and where
the focus of therapy should be.

PITTMAN, F., LANGSLEY, D., and DeYOUNG, C., "Work and School Phobias: A Family Approach
  to Treatment," Amer. J. Psychiat., 124, 1535-1541, 1968.
Eleven cases of work phobia (the patient experiencing overt anxiety associated with having to go to work or staying at work) are thought of as being "the adult form of school
phobia." Treatment goal is to allow the wife or mother to allow the man to separate.
One-year follow-up shows that five cases treated with conjoint family therapy were able
to return to work; the six in long-term individual therapy had not.

RAPOPORT, R., "The Family and Psychiatric Treatment," Psychiatry, 23, 53-62, 1960.
A conceptual framework for analyzing family relationships and role performance of psychiatric patients applied to a case. Three areas are considered important in conceptualizing role difficulties: familial position, personal and social norms, and personality
factors. This framework is applied to a case presented in detail.

RYLE, A., and HAMILTON, M., "Neurosis in Fifty Married Couples," J. Ment. Sci., 108, 265-
  273, 1962.
An investigation of 50 working-class marital couples to record the prevalence of neurosis as indicated by the Cornell medical index, the records of the general practitioner
with whom the families were registered, and the home interviews of a psychiatric social
worker. The information from these sources was compared and the presence of neurosis

was correlated with some aspects of adverse childhood experience, marital adjustment, consumer status, and social intergration.

SCHEFLEN, A. E., "Regressive One-To-One Relationships," Psychiat. Quart., 34, 692-709, 1960.
A description of regressive attachments between two individuals. The characteristics of these "gruesome twosomes" are: limitations of relatedness to others, decreasing gratification within the relationship, and the maintenance of the attachment by mutual exploitation of the partner's anxieties by such means as threats of desertion and arousal of guilt. Several variations of this type of relationship are presented and illustrated with four case histories involving differing sex and age combinations. There is a discussion of differentiating between neurotic and non-neurotic one-to-one relationships.

SNELL, J., ROSENWALD, R., and ROBEY, A., "The Wifebeater's Wife, A Study of Family Interaction," Arch. Gen. Psychiat., 11, 107-113, 1964.
A study of 37 families in which men were charged by their wives with assault and battery and who were referred to one of the psychiatric clinics which serve the courts of Massachusetts. Twelve of the families were studied in detail (both husband and wife being seen for three or more interviews). Four wives were in individual psychotherapy for "more than 18 months." In addition, some group therapy and "couple therapy" was attempted. A typical family structure is described: husband is passive, indecisive, and sexually inadequate; wife aggressive, masculine, frigid, and masochistic; relationship between the two characterized by alternation of passive and aggressive roles. An adolescent son may upset the equilibrium.

TABACHNICK, N., "Interpersonal Relations in Suicidal Attempts," Arch. Gen. Psychiat., 4, 42-47, 1961.
A description of the interpersonal context, largely familial, of the attempted suicide: "a product of reflection of over 100 cases of suicidal attempts studied by a team of social scientists at the Suicide Prevention Center at Los Angeles." One could deduce from the fact that attempted suicides are dependent and masochistic that the significant individuals in their environment would also be dependent and masochistic. Observation supports such an expectation, and in numerous situations both members of the unit are suicidal. Three cases are presented. Treatment suggestions are separation by hospitalization, and intervention to decrease the mutual dependence.

TITCHENER, J. L., D'ZMURA, T., GOLDEN, M., and EMERSON, R., "Family Transaction and Derivation of Individuality," Fam. Proc., 2, 95-120, 1963.
A report of an experimental method in research on family interaction. Subjects were families of patients who applied because of neurotic symptoms. Task was for the family to "reconcile their differences in opinion previously revealed in a questionnaire administered to each family member." The observers used tapes, films, and notes of direct observation to record the family transactions. The authors believe that "a young person elaborates an identity and develops his sense of it from the communicative interplay of the family." A case is presented in detail to illustrate.

VERON, E., KORNBLIT, A., MALFE, R., and SLUZKI, C. E., "Estructures de Conducta y Sistemas de Comunicacion Social" (Conduct Structures and Systems of Social Communication)," Acta Psiquiat. Psicolog.Argentina, 9, 297, 1963.
A conceptual model for the sociological study of psychoneurosis is described, including three strategic levels: individual, familial (group structure), and social stratification, including cultural structures. The recurrence of certain conduct structures in an individual, that is, of generalized ways of interaction, is the result of a meta-communicative process of learning, i. e., deutero-learning. The presence of recurrent ways of learning in a family group is a function of the family organization as communication system. The persistence of certain types of communication within the family group is a function of the sociocultural context which influences the family.

VIDAL, G., PRECE, G., and SMULEVER, M., "Convivencia y Trastorno Mental," Acta Psiquiat. Psicolog. Amer. Lat., 15, 55-65, 1969.
A sample of 1,322 patients were studied for family size, birth order of the patient, and family integrity (number of years the offspring lived together with both parents). The

hypothesis was that "the higher the amount of the family relationship the lower the severity of the mental disorder." Neurotics were expected to show smaller families,
first birth order positions and intact families, while psychotics would show larger
families, last birth order positions, and disrupted families. The hypothesis about
neurotics was confirmed but that about psychotics was only partially confirmed.

WHITAKER, C., "Family Treatment of a Psychopathic Personality," Compr. Psychiat., 7, 397-
    402, 1966.
From part of a summary of treatment of a woman identified as having "eight years of treatment, three psychotherapists, two near successes of suicide, and two successful divorces"
and her family, the author has evolved a theory of the development of the psychopathic
personality. The child divides a weak parental relationship and then adopts this approach to all situations in later life. A team approach is suggested.

WYATT, G. L., and HERZAN, H. M., "Therapy with Stuttering Children and Their Mothers,"
    Amer. J. Orthopsychiat., 32, 645-659, 1962.
A study of the therapy of stuttering children, indicating that therapy should start from
a sound theory of the interpersonal aspects of language learning in children. The techniques should be adapted to the age of the child, and the mother should be included in
the treatment program. Twenty-six children were included in the sample with some children seen in the presence of their mothers and some seen separately. Stuttering was considered to be the result of a disruption of the complementary patterns of verbal interaction between mother and child.

4.6 FAMILY — PHYSICAL HEALTH

ANTHONY, E. J., "The Mutative Impact of Serious Mental and Physical Illness in a Parent
    on Family Life," in E. J. Anthony and C. Koupernik (Eds.), The Child in His Family,
    New York, Wiley, 1970.
A report of a study of families where a parent figure has succumbed to a serious mental
or physical disorder necessitating hospitalization. Various views are offered of such
illness: as a disruption of family roles, as a crisis in accommodation, as a disconnection, and as a challenge. Family members were interviewed individually and in dyads
and triads.

BOSWELL, J., LEWIS, C., FREEMAN, D., and CLARK, K., "Hyperthyroid Children: Individual
    and Family Dynamics," J. Amer. Acad. Child Psychiat., 6, 64-85, 1967.
A retrospective study describing twelve children (ten girls, two boys; six black, six
white; four lower-, eight middle-class) who developed hyperthyroidism between the ages
of four and 14. Data were gathered from individual psychiatric interviews, psychologic
tests, parents, and from social agencies — but not from family interviews. Parents
were found to have given minimal care and expected maximum self-sufficiency from the
child. Children were found to be fixated at a pregenital stage.

BURSTEN, B., "Family Dynamics, The Sick Role, and Medical Hospital Admissions," Fam.
    Proc., 4, 206-216, 1965.
A discussion of how the medical hospital may be used in the service of family patterns.
There may be no organic difficulty or an organic difficulty can be combined with psycho-
social factors to resolve a family conflict. Case examples are given.

DYSINGER, R. H., "A Family Perspective on the Diagnosis of Individual Members," Amer. J.
    Orthopsychiat., 31, 61-68, 1961.
A discussion of the characteristic view of health matters by members of families containing a schizophrenic hospitalized as part of the Bowen study. Typically, mother,
father and identified patient are intensely involved emotionally over health issues.
Siblings are not included in the same way. Confusion over feelings, physical symptoms,
and definite illness exists, and attempts to do something effective about a health matter are often stalemated. Intense emotional problem in the parental relationship is

handled through a set of mechanisms that operate to support an inaccurate assumption
that the problem is the health of one child. The development of psychosis in the child
demonstrates the inefficiency of this displacement and also can become a focus for the
perpetuation of the family mechanisms.

GLASSER, P. H., and GLASSER, L. N. (Eds.), Families in Crisis, New York, Harper & Row,
     1970.
A collection of new material and previously published articles which includes discussions of families in poverty, disorganization of marriages and families, and families
in terms of physical and mental health. 405 pp.

GOLDBERG, E., "Difficulties Encountered in Assessing Family Attitudes," J. Psychosom.
     Res., 8, 229-234, 1964.
A discussion of studies made which attempted to assess family organization and functioning in relation to disease (such as chronic ulcers, schizophrenia, etc.). Problems of
methodology including interrelatedness of variables, objective assessment, comparisons,
and measurement in relation to the family are discussed.

GREENBLUM, J., "The Control of Sick Care Functions in the Hospitalization of a Child:
     Family Vs. Hospital," J. Health Hum. Behav., 2, 32-38, 1961.
The author hypothesizes that parents are more willing to give up control of instrumental functions involved in the sickness situation (medical tasks associated with care
and treatment of illness) than of the associated functions (merging socio-emotional
needs and socializing into desirable behavior). Interviews were conducted with 18
children suffering from paralytic polio and their parents. Fourteen families participated in two repeat interviews. The degree of dissatisfaction with various aspects
of hospital care was taken as an index of resistance to transfer of parental control.
In the acute phase of illness dissatisfaction is greatest regarding primary functions,
but decreases in the convalescent phase. Dissatisfaction regarding instrumental functions is low in the acute phase, and increases in the convalescent phase, especially
in regard to providing of medical information. Some problems arising in the posthospital period from the "trained incapacities" the child acquires through hospital experience are discussed.

GROTJAHN, M., "The Aim and Technique of Psychiatric Family Consultations," in W. Mendell
     and P. Solomon (Eds.), The Psychiatric Consultation, New York, Grune & Stratton,
     1968.
Two case reports are presented in support of a technique of consultation in which the
entire family is seen along with a referring physician in cases where the identified
patient has a medical problem. The consultation takes place in the internist's office.
Further management is left to the family and referring physician. Family psychopathology is usually the cause of the identified patient's problems.

JACKSON, D. D., "Family Practice: A Comprehensive Medical Approach," Compr. Psychiat.,
     7, 338-344, 1966.
The relationship of nonfunctional illness and the family is examined. Patterns of seeking medical care by families are listed; familial factors in relation to specific illness, e. g., ulcerative colitis and the "restrictive family" are discussed; and the family physician is encouraged to think of the patient's illness with the knowledge of the
family as a whole.

JACKSON, D. D., and YALOM, I., "Family Homeostasis and Patient Change," in J. Masserman
     (Ed.), Current Psychiatric Therapies, Vol. IV, New York, Grune & Stratton, 1964.
A case report of conjoint family therapy examines the hypothesis that "the schizophrenic
family is a specific system, which, when altered, results in a change in the identified
patient's symptoms and this change correlates with a noticeable alteration in the behavior of other family members." Specific techniques are described in detail — particularly "the therapeutic double-bind and prescriptions of behavior."

JACKSON, D. D., and YALOM, I., "Family Research on the Problem of Ulcerative Colitis,"
    Arch. Gen. Psychiat., 15, 410-418, 1966.
A study attempting to correlate parental behavior with the onset of ulcerative colitis.
Eight patients were intensively studied using four to 20 conjoint family therapy 90-
minute sessions. Identified patients were all children ranging in age from seven to
17. Sociality of the family was limited; they related in a "pseudo-mutual" fashion.
Suggestions for further study are made.

KELLNER, R., Family Ill Health, An Investigation in General Practice, Springfield,
    Charles C Thomas, 1963.
A report by a general practitioner concerning the incidence of physical and emotional
illness and its relationship to family dynamics. It includes a plan of the investigation, description of the cases, method of analyzing the data, results, and a summary.
112 pp.

LANGSLEY, D. G., "Psychology of a Doomed Family," Amer. J. Psychother., 15:4, 531-538,
    1961.
A report on a family suffering from an inherited renal disorder, all of whom face premature death. Of ten siblings, nine have been observed (six by a psychiatrist). Their
psychological defenses are discussed, with emphasis upon why one of them was more mature in facing death than were the others.

LINTON, H., BERLE, B. B., GROSS, M., and JACKSON, E., "Reaction of Children Within Fam-
    ily Groups as Measured by the Bene-Anthony Tests," J. Ment. Sci., 107, 308-325, 1962.
A study of 69 children in 28 families who were given the Bene-Anthony family relations
test in which they were asked to match statements with representations of family members.
The test scores were rated high or low on six qualitative variables in family life. The
child rated as sick by pediatrician and nurse was more involved with parent of the opposite sex, and in families with episodes of illness the children express a marked preference for mother. Significant patterns were found in boys and girls of different age
groups and in the group as a whole.

MABREY. J. H., "Medicine and the Family," in P. H. Glasser and L. N. Glasser (Eds.),
    Families in Crisis, New York, Harper & Row, 1970.
A consideration of family relationships in the promotion of health and the treatment of
illness. Included are medicine and family functioning, the family as a unit in medical
care, and the family's nursing function.

McCORD, W., McCORD, J., and VERDEN, P., "Familial Correlates of Psychosomatic Symptoms
    in Male Children," J. Health Hum. Behav., 1, 192-199, 1960.
Further study of data from the Cambridge-Somerville Youth Study (1935-1945). Data were
available on the physical condition of youths, their family backgrounds, and delinquent
activities. Hypotheses that children with psychosomatic disorders would have been raised
in families with a high degree of interpersonal stress and with anxious, hypochondriacal,
symptom-ridden parents were not confirmed. But when boys were cross-classified as extropunitive or intropunitive, some regularities are observed. It is concluded that degree
of extropunitiveness and nature of parental "sick-role" models are variables which affect
childhood diseases.

MacNAMARA, M., "Family Stress Before and After Renal Homotransplantation," Soc. Work, 14,
    89-98, 1969.
An essay from a renal transplantation unit where it was found that involvement of the
family of both donors and recipients prior to the transplant will avert complicated crises in the family and the patient.

MEISSNER, W. W., "Family Dynamics and Psychosomatic Processes," Fam. Proc., 5, 142-161,
    1966.
A discussion of the impact of patterns of family interaction on patterns of physical
health and illness, with a review of the literature.

MINUCHIN, S., "The Use of an Ecological Framework in the Treatment of a Child," in E. J.
    Anthony and C. Koupernik (Eds.), The Child in His Family, New York, Wiley, 1970.
A discussion of the three elements in the study of the child: the child as an individual, in his environment, and the linkage between. The ecological point is discussed.
A case of an adolescent with anorexia nervosa is examined in terms of his family and the
family therapy approach to the problem.

MINUCHIN, S., and BARCAI, A., "Therapeutically Induced Family Crisis," in J. Masserman,
    Childhood and Adolescence,Science and Psychoanalysis, Vol. XIV, New York, Grune &
    Stratton, 1969.
A report on a family treatment approach where a crisis is induced and resolved. A family with a child regularly hospitalized for diabetic acidosis was treated by assigning
tasks which induced a crisis situation to which the family members had to respond by
changing.

PURCELL, K., and METZ, S. R., "Distinctions Between Subgroups of Asthmatic Children:
    Some Parent Attitude Variables Related to Age of Onset of Asthma," J. Psychosom. Res.,
    6, 251-258, 1962.
A continuation of the authors' previous work with asthmatic children at the Children's
Asthma Research Institute and Hospital in Denver. Previous work had tentatively classified these 86 children as "steroid dependent" and "rapidly remitting" in terms of their
clinical course once at the hospital and separated from home. Parents' attitudes were
measured using the parent attitude research instrument. Positive findings of this study
were that within the group of rapidly remitting children relatively late age of onset
(after 12-18 months) was associated with autocratic and restrictive attitudes on the part
of their mothers. These findings were not found in the other group.

SERRANO, A. C., and WILSON, N. S., "Family Therapy in the Treatment of the Brain Damaged
    Child," Dis. Nerv. Syst., 24, 732-735, 1963.
The authors review their experiences with 34 children diagnosed as having organic brain
syndromes with behavior disorders. They emphasize including the evaluation of the total
family constellation (here using their multiple impact therapy method previously reported
on), in addition to the more traditional physical and psychological studies of the child.

SOJIT, C. M., "Dyadic Interaction in a Double Bind Situation," Fam. Proc., 8, 235-260,
    1969.
Marital couples were exposed to a double-bind situation to contrast parents of delinquents, ulcerative colitis patients, and normal controls. The couples were exposed to
the proberb "a rolling stone gathers no moss" and were asked to reach agreement about
its meaning. The responses were categorized and differences found.

TITCHENER, J. L., RISKIN, J., and EMERSON, R., "The Family in Psychosomatic Process: A
    Case Report Illustrating a Method of Psychosomatic Research," Psychosom. Med., 22,
    127-142, 1960.
A report of a study of a family in which one son developed ulcerative colitis. The
mother-child symbiosis is looked at in terms of the total family milieu. A detailed
case history is presented, and it is suggested that the object relations aspect of psychosomatic hypotheses can be more comprehensively investigated by inquiry into the patterns of interlocking relationships in the family.

TREUSCH, J., and GROTJAHN, M., "Psychiatric Family Consultations, the Practical Approach
    in Family Practice for the Personal Physician," Ann. Intern. Med., 66, 295-300, 1967.
In psychiatric consultations for patients with psychosomatic problems, the focus once was
on the presence of the psychiatrist in the internist's office with the internist in charge.
However, over the years it was recognized that the family seemed to be etiologic "in almost all psychiatric conditions likely to occur" in the internist's office. Techniques
of the family consultation are described.

4.7 LOW-SOCIOECONOMIC FAMILIES

ATTNEAVE, C. L., "Therapy in Tribal Settings and Urban Network Intervention," Fam. Proc.,
   8, 192-210, 1969.
A comparison of network therapy and interventions in a network-clan of a tribal minority
culture. An example of treatment with an Indian tribe is contrasted with urban network
treatment where the clan-like social structure must be reconstituted.

BARD, M., and BERKOWITZ, B., "A Community Psychology Consultation Program in Police Family Crisis Intervention: Preliminary Impressions," Int. J. Soc. Psychiat., 15, 209-
   215, 1969.
The second in a series of reports describing training of police in family crisis intervention with low socioeconomic class patients. Rationale for the program, methods of
selection, and techniques of training (which include use of family crisis laboratory
demonstrations and "human relations workshops") are presented.

BEHRENS, M., "Brief Home Visits by the Clinic Therapist in the Treatment of Lower-Class
   Patients," Amer. J. Psychiat., 124, 371-375, 1967.
A paper reviewing the author's experience with home visits. The sample was 80 patients
attending an out-patient clinic. These were chronic schizophrenics, the majority black
and female of low-socioeconomic class with certain exceptions. Home visits were made on
the average of one home visit per year per patient. At first the visits were done only
at times of crisis situations, later routinely. The visits have been found useful in
obtaining data about the patient and family, improving the relationship between patient
and therapist, and in decreasing rehospitalizations.

BEHRENS, M., ROSENTHAL, A. J., and CHODOFF, P., "Communication in Lower-Class Families
   of Schizophrenics," Arch. Gen. Psychiat., 18, 689-696, 1968.
The second part of a study of low-socioeconomic families of schizophrenics. The study
was done in the home where the family was focussed upon a task, particularly the Rorschach. Raters were asked to predict type of family from written transcripts. Results
indicate that communication and interaction patterns of lower-class families with a schizophrenic differ from families whose class background is similar.

CORNWELL, G., "Scapegoating: A Study in Family Dynamics," Amer. J. Nurs., 67, 1862-
   1867, 1967.
In a study of two lower-socioeconomic class families which included mother and son, the
following were described: how the scapegoating was done, how each member took mutually
reinforcing roles in the scapegoating, and how to change the process.

ELBERT, S., ROSMAN, B., MINUCHIN, S., and GUERNEY, F., "A Method for the Clinical Study
   of Family Interaction," Amer. J. Orthopsychiat., 34, 885-894, 1964.
Two methods are described to obtain data on family interactions which were developed by
the family research unit at the Wiltwick School for Boys. Families were from low-socioeconomic status with more than one delinquent child. The family interaction apperception
test is a TAT-style test consisting of ten pictures showing family members in different
activities. The family task is designed to permit observations of the family relations
and their interactions. The family is seated in a room and by operating a tape recorder
they hear six different tasks, which they must all discuss and answer together. During
the time they are discussing the tasks, a continuous report on nonverbal behavior is being dictated by an observer (looking through a one-way mirror). Verbal behavior is recorded by a tape.

GEISMAR, L. L., "Family Functioning as an Index of Need for Welfare Services," Fam. Proc.,
   3, 99-113, 1964.
A discussion of the need to have an objective means of assessing the need for welfare
services. A standardized method of evaluating family functioning is offered with a report of a study of families.

GLASSER, P. H., and GLASSER, L. N. (Eds.), Families in Crisis, New York, Harper & Row,
   1970.
A collection of new material and previously published articles which include discussions
of families in poverty, disorganization of marriages and families, and families in terms
of physical and mental health. 405 pp.

HOFFMAN, L., and LONG, L., "A Systems Dilemma," Fam. Proc., 8, 211-234, 1969.
A description of a man's breakdown in terms of the social systems within which he moved
and the attempts to intervene to bring about change. The ecological field of a person
is the area considered.

KING, C., "Family Therapy with the Deprived Family," Soc. Casework, 48, 203-208, 1967.
From the author's clinical work with delinquent boys at the Wiltwyck School, techniques
with working with low-socioeconomic class patients and their families are described.
Selection, rationale, and scope of family therapy is discussed. Basic techniques consisted of educational and therapeutic maneuvers focussed on clarity of communication,
and the teaching of parent and sibling roles.

LEVINE, R., "Treatment in the Home," Soc. Work, 9, 19-28, 1964.
A clinical report of treatment of seven low-income, multiproblem families who came to a
mental hygiene clinic for help with the identified patient, usually a child. Treatment
of the family rather than the individual was begun because it seems more economical, more
family members could be helped, and the therapist could be more accurate in understanding
problems. Treatment was done in the home. Techniques included talking, demonstration,
and family activity. The seven families were rated in terms of improvement.

MINUCHIN, S., "Conflict-Resolution Family Therapy," Psychiatry, 28, 278-286, 1965.
A description of a method of family therapy developed at Wiltwyck School for Boys in
which the therapist brings members of the family behind the one-way mirror with him to
observe the conversation of the remainder of the family. The procedure is said to be particularly effective with multiproblem families. The family members are usually asked in
family therapy to be a participant observer and in this method these two functions are
separated. "The one-way mirror maintains the emotional impact of interpersonal experiences, while it does not provide an opportunity for impulsory discharge." The family
members impulse to react with action, which is generally characteristic of the families
treated, is delayed and channeled into verbal forms.

MINUCHIN, S., "Family Structure, Family Language and the Puzzled Therapist," in O. Pol-
    lak (Ed.), Family Theory and Family Therapy of Female Sexual Delinquency, Palo Alto,
    Science & Behavior Books, 1967.
An approach to family therapy derived from treating low-socioeconomic families at the
Wiltwyck School for Boys. "We began to look anew at the meaning and effectiveness of
therapist interventions and to focus on two aspects of the family: family language and
family structure." Ways of challenging the family structure and other procedures are
described with illustrations.

MINUCHIN, S., "Psychoanalytic Therapies and the Low-Socioeconomic Population," in J.
    Marmor (Ed.), Modern Psychoanalysis, New York, Basic Books, 1968.
The failure of psychoanalytic therapies and psychotherapy to reach the low-socioeconomic
population is discussed in terms of the implicit requirements of those approaches and
the characteristics of the population. Alternate approaches such as living group therapy,
remedial learning therapy, and family therapy are discussed.

MINUCHIN, S., AUERSWALD, E., KING, C., and RABINOWITZ, C., "The Study and Treatment of
    Families that Produce Multiple Acting-Out Boys," Amer. J. Orthopsychiat., 34, 125-
    134, 1964.
An early report of experience with families of delinquent boys at the Wiltwyck School for
Boys in New York. The report focusses on some aspects of familial functioning, in particular "the socializing function of parental control, guidance, and nurturance." The
group's technique of family diagnosis and therapy with delinquent families is also presented.

MINUCHIN, S., and MONTALVO, B., "An Approach for Diagnosis of the Low Socioeconomic Fam-
    ily," in I. M. Cohen (Ed.), Psychiatric Research Report No. 20, Washington, American
    Psychiatric Association, 1966.
A report on the diagnostic techniques used in appraisal of the individual and the family
at the Wiltwyck School for Boys. The emphasis is upon communication style and affect.
Clinical illustrations are provided.

MINUCHIN, S., and MONTALVO, B., "Techniques for Working with Disorganized Low Socioeconomic Families," Amer. J. Orthopsychiat., 37, 880-887, 1967.
A paper describing some modifications of family therapy techniques useful for dealing with some families of low-socioeconomic class. The techniques include changing the family composition so that some members observe the family sessions through a one-way mirror, treating various subgroups within the natural family separately (e.g., all adolescents), actively manipulating these subgroups in relation to the whole family group, and finally helping the family to discuss what they want to act on.

MINUCHIN, S., MONTALVO, B., GUERNEY, B. G., ROSMAN, B. L., and SHUMER, F., Families of the Slums: An Exploration of Their Structure and Treatment, New York, Basic Books, 1967.
A book on a research project dealing with family treatment of low-socioeconomic class families where the identified patient was delinquent. Research strategy, rationale, dynamics, techniques, and assessment of results are presented. 460 pp.

POWELL, M., and MONOGHAN, J., "Reaching the Rejects Through Multifamily Group Therapy," Int. J. Group Psychother., 19, 35-43, 1969.
A clinical report based on use of multifamily therapy (two or more families meeting together). The setting was a child guidance clinic. Data were obtained from five groups, each consisting of three families. Each family included mother, father, and the identified patient, with siblings introduced when it was considered "appropriate." They were mostly of low-socioeconomic class. One group was reported on, and the results indicated that communication improved with all family members. Premature termination was not a problem.

RABINOWITZ, C., "Therapy for Underpriviledged Delinquent Families," in O. Pollak and A. S. Friedman (Eds.), Family Dynamics and Female Sexual Delinquency, Palo Alto, Science & Behavior Books, 1969.
A report on a family therapy approach to low-socioeconomic families. Includes a detailed description of the process of therapy with such a family based on work at the Wiltwyck School.

ROSENTHAL, A. J., BEHRENS, M. I., and CHODOFF, P., "Communication in Lower-Class Families of Schizophrenics," Arch. Gen. Psychiat., 18, 464-470, 1968.
This is the first part of a two-part report on low-socioeconomic families of schizophrenics. Groups compared were 17 black schizophrenics and their families, 11 in a black control group, and 11 white schizophrenics and their families. The procedure included observation in the home with tasks requiring the family to maintain a focus of attention on a specific topic. (For Part II of this study see Behrens, M.I., "Communication in Lower Class Families of Schizophrenics," Arch. Gen. Psychiat., 18, 689-696, 1968.)

SZALITA, A., "Deprived Families," Bull. Fam. Ment. Health Clin. J.F.S., 1, 5-7, 1969.
A clinical essay on the effect of poverty on families. Deprived families have a deficiency in leadership, in self-reliance, and self-esteem, as well as an inability to meet their needs successfully. If the family has been poor in earlier generations, later generations, although successful financially, often feel "insecure and unsuccessful." The therapist has to differentiate "his own sense of deprivation from that of the family he is treating.

5 LITERATURE SURVEYS

ALDOUS, J., and REUBEN, H., International Bibliography of Research in Marriage and the Family 1900-1964, Minneapolis, University of Minnesota Press, 1967.
An extensive bibliography of the literature on the family. There are sections on transactions within groups, family as a small group, mate selection, and many other subject classes. 507 pp.

BAILEY, M. B., "Alcoholism and Marriage," Quart. J. Stud. Alcohol., 22, 81-97, 1961.
A review paper summarizing and discussing the major literature relating to alcoholism
and marriage. Further research is said to be needed to attempt an integration of the
two hypotheses that regard the course of an alcoholic marriage as a manifestation of a
personality disorder or as a response to a particular kind of stress. "The past few
years have witnessed a general growth of psychiatric interest in total family diagnosis
and treatment, but this new emphasis has hardly begun to manifest itself in respect to
alcoholism." A bibliography of 46 references is included.

BATESON, G., JACKSON, D. D., HALEY, J., and WEAKLAND, J. H., "A Note on the Double Bind
     — 1962," Fam. Proc., 2, 154-161, 1963.
A brief comment by the Bateson group on the context of their 1956 paper on the double
find and further developments after that time. Includes a bibliography of project members arranged by subject with 70 references.

BAXTER, J., "Family Relationship Variables in Schizophrenia," Acta. Psychiat. Scand.,
     42, 362-391, 1966.
A complete review of the literature from 1892 to the present, with the focus on variables related to the family and child development. Topics covered are: (1) sibling position of the patient, (2) loss of one or both parents, (3) presence of a distressed
childhood in the patient's background, (4) atypical mother-child relationship, (5)
atypical father-child relationship, (6) emotional immaturity in the parents, (7) dominance and disturbances between the parents, (8) interpersonal conflict in the family,
(9) family-centered pathological behavior, and (10) special position of sib set for the
patient.

BAXTER, J. C., "Family Relations and Variables in Schizophrenia," in I. M. Cohen (Ed.),
     Psychiatric Research Report No. 20, Washington, American Psychiatric Association,
     1966.
An article reviewing the variables used in the study of family relationships of schizophrenics. Whether child or family is "causal" is discussed and the merits of one interpretation or the other is ambiguous at present.

BODIN, A., "Conjoint Family Assessment: An Evolving Field," in P. McReynolds (Ed.),
     Advances in Psychological Assessment, Palo Alto, Science & Behavior Books, 1968.
A resume of testing methods designed for use with families in the fields of both family
therapy and family research. Approaches have been individual, conjoint, and combined.
Subjective techniques include family tasks, family strengths, inventory, and family art.
Objective techniques include analysis of communication, games, and how conflict is re-
solved. A critique of these methods is presented.

BODIN, A., "Family Therapy Training Literature: A Brief Guide," Fam. Proc., 8, 727-279,
     1969.
The literature on training in family therapy is described and a bibliography of 32 articles listed.

BOWEN, M., "Use of Family Therapy in Clinical Practice," Compr. Psychiat., 7, 345-374,
     1966.
An extensive review of the history of the family therapy movement, dynamics of family
functioning, techniques of family therapy, and some of the clinical uses of family therapy. Current status and possible future of the "family movement" are discussed. The
family field is in a state of "healthy, unstructured chaos," and the future will see
much more research and further development of theory.

CUMMING, J. H., "The Family and Mental Disorder: An Incomplete Essay," in Causes of Men-
     tal Disorders: A Review of Epidemiological Knowledge, 1959, New York, Milbank Memo-
     rial Fund, 1961.
An essay called incomplete because it reviews only a portion of the very large number of
studies which attempt to relate mental disorder with the family. After a review of ideas
about the functions of the family unit, an attempt is made to provide a typology of family studies by surveying studies in the field with emphasis upon the structure and func-

tion of socialization processes. Relating the various studies to each other, the author concludes, "It is clear that organized study of the area of the family and mental illness is in a state of chaos."

FOUDRAINE, J., "Schizophrenia and the Family, a Survey of the Literature 1956-1960 On the Etiology of Schizophrenia," Acta Psychother., 9, 82-110, 1961.
In a thorough review of the literature, the author describes the development of the family point of view of schizophrenia and summarizes the works of authors who have published on this subject during this period. He explores the problem of attempting to conceptualize the function of the family as a whole and to connect pathological family structure with schizophrenia in the individual. A bibliography of 97 items is included.

FRAMO, J. L., "Systematic Research on Family Dynamics," in I. Boszormenyi-Nagy and J. L. Framo (Eds.), Intensive Family Therapy, New York, Harper & Row, 1965.
A review of family research relevant to family dynamics. Includes a discussion of small group research, family interaction studies, and methodological problems.

FRANK, G. H., "The Role of the Family in the Development of Psychopathology," Psychol. Bull., 64, 191-205, 1965.
A review of some of the literature on family influence as it relates to personality development and psychopathology. Studies of schizophrenia and neurotic problems are examined in terms of method of collecting data on family influence, including case history, psychiatric interview, psychological evaluation, and observation. The review concludes "we have not been able to find any unique factors in the family of the schizophrenic which distinguishes it from the family of the neurotic or from the family of controls, who are ostensibly free from evidence of patterns of gross psychopathology."

FREEMAN, V. J., "Differentiation of "Unity" Family Therapy Approaches Prominent in the United States," Int. J. Soc. Psychiat., Special Edition No. 2, 35-46, 1964.
A review and classification of family therapy with six "unit" or "conjoint" methods described, as well as eight closely related approaches. Similarities between methods are discussed in terms of frame of reference, family composition and activity of the therapist. A bibliography of 53 items on family therapy is included.

Group for the Advancement of Psychiatry, Committee on the Family, The Field of Family Therapy, New York, 1970.
A report on the field of family therapy which is meant to be a "snapshot" taken during the winter of 1966-67. Data are based upon a questionnaire answered by 312 persons who considered themselves family therapists as well as the opinions of the members of the family committee. The work deals with who the practitioners of family therapy are, how do families typically enter treatment, what are the goals and conceptual approaches, what techniques are used, and what ethical problems arise.

HADER, M., "The Importance of Grandparents in Family Life," Fam. Proc., 4, 228-240, 1965.
A discussion of the significance of grandparents in the life of young people and their significance to young people. The literature is reviewed on grandparents with a division between attitudes of positive and negative influences.

HALEY, J. (Ed.), Changing Families: A Family Therapy Reader, New York, Grune & Stratton, 1971.
A textbook bringing together 21 articles describing different approaches to family therapy. Both previously published and new articles are included. There is an extensive bibliography.

HALEY, J., and GLICK, I., Psychiatry and the Family: An Annotated Bibliography of Articles Published 1960-64, Palo Alto, Family Process, 1965.
An annotated bibliography of papers published from 1960 through 1964. Content includes articles on family therapy as well as family research studies which are relevant to psychiatry and psychology. Papers from the fields of sociology and anthropology were excluded unless they pertained directly to the psychiatric field.

HANDEL, G. (Ed.), The Psychosocial Interior of the Family: A Sourcebook for the Study
    of Whole Families, Chicago, Aldine, 1967.
An anthology of previously published articles on the social psychology of the family.
It includes sections on the family as a psychosocial organization, research methods,
the family as mediator of the culture, the meanings of family boundaries, the family
as a university of cognition and communication, patterning separateness and connected-
ness, and a review of family theories. 560 pp.

HANDEL, G., "Psychological Study of Whole Families," Psychol. Bull.,63, 19-41, 1965.
A review of family research and theory with an emphasis upon its development from a
psychological point of view. Includes the emergence of this area, family structure
descriptions, the interactional and interpersonal emphases, and research methods. A
bibliography of 100 references is included.

HILL, R., "Marriage and Family Research: A Critical Evaluation," Eugen. Quart., 1, 58-
    63, 1954.
An essay undertaking a critical review of the literature on marriage and the family, co-
vering trends in research, contemporary emphasis, and prospects for the future research.
The essay covers primarily the sociologic literature.

HILL, R., and HANSEN, D., "Identification of Conceptual Frameworks Utilized in Family
    Study," Marriage Fam. Liv., 22, 299-326, 1960.
An article which reports on a ten-year study attempting to inventory research on the
family in terms of: (1) findings, (2) research procedures, and (3) theoretical proposi-
tions derived from the research. Five different research approaches (interactional,
structure-function, situational, institutional, and developmental) and the disciplines
they are developed in are presented and discussed.

HORIGAN, F. D., Family Therapy: A Survey of the Literature, Psychiatric Abstracts No.
    11, Bethesda, Dept. of Health, Education and Welfare, 1964.
A selected, annotated bibliography of the literature of family therapy from 1949 up to
1964.

HOWELLS, J. (Ed.), Theory and Practice of Family Psychiatry, Edinburgh and London, Oli-
    ver & Boyd, 1968.
A collection of new material and previously published articles which includes discussions
of the theory and practice of family psychiatry; illustrations of the dimensions of the
family; individual, relationship, group properties, material circumstances, and community interaction; and illustrations of clinical practice, including organization, the presenting patient, clinical syndromes, and therapy. There is an extensive bibliography.
953 pp.

KLEMER, R. H., Counseling in Marital and Sexual Problems, Baltimore, Williams & Wilkins,
    1965.
A collection of new material and previously published articles which include discussions
of counseling in marital problems; counseling in sexual problems; other marriage problems; premarital counseling; and marriage counseling instruction in the medical curriculum. There is an extensive reading list. 309 pp.

LIDZ, T., "The Relevance of Family Studies to Psychoanalytic Theory," J. Nerv. Ment. Dis.,
    135, 105-112, 1960.
A lecture attempting to assimilate the theory of family dynamics into the theory of psychoanalytic psychology. There is a review of both the family therapy literature and the

psychoanalytic literature which discusses the family. Integrating family theory into psychoanalytic theory can lead to "a more dynamic and complete understanding of human behavior."

MALMQUIST, C., "School Phobia: A Problem in Family Neurosis," J. Amer. Acad. Child Psy-
      chiat., 4, 293-319, 1965.
In contrast to the traditional approach to school phobia, this essay puts forth the clinical notion that phobia can be seen as a reaction to family pathology. Four types for
characterizing disordered families that have been reported in the literature are: (1)
the perfectionistic family, (2) the inadequate family, (3) the egocentric family, and
(4) the unsocial family. How these family types relate to the symptom are discussed.
There is an extensive review of the literature.

MEISSNER, W. W., "Family Dynamics and Psychosomatic Processes," Fam. Proc., 5, 142-161,
      1966.
A discussion of the impact of patterns of family interaction on patterns of physical
health and illness, with a review of the literature.

MEISSNER, W. W., "Thinking About the Family — Psychiatric Aspects," Fam. Proc., 3, 1-
      40, 1964.
A review of the ideas and the literature produced by the shift from individual orientation to a specifically family-centered orientation. The family studies are reviewed in
terms of what has been said about mother, fathers, parental interaction, and total family constellations. The ideas of the major research groups are presented and analyzed.
Includes a bibliography of 135 references.

MISHLER, E., and WAXLER, N., "Family Interaction Processes and Schizophrenia," Int. J.
      Psychiat., 2, 375-430, 1966.
A critical and extensive review of the theories of the relationship between family interaction and schizophrenia with major space devoted to the work of the Bateson, Lidz,
and Wynne groups. Purpose of the review was to see how the theories could be tested and
used as guidelines for research. The major contributions of these groups are to the
theory of the etiology of schizophrenia by focussing on the family and its methods of
interactions, rather than on the individual. Critical evaluations by Bateson, Lidz,
Spiegel, and Wynne of the article and the various theories contained in it are included.

MISHLER, E., and WAXLER, N., "Family Interaction Processes and Schizophrenia: A Review
      of Current Theories," Merrill-Palmer Quart., 11, 269-315, 1965.
A review of the theories of schizophrenia and the family with special emphasis upon differences, and similarities between the Bateson, Lidz, and Wynne groups. A selected bibliography is included.

MOTTOLA, W., "Family Therapy: A Review," Psychotherapy, 4, 116-124, 1967.
A review of the literature of family therapy to this time. It is organized along problems of definition, history, examinations, issues, and research.

MURNEY, R., and SCHNEIDER, R., "Family Therapy: Understanding and Changing Behavior,"
      in F. McKinney (Ed.), Psychology in Action, New York, Macmillian, 1957.
A review of articles in a book of collected articles for psychologists. It describes
rationale, indications, methods, and theory of family therapy for the beginner.

NASHE, E. M., JESSNER, L., and ABSE, D. W. (Eds.), Marriage Counseling in Medical Prac-
      tice, Chapel Hill, University of North Carolina Press, 1964.
A collection of new material and previously published articles which includes discussions
of marriage counseling by the physician; premarital medical counseling; concepts of marital diagnosis and therapy; and marital counseling instruction in the medical school curriculum. There is an annotated book list. 368 pp.

National Clearinghouse for Mental Health Information, Family Therapy: A Selected Anno-
        tated Bibliography, Bethesda, Dept. of Health, Education and Welfare, 1965.
An annotated bibliography on the literature on family therapy up to 1964, which includes
general theoretical articles, therapy with adolescents, child oriented family therapy,
therapy in the home, therapy with families of psychiatric inpatients, marital counseling applications, therapy with schizophrenics, and training family therapists. 27 pp.

NYE, F. I., and MAYER, A. E., "Some Recent Trends in Family Research", Soc. Forces, 41,
        290-301, 1963.
The research literature on the family in four leading sociological journals from 1947-61
(N = 456) was analyzed. Changes in methodological aspects and substantive content are
documented. Problems remain regarding the failure to use research competence fully, inadequate communication among researchers, and lack of attention to methodological research per se. Special attention is given problems and potentials in the utilization
of theory, in control of extraneous variables, in the validity of data, in using third
variables as contingent conditions, and in longitudinal design.

POST, F., and WARDLE, J., "Family Neurosis and Family Psychosis: A Review of the Prob-
        lem," J. Ment. Sci., 108, 147-158, 1962.
A review of some of the work that has been done in social psychiatry — the psychiatry
of relationships. After discussing early studies investigating families of orientation
of various types of adult patients, the authors review the studies of the current families of child and adult patients. They conclude that even those studies of family events
and interactions occurring shortly before the patient became ill, and not years previously, are prematurely concerned with proving some basic theoretical construct. It is essential to discover the proportion and type of psychiatric cases in which there is a clear
link between emotional characteristics in relatives and friends and the patient's breakdown. A bibliography of 57 references is included.

RABKIN, L. Y., "The Patient's Family: Research Methods," Fam. Proc., 4, 105-132, 1965.
A review of family research with special emphasis upon the family of the schizophrenic.
Critical examination is done of case history studies, interviewing studies, psychodiagnostic testing, questionnaire studies, and observational research. A bibliography
of 99 references is included.

RUBINSTEIN, D., "Family Therapy," in E. A. Spiegel (Ed.), Progress in Neurology and Psy-
        chiatry, Vol. XVIII, New York, Grune & Stratton, 1963.
A review article of the literature on family dynamics and therapy for 1961 and 1962.
Articles are grouped in the following categories: (1) theory and research, (2) dynamics,
(3) technique, and (4) miscellaneous.

RUBINSTEIN, D., "Family Therapy," in E. A. Spiegel (Ed.), Progress of Neurology and Psy-
        chiatry, Vols XIX, XX, New York, Grune & Stratton, 1965, 1966.
In these two annual reviews of family therapy, the 1965 review emphasizes a shift to a
concern with the creation of a conceptual framework to understand the dynamics of the
family system. There were 54 references. In the 1966 annual review, there is a similar
emphasis with articles summarized under the following headings: theory and research,
dynamics, technique, and miscellaneous. Included are 54 references.

SAGER, C., "The Development of Marriage Therapy: An Historical Review," Amer. J. Ortho-
        psychiat., 36, 458-468, 1966.
An historical review of the literature on marital therapy and an attempt to integrate
current theoretical and therapeutic techniques. Transference from both a transactional
and psychoanalytic frame of reference is discussed and felt to be a valuable tool in
marital therapy.

SANUA, V. D., "The Sociocultural Aspects of Childhood Schizophrenia," in G. H. Zuk and
        I. Boszormenyi-Nagy (Eds.), Family Therapy and Disturbed Families, Palo Alto, Sci-
        ence & Behavior Books, 1967.
A discussion of methodological issues, research strategies, and the problems inherent in

studying parent-child relationships and interaction as an etiological factor in schizo-phrenia. Includes a review of the literature.

SANUA, V. D., "Sociocultural Factors in Families of Schizophrenics: A Review of the Li-terature," Psychiatry, 24, 246-265, 1961.
A review of family studies which includes problems of methodology, studies using hospi-tal records, interviews with relatives, data from psychotherapy, studies using tests, cross-cultural comparisons, European studies, and comparisons of the schizophrenic en-vironment and that of other pathologies. The author concludes that etiological factors fall into four general categories: (1) undesirable traits in the parents, (2) family structure — early parental or sibling deaths or broken families, (3) undesirable inter-personal patterns, and (4) genetic or constitutional factors. He points out the incon-sistency and wide variation in methodology and sampling, and the neglect of social vari-ables, and suggests an international research organization to coordinate research in mental illness.

SATIR, V.M., Conjoint Family Therapy, A Guide to Theory and Technique, Palo Alto, Sci-ence & Behavior Books, Inc., 1964.
A textbook on family therapy covering a theory of normal family function, communication theory, and techniques of family diagnosis and treatment. There is an extensive biblio-graphy. 196 pp.

SCOTT, R., "Perspectives on the American Family Studies in Schizophrenia," Confin. Psy-chiat., 8, 43-48, 1965.
A review of the American literature on family studies of schizophrenia with questions and criticisms. There is a selective bias in leaving out family history of schizophren-ics and focussing on interactional aspects. The concept of the double bind is ques-tioned and explained in a new way.

SPIEGEL, J., and BELL, N., "The Family of the Psychiatric Patient," in S. Arieti (Ed.), American Handbook of Psychiatry, Vol. 1, New York, Basic Books, 1959.
A chapter in a textbook on psychiatry dealing with sections on the history of the role of the family in mental illness; etiologic studies of parent-child interactions and de-velopment of various mental illnesses including schizophrenia, psychoneurosis, and act-ing-out disorders; the impact of mental illness upon the family; the family and treat-ment procedures, and new approaches to the family and its pathology, including family therapy. There are 238 references.

WINTER, W. D., and FERREIRA, A. J., Research in Family Interaction, Palo Alto, Science & Behavior Books, 1969.
A collection of some new and some previously published material dealing with studies and research on family interaction. There are sections on methodological issues in family interaction research; studies of individual family members; studies of family interaction: decision-making; studies of family interaction: studies, attitudes, and power; studies of family interaction: behavior; and studies of family interaction: in-trafamily communication. There is a lengthy bibliography attached.

ZUK, G. H., and RUBINSTEIN, D., "A Review of Concepts in the Study and Treatment of Fam-ilies of Schizophrenics," in I. Boszormenyi-Nagy and J. L. Framo (Eds.), Intensive Family Therapy, New York, Harper & Row, 1965.
A review of conceptual trends in family treatment of schizophrenics. Discusses the shift from parent pathology to nuclear family to three generational involvement.

6 BOOKS

ACKERMAN, N. W. (Ed.), Family Therapy in Transition, Boston, Little, Brown, 1970.
A two-part book, with the first part a series of papers on the theory and practice of

family therapy by different authors. The second part includes critical incidents with
discussion by different family therapists. 346 pp.

ACKERMAN, N. W., Treating the Troubled Family, New York, Basic Books, 1966.
A book concerned with techniques of family therapy including discussions of family crises, goals, the process of illness developing in the family, functions of the therapist,
treatment of husband and wife, treatment when the family includes children, and some
special techniques in dealing with the "scapegoat." 306 pp.

ACKERMAN, N. W., Psychodynamics of Family Life, Diagnosis and Treatment in Family Rela-
     tionships, New York, Basic Books, 1958.
A collection of new material and previously published articles which includes a discussion of the psychodynamics of the family, the relation of family theory to psychoanalytic theory, social role and personality, family dynamics, techniques in diagnosis, techniques of treatment and research. There are special sections dealing with disturbances
of marital pairs, parental pairs, childhood, adolescence, sociopathy, and psychosomatic
illness. 379 pp.

ACKERMAN, N. W., BEATMAN, F. L., and SHERMAN, S. (Eds.), Expanding Theory and Practice
     in Family Therapy, Family Service Association of America, New York, 1967.
A collection of new material on family therapy dealing with its future, need for a systems approach, family therapy as a unifying force in social work, intergenerational aspects, family therapy in the home, and multiple impact therapy. There are two panel
discussions, one on the classification of family types, and the other on communication
within the family. There are also papers on problems and principles, training family
therapists through "live" supervision, and an actual family therapy session with comments by the therapists on why certain interventions were made. 182 pp.

ACKERMAN, N. W., BEATMAN, F. L., and SHERMAN, S. (Eds.), Exploring the Base for Family
     Therapy, New York, Family Service Association of America, 1961.
A collection of new material on family therapy including papers on the biosocial unity
of the family, concept of the family in casework, family diagnosis and therapy, dynamics,
prevention, epidemiology, and research. 159 pp.

ALDOUS, J., and REUBEN, H., International Bibliography of Research in Marriage and the
     Family 1900-1964, Minneapolis, University of Minneapolis Press, 1967.
An extensive bibliography of the literature on the family. There are sections on transactions within groups, family as a small group, mate selection, and many other subject
classes. 507 pp.

ANTHONY, E. J., and KOUPERNIK, C. (Eds.), The Child in His Family, New York, Wiley, 1970.
Volume 1 in the series of the International Yearbook for Child Psychiatry and Allied
Disciplines. Included are papers from a variety of authors of different nations. The
sections include family dynamics, family vulnerability and crisis, chronic family pathology, and mental health and families in different cultures. 492 pp.

ARD, B. N., and ARD, C. C. (Eds.), Handbook of Marriage Counseling, Palo Alto, Science
     & Behavior Books, 1969.
A collection of previously published material on marriage counseling. There are sections
on the place of philosophy on values; theoretical issues; conjoint marriage counseling;
group marriage counseling; premarital counseling; special techniques; counseling regarding sexual problems; professional issues and ethics in marriage counseling; counseling
divorce; and technical assistance for the marriage counselor. There is an annotated
bibliography. 474 pp.

AUERBACK, A. (Ed.), Schizophrenia: An Integrated Approach, New York, Ronald Press, 1959.
A collection of papers oriented toward research in schizophrenia. Included is a paper
by Bateson on cultural problems posed by studying the schizophrenic process, and a paper
by Bowen on family relationships in schizophrenia. 224 pp.

BELL, J. E., _Family Group Therapy_, Public Health Monograph No. 64, Dept. of Health, Edu-
    cation and Welfare, 1961.
A manual of one approach to family therapy which discusses rationale and techniques
phase by phase from the first conference through the terminal period. 52 pp.

BELL, N. W., and VOGEL, E. S. (Eds), _A Modern Introduction to the Family_, Glencoe, Free
    Press, 1961.
A collection of new material and previously published articles by multiple authors which
attempts to provide a "sociology of the family." It includes a framework for a functional analysis of family behavior, study of different family systems, papers on the family
and economy, family and policy, the family and community, and the family and value systems. It also includes a section on how normal families function and now family function relates to personality development and maldevelopment. 691 pp.

BENNIS, W., SCHEINE, E., BERLEW, D., and STEELE, F., (Eds.), _Interpersonal Dynamics_,
    Homewood, Dorsey Press, 1964.
A collection of previously published material which includes discussions of the family
scapegoat, the family theory of schizophrenia, interpersonal relationships within the
family, and role conflict.

BERGLER, E., _Parents Not Guilty! Of Their Children's Neuroses_, New York, Liveright,
    1964.
A clinical report based on the notion that "there is no direct connection between acts,
words, or attitudes of parents on the child's behavior and later development." 283 pp.

BOSZORMENYI-NAGI, I., and FRAMO, J. L. (Eds.), _Intensive Family Therapy: Theoretical
    and Practical Aspects_, New York, Harper & Row, 1965.
A collection of new material which includes a review of the literature; theory of relationships; rationale, dynamics and techniques; family therapy with schizophrenia in
in-patient and out-patient settings; indications and contraindications, countertransference, and research on family dynamics. 507 pp.

BRODEY, W. M., _Changing the Family_, New York, Potter, 1968.
A personal view of families with many styles of family life described. "The stories...
are little descriptions of families mixed with just enough comment and contrast to tell
their own story and insist that you listen and feel...."

CHANCE, E., _Families in Treatment_, New York, Basic Books, 1959.
A report on a research study of families in treatment where the identified patient was
the child. Father, mother and patient were in individual treatment and there were no
conjoint sessions. One section of the book is on the differences in looking at the
data from the points of view of researcher, patient, and therapist respectively, and
the other section is on research design, descriptions of the families at the beginning
of treatment, the treatment relation, process of change, and interpretations of the
data. 234 pp.

CHRISTENSEN, H. T. (Ed.), _Handbook of Marriage and the Family_, Chicago, Rand McNally,
    1964.
A collection of new material on marriage and the family, including sections on theoretical orientation; methodological developments; the family in its social setting; member roles and internal processes; applied and normative interests including family
life, education, and the field of marriage counseling. 1028 pp.

COHEN, I. M. (Ed.), _Family Structure, Dynamics and Therapy_, Psychiatric Research Report
    #20, Washington, D. C., American Psychiatric Association, 1966.
A collection of new material which includes discussions of research methods, family
functioning, communication styles, dynamics, family myths, family relations where there
is a retarded reader, family relations where the patient has 14+6 cps EEG positive
spike patterns, family resistances, methods for family work-ups, techniques for dealing

with the low-socioeconomic class family, effects of videotape playback on family members, family therapy as an alternative for psychiatric hospitalization, use of heterosexual cotherapists, and multiple impact therapy as a teaching device. 234 pp.

COUCH, E. H., Joint and Family Interviews in the Treatment of Marital Problems, New York, Family Service Association of America, 1969.
A report of a project designed to collect data on rationale and techniques of caseworkers dealing with "troubled marriages." There are sections on special values of joint and family interviews for diagnosis and for treatment; conditions considered favorable and unfavorable to the use of joint interviews and family interviews; expansion of the circle of treatment participants and related experimental approaches; and summary and implications. 330 pp.

DICKS, H. V., Marital Tensions: Clinical Studies Toward a Psychological Theory of Interaction, New York, Basic Books, 1967.
A clinical research report investigating marital problems. Concepts of the study, rationale, social setting, individual setting, development of the study, evolution of concepts, symptomatology, diagnosis, treatment, and treatment results are reported. 354 pp.

DUVALL, E., Family Development, Philadelphia, Lippincott, 1967.
A book on the family for "preprofessionals" who work with the family. It focusses on family life style, tasks, how families reflect social changes, how families change with the introduction of children, and how families change after the children leave the family. 532 pp.

EHRENWALD, J., Neurosis in the Family and Patterns of Psychosocial Defense, New York, Harper & Row, 1963.
A collection of some new and some previously published material including chapters on family traits and attitudes, patterns of family interaction, patterns of sharing and parent-child symbiosis, a description of a family with obsessive-compulsive personality, dynamics from both an intrapersonal and interpersonal point of view, patterns of contagion, sections on the Mozart and Picasso families, psychiatric epidemiology, and interpersonal dynamics in family therapy. 203 pp.

EISENSTEIN, V. (Ed.), Neurotic Interaction in Marriage, New York, Basic Books, 1956.
A collection of new material which includes discussions (mostly from the psychoanalytic point of view) on a cultural perspective on marriage, the effects of marital conflicts on child development, neurotic choices of mate, analysis of interaction patterns, psychological assessment in marital maladjustment, changes as a result of treatment of one member, casework with a disturbed family, approaches to treatment of marital problems, and problems of prediction of marital adjustment. 352 pp.

FARBER, S. M., MUSTACCHI, P., and WILSON, R. H. L., (Eds.), Man and Civilization: The Family's Search for Survival, New York, McGraw-Hill, 1965.
A collection of new material given at a conference concerned with the changes in the family secondary to changes in society. It includes articles concerned with the "necessity of the family;" sacrifice of family structure; the family role; and new paths. 210 pp.

FISHER, E. O., Help for Today's Troubled Marriages, New York, Hawthorn Books, 1968.
A book on marriage counseling that covers the problems of marriage, aspects and procedures of marriage counseling, the problems of divorce and widowhood, and comments on remarriage. 288 pp.

FRIEDMAN, A. S., BOSZORMENYI-NAGY, I., JUNGREIS, J. E., LINCOLN, G., MITCHELL, H., SONNE, J., SPECK, R., and SPIVACK, G., Psychotherapy for the Whole Family: Case Histories, Techniques, and Concepts of Family Therapy of Schizophrenia in the Home and Clinic, New York, Springer, 1965.
A collection of new material based on a research project on treatment of schizophrenia using family therapy done in the home. The papers cover rationale, experience with the study families, results of treatment, and problems and concepts in treatment. There is a section on a search for a conceptual model of family psychopathology. 354 pp.

GALDSTON, I. (Ed.), The Family: A Focal Point in Health Education, New York, Interna-
    tional University Press, 1961.
A collection of material from a conference, with sections on a discussion of the family
in general; profile of the American family; psychological dynamics of the "familial organism;" an approach to the study of family mental health; education for personal and
familial living; education for parenthood; family and physician; social worker and family; family health maintenance; the anthropology of the American family; ethnic differences in behavior and health practices; and social differences in health practices.
216 pp.

GALDSTON, I. (Ed.), The Family in Contemporary Society, New York, International Univer-
    sities Press, 1958.
A collection of material from a conference on the family, with discussions of the previous conference on the family given in 1956; the history of the family as a social and
cultural institution; changing dynamics of the contemporary family: social and economic
basis; behavioral trends and disturbances of the contemporary family; homeostatic mechanisms within the family; and emotionally disturbed and healthy adolescents and their
family backgrounds. 147 pp.

GLASSER, P. H., and GLASSER, L. N. (Eds.), Families in Crisis, New York, Harper & Row,
    1970.
A collection of new material and previously published articles which includes discussions of families in poverty, disorganization of marraiges and families, and families
in terms of physical and mental health. 405 pp.

GOODE, W., The Family, Englewood Cliffs, Prentice Hall, 1964.
The author discusses sociological theory as applied to family relationships. He points
up the complex relationships between family systems and the larger social structure,
the biological basis of the family, legitimacy and illegitimacy, mate selection and
marriage, forms of the household, organized descent groupings, role relations, stratification, dissolution of family role systems, and changes in the family patterns. 120 pp.

GREENE, B. L. (Ed.), The Psychotherapies of Marital Disharmony, New York, Free Press,
    1965.
A collection of previously presented material on treatment of marital problems using
different approaches. There are papers on a multi-operational approach, sociologic and
psychoanalytic concepts in family diagnosis, marital counseling, the classical psychoanalytic approach, treatment of marital partners separately where the therapists collaborate, concurrent psychoanalytic treatment for the marital partners, conjoint marital
therapy, a combination of approaches, and the family approach to diagnosis. 191 pp.

GROTJOHN, M., Psychoanalysis and the Family Neurosis, New York, Norton, 1960.
A book based on the clinical experience which combined psychoanalytic as well as interactional factors in the etiology of mental illness. He covers the history and etiology
of the development of family therapy; psychodynamics of health and complementary neurosis of a family; treatment techniques, including the diagnostic interview, training analysis, and family treatment; and the dynamics of the therapeutic process. 320 pp.

Group for the Advancement of Psychiatry, Committee on the Family, The Case History Me-
    thod in the Study of Family Process, New York, 1970.
The purpose of this report is to demonstrate a systematic approach to modifying the traditional psychiatric "case history" for use in family diagnosis, treatment, and research.
There are sections on principles for compiling a family case history, a typical case is
presented and contrast made between a Puerto-Rican working-class and American middle-
class family. Contrast in values within the nuclear family as well as in the extended
family network are described. There is an appendix with a family case history outline.
380 pp.

Group for the Advancement of Psychiatry, Committee on the Family, The Field of Family
    Therapy, New York, 1970.
A report on the field of family therapy which is meant to be a "snapshot" taken during

the winter of 1966-67. Data are based upon a questionnaire answered by 312 persons who
considered themselves family therapists as well as the opinions of the members of the
family committee. The work deals with who are the practitioners of family therapy, how
do the families typically enter treatment, what are the goals and conceptual approaches,
what techniques are used, and what ethical problems arise.

Group for the Advancement of Psychiatry, Committee on the Family, Integration and Con-
    flict in Family Behavior, Report No. 27, Topeka, 1954.
A report by the committee on the family of GAP dealing with organizing data on the
study of the family. It discusses the relation of the family to the social system,
the system of values to which the family is oriented, and Spanish-American family patterns as well as American middle-class family patterns. 67 pp.

HALEY, J. (Ed.), Changing Families: A Family Therapy Reader, New York, Grune & Stratton,
    1971.
A textbook bringing together 21 articles describing different approaches to family therapy. Both previously published and new articles are included, and there is an extensive
bibliography.

HALEY, J., Strategies of Psychotherapy, New York, Grune & Stratton, 1963.
A description of a variety of forms of psychotherapy from an interactional point of view.
Includes chapters on marriage therapy and family therapy.

HALEY, J., and GLICK, I., Psychiatry and the Family, An Annotated Bibliography of Arti-
    cles Published 1960-64, Palo Alto, Family Process, 1965.
An annotated bibliography of papers published from 1960 through 1964. Content includes
articles on family therapy as well as family research studies which are relevant to
psychiatry and psychology. Papers from the fields of sociology and anthropology were
excluded unless they pertained directly to the psychiatric field.

HALEY, J., and HOFFMAN, L., Techniques of Family Therapy, New York, Basic Books, 1967.
A presentation of the work of five family therapists. Interviews were done with Virginia Satir, Don D. Jackson, Charles Fulweiler, Carl Whitaker, and a therapy team doing
crisis therapy. There is intensive examination of a first interview with a family to
illustrate their approaches.

HANDEL, G. (Ed.), The Psychosocial Interior of the Family: A Sourcebook for the Study
    of Whole Families, Chicago, Aldine, 1967.
An anthology of previously published articles on the social psychology of the family.
It includes sections on the family as a psychosocial organization, research methods,
the family as mediator of the culture, the meanings of family boundaries, the family
as a universe of cognition and communication, patterning separateness and connected-
ness, and a review of family theories. 560 pp.

HORIGAN, F. D., Family Therapy: A Survey of the Literature, Psychiatric Abstracts No.
    11, Bethesda, Dept. of Health, Education and Welfare, 1964.
A selected, annotated bibliography of the literature of family therapy from 1949 up to
1964.

HOWELLS, J., Family Psychiatry, Springfield, Ill. Charles C Thomas, 1963.
A collection of some new and some previously published material intended to be a textbook of family psychiatry. There are sections on theory and practice of family psychiatry; illustrations of the dimensions of the family; individual, relationships, group,
maternal circumstances, and community interaction; and finally, illustrations from clinical practice, divided into organization, the presenting patient, clinical syndromes,
and therapy itself. There is an extensive bibliography. 953 pp.

HOWELLS, J. (Ed.), Theory and Practice of Family Psychiatry, Edinburgh and London, Oli-
    ver & Boyd, 1968.
A collection of new material and previously published articles which include discussions

of the theory and practice of family psychiatry; illustrations of the dimensions of the family; individual, relationship, group properties, material circumstances, and community interaction; and illustrations of clinical practice, including organization, the presenting patient, clinical syndromes, and therapy. There is an extensive bibliography. 953 pp.

JACKSON, D. D. (Ed.), Communication, Family and Marriage, Palo Alto, Science & Behavior Books, 1968.
A collection of previously published papers covering early generalizations on family dynamics from clinical observations, papers on the double-bind theory, communication, systems and pathology, and research approaches and methods. 289 pp.

JACKSON, D. D. (Ed.), The Etiology of Schizophrenia, New York, Basic Books, 1960.
A collection of new material dealing with the etiology of schizophrenia. It includes a section on an overview of the problem, genetic aspects, biochemical aspects, physiologic aspects, psychological studies, and family theories of schizophrenia. 456 pp.

JACKSON, D. D., Myths of Madness, New York, Macmillan, 1964.
A discussion of madness emphasizing the different mythologies about it and expressing a more social view.

JACKSON, D.D. (Ed.), Therapy, Communication and Change, Palo Alto, Science & Behavior Books, 1968.
A collection of previously published papers covering psychotic behavior and its interactional context, the interactional context of other kinds of behavior, interactional views of psychotherapy, and conjoint family therapy. 76 pp.

JACKSON, D. D., and LEDERER, W. J., Mirages of Marriage, New York, Norton, 1969.
A book focussing on the nature of marriage, marital problems, and procedures for bringing about change. Illustrations of different problems are given. Exercises for a couple to work on their marriage are provided.

KELLNER, R., Family Ill Health, An Investigation in General Practice, Springfield, Charles C Thomas, 1963.
A report by a general practitioner concerning the incidence of physical and emotional illness and its relationships to family dynamics. It includes a plan of the investigation, description of the cases, method of analyzing the data, results, and a summary. 112 pp.

KLEMER, R. H., Counseling in Marital and Sexual Problems, Baltimore, Williams & Wilkins, 1965.
A collection of new material and previously published articles which includes discussions of counseling in marital problems; counseling in sexual problems; other marriage problems; premarital counseling; and marriage counseling instruction in the medical curriculum. There is an extensive reading list. 309 pp.

LAING, R. D., and ESTERSON, A., Sanity, Madness and the Family, Vol. I, Families of Schizophrenics, London, Tavistock, 1964.
A book describing a research project investigating 11 families in which the identified patient was a female with schizophrenia. The data were obtained from clinical interviews with family members both individually and together. "The behavior of schizophrenics is much more socially intelligible than has come to be supposed by most psychiatrists." Rather than having an illness, the symptoms are seen as a "strategy" invented by the person to live in an "unlivable" situation. 272 pp.

LAING, R. D., PHILLIPSON, H., and LEE, A., Interpersonal Perception — A Theory and a Method of Research, London, Tavistock, 1966.
A research project oriented toward understanding interaction of two persons. It includes sections on self and other; interaction and interexperience in dyads; the spiral

of reciprocal perspective; historical view of the method; the interpersonal perception methods (IPM); disturbed and nondisturbed marriages; study of a dyad; developments; and the IPM questions. 179 pp.

LANGSLEY, D., and KAPLAN, D., The Treatment of Families in Crisis, New York, Grune & Stratton, 1968.
A report of a research project where family crisis therapy was offered as an alternative to psychiatric hospitalization. Rationale, techniques of therapy, data on the patients, and results and implications are presented. 208 pp.

LENNARD, H.,and BERNSTEIN, A., Patterns in Human Interaction, San Francisco, Jossey-Bass, 1969.
A textbook on "clinical sociology" which discusses interaction processes, methodological problems in describing interaction processes, interaction patterns in the family, psychotherapeutic interaction, and functions of human interaction. Patterns of schizophrenic and control families are described. 224 pp.

LIDZ, T., The Family and Human Adaption, New York, International Universities Press, 1963.
A collection of three lectures dealing with the role of the family in normal development, the role of the family in a changing society, and specific requisites for successful family functioning: the parents' ability to form a coalition, maintain boundaries between generations, and adhere to their appropriate sex-linked role. Finally, the book covers the family's capacity to transmit the basic adaptive techniques of the culture by means of communication. Failures in these functions are explored in terms of an etiologic theory for schizophrenia. 120 pp.

LIDZ, T., FLECK, S., and CORNELISON, A. R., Schizophrenia and the Family, New York, International Universities Press, 1965.
A collection of new material and previously published articles by the Yale research group concerning their investigations of the intrafamilial environment in which schizophrenic patients grow up. The book includes the rationale for the study, some articles on the family environment of schizophrenic patients, a number of articles on the 17 study families (including aspects of casework techniques, family interaction, the hospital staff, familial dynamics, and psychological testing) and the implications of this data for a new theory of schizophrenia based on a disturbed intrafamilial environment. There is also a section documenting the type of thought disorder found in families with schizophrenic patients as seen on the object sorting test. There is an extensive bibliography. 477 pp.

LOMAS, P. (Ed.), The Predicament of the Family, New York, International Universities Press, 1967.
A collection of new material oriented toward the theme of psychoanalytic concepts of the family. There are articles on family relationships in contemporary society; mirror-role of mother and family in child development; family interaction and adolescent therapy; the family pattern of distress; simultaneous analysis of mother and child; the family and individual structure; and a study of marriage as a critical transition for personality and family development.

MacGREGOR, R., RITCHIE, A. M., SERRANO, A. C., SCHUSTER, F. P., McDANALD, E. C., and GOOLISHIAN, H. A., Multiple Impact Therapy With Families, New York, McGraw-Hill, 1964.
A report of a clinical project using a new technique for families who consult a child guidance clinic and who live a great distance away. The book includes a section on the development of family therapy, illustrations of the method; discussion of the method; and discussions of the family, family dynamics, therapeutic movement, the team, and results. 320 pp.

MASSERMAN, J. (Ed.), Science and Psychoanalysis, Vol. II: Individual and Family Dynamics, New York, Grune & Stratton, 1959.
In this book there are sections on familial and social dynamics. Included are papers

on survey of trends and research in the practice of family therapy, psychoanalytic approaches to the family, family homeostasis, family dynamics in schizophrenia, cultural aspects of transference and countertransference, techniques of family therapy, and a panel discussion and review on the family. 218 pp.

MIDELFORT, C. F., The Family in Psychotherapy, New York, McGraw-Hill, 1957.
A report of a clinical project involving family therapy and the use of relatives in the care of psychiatric patients on both an in-patient and out-patient basis. It discusses the purpose of the project, and the use of family treatment in schizophrenia, depression, paranoid illness, psychopathic personality, and psychoneurosis. 202 pp.

MINUCHIN, S., MONTALVO, B., GUERNEY, B. G., ROSMAN, B. L., and SHUMER, F., Families of the Slums: An Exploration of Their Structure and Treatment, New York, Basic Books, 1967.
A book on a research project dealing with family treatment of low-socioeconomic class families where the identified patient was delinquent. Research strategy, rationale, dynamics, techniques, and assessment of results are presented. 460 pp.

MISHLER, E. G., and WAXLER, N. W. (Eds.), Family Process and Schizophrenia, New York, Science House, 1968.
A collection of previously published articles which includes discussions of current theories; experimental studies; parents of the schizophrenic; dyadic interaction; parents with a schizophrenic child: pathogenic triad; parent and sibling: the family tetrad; and commentaries, which is a discussion by four family therapy theoreticians of the articles. 323 pp.

MISHLER, E. G., and WAXLER, N. W., Interaction in Families, New York, Wiley, 1968.
A report on a research project with the aim of systematically identifying distinctive patterns of interaction in families of schizophrenic patients. It includes background and aims of the study; research design; measurement techniques; strategy for data analysis; research findings focussed around expressiveness, power, disruptions in communication, and responsiveness; case examples of findings; and a review and implications of the study. 436 pp.

MUDD, E. H., The Practice of Marriage Counseling, New York, Association Press, 1951.
A study of the development of marriage and family counseling in the United States, and a description of its practice with case examples. It includes types of organizations and professions involved. 336 pp.

NASHE, E. M., JESSNER, L., and ABSE, D. W. (Eds.), Marriage Counseling in Medical Practice, Chapel Hill, University of North Carolina Press, 1964.
A collection of new material and previously published articles which includes discussions of marriage counseling by the physician; premarital medical counseling; concepts of marital diagnosis and therapy; and marital counseling instruction in the medical school curriculum. There is an annotated book list. 368 pp.

National Clearinghouse for Mental Health Information, Family Therapy: A Selected Annotated Bibliography, Bethesda, Dept. of Health, Education and Welfare, 1965.
An annotated bibliography on the literature on family therapy up to 1964, which includes general theoretical articles, therapy with adolescents, child-oriented family therapy, therapy in the home, therapy with families of psychiatric inpatients, marital counseling applications, therapy with schizophrenics, and training family therapists. 27 pp.

PARSONS, T., and BALES, R. F., Family, Socialization and Interaction Process, Glencoe, Free Press, 1955.
A collection of papers oriented toward the family and its relation to personality development, social structure, child socialization, role differentiation in a nuclear family and small groups, and the role of the family in the general culture.

POLLAK, O., and FRIEDMAN, A. S. (Eds.), Family Dynamics and Female Sexual Delinquency, Palo Alto, Science & Behavior Books, 1969.
A volume containing 18 previously unpublished papers, which had its origin in a seminar on the family system as it influences the personality and behavior of sexually-acting-out adolescent daughters. Sections include: family system theory, socioeconomic and cultural factors in sexual delinquency, psychodynamic factors in sexual delinquency, family interactional factors, and family therapy applications. 210 pp.

RIESS, F. B. (Ed.) New Directions in Mental Health, Vol. I, New York, Grune & Stratton, 1968.
A collection of articles on various psychiatric topics including papers on practice of family treatment in kibbutz and urban child guidance clinics; short term analytic treatment of married couples in a group by a therapist couple; the therapeutic field in the treatment of families in conflict; recurrent themes in literature and clinical practice; and patterns of interaction in families of borderline patients. 304 pp.

ROSENBAUM, S., and ALGER, I. (Eds.), The Marriage Relationship: Psychoanalytic Perspectives, New York, Basic Books, 1967.
A collection of some new and some previously presented papers focussing on the marital relationship from a family and psychoanalytic point of view. It includes discussions of communication; monogamy; femininity; resistance to marriage; mate choice; expectations in marriage; changing attitudes of marital partners towards each other; marital problems of older persons; the effects of children; effects of pathology of parents on the children; effects of sexual disturbances; effects of marital conflicts on psychoanalysis; different treatment approaches to marital problems including individual psychoanalysis, with different analysts, family therapy, group psychotherapy with couples, growth and maturation in marriage, and marital dissolution. 366 pp.

ROSENTHAL, D., The Genian Quadruplets: A Case Study and Theoretical Analysis of Heredity and Environment in Schiozphrenia, New York, Basic Books, 1963.
A case study in schizophrenia of a family in which quadruplets were schizophrenic. The book is divided into sections dealing with the case history, tests and studies dealing with basic characteristics in response processes, projective tests and their analysis, systematic analysis of observations of the family by the research staff and the community, conceptualization of the family members in their interrelationships, and a theoretical analysis of the heredity-environment problem in schizophrenia. 609 pp.

RABKIN, R., Inner and Outer Space, New York, Norton, 1970.
A book about social psychiatry with the emphasis on the shift from the inner space of the individual to social organisms. 215 pp.

RYLE, A., Neurosis in the Ordinary Family: A Psychiatric Survey, London, Tavistock, 1967.
A report of the author's study of the psychiatric health and personal relationships of 112 working-class families with children of primary school age. The study was done while the author was a general practitioner. It covers the methods of collecting data, social circumstances and characteristics of the population, parents' childhood, parents' psychodynamics, their parents' marriages, child rearing practices and their relation to other parental attributes, psychological disturbances in the children, parental factors associated with the disturbance in the children, family diagnosis, consultation and treatment, and evaluation and conclusions. 153 pp.

SAMPSON, H., MESSINGER, L., and TOWNE, R., Schizophrenic Women: Studies in Marital Crises, New York, Atherton Press, 1963.
A book on a research project studying family relations of 17 schizophrenic women who had to be hospitalized. The book discusses the crisis that led up to hospitalization and its context, the process of separation, becoming a mental patient in terms of family processes, and the crisis resolution in the hospital and posthospital period. A summary is presented, and implications of this study are discussed. 174 pp.

SATIR, V. M., Conjoint Family Therapy: A Guide to Theory and Technique, Palo Alto,
    Science & Behavior Books, 1964.
A textbook on family therapy covering a theory of normal family function, communication
theory, and techniques of family diagnosis and treatment. There is an extensive bibliography. 196 pp.

SCHEFLEN, A. E., Stream and Structure of Communicational Behavior, Behavioral Series
    Monograph No. 1, Philadelphia, Eastern Pennsylvania Psychiatric Institute, 1965.
A context analysis of a family therapy session by Whitaker and Malone. The examination
of the interview is in detail and includes kinesic, linquistic and contextual description.

SILVERMAN, H. L. (Ed.), Marital Counseling, Springfield, Charles C Thomas, 1967.
A collection of new material on marital counseling which includes discussions of psychological factors, ideological factors, scientific factors, and a summary of marital counseling concepts. 530 pp.

Social Work Practice, 1963, Selected Papers, 90th Annual Forum, National Conference on
    Social Welfare, Cleveland, Ohio, May 19-24, 1963, New York, Columbia University
    Press, 1963.
A collection of papers given at a social work conference which includes a paper on family diagnosis and treatment, family unit treatment of character-disordered youngsters,
and schizophrenia and family therapy. 255 pp.

STEIN, M. I. (Ed.), Contemporary Psychotherapies, Glencoe, Free Press, 1961.
A book containing a series of lectures about psychotherapy given in a seminar series.
In it are two papers by Ackerman on family therapy, and two papers by Jackson, one a
general paper and the other on family therapy where the identified patient is schizophrenic. 386 pp.

TOMAN, W., The Family Constellation: Its Effects on Personality and Social Behavior,
    New York, Springer, 1969.
A book describing a theory of the effects of the family constellation on personality
and social behavior. The theory is described, as well as the major types of sibling
positions and the major types of relations of the parents. Prediction of behavior is
based on six case examples. 280 pp.

THORMAN, G., Family Therapy: Help for Troubled Families, Public Affairs Pamphlet No.
    356, New York, 1964.
Rationale, indications, family dynamics, techniques and future trends are described in
this report.

VINCENT, C. D. (Ed.), Readings in Marriage Counseling, New York, Thomas Y. Crowell, 1957.
A collection of 52 articles on marriage counseling. The book includes sections on marriage counseling in an emerging and interdisciplinary profession; premarital counseling;
definitions, methods, and principles in marriage counseling; marriage counseling of individuals, couples, and groups; theories of personality formation and change applicable
to marriage counseling; research in marriage counseling; and questions related to marriage counseling as an emerging profession.

WATZLAWICK, P. J., An Anthology of Human Communication, Palo Alto, Science & Behavior
    Books, 1964.
A textbook and tape recording dealing with family dynamics, interaction, and communication patterns. Communication theory is outlined and there are sections on agreement and
disagreement, types of relationships, disqualifications, schizophrenic communication,
double binds, coalitions, and a suggested reading list. 63 pp. plus an audiotape.

WATZLAWICK, P. J., BEAVIN, H., and JACKSON, D. D., Pragmatics of Human Communication, A
    Study of Interactional Patterns, Pathologies, and Paradoxes, New York, Norton, 1967.
A book dealing with "behavioral effects of human communication with special attention to

behavior disorders." There are discussions of the frame of reference of the book, some
axioms of communication, pathological communication, the organization of family interaction, analysis of the play, <u>Who's Afraid of Virginia Woolf</u>, paradoxical communication,
paradoxes in psychotherapy, and existentialism and the theory of human communication.
296 pp.

WHITTAKER, C. (Ed.), <u>Psychotherapy of Chronic Schizophrenic Patients</u>, Boston, Little,
    Brown, 1958.
A transcript of a conference on schizophrenia in which there were eight sessions, each
oriented toward a particular topic in which no formal presentation is made, but rather
a general discussion with a moderator for each section was held. The book includes sections on diagnosis and prognosis, schizophrenic distortion of communication, orality,
anality, family and sexuality, countertransference, management of the patient, and
family management. 219 pp.

WINTER, W. D., and FERREIRA, A. J., <u>Research in Family Interaction</u>, Palo Alto, Science
    & Behavior Books, 1969.
A collection of some new and some previously published material dealing with studies and
research on family interaction. There are sections on methodological issues in family
interaction research; studies of individual family members; studies of family interaction: decision-making; studies of family interaction: studies, attitudes, and power;
studies of family interaction: behavior; and studies of family interaction: intrafamily communication. There is a lengthy bibliography.

ZUK, G. H., and BOSZORMENYI-NAGY, I. (Eds.), <u>Family Therapy and Disturbed Families</u>, Palo
    Alto, Science & Behavior Books, 1967.
A collection of new material and previously published articles which includes discussions
of family theory and psychopathology, relationships between family and sociocultural
systems, and specific techniques of family and marriage therapy. 243 pp.

7 FILMS

THE ENEMY AND MYSELF, 16mm., sound, black and white film, 50 min., by Nathan Ackerman,
    M.D., The Family Institute, New York, New York, 10021.
This film is a composite of four interviews with a family group over a period of one and
a half years. The family consists of four members, mother, father, and twin sons of
nine years, one of whom had made a suicide threat. Distribution: The Family Institute,
149 E. 78th St., New York, New York, 10021

FAMILY ASSESSMENT SERIES, 16 mm., sound, color film, 240 min.
A family is interviewed by four different family therapists. It is not a therapy inter-
view but a consultation, or assessment, which lasts 30 minutes. The interviewer then
spends 30 minutes immediately afterward discussing the interview and its implications
with the family's regular therapist. The interviewers are: Nathan Ackerman, M. D.,
New York, Murray Bowen, M. D., Maryland, Don D. Jackson, M. D., Palo Alto, and Carl
Whitaker, M. D., Madison. Distribution: Psychological Cinema Register, Pennsylvania
State University, University Park, Pennsylvania, 16802.

FAMILY IN CRISIS, 16mm., sound, color film, 48 min., by David R. Kessler, M.D., Langley
    Porter Neuropsychiatric Institute, University of California, San Francisco Medical
    Center, California.
The film is intended as an introduction to the understanding of family functioning and
family treatment. Material presented includes sequences of a family at home and in
therapy sessions, as well as of a professional seminar discussion group. The aim is
to highlight specifically a number of fundamental family concepts of general usefulness
to professionals rather than to present a chronological sequence of one family in therapy.
Distribution: Sandoz Pharmaceuticals, Hanover, New Jersey, 07936, or local Sandoz repre-
sentatives.

FAMILY THERAPY, 16 mm., sound, black and white film, by Walter Kempler, M. D., Kempler
    Institute, Los Angeles, California, 90048.
This film shows a family trying to work out their problems together in family therapy.
Distribution: Kempler Institute, 6233 Wilshire Boulevard, Los Angeles, California,
90048.

FAMILY THERAPY: AN INTRODUCTION, 16 mm., sound, black and white film, 43 min., by Ira
    D. Glick, M. D., University of California Medical Center, San Francisco, California,
    94122, and George J. Marshall, Sr., Medical College of Georgia, Augusta, Georgia,
    30904.
This film, designed for family therapists as an introduction to family therapy, is based
on treatment of a family over a 16-month period. The film demonstrates techniques (including videotape playbacks) and problems, but its primary purpose is to give an overview of the course of family treatment from beginning to end. Distribution: National
Medical Audiovisual Center, Atlanta, Georgia, 30333.

IN AND OUT OF PSYCHOSIS: A FAMILY STUDY, 16 mm., sound, black and white film, 120 min.,
    by Nathan Ackerman, M. D., The Family Institute, New York, New York, 10021.
This film deals with treatment of a family with a 16-year-old daughter, an only child,
who is mentally ill. The maternal grandmother is included in the family unit. Distribution: The Family Institute, 149 East 78th Street., New York, New York, 10021.

Author Index

*(The page numbers cited indicate only the first
appearance of each book or article listed in the bibliography.)*

Schweid, E. ------------ 16
Scott, R. D. ----------- 102, 152, 176, 227,
                         228
Searles, H. F. -------- 60, 76
Serrano, A. ----------- 7, 20, 22, 56, 80
Shapiro, M. I. -------- 78, 109
Shapiro, R. L. -------- 152, 242
Sharan, S. ------------ 119
Sharp, V. ------------- 199
Shaw, D. -------------- 26, 65
Shereshky, P. --------- 76
Sherman, A. ----------- 106
Sherman, M. H. -------- 119
Sherman, S. N. -------- 2, 4, 32, 33, 119,
                         152
Sherz, F. ------------- 152
Shoemaker, D. J. ------ 118
Shohan, S. ------------ 152
Shugart, G. ----------- 92
Shulman, G. ----------- 43, 59
Shumer, F. ------------ 25
Sigal, J. ------------- 28, 33
Silverman, H. L. ------ 53
Simmons, O. G. -------- 91
Singer, M. T. --------- 102, 122, 202
Siporin, M. ----------- 76
Skidmore, R. A. ------- 53
Skinner, A. ----------- 33
Slavson, S. R. -------- 76
Sluzki, C. E. --------- 33, 53, 152, 168,
                         229, 246
Smith, I. W. ---------- 33, 236
Smith, L. ------------- 34
Smith, V. ------------- 53
Smulever, M. ---------- 200, 230
Snell, J. ------------- 119, 241
Sobel, D. E. ---------- 177, 229
Social Work Practice -- 80
Sojit, C. M. ---------- 119
Solomon, A. P. -------- 76
Solomon, M. H. -------- 210
Sonne, J. C. ---------- 13, 34, 212
Sorrells, J. --------- 34
Spark, G. M. ---------- 34, 35, 56
Speck, R. ------------- 13, 34, 35, 212
Speer, D. C. ---------- 153
Spellman, S. ---------- 145, 240
Spiegel, J. P. -------- 35, 153, 154,
                         185, 229
Spitzer, S. P. -------- 84
Spivack, G. ----------- 13, 212
Stabenau, J. R. ------- 103
Stachowiak, J. -------- 26, 35, 116, 120
Steele, F. ------------ 132
Stein, M. I. ---------- 36
Steinhilber, R. M. ---- 238
Stennet, R. ----------- 103
Sternberg, D. --------- 39
Stockner, C. ---------- 92
Strean, H. S. --------- 36
Strodtbeck, F. -------- 120
Stuart, R. B. --------- 53
Stuckert, R. P. ------- 177
Sturges, S. ----------- 53
Stutzman, L. ---------- 42
Sumer, E. A. ---------- 186
Sussman, M. B. -------- 155, 186

Swank, G. ------------- 20
Swanson, R. M. -------- 84
Sweetser, D. A. ------- 177
Szalita, A. ----------- 61

Tabachnick, N. ------- 246
Taschman, H. ---------- 42
Tatsuoka, M. ---------- 106
Tauber, G. ------------ 61
Taylor, G. ------------ 22
Taylor, W. R. --------- 120
Terry, D. ------------- 95, 211
Teruel, G. ------------ 53
Tessman, L. H. -------- 155
Tharp, R. ------------- 36, 169
Thompson, P. ---------- 54
Thorman, G. ----------- 36
Timken, D. R. --------- 86
Titchener, J. L. ------ 36, 54, 121,
                         250
Towne, R. D. ---------- 101, 169, 227,
                         230
Treischman, A. -------- 71
Tribbey, J. A. -------- 177
Truuma, A. ------------ 80
Tubin, J. ------------- 103
Tyler, E. A. ---------- 80

Valantin, S. ---------- 183
Van Amerogen, S. ------ 77
Van Den Berghe, P. ---- 169
Vander Heide, C. ------ 121
Van der Veen, F. ------ 83, 103, 197
Van Houton, C. -------- 9
Van Sommers, P. ------- 88, 183
Vassiliou, G. -------- 36
Ventola, L. ----------- 42
Verden, P. ------------ 83
Veron, E. ------------- 246
Vidal, G. ------------- 200, 230
Vikersund, G. --------- 61
Vincent, C. D. -------- 54
Vincent, C. E. -------- 186
Viorst, J. ------------ 36
Vogel, E. S. ---------- 71, 132, 169

Wahl, C. W. ----------- 177, 230
Wainwright, W. H. ----- 103, 230
Wairi, M. ------------- 36
Wallace, J. G. -------- 18
Wardle, J. ------------ 129
Waring, M. ------------ 84, 230
Warkentin, J. -------- 36, 37, 54,
                         186
Watson, A. S. --------- 54, 182, 237
Watson, D. ------------ 230
Watzlawick, P. -------- 121
Waxenberg, S. --------- 113
Waxler, M. ------------ 116, 129, 147
Waxler, N. E. --------- 121
Weakland, J. H. ------- 17, 37, 85,
                         141, 204, 216,
                         231, 254
Weblin, J. ------------ 231

* * *